CORPORATE SOCIAL RESPONSIVENESS

The Modern Dilemna

CORPORATE SOCIAL RESPONSIVENESS

The Modern Dilemma

Robert W. Ackerman
Vice President, Finance and Administration, Preco Corporation
Former Lecturer, Harvard Business School

Raymond A. Bauer
Joseph C. Wilson Professor of Business Administration
Harvard Business School

RESTON PUBLISHING COMPANY, INC., Reston, Virginia
A Prentice-Hall Company

Library of Congress Cataloging in Publication Data

Ackerman, Robert W
Corporate social responsiveness.

Includes bibliographical references and index.
1. Industry–Social aspects–United States–Case studies. I. Bauer, Raymond Augustine, joint author. II. Title.
HD60.5.U5A29 658.4'08'0973 75-37636
ISBN 0-87909-137-1
ISBN 0-87909-136-3 pbk.

Case material of the Harvard Graduate School of Business Administration is made possible by the cooperation of business firms who may wish to remain anonymous by having names, quantities, and other identifying details disguised while maintaining basic relationships. Cases are prepared as the basis for class discussion rather than to illustrate either effective or ineffective handling of administrative situations.

10 9 8 7 6 5 4 3 2 1

Printed in the United States of America.

Contents

Preface

This is an effort to treat as a management issue one which has been treated predominantly as a social and/or ethical issue. The area of concern is one which usually has been labelled "corporate social responsibility," but which we prefer to call "corporate responsiveness." In order to position ourselves, we will have to present here as flat assertions a number of propositions which will be developed at length in the body of the book.

As has often been noted, while business has historically been viewed primarily as a provider of goods and services, at all times business has been expected to operate within the law and within prevailing norms, as well as to engage in a moderate amount of philanthropic activity. However, in the late sixties the notion of the responsibilities of business took a distinctive turn. The demands on business accelerated sharply and have continued at a high level. But, in the short period from about 1968 to 1975, the nature of those demands and the nature of business' response to them have changed in important qualitative ways. The contrast can be presented in the form of two outlines, one covering the business community in 1968, the other depicting the situation at the beginning of 1975.

In 1968, the business community together with the rest of the country was shaken by urban riots. A society which business had shaped had gone awry. Business leaders felt a sense of responsibility for the ills of society, and shared with others the belief that the vaunted skills of business could succeed in their solution where other institutions had failed. There was a commitment to solve problems which were external to business, with which business had little direct experience and, as it turned out, little capability to deal with. Money was committed and staff was added. Business was engaged in programs to save the cities and help the disadvantaged.

Equal employment opportunity legislation was on the books, but had little bite. Environmental issues were on the horizon. The consumerism movement was being launched and energy and materials were in good supply. The economy was booming.

By the beginning of 1975, the economy was not booming. Some–not many–social policy departments had been abolished, and a few staff persons were known to have lost their jobs. At least some urban or community affairs budgets had been cut. It had been years since hundreds or even scores of chief executives had attended a social responsibility revival meeting at the Waldorf, and businessmen were somewhat chastened by observers who contended that business had welshed on its commitment to social problems.

What the above brief scenario fails to mention is another scene that was happening simultaneously. To begin with, we will argue that the relationship between social responsibility and the profits or profitability of business is at best a marginal issue. This position becomes increasingly relevant as society at large formalizes its demands. Equal employment opportunities for women as well as minorities is an issue with teeth. So is pollution control. And compliance with the Occupational Safety and Health Act is becoming a serious matter. More than a score of consumer protection laws have been on the books since 1966. Since noncompliance with the law would undoubtedly be regarded as irresponsible, and since few companies are performing at a level which these laws demand, we cannot, as some do, conclude that these issues have been removed from the "responsibility" agenda of business by the passage of laws.

While adverse experience has tempered the more grandiose expectations of businessmen and others concerning the extent that business can readily solve our social ills, many voluntary activities continue. These activities are generally closer to the competence and interests of business firms than were some of those of the late sixties. A majority of firms surveyed in 1973 reported that they had shifted their activities toward urban problems. One finds good evidence of increasing efforts to purchase from and develop minority suppliers. Financial institutions increasingly develop services for the disadvantaged, and more of them include in their lending policies such considerations as pollution. Good community relations are seen as important from both a social and a business point of view. Concern with the quality of work life is growing—at least on a verbal level. By 1973, a majority of very large companies had in the past twelve months "audited" their social performance.

More importantly, as one follows (as we have) the developments within firms, one learns that they have been going through a prolonged experience of learning how to implement social policies and manage social programs. Even the selection of activities has taken on a management dimension as new structures, such as committees of directors and committees of operating managers, have been introduced to give coherence to the social aspects of companies' behavior.

The management aspect of corporate responsiveness has not been entirely neglected in the literature or at conferences for practitioners and students, and its importance is becoming increasingly recognized. Yet, this dimension has received relatively little attention compared to discussions of social issues, descriptions of activities, and philosophical questions of ethics and the corporate role in society. Since we have not yet defined what we mean by "management aspects," and since documentation of what is meant by "relatively little" would demand extensive data, we beg indulgence in the flatness of our assertion.

One of us (Ackerman) has recently published a book, *The Social Challenge to Business* (Harvard University Press, Cambridge, Mass., 1975), which we believe is the first full-length treatment of the topic as we are defining it here.

Case teaching materials which treat corporate responsiveness as a management problem are scarce. A search of the bibliography of the International Case Clearing House early in 1974 located close to a hundred cases which fit the rubric "social responsibility," but scarcely a dozen—other than those from our own research—which treated the issue as one of management rather than of ethical decision making or understanding of social issues.

Perhaps our position can best be made clear by reference to the two texts which, insofar as we know, come closest to this one. They are: *Up Against the Corporate Wall* by S. Prakash Sethi (Prentice-Hall Inc., Englewood Cliffs, New Jersey, 1971) and *Corporate Social Responsibility* by Richard N. Farmer and W. Dickerson Jogue (Science Research Associates, Inc., Chicago, 1973). Since the authors describe their own books so well, we will let them do so in their own words.

Sethi says of his book:

> The objective of this book is to expose the student, through a series of case studies involving business corporations, to a variety of problems that are increasingly becoming the prime concern of both business and society. It is aimed at developing in the reader a sensitivity to the issues involved, an awareness of the complexity of the motives of various parties, and a familiarity with the success and failure of their strategies and tactics. (p. x)

Farmer and Jogue tell the student:

> You must figure out what the ethical and economic issues are and then decide what should be done. Remember what seems right to you may not seem so to someone else. Your aim should be not to set down corporate policy, but to decide exactly why you want the company to do something. It is not enough to decide that a certain course of action is required. You must justify this action ethically, socially, and financially. (Preface, second of two unnumbered pages)

In the Sethi book, based on actual cases, the business firm is an organization under siege, bedevilled on a wide range of issues by a wide variety of factors. The organization itself is a virtual black box with only its external response depicted. Farmer and Jogue cover an equally wide range of issues, but from the inside of a single financial corporation. The incidents, while realistic, are also presumably fictionalized. The Sethi book, as promised, does illuminate the variety of issues with which the corporation is confronted and, by clear implication, the range of social problems to which the corporation is in one way or another relevant. The Farmer and Jogue book also lives up to its promise and gives the student a wide variety of exercises in making tough decisions of a largely ethical sort.

The problems of understanding the nature of social demands on the firm, the parties who represent these demands, and the ethical problems of making tough decisions in realistic response to those demands are important for students of management and for practicing managers lacking experience in these areas.

But there are many more characteristically managerial tasks which the foregoing do not cover. To begin with, one may structure and man an organization to relate better (or worse) to the range of issues and parties represented in the Sethi volume. The selection and training of personnel, the structure of the organization, its system of reward and control, may affect the outcome of decisions of the sort represented in the Farmer and Jogue volume.

Our research over the past several years has been on management issues such as the above and on additional ones such as: how to assess organizational performance on social issues and design information systems to monitor performance; the entire process of implementing social policies in large complex organizations; the identification of the stages that this process goes through and the characteristic problems and tasks associated with each stage; the evolution and/or design of structures and procedures for making the handling of social issues consistent with business strategies; the interaction of social and business issues; the roles of staff and line in the handling of social issues; and so on.

This book is aimed at three groups. The first and most obvious is students of management and, of course, their teachers. The organization of the book itself may suggest a separate course with a title such as "The Management of Corporate Social Responsiveness." This, however, is not necessarily an end we devoutly desire. The ideal, in our view, would be the integration of such material as this into the regular curriculum of management education, with some cases appearing in courses on human relations and organizational behavior and others in business policy, production or finance, personnel management, administrative systems, accounting and control, and the like. From a didactic point of view we would hope that the management of social issues would not be seen as something separate from the general problems of management. In all probability, we have not yet developed the material that is ideal for this form of integration, and other practical problems of curriculum revision may make a separate course preferable for the near future. But we hope that the doctrine of separate, even if equal, will be a transitional one.

The second group is practicing managers. We have learned much from them, and we have been encouraged by their response to our playback of what we believe we have learned. At minimum, we hope the case material will permit the manager to share the experience of others efficiently. Beyond that, we would be pleased if our interpretive text rings some resonant chords.

The third group is a grab bag of researchers, social critics, public policy makers, and regulators. Material of this sort has not been totally inaccessible to them, and many regulators have had first-hand contact—though usually in an advisary relationship. With the social critics in particular we have reason to anticipate that we will have a problem of credibility. Any exposition of the management problems of handling of social issues must of its nature make matters appear more complicated. To cite the reaction one of us got from a group of activists: "They were dismayed that a person of your stature has become an apologist for bureaucratic inaction." We have our own opinion of those who are so resistant to inconvenient truths and hope that critics of more substantial intellectual integrity will find some merit in having a more sophisticated image of the entity which they are trying to reform.

We have directed our attention to large, complex business organizations. The reasons are dual. Very large business organizations account for a majority of America's business activity, a high proportion of persons employed, and a high proportion of the impact of business on society. They also pose the most complicated administrative problems. We had to direct finite resources somewhere. If we had directed our attention at small businesses, we expect we would have found a contrasting picture, equally instructive, but not of the same practical consequence. Large organizations may pose more complicated managerial problems, but they also have more available resources and are generally less close to the brink of survival. Smaller ones are well worth attention. But, if man has a universal problem it is that he cannot attend to everything simultaneously.

Finally, we have the task of writing an empirically-oriented book in a field which is drenched with literature. Our reason for turning our attention to the empirical side several years ago was that we felt that the ratio of words to evidence was somewhat past the critical point. Ironically, however, this is a field in which the distinction between words and evidence is not clear. The same statement may be taken as "words" when uttered by a college professor, but as "evidence" when uttered by a bank president. Nor is the body of literature easy to define. There are, for example, dozens of newsletters that bear on the general topic or on the specific issues associated with business social responsibility. The Bank of America has now issued Volume IV of its *Bibliography: Corporate Responsibility for Social Problems* (San Francisco, California, May 1975). This bibliography includes conventional published writings, important speeches, and even corporate annual reports which cover topics of relevance. While it is restricted to items appearing in 1974, it nevertheless includes about 500 entries!

Quite obviously, this is not the book to bear the responsibility for a review of the "literature," however it might be defined. The reader for whom this is a new field can easily find his way into the literature by consulting *Business and Society Review* or the *Journal of Contemporary Business*, published by the University of Washington. The arguments, issues, and names will quickly become familiar.

Obviously, the published word is relevant to much of what we have to say, and we would stand naked and naive if we did not refer to it where appropriate. But we have opted for a policy of parsimony, which may leave our academic colleagues less edified than if we had chosen the opposite. The reason is not solely laziness, of which we have our share, but in the nature of the problems with which we deal and for which the literature gives scant help. For example, we will frequently be forced to make what are essentially statistical statements for which hard statistical data are not available. We have already done so with our outlines of the business community in 1968 and 1975, and with our assertion about the relative inattention to the managerial problems of responsiveness in the literature. We will be on similarly dubious grounds when we make assertions such as "increasingly informed observers are coming to realize that the important dimensions of corporate social impact stem from the firm's day-to-day operations, not from its philanthropy sacrificed from profits." Such a statement implies a statistical trend over time that could be documented only with great difficulty. And, quite obviously, we have defined an "informed" observer as one who agrees with our position, though we have probably included some subtle and complex calculations of astuteness and closeness to the scene of action which we would not be able to retrieve from our unconscious.

Having informed the reader of our choice on this matter, we will proceed to take the risks which it entails.

We end this preface on a personal note that has relevance to the practicality of what we have to say in this book. One of us (Ackerman) has as of the time of this writing spent approximately fourteen months as Vice-President-Finance and Administration of a medium-sized divisionalized company. In this context he has had to deal with these problems. If this experience had contradicted our findings in any major way, we would indeed be embarrassed. We are spared that trauma. But, has our research been useful? The answer to this question is a qualified yes. Little in our research gives guidance to specific solutions to specific problems—this demands invention. But, this author does find that he is able to diagnose problems more rapidly. He can more quickly understand the nature of the problem with which he is confronted and, therefore, can devote more time or an equal amount of time sooner to devising a solution. This circumstance complies with our belief that the notion that academics can provide practitioners solutions to specific problems in complex situations is both presumptuous and foolish. Such problems demand specific solutions tailored to the specific situation. The most we would aspire to, and this is considerable, is that we would improve the practitioner's understanding of the problem.

ROBERT W. ACKERMAN
RAYMOND A. BAUER

Acknowledgements

Our thanks extend to the many people who have contributed to our knowledge of the field and more particularly to the preparation of this book. All of the included cases were written at the Harvard Business School and, with a single exception, by either one of us or under our supervision. We are grateful for the professional competance and care in case development contributed by the following: Terry L. Cauthorn, (for Avon Products, Inc., FOODS Unlimited (A) and (B), National Bank and Trust Company (B), Parker Perry Systems, the Eastern Gas and Fuel Associates series, and Bordon, Inc.); Maureen Marlin (for National Bank and Trust (A)); Edwin A. Murray, Jr. (for the Golden Eagles and Metropolitan Development Corporation case series); and Ranee P. Warner (for the University of Pennsylvania case series). Our thanks go also to George C. Lodge for permission to use the Affirmative Action at Aldrich case prepared under his supervision by Rikk Larson. The field research was made possible through the cooperation of literally hundreds of managers to whom we are indebted for their time and trust.

More than three years were required to develop the conceptual material and collect the field data reported in the book. During that period, we benefited from the perceptions of numerous colleagues at Harvard and elsewhere who have a lively interest in corporate social responsiveness, including—Kenneth R. Andrews, Louis Banks, Norman A. Berg, Joseph L. Bower, C. Roland Christensen, Neil C. Churchill, Fred K. Foulkes, William C. Frederick, George F.F. Lombard, John B. Matthews, John R. Rosenblum, John K. Shank, George A. Steiner, Hugo E.R. Uyterhoeven, and Raymond Vernon. We were allocated the time for the larger research project of which this book is a part with the support and encouragement of Lawrence E. Fouraker, Dean of the Harvard Business School; George F.F. Lombard, Senior Associate Dean; and Richard E. Walton, Director of the Division of Research. Nancy R. Hayes, Saralee F. Irwin and Jeanne Lane were of invaluable help in preparing the manuscript for publication and managing the myriad of administrative matters that went along with it.

Financial support was generously provided from several sources: the Russell Sage Foundation, the Rockefeller Brothers Fund, and the National Science Foundation under grant number ERP73-02711. All opinions, findings and conclusions contained in this book are, of course, our responsibility and do not necessarily reflect the views of the National Science Foundation or the other funding agencies.

Part One

Chapter One

Corporate Responsiveness

About a decade ago a broad movement, probably of a revolutionary nature, began in the industrialized countries of the world. It is a movement to make institutions more responsive to human needs. On the negative side, it is a rebellion against measuring "progress" predominantly in economic and technical terms. Specific manifestations are the development of social indicators for measuring the performance of the society as a whole, and the development of technology assessment in terms of its probable social consequences rather than limiting the evaluation to more conventional technical and economic criteria.

The business firm is caught up in this stream of events as it is being pressed by public sentiment and legislative and regulatory action to respond to issues beyond its traditional task of producing goods and services at a profit. The list of issues is long and continues to grow. The nature of the pressure ranges from laws backed by enforcement agencies, through the vocal urging of special interests by organized groups, to the idiosyncratic consciences and values of individual executives. While the same general set of forces is impending on all institutions, the impact in the world of business is especially dramatic because the historic criteria for evaluating the performance of business have seemed so relatively simple and clear cut.

While there is a general recognition of these new demands on business, there is appreciable disagreement or confusion as to their underlying nature and stability. Time after time in the past few years the demise of social responsibility movement has been proclaimed. When Richard Nixon liquidated urban problems by verbal fiat, many critics and executives announced the heat was off–some with remorse, some with relief. The energy crisis of 1973 was signalled as the enemy of environmental protection. And, at the beginning of 1975 we have a recession in which public affairs budgets are being cut and some public affairs officers are losing their jobs. As workers were laid off it was feared that minorities and women would be the victims of lack of seniority.

There are eddies in every stream, and which way one thinks the water is running depends on his point of observation. The tendency has been to look at the new expectations of business in too narrow a perspective. Frequently, it is true, commentators note that business is not alone among institutions in public distrust and demands. Seldom, however, is this plight of our institutions put in the full perspective of the social movement alluded to above. It is only in that context that the nature and stability of the new demands on business can be adequately understood. For that reason we will step backward a pace to sketch what we see as the main dimensions of the broader movement as it was manifested in the United States.

The mid-1960s were pivotal years in the United States. The Vietnam War heated up. Key civil rights legislation was passed, including the law supposedly guaranteeing equal employment opportunity. We launched a War on Poverty whose history, apart from its intention, was not much more glorious than that in Vietnam. The Federal Government took important new steps in support of education and medical care for the poor and elderly.

Although the mid-1960s were a period of affluence, this was the time when confidence in our institutions began to decay. Confidence in all our institutions on which public opinion measurements were made had shown a steady upward trend since shortly after World War II. Suddenly, in the years 1965–1966 these measures began a downward slide from which they have not yet begun to recover. These same years marked the point of acceleration of interest in social indicators. One of us was working on a book which gave the name to this movement[1] and was taken off guard by the sudden popularity of what he was doing.

While the roots of the environmentalist movement date back to Rachel Carson's book in the early sixties, and former Congressman Emmilio Daddario began advocating technology assessment early in the sixties, the first big, dramatic opposition to the "technological imperative" (if you *can* do it, you *should* do it) arose in the mid-to-late sixties in the fight over the SST as a manifestation of the belief that advance in technology is a measure of "progress." The defeat of the SST (or perhaps even the strength of the opposition, if it had survived) is a signal of a change in man's relation to technology which is manifested more broadly in the now widespread practice of technology assessment.

By the beginning of the seventies, the consumer and environmental movements were in full bloom, and the desirability of economic growth for its own sake was being questioned.[2] In addition, a tradition of popular activism had developed in America (and abroad). There were two major streams that converged to form this issue. One stemmed from a sequence of major issues: the civil rights movements, followed by the antiwar movement, and then by the consumer and the environmental movements–with some of the participants trained in one movement passing on to the next, and then the next. The other stream came more from a general dissatisfaction of certain groups with the unresponsiveness of various institutions–students with educational institutions, neighborhood groups with planners and governments which imposed highways and develop-

---

[1] Raymond A. Bauer, editor, *Social Indicators*, M.I.T. Press, Cambridge, Mass. 1966.

[2] cf. *Toward Balanced Growth: Quality with Quantity*, A Report of the National Research staff, U.S. Government Printing Office, Washington, D.C., 1970.

ment projects on them against their will. These two streams not only created a core of activists and an activist tradition, they also reflected and articulated a growing demand that institutions be more responsive to the needs of people.

While we may have missed a piece or two, these are the main elements that form a mosaic of an agenda for a humanized society. Economic and technical measures of progress are questioned or even rejected. Emphasis is placed on the "quality of life"—the meaning of which is not clear except that it is not material prosperity alone. Measures of social performance are called for. The list of rights and entitlements (e.g. education, medical care, security) is expanded. And the people are not only demanding more from their institutions, but have developed techniques for persuading the incumbents of those institutions.

One may well ask how widely the vision we have sketched is shared. In one sense, probably not widely at all if we think of individuals adhering to each element as part of a coherent, thought-out view of the world. We are speaking rather of a *tacit* agenda to which there is no principled disagreement, one with which it is difficult to disagree in principle. It is graceless to favor pollution, poverty, sickness, inequality, or a poor quality of life. Furthermore, rights and entitlements once established are hard to reverse. Once they are acknowledged, the moral basis for opposing or denying them is gone. Seen in this context, it is difficult to see institutional responsibility as a transitory issue.

But, we have no disposition to deny that there are difficulties with, and sources of resistance to, this agenda. A portion of these is the subject matter of this book. But, more broadly, it is important to note that the agenda of a humanized society developed under conditions of actual or perceived affluence. In fact, the perception of affluence was in itself a stimulus to the development of the agenda. In 1969, the retiring Secretary General of the OECD[3] announced that since we had mastered the secret of economic growth we could now turn ourselves to directing the product of the economy better to improve the quality of such things as education and the environment. The National Goals Research Staff highlighted a quote from Nixon's 1970 State of the Union speech:

> In the next 10 years we shall increase our wealth by 50 percent. The profound question is—Does this mean we will be 50 percent richer in a real sense, 50 percent better off, 50 percent happier?[4]

It should further be remembered that even the present era of environmental concern was launched amidst the perception of affluence.

> Historically, our concern over resources focused on whether there would be enough food, energy, and materials to meet our needs. Today, in the United States, the concern is about the ability of the land, air, and water to absorb all the wastes we generate.[5]

---

[3]Thorkil Kristensen, "Problems of the Modern Society," *The OECD Observer',* #39, April 1969, pp. 5-6.

[4]*Op. cit.* p. 23.

[5]*Ibid.*, p. 27.

We have then the irony of an ambitious social agenda based on the assumption of affluence and, scarcely a half-decade later, an acute awareness of limitations of resources punctuated by an unusually problematic recession. These circumstances pose problems for the broad agenda and for the issue of corporate responsiveness which is the topic of this book.

There is an aspect of the agenda for humanizing society which could be adaptive in a resource-short world. The agenda is a call for the rationalization of society in human terms, and a need to conserve resources may stimulate the desire and perception of the need for such rationalization. Unfortunately, the rationalization of large complex social systems demands skills, knowledge, and disciplines (of character) which are in very short supply. In practice it may simply amount to the loading of additional, as yet unidentified, tasks on the business firm under the slogan of reducing externalities. And, one may worry that this will be done with little or no disciplined concern for the tradeoffs involved. In other words (and very abstract words at that), it would not be surprising that in a world of high prices and short supplies the basic function of producing goods and services might be prejudiced in the name of noble causes. Or, as Casey Stengel might put it, it may be that we ain't seen nothin' yet. We return to these issues in another context in the next chapter.

RESPONSIBILITY OR RESPONSIVENESS?

> Business enterprises, in effect, are being asked to contribute more to the quality of American life than just supplying quantities of goods and services. Inasmuch as business exists to serve society, its future will depend on the quality of management's response to the changing expectations of the public.[6]

The topic with which we deal is by now familiar. We have promised in the Preface to justify our preference for calling it "social responsiveness" rather than "social responsibility." This is the task to which we will now address ourselves. Our dissent goes both to process and content, and that is about all there is.

The connotation of "responsibility" is that of the process of assuming an obligation. It places an emphasis on motivation rather than on performance. And in so doing, it is consistent with the prevailing treatment of the topic in the literature. The earlier book by Ackerman was devoted to the thesis that motivation is not enough. Responding to social demands is much more than deciding what to do. There remains the management task of doing what one has decided to do, and this task is far from trivial. Since the present book is an elaboration of this theme, the reader will have ample opportunity to make his own judgement on this matter.

If our dissent were only with the inappropriateness of the label as a description of the process involved, we might feel guilty of semantic haggling. However, the concept of

[6] Committee for Economic Development, "Social Responsibilities of Business," A statement of the Research and Policy Committee, June, 1971.

corporate responsibility gives little guidance as to the content of what is to be done beyond "something more," and it deflects our attention from much that is important. Any attempt to produce a consistent definition of any operational usefulness leads to some form of ridiculous conclusion.[7]

There are three concepts which we can identify as having been used as a basis for finding consistency in the concept of social responsibility: the conscience of the executive, costs or foregone profits, and voluntary discretion. All perform as promised above.

There are few, if any, who would deny the desirability that executives have a conscience. But those who look to it to determine the content of social responsibility seem to assume that there is a definable bunch of good things a good conscience will inevitably lead one to. Henry Ford was unquestionably a man of strong conscience. One day recently we received from a friend an anonymous sheet entitled "A Most Ethical Businessman." It is pointed out that Henry Ford had, in fact, paid higher wages than those prevailing in the automobile industry. Consumerists of today might applaud his insistence on building a utilitarian automobile even though he lost customers. But, what about rejecting the self-starter because it would permit women to drive alone? Or maligning Jews, via the Dearborn *Independent*, for being responsible for many of the ills of society? Or hiring goons to break strikes because he thought the power of labor was not in the public interest?

Both Friedman and Lodge[8] have pointed out quite correctly that value setting is the function of politics, not of private business. While we must grant individual businessmen preferences of their own, just as we do to any other citizen, we would be ill-advised to urge them to use the power of their positions freely outside the established norms of the society. Conscience may be an effective sensitizer to those norms, but perhaps not more so than wisdom.

For some, among them David Linowes, the touchstone of "responsibility" is costs or foregone profits.[9] The slogan of many reformers is that business must forego some of its (presumably swollen) profits in order to serve social goals. Conservative economists argue that it is unethical to forego profits. And a sophisticated liberal economist such as Neil Chamberlin says there are not enough profits to forego to make much difference.[10]

Of these three positions, Chamberlin's is by far the soundest. Most activist reformers seem to vastly overestimate the amount of profits available for diversion to

---

[7]The reader who is not familiar with the prevailing literature can get started with Dow Votaw, "The Nature of Social Responsibility; You Can't Get There from Here," *Journal of Contemporary Business*, Winter 1973, pp. 1-20.

[8]Milton Friedman, "The Social Responsibility of Business Is To Increase Profits," *New York Times Magazine*, Sept. 13, 1970. George C. Lodge, "Business and the Changing Society," *Harvard Business Review*, March-April, 1974, pp. 59-72.

[9]David F. Linowes, *The Corporate Conscience*, Hawthorn Books, Inc., New York, 1974. Linowes proposes a system of measurement of social responsibility based on the marginal costs of activities beyond the regular costs of doing business.

[10]Neil Chamberlin, *The Limits of Corporate Responsibility*, Basic Books, New York, 1973.

good causes.[11] Furthermore, concentrating attention on those actions which a firm might undertake out of foregone profits diverts attention away from the social impact of what the firm does in its main line of business. "Social responsibility" via special programs, as implied by the notion of foregone profits, can never be more than a small part of the overall social impact of the business organization, and as this area of concern matures, it is becoming very clear that overall social impact is the issue—a point we will elaborate later.

Giving "brownie points" for marginal costs, as Linowes proposes, could at best relate to special socially intended projects or programs, and even in this area would produce anomalies. For example, in certain situations it would salute ineptness. A bank wrestled for seven years in developing a program for lending to minority entrepreneurs. At the end of that time it had a smoothly running program. The officers had learned how to manage this type of loan and had reduced losses. Furthermore, the handling of these loans had been transferred to regular loan officers, and as a result the assignment of overhead costs to this program would have been very difficult, and scarcely worth the accounting costs. In other words, precisely when the program was institutionalized into the regular operations of the bank the measured "social responsibility" of the bank would have approached zero.

This is by no means an exception. When pollution control equipment has been added to old processes, the capital cost is identifiable. But when new processes are designed which do not pollute, it is impossible to assess the cost of pollution control. And, if the process is more efficient, and pollution control is therefore profitable, should the firm be assigned a "responsibility debit"? The same logic applies to the design of safety into a plant, or of aesthetics which increase employees' gratification with their job. There is no way of isolating the "social cost."

Clearly, linking social responsibility closely with costs muddies as much as it clarifies. There is no doubt that many activities associated with new social demands have at least the initial appearance of costing money, though they eventually may not. And, in fact, virtually any expense can be rationalized in terms of long-run profitability. A high-technology company subsidizes the college education of minority engineers. This buys the business a certain amount of good public relations, it is a demonstration of good faith effort in complying with the spirit of equal employment opportunity, and eventually the firm will probably hire some of the engineers. Banks justify community development programs on the ground that their own welfare is linked to the welfare of the community in which they do business.

No business investment pays off instantaneously. So, unless the benefit appears in the same accounting period as the expense, or unless the expense is capitalized and carried forward into subsequent accounting periods in anticipation of future benefits, it appears on the books as a cost. If future benefits can be anticipated, then whether an expense is seen as a cost or an investment is arbitrary.

---

[11] There is the oft cited finding of the Opinion Research Corporation that the public believes that business earns 28% profits after taxes on the sales dollar whereas the correct figure is a little over 4% after taxes. Furthermore, there seems to be little awareness of the uses to which profits are put, and the dangers of a take-over to which a firm would expose itself if, as seems certain, its stock price were depressed because it diluted its profits substantially.

It should be seen by now that we have liquidated the apparently neat argument of the conservative economists such as Milton Friedman who argue against the propriety of business expenses that do not contribute to profitability. Their philosophical posture is clear, but it offers a bias rather than operational guidelines. Once the notion of long-range profitability is introduced, only paucity of imagination and a short time-horizon limit one's capacity to justify expenditures with no direct, immediate business benefit.

Another approach to assessing "social responsibility" is to confine that accolade to discretionary actions. This is reflected defensively in the behavior of business executives who point to the fact (or make the claim) that their behavior on such things as pollution control or repair of damage done by strip mining goes beyond the requirements of the law.[12] They expect to get little or no credit for "merely complying with the law." And, their critics are frequently heard to say: "Why should he get credit for that? He is only complying with the law."

There are two answers to this distinction between what is "discretionary" or voluntary and what is mandated. The first is simple and straightforward, namely that it does not apply in reverse. No one would argue that a businessman who broke the law is responsible, and few of the critics of business would contend that no businessmen break the law. Certainly we think better of those corporations whose executives refused (some did) to contribute funds illegally to election campaigns than we do of those who did contribute.

The second reason is that what is mandated is seldom clear cut, and what constitutes compliance is certainly not always clear cut. The eventual interpretation of the 1964 law supporting equal employment opportunity evolved over a period of eight years.[13] As of now, "compliance" means having an approved affirmative action plan, and compliance with pollution control standards also consists of submitting a plan. But "compliance" with product safety legislation, pollution, safety, or what have you, can and does proceed with varying degrees of commitment and skill. Should the existence of a law on the books keep us from attending to those differences? We think not. Furthermore, discretion is virtually never complete or absent. In a later chapter in which we make some proposals on the relating of social responsiveness to corporate strategy, we point out that there is a "zone of discretion" over which the amount of discretion diminishes over time, especially for an issue enacted into law. Discretion never becomes zero since everyone has the option of paying fines or going to jail.

The semantics of the term "social responsibility" and the discussions which accompany it are strongly loaded with the notions of intent, good will, sacrifice, and voluntary initiative. Such semantics were not grossly inappropriate when we were concerned with primarily philanthropic activities, though even here the semantics become questionable for those firms for which philanthropy is a part of corporate strategy. They have become progressively inappropriate as these issues have moved inside the firm and as

---

[12]For a further discussion of this, see S. Prakash Sethi, "Dimensions of Corporate Social Performance: An Analytical Framework For Measurement and Evaluation." Working Paper No. 2, Berkeley, California: Institute of Business and Economic Research, University of California, 1974.

[13]cf. Ruth G. Shaeffer, "Nondiscrimination and Employment: Changing Perspectives 1963-1972," Report Number 589 to The Conference Board, Inc., New York, 1973.

it has become apparent that what we are concerned with is the *social impact* of business rather than with a limited number of programs of overt social intent.

In effect, we are saying two things. The first is that most of the major social demands which have been placed on business in the past decade–pollution control, OSHA, truth in advertising, equal employment opportunity, quality of work life, product safety, fair warranties, and so on–all have to be implemented through the regular operations of the firm. They are not "external" programs. This is the thesis of Ackerman's article, "How Companies Respond to Social Demands,"[14] and of his subsequent book. Once that is accepted, then capability in implementation is of crucial importance, and it is only partially affected by the motivation of top executives; that is to say, motivation is not a sufficient condition for implementation.

It should be noted that the social issues with which corporations have been concerned over the past decade may be divided into three categories. The first of these refers to social problems external to the corporation which were not caused by any direct business action, or, if by direct business action (e.g., job discrimination), reflected flaws of the larger society. Poverty, drug abuse, decay of the cities are examples of problems in this category. They represent issues which stimulated corporate involvement in the late sixties. More traditional business concerns in this category are community relations and philanthropy.

The next category consists of the external impact of regular economic activities. Pollution by production facilities is one example. The quality, safety, and reliability of goods and services is another. Confusion or deception from marketing practices, the social impact of plant closings, and plant location are others.

The final category of issues occurs within the firm and is intrinsically tied up with regular economic activities. Included are equal employment opportunity, occupational health and safety, the quality of work life, and such emerging issues as industrial democracy.

Quite obviously, the second and third of our categories are of increasing importance in recent years and are intrinsically tied to the regular economic operations of business. Improved social performance demands changes in these operations.

While some other writers have been lamenting the waning of external programs of the first sort and the failure of chief executives to attend consciousness-raising conferences, we have been observing scores of firms at work on programs in all three categories. It is on the basis of these observations that we contend that the stream has not reversed direction.

It is in the second and third of these categories that legislation is concentrated. One might argue that it would be difficult to legislate business responsibility for problems on which it has no direct impact. And this is true. However, it should be added that the private syndicated research services which executives are seeing also tell them strongly that the public expects business to give priority to the latter two types of issues.

The second thing we are saying is the upside down version of the first. Whereas the major explicit social demands have to be met through the operations of the business, the operations of the business have social consequences whether intended or not. And

---

[14] Robert W. Ackerman, "How Companies Respond to Social Demands." *Harvard Business Review*, July-August, 1973, pp. 88-98.

frequently the latter category of social consequences are at least as important as the former. This second consideration, while in a sense obvious, asserted itself on us as we wrestled with the concept of a social audit.

In their article "What is a Corporate Social Audit?", Bauer and Fenn[15] made early attempts to define the territory for an "audit" of a firm's social performance. They argue for a "definable domain" without making too much of a case as to what it should be. As we worked with actual companies, the nature of the problem became clearer. A food company was very concerned over problems of nutrition. Was this a "social" program? Not in the ordinary sense. With a pharmaceutical company, the meeting of prevailing social demands would be no more than cosmetic in the light of the major issues of the social role of drugs, the product, marketing, and pricing policies of the industry. Obviously, what would concern a sensible person was not the motivation of the firm in engaging in a particular activity, but the consequences of the activity regardless of the intention.

A result of the foregoing is that many diligent students of "social accounting" are coming to the conclusion that the only conceptually adequate format for assessment of a firm's social performance is a matrix of the impact of all of the firm's activities on all of its constituencies.[16] Presumably evidence that a firm had been diligently responsive to each cell in such a matrix would be the ultimate test of social responsibility!

The notion of completing the entries in such a matrix is mind boggling. However, the notion of the matrix itself turns our attention in the correct direction. There is no conceptually clear way of identifying any of a firm's actions as not having a social impact regardless of intent. The categories "economic" and "social" are analytic distinctions which more often than not refer to different aspects of the same concrete phenomena. A job is an economic entity to the extent that it provides the funds whereby a person may feed oneself and one's family. It is a social phenomenon to the extent that it permits the members of the family to stand erect because the funds were earned. It is also a social phenomenon to the extent that it provides its incumbent gratification and opportunity to develop as an individual.

None of the above is in any way to deny that certain programs are not "social" in their initial intent; but they need not stay that way. To some extent there has been a realization that specifically social activities have an impact on regular economic activities. Too often, however, it has been assumed that this impact consists solely of a lessening of business profits.[17]

---

[15]Raymond A. Bauer, and Dan H. Fenn, Jr., "What *is* a Corporate Social Audit?", *Harvard Business Review*, January-February 1973, pp. 37-49.

[16]For example, we have had the privilege of seeing drafts of the report being prepared by the Committee on Social Measurement of the AICPA. This group has concluded that such a matrix is the *logical* format that an audit will eventually take. Being sensible persons, however, they regard "eventually" as a long way off.

[17]We have previously indicated that this is the perception of some social commentators. It is a virtually unanimous perception of line operators who are asked to undertake such activities. David Kiser's thesis on the implementation of consumer protection programs reveals that this perception produces distinctive distortions of the resource allocation process. c.f. David Kiser, "Allocating Resources for Consumer Projects: The Corporate Dilemma," unpublished doctoral dissertation, Harvard Business School, May 1975.

New business opportunities may be perceived. A bank devising a free checking service for the elderly found a way to fashion a profitable service for its business clients. (See "The Golden Eagles" case series). A telephone company found that recycling directories would be hopelessly expensive. But in considering this possibility, it considered the alternative of reducing to one the number of directories delivered to multiphone dwellings, while giving the occupants the option of requesting as many additional directories as they desired. This effected a considerable financial saving while also reducing solid waste.

A public utility organized community relations teams across its operating divisions on the working level. This opened up lines of communication that had not existed previously and facilitated the handling of business problems cutting across the operating division. In at least some instances, OSHA compliance has reduced accidents to the point that insurance premiums have been lowered. Affirmative action programs have, as often as not, stimulated a review of personnel policies. The chief immediate impact of affirmative action in many organizations is the improvement of the personnel function.[18]

The distinction between social and economic issues breaks down in still more ways. The status of the issues is often indeterminate. In some instances community relations activities may be virtually devoid of immediate business advantage. In others, the business aspect will be dominant. How are we to judge a life insurance agent involved in community activities? In most instances, activities can be viewed through a business lens or a social lens, or both–and it makes a difference. This can be said of equal employment opportunity, procurement from minority suppliers, branch banking in the ghetto, employee health and safety, consumerism, pollution abatement, even corporate giving–as our example of supporting the education of minority engineer students illustrates. A bank was discouraged from closing a ghetto branch by community pressure. Having decided to keep the branch open, it reconsidered it as a business operation. A year later, after the facility had been improved physically, it was clearly a profitable enterprise.

We are in no sense taking the pollyannish position that virtue inevitably produces economic rewards, that doing good means doing well. Rather we are arguing that there is little merit in treating social and economic issues as though they were clearly separable from each other. To miss what they have in common is to serve neither well.[19] Enforcing the discipline that ensures that social issues are seen in both perspectives is a management skill that our cases will document is far from universal.

Not only is any project or program begun in response to a social issue likely to have an economic component, the very execution of that project is likely to demand most of the skills and procedures required for the execution of regular business activities. The problem of scanning the environment for changing consumer values is not much different from scanning it for other emergent social demands. On the level of implementation, the

---

[18]cf. "University of Pennsylvania" case series.

[19]Admittedly, to fail to see what is distinctive is no more advantageous, but that fault is less frequent. However, Kiser did find in his study of the management of consumer affairs that line managers tried to fit new projects into old molds. This made them more acceptable and easy to handle, but ran the risk of distorting their purpose. In a later chapter we will again allude to the problems caused by the tendency to prematurely absorb social issues to existing practices.

institutionalization of *any* new policy has certain features in common with any other new policy in a given organization. The establishment of a corporate-wide purchasing policy faces many of the same organizational problems as does a policy of improved health and safety. From either, one can learn lessons applicable to the other. In one business firm, the staff person in charge of implementing equal employment policy had recently been in charge of establishing uniformity in the accounting procedures in the several divisions of the firm, many of which had been acquired in recent years. He commented: "Basically it is the same problem."

While our concern has been substantively with social issues, we believe that the general phenomenon which we have been studying is that of the modern corporation learning to institutionalize novelty. It may seem odd, given the age of the corporation as an institution, that such learning is necessary, but a majority of large firms have acquired new organizational forms in the last decade or so. They have little experience in institutionalizing corporate-wide policies. Where new organizational forms are not a consideration, the firm is required to acquire skills and knowledge that fall outside its regular competencies.

We are witnessing the development of a responsive corporation, which–if it is in fact learning–should be increasingly capable of handling new issues whether they be "business" or "social." It is reasonable to expect the development of a new breed of managers. They will probably have different values, as has been rather widely suggested. But, probably more importantly, they will be accustomed to and skilled at organizational change.

Finally, despite the fact that the society is insisting on evaluating business firms in terms other than their ability to deliver goods and services at a profit, the society is still dependent on the business firm for these same goods and services and, for that matter, on the profits, to the extent that they supply the necessary capital for the operation and development of the firm and supply taxes for the operation of the nonprofit sector. Social critics of the business firm have been reluctant to face this issue and have generally regarded it as a ruse for taking the heat off of the firm. Yet, it would be unwise to ask the corporation to do new things without attending to their impact on the corporation's ability to do that which is inescapably its prime responsibility.

THE EVOLVING CORPORATION AND ITS ROLE

When we talk about changing expectations of any institution, we are talking about a change in its role by the very definition of what a social role is. Classically, the existence of the business firm was justified if it delivered goods and services which customers bought under free market conditions. If it survived, it was filling its social role, and its existence justified itself. It is a matter of common and continuous observation that this condition has not existed for a very long time, minimally for many decades. Market conditions are admittedly imperfect. Price competition has been supplemented or supplanted by competition via product development, superior skills in distribution and marketing, and the like. Ownership and management have become divorced. And so on. And so on.

It is safe to say that no new rationale has been developed to take the place of the classical one,[20] and what remains of the classical rationale clearly is being challenged frontally. If there is anything unambiguous about today's criticism of business, it is that its existence is not deemed to be justified by its ability to provide and sell goods and services at a profit. It is true, as we have already noted, that there are conservative pockets of resistance to this critique, but they are of little guidance in a world in which they are becoming manifestly irrelevant.

Social philosophers, legal scholars, and economic and political theorists will undoubtedly continue an avid search for a new consistent rationale for the firm's existence. But in the absence of such a consensus on the firm's social role, there is unlikely to be a logically neat rationale for its responsiveness. Hence, we favor a more empirical approach. We would like to put forth the case that it may be more useful to proceed pragmatically, observing how the role of the firm in its corporate form is in fact changing, and extend the hope that this empirical understanding might also eventually facilitate our formulation of the rationale that does not exist.

A few things seem clear to us. One of these is that the business firm is being held responsible for the consequences of its actions in ways which have no clearly defined relationship to intention or to prior conceptions of its responsibilities. In a word, it is being held responsible for its social impact, but at present there are no guidelines which we can evoke with confidence to say what the limits of those responsibilities are or how they may be reached.

The implications of the above paragraph can be somewhat staggering. This is clearest if we think of it in the context ordinarily associated with business planning. Strategic planning is dominated by means-ends analysis. Viable objectives are established, and a strategy is devised to achieve them. If the firm is to take seriously the notion that it, or business at large, will be held responsible for the social impact of what it does, then means-ends analysis must be supplemented by cause-effect analysis: e.g., "If we do this, what will the consequences be?" In an article in the *Harvard Business Review* in 1965, Professor Robert Austin[21] argued that the historical failure of business to think in such cause-effect terms had resulted in large scale social impacts which in turn forced the body politic to turn around and regulate business in unsuspected and unpleasant ways.

The logic of cause-effect analysis of business actions is exactly that of the new art of technology assessment, which says that we should anticipate "all" the consequences of a new technology and evaluate them as well as consider "all" the alternate technologies for accomplishing the same purpose. Any person who has attempted this art—or is naturally gifted with common sense—will see that these are words more easily put on paper than into practice.

While our present perception of the scope of the potential social impacts of business has no boundaries, happily it has focuses. These focuses are the constituencies of business, most prominent of which are employees, customers, owners, vendors, the immediate community, and the larger community. One proposition that has been gaining

[20] For a classic statement of lack of a new rationale for the existence of the firm see Edward Mason, "The Apologetics of 'Managerialism'," *Journal of Business*, January, 1958.

[21] Robert W. Austin, "Who Has the Responsibility for Social Change—Business or Government?", *Harvard Business Review*, July-August, 1965, pp. 45-52.

currency is that the "social responsibility" of business may be defined in terms of its impact on these constituencies.[22] This is a position with which we can concur. We would extend this proposition further and contend that the future role of business will be found in the future relationship of business to these constituencies, and this "role" will be determined by the way in which these relationships are worked out.

Table A is a matrix, as complete as we have been able to make, that displays the areas of impact of the business firm on its constituencies. Perhaps the ultimate definition of business responsibility would be that a firm should have seriously considered the consequences of its actions in each of the cells of this matrix, and the ultimate in a "social audit" would be a matrix of this sort with all the entries in the cells completed[23]—another mind-boggling proposition to contemplate.

TABLE A

ACTIVITIES \ CONSTITUENCIES	EMPLOYEES	CUSTOMERS	OWNERS	VENDORS	IMMEDIATE COMMUNITY	LARGER COMMUNITY
PRODUCTS						
PRODUCTION						
MARKETING						
FINANCE						
FACILITY LOCATION						
R & D						
NEW BUSINESS DEVELOPMENT						
GOVERNMENT RELATIONS						
SPECIAL PROGRAMS						

Concentration on these areas of interaction between business and its constituencies will not only prove useful in the long run for understanding the evolving corporate role, it will also be useful in the short run in considering immediate problems of corporate responsiveness.

[22]This presumably will be the position of the AICPA Committee on Social Measurement when it completes its work.

[23]The origins, responsibility, and credit for many of these emerging ideas is impossible to document. There is an invisible college of corporate staff, professionals (particularly public accountants), and academics who have been sharing and shaping ideas in recent years to the extent that the assignment of individual credit would probably be inappropriate even where it conceivably could be done.

Basically, we are proposing a sociological rather than a legal or philosophical definition of the role of the corporation. It seems to us that the customary objective of a legal or philosophical definition is to define a single role for the firm in the context of one overarching entity, the society as a whole. Even though we have conveniently ignored the complication of multinationality, it seems to us that to attempt such a single definition flies in the face of what is happening.

It makes more sense to conceive of the business firm as the central element of a role set in which a new pattern of relationships among the elements is evolving. Each of the parties, either directly or via volunteer spokesmen (e.g., consumerists) is pressing its interests. Presumably, these various elements of the role set are moving toward some state of relative equilibrium. The firm will have to develop the capacity to manage this demanding set of relationships. In part, as we shall see in the chapter on staff specialists, this will consist of structural changes to provide for the internal representation of new interests and issues. It will consist also of the ability to monitor and anticipate the impact of the firm's actions on those interests and to negotiate conflicts between the firm's interests and those of its constituencies.

Chapter Two
The Fluid Scene

When we turned our full attention to the problem of corporate responsiveness several years ago, we wondered whether we were dealing with a transitory phenomenon which would within a matter of a few years be a rather interesting blip on the pages of history. We have been surprised on two fronts.

As our discussion of the humanizing and activizing of society clearly implies, we have concluded that social demands that business be accountable for a wider range of its impacts than has been traditional is part of a very general social trend which will occupy our attention for many decades. On the other hand, the specific substantive issues are very dynamic. New issues develop rapidly, and old issues change their nature. It is to this latter, dynamic character of the corporate scene that we turn our attention in the first portion of this chapter. We cannot pretend to give a definitive treatment of the changing corporate environment. We will concentrate more on trying to communicate the dynamic nature of the social demands, and of the issues involved. Later in the chapter we will speculate on the impact of the recession and a resource-scarce economy on corporate responsiveness, and on the compatibility of this movement with such an economy.

PROFITABILITY AND RESPONSIBILITY

Perhaps the most amusing of the changes we have observed had to do with the relatively free-flowing debate over the relationship of social responsibility of corporations and the profitability of corporations. Some commentators argued that since being socially responsible costs money, one should expect responsible companies to show a decrease in financial performance. This was the basis of Linowes's proposal that corporations be given credit for the costs of social responsibility. But others argued that only profitable companies could afford social responsibility, and therefore, social responsibility was a by-product of profitability. No, said, Messrs. Marlin and Bragdon in a famous article.[1] Companies are profitable because they are responsible. Responsibility is a symptom of foresight, and foresight means good and profitable management. Unwilling to let bad enough alone, we got into the fray. Ackerman suggested that expanding companies might be profitable because there were many opportunities for promotion and the line managers paid more attention to what the boss (who was more enlightened than they) said because they were looking for promotion. Bauer suggested that profitable companies might be more responsible because they were competently run, had the business side of the enterprise in hand, and had the managerial time and skill to address themselves to being responsible.

Milton Moskowitz, editor of the newsletter *Business and Society*, put the question to empirical test. He developed a portfolio of "responsible" companies (and later of "irresponsible" companies) and tracked the performance of their stocks. In the first issue of 1973, he heralded the performance of his portfolio with the headline: "Social Responsibility Stocks Outperform the Market." His stocks rose 16.9% in 1972 as compared to 14.5% for Dow Jones, 14% for the New York Stock Exchange, and 15.6% for Standard and Poor's. Virtue triumphs. But not for long. The first issue of 1974 bore the headline: "Social Responsibility Portfolio Collapses." His portfolio dropped 26.3%, as compared to 20.5% for the "irresponsible" companies, 16.6% for Dow Jones, 19.6% for New York Stock Exchange, and 17.4% for Standard and Poor's!

During 1974 one of his "responsible" companies, CNA Financial, continued to slip badly, until in December it was taken over. A week before Christmas the CNA Director of Social Policy was fired and his department wiped out. He commented, "I would have complained to my boss, but he was fired the day before, or I would have complained to the CEO, but he was fired the day before that."

While we were writing the first draft of the above passage a letter arrived from Mr. Moskowitz in which he announced that his newsletter would not appear in 1975 or thereafter because of rising costs. Since Moskowitz changed the makeup of his portfolio from year to year, we cannot know exactly what his verdict would be for the year 1974. However, we can get an approximation by looking at the 1974 performance of his 1973 portfolios. We find that the three major indexes each dropped 29%-30%, while the "socially responsible" portfolio dropped 46%, and the "socially irresponsible" portfolio only 13%!

One might be tempted by these data toward further speculation. We think it more sensible, however, to conclude that the tale we have recounted is best seen as reflecting simplistic thinking about a complex topic. Almost any one of the arguments introduced, and a few more that we refrain from raising, are sufficiently plausible that each must to some extent be relevant to some of the behavior of some of the multitude of U.S. corporations.

In this instance, changes in the underlying economy—to which we will return below in some detail—served to highlight the intellectual immaturity of this area of inquiry. As we study the phenomenon of corporate responsiveness, our perceptions change as our

---

[1] *Risk Management*, Vol. 19, #4, April 1972.

understanding increases. But the phenomenon itself is also changing. In this instance, change in the phenomenon showed that the initial perceptions were naive.

CHANGING NATURE OF THE ISSUES

We have treated the changing nature of the issues once before and we will treat it once more again. In the context of the first chapter, we dealt with the shift of emphasis from concern with societal issues for which the individual business firm could be considered only remotely responsible to issues which are the direct consequence of the actions of firms. We did this in part to show why some observers have missed the shift in issues, and in a larger part to justify our preference for the term "responsiveness" as better reflecting the close relationship between social issues and economic activities.

In Chapter 3 we will again deal with the changing nature of individual issues, specifically their passage through the zone of discretion, as a generic factor to be considered in the firm's response to them. Here we will concentrate more on some of the qualitative changes which are characteristic of the recent and current scene in order to communicate our perception of them to students and practitioners. We do this in the hope that this perspective will help orient them toward future changes and encourage teachers to include additional issues as they seem relevant.

Economic developments beginning with the oil crisis of 1973 have had a major impact on the issues, and we will turn attention to these developments shortly. Before that we will discuss, albeit in a somewhat discoursive style, some of the changes that characterize individual issues.

One might be tempted to argue that the present social issues impinging on the corporation are ones with long historical roots. This is an omnipresent temptation rooted in the desire not to be perceived as lacking in time perspective. But in this instance one is more struck by the discontinuities than by the continuities. A belching smokestack was once seen as the symbol of industrial prosperity and jobs for the community. In the early seventies one corporation which had a mural of its main plant in the lobby of its corporate offices had the smoke from the plant's chimney painted out. Reserve Mining, only a couple of decades ago, was cited very favorably for reviving the economy of the upper peninsula of Minnesota and for its care in dumping its tailings in a "safe" part of Lake Superior. Today, it is excoriated for poisoning the waters with asbestos–a danger that was once unknown.

Well within the memory of the older of the two authors, women were criticized for "taking a job that a man needs." Disposable containers were desirable until quite recently. Cheap and profligate (we can afford it!) use of energy was eulogized. Plastics were a triumph of our civilization rather than nonbiodegradable solid waste. In the market place, the doctrine of let the buyer beware has been replaced by the doctrine of let the seller beware. Employers were only recently forbidden by law to keep records of the race of their employees. Now it is required in order to develop affirmative action plans. One could go on, but we believe the point is made.

Probably the major *qualitative* reversals have taken place. They are consistent with what we labelled earlier as an agenda for a rationalized humane society. But changes continue to take place within the framework of this broad pattern. Some changes are logical extrapolations of previous ones. Equal access to jobs for minorities was logically followed by the demand for equal promotional opportunities. Demand for opportunities for minorities was followed by demand for opportunities for women, and now, for underprivileged ethnic groups. The notion that an employment system should be nondiscriminatory has been supplemented by the further notion that employment systems should compensate for past discrimination by special training and by hiring and promoting those who are "qualifiable," even though they are not at the moment "qualified."

Consumer protection legislation has proliferated, spawning more than two dozen Federal laws since 1966. This spread has been somewhat inhibited in the political process, as in the instance of stalled legislation for the establishment of some form of Federal consumer protection agency. But it is equally marked by a remorseless forward progress, which from some viewpoints seems constrained only by the ingenuity of consumer spokespersons in identifying new issues. One presumes, but cannot be certain, that this agenda is finite. However, in 1975 there were still a number of items for which legislation was being pushed.

One who follows the doings and thinkings of activists reasonably closely can be both edified and dismayed (sometimes simultaneously) at the ingenuity with which they can pursue logical extrapolations. Our favorite example is a proposal that the coloring of butter be prohibited because a richly colored butter is perceived as more nutritious than one less richly colored. On this basis, it was reasoned that artificial coloring of butter constitutes unfair economic exploitation!

For the future, the area in which logical extrapolation of the past may more likely be pursued is that of corporate disclosure. The topic of disclosure of corporate information is one of considerable scope and cannot be covered in detail here. But one thread of development can be used to illustrate our point. Information which in one sense is "social" in nature has been interpreted as being material to investment decisions. In the summer of 1972, the SEC issued a ruling that required corporations to reveal any substantial liabilities they had with respect to pollution control, whether these liabilities were a result of adverse legal or regulatory proceedings, or of existing inadequacies which made the firm vulnerable to such proceedings. Given this precedent, it took very little imagination to foresee that the same logic could be applied to vulnerabilities for failure to comply with equal employment opportunity regulations. By 1974, activist groups were arguing, and often successfully, before courts and regulatory agencies that information on minority and female employment were material to investment decisions as well as in the public interest, and, therefore, should be disclosed. This same logic could be applied to employee morale surveys as indicators of vulnerability to labor unrest, and to OSHA compliance information—particularly if a few companies suffer serious financial losses either from failure in OSHA compliance or in liability suits for accidents or occupational health problems.[2] The practitioner ought to assume that where a precedent has been set, someone will soon try to pursue its implications in new areas.

---

[2]On February 12, 1975, both *The New York Times* and *The Wall Street Journal* reported that the SEC would hold hearings on possible disclosure of "environmental and other matters of primarily social rather than financial concern." *The New York Times*, February 12, 1975, page 47.

Some changes represent the "logical" convergence of more than one issue. OSHA legislation has been on the books for several years. Until 1973, all sources, including our own interviews in companies, suggested that compliance was not being taken particularly seriously. Critics in general felt that OSHA inspection and enforcement capabilities were not sufficient to cause serious concern on the part of firms that chose to drag their feet.

In the meantime, the issue of the quality of work life has been a fairly lively one in various forms. The consensus until 1973 was, however, that it was not one over which labor unions were ready to fight with any militance. Quality of work life had been on the list of issues brought to the bargaining table, but it had invariably given way to higher priority matters of wages, pensions, and the like. But, by mid-1974, apparently some threshold had been overcome. The AFL-CIO was suing the Labor Department to enforce stricter conformance to OSHA. But a matter of somewhat greater novelty, a series of unions, led by the Oil, Chemical, and Atomic Workers, followed by the Rubber Workers, and the UAW, built health and safety into their contracts. The Oil Workers actually went on strike over the issue. The participation of the unions is very active. Illustrative of this activity is the fact that the UAW contract provides for full-time union health and safety officers.[3]

Thus skepticism about the seriousness of OSHA compliance had been widespread. But suddenly a new source of enforcement entered the scene, insofar as we can tell, in a surprising fashion, and the picture changed categorically for a number of major industries.

As issues get acted on their implications become clearer. In some instances this means that they gain additional support. One of our case series, The Golden Eagles shows how the issue of free checking for the elderly gained support as various officers of the bank began to see its business advantages. Some aerospace firms which are particularly skilled at handling affirmative action see it as a competitive weapon in bidding on government contracts.[4] More generally recognized, however, is that evolving implications generate opposition in the classic manner of thesis producing antithesis, and hopefully synthesis.

It is important to note here we are referring to reactions to the intrinsic implications of an evolving issue as they become clearer, and not to the impact of changing political and economic conditions on reaction to the issue. As we shall see shortly, the two circumstances often interact, but here we are dealing with that which has happened or may be presumed to have happened in the absence of a recession and a change in the national administration and government policies. Classic examples of what we are talking about are white male backlash to equal employment opportunity policies for minorities and females, communities protesting the closing of plants for pollution reasons, and Congress's revision of OSHA laws as they applied to small businesses.

In a sense, our case studies of the implementation of social policies in business firms are a special case of counteractions to the implications of social issues. Here we find mainly middle managers reacting to the implications for themselves and their operating units.

---

[3] See: "More Unions Devote Efforts to Eliminating Hazards in Workplace," *The Wall Street Journal*, August 19, 1974.

[4] "Acting Affirmatively to End Job Bias," *Business Week*, January 27, 1975, pp. 94-102.

What we are dealing with here is a form of dynamic conservatism. (The term "inertia", which is often used, is too passive to communicate the nature of this resistance.) Proponents of particular issues often view such resistances with apocalyptic dismay as though the entire cause has gone or is going down the drain. At a minimum, such dynamic resistances are natural phenomena to be expected. They pose problems of decision and/or management for those officials whose responsibility is to implement the issue or shape policy. At a maximum, however, such resistances must also be recognized as potential corrective forces responding to implications which had not been given adequate consideration in the formulation of the issue. We would take the EPA's policy of spelling out drastic plans for the implementation of air quality standards for various metropolitan areas as a deliberate but sly device for forcing a political reconsideration of the existing legislation by spelling out its implications.

Of these "antithetical" reactions we can, in summary, say a few things. They are inevitable and natural since no policy benefits everyone equally. When they occur, they represent legitimate problems which the policy maker and the executive must deal with as their responsibility. The extent to which such opposition should be met with overpowering force, mediated with, or capitulated to depends so much on the specifics of the situation that we can say nothing of a general nature about it. We can say this, however: in our perception, both supporters and opposers of issues have over-interpreted the outcomes of skirmishes or minor battles as the winning or losing of the entire war. To some extent, this is a reflection of a general underappreciation of the complexity and long-time perspective of such issues—a tendency that permeates all our contacts with the topic of corporate responsiveness.

CHANGES IN CONTEXT; RECESSION

But, as we have already noted, all these new issues affecting the corporation are being worked out in a social, political, economic context which is in itself dynamic. The impact of this dynamic context has been highly diverse. The most dramatic contextual change has been, of course, the worsening of economic conditions. Recessions are a recurring phenomena and much of what we have to say about the recession of the mid-1970s may prove to be relevant for those yet to come. It has generally been interpreted as dampening the "social responsibility movement."[5] This is simplistic.

The evidence cited for the negative impact of the recession on corporate responsiveness is of several sorts. In recent years several highly visible and popular corporate public affairs officers have left or lost their jobs. And, in early 1975, the grapevine is flowing with the news of the dramatic abolition of the CNA staff group and the dismissal of its popular and highly visible head, David Christensen. The incidence of such events is sufficiently low, and—even if their interpretation were unambiguous—they could be offset by counter examples. Some companies have stepped up their efforts.

There is a certain amount of data available, and it belies the idea of broad cutbacks. A personal communication from Douglas Ross of the Conference Board indicates that a

[5] cf., the editorial "A Social Lapse," in *The Wall Street Journal,* January 17, 1975.

survey of the public affairs officers of several dozen major corporations found the predominant state of affairs was a "holding pattern." The Human Resources Network surveyed its "Key 75" representatives of *Fortune's* 500. As of December 1974, about half were increasing their 1975 budget above the 1974 level, and less than one quarter were reducing their budgets.[6] It is not possible to make a complete calibration against inflation, but the maintenance of at least constant budget levels in the face of falling profits indicates something less than a full retreat.

The recession seems to be accelerating a trend that was on the way before the economy started on its way down, namely, the shift away from external problems of the society to those issues which involve the firm's operations more directly. On several issues involving the firm's operations, reformers have expressed pessimism. One is pollution control. There is no question but that there has been or is contemplated selective relaxation of control of pollution control standards, a deferral of deadlines on automotive emissions, a relaxation of emission requirements for utilities, the failure of stringent strip mining legislation, etc. We will defer our interpretative comments until a little later.

Another area which social critics view with pessimism is equal employment opportunity. There is a widespread exhibition of concern that the gains for minorities and women will be lost as employment slacks and layoffs occur. And this indeed has been a problem. Layoffs have been made according to seniority. But this trend has also met with opposition. Firms with commitments are usually trying to meet them despite adverse circumstances. And there seems to be no slackening of legal and regulatory action. Court suits continue, and regulators reaffirm their resolution.

One company faced with across-the-board layoffs realized that it had a considerable amount of dead wood among older employees. It realized that its slack personnel system failed to document the poor performance of these older employees and that they would therefore be subject to suits for age discrimination if these older employees were laid off.

The classic confrontation is that between affirmative action and the seniority provisions of union contracts. Here, again, yesterday's "good" becomes today's "bad." But it would be foolish indeed to contend that suddenly one should give zero value to the arguments which lie behind union seniority provisions and which were the cause célèbre of a previous generation of reformers.

The conflict between union seniority and equal employment opportunity and affirmative action has its origins well before the onset of the recession, and a number of quite celebrated and protracted cases have been involved in the resolution of this conflict. In the context of the recession, the regulatory agencies and the courts have been unwilling to bow before seniority rights without resistance.[7] The remedies suggested vary from monetary compensation to the construction of dummy seniority lists to reflect what might have been if there had been no past discrimination. Since many cases are still

---

[6]Human Resources Network, "Corporate Responsibility Key 75 Survey Report," Vol. 1, No. 1, January 1975, Philadelphia, Pennsylvania.

[7]A handy review which gives an informative coverage of various instances in which affirmative action has come in conflict with other rights, and a good notion of the issues involved will be found in "Job Discrimination, 10 Years Later." *The New York Times*, Section 3, p. 1, Sunday, November 10, 1974.

before the courts, the final resolution of this conflict is not clear. What is clear is that it is being worked out.[8]

At this point we will restrict ourselves to the limited evaluative comment that in the case of both pollution control and equal employment opportunity, the impact of the recession has been to accelerate and accentuate the confrontation of conflicting issues which were already in progress. Again, we defer broader evaluation until later.

Certainly, activists have not let up,[9] and in 1974 they had unparalleled success in persuading firms to disclose information that was previously withheld.[10] One of the consequences of the economic turndown has been to broaden the range of issues with which corporations are concerned. Suddenly, at the end of 1973, scarcity of energy and materials became a national issue and one of direct practical concern to most businesses. By April of 1974 "using up natural resources" jumped to a close second place–only four percentage points (54% as compared to 58%) behind the staid and true "discrimination against minorities"–in a poll of activists who were asked what problems business should work hard at.[11] By the end of 1974 conservation of energy and materials by business had become priority items for the general public.

The impact of these issues on corporations has been complex. Certain industries–the oil industry being an obvious one–have come under intense criticism. Energy labelling of products has begun and is likely to spread. The increased cost of energy and materials is a direct stimulus to their conservation in the process of producing goods and services. There are also various pressures toward producing products that use less energy and materials. Some of this pressure is in the form of threatened legislation, and some in the prospect that energy economy, at least, will be a competitive factor in the sales of products.

Obviously, the issues of energy and materials shortages are ones that invite a fine-honed debate over whether these are issues of social responsibility or of practical business importance. The reader will recognize that we have carefully positioned ourselves to reply that such debates are more of aesthetic than practical value. As a practical business matter they introduce new dimensions with which business traditionally has not had to contend. From a social point of view, they reflect a major national problem on which business actions will impact; they reflect social and political forces which will impinge on the conduct of business, and they have even stimulated some rather intense though minor sentiment for the nationalization of certain businesses in a society which has generally broadly resisted this notion.[12]

---

[8]As of the time of writing, seniority was winning in the courts. See: "An Anti-bias Drive Yields to Seniority," *Business Week*, February 7, 1975, p. 24.

[9]cf., "Minding the Corporate Conscience 1974," *Economic Priorities Report*, Vol. 5, No. 1, Council on Economic Priorities, New York, 1975.

[10]Ibid., p. 26.

[11]"Social Activists Views on Business and the Role of Corporate Boards of Directors," *ORC Public Opinion Index*, April 1974.

[12]Almost all poll data of recent years show that even while criticism of business has grown in intensity and universality, virtually no one favors nationalization. In a Harris poll of July 17-21, 1974, 82% said that if left alone, business would be greedy and selfish at the public expense, but only 11% of this sample favored government taking over most big businesses.

The recession has brought other issues to the fore. The agenda of one corporate committee meeting we attended in early 1975 was interesting in this respect. The first item of concern was retirement policy which took on some urgency because of a combination of recent Federal pension legislation combined with the prospect that the recession would probably prompt early retirement for certain personnel. Then the discussion went to the question of how to maintain affirmative action goals in the face of "negative hiring" and a strongly unionized workforce. Next, attention was devoted to the fact that the company had so little recent experience in furloughs, layoffs, and dismissals for general economic reasons that it had no established policies for such matters and was consequently getting into difficulties. The same was true of several plant closings which occurred rapidly as business fell off drastically. One or two plants had previously been closed because of pollution control requirements. These closures had been handled very satisfactorily from both the standpoint of the company and the employees, but this had been done when there was a lead time of a year or more. There was no policy to guide operating management when a plant had to be closed quickly. Finally, attention was called to the fact that employees who were furloughed could not understand why the company was not able to afford to continue to pay their insurance premiums while they were on furlough, although the corporation was continuing to give hundreds of thousands of dollars to philanthropy.

Admittedly, the above is a rather rich dose, but all these issues did come up in one two-hour meeting. While the response may be that of an unusually committed company, the agenda does illustrate our point that the impact of the recession has not been solely that of dampening the impact of issues on corporations. There is some dampening, some complicating, and some expansion of issues.

Up to this point we have been chary in our interpretation of the impact of the recession. We have noted descriptively several changes resulting from the recession. There does not seem to be any substantial net reduction in budgets and staffs devoted to external affairs. There is some selective easing of enforcement of pollution control requirements. It would not be surprising if there were easing of some other legislated requirements if difficulty of compliance could be directly linked to economic conditions. Compliance with affirmative action goals faces directly recession-linked difficulties, but this has resulted more in a sharpening of issues than a relaxation of pressure for compliance.

New issues have arisen as a result of material and energy shortages and of the recession. On the whole, we suspect that at this point many of these new issues can be ignored. Except as they are of practical importance for the organization, activist pressure is not likely to be effective. On the other hand, for committed organizations, they have increased the total organizational burden of being "responsive." In the meantime, additional consumer legislation is before the Congress.

What overall evaluation are we to put on these developments? We would say that at a minimum they cannot be interpreted confidently as a defeat for or reversal of the broad movement toward demanding of greater institutional accountability which we sketched out in the first chapter. There are, in movements of this sort, skirmishes represented by individual contested events, such as the fight over the Alaska pipeline. And there are "battles" which represent the conflict of major issues in a particular context. Here we may cite environmental protection vis-à-vis the need for energy and the need for economic recovery, or the desire for safe foods vis-à-vis the overall availability of food, industrial health and safety vis-à-vis the need for jobs, equal employment opportunity vis-à-vis job security for those with seniority, and so on.

In a situation in which two values are in conflict, it is no more than to be expected that the one which is under situational threat should be of increased concern. Those who see major social change as progressing in a linear uninterrupted fashion—whether they favor the movement toward corporate responsiveness or wish it would go away—are mistaken.

Major changes, such as those we seem to be witnessing, invariably run against other well-established values or institutional arrangements, many of which are, at least to some extent, necessary for the continuance of the society. As established values and institutions are threatened, there will be cycles of reaction. Even in revolutionary situations (witness the U.S.S.R. and China), the pattern of change is that of a secular trend in the new direction, but one that is characterized by cycles of backward and forward movement.

This is not to argue that major social movements are never reversed, but only that loss of a battle cannot, per se, be taken as the loss of the war any more than can the loss of a skirmish. At this stage of the movement for the humanizing of society, one needs to look at the relative strength of the underlying forces.

The strength of the movement lies, in part, in the moral basis for many entitlements which have come to be generally accepted and, in part, in better understanding of environmental and ecological issues, as well as of many health issues. The vulnerability of the movement for the humanizing of society lies in the fact that it is based on aspirations nurtured by a belief in affluence and virtually unlimited resources. The widespread perception of resource scarcity could not help but pose a challenge to this movement. But this challenge is not generally to the values of the movement, but to the practicality of its timetable and to its level of aspiration—at least in the short haul.

While an economic recession may slow the timetable of the movement, and even lower the level of some aspirations, it is difficult indeed to envision the circumstances which would reverse certain trends of the recent past: the recognition of equality of rights for minorities and women; our understanding of complex ecological processes and of the factors that have a long-term and subtle impact on health; the rights of consumers to be informed and to get safe and reliable products. In fact, all of these values, notions, and ideas are entirely compatible with and advantageous to the development of a reasonably rational allocation of scarce resources. Whether this will be properly perceived and implemented cannot be taken for granted, but it is reasonable to expect that at least by trial and error the new values and aspirations *may* eventually be integrated into a resource-scarce economy.

The present period cannot be seen entirely negatively by reasonable proponents of a humanized society. The liability of a perception of unlimited affluence is that it permits the preservation of the illusion that all values can be pursued as though they were absolute, as though there were no necessity for tradeoffs with other values. While such an illusion is never total, the recent perception of resource limitations has accelerated the recognition of many conflicts among the new values and older ones which are still cherished. For example, in a recent conference in Washington, a consumer spokesperson argued for absolute safety in food products. Other participants countered that the pursuit of absolute safety meant lesser available food production, and therefore increased starvation.[13] Whether the issue was properly posed or not, arguments of this sort are now taking place at an accelerated rate. Both sides as well as interested bystanders ought to facilitate the quality of such arguments rather than regret their existence.

Our personal expectation is that as the recession continues, those demands which are legislated will continue basically in force. The trend toward concentration on matters which are more directly associated with the firm's operations and perceivable self-interest will continue at the expense of corporate philanthropy and efforts to address social problems not directly related to the firm. We expect firms to emerge from the recession better equipped to deal with those social issues to which they are committed. To some extent, this will be facilitated by the recession itself. The added complications introduced by the recession have forced many firms to reassess their basic capabilities to handle many problems of personnel, quality control, product design, and the like. Whether from this consolidated base concerns will again expand to issues less directly related with the firm, will depend on specifics we cannot anticipate. To the extent that it does happen, we would guess it will be done with greater coherence with the firm's strategy and with greater organizational skill.

IMPLICATIONS FOR THE CORPORATION

Since we have discussed the impact of the state of the economy on the agenda for humanizing society, it seems appropriate to close this chapter with some speculations of the effects of humanizing society on the performance of the economy. One way of thinking about this latter impact is that we are building social value into the production of goods and services. If factories pollute less, we accrue benefits of health, aesthetics, and the longer term viability of our planet. Safer products mean less injury. More reliable products mean more satisfaction, and less haphazard costs incurred by the buyers of "lemons." Occupational health and safety means just what it says. Better community relations mean a more harmonious society. Equal employment opportunity means more than it says; it means also the wiping out of second-class status for some members of society, and corresponding adjustments–and hopefully a better self-concept–on the part of those who had been previously under-privileged. More truthful advertising, marketing, and warranty policies, again, mean a more efficient economy, a more harmonious society, and less exploitation of those who cannot protect themselves. Improved pension benefits increase personal security and provide a more dignified and satisfying old age. The reader can expand this list as he or she chooses.

While we will argue from time to time that discussions of "social responsibility" focus too exclusively on monetary costs (other resources, such as executive time, energy, and skill, are often more important), the fact is that in the net, these benefits involve at least short-term costs, are in varying degrees deferred and, to a large extent, accrue outside the system of production. While some efficiencies occur even in the short run, the net immediate effect of achieving such benefits must, initially at least, be to increase the cost of traditional goods and services. The Brookings Institution has estimated that the

[13] cf., report in, *Of Consuming Interest*, Vol. 8, No. 11, 11 December 1974.

costs of pollution control, health, and safety, over the next ten years will contribute 0.4% inflation per year.[14] If we were to add to this the operating costs of pollution control, product safety, and other social programs, we would venture the horseback guess that building social value into the production of goods and services must, in the near future, add about 1% to 2% per year to the Consumer Price Index. Presumably this is a "good thing" if it is recognized for what it is and not seen as inflation in the traditional sense.

This is not to argue that all the benefits are worth their costs or, conversely, that all the benefits cost what they are worth. These tradeoffs fall outside the market system, and to some extent they represent issues which are presently being fought out in the political arena. Nor is it to argue, as we shall shortly elaborate, that the short-term costs will not produce economic efficiencies. Rather the issue is that many of the efficiencies will accrue to the economy as a whole, and that many of those which accrue to the individual productive unit will be at least slightly deferred. As the cases in this book will illustrate, one of the consequences for operating managers who are called on to implement social policies is that they inevitably see the task as one that involves costs without foreseeable benefits to themselves (even though this is not always necessarily so). This very much colors the implementation process.

We have asserted previously that the agenda for the humanizing of society is compatible with the effective functioning of a resource-scarce society. With one version of the "humanization" of society, this is a tautology. Here we are referring to the program of those persons who advocate both a no-growth economy and a shift from material to nonmaterial values. Any net aggregate shift away from material values would produce a decreased demand for materials and energy by definition.[15] Hence, in this context, that particular version of a humanized society liquidates consideration of what we think is a more likely state of affairs, namely, that whatever the shifts in values may be, there will still be a sufficient demand for goods and services that limitations on economic resources will be an important issue.

Given an expanded agenda of "entitlements" in a situation of resource scarcity, the only conceivable place to look for a reconciliation of these two situations is through improved efficiency of those institutional arrangements that convert resources into the meeting of the human entitlements. Here, then, we must think of the society as a whole and of its individual institutions both in terms of their own efficiencies and of the efficiency of their role in the society.

This notion of increasing societal and institutional efficiency is far from a trivial one. If achievable, it will be difficult. We introduce it here only to indicate that it seems to be the only avenue to pursue that may reduce (but not eliminate) the pain of tradeoffs

---

[14] Various such estimates are reported in "The Surprisingly High Costs of a Safer Environment," *Business Week*, September 14, 1974, p. 103.

[15] There is one apparent exception, such as when a nonmaterial value demands the expenditure of resources of energy and materials. For example, to the extent that environmental protection is pursued for aesthetic reasons, and this involves an economic cost that would not otherwise be incurred, such a "non-material" value would pose demands of a material kind. From an economic point of view, such a value plays a role no different than the demand for bigger and better lollipops or weapons systems. To the extent that nonmaterial values require the consumption of energy and materials, the situation is identical to that which we deal with in the text.

in a resource-scarce situation, and to point out that it is at least in some respects consistent with the social demands being placed on business.[16]

We have hinted at some of these areas of compatibility. The "social values" which we referred to as being built into products and services produce systemic economic benefits, even though some may be fairly long deferred. The most deferred, of course, is the long-term viability of the ecosphere. Others pay off more quickly. More reliable and durable products, if the purchase of reliability and durability has been reasonably cost efficient, mean a more efficient overall economy. Safer products and workplaces and healthier environments, both at large and in the workplace, mean lower medical costs and a more productive work force. Equal employment opportunity means a more thorough and rational use of the skills of the work force. A better "quality of work life" may be a "directly consumable commodity," but the odds are that it will also produce a more productive work force.

To the extent that such benefits occur broadly, they would improve the efficiency of the economy in the overall. In part, they would also improve the efficiency of individual institutions including business firms.

There are additional ways in which the impingement of social issues on the firm bear on its economic efficiency and thereby on the efficiency of the economy as a whole. We use the term "bears on" because things may go either way, at least in the reasonably short run. A firm which bungles compliance with the law may incur lawsuits, economic penalities, and/or considerable internal dislocation. These may come about either through misjudgments as to whether or not they should comply and with what timing, and/or managerial ineptitude in carrying out their intention. Both the society and the firm pay costs for this. On the other hand, both benefit if these matters are handled expeditiously. To the extent that certain transformations are so nearly inevitable that they must be taken for granted, it is better for all parties if they are handled smoothly. In this context, social issues are not, per se, a source of institutional efficiency or inefficiency, but the development of managerial skills for handling them at least reduces the potential for inefficiency.

Some of the more important potentials for economic efficiency at the firm level are more indirect. As our cases will illustrate, grappling with social issues sometimes forces, and often encourages reexamination of regular business practices. There is no business function on which the handling of social issues does not impinge. We may begin with business strategy, go through production, product design, marketing, human resources, purchasing, quality control, public relations, government relations, community relations, and loop back to corporate philanthropy. In tackling some new social issue, the corporation often discovers that the business function which is relevant is deficient in the handling of its more traditional tasks. The social issues put the existing functions under stress and suggest ways in which their efficiency and effectiveness may be improved.[17]

---

[16] There is a considerable similarity between this argument and that developed by the Council on Trends and Perspectives of the U.S. Chamber of Commerce reported in *Economic Growth: New Views and Issues*, Washington, 1974. The arguments were developed independently.

[17] In this context we do not deal with such other consequences of dealing with social policies, such as the identification of new business opportunities. These opportunities are important considerations for the individual firm. However, they do not bear–or at least not very immediately–on increases in institutional efficiency, which is the matter we emphasize here.

This is not to argue that they always suggest the need or possibility of such improvements (though our guess is that it happens more frequently than not), nor are the opportunities always taken advantage of. We rest our case with an emphasis on the *potential,* since all we are arguing is the potential compatibility between the humanizing of society and a resource-scarce economy. Failure to recognize this potential may come either from unwise tradeoffs (paying for more than we get)—which is a matter for the political arena—or from lack of managerial skill and diligence in exploiting opportunities and avoiding undue costs. The latter of these problems is at least in part the subject matter of this book.

Lest our delineations of the *potential* for compatibility between the new demands on business under the banner of humanizing society and a resource-scarce economy be seen as simple-minded optimism, we should not leave this issue without a caveat. We mentioned in Chapter 1 the risk of prejudicing the basic business role of producing goods and services by overloading the firm with other responsibilities. The same applies to the economy as a whole. In the context of a resource-scarce economy, almost every one of the specific issues with which we are presently dealing has the potential for harm as well as for good. The potential for harm lies in unwise tradeoffs and it would be foolish to ignore the fact that that potential is real. Product reliability can be assured with gold-plated double-backup systems. Benefits which cost more than they are worth become increasingly disadvantageous as resources get scarce. And, there is a disposition for issue advocates to place an absolute or near absolute value on their cherished cause. The problem is, by definition, value laden, and will demand the utmost of discipline and skill.

Part Two

INTRODUCTION

This book is about the corporate response to the varied and changing demands of a complex society. It is written from a management perspective, not because we wish to criticize or praise those who direct business enterprises, but rather because the manager is ultimately the one who must shoulder the burdens of planning and implementing the corporation's response. Indeed, the overriding *responsibility* of the corporate leader to society and stockholder alike, in our view, is the development of policies and administrative skills that will enable the firm to respond effectively to social demands without destroying its capability to produce goods and services.

In Part Two we will describe the critical issues that should be considered in the discharge of this responsibility. Five in particular are significant.

First, social demands have strategic implications for the corporation that extend beyond the immediate costs of possible responses. Opportunities as well as risks may be apparent to the perceptive manager; an aggressive posture may be appropriate in some instances but not in others. Dealing with social change as though it were something apart from product-market policy is as confining as developing a marketing strategy without giving thought to potential competitive reactions.

Second, social responsiveness entails the management of a process through which public expectations are identified, placed in the context of other corporate concerns and, in some fashion, woven into the ways of doing business. The process itself is not readily apparent to the outside observer nor can it be understood by simply cataloging the firm's actions. The process is, however, amenable to influence by the manager who grasps the organizational implications of social demands.

Third, the management of social responsiveness calls for innovations in performance measurement. The social audit was first conceived as a means of public reporting analogous to the customary financial audit. In time, the difficulty of designing, conducting, and interpreting such audits has become apparent. So too has the paucity of appropriate information within the firm to guide the implementation of policy. Although less elegant than envisaged by some, social measurement systems are available in most large corporations today. How they are designed, introduced, and used raise important questions for the general manager as well as the systems expert.

Fourth, the corporation has had to contend with forces that at the outset it did not fully understand. Such a condition should not be surprising. Indeed, few social critics can claim a comprehensive knowledge of the consequences of their demands. A great deal must be learned about the issue—for ecology one must know how to measure pollution loads, what technologies to employ in treating effluent, what discharge standards to meet, and so forth. The corporation must monitor the issues, seeking new technical and administrative skills as public expectations change with time. Often these skills are provided by individuals whom we shall call "social issue specialists." The nature of their jobs, the constraints they work within, and the opportunities they have to exert influence are all vital considerations in securing flexible responses to social demands.

Finally, the response to most significant social issues requires the institutionalization of changes in the way decisions are made by operating managers in the field. Ultimately, if a revised corporate policy is to be implemented, what is expected of these managers must take that policy into account. Drawing an appropriate relationship between social responsiveness and executive performance measurement and evaluation is an extremely sensitive and difficult undertaking. This relationship—or its absence—exists, of course, in all organizations whether or not intended. The challenge for management is to insert and calibrate rewards and sanctions for social performance in a way that encourages the desired degree of responsiveness with as few unwanted side effects as possible.

The management of corporate social responsiveness involves attention to all of these factors, usually simultaneously. We have devoted a chapter to each as a means of developing the conceptual and practical skills particular to it. The material has been arranged to correspond approximately to the order we have observed issues to be raised in the corporation. Our intent is to achieve a cumulative impact structured in much the same way as learning takes place in the corporation. Nevertheless, the reader should not lose sight of the fact that the topics in each chapter are highly interrelated and he or she should not be surprised to find the cases following one chapter to be illustrative of issues raised in several other chapters as well.

Our vantage point within the firm will change from time to time. In some instances the view will be from the chief executive's window, looking out over the broad social environment and the full scope of the organization's relationship to it. In others, the perspective will be that of the lower level middle manager who has been caught between apparently conflicting demands on his time and resources. Social responsiveness has been likened to steering an ocean liner. Decisions made on the bridge to vary the direction and speed of travel are not immediately noticeable on the radar screen. Only in time does the ship respond. A complex management process is involved through which the activities of a great many people from the bridge to the engine room are organized and directed, and even then physical constraints impede the rapidity of movement. One cannot accurately understand how the ship operates by limiting investigation to reading the captain's log or interviewing the men firing the boilers.

A few words may be appropriate at this point on what may be expected from the text material in Part Two. If direct and clear-cut prescriptions are sought for reforming the social posture of the large corporation, the reader will be sorely disappointed. We would be naive to claim that we have hit upon a formula that assures a swift and painless means of assimilating the dictates of social change. On the other hand, we believe our approach has descriptive validity based on extensive field research, some of it summarized in Part One. The reader may not always find the corporate condition described herein appealing. However, our intention is to provide a foundation for understanding corporate social responsiveness, the diagnostic tools for analyzing specific situations, and an identification of the dilemmas and pitfalls that often accompany alternative remedies. A mastery of these elements should, we feel, be a prerequisite for the articulation of policy designed to align corporate behavior with public expectations.

Chapter Three

Social Demands and Corporate Strategy

The purpose of this chapter is to examine the relationship between the corporation's strategy and its response to social demands. Managers and business critics alike seldom give specific attention to this relationship, at least not until the economic consequences of the social forces have become manifest. This lapse is both surprising and unfortunate. The manager frequently concludes at the outset that acquiescing to demands imposed by government regulators or suggested by social advocates requires unproductive investments or activities which divert resources from the core functions of the business. Moreover, they are viewed as constraints to the exercise of management prerogatives; yielding to them may limit the manager's future alternatives as well as his control over the day-to-day direction of the enterprise. Resistance is the knee jerk response to social initiatives from an organization in which these perceptions predominate.

In some respects that resistance is entirely appropriate. Indeed, the advocacy system which underlies the formation of public policy in the United States depends on the effective presentation of both sides of an issue. Thus, without a clear understanding of the implications of consumer protection legislation obtained through industry's rebuttal, it is less likely that balanced and useful regulation will result. But automatic and unrelenting opposition seriously misses the mark for the competent business strategist. So too does the support of social programs for philanthropic reasons alone. Charity, of course, has value, and we do not wish to denigrate it. However, programs rooted in this soil frequently do not survive the heat of economic adversity. The commitment is often insufficient to provide them with sustenance during such times at the expense of the remainder of the business.

The development of an effective social posture, therefore, begins with the consideration of social demands in the context of the corporation's strategy. There is, of course, a great deal more to be considered before a comprehensive picture of corporate responsiveness emerges, as later chapters will indicate. Yet this first step is essential, for it forms the basis for setting priorities in the use of resources and securing the organizational support that is essential for policy implementation.

THE FORMULATION OF CORPORATE STRATEGY

The formulation of strategy is a central concern of general management. Alfred Chandler defined strategy as "... the determination of the basic long-term goals and objectives of an enterprise, and the adoption of action and the allocation of resources necessary for carrying out these goals."[1] The comingling of goals and objectives with action and decision making is an important facet of this concept, because the effective strategic plan is marked by close attention to the feasibility and means of implementation.

Although a corporation's strategy may not be explicitly stated or even fully understood by the organization, it can typically be identified in the firm's behavior over a period of time. With careful analysis, patterns are generally discernable in the products and services produced, the markets sought, the financing relied upon, and the managers recruited, which reflect the goals and policies guiding strategic choices made in the allocation of resources. The existence of such patterns does not, of course, guarantee that the strategy imputed to them has been consistently applied or is appropriate for the fulfillment of management's intentions. Yet the strategy represents an organizing theme around which day-to-day operating decisions have been made. It serves as a powerful management tool in the hands of a skillful general manager and an equally powerful prognasticator for the independent observer who recognizes that once a strategy has proven successful, the standard operating procedures supporting it are not easily shaken.

A particularly clear and consistently applied strategy has evolved at Avon Products, the subject of one of the cases in this book. This company has developed a broad line of moderately priced cosmetics and toiletries which are sold door-to-door by part-time female sales representatives. The target markets are low- and middle-income households which are visited on a continuing basis by the representatives, who are often women from the surrounding community. Direct selling is supported by extensive mass media advertising which stresses the Avon name and the convenience and economy of buying in the home—"Avon calling"—and a sophisticated distribution system designed to provide the rapid delivery necessary to compete with retail stores. A declared interest in growth has been pursued by extending the coverage and penetration of the sales force and increasing the number of products distributed through it In recent years this same basic formula has been implemented overseas.

The concept of strategy is widely recognized among managers and students of business policy as a useful means of translating corporate purpose into concrete plans for action. The process of determining strategy involves the analysis of several basic elements in a company's position, which in theory appears quite simple, but in practice requires difficult judgments and strong leadership.[2]

---

[1] Alfred D. Chandler, Jr., *Strategy and Structure: Chapters in the History of the Industrial Enterprise*, Cambridge, Mass., MIT Press, 1962, p. 13.

[2] Several texts are listed at the end of this chapter which offer comprehensive treatments of this subject. The reader is encouraged to consult one or more of them.

The first element is the corporation's environment. There is no revelation in the statement that an enterprise survives because it offers products or services which satisfy market needs. Were the environment stable, the task of identifying these needs would be straightforward enough. However, in a dynamic setting, the manager is confronted by a more complex assignment. Risks and opportunities to be considered in the determination of a strategy emanate from changes—some gradual, others precipitous—in the external forces that the firm must respond to. Those aspects of change which impinge directly on the operations of the business have characteristically received the most explicit attention. Thus, strategic planning is often focused on developing creative responses to trends in:

- Prices, interest rates, consumption, and other general economic indicators.
- Consumer preferences in markets served by the corporation.
- Channels of distribution available to reach these markets.
- Raw material supply and price.
- Competitive characteristics: entrance of new competitors, intercommodity displacement, etc.
- Technological developments related to the corporation's products and manufacturing processes.
- Demographic trends: growth of population, shifts in composition and physical location of the population, changes in educational and economic levels.

Sophisticated techniques have been developed in recent years to assist the manager in making forecasts in these areas. Simulations of the economy are perhaps the most widely recognized, though many firms also employ market research, technological forecasting, and commodity supply-demand models to name a few. The techniques themselves, of course, assume significance only as they offer conclusions that are relied upon to shape alternatives and define courses of action. If they are ignored or criticized, however, it is usually because the strategist chooses to rely on some other means of making judgments, not because these fields of inquiry are considered irrelevant.

The second element in the formulation of a corporate strategy relates to the resources available to prosecute opportunities and parry or surmount environmental threats. Most amenable to analysis are those reflecting financial condition; the firm's pattern of earnings, its access to capital, its outstanding obligations and so forth. A second resource lies in the firm's operational capabilities, including the configuration and condition of its facilities, the strength of its distribution channels, the value of its name, the state of its employee relations, the level and nature of its technical competence and the quality of its administrative systems. The third and perhaps most important resource is the depth and competence of its management group. Assessing the adequacy of a corporation's resources is a highly relativistic affair; whether it is well endowed or on the brink of calamity depends a great deal on the benevolence of its environment and the aggressiveness of the goals management hopes to achieve.

The strategy results from a matching of environmental conditions with financial and organizational resources. The ambitions, values, and tolerance for risk and uncertainty of the executive group have an important bearing on the outcome. Occasionally one encounters the Olympian decision that sets the course of an enterprise for years to come—the fortunate decision by the management of the Haloid Corporation to bet the company's future on the development of the xerographic process or the disastrous decision at the now defunct Underwood Corporation to attempt entry into the computer field. More commonly, the strategy evolves incrementally as the product of more numerous but less consequential choices made in response to environmental change.

In the broadest sense, then, the intellectual task of formulating strategy calls for a comprehensive understanding of the firm's environment and resources and is influenced by the personal inclinations of the managers responsible for determining policy. In subsequent chapters, the profound impact of organizational factors on the strategic process will be discussed at length. For the time being, however, the relationships noted in Figure A are sufficient for our purposes.

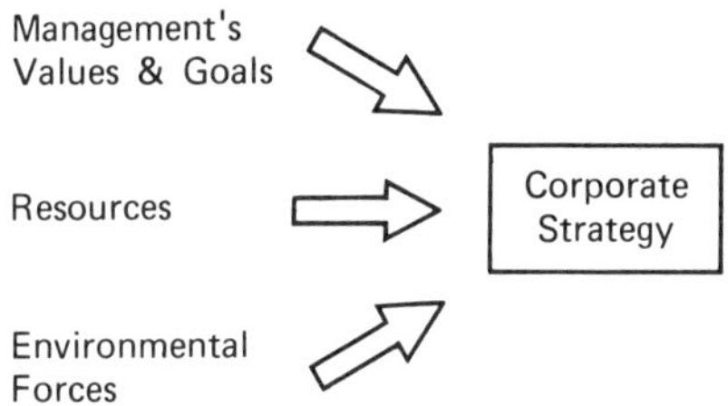

Figure A Elements in the formulation of corporate strategy.

PATTERNS OF CORPORATE SOCIAL RESPONSIVENESS

The large corporation is typically confronted by an array of social issues. It would be surprising indeed if one or more were not presently a factor in decisions effecting facility planning, manufacturing process design, product development, personnel administration, and marketing and sales policy. Grappling with them requires continuing infusions of energy and money and frequently prompts conflicts with established practices and business plans.

Yet as numerous and confining as social demands may seem, the chief executive retains an important freedom of choice in establishing the firm's pattern of response to them. Whether he exercises that freedom or permits it to lapse has strategic implications that may not be readily apparent at the time. Diagnosing the nature of the choices available requires a clear understanding of the firm's social context.

Most social issues follow a course that, in retrospect, appears to be quite predictable. There was generally a time when the issue was unthought of or unthinkable. In fact, social and economic sanctions are regularly applied to those fostering causes of some consequence that have no public support. However, should interest develop and be sustained, the issue enjoys a period of increasing awareness, expectations, demands for action and ultimately enforcement. At the end of this period, possibly measured in decades, it may cease to be a matter of active public concern. New standards may then have become so ingrained in the normal conduct of affairs that to behave otherwise would bring the social and economic sanctions formerly reserved for the contrary behavior. Thus, like the product life cycle, there is an analogous social issue life cycle.

The right to collective bargaining in the United States is an apt example. To have demanded, let alone countenanced, an independent union in the steel industry at the time of the Homestead riots in 1890 would have been viewed as folly, if not open subversiveness to the American way of life. However, over the next 47 years, a great deal happened to change that attitude. The workers in the steel industry were no longer easily intimidated immigrants, the depression raised massive unemployment concerns, the rhetoric of the New Deal nurtured the awareness of social inequities, and the passage of legislation favorable to labor made unionism socially acceptable and legally enforceable. In a sense, when Myron C. Taylor (then chairman of U.S. Steel) met privately with John L. Lewis (then president of the Committee for Industrial Organization) in the Mayflower Hotel on March 1, 1937 and agreed to recognize the Steel Workers Organizing Committee, he was acting out of logical consequences of social change in the country. Within nine years all of the major steel companies were unionized, and by the 1970's, the union-management relationship, while not always amicable, had become an integral part of doing business in that industry.

Managers, of course, do not have the luxury of responding to social demands in retrospect. On closer examination, issues of social concern present mammoth uncertainties to those who are forced to deal with them during the time in which they are vying for public acceptance. The uncertainties are of three types.

The first has to do with the urgency and durability of the issue. While the quest for equity and justice may be eternal, the current array of activists and the causes they champion are subject to change. Some will become enduring facets of business operations (such as child labor laws), others will fall by the wayside (such as prohibition). Predicting the strategic implications of social trends in the early days of public awareness may be no easier than assessing the economic significance of nascent technologies.

Second, acceptable standards of behavior are often difficult to determine, and they too change with time. What was greeted with praise yesterday may be tolerated today and considered reprehensible tomorrow. At some point, standards may be codified in law or regulation. However, even this formal statement may be ambiguous or changing, may differ among jurisdictions, and most significantly, occurs toward the end rather than the beginning of the cycle. Moreover, the equity and thoroughness of enforcement may be highly variable while the standards are new and very possibly for some time thereafter, as enforcement agencies struggle with funding and organizational problems of their own.

Third, the means of responding to social issues are generally unknown when the demands first arise. Technologies may have to be developed, new skills and knowledge acquired and so forth. "Getting on the learning curve" requires money and energy that can be no more confidently spent here than on basic research in the laboratory.

Thus, social issues pass through a period in which very substantial uncertainties exist in those factors of importance to the corporation in determining its response. However, uncertainty gives rise to discretion. The chief executive has a wide variety of options available for approaching the problem. Ultimately, these options will be narrowed or even eliminated as a new standard of behavior becomes generally accepted and thoroughly enforced through regulatory or other means. This *zone of discretion*, though of varying duration, is evident for most, if not all, social issues. Its presence affords the corporation the choice of how soon and in what way to respond.

The environmental analysis developed in Figure B permits the choices available to the corporation to be stated quite precisely. Fundamentally, the chief executive has to decide where the corporation is to be positioned relative to emerging social demands. Alternative policies may be stated in terms of the degree of lead or lag in responsiveness. The choice may not be made explicitly, particularly should there be a predilection to

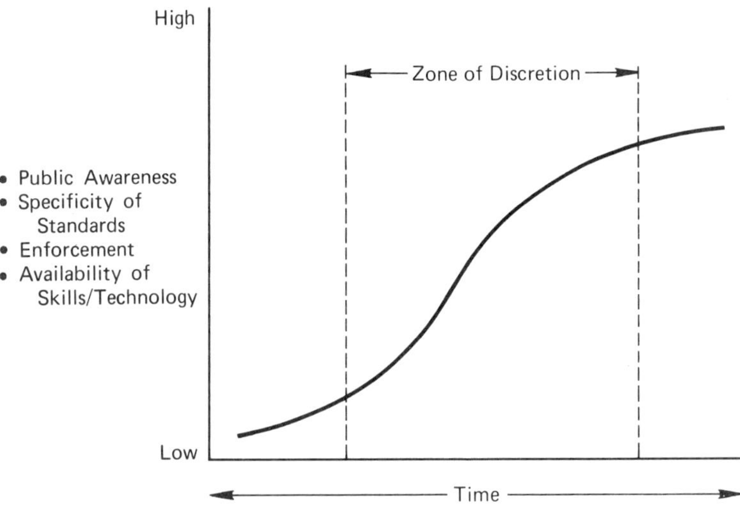

Figure B The social issue life cycle.

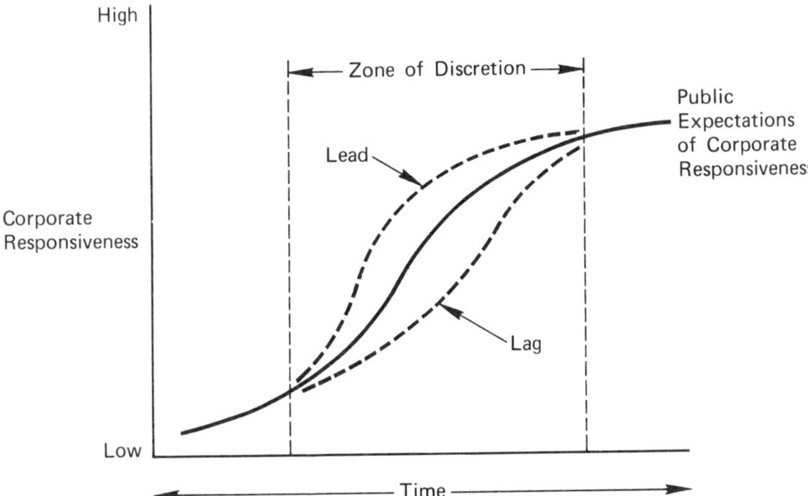

Figure C Patterns of corporate responsiveness.

withhold response until discretion no longer exists. Moreover, it may vary from issue to issue within the same corporation. Choice cannot, however, be avoided; the dynamics of environmental change force it on the manager whether or not he recognizes the implications of his stance at the time.

Although choice as it has been described in Figure C appears to be simple in concept, a closer examination reveals that complex judgments are required to unravel the consequences of a decision to lead or lag social expectations. For instance, by electing to respond early, the manager accepts the burden of acting under conditions of greater uncertainty as to the eventual dimensions of the issue and the appropriate means for dealing with it than would be the case should he delay. In addition, the corporation absorbs whatever costs may be involved at a time when the commitment of resources appears to be more nearly voluntary in the minds of investors and coworkers. In return, the manager may protect to some extent the flexibility to set policy without undue outside interference. He may also have the hope of benefits that will ultimately outweigh any immediate penalities. Such assessments are not made and acted upon without corporate and personal risk.

RELATING SOCIAL RESPONSIVENESS TO CORPORATE STRATEGY

Social forces may have an impact on the corporation's performance that is no less decisive than competitive conditions or technological developments. In one sense, they may upset the existing strategic equation by fundamentally altering the environmental conditions on which it depends. For instance, increased career opportunities for women may have a lasting effect on Avon's marketing program by extending the employment alternatives for the Avon Lady and drawing her traditional customers from the home. Or the resources required to maintain the strategy may be substantially increased, as many firms in basic industries have discovered in meeting pollution control regulations. In another sense, social forces may offer new opportunities and sources of competitive advantage to firms that adapt to them creatively.

Corporate social policy should therefore be guided by strategic considerations. The more clearly a social issue is related to the essential elements in the corporation's strategy, the more critical the response to it is likely to be. This does not mean that other issues should be disregarded or that the firm should attempt to assume leadership positions on all issues deemed to be of strategic significance. However, establishing the importancc of this relationship as an organizing principal yields two significant benefits for the chief executive in the management of social responsiveness. First, the strategy provides a basis for evaluating the firm's social initiatives and setting priorities in the allocation of resources to them. Some activities and expenditures for mature issues may be specifically required by law. However, more often than not, a sufficient amount of discretion is afforded the manager in the timing and extent of his commitments to permit a strategic assessment. Had such assessments been made, for example, the abortive efforts to establish manufacturing units in ghetto areas in the 1960s might have been avoided. Second, the corporation's strategy provides a measure of organizational cohesion, rooted in a common understanding of purpose that is essential for the implementation of social policy.

The policy questions before the chief executive are simply these: how should the response to social demands be incorporated in the firm's strategy, and specifically on which issues, if any, should the corporation seek to lead social expectations? The questions are of significance to the chief executive for two reasons.

First, by engaging emerging social demands as an element of strategy, the corporation may be better able to achieve its purpose. Some managers may dispute this statement. They may seek comfort in the belief that all parties effected by social demands will eventually be required to meet comparable standards, thus negating the opportunity for competitive advantage or the threat of that advantage accruing to others.

Such comfort is ill founded. For example, a sensitive understanding in the mid-1960's of the social issue life cycle as it applied to ecology would have prompted the prediction that expenditures for pollution control in some industries were likely to become a significant part of capital budgets. For the firm that gave strategic significance to this prediction, future benefits were possible from then current decisions on plant location and manufacturing process design. Early efforts to work with the issue may have produced subsequent cost savings that were not available to other firms which held back until action was forced by decree.

Second, the commitment to lead social expectations imposes burdens on the corporation, and these too should be considered in strategic terms. In one sense the early and aggressive response to social demands requires the subsidization of technical and administrative learning. This implies not only the costs of experimenting with new solutions to unfamiliar problems and the voluntary commitment of scarce resources. It also implies the costs of applying the organization to efforts that may drain time and attention from other more immediate operating problems. The funds available for social programs beyond those required by law, and the organization's tolerance for learning are distinctly limited. Care must therefore be taken to ensure that the corporation's portfolio of social commitments does not exceed its capability for implementation.

In another sense, the decision to engage a social issue should be influenced by whether the corporation has or can economically acquire the distinctive skills necessary to embrace the issue effectively. Thus, the company which has demonstrated a high degree of competence in product development relative to its competitors may find the opportunities in social responsiveness greatest for issues related to this competency. Conversely, the chief executive of a company having the bulk of its operations in rural communities will in all likelihood encounter only frustration should he seek an innovative posture on equal employment.

The formulation of social policy calls for analysis that is as rigorous as that given to the determination of product-market policy. For social issues of strategic consequence to the corporation the policy maker has the challenge of bringing data, analysis and judgment to bear on the following points:

- A prediction of the probable evolution of the social issue.
- An assessment of the impact it may have on the corporation's operations.
- A determination about whether the corporation may realize strategic benefits from anticipating the enforcement of public claims.
- An understanding of the problems likely to be encountered in implementing change and the price to be paid in overcoming them.

Naturally, the earlier in the development of a social issue such an analysis can be attended to, the greater the flexibility available to management in its response. We would be naive to contend that this task is easy. In fact, the forces acting on the manager encourage its delay, if not abandonment. The environment yields sketchy and sometimes misleading information, the implications may seem implausible (or unthinkable) and the response immediately costly and disruptive. Why bother?

Yet, there are often misconceptions about how policy commitments are formed in the large organization. Rarely are they made at one time on the basis of a "once and for all" feasibility study. Instead, they are typically fashioned bit-by-bit as managers attempt to understand the problems confronting the business and give direction to efforts to resolve them. The danger for the corporation is that it will drift into committed positions as social issues mature without giving specific, though inevitably partial, attention to their strategic implications.

We have stressed on several occasions that social responsiveness entails learning. This chapter has suggested a point of view that we believe is appropriate as a guide for making social policy commitments. In practice, the organization responds to social demands because it has been induced to do so, if not by its top management, then by environmental forces. As subsequent chapters will indicate, the implementation of social policy requires skillful management of a learning process through which organizational support for change is ultimately obtained.

SUGGESTED READINGS

1.–Uyterhoeven, Hugo E. R., Ackerman, Robert W., and Rosenblum, John W., *Strategy and Organization, Text and Cases.* Homewood, Ill.: Irwin, 1973.
2.–Andrews, Kenneth R., *The Concept of Corporate Strategy.* Homewood, Ill.: Dow-Jones, Irwin, 1971.
3.–Braybooke, David and Lindblom, Charles E., *A Strategy of Decision.* New York: The Free Press, 1970.
4.–Chamberlain, Neil. *The Limits of Corporate Responsibility*. New York: Basic Books, 1973.
5.–Kahn, Herman ed., *The Future of the Corporation.* New York: Mason & Lipscomb, 1974.

Case One

Avon Products, Inc.

> Their hours of work are comparatively easy and everything has been done to make their work pleasant and agreeable.
>
> Every report, every letter, suggestion, or request is considered carefully before it is answered. Our aim is to keep in the closest possible touch with you.
>
> We seek to assure complete customer satisfaction by offering quality and safe merchandise through prompt and courteous service, using the most ethical marketing methods.
>
> With the utmost confidence in our staff of dedicated employees—the crucial ingredient in our success—we look forward to another good year for Avon.

Which of these statements was written in 1903 and which in 1972? The fact that it is difficult to tell that the first two quotations predate the latter two by almost 70 years illustrates the consistency of Avon's business philosophy.[1]

In the early seventies, the top management of Avon became increasingly aware of the company's social role in the community and translated this consciousness into a series of research projects, presentations, programs, statements, and recommendations. In late 1971 and early 1972, the organization assessed its performance and in 1974, in a changed economic situation, continued to work at implementing its plans in this area. The coordinator of community and urban affairs explained in a memo to the manager of National Affairs, "We did not intend to put together a social audit, though that has been the net result."

THE COMPANY: PAST AND PRESENT

In 1886 David H. McConnell, Sr. founded the California Perfume Company and later described this venture:

> My ambition was to manufacture a line of goods that would be consumed, used up, and to sell it through canvassing agents, direct from the factory to the consumer.

[1]The first two statements are from "The Great Oak," written in 1903 by the company's founder, David H. McConnell, Sr.; the third, from Avon's "Statement of Corporate Responsibility," approved by the Board in the spring of 1972; and the fourth, from Chairman Wayne Hicklin's letter in Avon's 1971 *Annual Report*.

The company's name was changed in 1939 to Avon Products, Inc. By the 1970s it was a large and profitable company devoted to the manufacture and sale of cosmetics and toiletries with revenues in excess of $1 billion. The company's 1973 *Annual Report* described its "broad range of approximately 700 products" (not counting make-up shades), dividing them into four categories:

	Percent of Sales
Fragrances and bath products for women	40-45%
Make-up skin care and other products for women	25-30%
Men's products	10-15%
Other products: teen products, children's and daily need products, costume jewelry and ceramics	15-20%

Its newest ventures included a trial chain of 16 beauty salons, mail order clothing (Family Fashion by Avon), and plastic housewares sold by the party method. In this method the Avon Representative shows the housewares to potential customers in a social gathering at her home; they come to her "Avon party" and are given the opportunity to buy the Avon products.

Except for the first two of these last three efforts, the company's products were sold through the Avon Representative, an independent contractor universally associated with the two-toned doorbell and the familiar "Avon calling." *Business Week* described this system and the network of Avon ladies in the following way:

> As the world's largest cosmetics and toiletries company, Avon now has an army of 680,000 bellringers peddling 1,400 products to more than 85-million households in the U.S., Canada, and 16 foreign countries. In the U.S. alone, Avon commands 85% of the door-to-door market for cosmetics and toiletries and 20% of the total $5 billion market. . . .
>
> The Avon field system, as it has evolved over the past 87 years, consists of five levels. At the top is a general manager. He oversees one of seven branches across the country and two regional managers. The regional manager supervises eight divisional managers, each of whom keeps tabs on 18 district managers. The district manager recruits, trains, and works with an average of 150 bell-chiming Avon ladies.[2]

This unique system was a source of pride—and profit—to the company and one of the cornerstones of the corporate foundation. The letter from the president and chairman in the 1973 *Annual Report* expressed this faith: "As we view the future over the longer term, we always keep in mind the fundamental premise of our business—that the direct selling distribution developed by Avon is one of the most effective methods ever devised for permeating consumer markets." It also enabled Avon to maintain its large sales force with relatively low marketing and very low advertising costs,[3] thus contributing to

---

[2] "Troubled Avon Tries a Face-Lifting," *Business Week*, May 11, 1974, pp. 98 and 100.

[3] "Avon keeps its advertising costs low by rarely pioneering in new products—where both advertising cost and risk are high. In fact, Avon rarely advertises specific products at all, preferring to emphasize simplicity, wholesome good grooming, and the Avon name." "Avon Products: Is Its Beauty Only Skin-Deep?", *Forbes*, July 1, 1973, p. 21

very high profit margins, even in an industry known for high margins. By asset size Avon was not one of the largest companies, but as a *Forbes* article speculated:

> Thanks to this low-cost army of salespeople, Avon profits handsomely. Where it does its own manufacturing, its gross margins (before advertising and overhead) probably run up to 70% on the list price. Of the other 30%, packaging is the biggest single cost. One estimate puts the cost of the ingredients in a lipstick at 5 cents, with 35 cents going for the package. The lipstick would then sell for between $1.50 and $3. Imaginative packaging has become an Avon hallmark.[4]

These factors led to a spectacular earnings growth rate in the 1960's, a price/earnings ratio over 50 in 1973, and a *Forbes* designation as one of the "cult stocks, the elites, the vestal virgins."[5] The magazine elaborated:

> But it is in market value where Avon is truly a giant. At recent (July 1973) prices Avon's 8 million shares had a combined market value of $8 billion, more than that of the entire steel or airlines industries . . . Avon's earnings per share growth has declined gradually from an average of 22% a year between 1958 and 1962 to an average of 14% between 1968 and 1972. Yet Avon's P/E multiple has continued to climb.[6]

This growth pattern is evident from the financial data in Exhibit 1-1. In 1973, net earnings of $136 million (on sales of $1,150 million) were almost double those of five years earlier ($71 million on sales of $558 million). The next two largest cosmetic makers had 1973 sales of $506 million (Revlon) and $230 million (Max Factor).

During these years of rapid growth, the company attributed much of its success to its Representative. In the 1971 *Annual Report* she was described as "the most important person in the entire Avon world." Given this reliance on the Representative and her direct contact with the customer, Avon had always claimed to have been "people oriented." The 1971 *Annual Report* stated rhetorically, "What makes this kind of growth possible? Many, many things, but high on the list is people." In the words of one of its directors, it was a "cornball company." From McConnell onward, Avon declared that it cared—for its employees, its customers, and its products.

THE AVON AUDIT

PRELIMINARY CHANGES AT AVON: ORGANIZATIONAL AND PROCEDURAL: Although Avon had begun to look carefully at its social programs by 1969, no systematic review was attempted until the spring of 1971. At this point, the impetus came from the top and took a number of different forms.

---

[4] Ibid.

[5] *Forbes*, p. 20.

[6] Ibid.

Avon was organized into seven branches, each of them profit centers. The branch managers sent in monthly letters to headquarters. In the spring of 1971, the president requested that information on community affairs, social programs, etc., be included in this monthly report.

At the same time, Avon moved along other lines to change the structure as well as the procedures of the company. The Government and Public Affairs Department was combined with the Public Relations Department, the Community Affairs function expanded, and this newly organized Government and Public Affairs Department was placed under the direction of Robert R. McMillan. Robert Cortez, then Manager of Community and Urban Affairs, commented on the group's function:

> Community Affairs handles all aspects of home office, community, and urban affairs programs and serves as a resource to provide staff guidance for Avon associates in Government and Public Affairs (GPA) and for other home office departments.

McMillan felt that the "audit" may have been prompted by the growing consumer movement. But whatever the reason, in November 1971 he was instructed to find out exactly what was happening in the community and urban affairs area and then to make a presentation to top management on "where and what we are," and "where and what we should be," along with specific recommendations on how to implement proposed changes. William Corbett headed and supervised the staff that was instrumental in carrying out the audit work:

William Corbett, Group Manager, National Affairs
Robert Cortez, Manager, Community and Urban Affairs
Marcia Boles, Coordinator, Community and Urban Affairs
Joan Lawson, Media Affairs Writer
Donald Steller, Coordinator, National Affairs

THE AUDIT: BASIC FORM AND PURPOSE: The audit was to provide two results: a "Statement on Corporate Responsibility," and a much more detailed "Presentation on Corporate Social Responsibility," incorporating information from the "audit" and recommendations in a number of areas for McMillan to deliver to top management. The first was a general statement of policy. The second was a series of specific proposals for social programs based on an analysis of the issues in relation to Avon's policies and existing activities. The two documents were developed in parallel.

McMillan stressed that his aim was not to work for sudden or dramatic change. For example, he had no desire to alter radically the philosophical outlook of the suburban Avon executive. But rather, he hoped to show this employee that what was under discussion was the total system, of which both the New Canaan commuter and the Appalachian Representative are parts. McMillan hoped to demonstrate that the sorts of things social responsibility involved necessarily involved the whole Avon world: executives, employees, Representatives, and customers.

McMillan felt that the idea of "social responsibility" constituted no real break with the way Avon traditionally had talked and thought about itself and its activities. He noted that in some respects this continuity facilitated the audit. For example, department managers did not seem to fear that the audit would uncover embarrassing or potentially damaging intelligence and consequently were quite willing to supply information. Moreover, since top management had clearly accepted the idea of social involvement by initiating the project, the "auditors" did not spend a lot of time "selling" their work or providing theoretical justification for it. McMillan's staff did not agonize over what topics to include or why. They simply started to work on particular areas of obvious importance, some of which had been the focus of earlier or other ongoing Avon projects. As a result, the company was able to act with speed and efficiency. McMillan was given his task in November of 1971. By the end of January 1972, the presentation was ready.

PREPARATION OF THE STATEMENT AND RESEARCH

The preliminary research and drafting of the "Statement of Corporate Responsibility" was the responsibility of Joan Lawson, Media Affairs Writer. She also contributed significantly to the more extensive preliminary work that went into the preparation of the "presentation" and the "audit." The methods used in each case were similar.

For the "Statement on Corporate Responsibility" Lawson first compiled statements and pamphlets from other leading corporations which had been active in areas of social concern, and utilized the resources of the Public Affairs Council to determine what other companies had done in the way of defining their responsibilties. Material from company files, past statements and publications, and some input from top management were also included in the first draft statement. This draft was reviewed and revised by McMillan's staff. The second version was a consolidation of the first with further management input on consumer and community affairs, and this draft, again, was reviewed and edited. The third and final draft was a consolidation of the other two with specific areas defined–consumer, discrimination in employment, and environment. The final statement, shown in Exhibit 1-2, included contributions by David Mitchell, President of the corporation and S. Arnold Zimmerman, corporate Vice President and Secretary. It was formally adopted by the Board of Directors in March of 1972 and was subsequently widely circulated and publicized. For example, it was featured in the summer of 1972 edition of the company magazine, *Avon and You.*

The preparatory work on the "audit" resembled that on the "statement" but covered more areas. Again, the first step was research by Joan Lawson on the activities of other companies, on Avon's past involvement (obtained from company files and discussions with management), and on more general proposals of possible corporate social activities in the Public Affairs Council publication, "Social Responsibilities of Business Corporations." The legal side of the outline was prepared by Donald Steller, an attorney whose responsibilities included monitoring federal legislation on consumer protection, environmental quality, housing, social reform, manpower, minority enterprise, and social services.

An assortment of representative quotations on both sides of the social responsibility question was culled by Lawson, and a few of them were incorporated into the second draft, which also included additional managerial comment and criticism.

Concurrent with this research, staff work continued under Corbett's direction in various directions. For example, Lawson and Steller were developing policy positions and assembling norms—as defined by law and the activities of other firms—while others collected data on what Avon was doing. Marcia Boles, then Coordinator of Community Affairs, described this latter activity:

> Bob Cortez and I went to every department in the company as well as our own files to find out in hard facts what precisely the company had done to date in terms of environmentalism, corporate structure reform, minority affairs, equal employment opportunity, education and youth . . . This involved getting data on corporate contributions from our foundation and breaking it down into the above categories. It meant finding out from our Field Operations Department what our dollar sales were in the black community and from the advertising department what our advertising dollar was in the black community, etc. . . . At the same time we put together information for the departments on donations. At all times such data were gathered and thought of in terms of where we have been, where we are, and where we should be going so that each investigation has resulted in positive recommendations.
>
> In the area of cooperation from various departments and associates we encountered no opposition and from most associates full cooperation.

Such cooperation made it possible for the Government and Public Affairs (GPA) group to work very rapidly. The presentation was ready by January 28, but due to complications in the schedules of some of the vice presidents involved, it was not actually made until the end of February. This final outline was designed to be, in Lawson's words, "a definition of social responsibility, its total significance to the corporate world and its significance to Avon . . . . The final portion of the outline was devoted to recommendations for Avon's involvement—based on other companies' participation and input from Avon management."

OUTLINE AND ACTION

When McMillan made his "Presentation of Corporate Social Responsibility" to the top management group at the end of February, he covered five issues: Environmental Protection, Consumerism, Corporate Structure, Youth, and the Black Community. Comments on each issue were divided into sections on "areas of concern," "our posture," and specific "recommendations." The report is reproduced in Exhibit 1-3.

Unlike most documents labelled "social audit," here there was no section labelled "our performance." Rather, the GPA staff incorporated their estimate of Avon's performance into their "recommendations." Some such items were treated briefly with a comment such as "continue," and in part, this format reflected the staff's appreciation of what the officers already knew of Avon's activities. In general, the assessment function was done at the staff level and was reflected only indirectly in the "recommendations," or suggested obliquely under "our posture" (a section which included a mixture of policy statements and lists of activities).

McMillan concluded his presentation with the following remarks:

A.—We have not proposed drastic or expensive programs. We have tried to present materials responsive to a changing world. There are many other issues—education, the elderly, and so on; but we have only covered the major ones.
B.—As the social climate changes, we will have to make other adjustments.
C.—Positive action by Avon to demands for involvement in social issues:
  1.—Can be good business;
  2.—Can help penetrate youth and black markets;
  3.—Can gain us greater credibility in government affairs work;
  4.—Is urged by a large segment of the public and many of our shareholders; and
  5.—Is the right thing for us to do.

After McMillan's presentation, a staff meeting, called by Corbett, was held to review what had been accomplished and to assign priorities and work out timetables for what had been approved by the officers. A memo (Exhibit 1-4) was drawn up by Boles which listed the specific steps and reflected the decisions made at this time, April 26, 1972.

As Avon went to work on the specific implementation of its audit findings, one change in corporate posture was apparent. Corbett explained that some of the plans, such as the brochure on Avon's social involvement, represented a shift in company philosophy, since Avon traditionally had maintained a low profile and refrained from blowing its own horn. The company now wanted to make its efforts and achievements known, but still in a low key manner. He felt that Avon was not acting solely from financial motives, but neither was it trying to sacrifice dollars. Although no attempt had been made to cost out Avon's social programs, he was confident that in the long run "social responsibility" would pay off. Cortez echoed this optimism as he asserted:

> It (social responsibility) is our mandate—not just to adopt or live with this notion, but to capitalize on it and to turn it into a positive opportunity to prove that Avon is progressive and in tune with the changing times.

THE AUDIT AFTERMATH:

In the two years following McMillan's presentation there was definite progress with respect to some of the individual recommendations; i.e., a woman was added to the Board of Directors, and sales to the black community rose to about 12% of the total. However, Avon was concerned also with working out organizational mechanisms that would allow the implementation and integration of whatever specific programs or projects it was then committed to. Accordingly, a Social Responsibility Committee was formed, consisting of top management representatives from all the major departments including two blacks and two women. These were:

Executive Vice President, Chairman of the Committee (William Chaney)
Vice President, Vice Chairman of the Committee (Norman Haynes)

Manager, Community Affairs, Secretary to the Committee (Marcia Boles)
Group Vice President for Marketing
Senior Vice President for Field Operations
Group Vice President for Internal Affairs
Treasurer
Director for Personnel
Director of Purchasing
Director of Inner City Marketing

A staff memo described the early workings of this Committee:

> A corporate Social Responsibility Committee was formed which made one of its first projects a report from every department on what exactly it was doing in all areas of corporate responsibility from environmentalism to consumerism and minority affairs. This meant that every individual in the Government and Public Affairs Department was surveyed as to what his or her function was in those areas, and this was compiled.

Initially, the Committee met monthly and reviewed the progress in each operational area represented, but by 1974 it was able to reduce its meetings to every quarter. Between meetings, much of the work was carried on by Marcia Boles, now promoted to Manager, Community Affairs, working closely with Committee Chairman William Chaney. A complete "Social Responsibility Plan" for Avon was drawn up. This was a large loose-leafed notebook, consisting not only of philosophies and goals but also of progress reports and specific numbers in areas such as employment and purchasing. This plan went out as a procedure bulletin over Chaney's signature, initially to the officers and directors of the company. In the words of one member of the Committee, his method of distribution was designed to "carry a lot of weight."

Later a modified version of the plan was sent out to the branches and laboratories. In accordance with the Committee's desire to move these matters down into the line and to convey their importance, all branch and laboratory general managers were summoned to New York City in the spring of 1973 for a two and a half day meeting with top management devoted exclusively to the topic of "social responsibility." The last previous similar meeting (on another subject) had been three years before, and Committee Vice Chairman Haynes commented that a clear signal had been given. He added that the general managers might even have felt relieved; they now knew they really were expected to pay attention to these matters and were given direction as to how to relay it to the employees under them.

In many ways, dissemination of the Social Responsibility Plan was a communications effort, from corporate top management to the general managers at the locations and then to the management personnel there. Specific instructions, as well as a strong general emphasis, were conveyed. Goals were set for (and by) each general manager and monthly reports on minority suppliers, employment, and Community Affairs were required to be sent to the Committee. In addition, each branch manager's "State of the Union" letter to the president now included information in matters such as community relations, etc. When the information went to Boles, she used it to keep the plan current and monitored the progress of the various facilities by field visits as well as by checking the monthly figures. These measures were designed to make the plan not only important but also operational, to keep it, as she said, "an ongoing part of business."

FINANCIAL CHANGES: INTERNAL AND EXTERNAL

While these organizational developments were being worked out, both the national economy and Avon's financial condition changed significantly.

Business Week presented this flamboyant picture of the company's position:

> The spectacular sales and earnings gains of the 1950s and 1960s—often running 17% to 19% a year—are a thing of the past. Profit margins are being squeezed like an old toothpaste tube. Foreign expansion has run into problems. This has triggered a prolonged slide in the price of what had been one of Wall Street's highest flying glamor stocks. From a peak of $140 early last year, Avon's shares have tumbled to this week's $43 range.[7]

At the annual meeting (April 31, 1974) Chairman Fusee and President Mitchell presented a calmer assessment of Avon's performance, which by this time included a 10% drop in earnings on a 10% increase in sales for the first quarter of 1974. Table 1-1 presents these results.

TABLE 1-1

	Quarter ended March 31,		*Percent of*
	1974	*1973*	*Change*
Net sales	$242,188,000	$220,884,000	+10
Earnings before taxes	37,366,000	41,623,000	-10
Taxes on earnings	19,617,000	21,311,000	- 8
Net earnings	17,749,000	20,312,000	-13
Per share	31 cents	35 cents	

Some of this drop was attributed to the national economy, with skyrocketing inflation leading both to modifications in consumer buying habits and to much higher prices for supplies. The energy situation in late 1973 and raw material shortages were also contributing factors. Although admitting these results were "disappointing," the chairman reminded shareholders that Avon's performance was being measured against the previous year's record highs, and by other standards might not have seemed so weak. A *New York Times* article reported the following comments by Fusee:

> "This company is not sick. We're strong and we're going to move ahead again as soon as the inflationary spiral ends," Fred C. Fusee, chairman, told a long-time Avon stockholder who had journeyed from Chicago to get an opinion "on the worth of the stock in the future, say in 1974."

---

[7]*Business Week.* May 11, 1974, p. 98.

> Other shareholders pointedly asked about the sale of $10 million worth of Avon stock last year by top officers and directors before the slide began. The executives are defendants in two derivative shareholder actions alleging improper use of inside information.
>
> Mr. Fusee denied that he and his colleagues had "bailed out" as one stockholder charged.[8]

The president then outlined Avon's response to its changing environment. He noted, in part, the following programs:

> Consumers had become cautious in their buying habits and were avoiding, or buying fewer expensive gift items and more basics, where they felt they were getting good value for their money . . . .
>
> To offset the sales growth decline resulting from this substantial consumer shift, three major actions were taken early in the fourth quarter:
>
> 1.–The number of Representatives was increased to achieve better customer coverage.
> 2.–Two new incentive programs were introduced to spur customer activity, primarily among top-producing Representatives.
> 3.–A price reduction program (known as "Inflation Fighters") was begun to build sales volume . . . .
>
> As a result of these pressures on profits, Avon initiated a major internal cost reduction program late last fall. The first phase, which involved postponement of a number of capital projects, installation of new procedures in transportation and shipping, and improved preplanning to avoid air freight–resulted in a $15 million reduction in our preliminary 1974 expense forecast.
>
> The second phase, now being completed, involved the identification of other potential savings, setting of dollar objectives, and assignment of some of our top-notch management people to task forces to set up new procedures. . . . Hand-in-hand with our response to the profit squeeze has been the need to develop methods to handle the direct shortages . . . In the field, we are launching a Reduced District Size Program in June of this year. Six hundred Sales Districts from our current total of over two thousand were chosen for this program. We have also added 261 new Districts. As a result, over 800 of our total District Manager staff will have responsibility for fewer Representatives. Our most productive markets were chosen for this group, so we are adding strength on strength. . . .
>
> We know that Avon has the opportunity to reach a larger number of households. A broad survey conducted for us last year by a well-respected research firm revealed that out of 67 million U.S. households, almost half bought from Avon at least once in the previous year. However, 2/3 of these buyers did so only on an occasional basis. Therefore, we have growth potential by increasing the frequency of purchasing. (In addition, of the total non-buying households, 9 million expressed interest in having an Avon Representative call.)

---

[8] "Avon Blames Inflation; Predicts a Comeback," Marilyn Bender, *The New York Times,* May 1, 1974, p. 70.

Exhibit 1-1

TEN-YEAR REVIEW AVON PRODUCTS, INC. AND SUBSIDIARIES
(Dollars expressed in thousands except per share figures)

	1973	1972	1971	1970	1969	1968	1967	1966	1965	1964
Net sales	**$1,150,659**	$1,005,316	$873,153	$759,171	$656,660	$558,587	$474,814	$408,178	$351,990	$299,449
Earnings before taxes	**$ 267,648**	$ 254,827	$221,194	$197,144	$175,258	$152,734	$128,410	$109,246	$ 91,576	$ 82,276
% to net sales	**23.3**	25.3	25.3	26.0	26.7	27.3	27.0	26.8	26.0	27.5
Taxes on earnings	**$ 131,898**	$ 129,898	$112,057	$ 98,156	$ 90,965	$ 81,424	$ 63,027	$ 53,918	$ 44,007	$ 42,437
Net earnings	**$ 135,750**	$ 124,929	$109,137	$ 98,988	$ 84,293	$ 71,310	$ 65,383	$ 55,328	$ 47,569	$ 39,839
% to net sales	**11.8**	12.4	12.5	13.0	12.8	12.8	13.8	13.6	13.5	13.3
Shares outstanding (Thousands)	**57,991**	57,766	57,600	57,525	57,488	57,460	57,414	57,394	57,383	57,370
Per share of stock										
Net Earnings	**$ 2.34**	$ 2.16	$ 1.89	$ 1.72	$ 1.46	$ 1.24	$ 1.13	$ .96	$ .82	$ .69
Cash Dividends	**$ 1.40**	$ 1.35	$ 1.25	$ 1.07½	$ .90	$ .80	$ .70	$ .57	$ .45	$ .36
Working capital	**$ 273,548**	$ 227,399	$185,770	$164,914	$132,398	$124,424	$100,368	$ 87,899	$ 72,341	$ 59,823
Current Ratio	**2.24**	2.30	2.26	2.30	2.24	2.29	2.28	2.15	2.17	2.06
Property–Net	**$ 210,357**	$ 191,153	$169,992	$148,679	$134,502	$103,131	$ 85,518	$ 70,621	$ 57,749	$ 49,815
Capital expenditures	**$ 34,271**	$ 33,980	$ 33,155	$ 23,780	$ 40,400	$ 24,000	$ 22,100	$ 18,000	$ 12,500	$ 17,100
Total assets	**$ 711,488**	$ 598,647	$506,607	$440,840	$379,786	$331,683	$273,463	$245,230	$193,083	$166,318
Long-term obligations	**$ 31,696**	$ 37,529	$ 36,076	$ 34,788	$ 33,384	$ 30,310	$ 17,917	$ 18,524	$ 2,503	$ 4,676
Shareholders' equity	**$ 447,126**	$ 379,070	$317,083	$274,276	$235,224	$201,854	$175,123	$149,334	$126,833	$104,962
Shareholders	**34,800**	36,700	35,700	34,000	29,100	28,500	26,800	25,200	23,800	20,000
Employees	**26,800**	25,100	23,300	22,100	20,800	18,300	15,700	13,900	12,200	11,300

> The second area basic to our future business growth is our product line. Avon's basic strengths and greatest potential, however, is in its standard line of beauty and cosmetic products. . . . Some products will be packaged simply yet attractively to appeal to the expanding segment of the market which, because of age or attitude, is looking for the basics . . . .
>
> Another element in our plans for the future is our program of diversification. First, I want to comment on the beauty salon test we have been conducting for the past two years. . . . . We feel that the 16 salons presently being operated are perfectly satisfactory as individual units, and our present plans are to continue them in operation. At the same time, we have concluded that there is not a sufficient profit opportunity to justify a commitment to the beauty salon business, with the attendant investment and expenses, and therefore we have decided not to expand our test.
>
> Also in our plans for the future is the expansion of sales and earnings in our international markets. . . . To accomplish this growth, Avon's traditionally successful marketing tools in the areas of field, product, and pricing will be applied on a selective or modified basis depending upon the market. . . .
>
> In listening to my remarks today, I'm sure you feel that I am optimistic about Avon's future. You are correct—I am. Avon is inherently strong. Our method of distribution is not only viable in "good times," it also has allowed us to respond effectively to recent difficult challenges. Most of all it offers us a promising and rewarding future.

Exhibit 1-2

STATEMENT OF CORPORATE RESPONSIBILITY

As strong believers in the free enterprise system, we of Avon Management are keenly aware that by offering quality merchandise and by using ethical marketing methods, our Company has been able to earn a profit that provides a fair return to our thousands of shareholders, growth opportunities for our employees, more jobs for the community, and expanded earnings for Avon Representatives.

We also realize that success today is measured not only by corporate profits, but also by the corporation's degree of concern with the society and environment in which it functions.

We believe that the pursuit of profit and the pursuit of social objectives are compatible goals. Since the founding of our Company in 1886, Avon has always maintained a sincere concern for people and a firm commitment to responsible corporate citizenship. Through the years, the Company has made substantial contributions in resources and time to many programs and organizations devoted to the improvement of health, education, and welfare. We pledge Avon's continued strong support in these areas and encourage our employees to participate actively in organizations which are thus committed to serving society.

We further pledge our efforts in three specific areas which are not only of vital interest to society generally, but which also offer opportunities to apply Avon's special capabilities to make meaningful contributions:

THE CONSUMER. We seek to assure complete customer satisfaction by offering quality and safe merchandise through prompt and courteous service, using the most ethical marketing methods. We subscribe to the principle that all consumers should be informed. Therefore we shall take further steps to communicate to them information about our Company and our products, and to encourage their inquiries and comments.

DISCRIMINATION. We are committed to positive programs to prevent any discrimination whatsoever in hiring and promotion practices and in the treatment of people, because of their race, color, creed, sex or age. This not only applies to our dealings with employees and Representatives, but also to our dealings with suppliers of goods and services. We do not deem mere compliance with the law to be sufficient; we regard it as imperative that affirmative steps be taken throughout the Company to ensure that in every respect this policy of non-discrimination is actively followed.

ENVIRONMENT. To the greatest extent possible, we shall strive to eliminate the contamination of air and water, and to work toward the development of effective means for recycling disposable materials. We shall engineer our facilities for minimum environmental effects, cooperate with local, state, and federal agencies in developing improved systems of environmental management, and educate employees, Representatives and customers to the need for protecting our environment. We subscribe to, and encourage our employees to participate in, worthwhile programs that share these objectives.

We of Management make these pledges on behalf of every Avon employee. We expect complete cooperation—because we believe our employees have sound business sense and realize that by helping everyone in society to enjoy the highest quality of life, both society and Avon will benefit.

Exhibit 1-3

PRESENTATION ON CORPORATE SOCIAL RESPONSIBILITY

I. *Introduction*

A. Everyone is aware of public demand for corporations to do more than make a profit.

B. Two corporate views of social responsibility.

Our society and our system are for a fact threatened from within as never before. . . . by aggressively articulate masters of verbal violence . . . Business must respond to the idiotic and noneconomic nonsense put forth by our nation's self-appointed saviours.

John D. Harper, Chairman, Aluminum
Company of America—September, 1971

In our world today, there are certain responsibilities that business concerns do have. These are often described as the new dimension of business' social responsibility. We have concern for the preservation of our social and economic systems. Business helped create our societies and depends on their existence for its survival. We have tried for many years to practice good citizenship. Today, new approaches are needed to deal with new problems.

Dr. Louis K. Eilers, Chairman of
Kodak—November, 1970

C. Avon cannot follow the views of Mr. Harper.

D. Avon must assume a socially responsible role.

1. Nothing drastic or expensive is recommended.
2. We do not need to spend more time and give the subjects discussed more attention.
3. We should gradually improve what we are doing.

E. We react to many of the issues to be discussed from a government affairs viewpoint. This presentation will not deal with those efforts but is designed to provide positive recommendations for dealing with the issues.

II. *The Issues*—There are many. We will not be exhaustive, but will try to hit vital ones.

A. *Environmental Protection*

1. Areas of concern—
   a. Air, water, solid waste, noise pollution and beautification
   b. Industrial health (working conditions)

2. Our posture—
   a. Good working conditions
   b. Limited financial support for antipollution groups
   c. Limited involvement by executives in antipollution organizations
   d. Good practices in air, aesthetic, solid waste and water pollution in our facilities

3. Recommendations—
   a. Continue our close surveillance of antipollution measures at each facility
   b. Consider additional financial support for responsible conservation groups.
   c. Constantly search for biodegradable packaging materials because of growing government interest in disposable packaging and recycling of packaging.

B. *Consumerism*

1. Areas of concern—
   a. Safety of products and packaging

   b. Requests for more information about consumer products–formulas, ingredients, and safety testing
   c. Negative attitude of some towards door-to-door selling and invasion of right of privacy
   d. A better educated consumer

2. Our posture–
   a. Developing an information center to answer consumer inquiries and provide information
   b. Working with private consumer groups
   c. Providing limited amounts of literature to various groups and individuals requesting information about Company and cosmetics

3. Recommendations–
   a. Develop better test methods for the safety of our products and inform the public about these tests including acceleration in our basic skin research with emphasis on chemicals
   b. Give serious consideration to listing of ingredients and precautionary labeling (be out ahead of consumer movement)
   c. Develop consumer education materials designed to show quality control of our products and research efforts
   d. If Information Center test proves effective, expand it nationwide
   e. Continue and expand our program of showing positive side of door-to-door selling through Representative and Manager publicity
   f. Expand the role of GPA in assisting H. Q. Departments and Branches in responding to consumer demands and the importance of dealing with consumer matters promptly
   g. Consider a formalized program of Foundation grants to consumer organizations coupled with the establishment of communications between these groups and the Company

C. *Corporate Structure.* (While some issues here are the responsibility of Corporate Personnel, we do have some thoughts for consideration.)

1. Areas of concern–
   a. Women
   b. Blacks
   c. Other ethnic groups
   d. Physically handicapped
   e. Demands for consumer, youth, black and women representation on the Board and in top management

2. Our posture–
   a. Strides are being made in upgrading women in management
   b. Strides are being made in recruiting blacks for management positions
   c. Little is being done in other ethnic areas
   d. Little done in the physically handicapped area

3. Recommendations–
   a. More aggressive recruitment of blacks, women and various ethnic groups for management
   b. Develop programs at each facility for employment of the physically handicapped

c. Consider financial support of existing day care centers near our facilities
d. Add a black and a woman to the Board

D. *Youth*
1. Area of concern—
a. Better identification of Company with youth important from not only social responsibility area but also marketing
b. Distrust of free enterprise and feeling that corporations and establishment do not care
c. Failure of corporate executives to communicate with youth

2. Our posture—
a. Limited financial support for youth-oriented organizations
b. Teen program
c. Scholarship program

3. Recommendations—
a. Better job in publicizing our scholarship program
b. Help college students and youth to better understand the Avon approach to direct selling
c. Avon executives should be more accessible to requests from young people for interviews
d. Support for organizations trying to educate youth about the role of business in our society

E. *Black Community*

1. Area of concern—
a. Feeling of alienation from "white power structure"
b. Lack of adequate product line for blacks
c. Limited advertising in black media
d. Purchasing from black vendors

2. Our posture—
a. Limited black advertising
b. No black suppliers
c. Black bank deposits
d. L. R. Banks two days teaching at black university under Urban League program

3. Recommendations—
a. Accelerate efforts to make purchases from black suppliers
b. More black media advertising (presently under $100,000 a year)
c. Continue program of black bank deposits
d. Continue programs to recruit additional black management people
e. Develop black product line
f. Continue grants and continually evaluate grants from Foundation to black organizations
g. Accelerate efforts, where appropriate, to secure publicity for efforts in this area

III. *General Recommendations*

A. Summarize specific recommendations made in this presentation.

B. Whatever our *policies* and *actions* in this area be, they must be communicated to all levels of the Company, the Representatives, those concerned with each issue, and the general public.

C. We should publicize our Code of Social Responsibility when it is adopted by the Board.

D. Develop a brochure fully depicting our present efforts and future plans to deal with the entire social responsibility issue.

E. Provide for a "social audit" of our corporate responsibility activities in each annual report.

F. A continuing survey should be made to make sure that new issues are anticipated, analyzed and acted upon as they develop. We have the staff now for this.

IV. *Conclusion*

A. We have not proposed drastic or expensive programs. We have tried to present materials responsive to a changing world. There are many other issues—education, the elderly, and so on; but we have only covered the major ones.

B. As the social climate changes, we will have to make other adjustments.

C. Positive action by Avon to demands for involvement in social issues:
1. Can be good business;
2. Can help penetrate youth and black markets;
3. Can gain us greater credibility in government affairs work;
4. Is urged by a large segment of the public and many of our shareholders; and
5. Is the right thing for us to do.

Exhibit 1-4

TO: P. Lewis/R. Cortez April 26, 1972

FROM: M. Boles

Re: *MEETING WITH MR. W. CORBETT ON APRIL 25, 1972*

As a result of Mr. McMillan's presentation on Avon's Corporate Responsibility to top management, we have been directed to commence work on the following items:

1. By May 25, 1972—make a recommendation of what responsible conservation groups Avon should be contributing to.

2. Draft a letter to Harold Fulton, Charles Rowland for Mr. Corbett's signature on Mr. McMillan's presentation and top management acceptance of the recommendation that we be doing more research into the area of biodegradable packaging.

3. By May 10, 1972—prepare a list of suggestions concerning ways that we might promote environmental packaging by our Representatives. Some ideas might be to distribute the Avon Corporate Responsibility brochure to the Representatives

or put a message on their delivery bags, perhaps using our environmental ad. (The cost on this would have to be checked with the Purchasing Dept.)

4. Recommend a program to employ the physically handicapped. This would involve research within the company and with those groups who deal with handicapped–date by June 1, 1972.
5. Research through the branches, the availability of and desire for day care facilities in their communities for their employees.
6. Develop a program to publicize our scholarship program. This should be given priority since it would be employed by the time this year's awards are announced in June.
7. Research possibilities for making Avon executives more accessible to groups of young people–due date June 1, 1972.
8. Make a memo to call Fred Daley in the Purchasing Department monthly to obtain progress reports concerning the development of minority vendors.
9. Research and develop for the *Amsterdam News* a series of ads to be inserted once every other month. Topics for these ads should include Avon's Black Achievers, Black Suppliers, the opportunity for black representatives, equal employment opportunity at above representative level and our "Avon Cares" message.
10. Design a program to communicate Avon Corporate Responsibility to its employees and the public at large.
11. Draft a letter to Mr. Shook about the top management approval of the recommendation that we include some sort of social audit in our annual report.
12. Check with Mr. Kierney about a Corporate Responsibility issue of "Avon and You."
13. Have available for our various meetings with Norman Haynes a list of possible organizations to which we might donate that furniture which is being discarded as a result of our move.

In all of these projects, remember that the most economical proposals have the greatest chance of acceptance.

Marcia Boles

Case Two

Genco Inc. (A)

The situation that had enveloped the Elkhorn paper mill was perplexing. John Wilson, a lawyer in the Genco legal department, circulated a memorandum on September 14, 1972 summarizing his most recent conversation with a senior official in the regional Environmental Protection Agency (EPA) office. He wrote in part:

> 1.–If we do not agree by October 4, 1972, to meet the criteria in their June 9, 1972 guidelines, suit will be filed against us under the 1899 Refuse Act seeking to enjoin us from discharging in excess of those criteria.
>
> 2.–He acknowledged that the EPA cannot give us a permit under the Refuse Act under the present status of the law.
>
> 3.–He acknowledged that their statutory authority–except for the Refuse Act–is questionable but the law that passes[1] will provide for "best practical control" and he believes their guidelines can be shown to be the "best practical." If the regulations under the law that passes set limits lower than EPA's guidelines, he said that "something" will be worked out. Basically, his position is that he is certain their guidelines will be the new regulations.
>
> 4.–We were the first company he talked to. He has not been putting pressure on us and . . . is aware of the . . . plaudits we received [for the Genco record of achievement in pollution control] and recognizes that we have been cooperative.
>
> 5.–Apparently no one has agreed to their criteria yet but he believes they soon will. No suits have been filed yet. He is to send me the form of commitment letter they want. He said this is a national EPA program.
>
> 6.–If we want to negotiate, he suggests the following:
>
> The average daily production of our mill was used in their calculations. We can use maximum daily average production during the highest production week which will increase our allowable discharges about 20% in his opinion. No settleable solids will be allowed. Later on, they will want more reduction.

[1] The Water Pollution Control Act was then pending in Congress.

For over two years, managers in the Paper Products Division (PPD) of Genco, aided by the corporate Environmental Affairs Department and the legal staff, had been working with the State Department of Resource Conservation (DRC) to develop a program for reducing pollution from the Elkhorn mill. Just as that program was being implemented, EPA issued the guidelines referred to in the memorandum above and requested the "voluntary" compliance of firms in the paper industry, supported by a compliance schedule to be filed within 90 days (e.g., October 4). The EPA standards were considerably more stringent than the interim emission levels agreed to earlier with the DRC. The situation was further complicated by the uncertainties surrounding the Federal Water Pollution Control Act Amendments then pending before Congress; would the legislation be enacted and if so, in what form? Moreover, a definition of the "best practical control" technology and the resultant standards to be prescribed for the paper industry remained in doubt.

ORGANIZATIONAL FACTORS

PPD was one of six divisions in Genco, a diversified manufacturing company with sales in 1971 of approximately $2.2 billion and after tax profits of $81 million. PPD had sales of about $400 million, making it the second largest in the company, and after tax profits of $11 million. The divisions were managed independently with little direct involvement from the corporate offices in operating decisions. Each was held accountable for the attainment of an annual financial plan agreed to in the fall in carefully considered negotiations between corporate and division managers. PPD operated six integrated pulp and paper mills, one of them at Elkhorn, and over 30 box and bag plants, the latter converting much of the output from the mills. Major products included linerboard, corrugated medium, corrugated shipping containers, folding boxes, and multi-wall bags.

Wilson's memorandum about the Elkhorn mill was addressed to Elton Johnson, manufacturing manager of primary operations in PPD, and an early advocate of environmental protection. Since the late 1950s, first as a mill manager and later in his current position, Johnson had been actively engaged in proposing and implementing projects to upgrade the emission profiles of the PPD mills. The division's record in this regard was generally recognized to be outstanding among paper firms. In 1968 he was given responsibility for all six paper mills, and the mill managers reported to him. An organization chart is provided in Exhibit 2-1.

Johnson's efforts in environmental protection had been partially responsible for the stress given to such matters by Donald Mason, Chairman of the Board of Genco. During the mid-1960s, Mason became impressed by the pollution control activities in PPD and concerned about the ecological impact of Genco operations more generally. He also foresaw the growing public awareness of environmental issues and the increased governmental involvement likely to result. His response had been a strongly worded policy statement in 1966 followed by the creation of the Environmental Affairs

Department, initially that same year as a unit in the corporate engineering organization and in 1970 as an independent department reporting directly to the president.

The other managers receiving copies of Wilson's memorandum included most of those who had been actively engaged in the Elkhorn deliberations over the preceding two years. First, there was Peter Kruger, until recently vice president and division manager of PPD. Although Kruger had been appointed corporate vice president for administration on June 30, 1972, he continued to play an instrumental role in the management of the division while his successor, Dan Phillips, wound up his affairs as regional general manager in another division. (In fact, Phillips had had little to do with Elkhorn thus far and was not on the distribution list for the memorandum.) Then there was Fred Skinner, corporate vice president of environmental affairs, and Jim Peterson, manager of the seven-person corporate environmental control group. Also receiving copies were Ed Donaldson (vice president of public relations), Bill Comacho (a senior engineer in the PPD engineering department with special responsibilities in pollution control), Peter Fitchdorn (Elkhorn mill manager), and Dick French (Elkhorn technical director).

EARLY DEVELOPMENTS AT THE ELKHORN MILL

The original Elkhorn mill was constructed in 1888 and through the years had been expanded and modified on numerous occasions under a succession of owners. In 1972 it was a large (620 ton/day) facility utilizing a neutral sulfide semichemical process (NCSS) for pulp and paper production and employing 350 people. The technology is summarized in Exhibit 2-3. Shortly after Johnson became manufacturing manager in 1968, he made a presentation to corporate and division executives in which he outlined the history of pollution control expenditures for each of the PPD mills and the further investments that he felt would be necessary to maintain them within expected regulations. His comments on Elkhorn were in part the following:

> The Elkhorn mill was originally operated as a kraft specialty mill. The property was acquired by Western Paper Company in 1946[2] and by 1949 the first hardwood semichemical pulp for medium was produced. Waste liquor from the process was burned in the kraft recovery cycle to avoid discharge to the river. This marked the first commercial application for this process.
>
> In 1953 the last kraft operations were discontinued. In order to continue recovering the waste liquor, an installation of the Institute of Paper Chemistry Direct Sulfitation system was made. The use of this unique recovery system has allowed the Elkhorn mill to operate a semichemical process at a very low level of effluent discharge. In 1963, increased discharges of solids from the woodyard necessitated the building of 3 ponds to treat about 25% of the mill effluent. In 1966, they were further enlarged. . . .

[2] Western Paper Company was acquired by Genco in 1955.

In this state, both air and water pollution are under the jurisdiction of the Department of Resource Conservation. The Board is appointed by the Governor. The state has submitted criteria and classifications for interstate streams to the Federal Government. Hearings are being held for the purpose of classifying intrastate streams. Although the Elkhorn River is intrastate we feel that the interstate criteria will apply.

A general air pollution abatement bill has been passed by the state legislature. Standards have not been set as yet.

Pollution abatement expenditures to date at Elkhorn, based on 1967 replacement costs, have been $2,963,000. Anticipated capital expenditures for pollution abatement equipment for 1968-1972 amount to approximately one million dollars.

With the assistance of Bill Comacho, Johnson also constructed a pollution load chart for each mill which included the impact of specific abatement projects. The pollution load units were a composite of emissions into both air and water. For the

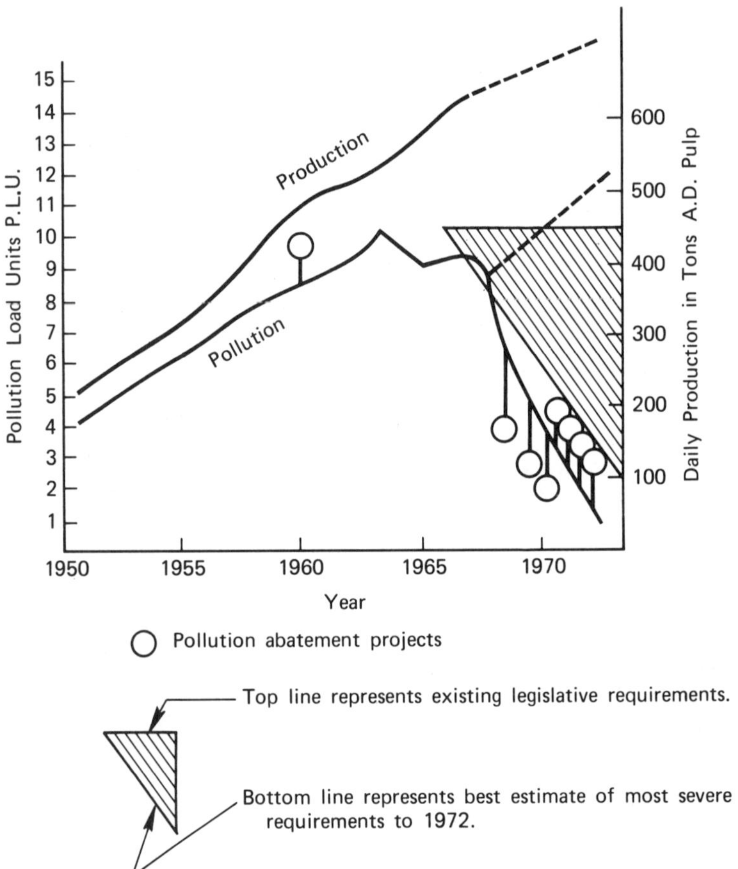

Figure 2-1 Elkhorn Mill—Load Chart—1968

Elkhorn mill, the most significant proposed expenditures were for enlargements and improvements in the holding ponds. These projects were to facilitate the removal of suspended solids and aeration to reduce the BOD[3] load prior to the release of mill discharge into the river.

DEVELOPMENT OF AN ABATEMENT PROGRAM

In August 1970, the DRC conducted public hearings on potential pollution sources on the Elkhorn River. Based on this and other data, the DRC issued pollution abatement orders on December 1 under state statutes to 64 municipalities and industrial concerns. A DRC official noted that over 90% of the suspended solids and BOD load were attributed to pulp and paper mills. He also said that pulp and paper production in the area had increased about 80% since 1960, while the BOD discharge remained fairly constant and suspended solids increased roughly 60%. The stated long-range goal was "to upgrade all waters to a quality suitable for the propagation of game fish."

Among the items contained in the DRC orders were the following: By January 1, 1971 the recipient was to submit a report of intention to comply together with a statement of alternatives; by June 1, 1971, detailed construction plans and specifications were to be submitted to the DRC; and by December 1, 1971, the facility was to be operating within the prescribed discharge limits on a "monthly average" basis. The DRC also indicated that petitions for review had to be filed within 60 days, to be followed by a public hearing.

The order sent to Genco was received by Fitchdorn and immediately circulated to other managers in PPD, environmental affairs, and the legal department. The daily limits prescribed for the mill were 11,160 pounds of suspended solids and 11,600 pounds of BOD, which compared with actual figures for 1970 of 21,565 and 15,865 pounds respectively.

By December 11, French developed a tentative plan for meeting the emission limitations encompassing four steps:

1.–Installing aeration in the pond system.
2.–Building a black liquor and evaporator cleanout surge pond.
3.–Installing sumps in the paper mill to collect press water.
4.–Installing a disc saveall-thickener in the waste system.

A plan based on these steps was duly submitted to the DRC. French also noted that an error had apparently been made by the DRC in applying the formula for suspended solids and that in fact the limit should have been 12,444 pounds. However, DRC officials indicated that a petition followed by a hearing would be necessary to amend the order. It was agreed within Genco that an appeal should be filed, recognizing that the hearing might result in some "poor publicity" from the particularly active conservation groups in the area.

[3]Suspended solids are materials floating in the water discharged from the mill. BOD is a measure of the oxygen needed to break down dissolved materials in the water.

By January 26, the abatement program had been further specified by French who also summarized for Johnson the assigned responsibilities for the engineering work. In each case the lead was to be taken by Elkhorn personnel, assisted in some instances by Comacho. Preparations were also made for the public hearing scheduled for April 1.

Then, on January 28 an environmentalist group petitioned the Attorney General of the United States to bring immediate action against nine industrial firms, among them Genco, ordering them "to desist from dumping harmful wastes into the Elkhorn River." The environmentalists further charged the DRC with being "permissive with the major pollutors of our [state] waterways." The regional United States Attorney met with the petitioners amid a clamor of newspaper stories on the issue, and subsequently with French and the company's local counsel.

In a later summary of Genco's record at Elkhorn prepared for the United States Attorney, French stressed that during the previous six years production had increased about 10%, while suspended solids had increased 11%, BOD had decreased 47%, and the water usage per ton of output had dropped 25%. He noted that the company had taken steps voluntarily to anticipate negative environmental effects and was actively involved in complying with a state order. The environmentalists remained adamant, however, and the United States Attorney indicated that he intended to follow the company's activities closely.

As French prepared for the April 1 public hearing, he discovered that one of the three paper machines in the mill had been shut down when the DRC tests were taken. As a result, the tests did not reflect the actual discharge from the entire mill. Based on this finding, French argued at the hearings that the allowable discharge should be considerably higher; specifically to 19,000 pounds of suspended solids and 15,000 of BOD per day. The DRC had until June 1 to respond to the Genco petition.

Meanwhile, with the approval of PPD, the Environmental Affairs Department, and counsel, the Elkhorn Engineering Department prepared and filed the detailed specifications for the treatment facilities on May 28. The program itself was not effected by the petition. French was also called upon to submit an air quality control program to the DRC by July 1, as well as file an application for the discharge of wastes into interstate waterways under the Federal 1899 Refuse Act.

The DRC did not act directly on Genco's petition for an increase in discharge limits. Instead, additional engineering data was requested within 90 days on the company's proposed treatment facilities. After conferring with the consulting engineers who had been engaged for the project, PPD officials concluded that this new DRC deadline could not be met. French then asked for and received an extension to February 1, 1972.

As Genco's relationship with the DRC developed over the following months, an understanding evolved on an approach to water pollution abatement at the Elkhorn mill. In essence, the discharge limits in the original order would stand and the company would seek to comply with them. However, because the improvements planned by Genco included some innovative measures, a one-year trial period would be granted from the time the operating permit was approved during which discharges in excess of the limits would not be considered violations unless considered unreasonably disproportionate by the DRC. At the end of that period the limits would be reviewed again.

The expanded water pollution control facilities were initially to be completed by September 1, 1972 at a cost of $750,000; however, because of weather and equipment delivery problems, the date was pushed back to December 1, 1972 with DRC approval. Also scheduled for completion on December 1, 1972 was the first phase of an air pollution control program—a precipitator costing $1.1 million to collect 99.5% of the particulates emitted from the recovery boilers. The second and third phase, each estimated to cost about $1.0 million, were to be undertaken during the succeeding two years.

ENTER EPA

On April 14, 1972, two officials from the regional EPA office visited the Elkhorn mill, stating that they wished to see a facility operating a secondary treatment system. They also indicated that the Region had requested approval from EPA in Washington to enter into voluntary agreements with major polluters, which would commit them to the same standards planned in the Water Pollution Control Act legislation then stalled in Congress. On May 22, Kruger received a letter from EPA requesting within three weeks information on the measures being taken to control the discharge of refuse into the Elkhorn River. It stated further that, "Your reply should be as complete as possible, and it is hoped that it will constitute a satisfactory voluntary commitment to an acceptable abatement program. In any event, the need for further action by this Branch will be evaluated in the light of your reply."

The EPA's actions were disturbing to Kruger. It was his understanding that state authorities were to have the responsibility for direct contact and negotiation with those in charge of individual facilities. In view of Genco's established relationship with the DRC, he objected to the need for dealing with a second regulatory agency. A second element in his thinking lay in the escalating cost of compliance. At Kruger's request, Comacho estimated that approximately $4.5 million in 1972 dollars would be required to have the "best available" technology for controlling water pollution by 1980, the guideline then being discussed in congressional deliberations. Kruger's reply to EPA on June 9 included the desired information as well as the following suggestion:

> I would respectfully submit that for us to attempt to work with both the state authority and the federal government on the same issues may tend to lead to confusion and all of us tending to work at cross purposes. Accordingly, we hope that your determinations on this matter will be in some manner channeled through the state Department of Resource Conservation.

On June 9, EPA issued voluntary emission level guidelines for water pollution control in the paper industry. French then met with regional EPA officials and was apprised of the specific limitations for the Elkhorn mill. In a letter of confirmation, EPA summarized its position: "We are seeking a firm program by your company to abate its violations of the Refuse Act of 1899 and the resultant pollution of the Elkhorn River. At the meeting, you were advised concerning the effluent limitations which we propose that your plant attain, and the means by which they were determined. We are inviting you to make a voluntary commitment to an undertaking to achieve such limitations." The average daily limits were BOD, 7,500 pounds and suspended solids, 4,600 pounds, both substantially less than called for in the DRC order. In addition, guidelines were proposed for oil and grease, iron and manganese which had not been explicitly covered heretofore.

PPD officials were highly upset by this turn of events. They felt that the demands continued to increase with little evident coordination between federal and state agencies. In addition, the mill had been shut down from time to time due to weakness in the market for corrugated medium, Elkhorn's primary product. By now Kruger was heavily involved in the day-to-day direction of the company's response. However, aside from the environmental affairs group (Skinner and Peterson) and legal counsel (Wilson), the deliberations remained within the division.

EPA had requested an answer to its proposal by July 8. On July 6, a reply was signed by French, containing the following comment written under Kruger's supervision:

> I am thus advising you that in the next 90 days you will receive a definite reply from an authorized officer of our Company on this subject matter. You understand that the economic implication of your request makes necessary an in-depth business evaluation of the mill, as well as the environmental considerations.

EPA responded to French's letter by requesting an answer by the end of August. After a brief review of the situation, the PPD management group concluded that the 90-day evaluation period promised originally was already tight enough. French then wrote to EPA that October 4 continued to be the earliest date that a reply could be expected. He also prepared the analysis and recommendations shown in Exhibit 2-2 as a basis for discussion on the eventual presentation to EPA.

On August 10, Johnson, Wilson, Skinner, Comacho, Peterson, and Peterson's senior water pollution control engineer met to establish a position on the Elkhorn mill. It was generally agreed that Genco should not accept a commitment beyond that made to the DRC. Moreover, rather than wait the full 90 days to answer EPA and possibly create the impression that such a commitment would be forthcoming, the group concluded that Wilson should sign a letter stating the company's position as soon as possible. Consequently, with the acquiescence of all concerned, including Kruger, Wilson wrote in part the following on August 22:

> As I understand the present federal-state water pollution control effort, the state intrastate water quality standards are the only standards applicable to our Elkhorn mill and the enforcement of intrastate standards is exclusively a state function. The state has diligently enforced its stringent intrastate standards for the Elkhorn River by a series of orders, including the order issued to our Elkhorn mill. Since we are in compliance with that order, under my view of the law, nothing more is required at this time. In addition, if we were to attempt to meet the standards you are proposing, revisions to our treatment system would be required which might delay our compliance with the state order.

Exhibit 2-1

PARTIAL ORGANIZATION CHART

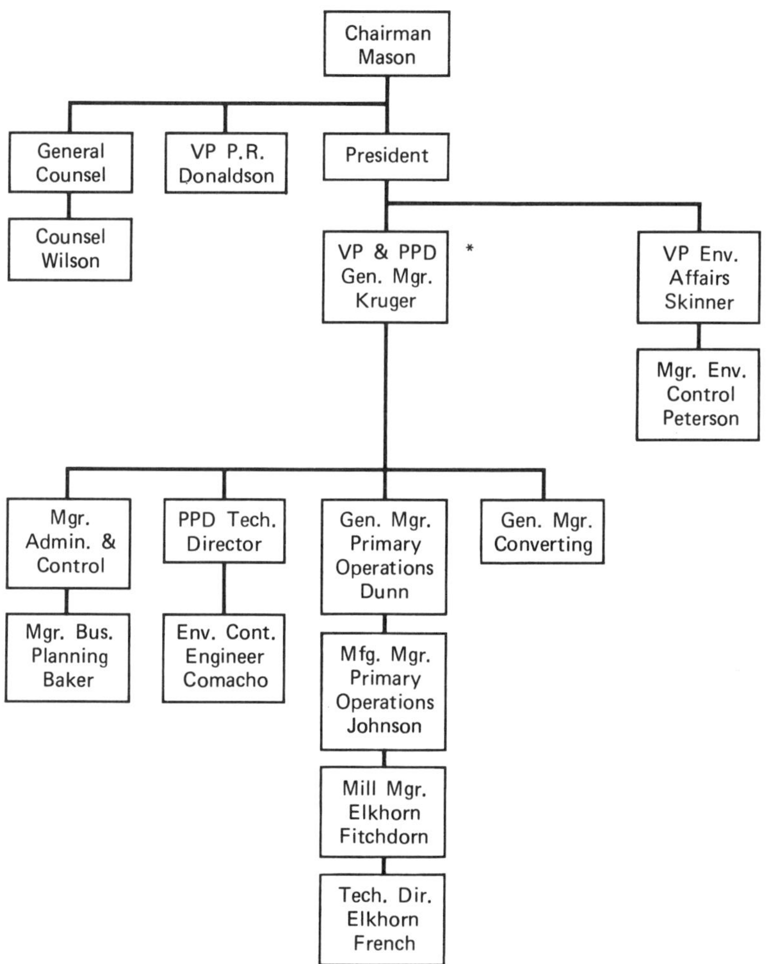

*As of June 30, 1972, Kruger was designated corporate senior vice president for administration. His place as general manager of PPD was taken by Phillips.

A POINT OF DECISION

Wilson's discussion with the regional EPA office summarized in his memorandum of September 14 (see page 61) was far from reassuring. A degree of urgency appeared to mark EPA's actions. An agreement had just been reached by the Senate-House conference committee on the Water Pollution Control Act and passage by Congress seemed assured.[4] Whether the President would veto the bill or, if he did, whether sufficient votes would be forthcoming to override his veto, were considerably less clear. Were the bill to become law, however, Wilson felt there was a reasonable chance that subsequent suits filed under the 1899 Refuse Act would be prohibited.

Managers at the mill tended to favor exploring the possibility of negotiating a settlement with EPA before the legislative issues were clarified. In this way, a more acceptable compliance schedule might result and, were it possible to obtain a five-year permit, some of the near-term uncertainty would be removed. On the other hand, Kruger maintained that if the legislation were enacted, the standards might well be less stringent; by accepting commitments now when others in the industry did not, the company might find itself at a competitive disadvantage. For his part, Wilson was not at all sure that EPA possessed the authority to negotiate an agreement or issue permits in the first place. Johnson, manufacturing manager of primary operations, wondered how his new division manager, Dan Phillips, would approach the problem.

Exhibit 2-2

Attention of Mr. E. B. Johnson
cc: P. K. Kruger
D. A. Phillips
T. A. Dunn
J. H. Wilson
W. S. Comacho
J. M. Peterson
P. G. Fitchdorn

Intra-Company Correspondence
July 23, 1972

RESPONSE TO EPA REQUESTS TO ELKHORN

The following are some facts, observations and possible approaches to be considered when answering the request from the EPA for a voluntary commitment to a long term pollution abatement program at the Elkhorn Mill.

BACKGROUND. There are three areas of concern involved in their request. First, an agreement to follow the state requirements as given in the DRC order to this mill. Second, an agreement to immediately lower the iron, manganese and oil content in our

---

[4] Under the Water Pollution Control Act, all industries discharging wastes into the nation's waterways would be required to apply the "best practical control technology" by July 1, 1977. By July 1, 1983 they would be required to use the "best available technology." Although no means of enforcement was provided, the Act specified further that discharge was to be eliminated entirely by July 1, 1985. The standards for particular industries and processes were to be specified later by EPA.

discharge. Third, an agreement to reach levels of 7,500 lbs./day BOD and 4,600 lbs. day of suspended solids by January 1, 1976 and to include an implementation schedule.

A commitment by this mill to meet the state order would of course change nothing technically as we are already involved in doing just that. There are two possible legal problems involved in adding a voluntary agreement to do the same with the federal government. First, I can conceive of this concession opening the door for all others by, in effect, admitting federal jurisdiction. Second, if we need to apply for an extension of our construction schedule, as now seems likely, we might have to obtain like permission from the EPA which would be time consuming.

The problem of iron, manganese and oil is potentially much more serious. Our pond revision is intended to handle surface oil and should do so. However, our one grab sample analysis made as part of our 1899 Act license submission showed apparent high oil contents in our No. 3 pond discharge. This was so in spite of there being no visible oil sheen on this pond. Further, a simple material balance of oil use within the mill versus apparent oil discharge indicates about ten times more oil being discharged than being used. The iron and manganese data also represents only one sample. Further, we have changed our pulping process which should decrease corrosion. We are now in the process of taking four composite samples of inlet water, No. 3 discharge and main mill discharge over a four-week period for analysis by the Institute of Paper Chemistry for iron, manganese and oil. Any further moves regarding these materials should wait on the results of these analyses.

It should be pointed out, however, that removal of iron and manganese would require a major investment in flocculation and settling equipment as there is no simple way to remove these materials.

The question of reaching the BOD and solids limits is best handled by a separate analysis. I do not believe that the BOD level specified will be difficult to reach. Our present system varies from 15,000 lbs./day in the winter to under 10,000 lbs./day in the summer. The enlarged system is intended particularly to lower the winter load to be more in line with state requirements.

I believe that it will be possible to meet the 7,500 lbs./day level through a continued program of collecting strong waste streams for complete treatment while at the same time removing all clean water from the strong collection points. In this manner, our Nos. 1, 2 and 3 ponds will operate at higher efficiencies. It may also be necessary to add some additional aeration after we have had time to analyze the operation of the enlarged pond system.

The solids limits of about 4,600 lbs./day may be difficult to reach. Whether it is attainable depends to a large extent upon the efficiency of No. 4 pond as a settling pond. It is difficult to predict as the majority of the material reaching that pond will be of very small size and will not settle rapidly. Recirculation of water within the mill will help as will possible filtration methods. It may well be, however, that in the final analysis some method of clarification will be necessary with recirculation of the solids removed back to No. 1 pond.

CONCLUSIONS. It is not possible at this time to design a least-cost treatment system for Elkhorn. Data is needed on the metals problem and on the operation of the expanded pond system. This information will not be available until late 1973.

If we were to commit the mill today to the 1976 goal *and* to specify how we would obtain it, I believe we would have to abandon our present approach and use a conventional system of clarifier, standard oxidation basis and secondary clarifier. This immediately implies an additional system for dewatering and burning sludge as we are too land limited to dispose of it by land fill. This additional system could include dewatering filters and presses, a predryer and a new furnace for burning the material.

RECOMMENDATIONS. I recommend that our next response to the EPA should comprise the following points:

1.–That we will continue to comply with the state order as it exists or as it is modified.
2.–That we will commit ourselves to reach the BOD and solids limits specified by January 1, 1976. (I don't believe that we would be conceding anything that won't be federal law long before 1976.)
3.–That all other points are to be deferred until we have had at least one year of operation of our new and enlarged system.

I do not believe that this type of reply will satisfy the EPA Region as they are presently operating; however, it is realistic with regard to our plans and system. It can be defended technically in my opinion. The danger of stronger legal action by the EPA does exist with this approach but that danger is present unless we concede to all of their requests.

It also may be that by the time our ninety days have expired this state and other states will have regained control by agreements similar to that made by Oregon. I must admit that I am somewhat pessimistic in this regard as it appears that the EPA has picked this state and particularly the Elkhorn River to make their big effort on.

D. L. French

Exhibit 2-3[1]

TECHNOLOGY, RAW MATERIALS, AND TYPES OF PAPER

PAPER MAKING TECHNOLOGY

THE MANUFACTURING PROCESS

The paper making process has two principal stages; the first involves converting wood to pulp, and the second is the conversion of pulp to paper. Ideally, pulp and paper making facilities should be located together, with pulp in slush form being pumped with high efficiency through pipes from one operation to the other at very low cost.

There are, however, a relatively large number of paper mills which do not have adequate pulp-making facilities to match their paper making requirements. These mills

---

[1]Adapted with permission from "A Note on the Paper Industry," prepared by Richard W. Moxon under the supervision of Associate Professor Robert B. Stobaugh, Harvard Business School, 1971.

purchase market pulp to make up their deficiencies. Market pulp is sold in sheet form, requiring drying, marketing, baling, and handling operations which are unnecessary in an integrated operation. Finally, after delivery to the mill, the bales are broken and individual sheets fed into the beaters in order to convert the dry sheets to slushy, free-flowing fibers.

PULP MANUFACTURE

Pulp is a crude fibrous cellulose raw material which, after suitable treatment can be converted into paper, paperboard, or rayon. Wood pulp is produced by: (1) mechanically grinding up logs (groundwood pulp); (2) chemical fibrization of wood chips (sulfate, sulfite, or soda pulp); or (3) a combination of chemical treatment and mechanical grindings (semichemical pulp).

Sulfate pulp, which accounted for about 67% of 1971 total U.S. pulp production, could be used in making most grades of paper. It is particularly suitable for producing packaging materials—heavy brown wrapping papers and paperboard. Since 1950, virtually all new pulping facilities had been constructed to utilize the sulfate process, both because recovery of chemicals make it a lower-cost process than sulfite, and because technological advances have made it possible to produce a good bleached (white) sulfate product. Sulfite pulp (representing about 8% of total U.S. pulp output) was once the most prevalent process. The pulp is light in color and especially well suited for the higher grades of writing and printing papers. Groundwood pulp (11% of the total) is much cheaper to produce than chemical pulps, since only about 7% of the raw material is lost in processing versus 55% or more in the chemical processes. But its low strength and coarse appearance limits its use to newsprint and low-grade tablet paper. The semichemical process (14% of total) was developed primarily to utilize hardwoods which initally were not well suited to the sulfate or sulfite processes. Semichemical pulp extracted a high yield from the wood input and produced a stiff, resilient paper best suited to corrugated medium, insulating board, egg cartons, and similar formed or molded products.

The cost of entering the pulp making business was high. Estimates in the early 1970s, gathered from various industry sources, placed the initial capital investment for pulp mills at somewhere between $140,000 and $160,000 per ton of daily output, exclusive of supporting forest lands with costs increasing at a rate of 10 to 15% a year. Many persons believed that the smallest economic size for a pulp mill was in the range of 350 to 400 tons a day, making $50 million a minimum capital requirement. Even such a small mill involved upwards of two years to construct and bring on stream.

PAPER MANUFACTURE

Paper is made by matting together wet cellulose fibers (the pulp obtained from one of the processes indicated above) to form a thin sheet of material which, when dried, has the desired strength, absorption, color, and flexibility specifications. In the modern day paper mill, the process begins in the beater, where pulp fibers, suspended in water, are mechanically cut, split, and crushed. During the beating stage, the fibers develop strong adhesive properties. When the pulp has been beaten and the necessary dyes, sizings, and resins added, the stock is refined and then allowed to flow onto the paper-making machine. The most widely used machine is the Fourdrinier, a machine that mats the fibers on an endless fine mesh screen, removes most of the excess water, and then dries the newly formed paper by passing it between a long series of steamheated cylinders.

The required capital investment for even a modest-sized paper mill was high, but not as great as that required for a pulp mill. There is a wide range of paper products that a firm may choose to make, and the choice of product line is the major determinant of the cost of entry. Paper machines designed to turn out huge quantities of standardized product, such as newsprint, might cost more than $20 million. On the other hand, a low-capacity machine, designed to make short runs of a specialty such as high-grade writing papers, could be built for less than five million dollars. The greatest restriction on construction of a paper-making operation of the latter type was the limited markets available for its output, rather than the magnitude of the investment.

Case Three

Genco Inc. (B)

On October 18, 1972, Congress overrode President Nixon's veto of the Water Pollution Control Act by a wide margin and it became law. In the preceding weeks, Genco officials had declined to negotiate a "voluntary" compliance schedule for the Elkhorn pulp and paper mill with EPA on the basis of guidelines proposed by the agency in June of that year. Genco's reply to EPA on October 4 was essentially a summary of its efforts to implement a program in satisfaction of the State Department of Resource Conservation's orders and an affirmation of the company's intention to maintain its cooperative posture on environmental matters. Genco was one of several that had been confronted with a possible suit under the 1899 Refuse Act for the discharge of wastes into navigable waters.[1]

After vacillating for several weeks on whether to initiate legal action, EPA decided against it. In fact, as soon as the legislation was passed, the company found the agency reluctant to discuss the standards to be applied for the "best available technology" required under the Act by July 1, 1977. As a result, the magnitude of the task ahead remained uncertain.

Toward the end of October, Peter Kruger, then in the process of disengaging from his job as division manager of the Paper Products Division (PPD) to become corporate senior vice president of administration, raised a number of fundamental questions. Should Genco invest upwards of $10 million for pollution control equipment over the next four years in the old Elkhorn mill which at the time had a book value of only $13 million? If this investment were made, was the corporation also implicitly committing itself to a subsequent expansion of the mill at a cost of $25 million? The division had proposed this expansion on two occasions during the previous six years, and both times the investment had been postponed. Was it not better to consider a new mill somewhere else? Were a new mill to be built, Elkhorn would be phased out and closed altogether prior to July 1, 1977, the date required for the installation of the "best practical" control technology.

---

[1] See Genco Inc. (A) case for background on these events.

Dan Phillips, the new general manager of PPD, was initially inclined to agree with the drift of Kruger's thinking. Rather than take a position on phasing out the mill at the outset, however, he obtained support for a full review of the Elkhorn mill. He was aware that managers in Primary Operations were strongly opposed to phasing out the facility. They maintained that it was a critical element in PPD's business strategy. Moreover, due in part to its low investment base, Elkhorn's after tax return on assets invested of 13.8% was three times the division average. On the other hand, Phillips knew that the chairman and president of Genco were both interested in the answers to Kruger's questions. In late November, responsibility for the study was assigned to Arthur Baker, manager of business planning in PPD. (See Exhibit 2-1 of the (A) case for a partial organization chart.)

THE ELKHORN MILL

PPD had a major market position in corrugated containers as well as the two products used to make them, linerboard and corrugated medium. The Elkhorn mill produced corrugated medium, and Baker noted that, despite the age of the paper machines, it was among the largest and lowest-cost facilities in this segment of the industry. He attributed the mill's advantageous position to a number of factors. First, the mill had been managed by highly capable managers over the previous two decades and consequently was well maintained and enjoyed fine labor relations. Second, company-owned woodlands were very convenient to the mill and capable of supporting half of its needs on a sustained yield basis, a high proportion for the industry. Third, the woodcutters in the area were as efficient as any in the country, thus providing relatively low cost raw material to the pulp mill.

Yet Baker and others in PPD were concerned that Elkhorn's leadership position in the industry would fade with time. Baker commented:

> There is one problem now that is likely to get worse. The three paper machines are old and relatively narrow. They don't trim as well with the newer, wider corrugating machines now being installed to make containers. A year ago we added some equipment to correct the width problem, but the process costs money and we sacrifice some in price. Our costs may have peaked out and at some point–it may be 2 or 10 or 15 years from now–they are likely to increase.

To preserve and extend Elkhorn's competitive position, PPD management had proposed a large paper machine to replace two of the existing machines and provide a 16% increase in capacity. Elton Johnson, primary operations manufacturing manager, was among the proponents of this plan. He commented:

> We applied for a new paper machine in 1969. It would have cost $13 million then against $25 million now. But we had just completed an $80 million integrated mill and the paper business was in the doldrums. The corporation said we were out of money and the project was turned down. Elkhorn has always been a low cost

> producer and that advantage is being lost. We've let the old machines go down hill in anticipation of a new one and our percentage downtime is beginning to show it. We've been starving the old machines—the mill manager feels it.

MARKET FACTORS: FALL 1972

In the fall of 1972, the paper industry showed signs of recovering from the slump that had marred the preceding several years. Prices appeared to be firming and operating rates and margins were improving, though in the last instance not to the levels enjoyed in the 1960's. As reflected in Exhibits 3-1 and 3-2, the industry's performance was closely related to the general economic condition of the country; from 1952 to 1972, tonnage increased at an annual rate of 4.4%, while real growth in GNP averaged 3.7%. Profits had been erratic, however, and overall had not kept pace with the growth in output. Selected statistics reflecting historical balance sheet and income statement trends for the industry are summarized in Exhibit 3-3.

Several explanations for the mediocre profit record among paper firms were typically offered. Central among them was the tendency for new mills to come on stream in waves, each wave creating excess capacity that was only absorbed in time for a new surge of expansion. Because of the capital intensive nature of the business and the relatively large number of competitors, producers opted for lower prices under these conditions in an effort to avoid reduced operating rates. Moreover, to obtain greater production economies, the average size and cost of the new installations steadily increased, thus placing greater competitive pressure on older mills. Price behavior is shown in Exhibit 3-4 and an indication of concentration in representative segments of the industry in Exhibit 3-5. There was also concern in some quarters about the intrusion of other materials, most notably plastics, into certain markets traditionally held by paper products, e.g., shipping sacks, throwaway cups, etc.

Semichemical paperboard, most of it used in corrugated medium, accounted for roughly 6.7% of the 55 million tons of paper and board produced in the U.S. in 1971 as shown in Exhibit 3-6. The markets for corrugated medium and linerboard were highly competitive, and producers had experienced considerable difficulty over the years securing price increases.

In late 1972, Baker described the corrugated market as a "paradox." An earlier forecast of supply and demand in each of the industry segments in which PPD competed indicated an expected weakness in operating rates for 1973 for semichemical mills that did not carry over to either linerboard or corrugated medium as a whole. Although PPD managers expected to outperform the industry, overall operating rates of 90% or less spelled trouble on the price front. These forecasts had been quite accurate in the past and were influential in shaping Kruger's thinking on Elkhorn.

On the other hand, by December 1972, Elkhorn production was edging toward practical capacity. Tom Dunn, Manager of Primary Operations, commented on market conditions:

> The market has gotten a lot stronger in the last few weeks. Right now I'd like to have that new machine at Elkhorn in operation. I could sell the increased output

OPERATING RATES

	Linerboard	*All Corrugated Medium*	*Semichemical Mills Only*
1966	96%	96%	96%
1968	94	90	92
1970	92	93	93
1971	93	95	95
1972	94 E	94 E	91 E
1973	95 E	93 E	89 E
1974	98 E	96 E	92 E

> this afternoon. We're even in danger of shutting down our own box plants because there isn't enough corrugated medium to supply them with.

Conclusive explanations for the discrepancy between forecast and actual conditions were illusive. The economic upturn was obviously one factor, though Baker was also aware that some mills were shut down or forced to run at reduced rates because unusual weather conditions had interrupted wood gathering operations in parts of the country. He also knew that one large new mill which was supposed to produce corrugated medium had been diverted to other products, at least for the time being, and possibly there were more in this category. Finally, semichemical mills were under pressure from pollution control regulations, and Baker suspected that a certain amount of capacity might have been lost as a result of mill closings. Prices were firm, but noticeable increases had not as yet been forthcoming, perhaps as a result of price control limitations.

Pollution control regulations were expected to have a significant impact on capital expenditures in the paper industry during the 1970s. Genco executives had taken special note of a study of the industry prepared by Arthur D. Little for the Council on Environmental Quality and EPA, and published in March 1972. The study indicated that roughly 45% of all U.S. paper mills, accounting for 15% of total capacity, were economically marginal and therefore susceptible to closure due to the costs of pollution abatement. Although only a fraction of these facilities were expected to shut down, semichemical mills were among those most likely to be effected. On the other hand, Elkhorn was well above the size considered by ADL to be marginal. Excerpts from this study are contained in Exhibit 3-8.

THE ELKHORN STUDY

The evaluation of the Elkhorn mill was completed in early January, 1973. Baker summarized the reasoning behind the study and the methodology employed:

> A number of people at corporate who are concerned about pollution control expenditures are asking in this case if they are not the tail wagging the dog. After we've doubled the book value of the mill, haven't we eliminated any choice on a new paper machine? The feeling that this is bad has been visceral, based on the

> belief that Elkhorn is an old mill and we might be better off starting all over again somewhere else.
>
> This department [business planning] hasn't been that deeply involved in pollution abatement except in a broad planning sense until this study. It's generally been Comacho[1] and people like that who keep track of budgets and activities. A financial analyst doesn't contribute much to technical decisions; if they say something is needed and Johnson and Dunn agree, we take their word for it. But the Elkhorn question is different.
>
> Our approach has been first to test the accuracy of the statement that after a new machine is installed, we would still have an old mill. We documented all the equipment behind the paper machines to determine its age, expected life, capacity and condition. We also evaluated the woodyard and asked how are the costs? Can it handle increased capacity? I believe we established that the mill is in good condition in most areas, though not all.
>
> Then, we compared the capital costs of various alternatives for the period 1973 to 1977. [The alternatives included (a) installing the pollution control equipment and certain maintenance projects without an increase in capacity, (b) making these investments and also eliminating a number of bottlenecks to increase production by 3.3%, (c) installing a new paper machine at Elkhorn, (d) building a new mill in the same area to take advantage of the Genco woodlands, and (e) building a new mill in another area.] The last step was to project a P and L for the next 10 years for each of these alternatives and calculate the incremental return on investment.

A summary of the study is contained in Exhibit 3-7. The results appeared to confirm one point that worried managers in PPD, as Baker commented:

> Returns on a new integrated pulp and paper mill installation are tough to show at current prices. You just can't get there from here. Numbers I've seen recently in the industry on new mills at today's costs yield a discounted cash flow of maybe 3%—not enough to begin to cover interest.

Johnson reflected on his view of the analysis:

> The study has shown that the three old machines are the only bad parts of the mill. The rest is good and the site is ideal. If we put in a new paper machine we'd have a first-rate mill. On the other hand, if we built another mill, we would have to install the "best available" pollution control equipment right away (not the "best practical") which might cost another \$4 or \$5 million. With an existing facility under the law, the best available isn't necessary until 1977 to 1983.

ADDITIONAL CONSIDERATIONS

Annual budgets and capital requests for the paper mills were generally initiated by managers in primary operations and reviewed in detail with the division general manager

[1] The chief environmental control engineer in the PPD technical department.

They were then submitted to the corporation for comment and approval. By early January, negotiations had been more or less completed throughout the company on the 1973 budget. Pending the outcome of the Elkhorn study, the assumption had been made in the PPD budget that the mill would continue in operation with future investments sufficient to execute the administrative order issued by the state and to keep up with required maintenance and replacement projects. Dunn reflected on his dilemma:

> We've been asked by the corporation to live within our cash flow as far as capital spending is concerned. Yet we're working against time limits on environmental control. That means I'm forced to take environmental control projects first and let capacity increases and cost reductions come later. The fellows at corporate won't tell you what to do; you hope like mad you're right.

Dunn's thinking on Elkhorn was complicated by the existence of another old mill in PPD having similar physical characteristics but a less secure woodlands position and generally lower returns. In this instance, environmentalist pressure had not been severe, though under the regulations to be promulgated under the Water Pollution Control Act by the states and approved by EPA, both mills would presumably have to meet a relatively uniform set of standards by July 1, 1977.

As the Elkhorn study was being circulated among PPD managers, the corporate planning office completed its consolidation and analysis of the division budgets. The figures revealed that the aggregate capital spending requests for all divisions for 1973 exceeded the president's guidelines by $18 million, or about 20%. It was unclear what, if anything, would happen as a result of this overage.

Negotiations were also proceeding with the State Department of Resource Conservation on a permit to discharge effluent into the Elkhorn River. In early January, the DRC drafted a permit for Genco review which provided for interim emission levels in line with the original state order, i.e., a monthly average not to exceed 11,160 pounds of suspended solids and 11,600 pounds of BOD. It also specified that by July 1, 1976 the company must comply with the levels suggested the previous June by EPA of 4,600 pounds of suspended solids and 7,500 pounds of BOD as well as limitations on iron, manganese, and oil and grease. The document stated further that the "permit is issued with the understanding that it does not stop the state or the U.S. EPA from subsequent establishment of further requirements for treatment or control at any time."[3]

The proposed permit was analyzed in detail by Dick French, Elkhorn technical director. His recommendations to Johnson included the following:

> I believe we should attempt to have the permit modified to reflect a July 1, 1977 date for achieving the operational levels and adjust the other compliance dates accordingly. It will be difficult, if not impossible, for us to make a least-cost solution with the schedule in this permit.
>
> We must object to the iron and oil limits as stated. A great deal of our hexane soluble material appears to come from our waste and pressure is on us to increase

[3]EPA had not as yet issued emission level standards for the paper industry under the Water Pollution Control Act.

waste percentage. If we are allowed credit for the river having iron then there would be no problem.

In some fashion we should clarify the question of what protection this permit gives us. It appears to be all one-sided.

A public hearing was scheduled for February during which Genco managers hoped these and other issues might be satisfactorily resolved. In the meanwhile, PPD managers had the task of planning for the overall future of the Elkhorn mill.

Exhibit 3-1

SELECTED ECONOMIC AND PAPER INDUSTRY STATISTICS

	Real GNP (billions)	*% Change*	*Paper Industry Demand/ Prod. (1) (000 tons)*	*% Change*	*Capacity Additions (1) (000 tons)*	*% Increase*	*Paper Industry Operating Rate (2)*	*Paper Industry Profits (1) (millions)*	*% Change*
1972P	$789.5	+6.4%	59,000	+ 8.9%	1,263	2.1%	96.2%	$883	+72.5%
1971	741.7	+3.0	54,180	+ 1.6	1,750	3.0	90.6	512	-28.8
1970	720.0	-0.6	53,329	- 1.6	580	1.0	90.9	719	-27.2
1969	724.7	+2.6	54,187	+ 5.7	2,131	3.8	94.6	987	+11.0
1968	706.6	+4.7	51,245	+ 9.2	2,262	4.2	93.0	889	+11.7
1967	675.2	+2.6	46,926	- 0.4	2,569	5.0	89.1	796	-12.6
1966	658.1	+6.5	47,113	+ 6.9	3,337	6.9	94.7	911	+ 4.8
1965	617.8	+6.3	44,080	+ 5.7	1,823	3.9	93.5	869	+15.3
1964	581.1	+5.5	41,703	+ 6.3	1,579	3.5	91.7	754	+18.9
1963	551.0	+4.0	38,230	+ 4.5	1,248	2.9	89.1	634	+ 1.0
1962	529.8	+6.6	37,541	+ 5.0	623	1.5	87.1	628	+ 7.7
1961	497.2	+1.9	35,749	+ 3.8	1,466	3.5	85.0	583	- 0.7
1960	487.7	+2.5	34,444	+ 1.3	1,102	2.7	84.5	587	- 5.2
1959	475.9	+6.4	34,015	+10.4	1,591	4.1	86.3	619	+34.6
1958	447.3	-1.1	30,823	+ 0.5	1,290	3.5	81.1	460	-11.7
1957	452.5	+1.4	30,666	- 2.5	2,330	6.7	84.7	521	-20.7
1956	446.1	+1.8	31,441	+ 4.2	1,852	5.6	92.2	657	+ 8.7
1955	438.0	+7.6	30,178	+12.3	996	3.0	92.4	604	+26.1
1954	407.0	-1.4	26,876	+ 1.0	990(3)	3.2	84.8(3)	479	+ 6.4
1953	412.8	+4.5	26,605	+ 9.0	1,324(3)	4.4	87.2(3)	450	+ 3.0
1952	395.1		24,418		1,141(3)	4.0	83.4(3)	437	
20-year Average (4)		3.7%		+ 4.4%					+ 3.1%

P – Preliminary
(1) American Paper Institute (API) data.
(2) Figured on average capacity that year. Computed from API data.
(3) Smith, Barney estimates based on API data.
(4) Computed by fitting log-liner, least squares trendlines to the figures in this 20-year period.

Source: Smith, Barney, *The Paper Industry–Another Decade of Disappointment?*, New York, 5/18/73.

Exhibit 3-2

APPARENT CONSUMPTION OF ALL GRADES OF PAPER AND PAPERBOARD

YEAR	*LBS./CAPITA*	*000 TONS PER BILL. $ REAL GNP.*
1899	57.9	
1904	73.7	
1909	90.8	
1914	108.8	N/A
1919	119.6	
1924	162.6	
1929	220.3	
1934	178.6	
1939	243.7	
1944	281.6	
1947	343.4	79.9
1948	355.9	80.6
1949	331.0	76.2
1950	381.1	81.7
1951	394.6	79.7
1952	368.3	73.4
1953	391.6	76.0
1954	385.0	77.1
1955	418.5	79.3
1956	432.2	81.8
1957	410.1	77.9
1958	401.6	78.5
1959	435.5	81.4
1960	433.3	80.3
1961	439.0	81.1
1962	452.7	79.7
1963	462.1	79.3
1964	483.6	79.8
1965	505.6	79.5
1966	536.2	80.0
1967	522.8	76.9
1968	554.7	78.8
1969	581.4	81.3
1970	563.8	80.2
1971P	566.6	79.3

Source: API, "The Statistics of Paper 1972," June 1972 p. 32

Exhibit 3-3

SELECTED FINANCIAL STATISTICS—PAPER AND ALLIED PRODUCTS 1950-1972

Year	*Capital Expenditures*[1]	*Fixed Assets as a % of Total Assets*[2]	*Debt/Equity Ratios*[3]	*Return on Sales*[4]	*Return on Net Worth*[4]
1950	299	41	13.7	8.8	15.6
1951	389	41	15.8	–	–
1952	371	43	18.2	–	–
1953	397	44	17.6	–	–
1954	533	45	18.2	–	–
1955	556	44	18.6	6.1	11.2
1956	750	46	22.3	6.1	11.4
1957	767	50	22.5	5.0	8.9
1958	618	51	23.7	4.5	7.3
1959	620	61	22.8	5.2	9.3
1960	644	64	23.3	5.0	8.4
1961	685	64	22.6	4.7	7.7
1962	750	64	25.1	4.6	8.1
1963	709	63	24.9	4.5	8.0
1964	901	64	23.7	5.1	9.1
1965	1,185	63	28.1	5.4	10.0
1966	1,422	65	35.6	5.4	10.5
1967	1,585	65	41.5	4.7	8.8
1968	1,238	67	45.1	4.7	9.6
1969	1,420	na	41.9	4.8	9.7
1970	1,397	na	46.8	3.4	7.0
1971	1,197	na	49.7	2.3	4.8
1972	1,421	na	46.8	4.0	8.9

[1] Source: U.S. Bureau of the Census. *Annual Survey of Manufactures,* various issues.

[2] Source: Department of the Treasury, Internal Revenue Service, "Statistics of Income, Corporation Income Tax Returns Annual Issues"; From API "A Capital and Income Survey," 1973.

[3] Source: Derived from Federal Trade Commission-Securities and Exchange Commission, *Quarterly Financial Report for Manufacturing Corporations,* 1950-1973.

[4] Source: FTC percentages calculated from "Quarterly Financial Report for Manufacturing Corporations," API, "A Capital and Income Survey," 1973.

Exhibit 3-4

WHOLESALE PRICE INDEXES OF PULP AND PAPER PRODUCTS 1961-1971
1957-1959 = 100

	1961	*1962*	*1963*	*1964*	*1965*	*1966*	*1967*	*1968*	*1969*	*1970*	*1971*
All industrial commodities	100.8	100.8	100.7	101.2	102.5	104.7	106.3	109.0	112.8	116.9	121.2
All pulp and paper	98.8	100.0	99.2	99.0	99.9	102.6	104.0	105.2	108.2	112.5	114.5
Woodpulp	95.0	93.2	91.7	96.1	98.1	98.0	98.0	98.0	98.0	107.4	109.8
Waste paper	80.5	97.5	92.2	92.4	99.4	105.0	78.1	101.5	108.3	97.6	87.4
Paper	102.2	102.6	102.4	103.6	104.1	107.3	110.1	112.7	116.6	122.2	125.6
Paperboard	92.7	93.1	94.7	96.4	96.4	97.1	97.3	92.1	94.4	98.4	99.6
Converted paper and board products	99.5	101.0	99.7	98.3	99.3	102.3	104.8	105.9	108.8	113.1	115.0
Building paper and board	100.8	97.2	96.2	94.0	92.7	92.6	91.9	92.8	97.1	92.8	94.6

Source: Bureau of Labor Statistics.

Exhibit 3-5

PERCENT OF VALUE OF SHIPMENT OF EACH CLASS OF SELECTED PAPER OR BOARD MILL OUTPUT ACCOUNTED FOR BY THE LARGEST COMPANIES

	Percent of Value of Shipments by			
	4 Largest	*8 Largest*	*20 Largest*	*50 Largest*
Tissue Stock				
1963	56	72	88	99
1958	57	69	83	94
1954	54	64	80	NA
Container Board-Kraft (26311-26312, exc. sp. fd. bd.)				
1963	32	54	82	99+
1958	37	57	84	99
1954	42	59	83	NA
Combination Paperboard: Shipping Containerboard (26314)–old designation as folding boxboard stock				
1963	31	49	75	98
1958	34	50	75	97
Combination Bending and Non-Bending Paperboard (26315, 26316)–once called set-up boxboard				
1963	37	52	79	NA
1958	28	48	78	NA

Source: U.S. Bureau of the Census. *Concentration Ratios in Manufacturing Industry 1963*. For Senate Subcommittee on Antitrust and Monopoly. Vol. I. pp. 168-169. 1966.

Exhibit 3-6

1971 U.S. PRODUCTION OF PAPER AND BOARD

	1971 (000's tons)		*1970 (000's tons)*	
All Grades		55,092		53,516
Paper		23,838		23,625
Newsprint, coated, book, and related papers	14,505		14,418	
Packaging & industrial converting papers	5,458		5,439	
Tissue	3,876		3,768	
Paperboard		26,121		25,477
Unbleached linerboard	11,321		10,962	
Bleached packaging	3,501		3,404	
Semi-chemical paperboard (corrugating medium)	3,717		3,414	
Combination shipping containerboard	1,391		1,523	
Combination boxboard	3,635		3,770	
Other paperboard*	2,547		2,404	
Construction paper and board		4,995		4,276
Wet machine board		138		138

*Total corrugated medium was 4,586 and 4,325 thousand tons in 1971 and 1970 respectively. In addition to semi-chemical paperboard produced through a sulfite process, medium was also produced through the sulfate or kraft process. This latter production is included in "other."

Source: Adapted from U.S. Department of Commerce, Bureau of the Census, "Current Industrial Reports," 1971.

Exhibit 3-7

ELKHORN MILL STUDY

I. Elkhorn Mill Alternatives–Capital Requirements, 1973-1977 (in thousands)

Mill Production-Tons/Day at 12/31/77[1]	*620 TPD*	*641 TPD*	*750 TPD*
Pulpmill			
Woodroom	$806	$806	$806
Digester Area	365	365	765
Washer Area	210	210	650
Recovery Area	290	290	290
Miscellaneous Capital (0-25M ea.)	3,250	3,250	3,250
Power Plant	755	755	755
Shipping	15	15	50
Pollution Abatement[2]			
Air	3,098	3,098	3,098
Water	2,033	2,033	2,033
Solids	825	825	825
Potential Projects	4,000	4,000	4,000
Subtotal Pollution Abatement	9,956	9,956	9,956
Refining and Stock Preparation	325	325	325
Paper Machines–Existing			
Minimum Expenditure	355	355	355
Maintain at 620 TPD	2,124	2,124	—
Expand to 641 TPD	—	2,557	—
New Paper Machine & Building	—	—	24,400
Total Capital	18,457	21,008	41,602

II. Percent After Tax Return on Incremental Investments

		1977	*1978*	*1979*	*1980*	*1981*	*1982*
(a)	Expansion to 750 TPD vs. no expansion at 620 TPD	6.4	7.6	7.8	8.1	8.3	8.6
(b)	Expansion to 641 TPD vs. no expansion at 620 TPD	10.4	8.0	8.0	7.9	7.9	7.9
(c)	Expansion to 750 TPD vs. expansion to 641 TPD	5.9	7.6	7.7	8.1	8.4	8.8

Exhibit 3-7 (continued)

III. Differential Profit Requirements—New Mill Versus Elkhorn New Machine (in millions)

	New Mill Same Area	*New Mill Another Area*
Investment	$67.3	$87.3[3]
Less: Elkhorn 750 TPD investment	41.6	41.6
Differential investment	$25.7	$45.7
After tax earnings required for 8% return on investment	$ 2.0	$ 3.6
Pre tax earnings required	4.0	7.2
Cost savings required in $ per ton	$15.24	$27.43

IV. Potential Cost Savings per ton Compared with Elkhorn

Tonnage—all at 750 TPD		
Wood	–	(Higher)
Waste	–	2.00
Chemicals & supplies	(Higher)	(Higher)
Labor	–	1.00
Electric Power	(Higher)	1.00
Fuel	–	1.00
Maintenance	2.00	2.00
Depreciation	(4.53)	(4.53)
Freight	–	(Higher)
Taxes	(Higher)	–
Net effect	(2.53)	2.47

[1] Several years are required to add new capacity. A new paper machine would not be in operation until 1977.

[2] In addition to identified abatement projects, it is possible that up to $750 thousand would be required in 10 years for replacement of existing abatement equipment. Another $1.5 million for pollution abatement might be required depending on the interpretation and implementation of the laws.

[3] Includes $20 million for the acquisition of timberland.

Exhibit 3-8

THE ECONOMIC IMPACT OF POLLUTION CONTROL PULP AND PAPER MILLS[1]

A. INDUSTRY STRUCTURE

About 45% of all U.S. mills, accounting for some 15% of total U.S. paper capacity, are economically marginal by current standards of efficiency.[2] In general, this means that they fall below the current minimum economic size for mills in their product sector. These mills will have the greatest difficulty in meeting the anticipated pollution abatement requirements. Table 3-1 on page 91 shows the distribution of these mills by product sector.

B. PROFITABILITY TREND

The paper industry's profitability is at its lowest point since World War II, with after-tax returns on total assets averaging about 4% in 1970. Profitability has declined further to about 3% of total assets in 1971, judging from the financial performance reported by 39 publicly held companies for the first nine months of 1971. . . . .

Our analysis points to improved operating rates in most sectors of the industry by 1973, assuming real GNP growth of 5% in 1972 and 1973. Significant overcapacity is expected to continue through 1973 in three product sectors: insulation board, semichemical corrugating medium, and special industrial paper. Mills in these sectors will have great difficulty in coping with additional pollution abatement costs because of weak prices and low profits. For the rest of the industry the market environment will generally provide increased mill utilization and be conducive to price increases in the absence of rigid price controls. Between 1974 and 1976 we expect operating rates to decline again judging from previous cycles in this industry. Industry profitability will follow the same cyclical trend.

C. PRICE IMPACT

To determine the price increases necessary to absorb the increased pollution abatement costs anticipated by 1976, we compared the abatement costs for efficient mills with the approximate median price of each product group. The major price increases

---

[1] Arthur D. Little, Inc., in *The Economic Impact of Pollution Control,* A Summary of recent studies prepared for the Council on Environmental Quality, Department of Commerce and Environmental Protection Agency, March 1972, p. 277 ff.

[2] In this report, except as noted, the term "mill" refers to a single facility that includes both pulp and papermaking facilities; that is, an integrated facility is considered a single mill.

relative to current prices will be in hardboard, newsprint and uncoated groundwood, bleached kraft pulp and unbleached kraft linerboard. Here, the price increases range from 6.5% to 10% of product value, depending upon the grade. Product sectors that will experience moderate price increases (3.5% to 6% of current product value) are: Bleached paperboard, semichemical corrugating medium, bag and wrapping paper, combination paperboard, insulation board, printing papers, and dissolving pulp. The other product sectors will require only modest price increases.

We anticipate that all of the above price increases will be obtained (in the absence of price controls) because of the tightening supply/demand balances projected for most sectors in 1972 and 1973. Beyond 1974, prices might well decline again should the industry enter another cycle of overcapacity.

In most cases, abatement cost levels for marginal mills will be appreciably higher than those for larger, more efficient mills since the latter benefit from economies of scale. This factor adds to the economic difficulties of the marginal mills.

D. MILL SHUTDOWN PROBABILITIES

Table 3-2 on page 92 summarizes mill shutdown probabilities between 1972–1976 with and without pollution abatement expenditures above current levels. It indicates the key impact areas are: sulfite and semichemical pulp, tissue paper, printing and writing paper, special industrial paper, and combination paperboard. In addition to these, we expect less extensive dislocations to occur in other product groups–mainly newsprint, uncoated groundwood paper, and packaging paper and board.

Some mills in all of the above sectors will close by 1976 strictly because of economic considerations, but the closure rate will be increased significantly by the requirement to expend capital to correct a pollution problem. In most cases, marginal, single-mill companies in these sectors will be unable to obtain capital for pollution control equipment because their return on investment is destined to remain very low. Most such mills are not integrated to woodpulp and will face a cost-price squeeze since prices for the market pulp or waste paper upon which they are dependent are expected to increase at a more rapid rate than the price of the end products which they produce. The life of many of these mills will be prolonged if they are able to minimize their capital costs by joining in a municipal water treatment system. For other mills, particularly tissue paper and special industrial paper companies, it is still questionable whether they can absorb the increased operating costs for pollution abatement since these costs are significantly higher for them than for large-scale producers.

TABLE 3-1 SUMMARY OF ECONOMICALLY MARGINAL PULP AND PAPER CAPACITY, 1971

		Economically Marginal Mills			
Production Sector	*Total No. of Mills*	*Size Criteria (under tons/day)*	*No. of Mills*	*Percent of Total Mills*	*Percent of Total Capacity*
Sulfite Pulp	37*	150**	12	33*	14
Semi-Chemical Pulp	41*	200**	9	22*	6
Tissue	102	50	49	48	18
Printing, Writing and Related	138	200	97	70	48
Special Industrial Paper	38	25	9	25	17
Combination Paperboard	170	100	78	49	27
Other Packaging Paper and Board	97	200–400	17	18	5
Newsprint and Groundwood	32	350	11	29	19
Construction Paper	47	100	31	60	36
Insulation Board	23	100	6	26	9
Hardboard	29	100	10	35	10
Total	752		329	44	15

*Nearly all of these pulp mills are integrated to mills making paper and paperboard.
**Includes some larger mills without chemical recovery systems.
Source: Arthur D. Little, Inc., estimates

TABLE 3-2 SUMMARY OF MILL SHUTDOWN PROBABILITIES, 1972-1976

		Probability of Closure		*Capacity Removal*	
Product Sector	*Marginal Capacity (000 tons/yr)*	*Status Quo* %*	*Additional Abatement %*	*Status Quo* (000 tons/yr)*	*Additional Abatement (000 tons/yr)*
Sulfite and Semi-Chemical Pulp	750	5-10	65	50	485
Tissue	650	15	50	105	345
Printing, Writing and Related	4,730	10	20	490	890
Special Industrial Paper	60	30	85	20	50
Combination Paperboard	2,030	10	25	200	540
Other Products	3,315	5	25	205	775
Total	11,535			1,070	3,085

*Assumes no additional pollution control expenditures above current levels.
Source: Arthur D. Little, Inc., estimates

Case Four

The Golden Eagles (A)

The Jefferson National Corporation, a one-bank holding company formed in 1968, was a diversified financial services company with total assets of approximately $5 billion. From a commercial banking history which could be traced to the 1700s, the holding company had, through mergers and acquisitions, expanded its activities into mortgage banking, investment management services, consumer finance services, leasing, and a number of other banking-related financial services. As shown in Exhibit 4-1, even though the company's commercial banking activities were not growing as rapidly as its other service categories, they continued to provide the bulk of both revenues and pretax income.

The Jefferson National Bank and Trust Company, the holding company's largest subsidiary, was a regional commercial bank with total deposits of over $3 billion. Through mergers with other banks and internal expansion, it had become the largest commercial bank in the metropolitan Cleveland area and ranked among the top 25 commercial banks nationally, as measured by total deposits. The compound annual growth rate of total deposits had been 12.7% from 1967 to 1972, and for the same five year period, loans had grown at a compound annual rate of 21.5% and total revenues at a rate of 26.6%. Earnings per share had grown by 12.9% per year and in 1972 the bank had achieved a return on equity of 16.1%.

The bank was considered an aggressive, innovative organization. For example, rather than concentrating on prestigious lending relationships with large prime-rate customers, the national banking group emphasized making loans to somewhat smaller (often local) firms in the "middle market," where credit arrangements commanded rates of interest higher than the prime rate. Jefferson National also had been one of the pioneers among banks in providing installment credit to consumers and small businesses. In support of these services and in order to expand its retail deposit base, the bank had launched an ambitious branch building program in the late 1950s. By 1973, it had 85 banking offices in seven contiguous counties of northeastern Ohio. Overseas, through its International Banking Group, the bank also had a London branch and representative offices in Mexico, Singapore, and Germany and participation in the ownership of a Mideast bank.

In addition to what was viewed within the banking industry as an impressive record of growth and financial performance, Jefferson National Corporation had come to be known as an industry leader in its responsiveness to social issues. As early as the mid-1960s, several of the bank's senior executives strongly advocated an increased institutional commitment to equal employment opportunities for minorities, commercial lending programs for minorities, and other community-oriented activities.

Typically, as was the case in most large commercial banks, top management had been selected from credit-trained officers inside the bank, and only seldom were senior executives recruited from the outside. Recently, however, this pattern had changed: Owen Taggert, Chairman, was an economist who had been with the bank only ten years; Walter Davis, President of the holding company, had been with the bank nine years and had had experience in an accounting firm and a manufacturing company; Benjamin Browning, Executive Vice President of the holding company, who had been with the organization for twelve years, had a background in retailing. There was also another notable exception to the usual progression of careers found in large commercial banks. Whereas the National Division (which handled the bank's "wholesale" lending relationships with large corporate customers) was frequently the route to top management, Taggert had risen through the retail banking organization where he had been responsible for the personnel function as well as branch administration.

A LETTER FROM THE GOLDEN EAGLES

On April 26, 1972, Peter Dawson, President of The Jefferson National Bank and Trust Company, received a letter from Miss Jennifer King, 67, representing the Action Alliance for the Aged (AAA), also referred to at times as the Golden Eagles, a coalition of senior citizens' groups in the Cleveland area. King called upon Jefferson National to "eliminate service charges on checking accounts for senior citizens and their organizations, eliminate fees for money orders for senior citizens who are customers, and revise the loan policy of the bank toward customers over 65." In addition, Dawson was invited to discuss his bank's policies at an AAA meeting scheduled for May 8.

THE BANK'S INITIAL RESPONSE

Dawson, in a letter to Miss King dated May 2, indicated that while he was "interested and concerned," he was "unclear as to the solution, if any," and moreover, he suspected that the problem must be "industry-wide rather than confined to one or two banks." However, he designated Stanley Johnson, Regional Vice President of the Metropolitan Department's Region VI, to represent him at the May 8 meeting. (An organization chart of the bank is provided in Exhibit 4-2.)

A spokesman for AAA denounced the response as insufficient. It was Dawson that the Golden Eagles wished to speak to, and if the bank would not come to them, they would come to the bank. Dawson then conferred with Bennett Turner, Chairman of the bank's Urban Affairs Committee, and John Kearney, the bank's Public Relations Officer, and agreed to meet representatives of AAA at the bank on May 16.

INITIAL ANALYSIS

Simultaneously, a "top of the desk" analysis of the senior citizens' three demands was undertaken. It was concluded that free checking was completely out of the question. All three bank executives were keenly aware of the situation which had developed in Pittsburgh two weeks earlier. There, a couple of the small commercial banks had attempted to chip away at the retail market share of the city's largest bank, Mellon National. When Mellon finally retaliated by eliminating individual checking account service charges, its geographical and market dominance in the Pittsburgh area, coupled with its influential role of "product" (or service) leadership, led swiftly to the elimination of checking account service charges for all Pittsburgh banks. In what one Jefferson National executive termed a "competitive nightmare," the Pittsburgh banks went from minimum balance checking to free checking within a month.

Mindful of this experience, Dawson, Turner, and Kearney vowed to avoid the initiation of any such "price war." If it happened in Cleveland, Jefferson National (as the city's largest bank) had the most to lose, and consequently would not advocate such a policy. For the year 1972, all categories of service charge income that potentially could be affected by bankwide free checking had totaled \$3.9 million—\$1 million for Jefferson National's regular checking accounts and \$2.9 million for its special checking accounts. Total pretax income for the same period was approximately \$70 million. (However, a "3-2-1" minimum balance checking plan[1] was being readied for use in the event of serious threats of free checking by competitors.)[2]

On the other hand, AAA's request with regard to credit standards for elderly people focused attention on a policy of apparently unintentional design. All personal loans, irrespective of age or any other criteria, typically were to be accompanied by some form of group credit insurance on the life of the borrower so that the bank would have a self-liquidating form of collateral should the borrower die. A few insurance companies would make group credit life insurance available to customers 65 years of age or older, but only for substantial increases in premiums. Several years earlier the bank had explored the feasibility of raising the coverage to customers aged 70, but it had been decided that the increase in premiums was too high to warrant further consideration.

---

[1] Under this plan, each personal checking account would be analyzed using the following service charge schedule: \$3.00 per month for an account in which the balance dropped below \$100; \$2.00 per month for an account in which the balance dropped below \$200; \$1.00 per month for an account in which the balance dropped below \$300; and no charge if a balance of \$300 or more was maintained throughout the month.

[2] Two small banks in the metropolitan area were already offering free checking.

A MODIFICATION OF POLICY

After considerable dialogue, it was agreed that, although it did not represent rigorous lending policy, in order to show good faith and blunt the thrust of the Golden Eagles' demands, management would instruct all loan officers to waive the group life insurance policy requirement for people over 65. Lending officers were encouraged to find some other way to obtain suitable collateral. Accordingly, an interdepartmental memo waiving the group credit life insurance requirement was distributed on May 15 to all Metropolitan Department lending personnel. An excerpt from that memo read:

> Our bank wishes to accommodate these senior citizens whenever possible and we ask that you look kindly on their loan applications and give them every consideration. If the individual applicant has sufficient income to repay the loan and can show evidence of some personal insurance coverage, you should take a positive approach providing, of course, there is no previous bad credit history. We would also discourage the acquiring of liens on real estate in dealing with senior citizens.

Whether this actually represented a departure from existing policy was not clear. Michael MacInnes, Senior Vice President of Marketing (but at that time in charge of installment loans) commented:

> The irony of the situation was that gradually, over a period of years we had, in fact, relaxed the policy. For people over 65, many lending officers were considering loan applications simply on the basis of the borrower's income and ability to repay. They were not relying on insurance. There was a gradual loosening without any real formal policy on it.
>
> Actually, you can't cast policy in iron. If you did that, we could have computers make all credit decisions. You'd simply have to ensure that certain ratios, projections, and quantifiable standards were met. Banking—and lending in particular—is much more complicated than that. That's why well-trained loan officers who can exercise sound judgment are required.
>
> Of course, when the formalized written policy was sent out about lending to elderly citizens, there probably were some lenders who saw it as a real go-ahead. Now, if they got into trouble on a loan to a senior citizen, they could point to a written policy as justification for their decisions.

THE FIRST MEETING

The next day, May 16, the Golden Eagles—represented by three spokesmen—were to meet with Dawson, Turner, and Kearney. Because of lending policy implications and the likelihood of discussions involving other retail banking policies, Earl Fairchild, Executive Vice President of United States Banking Group and in charge of all lending, was included. Kearney described the meeting:

> Approximately 10 minutes before the meeting, as I was approaching the Main Office Building, I saw a crowd of about 40 senior citizens. It was then that I realized we had an interesting meeting before us.

> Another surprise came when I spotted somebody I recognized; he was a reporter from one of the local newspapers. Then I saw pre-planned press releases being distributed, and I can remember thinking, "We've been had."[1]
>
> At the meeting itself, AAA's spokesman was Dr. Edmund Lundberg, a 70-year-old Lutheran minister. He pressed their appeal in such a heart-wringing, eloquent manner and summarized the bank's position as so crass that by the time he was finished, you wanted to give him the bank.

Nevertheless, the position taken by management at this meeting was that they were first and foremost responsible for the stewardship of depositors' accounts, and that to grant free checking accounts and free money orders for use by members of AAA would not be good banking policy. However, having had their attention called to the apparent inequity of lending criteria for senior citizens, it was the bank's intention to modify its lending policy, and this had already been done by waiving the group life insurance requirement for people over 65 years of age.

THE BANK'S POSITION REITERATED AND AAA'S REPLY

On May 18, Dawson sent a letter to Lundberg in which he reiterated this modification of lending policy for senior citizens. At the same time, the bank's firm position with regard to free checking accounts and free money orders was summarized as follows:

> . . . The subject of service charges on checking accounts and money orders represents only one element of the much larger and terribly complex issue of consumerism. Yet, despite our very real interest and empathy with the needs of aged citizens, it is impossible for us to justify denying free services to hundreds of very worthwhile interest groups, while granting this benefit to a single class of citizens.

The response from the Golden Eagles was ominous. Citing Dawson's reply as "not acceptable," AAA alleged "it shows that profit, not conscience, motivated your decision." Moreover, with regard to the bank's modification of its lending policy for elderly customers, AAA claimed "the fact that you admit and rectify a discriminatory policy on loans is not confirmation of a conscience–it says that the bank can concede something that will increase profits." Re-emphasizing what they viewed as the inherent legitimacy of their requests, AAA noted that if Dawson's letter represented the bank's final position, they would have "no alternative other than to take further action." Again

---

[1] In the press release, it was stated that AAA's leading spokesman believed that "special services for senior citizens go hand in hand with the new direction for bank policy outlined by President Dawson at the annual meeting of Jefferson National Corporation. At that time, Dawson stated, 'We view these two considerations, profits and social responsibility, so often portrayed as "either/or," as anything but mutually exclusive.' Said AAA's spokesman, "This is why we approach this man and this bank at this time. He wants to establish a scorecard for social performance, and we can show him where to begin."

a meeting with AAA leadership was suggested, and Dawson was asked to reply. (And, for the first time, a copy of AAA's letter was addressed to Owen Taggert, Chairman of Jefferson National Corporation, the bank's parent holding company.)

MANAGEMENT'S ASSESSMENT

Upon receipt of this letter, bank management became convinced that it had a "serious problem," but it was viewed as basically a public relations problem. Management had not changed its thinking about the appropriateness of its stand on the substantive issues of free checking accounts and free money orders. It firmly believed that if it gave in to the senior citizens, any number of special interest groups—conceivably even such controversial groups as the Vietnam Veterans Against the War and the Jewish Defense League—would have every right to request the same treatment. In the view of bank management, the situation could be reduced to two issues of major importance:

1.—Acceding to AAA demands would result in the forfeiture of service charge income from checking accounts and money orders, and thus would not represent good stewardship exercised on behalf of the bank's depositors and stockholders.
2.—Assenting to the demands of any one special interest group such as the Golden Eagles would be unfair to other "special interest groups." Exceptional treatment of one interest group would undoubtedly lead to justifiable claims of unfavorable discrimination *against* other groups.

Dawson expressed his views as follows:

> I personally have great difficulty with the free money orders and free checking. It is by no means clearly evident that senior citizens had any special claim to preferential treatment. Frankly, I have trouble distinguishing between the hardships of the elderly, the young, the handicapped, and others.
>
> We have seen the effects of free checking in other cities, and are quite fearful that our granting of free checking to the elderly would provide the opening wedge for city-wide free checking.

Senior bank management decided to stand firm on their convictions. Dawson replied to the Golden Eagles on May 30 that he saw "no purpose in further discussion" and concluded that "another meeting would be redundant."

PREPARATIONS FOR A CONFRONTATION

However, aware of the likely public relations repercussions that could arise from this posture, the bank set about preparing for what one executive termed "the blast." Feeling that AAA would try to trap the bank's branch personnel into concessions, an effort was made to inform and thus prepare contact officers in the branches. On

Thursday, June 1, Leonard Gorman, Senior Vice President in charge of the Metropolitan Department, issued a memorandum to all branch managers and regional vice presidents. Warning of the possibility of "demonstrations and picketing," Gorman urged branch personnel to call him or Metropolitan Operations for instructions before taking any action. He also stipulated that branch personnel were "not to make any public statement to a group, media representatives, or individuals either by phone or personally."

About a week after Gorman's memo had been sent out, King made an appointment with Taggert to present the demands and grievances of her organization. Shortly thereafter Taggert received a telephone call from Ralph Nader, the consumer advocate. Having been apprised by King of Jefferson National's resistance to AAA's demands, Nader asked if Taggert would give consideration to her case.

Exhibit 4-1

JEFFERSON NATIONAL CORPORATION

PROPORTIONS OF OPERATING REVENUES AND PRE-TAX INCOME GENERATED BY SERVICE CATEGORIES FOR THE YEARS ENDED DECEMBER 31*

	1972		*1971*	
	Revenues	*Income*	*Revenues*	*Income*
Commercial Banking	70%	72%	73%	68%
Consumer Finance	11	18	11	15
Real Estate Finance	17	10	13	13
Investor Services	2	–	3	4
Total	100%	100%	100%	100%

	1970		*1969*	
	Revenues	*Income*	*Revenues*	*Income*
Commercial Banking	80%	83%	81%	85%
Consumer Finance	11	10	11	10
Real Estate Finance	9	7	9	5
Investor Services	–	–	–	–
Total	100%	100%	100%	100%

*Certain services provided by the Investor Services group and holding company were previously performed by the Commercial Banking group and are reflected in its results for 1969 and 1970.

Exhibit 4-2

JEFFERSON NATIONAL BANK—PARTIAL ORGANIZATION CHART (1973)

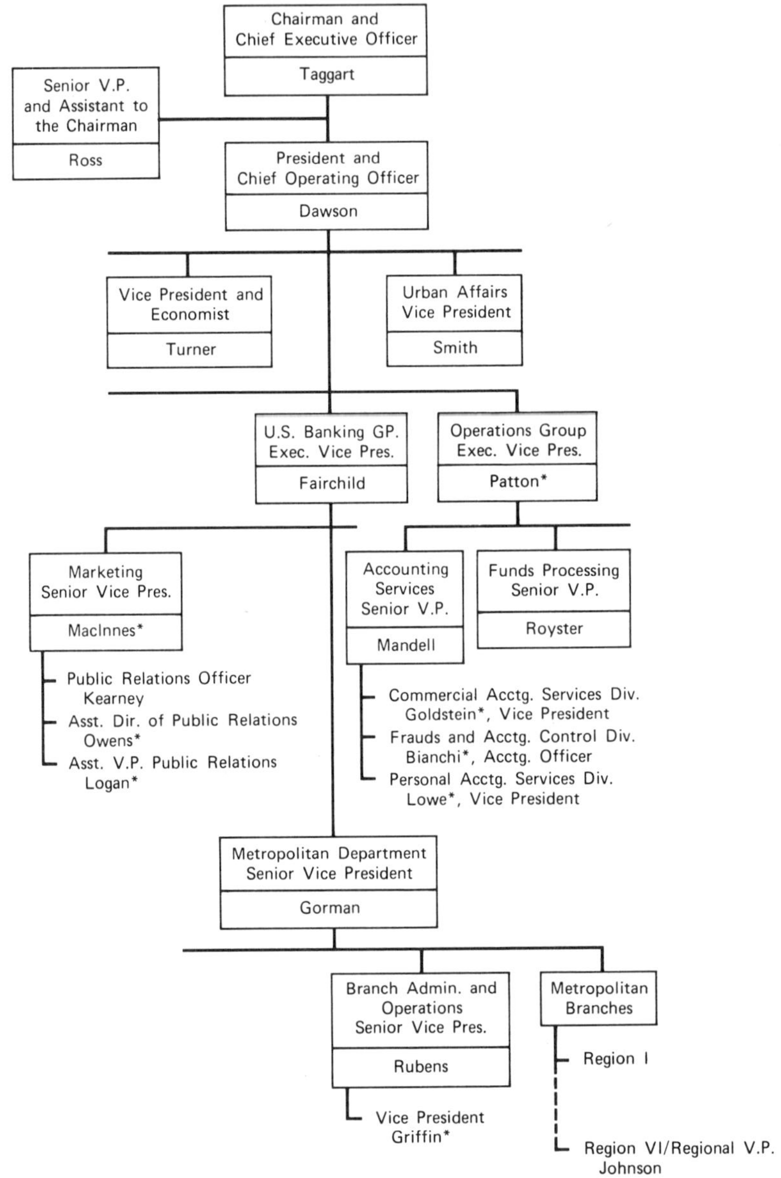

*Designates members of the Bank Task Force on Senior Citizen Checking

Source: Corporate records

Case Five

The Golden Eagles (B)

On June 12, 1972, Owen Taggert, Chairman of the Jefferson National Corporation, met with Jennifer King, representing the Action Alliance for the Aged, also known as the Golden Eagles. King reiterated her organization's position that the bank's response to the needs of the elderly was unacceptable. Taggert then agreed to establish a joint committee of bank personnel and representatives of AAA that would meet periodically to work out some form of solution.

THE FORMATION OF A TASK FORCE

Immediately after the Taggert-King meeting a committee of bank personnel headed by Robert Patton, Executive Vice President of the Operations Group, was appointed to deal with AAA's demands. According to Patton, who had undertaken other special projects in the past, this situation represented an "opportunity to get into the changing payments mechanisms associated with the trend toward a 'checkless society.'"

From his perspective, by working effectively with the senior citizens' group, the bank could translate the experience into a prototype for other business similar to the Cleveland Electric Company (CECO) Plan. This Plan, in existence since the mid-1960s, was a billing arrangement whereby CECO would send computer card decks to nine participating metropolitan banks each month. These cards, when processed by computers, would debit the checking accounts of those CECO customers who banked at the respective banks. Approximately two weeks prior to this automatic billing, CECO customers were advised by postcard of the charges to be made by the utility, permitting correction of erroneous charges and the posting of the charges in the individual's checkbooks. This type of billing arrangement not only greatly accelerated cash flow for the utility company, but at some point, if magnetic computer tapes could be substituted for punched cards, it was estimated that the bank's cost per billing transaction would decrease from about 9¢ to 2¢.

Taggert instructed Patton to form a group which could continue a dialogue with AAA, but at the same time "do something" for the bank. In forming the special task force, Patton looked to some of his "younger, more imaginative" officers as well as officers from other parts of the bank which would logically become involved in any introduction of special checking services. (Members of the task force are designated on the organization chart in the (A) case, Exhibit 5-2.)

In addressing the requests of AAA, Patton noted that:

> Primarily the senior citizens wanted to avoid what they viewed as the physical hazards of banking in person. Moreover, their real drive seemed to be toward free checking accounts, but if considered on a bank-wide basis, checking account service charge income represented about $4 million.
>
> We felt that our mission was to come up with something that would appeal to AAA without stampeding the other Cleveland banks into eliminating their checking account service charges in order to stay competitive with us.

GATHERING OF INFORMATION

In a survey of 11 "Exchanger Banks,"[1] it was found that only one bank was currently offering free checking to senior citizens, but that no statistical data were being kept to evaluate the program. In this same survey, the practices of the 11 banks regarding minimum balance checking[2] were compared. Of the six banks that rendered an opinion on the income effects of minimum balance checking service, five "felt" that they had lost income. (One of the banks acknowledged that its cost system was not adequate to tell the effects with any certainty.) The sixth bank, which had had a cost analysis system prior to the introduction of minimum balance checking, indicated that its service charge income had *increased* slightly.

From recent market research data, it appeared that Jefferson National had the lowest percentage of senior citizens in the Cleveland five-county market (see Table 5-1 on the next page). Applied "against actual 1971 changes," the estimated 5.6% of Jefferson National's customers believed to be 65 or over led to the projection of an annual potential decrease in service charges of $180,264 if free checking were offered to senior citizens.

Thus, upon first analysis, it appeared that the granting of free checking to senior citizens would cost the bank nearly $200,000 in foregone service charge income (as

---

[1]The Exchanger Banks were 11 geographically dispersed (and presumably non-competitive) banks with which Jefferson National regularly exchanged information regarding developments in the fields of lending, retail services, marketing, personnel administration, and so forth.

[2]Typically in this type of account, if checking account balances were kept above a specified minimum (or alternatively, if *average* bank balances were kept above a specified level), there were no service charges made against the account.

TABLE 5-1 AGE BREAKDOWN OF RETAIL CUSTOMER BASE IN METROPOLITAN MARKET BY THE LARGEST FIVE BANKS

REGULAR BANK	*SAMPLE* %Total*	*AGE OF HOUSEHOLD HEAD -25*	*25-34*	*35-44*	*45-54*	*55-64*	*65+*
Metropolitan Population Average	*100.0*	*8.8*	*24.6*	*23.0*	*21.6*	*12.9*	*9.1*
Jefferson National	13.7	10.2	29.9	21.2	22.2	10.9	5.6
Liberty Bank	10.5	12.0	24.9	26.6	17.8	10.9	7.8
Sumner Bank	10.2	7.8	27.6	25.5	18.0	12.0	9.1
Cleveland National	9.1	8.7	27.5	24.7	20.3	11.7	7.1
Erie National	5.2	10.0	27.4	19.9	22.8	12.8	7.1

*Total number of responses = 5,414.

compared with the spectre of $4 million.) By virtue of its relatively small clientele of elderly people, however, Jefferson National probably would suffer proportionately less foregone income than would its major competitors.

THE "GOLDEN OLDIES" CLUB

On June 13, Patton proposed to Steven Ross, Senior Vice President of the bank and Assistant to the Chairman, that a free checking account with a line of credit be offered to those senior citizens who joined a bank-sponsored "Golden Oldies" Club. The requirements for joining such a club were to be the provision of proof of age 65 years or older; the establishment of personal checking accounts only—no business accounts; and the stipulation that the individual must do all his banking with Jefferson National, sending all government and pension checks for deposit directly to the bank through the Mail Tellers Unit.

Members of the club would receive several benefits:

1.—There would be no charge for checks written and no monthly account maintenance charge.
2.—A reserve line of credit would be granted in $100 increments up to the amount of monthly income checks received (maximum $400.) No life insurance would be necessary on the reserve portion of the account.
3.—Free counseling would be made available regarding wills, estates, safe deposit boxes, and other banking functions.

However, Ross (who was responsible for keeping Taggert informed on the status of this project) responded by recommending a plan, first proposed by the Metropolitan Department, to offer four free money orders per month per person to be used only in conjunction with the bank's 4% passbook savings accounts. Although considerably less convenient to the customers than free checking, this plan was in accord with one of the original requests of AAA. Moreover, it was viewed as relatively safe from the standpoint of economic consequences—the number of money orders was nominal and limited, and in each case, their use would be tied in with a savings account. Thus, any form of free checking which could have potentially adverse effects on the bank's overall service charge income was avoided. The Ross Plan was accepted and new operating procedures were quickly drafted for issuance to the branches.

SENIOR CITIZENS' SAVINGS ACCOUNTS

On June 20, a press conference was held by Taggert to announce the creation of "new special savings accounts to meet the needs of senior citizens. Under this new program, anyone with proof of age 65 years or over will be qualified to open a special 4% passbook savings account." Effective July 1, passbook holders would be allowed to make up to four withdrawals a month via bank money order, enabling them to make major general utility and other payments without charge. Taggert also announced that Patton had been appointed to work with representatives of the Golden Eagles in "researching further innovations in direct payment of consumer bills by the bank."

On June 21, the new operating procedure describing the administrative details of the free money orders for senior citizens was distributed to the branches. All branches were instructed to submit weekly reports to the Metropolitan Department; these reports were to include the number of existing accounts and new accounts and amounts of initial deposits that had been marked as Senior Citizens' Accounts.

Although accommodating the demands of AAA appeared to have created new administrative work for the bank and some loss of service-charge income was expected, management felt that the arrangement was not entirely "one-sided." In addition to favorable publicity accruing to the bank, it was anticipated that a fresh inflow of deposit funds would stem from the newly created senior citizens' accounts. Moreover on the basis of the experiences of other banks, it appeared that the elderly generally maintained above average deposits in their savings accounts. In the case of Jefferson National, for instance, it had been confirmed that the average person 65 and older kept $1,300-$1,400 in his savings account, compared to about $900 maintained by the bank's average depositor. Moreover, as Patton maintained, dealings with AAA presented an opportunity to experiment with direct wire transfers. Senior Citizens' Accounts would be a sufficiently large base—yet of manageable proportions—to permit the testing of various techniques which could eventually lead to the development of bank-wide electronic funds transfer.

REACTIONS TO THE NEW PLAN

Reaction to Jefferson National's new service was swift. Within a day, Gerald Long, Vice President of the Federal Reserve Bank of Cleveland, called to question the legality of Jefferson National's new service. In a written reply to Long, the bank's counsel gave assurances that it was not the bank's intention, "in light of the provisions of Federal Reserve Regulation Q, to establish a bill-paying plan . . . for regular savings account depositors."

Competitive reaction was also quick, if somewhat subdued. The following week another major competitor, even without a formal request from AAA, began to offer certain free money order privileges similar to those provided by Jefferson National.

For their part, the Golden Eagles responded with guarded optimism. While they were pleased by the personal attention given to their requests by Taggert, they also indicated that the Free Money Order Plan was only a "first step."

Case Six

The Golden Eagles (C)

Among Jefferson National's first efforts to develop alternative checking systems acceptable to senior citizens was an examination of the bank's contingency "3-2-1" Checking System, a plan closely resembling in form the minimum balance checking plans employed by some of the Exchanger Banks surveyed. Charles Jorgenson, Assistant Vice President Project Management Division (a subunit of the Operations Group), on June 30 submitted a preliminary analysis to Patton.

Essentially, the impact of a bank-wide shift to the "3-2-1" system was analyzed. All of the bank's special checking accounts (118,534) and regular checking accounts (57,894), or a total of 176,428 "personal checking accounts," were costed out for the month of April using the "3-2-1" pricing structure. The report indicated that 113,672 (64%) of the personal accounts would pay service charges of $291,350 per month, while 62,756 (36%) of the personal accounts would have no service charges. For the same month, the bank's existing charge system for personal accounts had resulted in service charge income of $239,672. A change to the "3-2-1" pricing system would therefore represent a $34,521 (22%) increase in monthly service charge income. Moreover, because preliminary evidence indicated that many senior citizens kept balances in excess of $300, this plan was seen as a way of effectively offering many of them free checking.

In his report, Jorgenson discussed the analysis further:

> We are continuing to research the possibilities of developing "non-free" services for senior citizens which address their needs without negatively affecting the bank's income.
>
> Since the preliminary analysis does not take into account "switching" (accounts which would raise their balance to obtain lower service charges or low balance accounts who would leave), we are doing a more detailed analysis to evaluate potential effects in this area.

And as a by-product of this analysis, Jorgenson noted that:

> In discussing characteristics of potential services, it would appear that another customer group, college students, also meets a number of similar criteria (need for a

banking relationship, limited activity, banking by mail). They also represent excellent possibilities as a profitable post-graduate customer as their needs expand. This seems to represent some interesting possibilities for the bank.

FIRST ANALYSIS OF SENIOR CITIZENS' SAVINGS ACCOUNT ACTIVITY

On August 24, as consideration was being given to Jorgenson's report, the first survey of the newly developed Senior Citizens' Savings Accounts was made to determine both the number of converted and new accounts and the level of balances in each. Michael Bianchi, Accounting Officer in the Frauds and Accounting Control Division of the Operations Group and a member of the senior citizens task force, reported to Patton that after approximately seven weeks, there were a total of 180 Senior Citizens' Savings Accounts, of which 71 represented new accounts. Of the $334,000 total balances, $75,000 represented new business as shown in Table 6-1 below.

TABLE 6-1. SENIOR CITIZENS' SAVINGS ACCOUNTS AS OF AUGUST 24, 1972

	Total Accounts	*New Accounts*
No. of accounts	180	71
Total balances	$333,769.52	$74,724.97
Average balances	1,854.27	1,052.46
Median balances	543.70	158.85
Range	$4.21–$18,334.00	$5.50–$18,334.04

On September 11, at the second meeting of the bank's task force with the Senior Citizen Panel, the month-end statistical report as of August 31 was presented which showed 196 Senior Citizens' Savings Accounts with total balances of $373,000. The acceptability of the no-charge money orders was evidently increasing as indicated by the issuance of approximately 400 free money orders during August, up from about 200 issued in July.

In a memorandum to Fairchild dated September 13, MacInnes reported on the meeting:

> The meeting went well generally; however, some additional demands were made on behalf of old people:
>
> That the bank provide free checking account service for the aged. This request was completely rejected by Mr. Patton and both he and I did our best to explain why this could not be done. While most of the old people accepted our reasoning, they did not necessarily agree with it. There followed a second suggestion which was to

increase the number of free money orders on the existing savings account from four per month to ten per month. My feeling was that the old people would be agreeable to eight free money orders a month on a household basis. They did not specifically state this, but from their conversation I think that it would probably be agreeable. Mr. Patton left this question open and said we would discuss it internally, continue to track our experience and hopefully give them a decision at our next meeting which was tenatively set for October 13, 1972.

DATA GATHERING ON CHECKING ACCOUNTS

Meanwhile, specific responsibilities for the accumulation of statistics on senior citizens' checking and savings accounts were divided between the Metropolitan Department and the Operations Group. Bianchi assigned Metropolitan the responsibility for providing monthly raw data on the total number of free money orders issued and the number of money orders given to individual senior citizens. Operations, in turn, was to generate and distribute a report analyzing Senior Citizens' Accounts by branch.

A preliminary run-through was made on 72 Senior Citizens' Regular Checking Accounts to demonstrate the kind of information which would be generated. Total balances for these accounts amounted to $442,300, or an astonishingly high average of $6,143 per account. Estimating the income that could be generated from the balances and netting against it the costs associated with servicing the accounts (there were an average of 13.25 checks, 2.54 deposits, and 6.88 items deposited per account), the net profit for one month was calculated to be $260.47. Despite a probable bias toward large accounts of long standing, it was tentatively concluded that this particular group of Senior Citizens' Accounts would merit free checking:

> It must be realized that the information above was produced from accounts held with the bank for over 40 years (most likely placing them in the 65 or over category). The limitations to this survey are twofold: (1) Only regular checking was reviewed, since special checking does not get analyzed. (2) These accounts are long standing with the bank. Realizing these limitations, it is still interesting to see that this group of senior citizens show very high balances and would easily justify "free checking" in the group analysis plan. If we can attract this type of account from other banks, we would substantially increase overall balances while not adversely affecting service charge income.
>
> Also, it is highly probable that the Senior Citizens Group will carry balances well in . . . excess of our normal regular checking accounts based upon the balance position on the present Senior Citizens' Savings Accounts. Our normal 4% Savings Account customer carries average balances of $1,250.00, while our Senior Citizens average over $2,000.00 per account.

THE GROUP CHECKING PLAN

While the preliminary analytical work was being completed, the format for a Group Checking Plan was developed. Under this plan, the profit or loss, including regular service charges for Senior Citizens' Accounts would be calculated as a group. The profits on those accounts with "excess balances" would then be spread over the "loss" accounts by dividing the number of accounts in the loss category into the total profits. In this way, each of the loss accounts would have its service charges reduced by an equal amount. For those accounts with sufficiently high balances, there would be no service charges.

Offering the Group Checking Plan to the senior citizens was expected to result in several advantages for the bank. According to an internal memorandum:

> 1.–The plan does not specifically offer free checking, but it does give the Senior Citizens the ability to get free checking, or "lower cost" checking. It places the onus for its success on the Senior Citizens Group.
> 2.–The area banks cannot effectively compete with this plan since the opening of Senior Citizens Accounts at other banks will dilute the "pooled effects" of this group analysis approach.
> 3.–The plan does not compromise our position with other groups since the bank may justify it on the grounds of meeting a social problem. Also, the plan may be attractive enough for the bank to want to offer it to other groups based on their respective social problems or goals.
> 4.–The plan offers an opportunity for a large number of new accounts with a minimum effect on income. If only a small number of large balance accounts open, then the Senior Citizen Accounts will probably still be paying close to their usual service charge. If all of the accounts should fall into a "free checking" category, then this could only be through the attraction of a number of large balance accounts. If the latter should happen, then this would be to the bank's advantage.
> 5.–By having a checking account as the cornerstone for the Senior Citizen Plan, it can serve as the mechanism for introducing economies through advanced automation or introduction of "less-check" plans, such as CECO.
> 6.–The group analysis plan for the Senior Citizens should increase retail balances, which is presently an objective established by Marketing for 1973.

On October 11, Bianchi circulated an analysis of the bank's Davis accounts[1] to the bank's Senior Citizens Committee. In this report, detailing the profit and loss associated with over 1900 individual checking accounts affiliated with the industrial firm's corporate accounts and analyzed as a group, it was calculated that the average service charge per account would be $.73. It was also noted that the average balance needed per account to support the cost of free checking was $1,344. In discussing the application of a similar type of analysis to Senior Citizens' Accounts, Bianchi wrote:

> . . . In the case of the Senior Citizens, we would probably analyze each account, give free checking to those accounts showing a profit and then use the profit figure to reduce the charge to those accounts which showed a loss.

---

[1] Reference to a group analysis checking service offered to employees of Davis Laboratories. Under the plan, all Davis employees, by virtue of having their checking accounts at Jefferson National, got free checking. The difference between "credits" they received for their balance and the costs they incurred through activity-based service charges would be absorbed by Davis in its corporate account as an employee benefit. The bank had provided the service several years earlier at the request of Davis. Although the bank had since provided similar packages for a few other corporate customers, it had not promoted the service.

> Also, if the number of checks per account for the Senior Citizens was 10 per month, then the net loss figure could be reduced . . . lowering the service charge per account to 43¢ a month. . . . It is quite clear that by using this type of charge system the bank is not gaining any profit from the Senior Citizens, but merely recovering costs. If the balance were two-thirds of what is presently shown in the Senior Citizens Savings Accounts, all would receive free checking.

At the next senior citizens' meeting, on October 13, it was noted that the usage of money orders continued to rise (from 400 in August to 517 in September), but with the growth in the number of accounts, the average number of money orders per account dropped from 2.2 to 1.9. A memorandum summarized the meeting in these terms:

> Dismayed a little by these figures, the AAA representatives readily admitted the need to educate senior citizens in financial matters, breaking down old habits and explaining new services. I sensed that they still found this service a little eccentric and more difficult to advance than their earlier and constantly recurring demand, free checking.
>
> As an alternative, Bob Patton discussed with the panel an idea which all members of the bank's committee had agreed upon. Implementing a procedure currently used on the Davis accounts, the bank could offer to senior citizens a "group checking account." Each account would be analyzed separately, with profit accounts receiving free checking. But any . . . excess profits would be applied to the loss accounts.
>
> Early indications are that any cut in revenues suffered as a result of this service would be made up through acquisition of new accounts. The obvious advantage is that such a plan would encourage senior citizens to help other senior citizens by joining this checking pool. This service is, by the way, one which we could also implement for other groups should the need arise. The possibility of building retail trade is inherent.
>
> Making it absolutely clear that this idea had no official sanction, Bob indicated to the group that he would explore the subject further with management and subsequently be back in touch with Jenny King.

ANALYSIS OF THE GROUP CHECKING PLAN

By November 20, an analysis prepared by Bianchi showed the anticipated effects of the Group Checking Plan on service charge income. The major conclusions of this study were:

1.–The maximum possible service charge income that could be lost if all regular and special checking accounts that qualified for the Senior Citizen category switched to the new checking plan would be $195,090. (But this assumed no new business and was considered unrealistic.)

2.–Based upon experience with Senior Citizens' Savings Accounts to date, the anticipated service charge loss was expected to be no more than $872 a year.

3.–Again, based on experience to date with the Senior Citizens' Savings Accounts, it was thought that new accounts actually would result in an increased daily average balance of $179,212.

4.–Over the course of a year, this incremental daily average balance could generate an income of $12,903.

In his concluding remarks, Bianchi stressed the uncertainty inherent in several of the assumptions and data. He wrote in part:

> The preceding analysis is obviously based on many precarious assumptions and also the possible maximum loss to service charge income is highly unrealistic. However, due to our limited knowledge of age as part of the customer profile, this is the only type data presently available for such an analysis. It is our feeling that very few of our present profitable regular checking customers in the senior citizens age group will transfer to this account if it is offered. They have very little to gain by such a move–the benefits being social only. If those accounts with lower balances transfer (probably many from Special Checking), then they will receive a charge each month, since there will be few highly profitable accounts in the Senior Citizens' Checking Account group to affect their losses. The only way any high balance accounts can be attracted to the group is if pushed by AAA, and it is apparent that we would get as many accounts from other banks–thus new business–as would transfer internally. Therefore, the management decision must be based on the assumptions that this group analysis will follow the same basic pattern as the Senior Citizens Savings Accounts, and we will not lose any appreciable service charge income while gaining some new demand dollars.

The Marketing Department rendered its opinion on the proposed plan via a memorandum from MacInnes to Dawson. MacInnes, while "not certain that [the plan had] great Marketing implications" viewed the financial risk as nominal: " . . . if we were completely wrong [and] the loss of income was 3 times as much, it would still be less than $2,500 and the Public Relations benefit would be well worth that expense." Moreover, according to MacInnes, the attractiveness of this plan lay in its placing the "onus of developing the higher dollar amount customer on the senior citizens themselves and not on the bank." It was also felt " . . . from a Marketing viewpoint, that this plan might prove to be a usable test package and, should it prove successful, it would be sold to other groups. . . ."

Planning for the Group Checking Plan proceeded throughout the fall of 1972. On November 29, Bianchi circulated a set of guidelines to be used in tracking and analyzing the new plan when it was put into effect. At the same time, the level of Senior Citizens' Savings Account activity continued to be traced through monthly reports from Bianchi to Patton. The service continued to show growth, as measured both by the number of new accounts and levels of average balances.

By December 13, Advertising had developed a brochure for the Group Checking Plan, now renamed the Senior Citizens' Cooperative Checking Plan. Before final approval, however, Advertising asked that certain details be checked. It was requested that approval be obtained from the bank's Legal Department, and that the Metropolitan Department's Branch Administration group be contacted to verify that the new plan correctly assigned duties and conformed to procedures already established at the branch offices. In the meantime, the advertising copy was submitted by Patton to Dawson who, after some minor editorial changes, returned it with praise.

THE JANUARY 11 MEETING

On January 11, another meeting was held with the Golden Eagles. Louis Mandell, Senior Vice President of the Accounting Services Department (part of the Operations Group), chaired the session in Patton's absence. The cooperative checking plan was explained in detail to the AAA panel, but it met resistance because it excluded nonprofit organizations such as certain church and civic groups. The bank countered that its proposal was based on a survey taken with its regular checking senior citizen customers which had shown the potential number of participants to be high. Furthermore, the bank committee indicated that if nonprofit groups were to be permitted to join the plan, executive management would have to authorize it. The Golden Eagles agreed to discuss the plan and the bank's position on affiliating nonprofit organizations with their members and return with an acceptance or a rejection of the proposal.

Following this meeting, in a letter to Patton, Mandell registered strong opposition to the affiliation of any nonprofit institutions with the Senior Citizens' Cooperative Checking Plan. In particular, he was concerned about King's allusion to the Board of Pensions of the United Methodist Church, a customer having about a dozen accounts. Mandell noted that "this is a very profitable group, and I understand that average balances are in the neighborhood of $200,000 to $250,000." It was his recommendation that the bank "not consider affiliating such institutions with the AAA group, for this could certainly lead to many unpleasant and unprofitable ramifications." Specifically, Mandell was concerned about setting a precedent which could lead to demands for equal treatment by numerous other groups.

Case Seven

The Golden Eagles (D)

On May 17, in a confidential interdepartmental memorandum, Charles Schmidt, senior banking officer in the Branch Administration and Operations area of the Metropolitan Department, citing the "necessity of capturing a greater portion of the retail market," announced plans for the introduction of a package of new retail products in the fall of 1973, designed to counter the "recent intensified competition" experienced in Cleveland's retail banking market.

In what was to be "the most flexible, understandable retail package for both the customer and [managers] at the branch level," customers would be able to select, separately or in combination, a variety of plans for the bank's three main retail products–Checking, Revolving Cash (lines of credit), and Regular Savings. In Checking, for example, three pricing options would be offered to all customers–analysis, dime-a-time (10¢ per check), and minimum balance. In addition, most of the existing service fees which distinguished special checking accounts would be "eliminated to insure equal, equitable service for all."

This new retail product development effort reflected a growing concern over the apparent inevitability of minimum balance checking plans as a "stepping stone" to what was perceived to be eventual free checking for all customers. In early May 1973, Cleveland National Bank had introduced free checking services for those customers who kept a minimum of $200 in their checking accounts. Shortly thereafter, Sumner Bank had introduced "free" checking plus a number of other banking services in a single package, all for a fixed fee of $3 per month.

This prevailing competitive situation in retail banking led Patton to comment that the senior citizens checking problem had virtually "solved itself because of the economic climate." In May, the proposed Senior Citizens' Checking Plan was forwarded to AAA.

THE BRANCH SURVEY

Meanwhile, it was increasingly apparent that the Senior Citizens' Savings Accounts with money orders were proving to be an undesirable administrative burden in the branches. A number of complaints had been received from branch management. In addition, MacInnes had begun to have doubts about the proposed Senior Citizens' Cooperative Checking Plan. He commented:

> I don't think the Cooperative Checking will work. I feel that it will merely be an administrative exercise with no real benefit to either the bank or the senior citizens.
>
> In addition, it seems obvious that, based on experiences to date with the Senior Citizens' Savings Accounts, there are sufficient balances in savings deposits to take the chance on free checking. Furthermore, by this time we have some evidence that old people can be legitimately treated differently without encouraging all types of other special interest groups to demand the same treatment. The Metropolitan Transit System has recently reduced fares for elderly people, and no one seems to be offended by that form of special privilege.

Thinking that "maybe old people were entitled to a break" and that "we're going to do something anyhow—we may as well do it sooner rather than later," MacInnes requested that a survey of branch managers be conducted. In a May 1 memorandum to Walter Rubens, Senior Vice President of Branch Administration and Operations, MacInnes asked that the Metropolitan Department's regional vice presidents offer their opinions on the following four alternate courses of action:

1.—Do nothing at all and continue to offer senior citizens the savings account with free money orders.
2.—Offer senior citizens free checking as soon as possible.
3.—Offer senior citizens free checking providing they maintain a savings account with the bank (no minimum balance required.)
4.—Delay doing anything until the bank has a minimum balance account with a savings option tied in.

MacInnes reported the results of this survey to Fairchild on May 30:

> While four of six region[s] would prefer option #2, I do not think it would be difficult to get their cooperation in proposal #3. I think if we are inclined to adopt it, there could be some benefits in the social responsibility area.
>
> I do not intend to do anything further at the present time, but will leave it up to you. I think you have the option of making a decision or to make it with Peter [Dawson], whichever you see fit. . . .

In early June, this information was passed on by Fairchild to Dawson with the suggestion that free checking be offered to individual senior citizens on the condition that they each maintain a savings account at the bank (option #3). However, Dawson, aware of the new retail package being readied for introduction, wanted to wait until November before taking any specific action. For the time being, the matter was not pressed further. In part, this was because the Golden Eagles had not yet formulated a response to the bank's proposal for the Senior Citizens' Checking Plan.

A REVIEW OF SENIOR CITIZENS' SAVINGS ACCOUNTS

By July 1973, sufficient data were available to compile a summary of the bank's experience to date with Senior Citizens' Savings Accounts. Although the rate of attracting new balances had declined since the introduction of the plan, by the end of June, there were a total of 859 accounts with total balances of approximately $2 million (see Table 7-1 below.) At least $314,000 of this represented new balances.

TABLE 7-1. MONTHLY SENIOR CITIZENS' SAVINGS ACCOUNT ACTIVITY

	Accounts New to the Bank	*Total Accounts**	*Balances New to the Bank*	*Total Balances***
September 1972	74	268	77,000	540,000
October 1972	12	74	81,744	132,000
November 1972	18	68	32,347	168,385
December 1972	15	60	23,363	155,459
January 1973	N.A.	91***	–	237,963***
February 1973	34	91***	38,063	237,963***
March 1973	27	81	27,510	190,003
April 1973	N.A.	40***	–	114,079***
May 1973	12	39***	11,225	114,079***
June 1973	13	47	23,191	98,111
		859		1,988,040

*Includes both new accounts and existing accounts which were converted to Senior Citizens' Accounts.

**Includes both new balances and existing balances in accounts which were converted to Senior Citizens' Accounts.

***Average of two months, as report was not available in January and April.

N.A.–Not available.

Note: Based on the above, the average balance per account was $2,314.36. For new accounts only, the average balance per account was calculated to be $1,147.23. For comparison, the average 4% savings fund passbook account carried a balance of approximately $1,250.00.

Case Eight

The Golden Eagles (E)

Ultimately, the increased publicity given to the plight of old people combined with the growth of minimum-balance retail banking activity in the Cleveland area led Dawson to reconsider the bank's position on free checking for elderly customers. He commented:

> Whereas I had originally been opposed to the idea of free checking for senior citizens, I later came into the decision process and flipped my position. What I hadn't seen earlier was now quite apparent: elderly people were in fact perceived and treated as a distinct group with distinct problems.
>
> This greatly reduced our concern about free checking for senior citizens marking the opening round of a city-wide campaign leading to free checking for everyone. The fact that our major competitors were confining themselves to minimum balance checking plans tended to confirm our belief that they were reluctant to go to free checking.
>
> Also, in the interim we had an opportunity to analyze our data internally and find out how profitable the Senior Citizen Savings Accounts were.

Accordingly, Dawson advised Patton not to be adamant with the senior citizens at the next meeting because he had come to the conclusion that Jefferson National was definitely going to offer a minimum balance checking plan to meet the competition, although free checking per se was not mentioned.

The next meeting with representatives from AAA was held on July 30. The senior citizens formally rejected the bank's proposed Cooperative Checking Plan and reiterated their demand for free checking. Patton demurred and said that he would have to consult with top management.

At this point, the question of free checking was addressed by Dawson to Taggert. Taggert indicated that the bank had held off too long already and that management should now authorize free checking, with "no strings attached." Although as a matter of overall strategy, Taggert acknowledged that some delay may have been valuable, he also felt that some managers had misread his signals and that economic factors had been stressed too much.

Subsequently, at an August 17 news conference, Taggert announced that the bank would offer "regular checking accounts with no monthly maintenance charges" to the elderly. To establish their accounts, senior citizens were only required to present proof of age 65 years or over and to maintain a savings account with the bank. No minimum savings balance was required (but based on experience to date, it was thought that sufficiently large time deposit balances would result so as to offset administrative costs.

Public response was swift. In a letter dated August 21, the governor of Ohio offered congratulations to Taggert for the establishment of the "vital service" of free checking for senior citizens. And several newspaper accounts heralded the action as an exemplary demonstration of corporate social responsibility.

On September 17, a memo was circulated to all branches authorizing the closing out of the free Money Order Program. With the advent of the new Senior Citizens' Checking Plan, the Money Order Program was to be discontinued.

THE FIRST MONTH'S REPORT

The initial data on the Senior Citizens' Checking Accounts seemed positive. On October 4, Bianchi distributed the first Analysis Report for the month of September. The statistics cited were those shown in Table 8-1 below:

TABLE 8-1 SENIOR CITIZENS' CHECKING ACCOUNTS FOR SEPTEMBER 1974

Gross average balance	$1,980,600.00
Average available balance	1,851,100.00
Checks paid	16,898
Deposits	5,852
Number of Accounts	3,160
Average balance per account	$626.77
Average checks paid per account	5.34
Total service charge (based on regular personal analysis fees)	$ 25.96

Categorization of the accounts showed that for the first month of reporting, approximately 40% of the Senior Citizens' Checking Accounts were new. Based on this estimate, it was calculated that $792,000 of the gross average balance represented new money. That figure, less reserve requirements, left $657,360 that would otherwise have to be acquired at the estimated average federal funds rate of 10.75%. For a 30-day month, this cost of money was calculated to be $5,888.20, which was much more costly than the estimated "possible service charge loss" of $1,500 a month. (By visual inspection of the 3,160 accounts it had been judged that there were about 1,000 loss accounts, each one of which represented a cost of $1.50 to the bank.) Thus, the new checking service had resulted in a net monthly saving of $4,388 (i.e., $5,888-$1,500) in the acquisition of funds.

Chapter Four

The Implementation of Corporate Social Responsiveness[1]

The corporation's response to social demands has been a matter of controversy among businessmen and their critics for many years. Unfortunately, the controversy has all too often been phrased in moral or ideological extremes—as business irresponsibility or the unbridled use of corporate power on the one hand and a threat to private enterprise on the other. Both lines of reasoning, in our judgment, miss the mark. Worse, they obscure the important *managerial* dilemmas underlying the responsiveness of the corporation to its changing social and political context. The purpose of this chapter is to describe these dilemmas and the process that has developed for dealing with them. Whereas the previous chapter posed the question—how should corporate social policy be formulated?, this one addresses the equally difficult question—how should that policy be implemented? An example will set the stage.

The president of a consumer goods company and the manager of one of its divisions were confronted recently with different but equally uncomfortable problems. The former had been an early supporter of equal employment, especially in respect to minority hiring and training. He devoted much time to federal and state commissions locating job opportunities for minorities in the business community. The company from time to time had assisted minority enterprises in various ways and, on his initiative, had accepted a government contract to operate a job training center.

The president had communicated in strong terms his commitment to a policy of equal employment at all levels in his organization, and he had received general support for it. Despite these efforts, he felt that the company's record in hiring blacks and other minority group members and advancing them into management positions left much to be desired. He pondered how to close the gap between his public statements and the indications he received of actual performance. He also worried about the impact—tangible and intangible—of stricter government enforcement.

---

[1]This chapter draws from an article by Robert W. Ackerman, "How Companies Respond to Social Demands, *Harvard Business Review*, July-August, 1973. Portions reproduced with permission.

The division manager's problem was in some respects more difficult. He managed one of seven operating units in the company and was responsible for six plants, several dozen sales offices, and 2,200 employees. Each year, he and his management group assembled a plan that included a financial projection supported by an environmental analysis and a strategy for achieving the goals. After negotiations, top management and division management agreed on somewhat revised figures as the division's performance commitment for the coming year. Although the division manager took pains to keep the president and others on the corporate staff alerted to major strategic developments or changes in the forecasts, he was expected to take responsibility for managing the business.

The division manager understood and agreed with the president's position on equal employment. In view of the diversity of attitudes and values in his organization, he became convinced that the only way of implementing the president's policy was to agree on minority hiring and advancement targets with each of his manufacturing, sales, and administrative managers, and to hold them accountable for the results.

He had not, however, taken this step. He rationalized that the plants operated against very tight budgets; as long as a plant performed well on this measure, the plant manager knew he would win praise, earn pay raises, and preserve his relative autonomy. For several reasons, the division manager was unwilling to disturb this arrangement by appearing to put limits on the plant managers' autonomy in choosing their subordinates. He was equally reluctant to insist on the hiring of minority salesmen, thus risking damage to the sales managers' commitment to meeting volume targets. At least for the time being, the task of establishing standards and getting action was left to government enforcement agencies.

The illustration is not unique to this company or issue. By rearranging the situation, we could present comparable cases for other organizations struggling with pollution control, occupational health and safety, consumerism, and so forth.

MANAGEMENT DILEMMAS IN SOCIAL RESPONSIVENESS

Periodically in our history, the scope of corporate accountability has been extended. For instance, the rapid expansion of the labor movement in the 1930's is one obvious example among many manifestations of social change that businessmen had to assimilate during the Depression years. Why then, if the responsive corporation managed to adapt to them without serious damage, is not our problem today merely one of relearning the solutions to old problems? The answer lies not so much in the intensity of public expectations as in the radically changed configuration of today's large corporation.

According to recent studies, the divisionalized organization has rapidly replaced the functionalized organization as the dominant formal structure among the largest U.S. industrial corporations.[2] Table 4-A shows this transformation. Similar, though less marked, transitions may also be observed among financial institutions, insurance companies, and service organizations.

---

[2] Richard P. Rumelt, *Strategy, Structure, and Economic Performance*, Division of Research, Harvard Business School, 1974.

TABLE 4-A STRUCTURE OF THE *FORTUNE* "500" COMPANIES[3] IN THREE TIME PERIODS

Organization Structure	*Estimated Percentage of Companies* 1949	1959	1969
Functional	62.7%	36.3%	11.2%
Functional with subsidiaries	13.4	12.6	9.4
Product division	19.8	47.6	75.5
Geographic division	.4	2.1	1.5
Holding company	3.7	1.4	2.4
Total	100.0%	100.0%	100.0%

[3] *Ibid.*

Indeed, the only remaining bastions of the functional organization in the large corporation are found in the public utility and transportation industries, which, somewhat ironically, are among the most heavily regulated by government.

The adoption of the divisionalized structure, a result of the sharp swing toward diversification, has been accompanied by important modifications in the internal dynamics of the corporation and in the assignment of responsibilities for responding to environmental change. What is new about our situation today is that issues of social concern must now be managed by a large corporation that is *fundamentally different* than the ones which were called upon to respond to peaks of social involvement in the past. The results have not always been satisfactory. Social responsiveness does not fit neatly into the modus operandi of the divisionalized corporation. In its attempt to fashion flexible and creative responses to changing social demands, top management faces three dilemmas.

1. *The separation of corporate responsibilities is threatened.* In the illustration cited at the beginning of this chapter, the barriers between corporate and division offices had been built on mutual consent. The division manager, in exchange for the opportunity to run his own show and the promise of rewards if he did it well, had shouldered the responsibility for achieving agreed-on results. The president was then relieved of the task of formulating and implementing strategy in a number of (possibly unfamiliar) businesses and devoted his attention to matters of companywide interest.

However, as a result of the president's public statements and actions concerning equal employment, the world assumed he was responsible for seeing that it was accomplished in his organization. Successes or failures anywhere in the corporation reflected on him. Yet performance in employment opportunity—as in most areas of social concern—was closely related to operating decisions that had been delegated to managers down the line.

How can any president ensure an effective corporatewide response without interfering with his division managers? Should he choose to use the influence of his office, what effect would it have on the commitments he could expect for the achievement of corporate financial goals? Sharing the responsibility for social responsiveness may entail making traditional responsibilities more ambiguous. That is a result which most managers naturally want to avoid.

2. *The financial reporting system is inadequate.* Divisionalized companies rely heavily on sophisticated financial reporting systems to monitor the performance of operating units. Indeed the flow of plans, budgets, and accounting reports often constitutes the primary dialogue between corporate and division offices.

However reliable the reporting system may be in measuring operating unit performance against financial goals, not only is it ineffective in measuring social responsiveness, but by and large it is irrelevant. Analysis of a division's financial statements provides little indication of its effectiveness (however that may be judged) in controlling waste emissions, providing safe working conditions, or manufacturing safe products.

Accounting for the direct costs of programs related to social commitments is getting increased attention. For instance, one large packaging company isolates the projected expenditures for pollution control equipment in the capital budget (though the associated operating costs are not reflected in the projected income statement). A bank keeps track of expenses associated with its community relations program. The results, however, are at best incomplete, even on the cost side, and little progress has been made in the measurement of social benefits. We will return to the problems of social auditing in the next chapter.

The obvious alternative to the single financial reporting system is the creation of new measures of social responsiveness for each area of concern. Aside from whatever methodological problems such an attempt might pose, the result would be an enormous increase in the complexity of managing the organization—assuming that each reporting system was taken seriously. That, again, is a result most managers would prefer to avoid.

3. *The executive performance, evaluation, and reward process is challenged.* This dilemma is in part an outgrowth of the first two and is perhaps the most difficult to resolve. In the case of the company whose situation was described at the beginning of this chapter, the division manager participated in setting the standards to be used in evaluating the performance of his unit, and he secured commitments of support from his subordinates. He was not assuming that their behavior was predicated solely on the desire to meet the budget; their needs and satisfactions were defined in much broader and subtler ways. So he did not evaluate their performance solely in terms of the bottom line. Yet financial appraisal was an important tool for securing the subordinates' support in the pursuit of the division's strategy. The division manager was reluctant to insist on minority hiring and advancement quotas, which he felt would introduce new restrictions, ambiguities, and, possibly, discord into the process of evaluating his managers.

How can an organization obtain its middle managers' support for social responsiveness if their careers do not in some explicit way depend on it? One division manager in a large electronics company made the point very clearly: "Look, let's start with the idea that I don't need pollution control equipment or minorities to run my business. If the company wants me to do these things, they'll have to make it worth my while."

PATTERNS IN THE RESPONSE TO SOCIAL DEMANDS

These management dilemmas are not easily resolved, but neither are they intractable. In fact, a common pattern of response appears to have developed in corporations which have enjoyed at least a moderate degree of success in managing issues of strategic significance to their businesses. The nature of social issues naturally create differences, but the similarities are far more noticeable. There are three phases to this response process, spanning a period of at least six to eight years. The first two phases are necessary but insufficient in themselves for an effective response.

1. *The Commitment to Respond:* First, the chief executive recognizes the social issues as important. He may rationalize his interest as a matter of corporate responsibility or as far-sighted self-interest. Either way, it tends to be based on his personal conviction that the issue will be of continuing significance to the corporation rather than on his acquiescence to the petitions of subordinates. Even if managers down the line deem an issue to be worthy of an aggressive corporate response, the process seldom really gathers momentum until the chief executive's support has been obtained. Exceptions occur only occasionally when line managers see some strategic advantage for themselves and control the resources to exploit this advantage. Thus, the head of the aerospace division of an industrial firm may innovate on issues on which there is pressure through his government contract sponsors or which fit the skills and interests of the division's personnel.

The chief executive's involvement may be marked by several activities. Intially, he may begin to speak out on the issue at meetings of industry associations, stockholders, and civic groups. He may become active in organizations and committees involved in studying the issue or influencing opinion on it. He may also commit corporate resources to special projects such as ghetto businesses, waste recovery plants, and training centers. Soon he perceives the need for an up-to-date company policy, which he takes pains to communicate to all managers in the organization. Responsibility for implementing the policy is assigned as a matter of course to the operating units as part of the customary tasks performed in running the business.

The directives from top management, couched in terms of appeals to long-term benefits and corporate responsibility, almost invariably fail to provoke acceptable action or achievement. Heads nod in agreement, but the chief executive's wishes are largely ignored. Managers in the operating units lack evidence of the corporation's commitment to the cause, responsibilities are unclear, scorecards are lacking, and rewards for successes or penalties for failures are absent. The managers view as foolhardy any attempt to implement the policy at the risk of sacrificing financial and operating performance. And, of course, unless the chief executive is prepared to move beyond policy statements, they are right.

2. *The Acquisition of Specialized Skills and Knowledge*: The first phase may last for months or even years. The key event heralding the beginning of a new phase is the chief executive's appointment of a staff executive reporting to him or one of his senior staff to coordinate the corporation's activities in the area of concern, help the chief executive perform his public duties, and, in general, "make it happen." The new manager, often a specialist in his field, carries one of a variety of titles that have recently appeared

on organization charts: vice president or director of public or urban affairs, environmental affairs, minority relations, consumer affairs and so on.

The specialist views the problem as essentially a technical one that can be attacked by isolating it and applying specialized skills and knowledge to it. He begins to gather more systematic information on the company's activities in the area and matches these data with his assessment of environmental demands. For instance, if his responsibility includes minority relations, he gets personnel statistics from the operating divisions and attempts to pinpoint where problems exist in minority representation. He also develops methods for systematically collecting information, which later become the basis for planning and control systems. Finally, he mediates between operating divisions and external organizations, including government agencies, that are pressing for action.

But these efforts, while not without impact or merit, do not elicit the response envisaged in the corporate policy. The staff manager's attempts to force action are so alien to the decentralized mode of decision making that he becomes overburdened with conflict and crisis-by-crisis involvement. The only arrows in his quiver, aside from his own powers of persuasion, are the corporate policy and the demands of outsiders. But line managers may consider neither one credible. One environmental control director commented:

> We find ourselves in a "damned if you do, damned if you don't" situation a lot of the time. We get accused by the regulators of backsliding when we argue that the company is doing the best it can. Then when we argue for a program inside the company, we get accused of giving money away. The operating managers fail to see that if they don't take steps now, the cost in the long run could be a lot greater. They hear the wolves howling out there, but they only notice the ones that get in and not the ones we're keeping outside.

Consequently, if staff proposals interfere with its operations, middle management stands aside and lets the staff take responsibility (or blame) for the results. Faced with a choice between supporting his senior line executives (who have major operating responsibilities and probably a long history of sound judgments) and his new urban affairs vice president, the chief executive usually backs up the former.

Nevertheless, the job done by the corporate specialist is essential for the eventual implementation of the policy. He crystallizes the issue for top management. He also unearths and collects a great deal of information that serves to clarify what will be expected of the corporation in the future and the techniques or technologies that will be available to fulfill those expectations.

3. *The Institutionalization of Purpose*: The chief executive recognizes at this juncture that responsiveness entails a willingness to choose among multiple objectives and uses of resources. Fundamentally, such judgments are a general management responsibility. Top management sees the organizational rigidities to be more serious than previously acknowledged; they cannot be waved away with a policy statement, nor can they be flanked by a specialist. Instead, the whole organizational apparatus has to become involved. In this third phase, the chief executive attempts to make the achievement of policy a problem for all his managers.

In the cases we have observed, the chief executive's problem was not necessarily winning acceptance of the new company policy; in numerous instances, managers down the line were found who, from a personal standpoint, wished the policy had been stronger. Rather, the problem was in the institutionalization of the policy—that is, working it into the process through which operating decisions were made, resources allocated, and ultimately careers shaped.

A well-known characteristic of large organizations is that unless somehow provoked to do otherwise, they approach today's problems with yesterday's solutions, even though the context in which the new problems arise may be different. A study of the Cuban Missile crisis ascribed this phenomenon to "standard operating procedures" that are enormously useful in simplifying complex problems and organizational interaction.[4]

To illustrate, companies with strong unions and a long history of successful labor-management relationships develop routines for processing employee grievances that grow out of the union experience. If a complaint arises alleging plantwide discrimination, both union and management try to rephrase it in traditional terms; then they can handle it in their usual fashion. However, the minority employees may feel that their situation will not receive the special attention they believe it warrants if they rely on a decision-making process that has failed to satisfy their needs in the past. Consequently, they avoid the union and attempt to communicate directly with executives many levels above those managers normally responsible for employee grievances. The normal reaction in such instances is to rule the employees' tactic inadmissible and insist that they "play by the rules."

This phenomenon helps to explain the stability (stated negatively, the unresponsiveness) of most large organizations. For the chief executive of the decentralized corporation, the problem of securing responsiveness to social issues is compounded by the rules governing the interrelationships between corporate and division levels. The rules state that while the chief executive is obtaining and evaluating divisional results, he is not to meddle in the divisions' standard operating procedures. If he wants to change those procedures to coincide with the spirit of the new corporate policy, he presumably must attempt it indirectly by changing the standards for judging performance.

The chief executive does indeed try to play by the rules. This letter, written by one president to his subordinates, is a graphic illustration:

> The most significant change this year—the one that is basic to all others—is to place responsibility for achieving equal opportunity objectives where it rightfully belongs: with operating management, with each of us. Achieving these objectives is as important as meeting *any other* traditional business responsibility.
>
> It follows, of course, that a key element in each manager's overall performance appraisal will be his progress in this important area. No manager should expect a satisfactory appraisal if he meets other objectives, but fails here.

[4] Graham Allison, *The Essence of Decision: Explaining the Cuban Missile Crisis,* Boston, Little Brown and Co., 1971.

If one talks with operating managers shortly after such an announcement has been made, one finds an awareness of the policy but considerable skepticism about the corporation's will to enforce it. They detect gaps between pronouncement and performance. Since reporting on implementation of, say, a minority hiring quota cannot be integrated directly into the financial control system, it must be communicated separately. Consequently, it must compete for attention with the regular reporting system. In view of the technical problems likely to be encountered with the new procedure and the central position and historic importance of the old one, the competition may be very one-sided.

It may seem doubtful that a manager who has met his economic targets will be criticized, let alone severely punished, for failure to perform adequately in the area of social concern. The chief executive may be uttering strong words on appraisal, but it is the manager's immediate boss several layers down, not the chief executive, who appraises him.

In due course, a test case is encountered, though at the time it may not appear to be particularly significant. The institutionalization of purpose may hinge on the creative use of trauma. The trauma results not from the problem posed in the test case, but from the organizational dynamics through which the problem is resolved. Top-level executives suspend the rules governing their relationship with the operating divisions. For a brief period, division executives lose control of their operations; their decisions are countermanded and staff managers reporting to their superiors exercise inordinate influence in directing the outcome.

The whole affair is very unsettling for the divisions. Worst of all, questions are raised in the operating executives' minds about who really is responsible for managing the divisions' response and what the consequences may be if it is not they.

For instance, shortly after the letter quoted earlier had been sent, a smoldering controversy about minority relations erupted in a small service unit four levels down in a division. Eventually, no fewer than seven levels of line management, from the first-line supervisor to the chief executive, were involved with their associated staffs in attempting to settle it. For a two-week period, the normal chain of command was tenuously observed. Then, the chief executive intervened directly by issuing a decision that overturned the one announced by his subordinates. By his own forceful action, he dramatically illustrated the quality of management he expected in response to employee problems.

Intervention from the top level may not have been executed effectively in the test case, but that is not the issue. There were two very beneficial results:

1.–The managers in the division realized that to prevent such a fracas from recurring, they must be responsive to the issue in the future. That may mean incorporating action programs related to the issue into the division's strategy and modifying the process of evaluating the managers who are positioned to influence responsiveness directly.
2.–The company has provided clues to the new standard operating procedures that it wants adopted to establish the policy in the operating units. The policy has been tested and a precedent established that can serve as a guide for its implementation throughout the corporation.

The response patterns above may appear to be chaotic, and, in fact, they were often characterized as such by the managers involved. Yet there is underlying order and logic to the process.

Table 4-B illustrates how a policy problem is converted into a managerial problem through the process of institutionalization. During these three phases of involvement of the organization, concern for responding to the social issue spreads from the chief executive to middle-level managers. The awareness of a social need that produced the policy is enriched by the infusion of new skills and finally matures into a willingness on the part of middle-level managers to commit resources and reputations to responsible action.

The process receives strong impetus from the changing and increasingly demanding environmental conditions that often parallel the response pattern in this manner. We have referred to this phenomenon in the preceding chapter as the social issue life cycle.

UNDESIRABLE CONSEQUENCES

While this response pattern may eventually produce acceptable results, it is often inefficient and entails some undesirable side effects:

1.—If the six- to eight-year cycle observed in relatively successful instances is typical, the elapsed time required may be excessive. Unless social issues can be processed with reasonable speed, they may pile up and ultimately put the company in a position where it cannot function effectively in its traditional role as a producer of goods and services.

2.—Until the final phase, operating managers are not intimately concerned with the issue; specialists direct the responses. The legal staff and the environmental control director work out compliance schedules for pollution control, the minority relations specialist communicates with factory engineering managers about affirmative action programs, and so forth. But without middle-level management commitment, it is likely that the specialists will interfere with operating activities, misapply resources, or be ineffective in securing results. That is, in the two examples just cited, compliance schedules do not mesh with planned capital spending programs, and minority relations seminars are taken lightly. Deservedly or not, the specialist often shoulders the blame.

3.—Performance evaluation is usually skewed to distributing penalties for failures rather than rewards for successes. Moreover, the process is very unsystematic; it relates not so much to consistent performance against objectives as it does to poor handling of particular conspicuous situations. The manager cited for polluting a stream or charged with discrimination may find his career badly tarnished. His counterpart, who fails to construct and implement an effective environmental program or meet his hiring and advancement goals—but is not guilty of an overt action or is not so unfortunate as to have attention directed at him—may escape sanctions. The excuse normally given is, "We needed an example for the rest of the organization." Perhaps so, but it is unfortunate that such sacrifices must be made when the entire organization is trying to learn how to respond effectively to a new set of problems.

TABLE 4-B CONVERSION OF SOCIAL RESPONSIVENESS FROM POLICY TO TO ACTION

Organizational Level	*Phases of Organizational Involvement*		
	Phase 1	*Phase 2*	*Phase 3*
Chief Executive	Issue: Policy problem	Obtain knowledge	Obtain organizational commitment
	Action: Write and communicate policy	Add staff specialists	Change performance expectations
	Outcome: Enriched purpose, increased awareness		
Staff Specialists		Issue: Technical problem	Provoke response from operating units
		Action: Design data system and interpret environment	Apply data system to performance measurement
		Outcome: Technical and administrative learning	
Division Management			Issue: Management problem
			Action: Commit resources and modify procedures
			Outcome: Increased responsiveness

- *Phase 1*—social concerns exist but are not specifically directed at the corporation.
- *Phase 2*—broad implications for the corporation become clear but enforcement is weak or even nonexistant
- *Phase 3*—expectations for corporate action become more specific and sanctions (governmental or otherwise) become plausible threats.

THE SOCIAL RESPONSE PROCESS

In this chapter we have focused on the organizational requirements for implementing corporate social policy. Social issues arise not as discrete events, but as a flow of events which, whether or not closely related, share a common call on corporate attention.

They are at different stages in the zone of discretion. The outlines of some, such as air pollution control, have been well described, while the shape of others, such as "the new work force," is still murky. For example, referring to the evolving regulations covering noise levels, an experienced engineer in charge of applying federal environmental standards in his company commented, "If the company gave me $10 million to spend on getting noise levels down to 90 decibels, I wouldn't know how to spend it." He had neither the technology nor the directions for using it.

Therefore, from an organizational standpoint, the need is for a response process through which issues can be recognized and formed into policy, implications and possible solutions explored, and, finally, plans generated to govern action. The challenge for management is to facilitate a means of organizational learning and adaptation that will permit flexible and creative responses to social issues as they arise. In the divisionalized organization, that assignment will not be easy. The process for responding to social demands described in this chapter is a reasonable way of approaching a difficult mangerial problem. However, the process must be handled with care. In particular, there are four areas that require attention:

THE DANGER OF OVERLOAD. There is a real danger of overloading the process. The time and energy of the chief executive are limited, as are the organization's tolerance and capacity for wrestling with the environmental uncertainties. Top management should balance the numerous pressing social demands and the social goals it seeks, giving priority to those areas most likely to have an impact on the company's business. To ease the problems of implementation, top management must anticipate the transition from one phase to the next and clearly communicate to middle-level management the ground rules for managing the new phase.

THE EFFECTIVE USE OF SPECIALISTS. In the formative stages of its response the company must scan an unfamiliar environment, master new technologies, and collect and analyze a vast amount of information, both internally and externally. The staff specialist has the difficult task of developing approaches to this environment and designing systems to permit the planning and evaluation of programs for adapting to new needs.

The specialist also has a crucial, broader role in the organization. If he has managed his relationships in the organization well, he will be immensely useful in equipping it to respond to the future social issue. For instance, the specialist who has been concerned with air and water pollution has skills in engineering, environmental analysis, and government relations that may prove to be very useful in work with the occupational health and safety issue. He can become a multipurpose corporate change agent.

Thus, the effective management of the specialist's role is a vital part of the response process. Unfortunately, it is also frequently a weak link, not so much because the technical aspects of social demands can't be mastered as because the specialist finds it difficult or impossible to secure the necessary organizational response. These problems are discussed at greater length in Chapter 6.

IMPLEMENTING POLICY AT THE DIVISION LEVEL. To plan a rational sequence of activities in support of goals in areas of social concern, a response program is necessary. Placing the responsibility for formulating these programs with middle-level managers who are responsible for operations, exploits rather than subverts the organizational strengths of the decentralized company. The procedure of goal setting and program evaluation is second nature for both corporate-level and operating managers.

Insisting on a direct parallel between social response strategies and the more familiar business strategy yields three benefits:

1.—The response becomes anticipatory and not merely reactive.

2.—The response demands analysis that is too often lacking when resources are allocated to social problems. It may not be possible, or in the long run even worthwhile, to measure social costs and benefits in economic terms; however, requiring rigorous justification for the action to be taken makes the best use of the information and analytical tools available.

3.—The articulation of a strategy to govern response at the division level provides the basis for subsequent measurement and evaluation.

COMPLICATION OF THE EVALUATION PROCESS. This final point is, in our judgment, the most important but the least likely to happen of the four. It is commonplace to hear managers describe their jobs as being more complicated now than in the past. One division vice president summed it up this way: "Business used to be fun. But now there are so many people around demanding this and that, I just don't enjoy it any more."

Ironically, while the job of the manager—especially in the middle levels—has been growing more complex, the basis on which his performance is evaluated has often become simpler. The reason, of course, lies in the need for a lowest common denominator that can be used for allocating resources and making comparisons among units operating in different businesses and geographical environments. Financial performance serves well as this denominator.

If the corporation is to be socially responsive, however, top management may have to tolerate a greater degree of complexity in the measures it uses to evaluate the performance of middle-level executives. The path need not lead to more subjective or less results-oriented evaluations. Indeed, if attention has been paid to setting strategy in areas of social concern, the power of the results orientation may actually increase over a procedure that does not subject social programs to planning and analysis. Economic performance no doubt will always remain the dominant yardstick (and with good reason), but it should be augmented to reflect the greater complexity and scope of middle management's responsibilities.

SUGGESTED READINGS

1.–Chandler, Alfred. *Strategy and Structure*. Cambridge: the M.I.T. Press, 1962.
2.–Allison, Graham. *Essence of Decision: Explaining the Cuban Missile Crisis.* Boston: Little, Brown and Company, 1971.
3.–Zaleznik, Abraham. *Human Dilemmas of Leadership*. New York: Harper and Row, 1966.
4.–Bauer, Raymond A., and Gergen, Kenneth J. *The Study of Policy Formulation.* New York: The Free Press, 1968.

Case Nine

Xerox Corporation

On September 8, 1971, Mr. C. Peter McColough, then President and Chief Executive Officer of the Xerox Corporation, announced an experimental Social Service Leave Program to begin in January 1972. The program provided an opportunity for approximately 20 Xerox employees in the United States to take up to a one-year leave of absence, with full pay and benefits, and devote the time to working with a social service organization of their choice. They were also guaranteed the same or an equivalent job with the same pay, responsibilities, status, and opportunity for advancement upon return to the company.

In announcing the program to Xerox employees, Mr. McColough spoke of corporate and individual commitment and what the program represented for each:

> Xerox has always had a basic philosophy that we should be involved as a corporation in the problems of our society. We've encouraged our people to be involved. Social Service Leave is a logical extension of our commitment. We are determined to put something back into society.
>
> Many of our people share our commitment. But on a part-time basis, there is only so much they can do. A lot of them would like to really sink their teeth into a problem full time. We'll give them a chance to do this during the prime of their working careers, when they're best able to do it. They won't have to wait until they retire.
>
> Many of our best people would not be here today if Xerox stood only for profits.
>
> In the future, our conduct as corporate citizens will be even more important—if that's possible—as we try to recruit the best young people available. As a result of programs like the Social Service Leave, we think that the bright young people will be more apt to join us than some other big company.

By January 1972, Mr. McColough and others in management were beginning to evaluate the program to determine whether it ought to be continued and, if so, whether the scope, policies, and procedures underlying it were appropriate. As far as they could determine, it had been favorably received both inside and outside the company. Several overseas affiliates had evidenced an interest in a program of their own, usually to be operated under somewhat different policies. Moreover, it had so far been implemented according to plan and without serious mishap. On the other hand, a number of unforeseen organizational problems had already been encountered and the difficult tasks of responding to the needs of the men and women on leave and replacing them in equivalent career opportunities remained ahead.

The evaluation was accompanied by a degree of urgency. There was a general feeling among those closely involved in planning the program that the best time from the employees' standpoint to begin a social leave was in September, which, if adopted, would advance the announcement of a 1972-73 program to April or May.

XEROX HISTORY

In 1971 Xerox had sales of $1.94 billion and profits of $212.6 million, placing it among the largest 55 industrial corporations in the *Fortune* 500. Growth had been spectacular since 1959 when sales were $33.3 million and profits $2.1 million. In fact, from 1960 to 1970, earnings per share increased at a compound rate of 47.3% per year, highest on the *Fortune* list.

The primary source of growth for Xerox had come through the commercial development of an electrostatic-photographic copying process later known as xerography. Formed in 1906 in Rochester, N.Y. as the Haloid Corporation by Joseph R. Wilson and three associates to process and sell sensitized photographic paper, the company had struggled through the depression and emerged from the war years with sales in 1946 of $6,750,000 and profits of $101,000. That year Joseph C. Wilson succeeded his father as President. Confronted by increasing competition and decreasing margins in traditional product lines, the younger Mr. Wilson was eager to develop new products but lacked the resources to support a significant research effort. At this time the Battelle Institute, a nonprofit research organization, had been seeking industrial support for the development of a copying process patented by Chester Carlson in 1940 and since 1944 supported by the Institute. Although numerous corporations, including Kodak, IBM, and RCA, had turned the invitation down, Mr. Wilson in 1947 agreed to acquire from Battelle certain licensing rights in return for future royalty payments and an annual contribution of $25,000. A short time later, Xerox renegotiated the arrangement and became the sole licensing agency for all patents in the xerography field.

Xerox invested heavily in research during the next years, greatly expanding its patent position and yielding a series of specialized applications for xerography which by the mid-1950s contributed over half the company's revenues. From 1953 to 1960, over $70 million was poured into research, slightly more than half of it contributed by outside debt and equity financing. It was not, however, until 1960 and the introduction of the 914, the first fully automatic dry copier in the office equipment industry, that this investment really began to pay off.

On the strength of the 914, sales nearly tripled from 1960 to 1962 as Xerox became the leader in the copier field. The company sought to expand that position by aggressively broadening its product line to include desk top copiers and high-speed machines with expanded reproduction capabilities. As machine speeds increased and reproduction quality improved, the traditional distinction between the copying and duplicating fields became blurred. The pace of development and marketing efforts in office copiers and duplicators was intense as the partial list of product introductions below suggests.

Year	*Product*	*Feature*
1960	914	Basic console model (400 copies/hr.)
1963	813	Desk top model (330 copies/hr.)
1965	2400	Copier-duplicator (2,400 copies/hr.)
1966	720	Expanded version of 914 (720 copies/hr.)
1967	660	Expanded version of 813 (660 copies/hr.)
1968	3600	Expanded version of 2400 (3,600 copies/hr.)
1969	7000	Duplicator, expanded capabilities (3,600 copies/hr.)
1971	4000	Small console, expanded capabilities (2,000 copies/hr.)

By 1971, Xerox was estimated in the business press to have 65% to 80% of the office copier market in the United States. The company's record had encouraged competition from such large firms as Eastman Kodak, Minnesota Mining, Litton, Singer, and Sperry Rand and a variety of smaller ones. A recent entrant was IBM, which in April 1970 introduced a machine having much in common with the Xerox model 720. *Financial World*,[1] noting that some 70% of commercial and government establishments already contained a copier, was among those predicting increasing competition in the future. Nevertheless, Xerox 1971 revenues from copiers and rentals in the United States increased 12% over the previous year, with steady improvement relative to 1970 throughout the year.

In 1956, Xerox formed a joint venture with the Rank organization of London to manufacture and sell xerographic products in world markets, a relationship which in 1961 also led to the formation of a second joint venture between Rank-Xerox and Fuji Photo Film Co., Fuji-Xerox, directed specifically at markets in the Far East. Revenues overseas also increased dramatically after the introduction of the 914. Then in 1969 Xerox purchased the 51st per cent of Rank-Xerox and renegotiated certain royalty provisions in exchange for stock valued at $20 million.

During the 1970s, Xerox sought participation in several new fields. First, in 1963 Electro Optical Systems (EOS), an aerospace company involved in laser technology, solar power conversion, and space reconnaissance, was acquired to gain entry into the high technology, government-financed, R & D business. Then, beginning in 1964 and concluding in 1968 with the acquisition of a prominent textbook publisher, Ginn & Co., Xerox assembled an education group producing a wide range of materials and information services. Finally, in 1969 in exchange for approximately $1 billion in stock, the company acquired Scientific Data Systems, a mainframe computer manufacturer with revenues of $100 million, about 70% of it derived from scientific and engineering applications.

These new ventures had not as yet produced a record approaching that in office copiers. Cutbacks and reallocations in government programs had seriously affected the

---

[1] "Copiers: Competition Heating Up," *Financial World*, May 6, 1970, p. 6 ff.

aerospace business and dampened the growth in spending for education. The computer group, renamed Xerox Data Systems (XDS) had been subject to similar pressures and, in part due to more conservative accounting policies, had been operating at a loss. Revenues from computer products were off about 20% in 1971, and management indicated that losses were expected to continue through 1973.

A breakdown of revenues by product line was reported as follows:

	1969	*1970*	*1971*
Business Products	56%	58%	56%
International Operations	27	30	34
Computer Products	8	5	3
Educational Materials and Information Services	6	6	6
Government-sponsored Research and Military Products	3	1	1
	100%	100%	100%

Profits after taxes from international operations were $72 million in 1970 and $92 million in 1971, or 38% and 43% respectively of the corporate total. A financial summary is provided in Exhibit 9-1.

Xerox had a publicly stated goal of achieving continuing growth of 20% per year in earnings per share with a return on stockholder investment of 20%. This target was generally perceived in the organization to be a very demanding one. In 1971 Mr. McColough indicated that growth would be guided by two broad policies, the first directed toward industry leadership in the information industry and the second toward becoming a "great multinational company."

> We think that our field of interest is the business of supplying knowledge and information on a worldwide basis. It seems to me that this will be the fastest-growing business in the world in the 1970s. The demand for knowledge and information in every country of the world is increasing geometrically each year. There seems to be no limit to where we can go in that field if we apply ourselves to it in the right way. . . . I think in the middle seventies, you will see us bring [computer and imaging capabilities] together in combination to offer new services that will be very important to our business worldwide.
>
> One of our major objectives for the 1970s clearly has to be to make Xerox a great multinational company. Multinational. Not international. In the 1960s, as we spread our wings from the United States into the rest of the world through various partnerships we became an international company in the sense that we operated in many parts of the world.
>
> But in the 1970s we must become a multinational company. Among other things a multinational company must provide opportunities for all its people regardless of what country they come from. The young person who joins the company

today—whether in Milan or Sao Paulo or New York City—should have an equal opportunity to take my job in the future.

We must also put great emphasis in the 1970s on having manufacturing operations in many locations. We have to realize that if we are going to be large in the major countries of the world, we are going to have to contribute to those countries. We can't simply go in with products manufactured somewhere else; we must put something back in.

ORGANIZATIONAL STRUCTURE

Managing the company's growth constituted a formidable challenge for the Xerox organization. The number of employees grew from 9,000 in 1960 to 63,000 in 1971, about 25,000 of them overseas. Moreover, by the late 1970s this total was expected to more than double again. The average employee in the United States was estimated to be less than 30 years old, and about a third of them had been with the company less than three years. Xerox had entered the 1960s with a functional organization, but over the next decade changes at all levels were frequent as the company moved toward a divisionalized structure. The consequences of growth for individual managers were described by one personnel executive in the Business Products Group (BPG), which alone had 33,000 employees:

Xerox has the ability to make organization changes quickly. In BPG, going from $100 million to $1.2 billion in ten years has meant that just by staying in the same job, a manager's responsibilities increase dramatically. One of the rewards of my work is seeing people literally grow. Of course, some don't and we have had to move them down or aside. We no longer have employment contracts with our top managers but instead give them a six-month turnaround time should we decide to part ways.

Rapid growth had also prompted the company to seek managers for high-level positions from outside the company. Mr. Archie McCardell (45), President, who joined Xerox in 1966 from Ford[2] where he had held various jobs in the finance and control area, commented:

We have grown so fast that there has not been time for enough managers to come up through the ranks. We have brought in a number of outsiders at high levels and will probably continue to do so for another two or three years. With the pressures on our organization, getting sufficient attention devoted to management development has been a continuing source of concern for us.

---

[2]Other senior executives coming to Xerox from other companies since 1967 included Dr. Jacob Goldman (Sr. V.P., R & D) and Mr. James O'Neill (Gr. V.P., BPG) from Ford, Mr. Joseph Flavin (Ex. V.P.) and Mr. William Glavin (Gr. V.P., XDS) from IBM, and Mr. Robert Haigh (Gr. V.P., Education Group) from Standard Oil (Ohio).

In 1969, Xerox announced plans to relocate the corporate offices in Connecticut. On an interim basis, pending construction of a new office building in Greenwich, headquarters were moved to the neighboring town of Stamford, Connecticut.

In December 1971, a major rearrangement at the corporate level was announced to align the organization with the company's strategy for the 1970s. The announcement, although planned for some time, took place several weeks after the unexpected death of Mr. Wilson. Mr. McColough, who came to Xerox in 1954, rose through sales to Executive Vice President in 1962, President in 1966, and Chief Executive Officer in 1968, became chairman. Mr. McCardell, Executive Vice President since 1968, became President and Chief Operating Officer. All U.S. operations in computers, copying/duplicating, education, and aerospace were assigned to Mr. Raymond Hay (43), who formerly was responsible for BPG and, for a short time, overseas activities as well. Mr. Joseph Flavin (43), formerly Senior Vice President for Planning and Finance and then briefly in charge of XDS, was made responsible for international operations. The new organization is shown in Exhibit 9-2.

CORPORATE RESPONSIBILITY

Xerox management believed that the company was a social as well as an economic institution and had responsibilities to society beyond economic performance. Mr. Wilson articulated this attitude in a 1964 speech:

> The corporation cannot refuse to take a stand on public issues of major concern; failure to act is to throw its weight on the side of the status quo, and the public interprets it that way.
>
> Inevitably the corporation is involved in economic, social, and political dynamics whether it wills or not, and to ignore the noneconomic consequences of business decisions is to invite outside intervention.

There was a general feeling in the company that Mr. McColough's commitment to this point of view was also very strong.

The company had been involved in a number of programs which related to this social concern. In 1968 Xerox participated with local community organizations in Rochester in the founding of FIGHTON, Inc., a manufacturing company owned and managed by blacks in the inner city, and continued to be a major customer for its products and a consultant to its management. Investments and deposits had also been made in minority-owned banks. Internally, Xerox had instituted a minority hiring and development program that had substantially increased the number of minority employees. A pollution abatement control committee had also been formed to monitor the company's activities in that area.

The company had been active in sharing sponsorship of TV events of educational or cultural significance, among the recent programs being the "Civilization" series and "Sesame Street." In addition, charitable contributions of about $5.0 million were made during 1971, up from $4.4 million in 1970 and $3.7 million in 1969. The majority of the funds went to educational institutions; other recipients included Community Chests and

United Funds in locations having Xerox facilities and a wide variety of civic, legal, health, and urban affairs organizations. Asked in 1969 whether contributions should be cut back, 90.2% of the stockholders, representing 96.9% of the shares, voted "no."

THE SOCIAL SERVICE LEAVE PROGRAM—CONCEPTION AND DESIGN

In August 1970, Mr. McCardell and Mr. James Wainger took the night flight from New York to Los Angeles. Mr. Wainger, who originally joined Xerox in 1960 but left the company from 1966 to 1969 to teach and write plays, had been made Director of Personnel two months earlier.[3] The conversation turned to how Xerox might be more responsive to social and employee needs in the 1970s. Mr. McCardell suggested that the company consider making some of its people available to work on problems of their choosing. By the time the wheels touched in Los Angeles, a leave program had been outlined in some detail.

Upon his return, Mr. Wainger discussed the idea briefly with Mr. Sanford Kaplan, his immediate superior at the time, and Mr. McColough, receiving in each case enthusiastic support. He then described the program in a memorandum sent to corporate executives (see Exhibit 9-3).

Mr. McColough suggested one modification almost immediately: that the selection committee be composed of lower level Xerox employees rather than a prestigious outside board. He commented:

> Xerox is a very young company. Our average age is less than 30 and we will be hiring tens of thousands of young people in the next few years. Large corporations inevitably tend to be dictatorial, which runs counter to the needs of many young people. They would like to have a voice in policy and not have to wait until late in their careers. This committee is the first of a number of things that will involve our employees in either decision or advisory roles.
>
> I also believe that such a committee can do a better job of evaluating projects. Its members are probably more in tune with the needs that those applying for leave are hoping to satisfy. This procedure will erase any tinge that the committee is there to serve our [top management's] interests.

While the remainder of the top management group was positive about the leave program, there was some feeling that the fall of 1970 was not the appropriate time to initiate it. A soft economy in the latter half of the year was putting pressure on operating budgets, which in turn was forcing "modest" layoffs at headquarters and in Rochester. As one manager put it, "the psychology didn't sit right—to be laying off and at the same time doing this." Mr. McColough decided to delay the announcement of the program.

---

[3] Mr. Wainger recalled that his assignment had come as a surprise; "I told Peter [McColough] I had no experience in personnel, but he said what he was looking for was someone with a sense for the company in a society in evolution." He was elected vice president in1971.

Mr. Wainger began to reactivate the program the following spring. It was June, however, before the interview with Mr. McCologh which was to appear in the brochure describing it could be arranged. Then with summer vacations approaching and the desire to "do the brochure right," the announcement date was put off until September.

In the meantime, Mr. Wainger set in motion a procedure for selecting members of the Evaluation Committee. He first contacted the top personnel executives in each division and asked them to identify people in their units who were realtively young, had some background in social service activities, possessed an "intellectual and emotional affinity for social issues," and were not members of top management. He then reviewed the list with Mr. Robert Schneider, Assistant to the President and formerly Manager of Corporate Contributions, and selected from it those that appeared most appropriate, keeping in mind the desire for a representative group in terms of operating unit, race, background, and sex. The two men, individually, then visited these people in the field. Offers to join the committee were extended to and accepted on the spot by the first five interviewed. Messrs. Wainger and Schneider, as the two "old men," rounded out the committee shown in Exhibit 9-4.

The final ground rules for administering the program were also worked out for inclusion in the brochure. Xerox employees in the United States with three or more years of service were to be eligible for leave. No restrictions were to be placed on the type of projects acceptable except that they be legal, nonpartisan, and under the sponsorship of an existing nonprofit organization of some kind. In addition to describing how they proposed to spend their time, applicants were to have the written acceptance of the sponsoring agency. It was Mr. McCardell's original idea that to help insure the commitment of applicants to projects, the company should play no part in matching people and opportunities.

Applications were to be submitted directly to the Evaluation Committee; employee names, however, were not to be available to the committee during their deliberations. Employees would not be asked to seek permission to apply, nor were their superiors to be consulted at any time in the selection process. The brochure also noted that, "It's possible that in a rare case a person selected may be so essential in his work at Xerox that he cannot be released. If that should happen, the burden of proof will be on the manager and the final decision will be made by Peter McColough."

Mr. McColough commented on the reasons behind avoiding an "up the line" approval procedure:

> I do not want Social Service Leave to be looked upon in the organization as a reward for good performance. Nor do I want it, speaking pragmatically, to be a device for managers to get rid of people they don't want. There are other ways of doing these things, and this program should not be used as a substitute. I also do not want managers to be able to block someone from seeking leave. I would say O.K. to a manager who is emphatic about not losing a subordinate, but I could not do it lightly. Finally, putting the decision in the hands of an independent committee removes the inference that we have our own pet projects. I am able to tell agencies who call me directly that the choice is not mine.

Mr. Wainger added some further thoughts on the organization of the program:

> Having a multi-level approval process–God, doesn't that sound like jargon!–would dilute the corporate commitment to the project. This is *Xerox* doing something and not the units themselves, and the judgments should be those of the corporation. I favor functionalizing, not decentralizing responsibility for an activity such as this.
>
> A bottoms-up approach, I'm afraid, would introduce a lot of extraneous judgments in this case which would cut the heart out of the program. Worst of all, approval would be based on their [operations managers] view of the value of a project. That view could be influenced by administrative convenience–can't let a good subordinate go and so forth. That's especially serious when it comes to salesmen because so often those skills are what are most needed by social service agencies. We've gone to great lengths to involve on the committee the right people with right values to judge applications.

While the employees were on leave, their salaries, including a normal increase, were to be paid from a corporate account and not charged to the operating units. The aggregate cost was estimated at about $600,000.

ANNOUNCEMENT AND REACTION

On September 9, every Xerox employee in the United States was mailed a letter from Mr. McColough, the illustrated brochure and an application form (reproduced as Exhibit 9-5) which together described the program, the Evaluation Committee, and the procedures for applying. Thus, everyone in the company, with the exception of those few corporate executives who had been directly involved, was apprised of the program at the same time. Although he did not like the idea of a press release, Mr. Wainger had one issued to avoid the confusion and conflicting stories that he felt might reach the media from such a large mailing.

The outside reaction was "overwhelming." Newspapers all over the country carried stories about the Social Service Leave, a television network inquired if a special feature might be made of it, and numerous radio stations and magazine reporters called for interviews. Mr. Wainger spoke for many in the corporation when he said:

> I felt embarrassed about the attention this has received and did what I could to draw back from it. After all, the program is a very modest, experimental expression of our concern. Naturally, the publicity is good for our image, but that's not the reason we did it. Several hundred social agencies have also called, and we have had to send them a letter saying it's up to the employees, not us.

Within the organization, the response was described by one manager as that of "quiet admiration–a feeling that the company is really putting money and people behind its words."

From his vantage point, Mr. McColough said:

> The response I have had from the organization has all been favorable. In this case, that should not be surprising, of course, since it was clearly my decision and had

already been done. I am sure, on the other hand, that had the expense gone into the operating budgets, there would have been some opposition.

There being no further policy matters to attend to, for the time being, Mr. Wainger's office settled down to wait until November 1, the deadline for applications.

APPLICATIONS

There was little conversation in the organization during September and October about social leave. Mr. Douglas Reid, manager of personnel operations at BPG, received a few phone calls from applicants in need of information, which he referred to Mr. Wainger's office, and on one occasion from a manager in support of a subordinate's project. However, the period was an active one for those assembling proposals. Mrs. Frayda Cooper, an editor at Ginn and eventually among those selected for leave, recalled her experience:

> I had lunch with Mr. Baker's[4] secretary on September 9, and she told me about the Social Leave Program. It perked my interest. For some time I have wanted to work with the aged. That night I talked about it with my son, who encouraged me to try. When the brochure came a few days later I had mixed reactions, the committee didn't look very old—would they be interested in a program for the elderly? On the other hand, this field wasn't mentioned among the examples it provided—maybe if the committee tried to pick people in different areas, others wouldn't have thought of this one. Anyway, I decided to go ahead.
>
> I didn't talk about my plans in the company. The executive editor knew I was applying because I borrowed his brochure to write the proposal, having given mine away and being unable to find another one. Of course, out of courtesy, I had earlier told my immediate superior. I didn't have the sense that a lot of people around me were applying, but with 25,000 people eligible, there were bound to be a lot.

In the next three weeks, Mrs. Cooper talked during lunch hours and Saturdays with a variety of people in government and social agencies and at Brandeis University about the problems of the elderly and her interests and background. These discussions resulted in a letter of support, including a budget of $17,000 for various expenses, and a four-page work plan from the Massachusetts Department of Community Affairs, which Mrs. Cooper appended to her handwritten application form. Since a manuscript had recently been accepted by Ginn conditional upon her availability to edit it, she advanced the starting date in the leave proposal to April 1972.

Another sucessful applicant was Mr. Irving Bell, a salesman with Xerox Graphic Services. Referring to these weeks he said:

> I found out about the program by reading the AP story in the newspaper. I was interested—said to myself, "Now that's a good idea!" I have a few rich friends, and they never get a year to do their thing. I started to think about my background and

---

[4] Mr. Baker was President of Ginn.

> where I'd fit; I wanted to contribute more than the ordinary person working at night.
>
> This was right after Attica.[5] I have some friends who talked with me about the prisons in Massachusetts, and that got me thinking. A few years ago I had taught at a technical school, but unfortunately, teaching was a luxury I couldn't afford then. Nevertheless, it was very gratifying. It seemed to me that someone who wanted to teach in penal institutions could give a little dignity and a pride of accomplishment to some people who really need it.
>
> It was a lonely time, but working on this was such a personal thing. I thought my program was pretty good–I used to dream about it, I brought my plans up a little at home, but never mentioned them to my boss. Maybe I was hedging my risk–in case I didn't get it. I figured there would be an application from everyone who was eligible.

A few applications were received in Mr. Wainger's office in the first two weeks, but then the flow virtually stopped. By mid-October only 30 were in hand. However, the number began to increase rapidly during the last week; the total rose to 96 by Friday, October 28 and to 197 by November 1, including all those postmarked before midnight. Another 20 or so were postmarked after the deadline and were regretfully disqualified. Each application was given a quick review by the legal department to assess whether the project and agency involved was politically nonpartisan and legal. None was eliminated.

EVALUATION AND SELECTION

On November 1 the Evaluation Committee was convened at Xerox headquarters in Stamford. Since, with the exception of the two corporate managers, the committee members did not know one another, Mr. Wainger invited them to his house for dinner the night before to help them become acquainted with one another. The next morning, the group met with Mr. McCardell, who told them that the corporation was not going to give them instructions on who or what should be selected and that it was their responsibility to set standards to govern their choices.

The committee then read a dozen proposals and with this common background set about developing the evaluation process. After considerable discussion seven criteria evolved:

1.–Social impact
2.–Ability (of applicant to fulfill proposal)
3.–Commitments (of both individual and agency)
4.–Innovativeness
5.–Multiplier effect
6.–Continuity of program (after volunteer leaves)
7.–Realism

[5] There had been a violent end to a prison revolt at Attica State Prison in New York State in September 1971.

An eighth one—favorable or unfavorable impact on the corporation—was explicitly raised and set aside as not in the spirit of the Social Leave Program. The committee then agreed that each member should study each proposal and grade it high, medium, or low. After a batch of 25 or 30 had been read, the committee would then stop and compare notes before going on.

Mr. Wainger described the tenor of the ensuing deliberations in these terms:

> The discussions were very democratic. There was surprisingly little ego involved Although I acted as chairman to keep the book,[6] I consciously avoided dominating the discussion. In most cases there was a consensus on the low end. If there was wide disagreement, we would stop and talk it through, which often led to changes in opinions. As a result, some applications went quickly while others occupied us for two hours.
>
> After we had been through most of the proposals, it became clear that some of them were bubbling up as clear winners—seven in fact. We listed these by area of concern. Then someone said that they were all similar in that they exhibited a high intellectual content and were global in scope—proposals to set up programs or work on an institutional level. On the other hand, many of those we had given low evaluations to were one-on-one type projects. Someone else noted that all the pictures in the brochure showed people helping people in a very direct way. Was narrow bad? Was that what we had encouraged? The debate lasted a while and eventually resulted in a decision to go back and re-evaluate some of those we had rated poorly.

The committee labored with an increasing sense of cohesiveness from 9:00 A.M. until dinnertime from Monday to Thursday and concluded in the mid afternoon Friday. As the week progressed, the committee identified 38 proposals in 17 areas of social concern to be given special attention. A conscious attempt was made to spread the final choices across these areas of concern (15 were eventually included). In addition, a less explicit effort was made to use the salary information requested on the application to insure that a balanced cross-section of levels in the organization was represented.

Ultimately, 21 employees were selected, two of them requesting six-month leaves. Included in the group were three women and eighteen men. Their ages ranged from 26 to 60 and lengths of service at Xerox from three to ten years. Four had monthly salaries of less than $850 while one had a monthly salary in excess of $4,000. Thirteen were employed in BPG with the remainder spread among other line and staff groups. People and projects are described in Exhibit 9-6. Another five employees were named as alternates, with any substitutions to be made in the same field if possible. The alternates were not to be notified and remained identified by number only.

Before the committee adjourned, Mr. McCardell met with them again. He asked the group, "If you had another ten places, could you recommend individuals to fill them with

---

[6]The only record of the meeting was kept on a flip chart; one page devoted to criteria, two more to areas of social concern and employee proposals, and two to an analysis of those selected by age, salary, and operating unit.

equal enthusiasm?" The group said, "No." He then asked, "Are there five among the ones you have selected that you consider marginal?" Again the group said, "No."

That afternoon registered, special delivery letters of acceptance were sent to each of the winners. With the letter was a plane ticket and an invitation to attend a meeting at the Westchester Country Club near Stamford the following Friday and Saturday morning. The purposes of the meeting were to provide the participants with an opportunity to understand the policies to govern them while on leave, to share backgrounds, to meet members of the Evaluation Committee and to receive some advance counseling on the stresses and frustrations many of them were likely to encounter as they left the structured life of a large corporation. They were told to keep their selection in confidence until after the meeting, though it was anticipated that they might have to tell their managers in order to explain their two-day absence.

All 21 attended the meeting. Mr. McColough and Mr. McCardell mingled with the group and addressed them briefly on Friday. In addition to a considerable amount of time for informal conversation, the schedule included group meetings in which each participant described his program, and others in which an industrial psychologist and a "down to earth" urban consultant discussed potential problems. Company public relations officials also discussed how to handle press inquiries.

Mr. Wainger commented later on the relationship between Xerox and those on leave that he had stressed.

> I could have thought of a long list of dos and don'ts but didn't want to get into that. Basically I told them that they were still Xerox employees and we wanted them back and that we would try to help them personally if they needed it. While they are away, no reports will be required or evaluations made. Members of the Evaluation Committee will visit each person at least twice to see how the program is working, and we have asked for a report from the volunteer at the end of the year.
>
> There are bound to be situations we haven't anticipated. For instance, what happens if one of our people gets into legal difficulties in the course of his work? It's the agency's responsibility to back him up, but we'll do all we can to help. Or the Massachusetts Correctional Agency asks our man teaching in their prisons if Xerox will interview inmates for jobs when they are released. In such cases I told them to call me. The relationship between Xerox and the agency is a corporate matter. My suspicion is that we won't start lots of little programs to suit agencies. We have several major on-going ones initiated from the corporate level and new ones will come in the same way.

By Saturday noon, the mood was described by one man as "euphoric." Another said, "It was beautiful–the most moving experience of my life." Still another remarked, "I could sense a sigh of relief from the committee after they had been with us for a little while. By the end, we had been transformed from a bunch of individuals into a group with common bonds and a sense of purpose."

SEPARATION

Prior to the meeting at the Westchester Country Club, Mr. Wainger reviewed the list for anyone he felt might be considered indispensable. Although Mr. John Teem, Director of the Technical Staff in R & D would be difficult to replace, and Mr. William Gable was a senior executive at XDS, he anticipated no major problems securing their release. Then, on November 18 he sent a letter to each manager having a subordinate chosen for leave, formally announcing the selection and forcefully reminding the manager of Mr. McColough's guarantee of the same or an equivalent job for the employee after the leave. One of these letters is reproduced in Exhibit 9-7.

The employees were greeted with applause and admiration, although as one account representative related, it was not always universal:

> It's funny how people react. The first thing my boss said when I told him I was going to Stamford for two days was, "Who's going to look after your accounts?" Perhaps I'm expecting too much. After all, he has needs, and losing his best producer won't help.
>
> And the other night one of those who wasn't selected called me at 11:00 and said that he understood the Evaluation Committee had a tough job, but he couldn't see why they had picked my project rather than his. He had been with Xerox a lot longer than me and had really gone to a lot of work in putting his proposal together; it even included a letter from the governor.
>
> But the response I've gotten from others, especially my clients, has more than made up for it. They have a lot of respect for Xerox. It makes me glad I'm working here.

While Mr. McColough received no petitions claiming indispensability, a number of situations were uncovered during the next several weeks which reflected the complexity of administering the Social Service Leave Program and foreshadowed the problems to be encountered reinstating those on leave in the organization. In one instance, a manager was to have received a substantial increase in the scope of his job two days after he was notified of his selection by the Evaluation Committee. He had not known about the impending promotion prior to accepting the leave. In another case, one of the people chosen was to have been laid off. He was a specialist, very well thought of in his division, for whom no work was available because of government spending cutbacks. The company had tried for some time to relocate him in some other unit but had been unsuccessful. In fact, while the Evaluation Committee was meeting, the lay-off request was waiting on Mr. Wainger's desk for his approval.[7] Along with the others, however, he had been guaranteed an equivalent career opportunity when he returned.

A more difficult variation of the above situation also arose. A relatively senior man selected for leave was in the process of being terminated because his performance did not measure up to the standards set by the manager of his department, and other departments were reluctant to pick him up. He had accepted this fact and informally agreed during the fall to use the next 6 months to relocate. The department manager indicated that he was not aware of the social leave application until about the time the news broke.

A final case was described by Mr. Reid:

---

[7]Xerox maintained the policy that before an employee with eight or more years of service could be released, permission had to be granted by either Mr. McColough or Mr. Wainger.

> I got a call one day in December from a branch manager. That was unusual in itself since he was calling three or four levels up the line. He said one of his area sales managers had been selected for leave. He didn't have a replacement, and regional management told him that with the budgets cut to the bone there wasn't $5,000 to cover the relocation costs associated with moving someone else in. They then suggested that he put the sales planning manager into the ASM slot. The branch manager said that meant he would end up covering for the sales planning manager.
>
> I didn't like the sound of it so I called the regional personnel manager. It finally came out that they were interested in getting the branch manager more involved in sales planning and saw this as a good way of doing it. I told him that wasn't in the spirit of the program and some way of getting a replacement had to be found.
>
> A later discussion with the branch manager revealed that there was a good salesman there who could be made ASM. The branch manager was reluctant to do this because it would mean demoting him when the old ASM returned. I suggested that he could be moved to an ASM job elsewhere, but apparently he can't move for personal reasons for two years.

Mr. Wainger indicated that he had been informed that non-budgeted relocation expense might be involved. Rather than providing the money from corporate funds, however, he decided to leave it as a proper operating unit responsibility.

CONSIDERATIONS FOR THE FUTURE

In addition to worrying through the problems of specific individuals, corporate executives were concerned about how to measure the success of the Social Service Leave Program. Mr. McCardell noted four conditions he felt were important:

1.—The careers of people who have gone on leave do not suffer.
2.—They have a sense of accomplishment in their year away.
3.—They have a broadened perspective on the job and outside.
4.—The social agencies say their efforts have been useful.

Difficulties which he and others quickly acknowledged with such evaluation criteria were the lack of clear factual evidence and the long time span over which benefits were likely to occur.

Of more immediate concern were the number who returned to Xerox and the company's ability to reinstate them satisfactorily. A loss rate of 50% was generally viewed at corporate headquarters as "disappointing" and highly unlikely; 20% was thought by several to be "an acceptable price to pay," though again higher than expected. Mr. McCardell commented on reinstatement:

> This is probably the biggest problem we face, but with only 20 we can take a personal interest. That's why Peter's name was on the letters to the employees' supervisors. Of course, letters have been written before which have gone unheeded. A chief executive can't rule by fiat. We'll have to wait and see.

Aside from evaluation, several policy questions were raised at various levels in the organization. The first involved accounting for the costs; should they be allocated to the operating units or retained in a corporate account similar to that for charitable contributions? If the former were chosen, how far down in the organization should charges be allocated? Some difference of opinion existed among corporate officers though an immediate choice was not deemed necessary. Mr. Wainger indicated, however, that if the program grew, as he hoped it would, pressure would mount for doing away with a large, easily identifiable corporate budget item.

The second question related to the selection procedure. A senior manager in BPG put it this way:

> Had I been doing this, I would have put in more feedback from the organization and made it less a corporate-individual deal. That way we could have ironed out a lot of the administrative problems beforehand. A study of who goes on leave might be useful too. Are we encouraging the right type of people to work here? Are the ones who do this marginal? At this level—only 21 people—it isn't so bad, but if it gets any larger, I think we'll have some problems.

While most corporate executives favored direct employee access to the Evaluation Committee in the United States, for the reasons noted earlier, the issue was not as clear overseas. Mr. McColough described his dilemma:

> Just after the Social Service Leave Program was announced, I was in Europe talking with our people there. They were enthusiastic about it but asked why they weren't included. Aside from saying it was experimental, I told them this is the way we get into trouble. If we limit it to the United States, it's favoritism and if we spread our program worldwide, it's applying United States solutions to foreign problems. I told them if you want it, you must *ask* for it.

Inquiries had been received from a number of overseas subsidiaries including those in Holland, New Zealand, and Canada. In most instances the subsidiary leaned in the direction of an "up-the-line" selection and approval process. However, in January the nature and scope of overseas participation remained undefined.

As January drew to a close, the management group considered again the direction of the Social Service Leave Program. Mr. McColough's original charge had been expressed in the following way.

> Granting 20 people a leave isn't much for a company as large as Xerox. There are certain to be problems which can't be anticipated with precision beforehand. However, if we dwell on the problems, we will end up doing nothing. So, let's be cautious, but let's do it.

He now shared the task of interpreting that charge in light of the events of the previous four months.

Exhibit 9-1

TEN-YEAR STATISTICAL COMPARISONS

	1971[1]	*1970*[1]	*1969*[1]
Yardsticks of Progress			
Net Income Per Common Share	$ 2.71	$ 2.40	$ 2.08
Dividends Declared Per Share	$ .80	$ .65	$ .58⅓
Operations (Dollars in thousands)			
Total Operating Revenues	$1,961,449	$1,718,587	$1,482,895
Rentals, Service and Royalties	1,563,805	1,343,252	1,094,794
Net Sales	397,644	375,335	388,101
Payroll (Excluding Benefits)	590,744	514,172	419,888
Depreciation of Rental Equipment	245,164	200,189	183,187
Depreciation of Buildings and Equipment	38,999	36,149	29,888
Amortization[1]	20,070	21,406	17,449
Expenditures for Research and Equipment	104,137	97,524	83,682
Income Before Income Taxes	471,081	432,938	389,722
Income Taxes	217,600	211,800	204,500
Outside Shareholders' Interests	40,871	33,447	23,854
Equity in Net Earnings of Rank Xerox Limited	–	–	–
Net Income	212,610	187,691	161,368
Dividends Declared	62,834	50,935	43,969
Financial Position (Dollars in thousands)			
Cash and Marketable Securities	$ 197,921	$ 148,982	$ 56,836
Net Trade Receivables	347,768	326,623	311,997
Inventories	226,597	222,001	172,747
Current Assets	916,731	825,416	649,011
Rental Equipment and Related Inventories at Cost	1,633,207	1,345,303	1,104,506
Accumulated Depreciation of Rental Equipment	872,283	714,833	577,832
Land, Buildings and Equipment at Cost	541,817	431,624	352,951
Accumulated Depreciation of Buildings and Equipment	172,383	144,339	116,056
Total Assets	2,156,094	1,857,325	1,531,271
Current Liabilities	532,806	457,571	391,257
Long-Term Debt (Including Current Portion)	482,731	429,690	319,407
Shareholders' Equity	1,051,767	892,500	738,455
Additions to Rental Equipment and Related Inventories[4]	382,792	312,580	279,519
Additions to Land, Buildings and Equipment[4]	121,498	88,869	75,890
General and Ratios			
Average Common Shares Outstanding During Year	78,533,533	78,315,911	77,445,464
Shareholders at Year End	143,554	146,534	129,944
Employees at Year End	66,728	59,862	54,882
Income Before Income Taxes to Total Operating Revenues	24.0%	25.2%	26.3%
Net Income to Average Shareholders' Equity	21.9%	23.0%	24.1%
Current Ratio	1.7	1.8	1.7
Long-Term Debt to Total Capitalization[5]	29.4%	30.5%	28.3%

[1] The data include the accounts of Xerox Data Systems and of Rank Xerox Limited for its fiscal year ended October 31.

[2] The data include the accounts of Xerox Data Systems and of Rank Xerox Limited for its fiscal year ended in June.

[3] Amortization of deferred research and development, patents, licenses and other intangible assets.

1968[1]	*1967*[2]	*1966*[2]	*1965*[2]	*1964*	*1963*	*1962*
$ 1.68	$ 1.42	$ 1.20	$ .92	$ .68	$ .39	$ .24
$ .50	$ .40	$ .30¾	$ .20	$ .14¼	$ .08⅓	$ .04⅔
$1,224,352	$ 983,064	$752,508	$548,795	$317,840	$176,036	$115,220
896,673	673,548	477,954	327,814	184,157	114,077	65,847
327,679	309,516	274,554	220,981	133,683	61,959	49,373
336,602	289,009	223,855	160,725	93,921	55,112	36,653
175,692	135,975	97,221	69,110	37,295	20,236	12,454
26,747	23,779	18,519	12,637	7,243	4,338	3,267
12,304	8,437	6,026	5,439	3,695	3,070	1,570
59,888	50,806	53,329	38,170	24,050	14,609	8,547
309,096	226,500	182,113	138,872	86,800	50,423	30,779
164,020	108,576	86,490	68,199	44,598	27,850	16,801
16,126	11,540	8,923	–	4,984	–	–
–	–	–	–	1,523	428	(84)
128,950	106,834	86,700	65,689	43,725	23,001	13,894
34,363	28,555	21,996	14,698	10,788	4,895	2,688
$ 66,022	$ 70,670	$ 59,508	$ 26,289	$ 10,622	$ 6,933	$ 6,322
244,838	197,650	150,810	93,982	40,847	25,233	16,284
146,871	128,303	102,116	70,633	35,531	14,300	8,672
554,530	460,904	362,204	232,255	109,678	59,327	37,412
905,180	734,708	562,480	383,044	197,408	114,517	70,868
458,350	307,482	216,972	147,272	76,512	41,565	21,760
281,285	244,964	201,546	143,833	81,317	48,219	35,798
90,360	68,414	49,212	33,124	21,080	10,980	8,222
1,268,489	1,155,274	933,991	647,359	356,142	215,801	138,917
372,942	286,496	195,613	161,013	62,774	41,982	29,310
298,904	357,888	379,870	228,622	102,982	54,028	41,258
601,003	474,155	326,254	229,104	154,770	85,235	48,686
193,303	213,169	214,058	147,061	84,802	45,401	30,929
35,424	43,323	54,117	40,152	21,148	12,828	9,163
76,565,650	75,039,803	72,467,603	71,705,645	63,897,723	59,134,557	58,263,831
91,712	87,659	89,060	73,217	62,195	26,375	14,925
45,142	40,639	33,595	24,239	12,728	7,918	5,297
25.2%	23.0%	24.2%	25.3%	27.3%	28.6%	26.7%
24.0%	26.6%	31.2%	34.2%	36.4%	34.4%	33.4%
1.5	1.6	1.9	1.4	1.7	1.4	1.3
31.1%	40.8%	50.9%	47.4%	40.0%	38.8%	45.9%

[4] Additions prior to 1969 shown net of disposals.

[5] Total capitalization defined as the sum of long term debt (including current portion), in net assets of subsidiaries, and shareholder's equity. Common sahre data adjusted to reflect change of each common share into five common shares effective December 17, 1963, and the distribution of two additional common shares for each common share held at May 16, 1969.

Exhibit 9-2

ORGANIZATION CHART

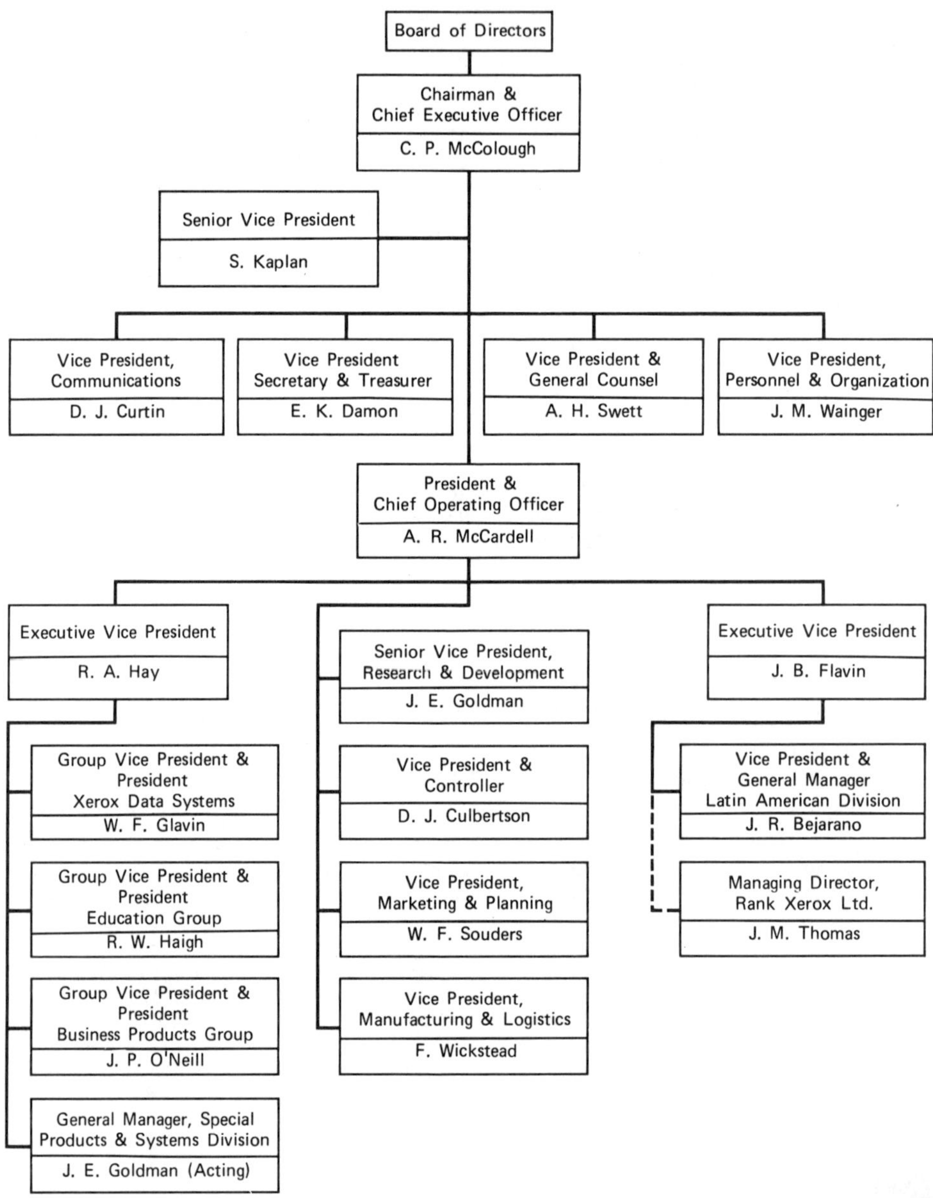

Exhibit 9-3

MEMORANDUM TO CORPORATE EXECUTIVES

TO:	See Distribution	Date:	August 7, 1970
FROM:	J. M. Wainger	Location:	HR 2
Subject:	Xerox Social Action	Organization:	Corporate Personnel

We have decided to institute, as promptly as possible, a program for Xerox employees which we think will have substantial positive impact internally and externally, both now and for our future.

We will offer to twenty Xerox employees, regardless of level in the Corporation (though excluding all of you), the opportunity to work for a year out of Xerox in some position that has high social value. As examples, the jobs might be with some community organization attacking urban problems, or some Federal Government agency, or a school, etc.

We plan to use the following approach. Through appropriate Xerox communications media, we will publicize the program and ask all those employees who are interested to submit a short description of the project they wish to work on and their reasons for choosing it. As part of their submission, they must include assurance that they have agreement from the prospective employer to take them on if they are freed up. We hope to receive many submissions.

All of these submissions will be screened by an impartial, outside board of prestigious men who will choose the twenty they consider to be most worthy according to the social criteria we've established.

The twenty selected employees will then be given a year to work at their chosen task. We assume they will return to Xerox at the end of that time, though no guarantee can be exacted. We will require that the projects they select be in or near their present communities. In other words, this program should not carry with it relocation subsidies for attractive long-range trips to such places as Los Angeles, Washington or Hawaii.

Xerox will maintain the employees' total compensation at the rate prevailing at the time they left Xerox by paying them the difference between whatever they receive from their outside job and their then Xerox salary.

We need to set up our outside screening board as soon as possible. I need your help. Would you please submit to me as soon as possible the names of one or more people you deem suitable to serve. The names you submit should be of people you feel fairly confident you can "deliver" if asked to contact them directly. I anticipate a board of perhaps five men, disparate in background but uniform in quality.

I recognize that there are problems inherent in this program, and I'm sure you do too. However the results will more than justify taking the problems on. We will benefit and, by leading, we will influence.

You will, of course, be apprised of the details of the program as it is shaped up. May I have your nominees for the selection board as soon as possible.

(signed) Jim

JMW/sd

Distribution: D. J. Curtin
J. B. Flavin
J. E. Goldman
S. Kaplan
A. R. McCardell
C. P. McColough
J. W. Rutledge
J. C. Wilson

Exhibit 9-4

EVALUATION COMMITTEE

EUGENE R. ALLEN, director of international operations of the Xerox Education Group in Stamford, joined XEG in 1970 following three years as director of urban education at Litton Industries. Allen, 37, was born in Sacramento, Calif.

ROBERT M. FLEGAL, 29, is a scientist in the computer science laboratory at the Palo Alto Research Center. He served in the Peace Corps in Ghana for two years. He is a native of Salt Lake City, Utah. He joined Xerox in 1970.

ERROL L. FORKNER, 29, a commercial analyst in the product management department of Xerox Data Systems in El Segundo, is working for an MA in computer sciences at UCLA. He came to XDS in 1969 after three years with IBM.

JANET L. KNIGHTON is an educational and training specialist in the Business Products Group in Webster. Before joining Xerox in 1970, she had been assistant director of the adult department of the Rochester YWCA.

ROBERT M. SCHNEIDER, assistant to the president of Xerox in Stamford, was manager of corporate contributions for three years before assuming his present post in 1969. A native of Passaic, N.J., he is 40 years old.

ROLAND A. STENTA, 31, is national accounts manager of the Philadelphia branch of BPG, following work in personnel and sales. Born in Brooklyn, he joined Xerox in 1968, from the Office of Economic Opportunity in Washington.

JAMES M. WAINGER is corporate vice president, personnel and organization, in Stamford. He joined Xerox in 1960, but left from 1966 to 1969 to teach English in high school and write plays. He's 44, and a graduate of Harvard Law.

Exhibit 9-5

APPLICATION

To be returned to:

Evaluation Board,
Social Service Leave Program
Xerox Corporation
Stamford, Connecticut 06904

My name: ____________________
(print) first middle last

Home address: ____________________

Phone: ____________________
Home Xerox

Xerox Group/Division: ____________________ Location: ____________________

Present Position: ____________________ Employee Number: __________ Date Hired: __________

don't write here Application No.:

---

don't write here Application No :

In one sentence, what I Want to do is: ____________________

____

Time desired: ____________________ Dates desired: ____________________

This is the organization I'll work with: ____________________
(name)

____
address department name & function I would report to

Phone: __________ Acceptance Letter attached ☐

Salary, if any, I'll recieve from the organization: __________

These are the details of the program I want to work on: (goals, history, scope, program, people affected, other workers involved, nature of activities, budget—*very specific description, please* that will help us understand the project; attach any literature or reports or clippings that will help)

____

____

____

____

My specific work will be: (what skill, what function, what tasks, what aims—or programmed results, if these can be stated in advance)

____

I am specially qualified to do this by: (cite specific experience, training, skills, prior involvement, personal history—or just gnawing desire)

This is why I want to work on this project and this is what I hope to accomplish:

My present monthly salary is: $____________________

Circle Highest Grade Completed:

High School	College	Graduate
9– 10– 11– 12	13– 14– 15– 16	17– 18– 19– 20– 21– 22

College or University Attended	Degree Awarded	Major Subject

Please use as many extra sheets as you need to answer the questions fully.

Exhibit 9-6

1972 RECIPIENTS

Name & Xerox Job	*Age*	*Years with Xerox*	*Project*	*Agency*
Joel N. Axelrod Business Products Group Group Program Manager	39	5	Develop and implement techniques for evaluating training programs funded under the Drug Abuse Act	U.S. Office of Education
Oswaldo Aymat Xerox Reproduction Center Quality Control Supervisor	35	11	Counsel and guide Puerto Rican college students with the objective of reducing the high dropout rate.	Aspira of New York
James E. Bales Business Products Group Technical Representative	35	10	Manage the development of a literacy program	Greater Little Rock Literacy Council
Irving C. Bell Xerox Reproduction Center Sales Representative	43	4	Teach mathematics to inmates in two prisons and instruct them in building trade skills	Massachusetts Department of Correction
Robert P. Britton Business Products Group Technical Representative	29	6	Set up and teach an entry level course in electromechanical job skills for unskilled and unemployables	Opportunities Industrialization Center
Frank V. Cliff, Jr. Business Products Group Account Executive	43	9	Work with minority businessmen	Economic Development Corporation of Greater Detroit
Frayda F. Cooper Ginn and Company Elementary Mathematics Editor	47	4	Organize an experimental program to provide services to the aged in a multi-town area where no such service is now available	Massachusetts Department of Community Affairs
Robert B. Cost Business Products Group Account Representative	26	5	Teach and counsel in a drug rehabilitation center service high school age children from New York City.	Pius XII School

Joe A. Duardo Electro-Optical Systems Physicist	40	9	Counsel hard-core youth in a Mexican-American area	Abraham Lincoln High School
William Gable Xerox Data Systems Vice President	43	3	Assist low-income families in black neighborhoods in achieving home ownership	Protestant Community Services
James P. Herget Business Products Group A Regional Marketing Manager	27	4	As the agency's director of marketing, guide and assist minority-owned businesses in developing their marketing capability	Interracial Council for Business Opportunity of Greater Washington
Robert S. Huddleston Business Products Group Technical Representative	44	9	Expand work of agency devoted to assisting former convicts in their return to life in communities	The Seventh Step Foundation Topeka, Kansas
Paul S. Israel Business Products Group Area Sales Manager	38	8	Direct an effort to build a model classroom for teaching mentally retarded preschoolers	The Arizona Preschool for Retarded Children
Esther E. Kapuschat Business Products Group Staff Nurse	60	7	Serve as director of nursing in an interdenominational crippled children's hospital	The Holy Land Christian Mission Kansas City, Missouri
Kenneth R. Lane American Education Publications Special Education Department Editor	41	3	Establish an in-service training program leading to accreditation of house-parents in residential schools for the deaf	Conference of Executives of American Schools for the Deaf, White Plains, New York
Frederick Lightfoot Business Products Group Multiple Drill Operator	36	3	Work as a community organizer in central city area	Action for a Better Community Rochester, New York
Raymond E. Poehlein Business Products Group Development Engineering Manager	33	5	Help develop physical science curriculum and teach in a secondary school for Aglala Sioux Indians	Red Cloud Indian School
Lionel E. Reim Business Products Group A Regional Marketing Manager	28	3	Serve as business manager for an on-going coffeehouse and medical clinic for youth	General Conference of Seventh Day Adventists

1972 RECIPIENTS (continued)

Name & Xerox Job	*Age*	*Years with Xerox*	*Project*	*Agency*
Michael I. Slade Corporate Research Physicist	30	5	Provide research and develop information bulletins on ecology problems (transportation and water)	Rochester Committees for Scientific Information
John M. Teem Corporate Research and Development Director of Technical Staff	46	13	Develop and teach a science curriculum in an experimental "school without walls"	Alpha Learnings Community School
Jean G. Williams Business Products Group Programmer	26	4	Tutor and counsel minority college and pre-college students to reduce dropout rate	Project Equal Opportunity University of Colorado

RECAPITULATION

Division	
Business Products Group	13
Corporate Staff Group	2
Education Group	2
Xerox Reproduction Center	2
Electro-Optical Systems	1
Xerox Data Systems	1
	21

Salary per Month	
850 or less	4
850-1,250	5
1,251-1,600	6
1,601-2,000	2
2,001-3,000	1
3,001-4,000	2
Over 4,000	1
	21

Exhibit 9-7

MEMORANDUM TO SUPERVISORS

November 18, 1971

Dr. J. E. Goldman
Xerox Corporation
Corporate Headquarters
Stamford, Connecticut 06904

Dear Jack:

John M. Teem, who is employed in your organization, has been selected to receive a Xerox Social Service Leave. Based on his application, he will be engaged full time away from the company for the next year on a voluntary social program of real value. Xerox is proud of the commitment of this employee, and I'm sure you share that pride.

As you know, Peter McColough has assured all employees that those who are chosen for Leaves are *guaranteed* that on their return they will return to their former job or one of equal pay, responsibility, status and opportunity for advancement. Peter and I will review each returning employee's job placement to make certain that this guarantee is fully honored.

Therefore, as you plan for the carrying on of John's work, I'm sure you'll want to keep in mind this essential provision of the Social Service Leave policy. If the job of the person going on leave is one of many jobs of the same type, I'd expect no special provisions need be made at this time.

If, however, the job is relatively unique, I suggest that you give consideration to designating any replacement as "acting." Certain jobs may even lend themselves to developmental use, permitting the rotation of several people in them during the period of the Social Service Leave.

I'm asking relevant Personnel Departments to monitor and approve the method used to fill each job vacated, and I'm requesting, too, that Personnel Departments inform me of the action taken to fill each job vacated by an employee going on leave.

Sincerely,

(signed) Jim
James M. Wainger
Vice President
Personnel & Organization

JMW/sd
c: C. P. McColough
A. R. McCardell
G. F. Wajda

Case Ten

Foods Unlimited (A)

The Freshman, away from home for the first time, wanders into the College Cafeteria, grabs a plate, starts down the wrong end of the line, and drops the plate on the Dean's toe. . . .

The hijacker decides to eat first and removes the cellophane wrapping from his ham and swiss cheese sandwich (alternating layers of light and dark bread). . . .

The bride smilingly poses in front of the 10 ft. plastic replica of the wedding cake, cuts a piece of the real cake, and feeds it to the groom as the 400 guests applaud politely. . . .

13 yr. old Peter Jones sets a new record at the "All You Can Eat" Wednesday steak sandwich specials at his favorite restaurant, FOODS Fantasia. . . .

THE COMPANY

What do these people have in common? They are all about to become customers of FOODS Unlimited (Food: Ordering, Operating, Dining, and Serving) and partners in the gustatory enterprise linking much of America's life and leisure. If the way to a man's heart is through his stomach, FOODS Unlimited is the way to many a man's stomach.

This corporation, founded at the turn of the century as a modest cafeteria in a modest section of Philadelphia, encompassed a wide range of services and activities, all of which basically concerned people and eating. Williamson's Cafeterias and Suppliers (the name was changed to Williamson's Foods in 1935 and to FOODS Unlimited in 1951) first expanded into the institutional market and became more involved with factory lunchrooms than commercial cafeterias. And, in the late 1920's and 30's, Williamson's was one of the first companies to take advantage of the developments in vending machine technology. Consequently today, from subway stations, to restrooms, to the basement hallways of Harvard Business School, FOODS is there, offering coffee, doughnuts (and much more than coffee and doughnuts) for nickels and dimes (and much more than nickels and dimes) placed in a slot.

The R & D work, which went beyond developments in vending machines to the sophisticated reaches of automation in cooking and serving, was carried on by Lexington Laboratories, a separate, wholly owned subsidiary of FOODS. Lexington Laboratories existed "to serve the changing needs of FOODS Unlimited," and in recent years especially, it often had led the way in changing these needs. For example, the KWIK-KOOK franchises were an outgrowth of discoveries of Lexington Laboratories, and in many communities a household could call up and have a complete roast beef or turkey dinner delivered within an hour.

The service side of the business was separated from the more technical works at the Labs, and for these operations FOODS was organized geographically. There were 156 local units throughout the country, each with a staff of service people in the familiar yellow and black FOODS uniforms, driving yellow and black FOODS trucks, stocking and repairing vending machines, servicing airplane cabins, serving lunches for construction workers and Boards of Directors, delivering 6,000 cucumber and asparagus sandwiches for the Annual DAR Tea in Richmond, Virginia, and manning FOODS Fantasia restaurants. In any one locality, FOODS would be involved in several of these activities.

THE ISSUE

FOOD'S total revenue for 1973 was $1,466,617,000 (up 8% from 1972), and its net income was up 10% from 1972 to $48,170,000. In spite of this growth, however, FOODS had become a popular target for criticism and public outcry. The Justice Department had objected to FOODS' proposed acquisition of another supplier of airline food, and there had been both internal and external problems with that elusive reality of "image." Some of the younger employees especially objected to what they felt was the paternalistic spirit of the company, and a series of jokes stemming from a fifth-grader's identification of the uniformed FOODS man as a "yellow-bellied sapsucker" had made the company an all too familiar household word. In addition, the rising consumer movement had focused attention on machines which swallowed quarters and delivered cold or tasteless food and spoiled milk.

Partly in response to such sentiment and the increasing number of complaints, the Community Activities Department had become an increasingly active and concerned part of the company. David Andrews, manager of this department for Lexington Labs hoped to learn how to deal with some of these problems from Jonathan Dils and Ben Crawford, responsible since 1968 for coordinating the community activities efforts of the 156 FOODS regional organizations. Although there were far fewer Lexington facilities than FOODS organizations and contact with the community was less direct, Andrews hoped that his colleagues' experiences with a Community Activities Review function might constitute a viable and transferable approach.

Andrews called the tools and available methods for ascertaining where Lexington Labs stood "relatively unsophisticated" and was not confident about his past efforts in this field. Several years ago he began collecting data from each autonomous operating unit, in an attempt to describe the company's ongoing social programs and to measure the extent of the company's participation and the cost. However, Andrews encountered numerous problems in collecting and evaluating this information and was additionally frustrated by not being able to utilize the material for a genuine audit as he had hoped originally. He found that people did not want to tell what they were doing. They became proprietary–or unaccountably ignorant–about this information. They clearly did not want the "boss" to know the costs involved. Andrews said it was extraordinarily difficult to "weed out the puffery" since, "you simply cannot rely on people to do it right when you just give them a letter with an outline, requesting them to fill it out." Accordingly, he was forced to settle for just an overview, not an assessment, and declared himself generally "unsatisfied" with these results. At this point he decided to turn to the men from FOODS for guidance.

DILS' AND CRAWFORD'S INVESTIGATION

Faced with the same problem of finding out just what was going on, Dils and Crawford told Andrews that they opted for in-depth, on-the-spot evaluations. They came to this idea (and to their present roles) via the Community Activities Department and their gradual realization that no one really understood what that concept meant. The standard procedure for reporting on social programs seemed to be for a unit to take the previous year's account and increase by 10% the number of meetings, contributions, etc. In fact, a good deal of money was being spent and a number of worthwhile programs were in operation, but there was no way to know that these matched the community's needs.

So, with the help of three task forces in this area and an extensive Roper survey to see just how communities did regard FOODS, Dils and Crawford drew up a Community Activities Manual. This in turn led to their present practice of spending Monday through Friday at a FOODS unit in close contact with the activities of that center, culminating in an oral report to the local FOODS management group.

Both Dils and Crawford stressed the need for FOODS to be problem oriented. Moreover, (and the Roper study confirmed this view) they felt strongly that the role of FOODS in the community was not a matter for debate. By its very nature, the company had a unique role; the community saw this service as imperative, (even if the company might still consider other aspects of social responsibility a nice but not necessary option). Crawford and Dils added that by highlighting the need to discover what problems existed in the community (especially those which FOODS might already have the competence to alleviate), some of the semantic and cultural "hang-ups" evoked by a term like "social responsibility" could be avoided.

Exhibit 10-1, "Urban Affairs at FOODS," suggests some of the reasons FOODS felt compelled to face these problems. In the past, FOODS' trucks had been prevented from entering certain urban neighborhoods, or windows had been smashed and tires slashed while FOODS servicemen made their rounds. The company claimed to offer 24-hour service, yet some workers refused to travel at night to installations in inner city areas. In some regions (around New York and Washington, D.C.) extra employees had been hired so the men could travel in pairs. In addition, night workers in these districts were supplied with an extra $5 (mug money) in case of a robbery. Customers' complaints about inequitable and often poor service had doubled in the past two years, and employees were becoming reluctant to accept certain undesirable or dangerous jobs.

Crawford and Dils were emphatic on the point that the communities' problems were FOODS' problems and possibly FOODS' opportunities as well. Their field investigations reinforced this emphasis in the local, specific, and immediate, rather than abstract terms.

Their program of visits spawned its own problems, of course, and the results were both expected and unexpected. The men had been able to visit about one out of the 310 sales areas a month.[1] However, they hoped to be able to put together a sort of "training package" so others could cover more areas. Generally, the particular unit requested the visit, sometimes out of pride—which often turned out to be mistaken—or out of concern. And the initial announcement of an impending visit generally caused a great deal of preliminary "scurrying" to set the house in order. In fact, the examination could thus be said to begin before the visit, and Crawford and Dils thought this activity might have beneficial effects in making the location aware of itself even before their arrival. At times there were difficulties arising from the necessarily pressured and intimate association among groups hitherto strangers. Crawford and Dils wished to avoid the impression that they were men from the front office coming to tell the field units what to do. Consequently, they placed great emphasis on the confidentiality of material—both the material given to them and the feedback they presented. The report was made on Friday to the local management, but no copy was sent back to the Head Office. Crawford and Dils then wrote a report, but only to send back to the cooperating field unit.

Their efforts were not concerned with training and hiring programs and policies, which fell under the aegis of the Personnel Department, but did cover a great many aspects of what was generally considered to be the urban affairs, community relations, service, and social responsibility area. Indeed, one of the problems they encountered was the overlap of programs, due in part to the size of the company and the fragmentation of responsibility. As an extreme example, they suggested that it would have been possible for five different FOODS representatives from the same area to be speaking at the same school on the same day, each ignorant of the others. So, some of Crawford and Dils' work involved telling the right hand what the left hand was doing. In each case they dealt with certain specific topics, discussed what FOODS was doing in that area and included comments and analysis as well as ratings. Thus, based on the outline in the Community Activities Manual, (see Exhibit 10-1), their reports corresponded to the following form:

Top Management Support and Concern
Community Activities: Coordinator and Staff Support
The Community Activities Field Unit
Service Considerations

---

[1] The small number of areas audited was in part a function of the number of "auditors" to do this job. It was also a function of the reluctance of many of the regions to allow the auditors in. Many areas said, "Don't audit us now. Wait until next year when we have things straightened out."

The Community Activities Program (what, why, and how it relates to the community's problems)
Employee Information Programs
Public Information Program
"Influentials" Interview Program
Company-Sponsored Memberships
Employee Participation in the Community
Community Activities

These were broken down into more detailed topics to suit the situation, and the reports concluded with recommendations. The checklists from the FOODS Community Activities Manual in Exhibit 10-1 offer a more complete picture of this corporate review function and suggest what specifics they looked for and what criteria they used.

Crawford and Dils gave out suggestions and information, but in turn they also learned a great deal from these sessions. For example, they found out that the FOODS truism that good service guaranteed a good image simply did not hold. There were centers with excellent service, but poor images in the community, and, conversely, they visited one unit which simply did not offer first class service but ranked high in the eyes of the community anyway.

As these examples suggest, one of the things Crawford and Dils learned was the danger of generalization. What worked well in one area might not work in another; the needs and expectations of customers varied in different communities. This lack of transferability was another good reason for confidentiality; it was important to keep a center from trying something just because they heard about it succeeding someplace else. One area they visited seemed to be doing all the right things without conscious effort and Crawford and Dils had to work to keep them from adopting unnecessary programs. Sometimes well-meaning attempts backfired; one particular center gained more resentment than goodwill when it gave away Christmas baskets of food to some, but not all, of the local residents. Dils and Crawford found no cure-all or easy answers which could be applied to all FOODS centers.

Dilemmas concerning costs and benefits in a social context continually surfaced. There were from city to city vast variations in the amount of damage done to FOODS vending machines. How should one evaluate a situation where FOODS personnel need to travel in pairs because of the high crime rate? A worker is just as anxious for his coffee break at 3:00 A.M. as at 3:00 P.M., but factories or banks lose 24-hour service because FOODS servicemen will not go there at night. In some communities FOODS trucks servicing vending machines were vandalized; in others, they were welcomed friends. Some operators of FOODS Fantasia franchises refused to stay open after 11:00 P.M., although country-wide advertising continued to proclaim a policy of around-the-clock service.

The company was able to enter on its balance sheet the $5 a day some FOODS workers were given (to hand over if robbed), but the factors which necessitated this action were more complicated, harder to account for, and probably more costly in the long run. There was no column marked "Ambiguous expenses," although there were many ambiguous situations. It was recently decided that guards were necessary for the home office building. On the one hand, this was an additional expense for the company. On the other hand, this situation created many job opportunities for minority workers.

Dils and Crawford encountered encouraging signs as well as confusing ones. Although there was no formal follow-up program, many of the local centers seemed to be ahead of the home office and continued to send in recommendations and new ideas after the initial probing. The most successful efforts seemed to be those concentrating very immediately on the local community and its problems—work on drug programs to get at the root of the crime or educational exposure to present the FOODS employees as friends. Dils and Crawford maintained that this policy of strong local involvement could work; they cited a Washington community where even during riots FOODS workers who lived in a ghetto area traveled freely in FOODS trucks.

However, the problems remained sizeable, and Dils and Crawford acknowledged the difficulties even as they continued to struggle. A 1973 document, "Urban Affairs at FOODS," (see excerpts in Exhibit 10-2), reflected their current thinking and reiterated again the importance of FOODS' role in the community, of the need for "providing service based on the service needs and expectations of the customers."

THE CONCLUSION

Andrews sipped coffee from a yellow and black FOODS cup and contemplated his next move, reviewing what he had learned from Dils and Crawford. Clearly, he saw that the FOODS program was more comprehensive and thorough than many others. The on-the-spot visit and in-depth evaluation seemed to be a strong alternative to the mailed questionnaire, especially for a company with many scattered operating units. Dils and Crawford's caution and pessimism concerning their work might be signs of strength, not weakness, and such attitudes might be more productive than an unrealistic optimism or overly ambitious program. However, while Andrews hoped to use some of Dils and Crawford's ideas and techniques, he continued to despair of actually being able to cost out these programs and draw the fine lines required for a comprehensive evaluation.

Exhibit 10-1

COMMUNITY ACTIVITIES ANALYSIS

A. Top Management Support and Interest	YES	NO	COMMENTS
1. Area management representatives periodically attend local Community Action Group[1] meeting?	____	____	____________
2. Are CA Group members personally encouraged, by at least an assistant resident manager, to take the time necessary to effectively carry out their CA responsibilities?	____	____	____________
3. Are there CA Groups at resident head or assistant level?	____	____	____________
4. Is the CA Group program reviewed and approved at the regional or area level?	____	____	____________
5. Are company and area CA objectives communicated to the local CA Groups prior to the preparation of their annual program?	____	____	____________
6. Is there tangible evidence that each department recognizes their employees for their contribution to CA?	____	____	____________
7. Do local Action Group members feel they have the support and interest of their boss for the time they spend in CA?	____	____	____________

B. Community Activities Coordinator and Staff Support	YES	NO	COMMENTS
1. Does the local CA Group have a coordinator?	____	____	____________
2. Is he a participating member of the CA Group?	____	____	____________

[1] Each unit in the FOODS organization was to have a Community Action Group which was responsible for implementing and, in many cases, developing the company's social programs in the community.

Source: FOODS "Guide for Community Activities" (internal document for the guidance of FOODS Community Activities reviews and evaluation).

Exhibit 10-1 (continued)

	YES	NO	COMMENTS
3. Does he or a staff representative assist the CA Group in planning and implementing their program?	____	____	____________
4. Does he attend most Group meetings?	____	____	____________
5. Has he been trained on the use of their CA Guide?	____	____	____________
6. Does the CA Group receive information about what other Groups are doing?	____	____	____________
7. Does the home office staff provide assistance in training new Group members?	____	____	____________
8. Have corporate objectives been provided to CA Groups?	____	____	____________
9. Has a CA Manual or guidelines been provided to CA Group?	____	____	____________
10. Is the Group kept informed of what others are doing within the company on CA activities? i.e., Educational Relations, Urban Affairs, Public Affairs, etc.	____	____	____________

C. Community Activities Group	YES	NO	COMMENTS
1. Is the Group formally organized?	____	____	____________
2. Is it interdepartmental in makeup to the degree appropriate?	____	____	____________
3. Does it meet on a regular schedule?	____	____	____________
4. Have the majority of Group members been on the team for more than 1 year?	____	____	____________
5. Does the chairman have a copy of the company CA Manual?	____	____	____________
6. Are minutes prepared for each Group meeting?	____	____	____________
7. Are regular minutes of the Group meetings submitted to higher management?	____	____	____________

Exhibit 10-1 (continued)

	YES	NO	COMMENTS
8. Are individual Group members responsible and accountable for specific CA projects?	____	____	____
9. Are new CA Group members familiarized with their CA Manual and trained within 1 month after their appointment to the team?	____	____	____
10. Has the Group Chairman been formally trained on his responsibilities?	____	____	____
11. Does the CA Group have a formal method of determining local public attitudes?	____	____	____
12. Does the CA Group regularly review customer complaints to higher management?	____	____	____
13. Are the members of the Group the appropriate ones to represent their departments?	____	____	____

D. Service Considerations	YES	NO	COMMENTS
1. Have the service problems which are or could be affecting company reputation been identified? i.e.	____	____	____
• Service problems caused by the company	____	____	____
• Service problems caused by the customer	____	____	____
• Service problems caused by the community	____	____	____
2. Have programs been developed which deal with identified service problems?	____	____	____
3. Have programs, formal or informal, been designed to improve the community's understanding of service goals?	____	____	____
4. Do group members understand the relationship between service and community relations?	____	____	____

Exhibit 10-1 (continued)

E. Community Activities Program	YES	NO	COMMENTS
1. Are local objectives developed into a formal program?	____	____	____________
2. Is a written program prepared annually?	____	____	____________
3. Was the program developed through formal fact-finding procedures?	____	____	____________
4. Is the program forwarded for higher management review?	____	____	____________
5. Are corporate objectives reflected in formal programs?	____	____	____________
6. Is there any indication that the program has been approved by higher management?	____	____	____________
7. Is the program reviewed and followed up at Group meetings and progress noted in the minutes?	____	____	____________
8. Is responsibility assigned to specific individuals for program projects?	____	____	____________
9. Is the program coordinated with other FOODS divisions?	____	____	____________
10. Is there an attempt made to periodically evaluate the effectiveness of the program? (i.e., have they accomplished their objectives?)	____	____	____________
11. Does the CA Group submit a budget in connection with its annual program?	____	____	____________
12. Is it itemized by projects?	____	____	____________
13. Is an accounting made of the budget at the conclusion of each project?	____	____	____________

F. Employee Information Program	YES	NO	COMMENT
1. Are company CA activities regularly reported to all employees?	____	____	____________
2. Are service improvement programs being publicized to employees?	____	____	____________
3. Is company participation in the community being publicized to employees?	____	____	____________

Exhibit 10-1 (continued)

	YES	NO	COMMENT
4. Does the local CA Group have an organized method of determining the kind of information employees want to receive?	____	____	____________

G. Public Activities Program	YES	NO	COMMENT
1. Are news releases being localized where appropriate?	____	____	____________
2. Are service improvement programs being publicized to the public?	____	____	____________
3. Is company participation in the community being publicized to the public where appropriate?	____	____	____________
4. Does the company spokesman regularly meet with local news media to discuss mutual objectives?	____	____	____________
5. Has formal press relations training been given to the person responsible for news media contacts?	____	____	____________
6. Are the CA Group members familiar with school activities that are offered in their area?	____	____	____________
7. Are CA Group members familiar with company films, exhibits, displays, talks, booklets?	____	____	____________

H. "Influentials" Program	YES	NO	COMMENT
1. Is there a formal list of community "Influentials"?	____	____	____________
2. Is it updated at least annually?	____	____	____________
3. Is there a formal program for "Influentials" scheduled at regular intervals?	____	____	____________
4. Are interviews with "Influentials" scheduled at regular intervals?	____	____	____________
5. Are records of interviews kept?	____	____	____________
6. Are interviews reviewed by the CA Group?	____	____	____________
7. Are interviewers formally trained?	____	____	____________

Exhibit 10-1 (continued)

	YES	NO	COMMENT
8. Do interviewers represent a cross section of local management?	_____	_____	_____________
9. Does the Group have any responsibility for suggesting names for inclusion on "Influentials" list?	_____	_____	_____________
10. Do appropriate members of CA Group have responsibility for "Influential" contacts?	_____	_____	_____________

I. Company-Sponsored Memberships	YES	NO	COMMENT
1. Is there an up-to-date list of all community organizations?	_____	_____	_____________
2. Does the CA Group maintain a list of Company-Sponsored Members?	_____	_____	_____________
3. Is an annual review of membership made for appropriateness of continuing, adding, or dropping memberships?	_____	_____	_____________
4. Are new members *formally* oriented on their responsibilities prior to becoming members?	_____	_____	_____________
5. Does the Group periodically meet with Company-Sponsored Members?	_____	_____	_____________
6. Do Company-Sponsored Members regularly provide feedback to the local CA Group?	_____	_____	_____________
7. Is this feedback discussed at regular Group meetings?	_____	_____	_____________

J. Employee Participation in the Community	YES	NO	COMMENT
1. Does the Group have an up-to-date list of employees participating in community activities?	_____	_____	_____________
2. Is there a formal program to encourage employee participation?	_____	_____	_____________
3. Is local recognition given to employees who participate in community activities?	_____	_____	_____________
4. Are employees active in the community encouraged to provide feedback to the local CA Group?	_____	__________________	

Exhibit 10-1 (continued)

	YES	NO	COMMENT
5. Is their feedback discussed at the regular CA Group meeting?	____	____	________

K. Community Activities	YES	NO	COMMENT
1. Is there a record of community activities and projects in which the company is participating?	____	____	________
2. Is company participation based on clearly defined community problems and established priorities?	____	____	________
3. Does the Group clearly understand the reasons for participating in each project?	____	____	________
4. Is there a formal procedure for reviewing and evaluating activities on an annual basis?	____	____	________
5. Are requests to participate in new community activities being considered by the local Group?	____	____	________

Exhibit 10-2

URBAN AFFAIRS AT FOODS *(EXCERPT)*

FOODS companies experience unique operating problems in urban communities.
Key Points to be covered:

A. *Customer Service Expectations*

1. Customers depend on FOODS service more than in other areas.
2. Customers want the same high quality service we provide in other communities regardless of high crime rates or vandalism.
3. They want more vending machines and better vending machine maintenance.
4. Want to be sure they are getting a fair shake
   - No talking down to customers because they are minorities, or poor.
   - No inferior service or special requirements because they are poor or belong to minority groups.
5. Expect us to provide service based on their needs. If they speak only Spanish—that's our problem in their opinion. We respond to the particular needs

Source: "Urban Affairs at FOODS," internal document circulated in 1971.

of business customers, college students, and the handicapped. We are expected to do the same for the Blacks and Spanish-surnamed.

B. *Problems in Serving Urban Customers*

1. Higher costs of providing service.
2. Harrassment of vending machine installers and repairmen.
3. High maintenance due to vandalism.
4. Vandalism of employee property.
5. Customers' inability to speak English.
6. Employees' inability to speak Spanish.
7. Difficulties in installing machines in housing developments.
8. Safety of employees on the job and going to and from work.
9. Difficulty in gaining access to make installations and repairs.

C. *Short- and Long-Range Solutions*

Key Points to be made:

1. Urban affairs activities should be geared to respond instantly to both short-range and long-range problems.
2. There is no question that employee safety, for example, demands immediate attention. However, protective measures such as two-man teams, walkie-talkies, reduced hours of work, etc., can result in community resentments.
3. Urban affairs activities, then, should also be geared on a long-range basis to get at the root causes of community problems that inhibit our ability to serve.

Case Eleven

National Bank and Trust Company (B)

The National Bank and Trust Company, with total assets of $15 billion, deposits of over $11.25 billion, and net income close to $65 million, was the largest bank in Connecticut, and one of the 25 largest in the country. (See financial data in Exhibit 11-1 and Exhibit 11-2 for the table of organization.) Its headquarters were in Hartford and it had scores of branches throughout the state. For decades it had been known as a progressive bank, pioneering in many innovative banking services and showing a high level of public involvement. In recent years, its President, Phineas Bailey, had made a number of well-publicized and well-received statements on the social responsibility of business. During the period of student unrest in the spring of 1970, the bank was the target of demonstrations by students, chiefly Yale students in New Haven. Observers judged that the bank drew this attention more because of its size than because it had a particularly bad record. In fact, Bailey, in reviewing these events, decided that while he felt that the bank had been relatively more responsive than other banks and Connecticut business in general, he would make them the occasion for further consolidating the bank's social commitment.

To ensure that the bank's future behavior would be that of a good corporate citizen, Bailey established a Public Affairs Department and appointed Richard Trumball to head it. Since Trumball was a well-respected senior operating officer of the bank, this was an unusual token of Bailey's intention.

One of the promising young officers assigned to Trumball's department was Bob Baron, who had joined the bank after a period of public service. One of Baron's first assignments was to consider the possibility of a corporate social audit. The bank had already made one fairly successful attempt at identifying those of its activities with a direct social impact and assigning costs to them. (See National Bank and Trust Company (A)) Baron felt that this effort could be improved. He read available literature, attended several conferences, and talked widely with people active in the field. He began to look at social auditing, or social accounting, as a way for bringing some coherence to the bank's efforts in the social area. He hoped that some form of social audit would help rationalize the bank's decision making and actions.

In an effort to explore this possibility, he hired three students to work with him during the summer of 1972. He decided initially to focus on three of the bank's special loan programs: the Low Income Mortgage Program, the Small Business Minority Enterprise Program, and Federally Guaranteed Student Loans.

The minimum target set was that each student would produce a detailed plan for evaluating one program. This plan would begin with an assessment of the origins of the program in the bank. This step was justified on the grounds that if the bank did not understand how it got into activities of this sort, it could not very well hope to do such things rationally in the future.

The students completed their work and turned it in to Baron in the last week of August 1972. The first item he read was a report on the origins and history of the Federally Guaranteed Student Loan Program. He wondered what he should make of it. Should he consider it a part of the larger auditing activity and hold on to it until its findings could be incorporated in an overall audit? On the other hand, it seemed to pose some interesting questions about the bank's efforts to improve its marketing to college students. Should Trumball see it? Should it be forwarded with recommendation that it be referred to Bailey? Should it be accompanied by policy recommendations? If so, what should they be?

THE HISTORY OF THE FGSL AT NATIONAL BANK AND TRUST

This history of the FGSL at the bank was based on interviews with the bank's officers and a survey of the relevant bank files. Since many officers expressed uncertainty about events which occurred a few years ago, and the memories of some conflicted with those of others, it was felt that documentation should be confined to those materials found in the files.

THE BANK AND THE CAMPUS BEFORE FGSL. In the early sixties, the bank was concerned about its relative lack of attraction to upper-income and upper-status groups. A survey conducted for its research department in 1962 had shown that among lower income families with checking accounts, about 40% had their accounts with National; in the middle income group this proportion fell to 30%, and in the upper income group it fell still further to about 25%. A memorandum of February 1964 from the Secretary of the Marketing Research Committee to the Senior Vice President, Donald Sindal, who also served as Chairman of the Marketing Research Committee, forwarded a report that contained such passages as these:

> One may speculate, that the $10,000 and over group is comprised of individuals who desire Tiffany-type banking service. Should we fail to improve our penetration among this segment of the population, the detrimental effect on our competitive position could be material.

> In order to keep pace with the forecasted market changes, it seems reasonable to consider special efforts directed at two groups:
>
> 1.–The young people who have the best potential for upper class income, i.e., college students.
> 2.–The population currently in the upper income groups.
>
> One may reason that the college student of today has the best opportunity to be in the upper socio-economic groups in the future. If we can foster a favorable image among these young people–who have established banking relationships within a few years–then we have an opportunity to gain and retain the relationships as they progress financially. This may require special efforts.

In early September 1965, David Beer, Senior Vice President and Cashier, directed a circular to branches in the vicinity of college campuses in anticipation of the beginning of the school year, urging "personalized service" and "intelligent financial guidance" for the incoming students despite the fact that "very few of these young men and women have sufficient funds to make them substantial customers." The steps recommended included: extended closing hours, additional staff during peak registration times, and "a lobby hostess." Branches which did not have a lobby hostess were told to train a member of the staff. Branch managers were instructed to extend every possible courtesy including the sending of a "Thank You Card for New Depositors." The manager was also told to waive the student's first overdraft charge and to give him personal counseling.

The circular closed with the following paragraph:

> In May 1966, a circular will be issued outlining steps to be taken to encourage returning students to keep their accounts open during the summer months. In addition a plan will be presented for retaining the business of graduating students.

A memo dated later that month reveals a 23-step chronology of the work of the Committee on the College Student Marketing Program from February 1964 to the issuance of the circular mentioned above early in September. These 23 discrete steps ranged from research into the college student market to various mangagement meetings out of which the policies mentioned above evolved.

STUDENT LOANS PRIOR TO FGSL. Toward the end of October, Mr. Bailey received a memorandum with the title "College Student Program" from Vice President Art Gillespie. This document reaffirmed the importance of the good will of students, citing research to the effect that the bank's image was poor in that quarter. Gillespie also noted that Sindal did not think the policies outlined in the September circular went far enough. Apparently, other officers in the bank had put the brakes on him. Gillespie further complained of inadequate participation of the Marketing Committee. "There is little indication of a strong senior force pressing consistently for an obviously liberal college program." The Managing Committee was cited in particular as an inhibiting factor.

One of the items of concern in wooing the student population was, of course, loans to students. In 1962, the bank adopted the United Student Aid Fund loan program. USAF was a nonprofit organization supported by philanthropic funds, charges made against the college for loans made to its students, and minimal charges for administrative costs levied against the students. Interest under this plan, in which the bank still participated, was assessed during enrollment in school, but actual payments were deferred until after graduation. The interest was 7% simple.

The USAF loan program had not been particularly popular with either the students or the bank. In August 1964, Kirk James, New Haven Regional Vice President for Personal Loan Administration, received a memorandum from one of his assistants criticizing the USAF program. It was argued that the administration of the program was complex and confused. It closed as follows:

> Taking everything into consideration, the Plan has become very costly and time taking. Branches, unless they have volume are always confused and require guidance. Bank image is blackened by unhappy students.
>
> My recommendation is to drop the Plan.

A pencilled note read, "Recommendation Reluctantly Rejected."

In the meantime, other loan programs were being proposed. The Johnson administration was considering a Federally Guaranteed Student Loan Program. The administration's move appeared to be a counter to Senator Ribicoff's proposal for an income tax rebate for the costs of higher education. A release from The American Bankers' Association on March 18, 1965 revealed that that organization was opposed to such a loan program on the basis that "State and private loan-guarantee programs have evidenced their ability to meet the supplemental demand for such loans."

At the same time, a bill was introduced in the Connecticut legislature for a loan program under which students would reimburse the state for the costs of their education. First knowledge of this proposal came in the form of a letter from the sponsoring state legislator to Mr. Bailey, the President of the bank. There is no indication of any economic analysis or that any was even done of the potential impact of such a program on the bank. However, Mr. Bailey did refer the matter to the bank's outside lawyers, while having a polite letter of acknowledgement drafted for his signature by a member of the staff.

Legal counsel found that "this bill neither conflicts nor coincides with any association policy since, as far as I can see, there is no relationship to banking." He also commented: "I see no particular harm in being cited as interested in this new approach . . . particularly as there seems little prospect for its passage . . ." Whether or not this particular legislation would have passed, it was soon made irrelevant by the passage of a federal law.

THE BEGINNING FGSL'S. On November 8, 1965, President Johnson approved the Higher Education Act of 1965, which, among other things, created a program of low interest guaranteed loans for students of higher education. It was expected that this would gradually bring about the phasing out of the National Defense Student Loan Program which had been administered through the colleges.

On November 11, 1965, Mr. Knut Lake, Vice President, Personal Loans, Hartford Headquarters, received a resume of the Higher Education Act from the Governmental Relations Officer. The most relevant portion of the Act for the bank was the FGSL's:

> For students from families having adjusted family income less than $15,000 the Federal Government would subsidize *all* of the interest while in school and 3% thereafter; for students from families having higher incomes there would be no interest subsidy but the insurance would cover loans to such students.

The interest to be charged would be "no higher than 6% annual interest on the unpaid balance," and repayment would begin no earlier than 60 days after the completion of study. This plan would obviously be more attractive than the USAF program to students eligible for the subsidy, since they would have to pay no interest against the time during which they continued schooling, and only the difference between the 6% maximum and the 3% subsidy after they completed school. This contrasts with the USAF plan's 7%, which would be subject to interest from the moment the loan was made, even though payments would be deferred until after the student left college. Under the FGSL provisions the state and private programs which would be set up had to be authorized to insure loans for not less than $1,000 and not more than $1,500 for at least 6 years. The government would cover 100% of unpaid principal to a maximum aggregate of $5,000 for undergraduates and $7,500 for graduate students.

On November 15, Mr. Lake wrote to Mr. Fred Dunn stressing the growing importance of student aid funds and student loans and suggesting "the establishment of a committee, having as its sole function the study and analysis of these interesting forces. . . ." Four days later, on November 19, Mr. Bailey sent a letter to Mr. Saunders, Senior Vice President, New Haven. The first paragraph read:

> In New Haven I omitted to speak to you about the special college program which was assigned last February and supposed to have been completely set up and ready to go with the opening of school in September. As you know, it fell between the cracks somewhere.

In February of 1966, a memorandum went from one Executive Vice President to another calling attention to the need to prepare for servicing students enrolling for the spring semester. This was accompanied by a new circular laying out policies somewhat more liberal than those of the prior September. For example, "selected branches were authorized to waive the 50¢ quarterly maintenance charge on . . . accounts of students." Also, the policy of waiving overdraft charges was extended from one overdraft to two.

In July 1966, the bank received a letter from Allen P. Stults of the Association of Reserve City Bankers announcing that the ARCB had decided to support the Higher Education Act. In late October 1966, somewhat more than eleven months after the passage of the Act, Mr. Bailey received a handwritten letter, which read in full:

October 22, 1966
Milford
Conn.

National Bank and Trust Co.
Hartford, Conn.

Attn: Mr. Phineas Bailey, President.

Dear Sir:

Please will you be the lender for State Guaranteed Loan at 6%?

If so, I can qualify and attend a State College near my home in Danbury, Conn.

This refers to Higher Education Act 1965 OE-1071 (6-66) Federal Student Loan Program P.L. 89-287 Budget no. 51-R572 for adjusted family income less than $15,000.

I hope you will complete my borrower's application for these Federal interest benefits.

Very truly yours,

Robert Cromwell

P.S. Your branches here are not interested—says they prefer higher interest loans.

On November 3, Knut Lake replied to Mr. Cromwell.

Dear Mr. Cromwell:

Your letter to Mr. Bailey has been referred to me since my installment credit repsonsibilities embrace the student loan program of National Bank and Trust.

We have not as yet signed an agreement with the Connecticut State Scholarship and Loan Commission to originate student loans under the Higher Education Act of 1965. We believe it probable that such an agreement will be signed in the very near future and that certain branches, including Danbury, will be designated as points where such applications will be accepted.

I would suggest that in a few weeks you again contact the New Milford Branch for further information on the plan.

Cordially,

Knut Lake
Vice-President

On November 9, approximately two weeks after the receipt of Mr. Cromwell's letter, the Managing Committee received a memorandum entitled, "Student Education Financing, Federal Higher Education Act of 1965, Connecticut Student Guaranteed Loan

Program." It was signed by four officers, one assistant vice president, and three vice presidents, among them Mr. Lake. It requested approval for a loan program which would meet the terms of the Higher Education Act. The relevant portions of the memorandum that bear on the goals of the loan program are the following:

> This program is not a directly profitable operation. There are, of course, certain advantages to the bank, namely linking the young student to services he can use while in school and more important, services available to him as a consumer and businessman. Our Studyplan Program is profitable and is an ideal supplement when additional funds are needed. This school study plan can be enhanced by our participation in this government program.

The memo then went on to identify three competitors who were in the process of setting up such loan programs, and to identify one other which had decided not to. It continued:

> It is understood by all lenders that although this program is not profitable, the Federal Government would step in to run the program much along the line of the National Defense Education Act of 1959, if private lenders did not participate. In addition, publicity for the bank, as well as a moral obligation to the student, should be taken into consideration.

On the same day that this proposal went to the Managing Committee, the Dean of the Yale Law School wrote Mr. Bailey. In a two-paged, double-spaced letter, the Dean outlined the problems of financing students through law school education. Toward the end, he called attention to the fact that the state of Connecticut had already formed a loan program with Federal funds under the Higher Education Act, but that few banks were processing such loans. He did mention, however, that one of the Bank's major competitors was in fact already doing so, but only to students whose parents were already depositors of that bank. He concluded:

> It is my sincere hope that the National Bank and Trust Company will find it possible to participate, and the purpose of this letter is to point out that time is of the essence.
>
> Anything you can do to assist us in this matter will be most sincerely appreciated, not only by the administrative officers of the school, but also by the overwhelming majority of the students.

The minutes of the Managing Committee of November 14 report that the committee had received a report on student loans from Mr. Lake, and decided "that our efforts be aggressive in soliciting loans from students attending schools with high academic standards and that we accommodate loan requests from students in schools with lesser standards but without an aggressive approach." On November 17, the Subcommittee on Loans of the General Finance Committee announced the approval of the loan program with provisions conforming to the Act. There were no restrictions in these provisions other than those inherent in the Act. The purpose of the program was described simply as "to assist (students) in meeting educational costs. . . ."

It was not until five days after this that Mr. Lake responded to the Dean of the Yale Law School in Mr. Bailey's name. However, by this time he was able to assure the Dean that the bank had approached the state government and that a program should be in effect within a matter of a few weeks. That same day, a circular announcing the program was sent to all branch managers. A copy of the circular was forwarded to Mr. Bailey. Attached to it was a buck-slip from a bank official assuring Mr. Bailey that another officer had already phoned an officer of Yale to assure him of the bank's plan to participate.

During the next several months the bank received a number of messages from the Association of Reserve City Bankers urging its members to support FGSLs, citing President Johnson's personal interest in the program, and the American Bankers' Association's support of the program it had once opposed. On April 11, 1966, Johnson himself wrote a letter of congratulations to the ARCB on its part in the program. However, a year later, by April of 1967, the *ARCB Newsletter* reflected some complaints. One New England banker protested: ". . . it serves to spin a web around the banks from which they cannot extricate themselves without bad public relations. . . ."

On June 15, 1967, the Subcommittee on Loans (of the Managing Committee) set an increase in the maximum amount that could be loaned to graduate students per year as $1,500 as compared to the previous limit of $1,000. This raised the aggregate total from $6,000 to $7,000. However, an unidentified memorandum some time that summer began raising some notes of concern. The central issue was the lack of a requirement of need. It was pointed out that students from families with adjusted incomes of $15,000 were eligible even though some such families had programs for financing the education of their children. It was also pointed out that a student who had received a National Defense Educational loan could also qualify. In August, the President of the ABA made a speech in which he complained that the banks were losing money on the FGSLs and asked for several amendments to the original Act. He further suggested that arrangements be made for bank officers to give financial consulting to students.

On September 1, 1967, Mr. Lake summarized the first six months' experience for Mr. Bailey. He pointed out that there were about $2 million in loans outstanding. He estimated that the FGSLs might reach $13 million in a few years and perhaps $50 million within a decade. He said: "We have taken a prominent position in this field and I am confident it will pay substantial future dividends." He finished his memorandum by stating that he had been working with "certain governmental agencies" and expected that "in the not too distant future" additional subsidies "should add about 1% additional to our gross yield."

DOUBTS ABOUT FGSLS. On March 4, 1968, Vice President S. Smythe in the Hartford Personal Loan Office wrote to Mr. Bailey and Senior Vice President Saunders to warn them "of the tremendous rate at which guaranteed student loans are increasing. In slightly over one year we have increased our outstandings for all student loans over $8.5 million." The bulk of this increase by far was in FGSLs which accounted for about $8 million of a total of $10 million outstanding. He projected a doubling of outstanding loans by the middle of 1968 and said that he had been advised that the bank was making about 70% of all guaranteed student loans in Connecticut. He concluded:

> The Comptroller's Department figures indicates these loans are not particularly profitable, although the personal loan section is presently probing several avenues to increase our gross yield.
>
> In the absence of an indicated revision in our present policy, the personal loan section will continue to promote the guaranteed student loan program.

About two weeks later Saunders wrote to the Comptroller, referring to the FGSLs as "not particularly profitable" and growing at a "geometric rate." He asked for an up-to-date cost analysis.

During the next months several memoranda circulated, using about the same figures as those presented by Mr. Smythe and expressing anxiety about the growth of these relatively unprofitable loans. Some discussed possible prospects for more favorable terms for the bank. One, on April 7, 1968, suggested the possibility of an overall ceiling of outstanding loans in the vicinity of $17.5 million. In *none* of these memoranda was there any discussion of the goals of the FGSL program or of the effect of expansion or restriction of the program on those goals. In addition, none of the files which were searched, including that of the President, Mr. Bailey, revealed during this time a trace of the economic analysis that had been requested of the Comptroller.

Finally, on May 14, the Subcommittee on Loans approved a proposal that FGSL loans be restricted to the bank's own depositors, specifically to those who had an account six months prior to the loan application. A few exceptions would have the deposit requirement waived if the vocational school had substantial deposits at the bank.

At the same time, other divisions of the bank continued to exhibit concern for campus good will. On May 24, the Contributions Committee decided to maintain but not increase its $80,000 Aid to Higher Education Program of gifts to Connecticut colleges. However, they were considering an additional matching gifts program to supplement the Aid to Education Program.

On May 28, Mr. Beer, the Cashier, confirmed the restriction on loans to depositors, spelling out such details as that the deposit account must be that of the student's parents "unless the student is married and self-supporting." A memo from Vice President Smythe to Senior Vice President Saunders of August 12 contained the first traceable reference to the Comptroller's analysis. The key sentence of the August 12 memo was: "The salient point brought out by this estimate reveals that "if $10 million is invested in loans averaging two study years at $750 per year with the cost of funds 3.99% (during maturity of the loan), the bank would lose $590,000'." Mr. Smythe interpreted this to mean that there would be an opportunity loss of about a quarter of a million dollars after taxes over a three-year period.

A circular of September 12 to all branch managers announced that the government had raised the interest rates on FGSL loans from 6% to 7%. Branch managers were instructed to process all loans at 7% "if the interim disbursement was made on or after August 3, 1968." There was some liberalization of the deposit requirement at the manager's discretion if for one of a number of reasons, such as enrollment in a professional school, the applicant looked like a good long-term business prospect.

Mr. Sindal seems to have been slow in getting to Smythe's memorandum of August 12, because on November 26, 1968, he wrote to Senior Vice President Saunders as follows:

> I have just finished reading Sam Smythe's report regarding the dollar outstandings and other comments.
>
> I did not get too excited about the report until I got to the bottom of the first page, where it is indicated that the Comptroller's department contends that we could lose $1 on each $20 loaned. It was my understanding that we couldn't lose anything on these except our time.
>
> Then I got into the second page and found the delinquency ratio for other lending institutions is about one-third of what ours is, so they must be doing a better job of screening.
>
> The main reason for writing this memorandum, Freddie, is that I have a most vivid recollection of how we got out of Government Guaranteed Rehabilitation Loans. We were accused by the FHA of deliberately taking substandard applications and processing them. In fact, FHA in 1955 sued the bank for over $1 million. The suit was settled out of court, and it is my recollection that it cost us about a half million dollars. . . . A new administration might become very critical of us if we developed something like $10 million in losses under the guaranteed program.
>
> I think this is something that should be discussed by you at a meeting of the Managing Committee so that everyone may have their eyes opened.

There is no record of the response to Mr. Sindal's proposal.

In March of 1969 another analysis was made of the student loan program. By this time, $26 million were outstanding, 80% of which were FGSLs. A comparison was made between FGSL delinquencies and delinquencies on student loans prior to FGSL. The prior delinquency rate was 2%. Under FGSL it rose to 12.3% in the period ending December 31, 1967, and droppped slightly to 10.88% in the following year.

The history of the federal program was reviewed. The two most significant items were the rise in the interest rate from 6% to 7% and the raising of the maximum annual loan from $1,000 to $1,500 for undergraduates. The following paragraph is especially pertinent:

> Our guaranteed student loan program has not been in operation long enough to gain sufficient information to analyze the profitability of the program according to a study done by the Comptroller's Department. We need additional experience to determine the mix in loans by dollar amounts, years of study to be financed, and period over which the payout loan will be amortized. The present rate of 7% simple interest is applicable to only those student loans made after August 3, 1968. Previous to that time, the maximum rate was 6% simple. We thus have the major share of our current outstandings on our books at 6%. It should again be mentioned that we are "locked in" to this interest rate for a period of up to 15 years.

Several months later, in July, the Subcommittee on Loans approved a new policy which had the following additional restrictions: a student must be in at least the second academic year of school; loans were to be restricted to periods of the year corresponding to the quarterly or semester system; maximum advance for the year would be the federal limit of $1,500 for a student in a four-year college, but limited to $1,000 for a junior college student; further advances would be made only if parents maintain a satisfactory balance in their accounts or for a few exceptional circumstances; and loans would be limited to undergraduates under 25 years of age. All other former requirements were maintained.

On February 6, 1970, the maximum limit was lowered to $1,000 for four-year undergraduates and graduate students and $500 for junior college students. All former restrictions were retained and a few additional ones added, such as that the applicant must be interviewed personally by a branch officer, be a resident of Connecticut, possess a social security number, be taking 12 units, and be in good academic standing. The items which were found in the files during this period again contain no discussion of the impact of these restrictions on the goals of the FGSL program. However, once more they contained evidence of the concern of other portions of the bank for the college market. One memo of February 24, 1970, revealed that a task force reaffirmed the priority to be given to the college youth market and stated, "It can only receive this priority from senior management." It recommended an ambitious program of research, services for the college market, and advertising to that market. One statement in the memorandum reads: "Image building and personalized service can be our most important assets during this period in a young customer's life." While the documents pertaining to student loans made no reference to the campus market, it is equally interesting that in the document on the campus market there was absolutely no reference to student loans in this single-spaced, two and a half page document.

THE LEGACY OF THE SPRING OF 1970. The spring of 1970 was as tumultuous for the National Bank and Trust Company as it was for the country at large. The bank had long been closely associated with the manufacturing industries of Connecticut. It had financed much of the work of the General Dynamics ship-building yard and had been the long-standing source of funds for a number of firearms manufacturers. In the student uprisings following the Cambodian invasion and the shootings at Kent and Jackson State, the bank became the special target of student radicals, some of whom occupied a bank-owned office building in downtown New Haven. These students set a fire in the building which got out of control and resulted in several hundreds of thousands of dollars damage.

Bank officers began a series of dialogues with students from Yale, the University of Connecticut, Connecticut College for Women, and a number of state and junior colleges. A memo of June 11 from Philip Stevens, Vice President, to the Managing Committee urged that the bank seize the initiative by "challenging constructively concerned youth with programs of our own, rather than reacting to their leads." He suggested that the Managing Committee take responsibility for coordinating the bank's response in line with recent statements made by the chairman and president.

Events within the bank seem to have moved rapidly over the next several weeks. By the beginning of August, a Student Affairs Committee and an Ad Hoc Committee on

Social Priorities were established. On August 4, the Student Affairs Committee met. Two new names of interest appeared. One was that of Richard Trumball, who had been a senior operating officer of the bank and was to become the head of the Public Affairs Department. The other was Bob Baron, who at the time had the title of administrative assistant. Neither name had previously appeared either as participant or as addressee in any of the correspondence bearing either on student loan policy or on the development of the campus market. The issue had broadened.

The first substantive paragraph of the minutes of the August 4 meeting struck a vigorous tone and for the first time linked the bank's loan policy explicitly to its other efforts to woo the campus youth:

> Our credibility with youth is poor, and deteriorating. Youth–and others–are frustrated by the lack of responsiveness of "establishment" institutions, and by the apparent contradictions between our saying and our doing. For example, we want to appeal to youth, but have made student loans more restrictive; we say war is bad for business, yet we are seen as actively financing and prospering from the war . . . and, apart from our Chairman's words, not doing anything to end it.

The committee called for a coherent pattern of action for the bank as a whole and for undertaking "the formidable task in 'sensitizing' our total staff, many of whom are as alienated from the youth as they are from us." Within a few days of the circulation of the minutes of the committee (August 10) Duke Morgan, Regional Marketing Officer, and Don Perkins, Vice President, submitted a proposal for a program, "Communicating our Commitment to our Staff and Branch Personnel." Nine specific steps were proposed; among the more interesting were: structuring the 1971 Management Conference around the theme "Changing Business Values"; statewide sensitivity training for all 3,500 bank officers; establishing regional councils on social responsibility; and including social performance on the branch officers' performance reports.

The writers of this proposal were by no means overly optimistic about the bank's credibility. Apropos of contact between branch managers and the campus youth, they said, "For one thing, we feel receptivity to the idea by most branch officers would be at an all time low. Secondly, we fear that an unsensitized officer might do more to alienate moderate students than communicate with them."

Finally, in September 1970, a Student Affairs Subcommittee addressed the issue of loans directly, linking them explicitly to the overall problem of campus relations and suggesting a review of policy. In going over the history of participation in FGSL, the Subcommittee made a number of points. In the first years of the program, the yield had been 5% to 7%. "The yield is now 9¼% including a 2¼% subsidy." It then listed the various restrictions which progressively were put on these loans between June 1968 and February 1970. As these restrictions were imposed the bank's share of student loans in the state fell from over two-thirds to about one-third.

The Subcommittee suggested three objectives for the program: a) help assure that no one in Connecticut is deprived of an education for financial reasons, b) establish potentially profitable relationship with a group of college students and c) let it be known that we are the leader among Connecticut banks in the activity. A bank officer scrawled in the margin a fourth objective, "ongoing communication with student holder of loan frequently." He also wrote: "Convey to staff why we are in program—1) potential student customer, 2) philanthropic, 3) first relationship."

In suggesting a review of the student loan program, the Subcommittee assumed that there would be a limit on the amount of resources the bank could commit to it. They projected that within two years the total outstanding would be $67 million. Their suggestion was that all arbitrary restrictions be removed, but that limits on total loans be maintained by introducing a criterion of need about which the government legislation had nothing to say. It was further suggested that the bank attempt to benefit from this lending relationship by attempting to interest students in other bank services, both currently and after graduation.

The Subcommittee's last remark on the subject of loans was to note with dismay the instructions in a bank circular of 2-6-70 to "judge the appearance and character of the student," noting that this was an invitation for the loan officer to exercise prejudice. The minutes of the Student Affairs Committee as a whole in reviewing the work of its subcommittee and passing its own recommendations to the bank had only this to say:

> Agreed that (1) student loans should be subject to need test, (2) criteria for this should be developed, plus a recommendation of the total program to recommend level of total resources to be committed, types of schooling that should be considered, and restrictions, if any, that should apply.

However, the committee did pass along a wide range of recommendations for bank policy including the elimination of the booklet, "How Should I Dress on the Job?"

Three months later, on December 7, the Student Affairs Committee sent a summary of its work and recommendations to the Managing Committee. The Student Affairs Committee once more stated that the student loan policy had been too restrictive. It recommended raising the maximum loan to $1,500 for four-year colleges and $1,000 for junior colleges; allowing freshmen to participate; and removing the six-month deposit requirement for the initial loan, but requiring the student to have maintained an account to qualify for subsequent loans. There was no reference to a need qualification. (A marginal note indicates that this matter was referred to the Loan Policy Committee by the Managing Committee.)

The Student Affairs Committee forwarded some dozen recommendations ranging from training of officers, through the establishment of regional councils to achieve better community relations, to minority hiring and minority scholarships, and even the suggested abolition of a code of dress for bank employees. Perhaps its most important recommendation was a support of the proposal of the Ad Hoc Committee on Social Priorities for establishing a Public Affairs Officer.

AFTER THE DUST SETTLED. In February of 1971, the cashier issued a circular on student loans which was described as an "operational guide for student loans." It dealt only with procedures to be used and made no reference either to the lifting of restrictions or revision of the maximum amounts of loans. This did not happen for more than another year.

A newsletter, "Washington Banktrends," of July 24, 1972 predicted that there would be a substantial reduction in the number of students who would qualify under the

HEW regulations. This reduction would be caused by strict requirements for documentation of need. "The basic thrust of the new aid program is the channelling of government student aid toward lower-income families and away from the more affluent." However it also announced that "the ceiling for the interest-free loan program has been raised from $1,000 to $2,500. The maximum career total will now be $10,000, an increase of $2,500."

On August 2, 1972, managers were informed, via a circular from the cashier that the deposit requirement had been eliminated and that maximum loan advances had been set at $500 for community and junior college, $1,000 for colleges and universities and $500 additional for summer school. Loans were not to be made to students who had loans from other lending institutions, undergraduates over 25, nor freshmen. Finally, the criterion of financial need was established:

> Give primary consideration to students with greatest financial need. Always determine if parental help or self help is available. Student's expenses and income must be accurately reported. Both should be reasonable and in line with those of other students at his campus.

On August 15, 1972, a new circular followed on the heels of that of August 2. It stated that "effective as of July 1, 1972, the Higher Education Act of 1965 has been amended." One of the amendments was: "Legal maximum loan amount increased and additional $500 loan advance for summer school eliminated." Under "Bank Policy" the parallel statement was: "Maximum loan amount remains at $1,000 for colleges and universities and $500 for junior colleges, per academic year, but $500 additional for summer school has been eliminated."

Exhibit 11-1

FINANCIAL HIGHLIGHTS (CONSOLIDATED DATA)

FOR THE YEAR	*1971*	*1972*	*Change*
Operating Income	$ 506,935	$ 550,431	8.2%
Operating Expenses	447,468	487,433	8.9
Income before Securities Transaction	59,467	62,998	6.0
Net Income	61,029	64,149	5.3
AT YEAR'S END			
Resources	$11,328,635	$13,629,483	20.4
Deposits	9,691,100	11,695,044	20.3
Loans	5,672,013	3,226,254	13.8
Securities	1,115,855	1,141,158	2.3
Capital Funds	237,950	280,087	17.7
Reserves for Possible Loan Losses	46,035	49,229	6.9

*All numbers indicated are in thousands.

Exhibit 11-2

PARTIAL ORGANIZATION CHART

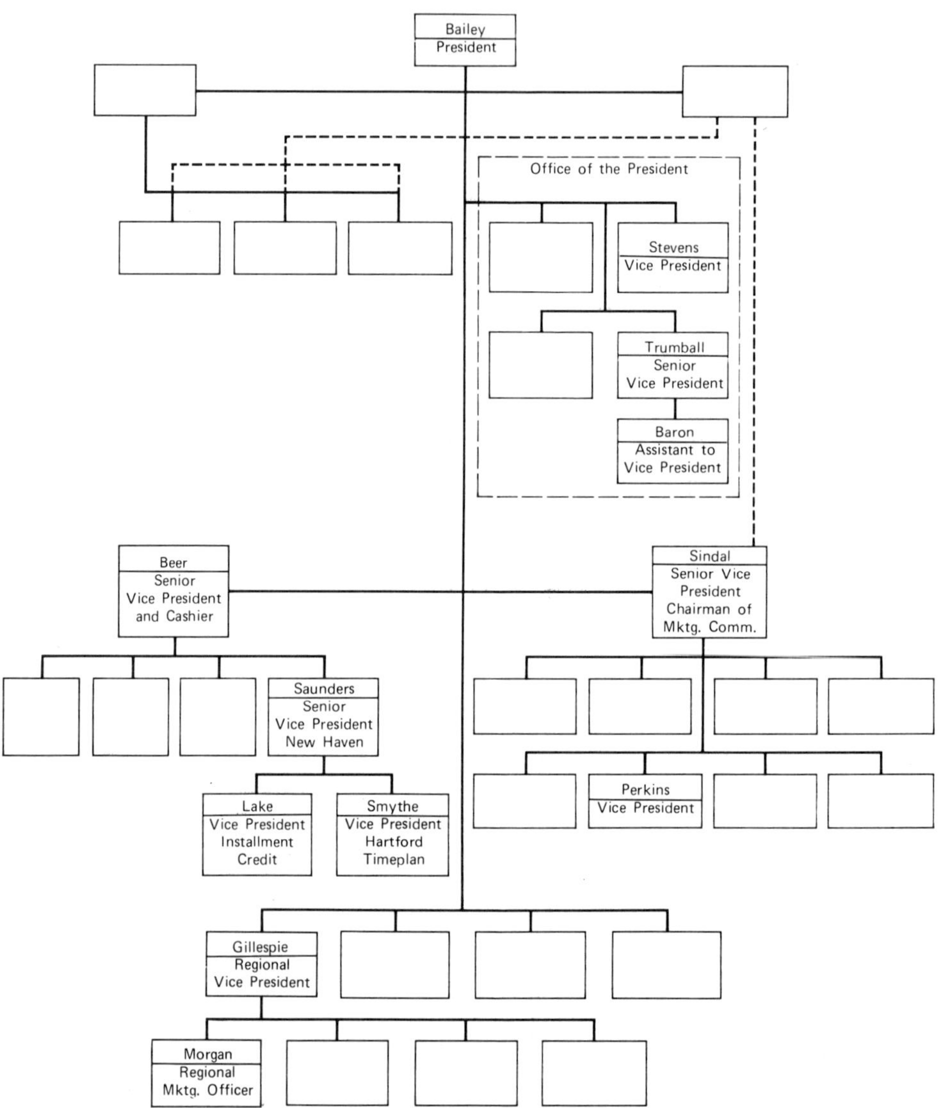

Case Twelve

The Metropolitan Development Corporation (A)

The Metropolitan Development Corporation (MDC), designed to be "a private corporation for pecuniary gain and profit" was formed in Norfolk, Virginia in June 1968 as a wholly owned subsidiary of the Continental Bank and Trust Company. According to MDC's charter:

> The general nature of the business to be transacted shall be the promotion of small businesses and job opportunities for the poor and needy; slum clearance and the provision of adequate and proper housing for the needy; the development of plans to be followed by other cities in connection with the social, vocational, educational and economic development and rehabilitation of urban property and residents; and in connection therewith, the borrowing and lending of money, whether or not the loan be secured or subordinated to other creditors; the purchase and development of real property; the development of modern and pilot programs; the purchase and lease, reworking, development, improvement, and sale or rent of personal property or real property.

Because this profit-making organization was formed to make second-mortgage loans to enable low-income people to get the funds to make a down payment on a small business or home, it was organized as a subsidiary of the bank; federal banking laws prohibited national banks from making second-mortgage loans. Initial capitalization of $1 million was supplied by the bank from its undivided profit account in return for MDC's authorized 1 million shares of $1 per value common stock.

THE CONTINENTAL BANK AND TRUST COMPANY

The Continental Bank and Trust Company (CBT) was a large, regional, commercial bank heavily oriented toward retail banking with total deposits of approximately $2 billion. Originally incorporated in the late 1800s as a commercial bank, CBT had grown through mergers and acquisitions, so that by 1972 it had 100 offices across the state of Virginia with over 30 in the Metropolitan Richmond area, where it was the largest commercial bank. In addition, it operated service offices in four U.S. cities, an office in Nassau, and two representative offices in South America. Through its wholly owned subsidiary, Continental (or CBT) Holding Company, the bank had purchased minority interests in a large number of other banks and bank holding companies as well as participating in a variety of diverse financial services. It was involved in activities such as sales finance, asset management, investment counseling, factoring, life insurance, export financing, mortgage banking, consumer finance services, and travel services. Despite its rapid growth, however, in 1972 the holding company still accounted for only about 5.6% and 5.0% of the bank's total income and net operating earnings, respectively. The bulk of both revenues and income continued to come from commercial banking.

In the ten-year period ending in 1972, the bank overall had achieved an annual compound growth rate of 10.6% for total deposits. Total operating earnings had increased at an annual compound rate of 18.9% and net operating income before securities gains and losses had climbed 13.8% a year. Earnings per share had shown an annual compound growth rate of approximately 12% over the past decade, and by the end of 1972, return on average stockholders' equity amounted to 14.3%. These growth rates had placed CBT in the nation's top 50 banks as measured by total deposits and had contributed to its reputation throughout the industry as an innovative, aggressive bank.

Emphasis had been placed on optimizing the bank's long-term financial performance by striving for quality loans that would yield a targeted rate of return. To meet this broad objective, considerable attention had been devoted to the development of entrepreneurial young lending officers who would be able to respond quickly and creatively to customer loan requirements. In support of this approach, all lending officers throughout the bank were authorized to lend the "house limit," an amount in excess of $7 million. Control of the bank's loan portfolio quality was maintained chiefly by the Credit Administration Department, which would participate in various bank Credit Committee meetings to "coach" and monitor loan decisions and follow-up procedures.

Traditionally, top management had been selected from within the bank, and only seldom would senior executives be brought in from the outside. Mobility within the organization was extensive, however, with promising executives being reassigned frequently. Top management emphasized informality and promoted the free flow of information among various functional areas of the bank. (An organization chart is provided in Exhibit 12-1.) One senior executive said, "We believe in operating in each others' backyards." In part, this resulted in a high degree of flexibility with regard to executive career paths. For example, the current President and Chief Executive Officer, Mr. Jeffrey Rhodes, had started in 1958 as a trainee in the bookkeeping department. He then rose swiftly through the positions of assistant cashier, operations officer, assistant vice president, vice president, and assistant to the president to become executive vice president of the bank's Norfolk offices in 1968. In 1971, 13 years after joining the bank, he was made president at the age of 35.

Operating performance was guided by a comprehensive annual budget with broader plans developed for the following four years. For the first time in 1970, bank management had developed a longer range 10-year strategic plan for the 1970's. After key executives within the bank had defined the organization's "business values," strategy teams headed by executive vice presidents formulated specific goals and plans to achieve those objectives. Central to the bank's future operations was achievement of a 23%

average return on projected equity over the next 10 years. According to forecasts, this meant that over the next five years, an additional $35.8 million in pretax earnings would be required. In management's view, this called for a selection of only those projects in the future that would yield 30% return on investment and a minimum pretax contribution of $1 million over five years.

To maintain and accelerate the bank's historically high growth rates, top management had also established ambitious, performance-oriented criteria for officers. Incentive compensation was awarded annually to managers in the form of bonuses distributed on the basis of achieving mutually agreed upon objectives and performance against budget. Branch managers, for example, were evaluated according to four "goal posts" which were reported quarterly: dollar level of deposits; dollar volume of loans; profit development (cross-selling of related services such as trusts and insurance, or other business development activities such as referring customers to the real estate department); and personnel development (generally in the form of on-the-job training.)

CREATION OF THE MUNICIPAL DEVELOPMENT CORPORATION

When first created, MDC was considered part of what originally was called the "Norfolk Plan." James Hale, grandson of the founder of the bank and for 25 years its president, had begun in late 1967 an aggressive program of "paying his back rent" to society. While driving through sections of Norfolk, Hale had become appalled at the slum conditions in which many black people were living. He became convinced that his bank should become deeply involved in increasing both home ownership and black capitalism in such deprived areas.

In October of that year, Hale had been approached by 20 local black leaders who expressed their concern about substandard housing, unemployment among blacks, and a lack of recreational facilities for black children in Norfolk. At this meeting Hale suggested that instead of demanding the government act on the city's problems, CBT and the blacks jointly undertake an extensive cleanup of some of the slums in an effort to initiate a self-help revitalization of living conditions. One corporate account of this project noted that:

> Hale wanted the developing Norfolk Plan to be a practical demonstration to show that, without federal financial assistance, any community could revitalize both its living and business environment by utilizing its most basic institutions—the home, the church, and the school—on a voluntary basis.

After a series of meetings, it was agreed to mount such a clean-up campaign on a weekend in May 1968. Douglas Fredericksen, Assistant Comptroller in the Purchasing Department of the Richmond office, was designated by Hale to direct and coordinate the project.

Ultimately, approximately 10,000 volunteers—school children, college students, civic groups, church congregations, and residents of the affected areas—cleaned up 109 blocks where 3,100 black and white families lived. Awards of $5,000 were offered to the college, church, and school doing the best jobs in the cleanup. Special buttons, T-shirts, and hats were donated as were refreshments, fencing, and tools, and the bank gave a new garbage can and American flag to every participating family in the target areas. For those two streets whose residents had done the best job of cleaning up, the bank paid the citizens' share of having their streets paved. The total cost to the bank for the spring cleanup was approximately $70,000.

According to Hale, "The Norfolk Spring Cleaning operation was designed only as a first step toward a repeat of the same cleanup in all other areas of the city, and then the beginning of short-range and long-range plans for the improvement of existing housing, new housing, job training and job opportunities." More spring cleanups were planned in the following years. In 1969, spring cleanups were conducted in 12 cities where the bank had branches or affiliates, and by 1970 the "Norfolk Plan" had spread to 47 cities and towns in the state.

MDC, which marked the formal beginning of the Norfolk Plan, was part of Hale's and the bank's longer-term commitment to making available improved housing and providing capital for minority business enterprises. CBT considered the MDC to be "a research project in financial assistance as an effective, private, profitable way to revitalize and rebuild the urban environment." In a November 6, 1968 memorandum describing the objectives of MDC, Hale wrote:

> We have a belief that society is built from the bottom up—that money, both on the income side and the expenditure side, is the most important material thing in a man's existence. We feel further that all the money in the world, no matter from what source it comes, cannot make a model city—only people can do this. We feel, also, that private industry, especially banking, has a greater sense of community responsibility as the custodian of the community's wealth and a greater ability to tackle all money problems. We believe that profitable activities of the Metropolitan Development Corporation can be demonstrated. We believe it is something that could be repeated in communities throughout the United States with telling effect. We think that we can match sweat equity of individuals with dollars to improve business and living conditions.

Several areas in which MDC initially concentrated its efforts were as follows:

1.—A block of property was purchased as a "research project" to "discover whether rundown property can be rehabilitated and resold as a family living unit to individuals of low income on credit at a price that would return a gain after the cost of property and the cost of rehabilitation."

2.—MDC designed, had built, and sold new family dwelling units on a parcel of vacant land in a low-income area as an experiment to see if "a house can be built and sold that will return a gain and yet can be sold at a price that a family in the low-income group, below $5,000, can afford to purchase and make regular monthly payments for the purchase."

3.–The provision of second-mortgage loans (for down payments on houses) on a "sound basis that would enable low-income families to obtain first mortgages at our own bank."
4.–The building, selling, and financing of small shopping centers in low-income areas as a "research project" to determine if retail trade in such areas could thereby be stimulated.
5.–The "expansion of small business units by providing management assistance (and) capital loans for improvements and expansion" and the "formation of new business units."
6.–Demonstration projects which would lead to the "health, education, welfare, training and development" of all age levels in the low-income group. A building was purchased and renovated for use as a day-care center for children.

With regard to financing, Hale noted that because MDC was viewed as a research project, the initial capital of $1 million was charged off as a reduction in bank assets without a tax deduction. However, MDC's ultimate goal was "to see that the capital . . . remains intact, (and) produces a return that can, in turn, finance additional research projects in the broad field of its total activities." Overall, a total bank commitment of $10 million was established although it was not to be considered a ceiling according to Hale, who said that the bank would "allot whatever is necessary to do the job."

Hale also addressed the interests of the bank's stockholders:

> For the stockholders of the Continental Bank and Trust Company, the goals are long range, a part of enlightened self-interest based on the realization that if the environment for living and business in urban areas is to be improved, the private incentive method is the best—that people have to develop pride, character and ambition. The method of operation of the Metropolitan Development Corporation is to help people help themselves, not to offer charity with nothing in return.
>
> Surely, if the Metropolitan Development Corporation can help build a better community, then the bank itself will grow and prosper with the community and this, in turn, will represent the tangible rewards to stockholders of the bank.

Addressing the integration of this novel type of community development effort into the operations of a commercial bank, Hale noted:

> As a practical matter, an urban development corporation to be successful, would have to be one with minimum capital requirements that perhaps only the major banks of the country would be able to provide. Probably, also, only in the major banks of the country would you find the managerial capacity to manage an urban development corporation and to interrelate its activities with the . . . mortgage lending and term business lending of the bank . . . .

Initially, MDC operated in Norfolk. Jeffery Rhodes, then Executive Vice President in charge of the bank's Norfolk offices, was named President, and Fredericksen was designated Secretary-Treasurer and Operating Director. Assisting Fredericksen were two young, recent graduates of the bank's credit training program. Focusing their efforts on the Norfolk area, they concentrated on four programs: home-ownership loans, home-improvement loans, equity financing, and demonstration housing projects.

THE DEVELOPMENT OF NEW PROCEDURES

In order to take into account the unusual situations of their clients, MDC officials were unable to operate according to standard lending regulations. Rather, a high degree of judgment was required, and during the first 18 months special criteria and procedures were developed. By doing this, MDC lenders were able to begin immediately to make home loans at standard interest rates with terms for repayment structured to meet their clients' budgets. It was considered essential that MDC act quickly on the loans because there was widespread suspicion and doubt—especially among blacks—about the sincerity of CBT in this effort.

Despite considerable flexibility for MDC and bank officials to grant loans—any lending officer in any branch could approve a loan, but it required at least two negative judgments by members of a central committee to turn one down[1]—it was always specified that the loan was to be repaid, and that the funds were not a gift. Definite repayment schedules were called for, although they could be tailored to an individual's or business' circumstances. (Often, the schedules were extended so as to permit smaller, and more manageable, installment payments by the borrower.) Moreover, CBT and MDC officials were to give assistance in developing family budget plans, and in the case of business loans, income and expense projections. A policy statement that "additional patience, understanding and administrative time will be required to make the loans and to service them"

In terms of handling applications, "everybody in the bank who normally handles loans" was to be involved in this lending program. Moreover, "buck passing" was forbidden. Whoever was first contacted with regard to the loan was to handle the application. The administration of Norfolk Plan home improvement loans were described further in a June 1968 operating bulletin:

> . . . We propose to handle Norfolk Plan home improvement loans using the same forms, procedures and general operating techniques as are presently used in making this type of loan, with modifications to fit the circumstances. . . . Modifications include revision of terms and credit standards to some degree, but most importantly, spending the time that is necessary to qualify as many applicants as possible.

On the other hand, one-stop loan service was viewed as impractical for Norfolk Plan loans:

> . . . Of more importance than speed are the fundamentals of getting a full credit statement and conducting [a] credit investigation as needed, including the making of a personal visit to the applicant's premises to help form the decision.

---

[1] Business loan applications were routed to the central office where they were reviewed with guidelines more liberal than normal credit standards.

REGULATORY PROBLEMS

Initially, permission to establish the MDC was obtained from the district Federal Reserve Bank and the Comptroller of the Currency, but after MDC had been formed, federal examiners in an annual audit of the bank's loan portfolio criticized the MDC portfolio. This in turn led the Federal Reserve Board to order a cessation of MDC's activities. However, Hale, Eugene Dunn (First Vice President of the bank and Chairman of the holding company), and Fredericksen, in a three-hour meeting convinced the Federal Reserve's Board of Governors of the propriety and legality of MDC's activities. Nevertheless, noting that all other banks engaged in such activities took advantage of Small Business Administration (SBA) loan guarantees, the Federal Deposit Insurance Corporation required that all MDC loans—characterized as "high risk"—were to be charged off as soon as they were put on the books.

As a matter of policy, the bank and MDC had decided not to participate in the SBA loan guarantee program. Fredericksen explained:

> A government guarantee doesn't make a bad loan any better. If they knew the SBA would bail us out, our loan officers wouldn't try so hard to save their loans. As for loan volume, that poses no problem for us because we have Jim Hale, Jeff Rhodes, and myself urging our officers to put on these kinds of loans.
>
> Part of the SBA's problem is that SBA loan officers are not judged on how many loans go bad. Rather, they are evaluated based on how many loans are on the books. Therefore, they tend to be volume-oriented, regardless of the quality of the loans.

EARLY GROWTH AND DEVELOPMENT OF MDC

Following the May 1969 Spring Cleaning project in Norfolk,[2] MDC offices were established in ten other Virginia cities. Because many of the chosen cities did not have sufficient potential volume of MDC-type loans, full-time MDC officers were not designated in all locations. Instead, the executive officer in charge of that location's branches would appoint a local lending officer to whom MDC lending would be assigned as a collateral responsibility. MDC headquarters in Norfolk coordinated activities by issuing lending guidelines and collecting data for reporting purposes.

By the summer of 1969, 12 months after it began operations, MDC had loaned over $2 million to restore over 800 houses, to provide capital for 24 businesses (both white and black), and to enable over 40 families to buy their homes. Moreover, in a period of tight money, MDC was the only area of Continental Bank that did not reduce its loan activity. In January 1970, another $1 million of capital was invested by the bank, and at least $10 million more was committed for first-mortgage loans to "high-risk," low-income people.

By the end of 1970, over $5 million had been committed to MDC's four program areas:

---

[2] Hale had elected Fredericksen, by then a vice president, to coordinate these projects statewide.

Home Ownership—More than 350 loans—275 of them in Norfolk—had been made by the MDC for down payments on homes. The loans totaled over $600,000. Terms for each loan had been adjusted to individual needs and family budgets so that first mortgages could be obtained either through CBT or a savings and loan institution. Average home loans were for $11,000, with one as high as $14,000 and one as low as $1,200.

Home Improvement—Loans for the repair of over 3,000 substandard units—most of which were for renovation, painting of houses, replacing of faulty wiring, providing inside toilet facilities, and repairing plumbing—totaled $2 million.

Business Ownership—By the fall of 1970, 136 "high-risk" business loans had been made, totaling $1,578,000. Of these loan situations, only four businesses had failed. Loans ranged from $2,500 to $60,000, with the average loan at $15,000.

Demonstration Projects—In its largest single project, MDC purchased a 132-unit "temporary" housing project which had become a slum area for low-income white tenants. After purchase of the property for $245,000, a three-year, $700,000 remodeling project was initiated. By the end of 1970, MDC was losing about $21,000 per year on the project, but it was expected that by 1973, debt servicing would begin and within 12 years the project would be free of debt.

In evaluating MDC's operations and performance, senior management of the bank expressed satisfaction. Charge-offs through 1970 had been only $14,670.[3] "Cumulative profits" were just over $77,000, and state and federal taxes paid were $75,000, leaving a net profit of approximately $2,000. Income statements did not include as expenses the salaries of MDC personnel and certain overhead items, but it was believed that offsetting these expenses was the "additional income gained for the bank through first mortgage loans, savings accounts, checking accounts, and other services generated by MDC activity."

By the end of 1970, Dunn felt that the Norfolk Plan might be viewed in the future as the "most important thing this bank did in the '70s" to provide long-term dividends for the bank. Moreover, it was thought that the program had evolved to the point that it could serve as a model for other banks across the country.

A CHANGING STRATEGY

In late 1970, a three-year effort to determine and articulate the bank's "Business Values" and strategies to support those values was completed. Originally, seven values were agreed upon for presentation to officers and management associates:

- Customer Service
- Organization
- Employee Relations
- Innovation
- Recognition

---

[3] A charge-off ratio of 1% on outstandings was considered about average for traditional lending to small retail and service operations. For commercial lending overall, an average charge-off ratio of 0.5% or less was considered normal by most large urban banks.

- Growth
- Immediate Earnings

Later, an eighth value, "Citizenship" was added. It was described as "an essential value encompassing all others":

> We define citizenship as the reinvestment of our leadership and corporate resources to improve the economic climate from which we ultimately expect a profit.

Three justifications were offered for the bank's pursuing citizenship-oriented activities:

1.–Such activities would dissuade critics of business from the notion that businessmen were "more concerned with selling useless items at a profit than improving the quality (of life) for the American citizen."
2.–Schools–the source of bank employees–were viewed as denigrating the role of the businessman in society. Consequently, unless signs of increased commitment to the community were forthcoming from business establishments, it was reasoned that "business as we know it will be destroyed by the poor, the underprivileged, the militant and the (disenfranchised)."
3.–"There exists a very real potential market, size unknown which, if developed, could significantly contribute to the economic growth of our region and our bank."

CREATION OF THE PUBLIC AFFAIRS DEPARTMENT AND REDEFINITION OF MDC

In order to "implement greater achievement in the citizenship value," a Public Affairs Department was established to be headed by Fredericksen who was to report directly to Hale and, when Hale became chairman, to Rhodes. This department was to establish and develop relationships with governmental agencies in addition to overseeing and coordinating MDC's community development efforts.

With regard to MDC, the bank's major effort to date, the strategy statement noted that after three years of operation: "An impressive record has been achieved thus far . . . and yet no other businesses or banks have taken the risks *or* seen the opportunity to invest in its ownership. . . . We can't do the job alone." Stressing that "businesses which derive their income from the community have a responsibility to the overall economic growth of the community," the statement concluded that if community needs were not met locally, "we face the alternative of government intervention and high spending, community unrest, and overall deterioration."

To meet this broader challenge, the strategy for the bank's social activities was enlarged as Fredericksen commented:

> Our 1970 Citizenship Strategy paper stressed the need to look beyond MDC, which until that time had been mostly a black-oriented effort. Most of our community on a state-wide basis is white, and community development efforts realistically should include more than just urban affairs.

> Considering activities related to government, educational programs, transportation, and greater participation in the community in general led us to broaden the bank's charter in this area. A Public Affairs Department meant *more* than just the MDC.

A new corporation, the Virginia Development Corporation, was to be formed, to extend the work of MDC and enlist the support of the business community in Virginia. The goals of the restructured development corporation would be:

> 1.—To invest dollars in under-capitalized Virginia businesses.
> 2.—To actively seek out and bring in those companies willing to locate plants in or near under-developed communities throughout Virginia.
> 3.—To construct housing developments and actively work to improve housing and living conditions throughout Virginia.
> 4.—To own and operate Child-Care Centers within disadvantaged areas.
> 5.—To implement job training programs and obtain the commitment of the state's largest employers to actively increase minority employment.
> 6.—To seek out problem pockets within impoverished areas throughout the state and endeavor to find and implement solutions.
> 7.—To develop and promote the "Community Reinvestment Index" and other recognition programs to increase public awareness and understanding of community programs.

The Virginia Development Corporation was thought to require initial capitalization in the amount of $5 million. To supplement the $2 million already invested by CBT in MDC, national companies operating in Virginia would be approached for debt or equity financing in $100,000 certificates with interest paid at "market rates."

It was also envisioned that the corporation would have a broadly based board of directors and that those companies investing in the stock would provide staff managers of various functions on a loan basis for two or three years. "The stockholder would then receive a much better executive after the loan period as his return on investment." Corporate "stockholders" would also be expected to "coach" clients of the Virginia Development Corporation by providing business assistance, offering job training, aiding in personnel placement, or purchasing of products or services.

While these programs were being discussed, MDC was kept intact but moved from Norfolk to Richmond (where the bank's headquarters were located) in March 1971.

FUNCTIONS OF THE PUBLIC AFFAIRS DEPARTMENT

By April of 1971, Fredericksen had developed a more formalized statement of functions and responsibilities for the Public Affairs Department. In an April 21 memorandum to Hale, he indicated those activities for which he sought specific responsibility. They were:

> 1.—To coordinate bank officers in a "team" approach to community problems involving rapid transit, consolidation of government, education, housing, and environmental matters.

2.–To work closely with Mr. William Teale (assistant president of the bank and president of the CBT Holding Company) in the political activities of the bank.
3.–To decide on bank contributions.
4.–To work with the Marketing Department in developing a program of economic education and student liaison.
5.–To coordiante Public Affairs groups, led by CBT executive officers, throughout the state.
6.–To develop information center files on community groups, public issues, and appointed and elected officials.
7.–To serve as liaison between the bank and MDC.
8.–To coordinate the bank's voter registration and responsibility program.

Primary responsibility for other areas of activity discussed in the Citizenship Strategy paper should be lodged elsewhere, according to Fredericksen. For instance, in the Real Estate Finance Department, it was suggested that a task force be formed to "aggressively encourage development of low-income housing." It was also recommended that a small business training program be developed by the Term Loan Department and that personnel policy changes in fulfillment of the bank's "citizenship responsibility" be undertaken by the Personnel Department.

Despite efforts to launch the Virginia Development Corporation, in July 1971 MDC remained largely unchanged in its composition and functions. Fredericksen, having been made an executive vice president of the bank, became President of MDC, and Russell Burke, an assistant vice president with a background of credit training and line lending experience, was given responsibility for the unit's system-wide operations as well as those of the Richmond office. (For an organization chart of MDC, see Exhibit 12-2.) MDC's two primary operations were still described as the provision of funds for home ownership and equity capital for new, small businesses. Additionally, MDC continued to build housing projects in an effort to demonstrate what could be done to provide suitable homes at costs that were manageable for low-income families.

OBJECTIVES FOR 1972

On December 7, 1971, in a letter to Rhodes, Fredericksen delineated the objectives for the Public Affairs Department in 1972. In discussing MDC, two "concrete improvements" were set forth for implementation in 1972:

a.–Complete the concept and organizational changes per Citizenship Strategy paper to enable corporate accounts department to sell $5 million in stock.
b.–Reduce loan losses by 25% of 1971 level by improved controls and communication of new loan guidelines and increased management assistance to the businesses.

Fredericksen's comment regarding the extent of loan losses marked one of the first manifestations of concern among management about MDC's operations. On January 4, 1972, Burke presented his goals for the state-wide MDC system as well as those for his own office in Richmond, and, in part, these reflected Fredericksen's objectives. Particular emphasis was accorded the management of loans and profits. Total loans outstanding (including short-term loans and discounts–L&D, term loans, and real estate loans) were to be increased to $3,710,000, up 25% from 1971's balance of $2,967,100. At the same time, attention was to be focused on follow-up procedures so as to control delinquent loans. Expected and actual performance were described as shown in Table 12-1:

TABLE 12-1 MDC PAST-DUE LOANS AS A PERCENTAGE OF OUTSTANDINGS

Type of Loan	*1971 Actuals*	*1972 Goals*
L & D	26%	5%
Term	21%	10%
Real Estate	5%	5%

In order to achieve these levels, management assistance was to be "significantly" improved by "assigning a qualified officer or management associate as advisor for each MDC business."

Partially as a result of fulfilling the objectives set forth above, it was anticipated that MDC could generate a "profit" of $94,000 before taxes and reserve for losses, up 56% from $60,000 in 1971. In addition, Burke sought to reduce loan losses to $116,000 for the year, a 25% reduction from 1971's charge-offs of $155,484 (including losses of $108,000 written off on January 2, 1972).

NEW MDC POLICIES

In order to meet these projections for 1972, Burke formulated a more comprehensive and rigorous set of guidelines for all MDC lending activities than had existed previously. In a policy statement issued February 22, 1972 to all MDC directors in CBT offices across the state, several new criteria were established:

(a)–No working capital loans were to be made unless current balance sheets and income statements were provided.

(b)–No more overdraft financing was allowable for any reason. (If overdrafts occurred, they would become the responsibility of the branch managers.)

(c)–Demand loans were prohibited, and for any new business loan requests, the applicant would be required "personally [to] invest 100% of whatever he has available. . . ."

(d)–All MDC customers were to be identified in credit information files, and all MDC loans were to be reviewed with "top management" in credit committee meetings on a regularly scheduled basis, with minutes of those meetings to be sent to Burke in the Richmond office.

(e)–Quarterly, each MDC office was to audit its own loan portfolio and send a report of that audit to Richmond.

In addition, standardized MDC term loan agreements were to be used for all new business loans, and business loan applications were to be screened with a specific "customer market" in mind, as shown in Table 12-2.[4]

TABLE 12-2 NEW BUSINESS LOAN CATEGORIES

Perferred Business	*"Red Flags"*	*Not Acceptable*
Small Manufacturers	Franchises	One-man Businesses
Medium and Large Retailers	Barber Shops	Part-time Businesses
Asset to Community	Beauty Shops	Liquor Stores
	Lessee Truckers	Social Clubs
	Mom & Pop Cafes	Night Clubs
	Mom & Pop Groceries	
	Service Stations	
	Printing Businesses	
	Small Retailers	
	No Owner Investment	

A "qualified officer or management associate" was to be assigned to all MDC businesses by April, and each MDC office was to work with its local advisory board, business leagues, Office of Minority Business Enterprise (OMBE) office, bank customers, and branches in order to seek the "best possible" MDC business applicants. However, it was stipulated that, "[in] dealing with bank branches and departments, the same person should not make lending decisions for MDC and for the bank." In order to clean up bad debts and potential charge-offs, more thorough and frequent follow-up visits and documentation were ordered.

Finally, the maximum lending guideline on all MDC business loans was restricted to $50,000; any greater amount required the written approval of Fredericksen. Moreover, all new business loans exceeding $20,000 were to be reviewed with the term loan department with any portion of the loan in excess of that amount offered to term loan as a participation.

ASSESSMENT OF MDC

In April 1972, there was further evidence of top management's concern about the status of MDC. Its operations were the topic of discussions within a number of the bank's

---

[4]This "customer market" reflected those factors associated with success or failure on the basis of an analysis of the profiles of 12 successful businesses, 19 charge-offs, and 5 potential losses. Data were compiled from MDC offices across the state. In addition, it was noted that, "In almost every case, failures were a result of simply not following good lending procedures and judgment."

executive management meetings, and scrutiny of the unit's performance persisted throughout the summer. At Rhodes' request, a summary of MDC's lending experience to date was compared with the charge-off histories of other banks with similar programs. Compared to an average loss ratio of 12.8% on outstandings (i.e., gross charge-offs as a percentage of loans outstanding) for all banks surveyed, MDC's charge-off ratio was 14.5%. (Cumulative charge-offs since the inception of the program had grown to $348,000.) In his report, Fredericksen noted that, "All [banks] report undergoing the same internal re-examination, heavy losses, and high delinquencies. Many 'early loans' have been charged off. All report the economic slump (of 1970 and 1971) hit their minority loan business hard."

Despite the infusion of another $1 million in capital during 1972, there continued to be mounting concern over the level of losses and indications of more charge-offs to come. Top management continued discussions about the future of MDC. It was generally felt that insufficient attention had been given to the need for experienced, credit-trained officers.

Fredericksen, with expanded responsibilities for the Public Affairs Department, had been able to devote increasingly less time to MDC's operations. For instance, earlier that year he had been encouraged by Hale to accept a vacancy on the city school board, a job which eventually occupied about 60% of his time. (Fredericksen's only staff assistant was similarly absorbed in matters external to the bank.) Fredericksen commented:

> With many other commitments in the public affairs area, I need to back off from MDC. I have less and less time for actual supervision of our lending, in addition to which my strengths are not in the lending area. Also, detailed follow-up and supervision become more difficult as our MDC lending expands. This is becoming apparent as some of our first losses begin to come in. We started the operation with relatively young management associates, but some of them have gotten so carried away with the program that they put on poor loans which eventually end up as charge-offs.

Exhibit 12-1

PARTIAL ORGANIZATION CHART—1972

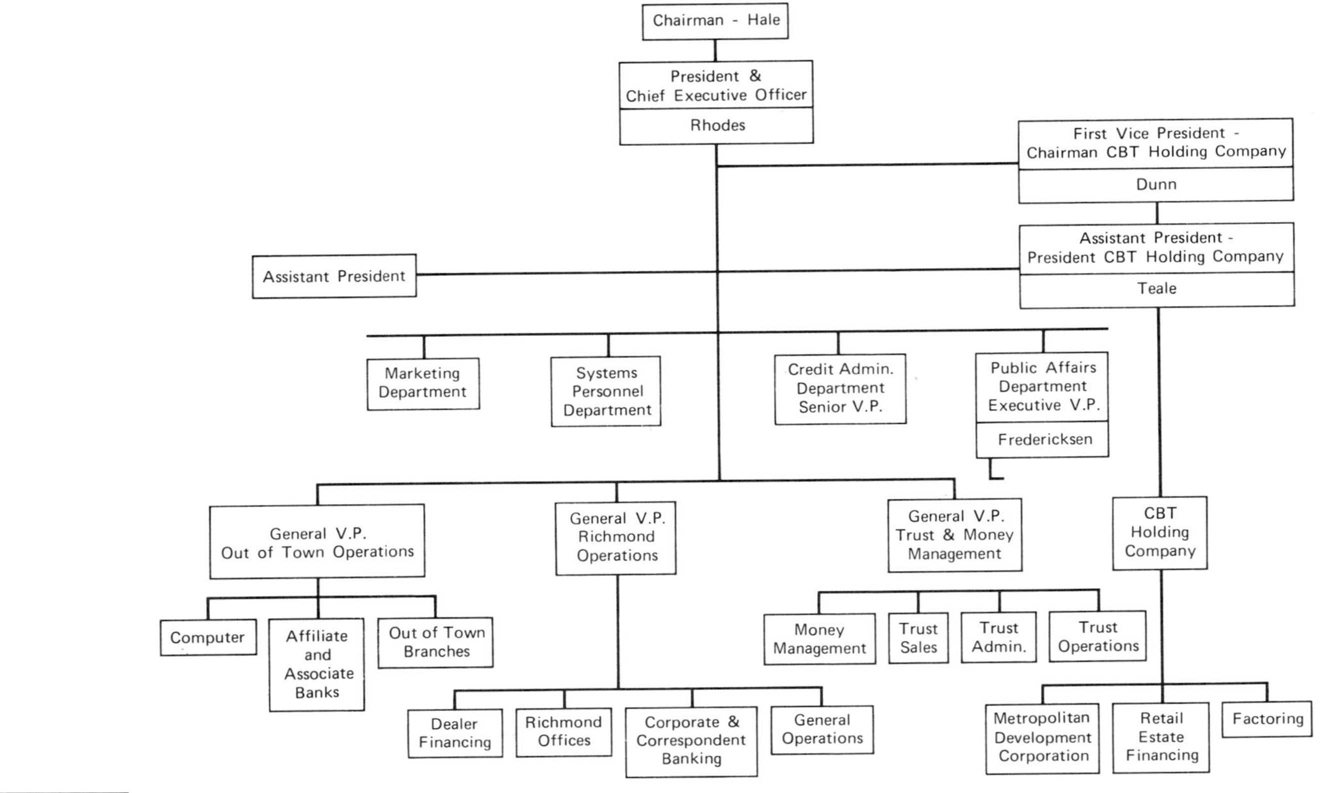

Source: Researcher's interview notes.

Exhibit 12-2

METROPOLITAN DEVELOPMENT CORPORATION ORGANIZATION CHART—JULY 1971

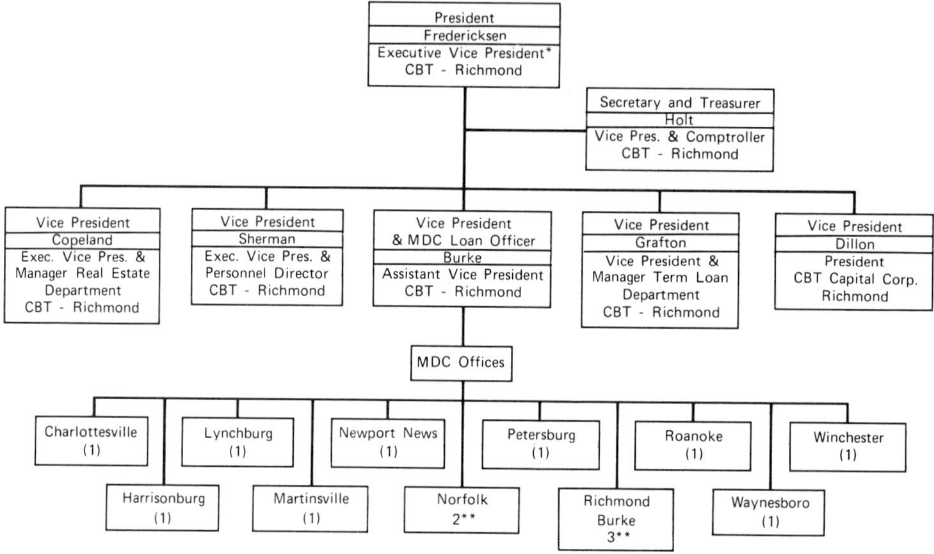

*In July 1971, Fredericksen was promoted to executive vice president.

**Full-time professional staff members. Numbers in parentheses indicate part-time staff.

Source: Researcher's interview notes.

Case Thirteen

The Metropolitan Development Corporation (B)

In October 1972, responsibility for MDC was reassigned from the Public Affairs Department to the Term Loan Department, and Burke, who was in charge of MDC's operations, began reporting to Frank Simm, Senior Vice President and head of Term Loan (see Exhibit 13-1). It was generally conceded that the best source of supervision for commercial lending to small minority businesses could be found in the corporate accounts area of the Term Loan Department. Through this reorganization top management in the bank hoped that MDC would have access to greater expertise in credit analysis, thus making it more responsive to its clients. Fredericksen noted:

> One immediate benefit of being tied to the Small Business area is MDC's participation in the weekly Term Loan credit committees. This gives MDC's lending officers a chance to perform for a larger group and get some recognition as well as advice. Also, a person from the Credit Department sits in; that and the credit rating system helps assure us of greater consistency in our lending policies.

Fredericksen continued to coordinate the operations of MDC. He also represented its activities to the community at large. For example, in October 1972, he cited its "track record of 216 going businesses, approximately 300 new homeowners, and 5 demonstration housing developments":

> Only 30 businesses have failed and there have been only 6 mortgage foreclosures. We believe two factors have contributed to the success record: first, the Metropolitan Development Corporation works without any type of government guarantees; there's no one to "bail us out" if a loan goes sour. This ties directly to the second reason: management assistance. Every effort is made to assist the businessman and to lend financial and operational know-how through on-the-spot counselling. Volunteers drawn from the bank's management training school are assigned to each business to provide assistance when requested.

PERSONNEL CHANGES

In November 1972, Stephen Cole, Senior Vice President, was designated the officer in charge of the Term Loan Department, replacing Simm, who in turn assumed responsibilities for the Corporate Banking Department. The following month, Burke, who had headed up MDC operationally, was replaced by Allan Fuller, Commercial Officer, who had been in the Term Loan Department for two years and had most recently directed the Enterprise Term Loan area. In this capacity he had specialized in lending to small businesses and entrepreneurs. Earlier, Fuller had specialized in credit analysis.

One of Fuller's first priorities was the "clean-up" of MDC's loan portfolio. A number of the loans booked in earlier years had been chronically delinquent, and a conscious effort was undertaken to realign the loan portfolio so as to purge these dubious credits. By February 1, 1973, cumulative charge-offs since the inception of MDC had mounted to a total of $753,240. Of this amount, $501,000 had been written off in Norfolk, and $160,000 in Richmond. In part, these charge-offs (totaling over $600,000 in 1972 alone) were a consequence of Fuller's plan to "improve the quality" of the MDC loan portfolio. This objective, along with the goals of increasing the volume of loans outstanding and developing business through the cross-selling of other bank services, formed the basis for his broad strategy for MDC's operations in 1973. In a March 7, 1973 statement of goals for MDC, specific objectives were established in these areas as indicated in Table 13-1.

1973 OPERATIONS

By May 1, 1973, there were indications of progress in MDC's drive to improve the quality of its loan portfolio. In a "rated loan" report which reviewed all commercial credits over $5,000 where there was a potential loss or need for continuous attention, it was noted that "total rated loans dropped in dollars and as a percentage of total outstandings. . . ." This was also partially attributable to increasing loan volume and the charge-off of previously rated loans. (See Table 13-2 for MDC's rated loan trend.)

REASSESSMENT OF MDC

In May 1973, Cole approached Gordon Kuhnemann, Vice President in charge of CBT Holding Company's leasing subsidiary, with a request that he head up a task force of seven persons to evaluate the accomplishments, shortcomings, capitalization, and financing of MDC and prepare appropriate recommendations for top management. The composition of this task force was thought to represent a broad cross-section of the bank: there were Richmond and non-Richmond managers, blacks and females, and commercial and retail managers involved.

Cole said:

When I first came in to Term Loan, there had been a number of changes made in MDC. As a consequence, we began to see more and more people in the bank not knowing what MDC was all about. Because of this, I asked Gordon Kuhnemann to head up a strategy team for the purpose of assessing MDC and its goals. It was clear to us that the situation in 1973 was a lot different from that in 1968.

TABLE 13-1 MDC ACTUAL DATA FOR 1972 AND GOALS FOR 1973*

Objectives (and indicators)	*1972 Actual*	*1973 Goals*
I. Improve the quality of the MDC portfolio		
A. Ratio of dollar past due loans/outstandings	18.0%**	10.0%
B. Ratio of dollar rated*** loans/outstandings	20.4%†	19.0%
C. Ratio of dollar charge-offs/outstandings	27.6%††	5.2%
II. Increase the amount of help we provide businessmen and homeowners		
A. Commercial		
Richmond	$300(20)	N.A.
Outside Richmond	150(10)	N.A.
Total	$450(30)	$1,796(186)
B. Real Estate		
Richmond	$200(66)	N.A.
Outside Richmond	250(83)	N.A.
Total	$450(149)	779(294)
Grand Total	$900(179)	$2,575(480)

*Dollar amounts in thousands. Numbers of loans in parentheses.
**Last 5 months of 1972.
***"Rated" loans were "trouble" credits, or considered to be potential charge-offs, thus requiring special attention and follow-up.
†As of February 1, 1973.
††Based on outstandings at year end.
N.A.–Not available

TABLE 13-2 MDC'S RATED LOANS FOR FEBRUARY AND MAY 1973

	Feb. 1, 1973	*May 1, 1973*
Total Loans	$2,609,022	$2,979,576
Rated Loans	531,483	528,671
% Rated Loans to Total Loans	20.37%	17.74%
Number of Rated Obligations	22	20

Fuller also had been concerned about the operations of MDC, and after six months in charge of both its system-wide operations and the Richmond office, he presented an analysis of its activities to Cole, with a copy to Kuhnemann and his task force. In a June

1973 memorandum he noted that in MDC cities other than Richmond and Norfolk, existing loan volume did not justify the assignment of a full-time loan officer. Although a "coordinator" was designated to file reports, the responsibility for making and servicing MDC loans did not rest entirely with him. Other commercial lending officers were assigned specific MDC loans for servicing and had authority to make such loans. According to Fuller, this often resulted in several problems:

> 1.–Existing accounts do not receive proper attention because the officers' primary functions demand more time.
> 2.–MDC loans are frequently assigned to inexperienced management associates because these credits are normally smaller in dollar amount.
> 3.–Insufficient control is maintained over MDC accounts because I lack direct authority over the account officers and coordinators.
> 4.–Minimal contact is maintained in the black community because MDC is not a primary full-time function and does not receive a personal commitment.

Fuller suggested that the above problems might be overcome by the implementation of a "circuit rider" concept. An experienced lender, located in a central office such as Roanoke, could serve that central city as well as other CBT offices in neighboring communities. He would have direct responsibility for the MDC portfolio in his area and report to Fuller in Richmond. The "circuit rider" would thus be free to devote his time to problem loans and the development of contacts in black communities.

Fuller wrote:

> By making [the circuit rider position] a full-time job under my authority, we could more easily ensure that proper control is maintained over a portfolio, and that the proper amount of interest and expertise is available. Furthermore, we could generate goodwill and loan referrals for the Metropolitan Development Corporation by freeing loan officers from what is generally considered a distasteful task. Lastly, we could more easily determine total administrative expenses. The results should be a greater contribution to the community, more and better loans for MDC, increased credibility and goodwill, and a more smoothly run organization.

Mindful of the organizational implications of his proposal, Fuller noted that his concept might "deprive" the executive vice president for a city of his community action responsibility. Acknowledging that this would be undesirable, he suggested that the circuit rider idea should not be forced on any executive vice president who found it unacceptable. In general, however, Fuller felt the circuit rider concept would in all likelihood be welcomed by officers throughout the system:

> [The executive officer] would not have to relinquish any community involvement, but would merely use the MDC man to do business in a manner similar to the way the Trust Department circuit rider has been used. The EVP or president would be measured by and awarded recognition for the number of referrals his office provided. Of course, his office would continue to receive checking account balances and any other services that might be sold. If his only responsibility is finding good deals and not worrying over workouts, he may be stimulated to produce more business.

IMPROVEMENTS IN OPERATIONS

In the meantime, more funds were needed to support a loan volume that was expanding in accordance with projections. Based on this and further indications of improvement of the quality of MDC's loan portfolio, top management of the bank in June 1973 authorized the infusion of another $1.1 million in capital. (Also in June, several of the bank's black employees walked out on strike, alleging racial discrimination. Even though the strike lasted until September 7, it did not materially impair bank operations.)

Further confirmation of an improving credit situation at MDC was documented during the week ending July 13 when a credit examination of MDC's loan portfolio was conducted by internal auditors. All borrowing relationships totalling $5,000 or more were reviewed as well as those debt situations in which past due loans were involved. Of the $3,443,601 in loans outstanding, loans totalling $2,312,314 (67% of the total loan portfolio) were examined. In a statement of condition, the examiner disclosed the data shown in Table 13-3. The total portfolio had increased 16% in volume, from $2,950,000 to $3,444,000 over the past year. At the same time, both demand and time loans were decreasing in number, amount, and as a percentage of the portfolio. The greatest growth was found to be in real estate loans with a 73% increase in volume from 1972 to 1973. By and large, this was attributed to the considerable success of the MDC office in Norfolk. It had experienced a delinquency rate of only about 5% of outstanding loans, and charge-offs were considered negligible. In this office in particular business lending had been deemphasized in favor of first- and second-mortgage loans.

TABLE 13-3 MDC'S LOAN PORTFOLIO AS OF JUNE 30

	1972			*1973*		
Loan Type	*No.*	*Amount*	*%*	*No.*	*Amount*	*%*
Demand	24	$ 102,073	3	2	$ 41,361	1
Time	57	615,774	21	40	256,545	7
Term	160	1,460,495	50	150	1,813,177	53
Real Estate	274	771,854	26	343	1,332,518	39
Grand Total	515	$2,950,196	100%	535	$3,443,601	100%

For MDC as a whole, a dramatic turnaround had been achieved in charge-offs as evidenced by an analysis of the charge-off and recovery experience on all MDC loans from 1970 through the first six months of 1973. From a charge-off ratio of .84% in 1970, losses had increased to over 26% in 1972, but in the first six months of 1973, recoveries had actually exceeded charge-offs, as shown in Table 13-4. This was believed to stem largely from the heavy write-offs deliberately taken in 1972 and intensified collection efforts mounted in 1973.

The credit examiner also made a number of more general comments about the overall structure and operations of MDC. It was noted, for example, that "management is now

TABLE 13-4 MDC CHARGE-OFFS AND RECOVERIES FOR ALL LOANS

	1970	*1971*	*1972*	*1973 (thru June)*
Amount Charged off	14,670	155,544	602,700	42,259
Recovery	41	–	7,852	58,120
Charge-Off, Net of Recovery	14,629	155,544	594,848	(15,861)
Avg. Loan Outstanding Less Unearned Interest & Participations Purchased from CBT	$1,731,325	$2,423,141	$2,242,046	$2,334,046
Charge-Offs as a % of Avg. Outstanding Less Unearned Interest & Participations Purchased	.84%	6.42%	26.53%	–

exercising more caution in making MDC loans." This resulted in the more recent loans being of a better quality.

The examiner observed further that only in Richmond and Norfolk was the MDC operation large enough to warrant assigning MDC as the primary responsibility of one or more individuals. In the other offices, responsibility for MDC was of secondary importance, and the program did "not appear to fare as well" or "receive the impetus" that it did in Richmond and Norfolk. Consequently, the lending personnel of these larger offices appeared "attuned to the needs of their customers" and had a "good concept of the lending philosophy of MDC," while the outlying offices were only "holding the line" or giving "limited attention" to the MDC program.

Moreover, in the area of communications, the examiner found a general need for defining or redefining MDC policy in terms of the overall goals of the program and specifically the type loans to be sought and the degree of diversion from standard lending procedures to be permissible. Since it was the bank's policy to "try to find a way to meet any loan request," there remained "only a very small area left between a bankable lending situation and a loan which should not be made by any agency."

TAKING THE LID OFF

By July 1973, the bank had so exhausted its supply of loanable funds bank-wide that the decision was made to cut back all loan portfolios 10% through attrition rather than seek more high-cost purchased funds in the money markets. But shortly thereafter, on August 10, Rhodes notified Fuller that he would "like to take the lid off MDC loans" and make a "special effort to go after quality MDC loans." Subsequently, on August 15, Fuller distributed to all senior lending officers throughout the bank and MDC office coordinators the following memorandum:

> The bank-wide lending curtailment has been in effect for slightly over one month. Until now the Metropolitan Development Corporation has been expected to adhere to the cutback policy.
>
> Jeff Rhodes believes the objectives of MDC are important enough to justify an exception in this lending area. Therefore, he is releasing MDC from the general lending prohibition and is directing us to make a special effort to make good quality MDC loans.
>
> We are seeking small (under $50,000) term loans (less than seven years) primarily, but not exclusively, to minority-owned businesses, that would finance start-up situations, acquisitions, or expansions. The borrower must be strong in integrity, motivation, and experience, but he is not expected to be able to provide the normal capital investment or security. Obviously, he should show a good market and strong profit potential. We also want to expand our business in financing down payments for the purchase of low cost (under $30,000) housing.
>
> Our capital base has recently been increased by $1,100,000. Emory Clarkson, our staff accountant, and I are ready and willing to do anything we can to help your office put on some good business.

Nevertheless, reaction throughout the system was minimal. The Richmond office prepared and analyzed month-end lending volume reports comparing 1973 and 1972 year-to-date data. As shown in these reports, in addition to the existence of very uneven lending performance among MDC offices, there were indications that loan activity was actually declining in some of the offices. (See Exhibit 13-2 for August's month-end data.)

Exhibit 13-1

PARTIAL ORGANIZATION CHART—OCTOBER 1972

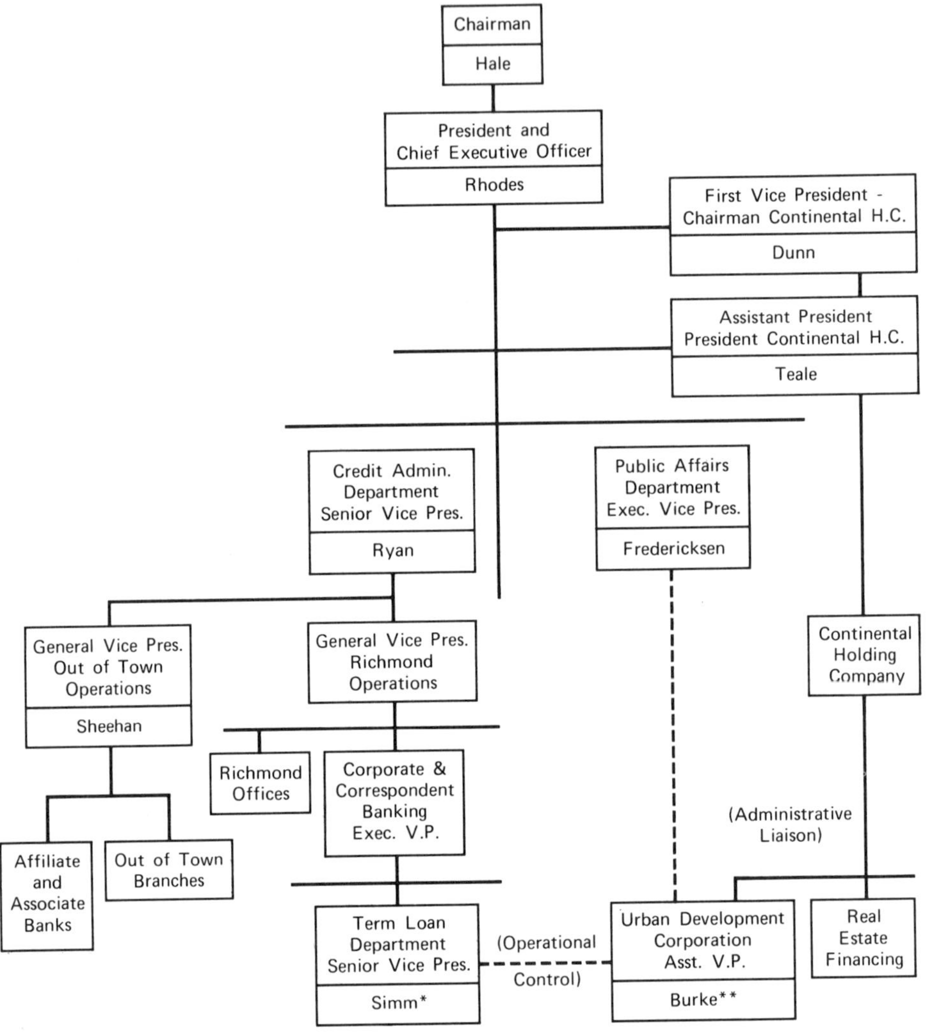

*Until November 1972, then Cole.
**Until November 1972, then Fuller.
Source: Researcher's interview notes.

Exhibit 13-2

DATA FROM MDC'S MONTH-END VOLUME REPORT FOR AUGUST 1973

		Volume			
		1972 Year-to-Date		1973 Year-to-Date	
		No.	Amount	No.	Amount
Charlottesville	– total	6	$ 71,159	–	$ –
	rejections	3	105,000	–	–
Harrisonburg	– total	–	–	1	16,900
	rejections	–	–	–	–
Lynchburg	– total	1	1,126	1	1,669
	rejections	–	–	–	–
Martinsville	– total	5	9,637	7	63,193
	– rejections	–	–	–	–
Newport	– total	7	17,797	–	–
News	– rejections	–	–	–	–
Norfolk	– total	94	422,593	173	1,198,769
	– rejections	17	129,039	12	83,950
Petersburg	– total	2	11,986	4	27,970
	– rejections	–	–	–	–
Richmond	– total	55	448,624	77	795,302
	– rejections	61	1,291,700	N.A.	N.A.
Roanoke	– total	3	32,784	2	54,009
	– rejections	–	–	–	–
Waynesboro	– total	4	18,496	2	6,949
	– rejections	–	–	–	–
Winchester	– total	1	4,044	–	–
	– rejections	–	–	–	–
Grand Total Loan Values		177	$1,034,202	284	$2,164,761

N.A.–Not available
Source: Corporate records.

Case Fourteen

The Metropolitan Development Corporation (C)

During the late spring of 1973, Fredericksen became convinced of the desirability of a bank-wide inventory and performance report on community-related activities to identify areas in which the bank was active and measure the magnitude of its social contributions. A professor from a nearby graduate school of management was engaged as consultant to perform the audit. Working throughout the summer, he and the Public Affairs staff developed a report that showed 1972 cash expenditures by sources and uses. Whereas precise measurement of costs was professed to be a problem, it was estimated that at least $1.1 million had been expended. Of that total, $632,000, or 58%, was accounted for by charitable contributions dispersed through the CBT Fund, $255,000, or 24%, represented costs incurred by the Public Affairs Department (including the salaries of MDC personnel), and $56,000, or 5%, was attributable to loan losses absorbed by MDC.

The consultant noted that the actual cost to the bank's stockholders necessarily included the associated opportunity costs. Depending on the rate used (estimated to be between the bank's average lending rate adjusted for taxes and its after-tax rate of return on equity), he concluded that the bank's stockholders had "given up no less than $1.1 million and no more than $1.7 million in 1972 in order to engage in activities for the benefit of society." This represented between 4.5% and 7% of the bank's net operating earnings before securities gains and losses for the year.

The report was submitted to Rhodes and executive management on September 13. At that time, the following recommendations concerning the bank's "citizenship program" were made:

1.–Rhodes should "enunciate the policy of involvement and indicate his direct commitment to having it carried out."[1]

2.–Action programs for citizenship activities should be formulated and carried out by branches and departments.

[1]Up to this point, in keeping with management's orientation toward informality, there had been no written statement of social policy promulgated within the bank.

3.–Evaluation of "civic performance" should be made at the end of each year.

4.–Promotions, bonuses, and other benefits should "take into consideration . . . civic performance as well as . . . profit performance."

No specific actions were taken as a result of the audit report other than to plan for another audit of 1973's social performance.

THE MDC TASK FORCE REPORT

On October 30, 1973, after a five month investigation, the task force headed by Kuhnemann[2], submitted its 35-page report to Cole, Simm, Fredericksen, Rhodes, and other members of senior management. Although the MDC was evaluated as having made some solid contributions to the communities it served, three prominent shortcomings were found to have culminated in a "serious lack of cooperation and support for MDC around the system."

1.–*Low volume*. In most cities, emphasis on minority enterprise loans generally had been "sporadic." Several reasons were cited: (a) loan officers tended to generate MDC loans only when "under pressure" to do so, and top management had not supplied sufficient incentives or applied enough emphasis regularly; (b) goals had not been defined specifically and communicated throughout the system, especially to loan officers; and (c) there had been inadequate external communication of MDC's operations to the minority community and others who could favorably influence the program's atmosphere by referring good prospective borrowers.

2.–*Poor credit judgment*. Both the low number of loans and the large number of charge-offs suggested a general lack of expertise in committing loans and servicing clients. Although charge-offs for real estate loans had been virtually nil, $811,000, or 21% of MDC's cumulative dollar business loan volume, had been charged off over the course of the past five years (see Exhibit 14-1). It was noted that MDC had been staffed by relatively inexperienced lending personnel. In most areas of the state, the MDC administrator had been a management associate with little or no knowledge of commercial lending. In Richmond the MDC administrator was currently an experienced loan officer, but junior personnel had been inexperienced. This situation had in part led to the high charge-off ratio experienced by MDC.

3.–*Insufficient coaching*. Many MDC loans required specialized help in such areas as accounting, legal, and marketing, which, with few exceptions, MDC had not had the capability to provide.

The task force had also conducted structured interviews with the designated MDC officers and the area executive officers in each CBT branch bank city and all affiliate banks outside the Richmond area. In summary, their survey revealed that:

---

[2] See Metropolitan Development Corporation (B).

> . . . in most cities regard for the MDC program is low. In fact, informal conversations between committee members and staff personnel other than questionnaire respondents indicate a serious and widespread feeling that the program is not worthwhile. Moreover, operational procedures are not consistent.

More specifically, over half of the respondents felt that specialized legal and accounting assistance should be made available to MDC customers. They also indicated that such management assistance was usually lacking because of a shortage of staff time and expertise. Moreover, while management associates were usually assigned to MDC activities because it was "good training," it was generally conceded that MDC lending personnel should be the "most capable people in the bank" because equity type loans were the "most difficult ones to make."

Exacerbating the problems associated with the assignment of relatively inexperienced lending officers to MDC loans was the frequent discontinuity found in the servicing of the loans, from initial receipt of applications through processing and collection. In several instances it was found that an application was processed by any lender or a designated MDC person and then the approved loan was passed on to another person for follow-up and collection.

Finally, a number of respondents suggested that top management emphasis be increased by making minority lending activities a part of the performance appraisal of each executive officer who supervised lenders. This had not been done in the past, and the lack of enthusiasm for MDC programs among lenders was believed to reflect the degree of emphasis given MDC lending by the bank's executive officers.

Following a discussion of the lending programs of other banks and the SBA, the task force recommended the following changes:

1.–The missions and goals of the MDC should be stated "more crisply" and communicated clearly to all employees, particularly all loan officers.

2.–In order to place greater emphasis on minority lending activities "each executive officer supervising MDC personnel should accept specific goals and be measured by attainment of these goals."

3.–The program should continue to be operated independently of other banks to ensure control, but outside specialists should be engaged as needed in counseling clients.

4.–a. All MDC loan officers should be "well-rounded in financial analysis and other aspects of credit" as well as experienced in commercial lending. In addition, MDC personnel "should be made aware that the department can be . . . part of their career growth, and these personnel should be 'promotable' within MDC and not just after they have left the department."

b. Where full-time MDC administrators could not be justified, "circuit-rider" administrators should be assigned who would report to the local executive officers.

5.–Each executive officer supervising a MDC administrator should agree at the beginning of each year with top management on a target level of outstanding loans for the executive officer's city, and that agreement could help form the basis for the MDC portion of his performance appraisal at the end of the year.

6.–Since MDC never had been profitable and was unlikely ever to be profitable on a fully allocated cost basis, the uncontrollable cost of funds should be split out and MDC objectives set in terms of achieving a "break-even." Personnel expenses should be included as part of the overhead to be charged to the local MDC offices, and since they were "at least partially controllable by the department," used in performance appraisal.

7.–Participation with the SBA should be initiated so that in the event of loan losses, guarantees would increase the loanable funds available for reinvestment. The guaranteed portions of the loans should be used as pledges against certain secured deposits of the bank, including the treasury tax and loan account. This procedure would permit some of the bank's securities portfolio currently pledged to be replaced by guaranteed portions of loans, thus providing more liquidity for the bank.

8.–The services offered by MDC should be promoted throughout the black community, including real estate groups, attorneys and other business leaders, as well as among packaging houses and governmental agencies.

Exhibit 14-1

VOLUME AND CHARGE-OFF REPORT
INCEPTION THROUGH SEPTEMBER 18, 1973

City	O/S[1] #	Vol. #	C/O[2] #	%	O/S $	Vol. $	C/O $	%
BUSINESS LOANS								
Charlottesville	13	21	4	19	164,355	186,927	37,220	20
Harrisonburg	1	1	–	–	15,210	13,000	–	–
Lynchburg	4	11	1	9	3,738	17,678	777	4
Martinsville	6	4	1	25	59,191	56,341	1,120	2
Newsport News	15	20	6	30	159,830	412,184	45,418	11
Norfolk	49	60	25	42	308,510	1,495,885	505,644	34
Petersburg	12	14	3	21	66,754	123,576	27,441	22
Richmond	82	94	23	24	1,163,309	1,426,741	191,087	13
Roanoke	7	11	2	18	91,297	142,114	2,111	1
Waynesboro	3	3	–	–	34,361	34,178	–	–
Winchester	2	3	1	33	4,290	9,095	656	7
	195	240	66	28	2,070,845	3,874,286	811,474	21
REAL ESTATE LOANS								
Charlottesville	1	3	–	–	9,230	13,700	–	–
Lynchburg	–	2	–	–	–	7,300	–	–
Martinsville	28	31	–	–	34,797	46,257	–	–
Newport News	1	2	–	–	751	3,546	–	–
Norfolk	282	297	1	–	1,302,391	942,243	1,901	–
Petersburg	5	5	–	–	101,070	32,213	–	–
Richmond	36	42	1	2	133,864	170,750	2,975	2
Roanoke	7	9	2	22	63,789	65,781	3,657	6
Winchester	1	6	–	–	12,301	15,000	–	–
	361	397	4	1	1,658,193	1,296,790	5,558	–
Total Business & Real Estate	556	637	70	11	3,729,038	5,171,076	817,032	16

[1]O/S–Outstanding
[2]C/O–Charge-Off
Source: Corporate records

Average Loan Size
Business $16,143
Real Estate 8,118

Case Fifteen

The Metropolitan Development Corporation (D)

On December 18, in a letter to Kuhnemann, Fredericksen responded to the task force report on MDC. Whereas he was surprised that some senior officers would interpret MDC's efforts as merely a public relations gesture and a "giveaway," he did acknowledge problems of credibility which had led to a degree of system-wide apathy:

> I believe this has happened because of negative feelings created because of our heavy losses, a general change of attitude throughout the bank and the country toward programs and activities such as MDC, and a lack of visible top management continuing commitment being interpreted as a lessening of commitment. Further, I think our performance goals and incentive system create a conflict of goals (MDC loans vs. losses and community projects vs. earnings). Jeff [Rhodes] has been giving some thought to how these conflicts might be best resolved.

With regard to the recommendation that circuit riders be used, Fredericksen thought that "this would be a step in the wrong direction." It would present an easy way for executive officers in each city to "pass the responsibility" instead of increasing both their commitment and participation.

Addressing the question of SBA participation, Fredericksen cited recent controversy surrounding the SBA as evidence to reinforce management's belief that many banks used government guarantees for the wrong reasons.[1] Enumerated as additional negative factors were the "political pressures, the 'crutch' syndrome, and the additional administrative burdens (paperwork and bureaucratic entanglement). . . ." Additionally, Fredericksen felt that there was a "negative relationship" created between the lending officer and the customer, and that between two problem loans–one guaranteed and one not–the lending officer and the support staff of the bank would tend to concentrate harder on saving the nonguaranteed loan. He still was not convinced that the bank should participate with the SBA.

---

[1]During the spring of 1974 several regional officers of the SBA were being investigated for alleged conflicts of interest in the approval of loans.

With respect to MDC profitability, Fredericksen noted that the bank's policy had been to underwrite the operating cost of MDC and have the loan income applied against losses, real estate development projects, and specific expenses related to MDC loans (filing fees, etc.). This was done because management "fully recognized that the administrative costs and other operating expenses would be greater than the loan income without even considering loan losses." If all expenses were applied to MDC, the bank constantly would have to add more capital—"an exercise that would not make sense from the tax standpoint or any other."

In January 1974, Cole, Senior Vice President in charge of the Term Loan Department, commented on the MDC task force report:

> One of the most positive aspects of the report, in my opinion, is the recommendation that specific goals be set for MDC type loans in our various offices. What I've been trying to get Jeff [Rhodes] to do, and what he's doing for the first time this year, is set goals for MDC-types of loans by office location.
>
> Our big problem has been that this past year both Jeff Rhodes and Ted Sheehan[2] have been telling our offices not to make new loans, reduce their credit losses, and get more deposits. At the same time, we in MDC are telling them to make loans they generally wouldn't make even under normal circumstances. What we're saying goes directly against the other three directives from top management, but their bonuses and salary increases are based on those three things.
>
> Their response is, "What you're telling me to do is contrary to what my boss is telling me to do!" Jeff Rhodes understands this, and now I think they've got a proper incentive. We will be asking them to establish and meet specific goals for MDC loans.
>
> Since Jim Hale retired, MDC has not been as visible throughout the system. The only part of MDC that people outside Richmond saw was the MDC monthly charge-off report by our Credit Department. People would just shake their heads and say, "My gosh, they're charging off another $50,000 this month. Last month they charged off $50,000 and last year they charged off $600,000!"

Rhodes, President of CBT, also remarked on the report in the course of a discussion centering on MDC and its operations:

> We've made a lot of mistakes, and one of these was getting carried away by some of our early successes. Although we learned our lesson in MDC, we lost a ton of money doing it. One mistake was in using our least experienced people instead of those with the most experience.
>
> . . . This year, 1974, part and parcel of our executive officers' goals will be a citizenship project for their respective communities and specific objectives in

---

[2]Edward Sheehan, General Vice President in charge of all offices in the state outside Richmond.

MDC-type loans. These will also form a portion of their performance review and evaluation which we will be establishing for the upcoming year. Unless you make it part of their goals, it gets lost in their list of priorities.

. . . The only problem with this recent report on the MDC was the suggestion that we use SBA guarantees. Frankly, a government guarantee doesn't make a bad loan any better, and the SBA is just too cumbersome to deal with administratively. If they would be willing to grant us a $25 million line of guaranteed credit, I'd accept the guarantee–just as long as we were free to manage the actual loans ourselves. From recent published accounts, we estimate that we can do better in terms of delinquencies and charge-offs than SBA-guaranteed programs.

1973 YEAR-END RESULTS FOR MDC

On January 25, 1974, Fuller submitted a memorandum to senior management reporting the lending performance of MDC for 1973. Overall loan volume had exceeded the year's goals by 19%, and, as illustrated in Table 15-1, total outstandings had increased 55.3%, with commercial loans rising by 28.8% and real estate loans by 116%.

TABLE 15-1 OUTSTANDING MDC LOANS AS OF DECEMBER 31

	1972		*1973*	
	No.	*$*	*No.*	*$*
Commercial Loans	186	$1,796,648	214	$2,314,367
Real Estate Loans	294	778,717	364	1,685,479
Total	480	$2,575,365	578	$3,999,846

However, uneven performance among the various MDC offices was still evident, and Fuller addressed himself to this when he wrote, in part:

It should be noted that Norfolk and Martinsville were the only MDC offices active in real estate lending in 1973. Norfolk, in particular; should be commended for its efforts.

Martinsville and Richmond were the only MDC offices with substantial increases in commercial business, and we encourage other offices to become more involved in making good quality commercial loans, as well as down payment residential real estate loans. . . .

In addition to growth in volume, progress had been achieved in reducing charge-offs. For 1973, net charge-offs as a percentage of average outstandings were 2.1%. This compared favorably with the ratio of net charge-offs to cumulative net outstandings from 1968 through 1973 of 15.1% (See Table 15-2.)

TABLE 15-2 METROPOLITAN DEVELOPMENT CORPORATION CHARGE-OFFS AND RECOVERIES FOR ALL LOANS

	1970	*1971*	*1972*	*1973*	*Cumulative Total*
Net Charge-Offs	$ 14,629	$ 155,544	$ 594,848	$ 69,345	$ 834,366
Average Loans Outstanding Less Unearned Interest & Participations Purchased	$1,731,325	$2,423,141	$2,242,046	$3,353,216	$5,542,602
Net Charge-Offs as a % of Avg. Loans Outstanding	.84%	6.42%	26.53%	2.10%	15.10%

LOOKING AHEAD

Despite the progress made in 1973, forecasts for 1974 did not look promising. On projected average outstanding loans of $4 million, gross charge-offs of $306,000 or 7.6%, were anticipated. Fuller stressed that "these are . . . problems that have had our attention for some time; nevertheless, our highest priority for 1974 should be to provide even closer attention to our potential losses and problem situations."

Past due loans also loomed as a potential problem. Despite efforts during 1973 to achieve a ratio of 10% past dues on dollar outstandings, they had averaged approximately 12%. Furthermore, since August, there had been a "worsening trend" so that by the end of the year, $573,000 in loans, or 14% of outstandings, were past due. Despite what were viewed as "more serious credit problems" in 1974, MDC would attempt to keep past dues at or below 12%.

Rated loans had been kept to an average of 18.6% of outstandings for the year versus MDC's goal of 19%. However, in the fourth quarter of the year, rated loans had increased by $159,000 to $774,486, so that rated loans as a percentage of outstandings had increased from 16.8% in the third quarter to 19.6% in the fourth quarter.

By the end of 1973, it had also become clear that new pressures for improved financial performance had developed throughout the entire bank. Net charge-offs within the CBT's regular commercial and real estate loan portfolios had been unexpectedly heavy for the year, representing a 125% increase over 1972's write-offs. These losses had in part been responsible for a 5% decline in CBT's net income before securities gains and losses, marking the first downturn in earnings in over 15 years. Top management believed that two important contributory factors were to be found in the relative youthfulness and inexperience of the bank's lending officers and their rapid internal mobility (both of which were attributed to the bank's rapid growth and expansion.) The frequent reassignment of personnel often led to discontinuities in credit relationships with customers which in turn sometimes hampered appropriate follow-up and loan servicing.

Top management had moved to cope with the perceived lack of experience in their branch lending personnel by creating in August a new layer of supervisors known as "zone managers" in the Richmond area. These executives were seasoned branch managers who were made responsible for five or six neighboring banking offices in addition to their own branches. The managers reported for their zones directly to the head of all Richmond offices.

To deal with inadequate loan servicing and follow-up, senior management beefed up its credit administrative function. Rhodes authorized the formation of four two-person teams to aggressively pursue and retrieve, or "work out," the bank's loss situations. These teams were to report directly to the head of the Credit Department. Fuller, described by one executive as "one of the best young scramblers in the bank," was chosen as the senior member of one team. The other member of that team was from the Public Affairs Department staff.

THE SECOND SOCIAL AUDIT

By late January, the consultant to the Public Affairs Department had compiled the data necessary for an audit of the bank's social performance during 1973 (see Exhibit 15-1.) Despite some noncomparability of figures from one year to the next, preliminary data showed that total expenditures for social programs had increased by 11%, from about \$1.1 million in 1972 to approximately \$1.2 million in 1973. However, community development projects, over which system executive officers and presidents of affiliate banks had primary control, were found to have decreased from \$96,990 in 1972 to \$72,297 in 1973, a decline of 25%.

On the other hand, expenditures of the Public Affairs Department–largely administrative expenses, but including some program expenses–had increased 41%, from about \$255,000 in 1972 to approximately \$360,000 in 1973. It appeared that whereas overall dollar expenditures for social programs in the bank's communities were increasing, outlying offices and branches were reducing their participation at the same time those expenses controlled by the Public Affairs Department were increasing.

Exhibit 15-1

SUMMARY OF CBT CITIZENSHIP EXPENDITURES

	1973	*1972*	*% Change*
SOURCE OF EXPENDITURES			
CBT Fund	\$ 537,179	\$ 631,925	- 15%
Community Development Projects	72,297	96,990	- 25%
Other Contributions	16,514	Not Avail.	
Metropolitan Development Corp.	76,680+	56,260	
Public Affairs Department	359,568†	254,914	+ 41%
Tuition Refunds	27,787	30,400	- 9%
Educational Assistance Program	12,767	Not Avail.	
Matching Educational Grants	31,919	14,869	+115%
Hale Chairs in Banking	74,500	Not Avail.	
TOTAL	\$1,209,211*	\$1,085,358	+ 11%

SUMMARY OF CBT CITIZENSHIP EXPENDITURES (continued)

	CBT Fund	*Community Development*	*Contributions*	*MDC*	*Public Affairs*
USE OF EXPENDITURES					
Health & Welfare	$231,987	$ 6,300	$ 3,034	$–0–	$ 8,208
Education	196,204	1,169	3,557	–0–	15,167
Culture	25,295	–0–	1,550	–0–	1,800
Civic Causes	52,175	33,828	4,635	32,206++	12,995
Religion	21,868	–0–	815	–0–	5,450
Business Organizations	4,600	31,000	2,848	44,474++	38,500
Other	5,050	–0–	75	–0–	13,596
TOTAL	$537,179	$72,297	$16,514	$76,680	
Administration					$263,852
TOTAL					$359,568

	Educational Assistance	*Tuition*	*Educational Grants*	*Hale Chairs*	*Total 1973*	*Percentage*	*Total 1972*	
Health & Welfare	$–0–	$–0–			$ 249,529	21%	$ 246,006	23%
Education	12,767	27,787	$31,919	$74,500	363,070	30%	396,749	36%
Culture	–0–	–0–			28,645	2%	12,288	1%
Civic Causes	–0–	–0–			135,839	11%	96,524	9%
Religion	–0–	–0–			28,133	2%	12,288	1%
Business Organizations	–0–	–0–			121,422	10%	35,017	3%**
Other	–0–	–0–			18,721	2%	298,774	–0–
TOTAL	$12,767	$27,787	$31,919	$74,500			$1,085,358	
Administration					$ 263,852	22%		27%
TOTAL					$1,209,211	100%		100%

+Change in reporting techniques make these figures not comparable. The 1972 figure is based on direct cash outflows only, whereas the 1973 figure is the operating loss reported by the CBT Comptroller for that department.

†The 1973 figure is composed of 95,716 of community development expenses and the $263,852 of administrative expenses. The 1972 figure is composed of $47,465 community development expense and $207,449 of administrative expenses.

*Inclusion of two programs not previously reported (Educational Assistance Program, $12,767, and Hale Chairs in Banking, $74,500) and more comprehensive reporting of expenditures by Correspondent Associates cause 1973 figures to show an unwarranted increase over 1972 figures. Because of these changes, the two years are not directly comparable.

++MDC loans were made for residential or commercial purposes as of December 31, 1973. The portfolio consisted of 214 commercial loans for $2,314,367 (58%) and 364 residential loans for $1,685,479 (42%). MDC loss was allocated 58% to business organizations and 42% to civic causes.

**The main vehicle for contributions to business organizations is the Community Development Expense Account of Departments 510 and 943. In 1972, records are not available to allocate this according to use. As a result, this amount ($38,500 in 1973) was not broken out of the public affairs department expenses, all of which was shown in the "Other" column.

Source: Corporate records.

Chapter Five

Assessing Performance

Information is essential for effective managerial action. However, the established information systems used for monitoring performance in divisionalized companies focus on financial performance. They do not report centrally on waste emissions, safe working conditions, equal employment opportunity, or community relations activities. To some extent this picture is changing as executives find it necessary to develop assessment systems to supplement the system of financial reporting.

At the same time, activist reformers—and to a lesser extent investors—are seeking information on the social performance of corporations for purposes of litigation, moral suasion, or the granting of good or bad publicity. The cases which follow are centrally concerned with these issues, but they also will be found running through many of the cases throughout the book.

In the Eastern Gas and Fuel Associates case, Goldston tells of the difficulty of getting good data on the status of minority employees in just one of his operating companies in the late sixties. He was told that there were four minority employees of the gas company. "Persisting, I then discovered that the four included myself, because I was Jewish; an Irish fellow who was dating a Chinese girl; and a black fellow who had retired a few years back. The fourth was never found."

In 1970 when the Council on Economic Priorities measured the pollution control performance of a number of paper companies, several of the companies were surprised—some favorably and some unfavorably—by the findings for their own firms. Until the early years of the seventies, very few corporate executives of large firms (we actually know of none) would have had a detailed picture of their firm's social performance, and many find the picture deficient to this very day.

THE CORPORATE SOCIAL AUDIT

Beginning in 1971, the concept of a corporate social audit got a good deal of attention very rapidly. It was said that within five years or so firms would report their social performance as formally and as regularly as they report their financial performance.[1] Rather elaborate and ambitious proposals were made for "social balance sheets," numerical scale ratings of various dimensions which would then be combined into a single weighted index of social responsibility, cost/benefit analyses of social programs, calculations of the contribution of a firm's social programs to its long-term profitability, and so on.

In early 1972, Bauer and Fenn were able to locate about a half dozen firms that had made some sort of audit.[2] Undoubtedly there were other firms which had done so, but it was rare. However, 1972 saw a rapid acceleration of various means of assessing social performance. When Corson and Steiner conducted a survey at the end of 1973, 76% of the firms which replied indicated that they had done some form of "social audit" since January, 1972.[3]

However, what has evolved so rapidly is a far cry from what was envisaged in the programmatic statements of a few years ago. As a matter of fact, a knowledgeable observer labelled 1974 as the year of "the terminal illness of the social audit."[4] He is referring, of course, to some of the more grandiose schemes of a few years back. Paluszek goes on to say:

> A number of worthy, if less ambitious, alternatives appear ready to replace the audit concept. Called variously process audits, performance reviews, social progress reports, or any of a number of other things, these efforts aim at the attainable and the utilitarian. They are mainly attempts to measure one, several, or all of the company's socially oriented programs in terms of goals and progress being made toward those goals.[5]

Not only are these methods of assessment less grandiose, formal, and uniform than some of the early proposals, but they lack the external attestation that is implied by the term "audit." But, perhaps most surprising is the fact that such measures as are made are seldom primarily to report to the public, but to inform management of the performance of their own organization. Corson and Steiner asked why the various firms had made an "audit." Only 17% cited any reason associated with external reporting as the purpose for

---

[1]This early history is captured in Raymond A. Bauer, "The State of the Art of Social Auditing," in Meinholf Dierkes and Raymond A. Bauer (eds.) *Corporate Social Accounting,* New York: Praeger Publishers, 1974.

[2]Raymond A. Bauer and Dan H. Fenn, Jr., *The Corporate Social Audit,* New York: Russell Sage Foundation, 1972.

[3]John J. Corson and George A. Steiner, *Measuring Business's Social Performance: The Corporate Social Audit,* New York: Committee for Economic Development, 1974.

[4]John Paluszek, "The Top Ten Social Responsibility Happenings of 1974," *Business and Society Review,* Winter 1974-75, No. 12, pp 26-29.

[5]*Ibid,* p. 27.

making the "audit," while 59% gave reasons which amounted to finding out how the firm was doing or to gathering information to aid in the implementation of policy—essentially the same thing.

This finding should be "surprising" only in the context of the early literature on social auditing which placed so much emphasis on public reporting of corporations' social performance. In fact, there is a good deal of social reporting and disclosure of previously closely guarded information, and almost half of the "audits" identified in the survey by Corson and Steiner did result in some form of public report. However, the internal needs for measuring social performance are more compelling. In some instances there is a desire to be informed of the firm's performance before its officers are caught by surprise by outside activists. In many other instances some or most executives want reassurance that they will be able to assess the findings before there is any commitment to tell all to the public. Finally, if corporate officers are committed to enforcement of policies in the firm's operating units, they must have an assessment of performance broken down by operating units. This "auditing" for internal purposes is the beginning of a management information system, and in the past few years such regular reporting systems have been developed in many firms with a quarterly or even a monthly reporting of affirmative action information becoming quite common.

SOCIAL REPORTING AND CORPORATE DISCLOSURE

Much information on corporate social performance is reaching the public. In recent years a majority of major corporations regularly report on some dimension of performance either in their annual reports or in some separate publication.[6] But in form they are not markedly different from what the early advocates of social auditing derogated as "P.R. reports." The social audit movement has made such reporting increasingly more complete and informative. Norms of interpretation of data are more frequent, historical trends reported, and occasionally future goals are announced.

This increased social reporting results in part from a general sense of the times. It is facilitated, however, by an increasing realization of the difficulty of avoiding disclosure. Requests of activists for information responded to voluntarily, and/or abetted by orders from courts or regulatory agencies including the Securities and Exchange Commission, are bringing forth information on pollution control, affirmative action, strip mining, health and safety, international operations, and the like that only a few years ago corporations regarded as confidential.[7]

---

[6]There are many such separate publications such as General Motors' "Report on Progress in Areas of Public Concern." Quaker Oats, Bank of America, and other large corporations also have several such reports.

[7]cf. Nancy H. Treverton, "Trends in Corporate Disclosure, Part I," unpublished manuscript, Harvard Business School, 1975.

It is difficult to imagine a reversal or even an abatement of the trend toward more extended social reporting and disclosure of "social" information.[8] Except where there are official reporting requirements, as with affirmative action, we expect little initial uniformity, though one must assume that increased uniformity will evolve. The trend of events is such that most large corporations are coming to the conclusion that there must be a presumation of openness, and a bias toward disclosure of information unless there are compelling reasons to the contrary.[9] With this as an evolving position, it seems only reasonable that there will come to be a premium on disclosing information voluntarily before being coerced into doing so.

ORGANIZATIONAL PROBLEMS

Assessment of social performance demands information about activities that occur at widely dispersed places in the organization, and it reflects on the performance of persons equally widely dispersed. It engages in an unfamiliar task staff persons who already have a fulltime job and demands gathering of information in areas that are the province of other staff functions. Even executives whose own performance is not being assessed may think the whole idea is dangerous nonsense. Also, skills may have to be recruited from various parts of the organization.

The potential for organizational difficulties is great and seldom fails to be realized. Three incidents will illustrate the point. In one firm, corporate staff "wisely" invited the operating divisions to take part in designing the survey instrument to be used; after due consideration, the operating divisions announced that they did not want to be "audited." In another organization, the director of urban affairs was asked to survey the company's social performance; corporate personnel staff refused to assemble the required employment data on the grounds that such data had nothing to do with urban affairs. A staffer had difficulty getting data from another staff person despite the fact that she was acting on the direct orders from the C.E.O.; she found that her colleague had prepared a presentation of the data in question and had been trying to get an audience for the presentation for several months.

Very recently the C.E.O. of one of the Fortune 500 companies assigned a team to assess its social performance. The team is chaired by a senior financial officer who has been with the firm for decades and recently headed one of the operating divisions. A second member has similar senior status, and recently headed an operating division. His specialty is marketing. The third member, also a senior vice president, has been in charge of manufacturing for the largest of the operating divisions. The formation of the team

---

[8] In the Spring of 1975, the S.E.C. held hearings to explore the possibility that it might require more extensive reporting of performance on social dimensions. Private sources in both France and Germany report that there are serious moves in both countries to require formal standardized reporting on corporate social performance. It is not anticipated that such legislation will pass immediately, but rather that the present move will initiate discussions from which some concensus will be reached.

[9] cf. Nancy H. Treverton, "Trends in Corporate Disclosure, Part I," unpublished manuscript, Harvard Business School, 1975.

and a statement of its mission was announced in a memorandum signed by the C.E.O. and sent to all senior management.

What is unusual about the foregoing is that every element, including the announcement by the C.E.O., the senior line status and range of competencies of the team members, is individually rare. The combination, therefore, is all the more so. The modal pattern is to assign the assessment task to one or more staff people, frequently new to the job and even the company, without the support of the chief executive officer, and often without his explicit concurrence. The consequence of this modal response is prolonged delay, frustration, and friction. By now, the politics of "social auditing" have been reasonably well publicized, and no one should be surprised to encounter them. While no arrangment will nullify organizational problems entirely, the assignment of a team of senior line executives of diverse competencies, with an explicit mandate supported overtly by the C.E.O. should go as far as possible toward keeping them to a minimum.

PROCESS AUDITING

A major financial institution proposed that its lending officers screen business clients for bond issues on the basis of their social responsibility. One of the criteria suggested that prospective clients should not have marketed dangerous or harmful products. A consultant pointed out that this was not a very fruitful way of looking at things. The probability of any one firm having marketed a clearly dangerous or harmful product in the recent past is quite remote. And, if a firm had done so recently and the occurence had received wide publicity, they would probably now be highly traumatized and unlikely to repeat that particular sin. The information that one would want would be a description of the systems the organization used to avoid producing and marketing such a problem product. Given the existence of luck, both good and bad, one would be better advised to judge a firm by how it handled the problem rather than by how it fared in a chancey situation.

Both our own experience and that of others has led us to attend increasingly to the processes with which organizations address social issues. Bauer and Fenn were first led to this position[10] by virtue of the fact that some results of a firm's policies and actions are long deferred, complex in causation, and, for various other reasons, difficult to measure. Accordingly, it was suggested that attention be directed to the processes by which issues were handled. A process audit in our original way of thinking would consist of a description of a social program in terms of its objectives, the proposed course of action and the rationale that linked that course of action to the objectives, and finally, a comparison of what actually was done and what had been planned.

In retrospect, our early version was suited to special programs of limited scope, such as a bank's program for lending to minority businesses. As a matter of fact, it was just such a program that taught us the distinction between one person learning the technical task of lending to minority business persons, and the quite different task of

---

[10]The evolution of our thinking is sketched out in Raymond A. Bauer, L. Terry Cauthorn, and Ranne P. Warner, *Management Process Audit Guide*' # 9-375-336, Intercollegiate Case Clearinghouse, Boston, Massachusetts, 1975.

learning how to get lending officers to undertake making such loans on a bank-wide basis. We called the first type of learning "technical" and the second "administrative."[11] Quite obviously, our research on the institutionalization of social policies has been concerned with "administrative" learning. If progress in policy implementation demanded the accomplishment of certain managerial tasks, then the accomplishment of those tasks could be taken as a measure of progress or, if you will, of the organization's capacity to handle the policy issue.

In accordance with the foregoing reasoning, Bauer, Cauthorn, and Warner developed a Management Process Audit Guide[12] as a manual for organizational assessment. The basic notion is to apply our research-based understanding of the implementation process for diagnostic purposes. And, to a large extent, that is the function of this book insofar as it is concerned with policy implementation. In essence, a management process audit locates an organization in terms of the progress it has made in the several stages of implementation laid out in Chapter 4. To the extent that this procedure is applied to the cases in this book, it not only measures the organization's capacity to perform, but clearly implies what next steps may be required.

The development of management systems for handling policy implementation is necessary, but not sufficient. That is why we refer to such an assessment as one of "capacity to perform" rather than of performance per se. It is our judgement that both measures are required for a complete assessment. It is obvious that one would like to supplement a measure of capacity with one of actual performance. Less obvious, but equally important, is to know whether actual performance is supported by systems which ensure its continuance and development. Regrettably, since performance measures are often very difficult to obtain, and since either requires considerable expenditure of resources, we often have to choose between one or the other.

THE TREND OF DEVELOPMENTS

The cases in this section reflect early efforts at assessment of social performance. As such, they present a considerable variety of purpose, method, and ambition and reflect the political problems of getting organizational support for making an initial assessment. If anything, they understate the political problems, as well as those of getting consensus on which topics to include in the "audit," what measures to use, and so on.

Any collection of cases illustrating attempts at "social auditing" would reflect a rapidly evolving recent history of that concept and, therefore, to some extent depict events that are not likely to be repeated in the future. If we take 1971 as a baseline, we may say that by 1976 a number of things had changed.

1.—The necessity of *some* form of stock taking on social performance is accepted at the top of virtually every large corporation.

---

[11]The actual terminology was contributed by Murray, cf. Edwin A. Murray, Jr., *The Implementation of Social Policy in Commercial Banks,* unpublished DBA thesis, Harvard Business School, Boston, Massachusetts.

[12]Bauer, Cauthorn and Warner, *op. cit.*

2.–The reasons are practical and immediate rather than concerned with the devising of some ideal method of "social accounting."
3.–There is a rapidly widening appreciation of the inevitability if not the desirability of disclosure of information on corporate policies and actions that a few years ago were regarded as confidential. This has come in part from the actions of the SEC, of the courts, and generally from the success of activists in getting the information they are after.
4.–There is a less wide but growing appreciation that assessments of social performance cannot be limited to special programs and activities but must include–in principle at least–the impact of all of the organization's activities. There now exist internal monitoring and/or auditing systems for reviewing the impact of various regular business activities. To some extent, these are extensions of traditional monitoring systems such as quality control, but they are an explicit recognition of new expectations of accountability for corporate performance.
5.–Some elements of what might have been considered a "social audit" a few years ago have become components of a changed system of control and information. For example, it is now commonplace for equal opportunity employment information to be reported for each meaningful operating unit on a quarterly or even a monthly basis. Less widespread, but identifiable, are attempts to create a regular flow of information to monitor the performance of operating units on pollution control, OSHA, community relations, and consumer relations.
6.–Our notion of a management process audit seems to be gaining embryonic acceptance as it becomes clear that one can specify the sorts of management and administrative arrangements that facilitate policy implementation.

On the whole, the area of activity which was labelled social auditing several years ago has quickly developed into one of practical concern directed to the two major objectives of internal control and external reporting. The measures that have been used have been simple and descriptive. Sophisticated methods may be developing gradually, but they are developing in response to concrete problems, and not through the importation of models such as balance sheets and cost/benefit analysis developed in other fields to suit other purposes.[13]

SUGGESTED READINGS

1.–Bauer, Raymond A. and Fenn, Daniel H., Jr., *The Corporate Social Audit.* New York: Russell Sage Foundation, 1972.
2.–Bauer, R. A. and Dierkes, Meinholf, *Corporate Social Accounting,* New York: Praeger Publishers, 1974.
3.–Van Pelt, III, John V., "The Social Costs of Social Benefits, *Management Accounting,* October 1974.

---

[13]cf. a tool for analyzing and planning affirmative action programs developed by our colleagues Neil Churchill and John Shank, "Accounting for Affirmative Action, *Accounting Review,* in press.

Case Sixteen

Parker-Perry Systems

In 1969 Parker Systems, a giant New York-based electronics firm, acquired the smaller but more profitable Perry Industrial Suppliers with home offices in Cleveland, Ohio. The following year the corporation was renamed Parker-Perry Systems, and four market-oriented divisions created. These (with the number of plants in each division) were:

Division	*Plants*	*Predecessor Corporation*
Electronics	(22)	Parker Systems
Systems	(7)	Parker Systems
Industrial Components	(14)	Perry Industrial
Vehicle Equipment	(8)	Perry Industrial

The company described itself as a "technically oriented manufacturing company" which offered both "products and performance systems" for a wide range of uses. Long associated with the glamorous electronics industry, PPS nonetheless manufactured ball bearings and metal cutting tools as well as sophisticated computers.

Sales for the combined company had declined slightly since 1967, reaching the $1.7 billion mark in 1971, while earnings edged upwards towards $50 million. The two electronics divisions had been most imperiled by recent economic trends, the competitive situation within the industry, and the cutback in government military spending. Consequently, in 1971 they were outperformed by the smaller industrial equipment divisions, which contributed over half (55%) of the company's pre-tax profits on only 40% of the sales. To reduce the financial exposure and to achieve a closer fit among divisions, management had recently begun to move away from reliance on huge electronics systems and to diversify into smaller and more stable markets. This change in policy was not inflexible, of course; for instance, PPS won a billion dollar contract from the French government to develop a Pan-European computer system to challenge the near monopoly of IBM. With this contract, however, PPS management maintained even more strongly that the company should break away from its industry mold and seek growth in new fields with greater stability.

THE SOCIAL RESPONSIBILITIES INVENTORY

Shortly after the reorganization, Mr. Horace F. Wood, an engineer trained at MIT and employed for several years in the electronics segment of the company, was appointed Director of Urban Affairs. Although he was successful in gaining some understanding of PPS's social performance from a corporate level perspective, by late 1971 Mr. Wood felt the need for a more systematic review of activities in the company's diverse and scattered operating units. The vice president of public relations, to whom he reported, was sympathetic to this need, and, together with the vice president of personnel and Mr. Wood, approached the president with a proposal to initiate some sort of social audit activity in PPS. The proposal was accepted, and the three men were appointed to a committee and given permission to proceed with a survey.

During the next several months, Mr. Wood drew up a questionnaire, based on a model developed by The Public Affairs Council, a national association of public affairs officers, to be sent to all PPS plants. Many of the questions were factually straightforward. They concerned the types of contributions made or programs underway in the areas of employment, charity, education, training, loaned employees, pollution, local government reform, housing, economic development of the local community, and transportation for employees. Other questions called for an interpretation of "pressure" or "effort" such as those on plant location: "Has the impact of the disadvantaged been a factor in selecting plant sites?" and "Has there been pressure to locate or not to locate a plant in a particular area?" However, no requests were made for estimates or expenditures.

The document, entitled "An Inventory of Practices, Problems and Issues Pertinent to Corporate Social Responsibilities," was approved by the committee and distributed to each plant manager in May 1972, accompanied by only a short cover letter. No detailed instructions were given for completing the seven-page form; the plant manager was simply requested to fill it out and return the form to Mr. Wood.

ANALYZING THE RESULTS Two months passed before the last of the 52 questionnaires was returned. Mr. Wood attributed the delay to natural inertia, however, rather than resentment or protest. In fact, he sensed no negative reactions to the inventory at all, which led him to suspect that it was viewed as "noncontroversial" by the operating managers. Nevertheless, he was pleased to find that, with few exceptions, the document was signed by the plant manager. A sample questionnaire, including a statistical summary of the responses, is shown in Exhibit 16-1.

On the basis of his detailed review, Mr. Wood prepared the summary of the inventory reproduced in Exhibit 16-2 and circulated copies to senior line and staff managers. He recognized that many of the questions, such as those related to the company's image in the community, called for subjective judgment. In these instances the possibility of bias was increased in the likely event that only the respondent's opinion was represented. To provide a greater depth of understanding about the company's standing in the community in terms of employment and social contributions, Mr. Wood briefly considered an outside survey. However, the expense involved (estimated at $100,000) and the difficulty of getting the job done correctly led him to reject this possibility. Even were the cost cut to $50,000, Mr. Wood indicated that he would not be willing to sponsor such a project.

Mr. Wood was aware that some managers felt that social issues were less relevant to PPS than to consumer-oriented firms. Historically, the company, like others in the electronics and industrial products area, had few dealings with the public and was consequently less concerned about image. Mr. Wood considered this attitude (and PPS certainly was no worse than "typical" in his view) to have been an error. In fact, he contended that the company did relate to the consumer and that the product line might even be vulnerable to a Nader-like attack, for example, on the grounds of supplying the valves for the cars General Motors then recalls. Although the 1970 merger appeared to change the company's posture for the better, he at times felt that his was a voice crying in the wilderness, or "at least in a large forest."

Mr. Wood was relatively satisfied with the questionnaire, but not necessarily with the overall impact of his work. He believed that PPS's record was very good in terms of minority employment (where detailed records were required by the government), pollution, and health and safety. He said he was a little surprised, however, by the lack of involvement in community activities by some of the plants in the "hinterlands." The plants were anything but uniform in their policies and practices. Mr. Wood hoped his study would prevent contributions from being made in a vacuum and perhaps be an incentive to further socially oriented programs. In that sense, any effort was better than none. Yet within the total company, response to the survey seemed to have been negligible thus far, and Mr. Wood acknowledged that the problems to be overcome included those of securing time and money and getting top management to move. A month had passed since his analysis had been distributed and Mr. Wood wondered what to do next.

Exhibit 16-1

AN INVENTORY OF PRACTICES, PROBLEMS AND ISSUES PERTINENT TO CORPORATE SOCIAL RESPONSIBILITIES

I. *IDENTIFYING INFORMATION*

A. Name and address of division or plant

52 divisions or plants responded to questionnaire.
____

B. Name and title of executive completing this questionnaire.

____

II. *PRACTICES*

A. *Contributions*

Give names of organizations to which your division and/or plant contributes surplus material, equipment or cash (other than direct corporate contributions).

46 reported contributing.

6 reported they did not.

(Include contributions to civic, charitable, religious, educational, and other similar organizations.)

B. *Employing the Disadvantaged*

1. Does your division or plant have a pledge with the National Alliance of Businessmen to employ the disadvantaged?
   Yes 7 No 45
   a. If so, how many have you hired? 426 (+334 "CHANCE")
   b. What percent of the work force? ______
2. Does your division or plant have a contract under the JOBS program with the U.S. Department of Labor? Yes 2 No 50
   a. If so, which program? ______
   b. How many trainees are covered? ______

C. *Education Training*

1. Has your division or plant participated in community efforts to improve local schools? Yes 29 No 23

   If so, please describe the type of effort. ______
2. Does your division or plant?
   a. Tutor students? Yes 7 No 45
   b. Counsel students? Yes 17 No 35
   c. Other (describe) Yes 24 No 28
3. Does your division or plant give extra or special aid or assistance to schools in disadvantaged areas? Yes 10 No 42

   If so, please describe ______

D. *Loaned Employees*

Does your division or plant make available employees to social agencies or government agencies in the social field, full time or part time, with salary paid? Yes 13 No 39

Please list the names of such employees, indicating the time off, allowed, and the name of the agencies.__________

E. *Quality of Urban Life*

1. *Curbing Pollution*

a. Has your division or plant had adverse publicity, formal or informal charges of polluting the environment? Yes 10 No 42

If so, attach copies of clippings and other reports relating to such charges or give brief descriptions of facts surrounding the situation.

b. What actions have been taken to curb pollution?

Taking Action 37

Not Taking Action 22

2. *Local Government Reorganization or Reform*

Has your division or plant been involved in such programs? If so, describe Yes 10 No 42

3. *Housing*

a. Does your division or plant help its employees (particularly low-income or minority employees) to find adequate housing? If so, please describe Yes 15 No 37

b. In what ways, if any, is your division or plant involved in community efforts to improve housing available for low-income families in the area?

4 involved

48 not involved

c. Has your division or plant given any type of support to open or fair housing programs in the area? Yes 6 No 46

If so, please describe ____________________

4. *Economic Development*

a. Has your division or plant participated in efforts to expand the economy of the disadvantaged community? Yes 15 No 37

If so, please describe ____________________

b. Has your division or plant participated in efforts to facilitate the establishment of minority business enterprise? Yes 6 No 46

If so, please describe ____________________

c. Has your division or plant made special efforts to increase purchases from minority suppliers? Yes 10 No 42

If so, please describe ____________________

5. *Transportation*

Has your division or plant participated in community efforts to improve public transportation? Yes 10 No 42

If so, please describe ____________________

6. *Plant Relocation or New Plant Location*

a. Has the impact on the disadvantaged been a factor in selecting plant sites? Yes 3 No 49

If so, please describe the situation and name the plant(s) affected

____

b. Has there been community pressure to locate or not to locate a plant in a particular area? Yes 7 No 45

If so, please describe ____________________

F. *The Company Image in the Community*

1. Please list the top three companies in terms of employment in your community 1st–13; 2nd–5; 3rd–8; 4th–3; 5th–1; 6th–10th – 6; Over 10th–11; don't know or not ranked–5.

2. Please rank the above companies in the order in which you think they have an impact on the community in terms of social involvement.

   1st–15; 2nd–9; 3rd–3; 4th–2; 5th–0; 6th–10th – 5; Over 10th–7; don't know or not ranked–11.

   ____

3. How do you rate the image of your plant or facility in your community? Excellent 22 Average 27 Poor 1 Don't Know 1 No Answer 1

4. How well recognized in your community is the product manufactured by your plant or facility? By 100% of the population 6 75% 17 50% 13 Don't Know 15 No Answer 1

5. Does your plant have an active program to publicize company activities in behalf of the community? Yes 23 No 29

   Should this be expanded? 26 Remain the same 13 Reduced 0 No Answer 13

6. In your opinion are the social responsibility activities of your plant or facility known by members of your community? Yes 22 No 19 Don't Know 11

   In your opinion how can they be improved? ______________________________

   ____

   ____

G. *Other Social Activities*

In what other type of social support activities not covered in the foregoing questions is or has your division been engaged?

____

____

____

____

____

III. *COMMUNITY ISSUES AND OTHER CONFLICTS*

A. What community pressures relating to the quality of the environment, consumer demands and social responsibilities has your division experienced from:

1. Employees (describe) 9 Affirmative Responses

2. Community at large 13 Affirmative Responses

3. Special interest groups (Please describe and give the names of such groups) 11 Affirmative Responses

B. Do you anticipate any new community pressure? ______ If so, please describe 11 Affirmative Responses

C. What steps do you believe your division should take to prepare for or reduce the impact of anticipated community pressures? 24 Responses

Exhibit 16-2

A SUMMARY OF PRACTICES, PROBLEMS, AND ISSUES AT PPS DIVISIONS AND PLANTS RELATING TO CORPORATE SOCIAL RESPONSIBILITIES

In May 1971 all operating divisions and plants (field offices were excluded) of the company were sent a social responsibility questionnaire to complete and return to the Corporate Offices.

Completed questionnaires were received from 52 company locations. Broken down by group, questionnaires received were as follows: Corporate–1, Electronics–22, Systems–7, Industrial Components–14, and Vehicle Equipment–8. The following summary of the responses was prepared in the same order and with the same section heading as in the questionnaire. This summary starts with item II, because item I is not subject to summarization.

II. *PRACTICES*

A. *Contributions*

Forty-six (46) plants (the term "plant" will be used hereafter to refer to any company establishment reporting) reported making some kind of contribution (cash or surplus material and equipment) to community organizations. Only six (6) plants left this question blank, indicating no contributions of any kind.

The organizations to which contributions were made cover a wide range, but most are typical of those supported by United Funds and similar agencies, such as the Red Cross, Boy Scouts, Salvation Army, local schools, YMCA, Hospitals, Heart Fund, Cancer Society, Police and Fire Benefit Associations, etc. Except in major cities, there were relatively few contributions to minority organizations or projects, (i.e. those organized solely or primarily for the benefit of minorities).

B. *Employing the Disadvantaged*

1. *National Alliance of Businessmen–Pledges and Hires*

Seven (7) plants have made pledges to the National Alliance of Businessmen to employ the disadvantaged at some time since NAB was born. Except for the CHANCE Program in St. Louis, there are almost no current NAB pledges. Even in past years most of the pledges as well as the hires occurred in St. Louis under CHANCE where 334 disadvantaged employees have been hired since June 1968. The Aeronautical Division pledged and hired 62 in 1969 (because of work force reduction only 10 are still employed).

The Systems Group has hired 50 under the NAB pledge program–18 are still employed. The Automobile Products Division hired 26 in 1969 and a Computer Center Facility has made 24 NAB hires. Most of the other plants participating have hired less than a dozen employees each under the NAB "permanent" hiring program.

In addition to the "permanent" program, some plants have participated in the NAB summer hiring program. The Los Angeles Division hired 103 disadvantaged youth under the NAB program during the summers of 1968 and 1969. The Aeronautics Division hired 110 in 1968 and 67 in 1969. Other divisions also participated in the NAB summer programs to hire disadvantaged youth in 1968 and 1969. However, because of reduced business and work force cut back, most of the plants have discontinued or drastically curtailed their NAB programs since the summer of 1970. As previously stated, the only exception is at St. Louis where most of the production workers continue to be drawn from the ranks of the disadvantaged.

An equipment plant in Rochester, New York has a free training program for the unskilled, but no NAB pledges. In addition to hiring the disadvantaged, some plants have supported NAB by lending executives to the program part time or full time. Johnson Morris, Vice President of Administration, served as NAB Metro Chairman for New York in the year 1969-1970. D. F. Davis, President of the Electronics Group, is the current NAB Metro Chairman of Essex County. James Donaldson of the Electronics Group has been on leave with full pay loaned to the Essex County NAB as Staff Director. Robert Hendry from the Systems Executive Office was loaned at full pay to the Seattle NAB Metro Staff in 1969-1970.

2. *JOBS Contracts–U.S. Department of Labor*
Only two (2) plants have signed JOBS type contracts with the U.S. Department of Labor. St. Louis had employed 163 under MA-2, 32 under MA-5, and 7 under MA-6. Tulsa has MA-6 contract Option B (training for upgrading current employees) covering 10 "slots." However, no employees are currently enrolled because of a downturn in business. Ames Chain has a JOBS 70 contract covering 4 trainees.

C. *Education and Training*

1. *Participation in Community Effort to Improve Local Schools*
Twenty-nine (29) plants answered this question in the affirmative. Many plants have provided speakers for career day appearances, made their facilities available for plant tours, loaned executives to serve on curriculum planning committees to help make the courses of study more relevant to industry needs, and provided employees to instruct special classes. Many divisions donate surplus materials and equipment to local schools.

A few plants appear to have become quite deeply involved in programs to support and improve local schools. For example, the Valves & Bearings Plant in Allentown assisted in new building programs in behalf of Allentown Public Schools and organized an effort to establish an area community college.

Several plants have given executives time off to serve part time on school boards and advisory committees to local colleges and secondary and primary schools.

2. *Providing Employees to Tutor, Counsel, or Give Other Assistance to Students Attending Local Schools*
Seven (7) plants reported that they made employees available to tutor students in local colleges and high schools.

Seventeen (17) plants provide employees as counselors to students.

Twenty-four (24) indicated they gave assistance to students in addition to tutoring and counselling. Such assistance took the form of classroom assistance to regular teachers, participation in seminars, plant tours, student co-op programs, sponsoring of junior achievement projects, assisting Science Fairs, and giving awards for outstanding performance in various school projects.

A program deserving special mention is ABC (Advancing Business Communication) which was initiated by the Electronics Division and currently is being instituted at other divisions in the New York area. ABC provides educational enrichment and serves as a bridge between the classroom and industry.

This program has provided training for more than 350 high school junior and senior students over the past two semesters. More than 95 per cent of the students are from racial minority families. The in-plant classes are held each Tuesday and Thursday between the hours of 5:00 and 7:00 p.m. Instruction is provided by volunteer employees, all highly skilled professionals in their fields.

During the first semester eight courses were offered: Technical Illustration, Writing for Industry, Magnetic Tape Selectric Typing (MTST), Television and Speech, Industrial Photography, Photo Lab Processing, Offset Printing, and Television Electronics. Three school districts were involved, all near a PPS facility.

At the start of the second semester the class sizes were increased and six new classes added: Microfilm Techniques, Electricity and Its Application in Industry, Materials and Their Application in Industry, Introduction to Business Operations, Production Typing, and Computer Programming for Industry.

Most of the New York divisions have established some form of the program (although not necessarily identified by the same acronym) to give special assistance to schools in disadvantaged areas.

3. *Special Assistance to Schools in Disadvantaged Areas*
Ten (10) plants said they gave extra or special assistance to schools in disadvantaged areas.

Various types of assistance provided by PPS plants include such efforts as: lending computer equipment, donation of surplus electronic equipment ($26,000 by the L.A. Division to the Watts Skill Center), lending employees as instructors to schools and skill centers (such employees are placed on leave without pay and the school pays the salary).

One interesting example of special assistance to the disadvantaged is at the Transmission and Axle Division where for the past 10 years training materials have been given to a nearby State Prison for its mechanical training classes.

Several divisions in southern states cooperate with the National Alliance of Businessmen in support of the NAB "College Cluster Program" for Negro Colleges.

D. *Loaned Employees*
Thirteen (13) plants reported they had loaned employees on a full time or part time basis to social or government agencies, with salary paid. The agency

named most frequently as a recipient of a loaned employee was the United Fund. Other agencies reported were: National Alliance of Businessmen, College (Negro) Cluster Program, Urban League, Skill Centers, Youth Motivation Task Force, Human Relations Committees, Model Cities, Selective Service Boards, Green Power Inc., and Economic Development Corp.

E. *Quality of Urban Life*

1. *Curbing Pollution*

a. *Adverse Publicity, Formal or Informal Charges*
Ten (10) plants have received either adverse publicity, formal and/or informal charges of polluting the environment. Six (6) of these were in the Industrial Components Group and four (4) of them were in the Vehicle Equipment Group. In most cases adverse publicity was experienced. At six (6) plants only informal complaints were received, (i.e. complaints from local residents or citizens without any formal action by a governmental body). At least three plants have had a formal charge from a government agency filed against them and in at least one (1) of these cases cash fines were levied. One case was reported where citizens took their complaint against the Company to court.

b. *Action Taken to Curb Pollution*
Many plants have taken action to curb pollution even though they have no complaint of any kind charging pollution of the environment. Whereas only ten plants reported receiving any kind of complaint concerning pollution, thirty-seven reported they had instituted programs to curb pollution, some of which are quite comprehensive.

2. *Local Government Reorganization or Reform*

Ten (10) plants indicated some involvement in local government reorganization or reform. The most typical involvement was service by company executives and employees on city councils, boards, committees, and planning commissions. Four (4) plants reported that their executives and employees have been active in planning, campaigning, or supporting some type of change in the form of the local government.

Several plants reported that their employees served as Mayors, City Councilmen, School Board Members, and Planning Commissioners.

3. *Housing*

a. *Helping Employees (particularly low-income and minority employees) to Find Housing*
Fifteen (15) plants reported that they give some kind of assistance to their employees in finding adequate housing. Typical of this assistance is to provide a referral service to housing sources, as real estate agents and rental agencies. For minority employees, contact with local fair housing councils is provided.

Several plants provide letters of introduction to real estate and rental agents for minority employees. One plant provides a personal escort and transportation for minorities seeking housing if they desire such service.

Some plants provide the housing service only for new and transferring employees who are relocating from another area.

b. *Involvement in Community Effort to Improve Housing for Low-Income Families*
Four (4) plants reported some involvement in community effort to improve housing for low-income families. In most cases, however, this involvement does not go beyond serving on planning boards and advisory committees.

c. *Support of Open or Fair Housing Programs in the Local Area*
Six (6) plants said they had supported fair housing programs in their area. Typical of such support is to contact (i.e., a letter from the division president) real estate brokers, rental agents, and apartment house operators to obtain a commitment in writing from them that they will offer their property to any qualified person without regard to race, creed, or color.

At some plants employees serve on fair housing councils. Another form of support by some plants is cash contributions to the local fair housing councils.

4. *Economic Development*

a. *Participation in Efforts to Expand the Economy of the Disadvantaged Community*
Fifteen (15) plants reported efforts to assist economic expansion in the disadvantaged community. The most frequently mentioned types of economic assistance were: technical and financial assistance to minority business enterprises, increased purchases from minority suppliers, and service on economic planning committees. Typical of the latter is the Aeronautics Division's assistance given to organize and manage the Economic Development Union of Camden (EDUCAM). This is a union of the Mayor's Office, the Chamber of Commerce, local business leaders (including PPS's), and the local Junior College. Other plants have engaged in similar activities.

b. *Participation in Efforts to Facilitate the Establishment of Minority Business Enterprises*
Six (6) plants reported they had provided various types of help and assistance in the establishment of minority business enterprises in their community. Such assistance included the organization of a separate company (which was located in the central city and operated by minority managers), cash contributions, loans and gifts of surplus material and equipment to new or established

minority businesses, and provided consultation in management and technical matters.

c. *Efforts to Increase Purchases From Minority Suppliers*
Ten (10) plants reported making special efforts to increase their purchases from minority suppliers. To support this effort various plants took such action as: providing buyers with listings of potential sources of minority business, holding special meetings with local minority businessmen to offer advice on how to participate as subcontractors and suppliers, placing minorities on the buying staff, and seeking out qualified minority suppliers.

5. *Transportation–Efforts to Improve Public Transportation*
Ten (10) plants reported on efforts to improve public transportation in their community. In a few instances such efforts were primarily for the purpose of improving the transportation service to and from work for the Company's employees. In most cases, however, the company representatives participated in broadly based activities in the total community, which only incidentally would benefit company employees. Such participation included membership of company executives on community and state-wide committees and cooperation with Chamber of Commerce transportation activities.

One division made special arrangements with a private bus company to provide transportation between Los Angeles and Anaheim for low-income minority employees. This service became necessary when the plant moved and many of the minority employees could not find housing at the new location and did not have adequate transportation of their own.

6. *Plant Relocation or New Plant Location*

a. *Impact on Disadvantaged–A Factor in Plant Site Selection*
The impact on the disadvantaged has been a factor in selecting plant sites for at least three (3) plants. They include facilities located in depressed areas or near centers of disadvantaged minorities in St. Louis, West Virginia, Oklahoma, and Ontario.

b. *Community Pressure to Locate or not to Locate in a Particular Area*
Seven (7) plants reported that they had experienced some degree of pressure to locate or not to locate a plant in a particular area. Most of such "pressure" reported was of a positive nature, that is, encouragement *to* locate in certain areas from such groups as the Chambers of Commerce and other community industrial development organizations. Negative pressures have come from communities where plants have indicated plans to move away.

One case was reported of litigation being brought against a planned move of a scientific laboratory into an area adjacent to residential housing.

F. *The Company Image in the Community*

1. *Rank of PPS in Community in Terms of Employment*
Thirteen (13), or 25% of the PPS plants rank first in their community in terms of employment. Twenty-six (26) or 50% of the plants rank 3rd or better in their community in terms of employment.

2. *Rank of PPS in the Community in Terms of Social Involvement*
Fifteen (15) or 28% of the plants reported that they felt that they ranked number one in their area in terms of social involvement. (This was a difficult question for many of the plants because of lack of objective criteria for evaluation.)

3. *Self-Rating of Image of Plant in the Community*
Plants reporting rated their image in the community as follows:

Excellent	22
Average	27
Poor	1
Don't Know	1
Didn't Answer	1
Total	52

4. *Recognition of Local PPS Plant's Product in Community*
Concerning how the local community at large recognized the product(s) produced, the plants reported as follows:

Percent of Population Recognizing Product	*Number of PPS Plants*
100%	6
75%	17
50%	13
Don't Know	15
Didn't Answer	1
Total	52

5. *Programs to Publicize Company Community Activities*
Twenty-three (23) plants reported that they had a program to publicize their community activities.

As to whether such programs should be expanded, the plants commented as follows:

Should be expanded	26
Remain the same	13
Reduced	0
No answer	13
Total	52

6. *Community Knowledge of the Local Plant's Social Responsibility Activities*

Knowledge of the community concerning responsibility activities were reported by the plants as follows:

Social Activities are known by community	22
Not known by community	19
Don't know	11
Total	52

How Can Community Knowledge of the Plant's Social Activities be Improved?

Eighteen (18) plants had some comment on how the community knowledge of the Company's Social Responsibility activities could be improved.

The various answers given to this question were: "More publicity," "more active participation by senior executives," "expand efforts to get coverage in news media," "appoint community relations representatives," "more intensive coordination with minority news media," "better use of the minority Equal Opportunity Advisory Committees," "expansion of public relations activities."

G. *Other Social Activities not Covered in the Questionnaire*

Twenty-six (26) plants reported some kind of other social activity in response to this section of the questionnaire.

The "other social activities" reported do not appear to be very different from those reported in other parts of the questionnaire. Rather, they appear to be an extension of such activities. The typical activities reported were the support of various recreational, sports, social, and club activities such as: little league teams, Boy Scouts, Welcome Wagon Club, Exchange Clubs, community recreational parks, hospital drives, medical centers, Urban League, NAACP, Mexican American Opportunity Foundation, etc.

An unusual activity report was the Tulsa Division "Operation Frosty"—an airlift of foodstuffs, clothing, and medical supplies to two Indian tribes in December of 1970.

III. *COMMUNITY ISSUES AND OTHER CONFLICTS*

A. *Community Pressures Relating to Social Responsibilities*

1. *Pressures from Employees*

Nine (9) plants reported some pressure from employees, but most of those reported did not appear to be serious or significant from a broad social point of view.

2. *Pressures from the Community at Large*
   Thirteen (13) reported some kind of "pressure" from the community at large. Some of the so-called "pressures" were merely requests to support various worthy causes. More serious pressures from the community relate to quality of the environment such as air, water, and noise pollution. At least half of the plants reporting community pressures described this type of concern.

3. *Pressures from Special Interest Groups*
   Eleven (11) reported some kind of pressure from special interest groups in the community. These "pressures" related to: quality of the environment (air, water, and noise pollution), employment of minorities, and requests for contribution to worthy causes.

B. *Anticipation of New Community Pressures*

Eleven (11) plants reported that they anticipated new community pressures. Eight (8) plants anticipate pressures relating to the quality of the environment. Two (2) indicated the pressures would come in the form of a drive to provide more jobs and better housing for minorities. One mentioned continued pressure for the contribution of dollars. Another suggested unemployment would become a serious issue locally.

C. *Steps that Should Be Taken to Prepare for the Impact of Anticipated Community Pressures*

Twenty-four (24) plants responded to this final question and offered suggestions of steps that should be taken to prepare for anticipated community pressures.

Their comments were many and varied, but the frequently repeated ones were: Increase the Company's participation in civic and community activities, make certain that we set realistic goals for the employment of minorities, then follow up with a good faith effort to meet them, maintain rapport with representative minority organizations, and anticipate and correct any pollution or other type of community problem before complaints can be made.

Prepared by: Horace F. Wood
Urban Affairs

August 20, 1972

Case Seventeen

National Bank and Trust Company (A)

In April of 1970, the National Bank and Trust Company, with headquarters in Hartford, Connecticut, and branches throughout the state, assigned its Controller's office the responsibility for inventorying its social activities and determining their costs to the bank. In March 1971, a report of National Bank and Trust's social activities was submitted to the bank's President, Phineas Bailey (see Exhibit 17-1, 17-2, and 17-3).

The following discussion, held in June 1972, focused on the method used by the bank in assigning true costs to its social relations program. Participants included: O'Hennessey, of the Controller's office; Baron, from the Urban Affairs section; two MBA students working at the bank during the summer (Clarence and Darrow); and a professor from a well-known eastern business school acting as a consultant. The initial discussion focused on the general cost accounting methods employed by the bank and then its applicability to loans to minority-owned small businesses, new low-income home loans, and loans to students.

Consultant: Can you tell us—in general terms—how you determine the true cost of a given activity.

O'Hennessey: [Comptroller] We use time-motion studies to determine the cost of an activity. For example, we take an account from the time a deposit is made at the window to the time it's credited to a customer's account and the deposit slip is filed away. There's a certain routine one has to go through, and for each step along the way we note how much time it takes. We add up all of those which would be the direct minutes.

We know the level of person who's doing the work, so we extend out by the salary costs for that level of person times the number of minutes he or she takes to do it. In that way, we get the direct salary costs and the direct time for each activity. We then add so much on for branch supervision, employee benefits, social security taxes, and branch overhead.

On top of that, we add something for administrative overhead—controller's department, administration, and things like that. This will vary according to the type of function. If it's a commercial deposit, this administrative expense may be 12% to 15% of total costs. If it's a commercial loan, it may be 30% to cover the additional costs of the finance committee, supervisors, and things like that. Generally, it's supposed to cover all costs.

Consultant: What would the overhead be currently on loans to new low income and minority homeowners?

O'Hennessey: Maybe about 20% or 22%. I'm just guessing. You have costs of the real estate appraisers, the loan supervisors, and maybe the regional loan supervisor, which would have to be tacked on.

Consultant: I suppose the various conventions for assigning overhead would not drastically change one's picture of the cost of the loan.

O'Hennessey: No. The largest direct cost is actually the cost of servicing people at the start, because most of them had never borrowed money before. You have to sit down and very slowly explain the lending process and the various repayment plans available to them. Thus, it takes considerably longer to get minority loans on the books than it does a conventional loan.

Baron: [Urban Affairs] Then the differential in servicing costs for these special loans is actually greater than the differential in interest earned?

O'Hennessey: No, the interest is also a big factor. In fact, the loss of interest would be the biggest non-controllable cost factor in the whole bunch.

Baron: Let me ask you this. The three loans we are most specifically concerned with are loans to students, to new low-income homeowners, and to minority-owned small businesses. Now let's look at the low-income home loans. You've got the interest in percentage points which would be charged for this special type of loan. With what would you compare this rate of return to determine sacrificed income?

O'Hennessey: We could use several types of loans for comparison. We decided to use FHA and conventional real estate loans for comparative purposes. This did raise some questions. We could have lent it out higher if we'd put it out in commercial loans since, at that time, there was a big market for commercial loans.

Baron: I just want to isolate the alternatives that could have been used. You could use a similar type of loan (such as normal FHA loans); or the rate attached to an alternative type of loan that would have a higher yield; or to the "pool" rate of return which is an average of all uses of funds.

O'Hennessey: I don't think you want to relate it to the pool because the funds that went into these special programs wouldn't have gone into one pot. At that time money was tight and we could have put the funds into commercial loans. Then, we were buying Eurodollars and paying more for them than we were earning from our low-income homeowners loan program.

Baron: In a soft money market you might not be able to lend the money out at all. If there were no special loan program, those funds would probably be invested in securities. This would argue for comparing the special program loan rate with the average rate of return on securities investments.

O'Hennessey: This decision depends on where we're putting our money currently and, as such becomes a money market and policy investment problem which is out of our department.

Consultant: Would you say that because we're currently in a loose money period, there would be no way to put the money in the bank's regular loan business?

O'Hennessey: That's right. I think right now we might be doing better by putting our money in the special program. When we looked at the problem originally in 1970-71, there was a tight money market, so we said we could have put it in alternative types of loans.

Baron: Is there such a thing as an average rate of return on a non-loan investment?

O'Hennessey: Well, you can take the pool or you can take the average rate we are getting on the securities. Although most of the money is going into commercial loans at this time, I think a considerable amount is also going into securities.

Baron: This is an angle that hadn't occurred to me before this morning, but, in making this cost estimate and in evaluating the effectiveness of these social programs, you have to take some sort of time slice.

Clarence: [summer student] To evaluate this program you're going to have to accumulate costs and income data over several years since there are going to be months when you're losing money and months when you're gaining money. It gets to be much more intricate than I thought.

O'Hennessey: I think you have to take some sort of average and run it out. If you try and adjust it too often, you never get through with the problem.

Baron: On the loans to low-income homeowners you compare the interest rate with that charged on regular FHA loans. On the minority small business loans do you use the rate on regular Small Business Administration Insured loans for comparative purposes?

O'Hennessey: Yes. And in this area of loans to minority small business, I don't think we lost too much in interest. I think in these loans about all we lost was expenses.

Baron: How come you didn't match these loans against the average commercial loan rate?

O'Hennessey: Because we're getting the same rate for non-minority SBA loans. Actually, you could match it against anything, but at this point, all we're trying to do is see how much more these loans are costing us than the same type of loans made to somebody else.

Baron: You didn't feel that the regular SBA program was any special socially motivated program. So why do you feel that SBA loans to minority businesses are something special?

O'Hennessey: Even though the rate is the same, the ground rules are a little bit different, a little bit more lenient. We have made some real concessions in normal credit requirements.

Baron: I notice that there's nothing in here for added costs of followup and delinquency costs.

O'Hennessey: We were just about getting started on this. This is a new program and we didn't have a good picture of how the delinquencies were going to run. This was what we said at the time, in our report to the president, "The interest rate on these loans was similar to regular SBA and commercial loans. We do not have enough experience on delinquent loans to make any estimates of costs or probable losses in this area."

Let me shift to the third area you mentioned–student loans. We made a study of our consumer loan portfolio, in which we also include student loans. Student loans, taken as a whole, returned about 1½% less.

Consultant: Is it conceivable that those loans would look different today? In a loose money market, would these student loans appear relatively more profitable?

O'Hennessey: I don't think so. Because most of it is the cost of service, and this has very little to do with interest costs. The only thing where it would be different is the amount of money we would be getting back in insurance support from the government.

Consultant: Can you explain item IH on the cost sheet? It says "Advertising–New Haven."

O'Hennessey: That's where we had all the trouble during the invasion of Cambodia. We put a lot of advertising in the newspapers explaining our bank position on peaceful dissent.

Consultant: It was just plain straight public relations?

O'Hennessey: Just public relations. We also put out a number of booklets and other material.

Consultant: What's Item IIB under security–refurbishing buildings?

O'Hennessey: Oh, that's for repairing the damage to a New Haven office building we own that was in the riots.

Consultant: Do you have an overall criterion that you use for including or excluding a program in that list?

O'Hennessey: That's when we sat down with John Rogers, Vice President of Public Relations, who had already compiled an inventory of all the bank's social activities. Nobody before had ever worried about trying to bring all these diverse programs into one pot. There were people in all divisions and all branches involved in these programs and we had to go find these people and find out what they were trying to do and how much time they were spending. We think we got almost all of it, but there could have been some bits and pieces we didn't get.

The administrative staff told us anything that had to do with social affairs of any type and ecology should be included. That's when we sat down with John Rogers and his inventory. We figured he was going to be the person to write the final report if anything was published. So we sat down with him and said, "John, what do you want in here and what do you want to exclude?" He was the one who made the decisions.

Consultant: Can you explain item IG on the cost sheet–Administration?

Baron: Yes. This is the salaries paid to special people–such as our Urban Affairs officers who work in this area full time.

Consultant: How about your salary? Does that go in here?

O'Hennessey: No, we didn't attempt to separate out the salaries of those who only do a few special projects on a part-time basis.

Consultant: I see that these salaries ran $66,000 in 1970 and you're projecting $87,000 in 1971.

O'Hennessey: Well, we're just making a good guess there. We talked to people and tried to build what we thought it would cost to run the Urban Affairs office in the next year.

Darrow: [summer student] I want to go back to the SBA program. You said that the chief area of cost in the program is the added servicing that's required. Is that right?

O'Hennessey: Right. Everybody we talked to said it took 50% longer to put the minority-type SBA loans on the books than to put a normal SBA loan on the books.

Consultant: It seems to me that you can probably look at cost two ways: One is total cost and the other is the incremental cost. I think that when Darrow gets to totaling up his evaluation of the minority SBA program, he will want to display both total costs and incremental costs. What you have here are incremental costs.

O'Hennessey: Right.

Consultant: That will not show the total costs of the program.

O'Hennessey: It wouldn't be the total costs, that's right. This is only the difference between making this type of loan and making a regular loan.

Consultant: Right, but I think to get a total picture you'll want both types of costs.

O'Hennessey: Our cost section can give you an idea what it actually costs to place an SBA loan on the books based on the time and motion studies we have done of our normal business activities.

Clarence: On this total figure you have here $5,600 for the SBA acquisitions.

O'Hennessey: On the first page of our report we pointed out to management that because of the time restriction set as to when the final report was desired, there were varying degrees of accuracy in the data presented.

Definite were items where you could go to the bank's records and find the specific item of expense, such as the $204,500 for advertising. Here the exact bill and its payment could be identified.

Indefinite were items where we came to the conclusion after talking to people that the time taken to do the specific job took a certain percentage of time over and above our regular standard time allowance. Or they were estimates made by the people doing the job where we had no current time studies.

Guesstimates were where we made a specific decision as to the cost or loss of interest based entirely on our own past experience.

In other words, we wanted to let management know how reliable the various figures were so that they would know what they might be basing their decision on.

Consultant: How did you arrive at the 50% differential between regular and minority SBA loans?

O'Hennessey: We had something to base it on. We knew what it cost us to put a regular SBA loan on from our time and motion standards. We didn't go make any new time studies for the minority SBA loans. We just talked to a lot of people and—to the best of their ability—they made estimates which, on the average, came out pretty close to 50%.

Consultant: Could you get upper and lower bounds on the guesstimate to be considered firmer? The $170,000 for lost income and interest. I'm wondering if it would be useful to somebody confronted with that figure to know within reason what amount was at risk through losses?

Darrow: We didn't have a very good feel for losses at that time because the minority business program had just started so we would have been hard pressed to develop these bounds.

Consultant: But do you think you could get there now that you've been given some time?

O'Hennessey: Yes you could now. I think you could make a good guesstimate now. We've had enough experience right now knowing they've been on the books a long enough period of time and the delinquency ratio has developed a fairly stable pattern.

The discussion then shifted to special minority hiring and training policies and programs.

Consultant: Now, what I'm interested in is some of the training. Training doesn't tell you the total costs of having a good minority hiring policy, does it?

O'Hennessey: No, the training costs considered were only for the hard-core unemployables. Under our normal minority hiring procedures where they come in and file an application and we hire them, even though they require some training before they can do the job, none of this expense was considered in our cost. The only costs we put here were the ones we're incurring when we run the special training programs. That is, when we take the hard-core people that nobody else will hire, bring them in and put them through a course of training, and try to fit them into the system. We also bring these people back later and put them through another program to try and upgrade their capabilities.

Consultant: You wouldn't have any costs here for handling them on the job? After they've been put in regular jobs at the bank? Are there costs associated with this?

O'Hennessey: Yes, there are some on-the-job training costs, but we figured this was normal for a new hire and did not include it. In this particular program, we have some time allocated for follow-up counseling. There's also one full-time person who does this and also counsels their supervisors before and after these people are placed on the job.

Consultant: All right, how about something that falls outside the training program—say taking special initiative to get blacks, Puerto Ricans, and other minority groups to apply for jobs and taking more time to process them—interviewing, hiring and so forth. That wasn't considered at this time?

O'Hennessey: No, we only took the hard-core people.

Consultant: That might be something to think about. Suppose the bank has ads on black radio or Spanish language radio stations saying that the National Bank and Trust Company is an equal-opportunity employer. That I would think would be a legitimate expense. What if, for example, you have to interview, say, four people where previously you only had to interview three people in order to fill a slot.

O'Hennessey: We didn't worry about that at all. This was one of the things we kicked around at the beginning and threw out. Considering our time constraints and the fact that this is a pretty murkey area, we figured all we wanted were the costs of the hard-core training programs alone.

Baron: Then, this hard-core training is straight out-of-pocket costs. There's no deduction for the cost of training an average guy.

O'Hennessey: No, this is just what it costs to get this person so he or she can do a job.

Consultant: You want to get him to come up to the point where you think the average guy would be when you hire him?

Baron: Is that right?

O'Hennessey: Yes, but the hard-core people, even when they finish training and go into the branches, generally take longer to do a job than somebody you would hire normally.

Consultant: So you don't have that quantified?

O'Hennessey: Not yet.

After this brief discussion of the costs of training and hiring minority personnel, the discussion shifted to more general methodological issues regarding the conduct of the social audit.

Consultant: We've been thinking, for the immediate future of Baron's activity, to concentrate on explicit socially directed activities.

Baron: That does not exhaust an understanding of the bank's total social impact. A lot of that comes through right in the business activity. The bank's total social impact is something that should be looked at down the line. One of these areas of impact would be, of course, concern over the nature of loans as to whether or not they were "socially desirable." I suppose it would be possible to find out from a loan officer what portion of his time is spent prowling around to develop "socially desirable" loan applications.

O'Hennessey: Now you're talking about ecology, for example.

Baron and Consultant: Yes.

O'Hennessey: First, we had thought we would include that. But you get into very grey areas. Somebody's got to sit down in the very beginning and make some definitions as to what you mean. The problem you run into is that most loans we make are general–purpose lines of credit. If we lend $15 million to an oil company, some little bit of that goes to improve a refinery so that it doesn't throw so much smoke and sulfur in the air. Some other part is always going to go somewhere else. Well, how much do we charge to the ecology part of it?

Baron: By and large we are not directive with regard to the use of funds.

Consultant: Would it be possible to pull our a number of loans–a sample of loans–then decide for which of these it might be a good idea for the bank to look further into the social impact of these loans.

O'Hennessey: Yes. The measurement would be the result of making the study and then developing a policy and then measuring against this standard. On our commercial loan computer program, for example, one of the last things I had them do was to leave a two-digit space in case we wanted to code our loans for ecology purposes. But then, as I say, we got down to talking to the loan people and they said, "O.K., you get somebody to sit down and give us definitions of what you mean by each of these, then we'll put them into the slots."

Baron: I have a thought which just might be workable. Take maybe one to two categories of loans that are generally directed and probably do have ecological impact–maybe new real estate development or capital equipment loans–and establish a policy that for these limited number of loans your loan officer will complete an added section of credit application that calls for their view of the environmental impact of granting this loan. We could then have somebody in the regional office with responsibility for reviewing these and judging the officer on the thoroughness of how well he answered these questions. An accounting system could be developed to quantify the amount of time and energy spent reviewing these factors and possibly the cost that would be incurred to us not only of the time but the lost revenue of any loans we turn down on this basis. But as I say, we've got to get better definitions so the loan officers can handle the assessment.

As part of the its concept of the social responsibility of business in regard to serving the community, National Bank and Trust had already established two branches in ghetto areas and was in the process of building two more.

Baron: What's the story on the costs for ghetto branches (Item IIA on cost sheet)?

O'Hennessey: In our regular branches, we'll just say that to take in a commercial deposit, it takes x number of minutes. In the ghetto branches, it takes x plus some minutes because many of the people coming to be served are slower and we are often breaking in new tellers who don't work as fast. So it takes maybe 30% more staff to produce the same amount of work. It's not only because the staff is slower, but it's because the customers are slower.

Baron: By including all that difference, it assumes that you could have placed a similar branch somewhere else in Connecticut and had normal operations.

O'Hennessey: It costs the ghetto branch much more to operate with a given volume of work than if we had this branch in a non-ghetto area.

Baron: But the point is that if there were an opportunity to place a branch in a non-ghetto area and it could operate profitably, we'd have placed a branch there.

O'Hennessey: We only put these branches in the ghettos to bring banking service to the people. For most of these branches it will be some time before we are able to make a profit.

Baron: What kind of information has been released through some form or another regarding the fact that some of these branches are not making money and the reason that they were still in operation was that there was an explicit policy on the part of the bank to provide a public convenience.

O'Hennessey: We thought about it, I don't think we wanted to make a big thing out of it.

Clarence: Sure, it's been in the annual reports, "In addition, last year we opened two branches: the first branches ever in East Hartford and Westford and while we recognize that these won't be profitable for a long time we do think they will. . . ."

Following this exchange, the conversation shifted to National Bank and Trust's use of minority suppliers and contractors.

Clarence: I remember reading about black architects working on the construction of the East Hartford branch and about how they utilized local talent and all that, but I don't recall reading about it being unprofitable.

O'Hennessey: When any de novo branches are opened, we generally expect them to be unprofitable for one to two years. These branches were in that class and have not been opened long enough to tell when they will be profitable. This is the reason there was no mention as to whether or not these branches were profitable or unprofitable.

Another problem is that we used the black architects and all local workers in East Hartford, and then to my knowledge they never got on our bid lists afterwards. I don't think we've ever used them again even though they did a good job.

Baron: Why didn't we?

O'Hennessey: I'm not sure of the exact circumstances at all. I don't think there was any malice involved. We just didn't think about it. We went back to the old bid lists for our other jobs. We have some people now looking into the whole issue of encouraging minority contractors and suppliers. This is a major area of social concern, and I'm sure we'll rectify the situation.

Consultant: Now supposing you do have an aggressive program of picking up minority suppliers and you find out from your jolly accountant, O'Hennessey, that you're losing some money that way. At the same time, you start going public with your social audit. Further, suppose another part of your social audit says it costs us more to do a certain volume of business in minority areas because the people are slower and the workers are slower. You're going to catch some flack!

Baron: Well, now, there's another fact too–I'm being perfectly frank with you–who made the decision on the time motion standards being 1+?

O'Hennessey: Time studies were made in the branches, those in the minority areas showed higher time requirement than in our branches with a more mixed type of customer.

Baron: In other words, this is based on actual experience?

O'Hennessey: Oh yes, it's actual data. We went out and made new time studies, and from these new studies a different set of time standards were set for these branches than were set for the others.

Baron: I hope they're substantiated–that nobody just pulled them out of the air.

O'Hennessey: Oh, no, no! They went out and actually time studied the jobs at some of these branches.

Consultant: Your position reminds me of arguments I used to have with my daughter when she was young and she would say, "But I'm right," and I would reply, "That's no excuse." The mere fact that you write it and document it is not going to get you off the hook.

Baron: There's a time for diplomacy.

O'Hennessey: Yeah, but here again all we were trying to do was to get our management alerted to this, provide them a picture, and then hope they would do something–which they're now doing.

Baron: But you know I have mixed feelings about the social audit thing. Although I think it's time for diplomacy with the social audit, I think you can afford to be explicit on some of these things. I don't think the bank ought to, in the long run, attempt necessarily to cover up these things, although there might be times to discuss it and times not to.

Darrow: The objective in the ghetto branches would ultimately be to close the gap, to make them branches like every other branch. So if you've got a time series on the thing, you show that when you first opened up it really wasn't bankable, that people didn't know anything about banks and, as a result, it took longer to educate them and whatever.

Clarence: You'd have a real sense of accomplishment from this.

Darrow: Right. And after a year if you did another time study, it might show an improvement.

O'Hennessey: Yes. That's right. But we now get a report each month of the activity, and the trend is still not running down. They're still over standards, even the standards for their particular branch.

Consultant: As long as we're asking nasty questions, there's a logical linking step here. Do you make time studies on minority employees versus non-minority employees in your regular branches?

O'Hennessey: We don't segregate them.

Baron: Branch-wise you mean?

O'Hennessey: We just make so many samplings, and there may be some minorities in there as well as the others.

Consultant: But the logic of your position for East Hartford suggests that with a very slight extension and with no distortion of the logic that the bank should get credit for hiring minority people in those branches, if the minority people are slower workers than the non-minority people.

O'Hennessey: Well, I don't think we've ever tried that.

Darrow: And are paid the same.

Consultant: Yes, and are paid the same.

Baron: They may not be advancing the same.

Consultant: Now you see when you extend it that far I think you're really getting yourself in a risky public relations position. But I think internally I would like to know that.

Baron: I think probably the reason the time-motion studies, for the ghetto branches, have higher time ratios is more due to the nature of the serving area than the nature of the employees in the branch.

O'Hennessey: Yes. I think it's some of each.

Baron: Yes, some of each, but the community requires different services.

Exhibit 17-1

March 4, 1971

MEMO TO: Phineas Bailey, President
SUBJECT: Survey of Social Relations Programs

This survey attempts to determine the full extent of our bank's involvement in social relations programs and to establish related expense. Social relations programs or social affairs involvements include five primary areas:

1. *Minorities*

   Racial
   Ethnic
   Other

2. *Youth*

   Students
   Minority Sub-groups
   Educators (Facilities, School Districts, School Administrators)
   Employment Assistance (N.A.B., etc.)

3. *Community Activities*

   Service Organizations
   Charitable and Social Service Agencies and Associations
   Other Community and Trade Organizations

4. *Physical Environment*

   Transportation
   Housing
   Ecology

5. *Government*

   Federal, State, County and Local

Our investigation revealed no centralized source of information regarding the bank's involvement and that both communication on and coordination of the bank's efforts were inadequate. Extensive research was required to determine costs since many branches and administration departments were participating in social relations programs in varying degrees and incurring varied types of costs ranging from foundation grants to loans to capital expenditures or operating expenses.

In order to segregate expenses in a more meaningful manner, they were classified into three groups based on their relationship to social problems. Because of the varying degrees of accuracy of the data, further classifications of expense were made on the basis of definite, indefinite or guesstimate.

SUMMARY OF EXPENSES FOR SOCIAL RELATIONS PROGRAMS (MILLIONS OF DOLLARS)

Expenses Incurred	*1970*	*Cumulative through December 31, 1970*					*Est. 1971*
		Total	*Definite*	*Indefinite*	*Guesstimate*		
I. Because of current social relations problems	2.1	2.4	0.7	1.6	0.2		2.0
II. Either because of social relations problems or for security reasons	2.0	3.1	1.3	1.8	–		1.8
III. Through contributions to help solve social relations problems	0.8	0.8*	0.7	0.1	–		0.8
Total	4.9	6.3	2.7	3.5	0.2		4.6

*1970 only. See Footnote 8, Exhibit 17-2.

The National Bank and Trust's involvement in social relations programs is extensive and expensive as is demonstrated by the $4.9 million spent in 1970 and the estimate of $4.6 million for 1971. The detailed breakdown of these expenses summarized above are presented in the attached Exhibits 17-2 and 17-3. Before using any of the data, reference should be made to the extensive, explanatory footnotes on Exhibit 17-2.

SUMMARY

1.–Both the dollars of expense and the sensitivities involved in social relations programs demand much closer evaluation and direction from top management.

2.–The extent of our bank's involvement in social relations programs makes mandatory the establishment of a master coordination and communication control center.

3.–Despite our good intentions and substantial dollar outlay, our ineptness, in some instances, has created additional social problems and negative public relations.

4.–We must reexamine our approach to Management Information Systems in order to provide an entirely new type of basic data that will bring into focus our economic involvement in social relations programs.

O'Hennessey
Controller

Exhibit 17-2

SOCIAL RELATIONS PROGRAMS (ESTIMATED COSTS–CONTRIBUTIONS)

		Cumulative Cost to Date (Including 1970)			
	1970 Cost	*Total*[1]	*Definite*	*Indefinite*	*Guesstimate*
I. Expenses Incurred Because of Today's Social Problems					
A. Premises Loaned					
1. Shadowbrook Youth Association	$ 1,750	$ 3,000	$ 3,000	–	–
2. Urban Training Center	22,000	51,500	51,500	–	–
	$ 23,750	$ 54,500	$ 54,500	–	–
B. Training					
1. NAB Summer Program	$ 44,446	$124,400	$124,400		
2. Loaned Executives to Summer Program	7,500	7,500	7,500		
3. Hard-Core Training	75,000	150,000	44,000	106,000	
4. Appraisal Dept. College Scholarships	10,000	14,225	14,225		
5. Other Appraisal Dept. Scholarships	300	300	300		
6. Opportunity Job Training (Hartford)	3,000	3,000		3,000	
7. "52" Association	1,390	1,390	1,390		
8. Hartford Jr. College	5,250	5,250	5,250		
	$148,986	$306,065	$197,065	$109,000	–
C. Education					
1. Parent-Child (New Haven)	650	650	650	–	–
2. Taylor High (Hartford)	1,150	1,150	1,150	–	–
	1,800	1,800	1,800	–	–

Exhibit 17-2 (continued)

SOCIAL RELATIONS PROGRAMS (ESTIMATED COSTS–CONTRIBUTIONS)

			Cumulative Cost to Date (Including 1970)			
		1970 Cost	*Total*[1]	*Definite*	*Indefinite*	*Guesstimate*
D.	Bank–Sponsored Loan Agencies					
	1. Business Ownership, Inc. (Hartford)	$ 50,529	$ 77,908	$ 77,908	–	–
	2. Business Ownership, Inc. (New Haven)	8,125	8,125	8,125	–	–
		58,654	86,033	86,033		
E.	Bank Loan Programs					
	1. "Own Your Home" Program					
	Advertising		19,750	19,750		
	Acquisition	43,500	65,000		65,000	
	Servicing	13,500	18,450		18,450	
	Lost Income (Interest)[2]	170,000	170,000			170,000
	2. SBA–Minority Enterprise–Acquisition Cost	3,750	5,600		5,600	
	3. Small Business Publications	5,000	5,000	5,000		
	4. Student Loans[3]	1,375,000	1,375,000		1,375,000	
		1,610,750	1,658,800	24,750	1,464,000	170,000
F.	Regional Urban Affairs					
	1. Coordinators	10,000	10,000	10,000	–	–
G.	Administration					
	1. Salaries, Etc.	66,000	87,500	87,500	–	–

Exhibit 17-2 (continued)

SOCIAL RELATIONS PROGRAMS (ESTIMATED COSTS–CONTRIBUTIONS)

		Cumulative Cost to Date (Including 1970)			
	1970 Cost	*Total*[1]	*Definite*	*Indefinite*	*Guesstimate*
H. Advertising					
1. New Haven	204,500	204,500	204,500	–	–
Total I:	$2,122,440	$2,409,698	$666,648	$1,573,050	$170,000
II. Problems Incurred–Some Due to Social Problems, Others for Bank Convenience					
A. Branches					
1. New Branches[4]	430,835	430,835	430,835		–
2. Special Time–Ghetto Branches[5]	309,120	309,120		309,120	–
	$739,955	$739,955	$430,835	$309,120	–
B. Security					
1. Guards	636,000	1,080,000		1,080,000	–
2. Precaution Equipment[6]	167,000	877,000	877,000		–
3. Refurbishing of Building[7]	382,005	385,387		385,387	–
	$1,185,005	$2,348,387	$877,000	$2,471,387	–
Total II:	1,924,000	3,088,342	1,307,835	1,780,507	–

Exhibit 17-2 (continued)

SOCIAL RELATIONS PROGRAMS (ESTIMATED COSTS—CONTRIBUTIONS)

		Cumulative Cost to Date (Including 1970)			
	1970 Cost	*Total*[1]	*Definite*	*Indefinite*	*Guesstimate*
III. Contributions—A Good Portion For Social Problems—Some Recent, Others Past[8]					
A. Organizations					
1. Youth	7,297	7,297	7,297		
2. Hospitals	17,224	17,224	17,224		
3. Ecology[9]	10,913	10,913	10,913		
4. Community Involvement	27,732	27,732	27,732		
5. Aid to Education[10]	115,820	115,820	115,820		
6. Other	13,920	13,920	13,920		
7. United Fund and Community Chest	507,530	507,530	507,530		
	$700,436	$700,436	$700,436		
B. Cost to Collect Annual Charity Contributions[11]					
1. Inside/Outside Bank	60,000	60,000		60,000	—
Total III:	$760,436	$760,436	$700,436	$ 60,000	—
Grand Total:	$4,907,836	$6,258,476	$2,674,919	$3,413,557	$170,000

Exhibit 17-2 (continued)

[1] Previous years' cost figures were obtained in some categories; however, in other categories records of previous years' costs were either vague or unavailable to make good estimates.

[2] Although the "Own Your Home" Program has been in operation since 1968, the estimate for lost income was for the period January-October, 1970. The lost income was the difference between prime rate and the rate charged "OYH" Program borrowers for the above period. To determine previous years' lost income would be very difficult.

[3] This estimate was for 1970 and was the difference between the normal personal loan rate and the return on Student Loans.

[4] Two branches were completed in 1970. Two more should be completed in 1971-1972

[5] Special time allowance for ghetto branches in 1970. Estimates for previous years were unavailable.

[6] Precaution equipment that has been installed in the East-West Computer Centers, New Haven Master-charge Center, and the Hartford Stock Transfer Department. Some equipment was installed for the bank's convenience; other, due to today's social problems. This amount is a capital expenditure.

[7] This cost was to repair damaged buildings caused by the student disturbance at Yale and should not be considered a capital expenditure.

[8] Contributions made in 1970 are thought to apply to today's social problems although in some cases the bank has been contributing to these organizations for many years.

[9] A good portion of this amount was used to support election propositions, which contributed to community betterment.

[10] All of this amount involves contributions to schools, colleges, and universities. Here again the bank has been contributing to educational institutions for many years.

[11] This amount is an estimate of the cost to the bank of our employees, who assist with major annual charity collection drives. No previous records were available, and the 1970 estimated cost was obtained through a survey.

Exhibit 17-3

SOCIAL RELATIONS PROGRAMS (ESTIMATE 1971)

				Estimate 1971
I.	Expense Definitely Incurred Because of Today's Social Problems			
	A.	Premises Loaned		
		1.	Shadowbrook Youth Association	$ 1,750
		2.	Urban League Training Center	18,000
				$ 19,750
	B.	Training		
		1.	NAB Summer Program	$ 42,500
		2.	Hard-Core	80,000
		3.	Appraisal Dept. College Scholarships	14,000
		4.	Other Appraisal Dept. Scholarships	300
		5.	Opportunity Job (Hartford)	3,000
		6.	"52" Association	?
		7.	Hartford Jr. College	4,500
				$ 144,300
	C.	Education		
		1.	Parent-Child (New Haven)	?
		2.	High Schools (Hartford)	?
	D.	Bank Sponsored Loan Agencies		
		1.	Business Ownership (Hartford)	$ 62,500
		2.	Business Ownership (New Haven)	12,500
		3.	M.E.S.B.I.C.	?
				$ 75,000
	E.	Bank Loan Programs		
		1.	"Own Your Home"Program	
			Advertising	?
			Acquisition	$ 35,000
			Servicing	15,000
		2.	SBA Acquisition	5,000
		3.	Small Business Publications	?
		4.	Student Loans	1,500,000
				$1,555,000
	F.	Regional Urban Affairs		
		1.	Coordinators	$ 50,000
	G.	Administration		
		1.	Salaries, Etc.	$ 87,500
Total I:				$1,931,550

II. Expense Incurred–Some Due to Social Problems, Others for Bank Convenience	
A. Branches	
1. New Branches	$ 248,000
2. Special Time–Ghetto	310,000
	$ 558,000
B. Security	
1. Guards	$ 675,000
2. Precaution Equipment	?
3. Refurbishing of Branches	?
	$ 675,000
Total II:	$1,233,000
III. Contributions–A Good Portion for Social Problems–Some Recent, Others Past	
A. Organizations	
1. Youth	$ 10,000
2. Hospitals	17,500
3. Ecology	17,500
4. Community Involvement	30,000
5. Aid to Education	150,000
6. Other	15,000
7. United Fund and Community Chest	510,000
	$ 750,000
B. Cost To Collect Annual Charity Contributions	
1. Inside/Outside Bank	$ 60,000
Total III:	810,000
Grand Total:	$3,974,550

Case Eighteen

Eastern Gas & Fuel Associates (A)

> A diversified energy company engaged in the production, transportation, and distribution of the raw materials of energy. Major operations are in bituminous coal, gas utility, and inland and coastal marine transportation.[1]

> But they [social problems] will not get solved unless innovative business men, who sense a changing world and feel challenged rather than threatened, react in a fashion likely to produce profit as well as imaginative response to social need.[2]

With the threat of an energy crisis becoming a reality and the persistent problems of "Black Lung" disease and minority employment, the company described in the first quote above seems to be an unlikely candidate for committing itself to the type of action recommended in the second. However, Eli Goldston, President of Eastern Gas and Fuel, described his two-fold task in the industrial and social arenas in the following manner:

> In the last decade I have had the task—and fun and excitement—of trying to lead a large diversified energy corporation not only toward technical innovation and profitability, but also toward social innovation in response to changing public expectations of corporate conduct.[3]

This case will examine one specific aspect of Goldston's attempt at "doing well while doing good":[4] the question of whether EGFA should conduct some sort of social

---

[1] Eastern Gas and Fuel Associates, 1972, *Annual Report.*

[2] Eli Goldston's statement as candidate for Harvard Board of Overseers, quoted in Harvard Business School Association of Boston, Business Statesman Award Announcement, 1973.

[3] *Ibid.*

[4] *Ibid.*

audit of its operations. It will focus on that point when the decision was to be made, when Mr. Goldston returned to the company in the second half of 1972 after a six month leave of absence.

THE COMPANY

Although the company had some difficulties with the profitability of its coal company in the early 1970s, in general EGFA had proven it could "do well." In 1972 it ranked 368th in sales among the *Fortune* 500[5], and its annual revenues were over $330 million, and it supplied over 1½% of the national energy consumption (counting coal produced, brokered, or barged, oil barged, and gas distributed[6]).

EGFA, a Massachusetts voluntary association,[7] was formed in July 1929. Headquartered in Boston, the company's important subsidiary operations were in coal (Eastern Associated Coal Company), gas (the Boston Gas Company), marine (Midland Enterprises), plus a coke plant in Philadelphia and over one-third ownership of a natural gas pipeline (see Exhibit 18-1 for complete list of subsidiaries.)

The company's annual Form 10-K report to the SEC for the fiscal year ended December 31, 1972, gave this description:

> Eastern and its principal subsidiaries are engaged in the production and sale of bituminous coal, water transportation . . .,and the distribution of natural gas in eastern Massachusetts. Eastern and its subsidiaries also conduct other marine operations and operate a coke plant, several docking facilities, and a shipyard.[8]

Overall, the company had a good financial record with net sales and operating revenues increasing steadily to $331,022,000 in 1973 (up 13% from 1971). However, 1970 was the peak year; net income before extraordinary items soared to $22,248,000 (up from $12,410,000 the prior year), and earnings per share were $2.09 (up from $1.18). Unfortunately, in 1971 and 1972 earnings in the coal company dropped sharply bringing total EGFA income before extraordinary items down to $16,950,000, or $1.75 per share (for detailed financial data see Exhibit 18-2). Since each of the quite independent and distinct subsidiaries faced diverse problems, it is useful to look at the different businesses and their recent performance records separately (Exhibit 18-3 presents the financial data broken down by subsidiary).

---

[5]Other *Fortune* rankings include 226th in assets, 280th in net income, 165th in net income as a percent of sales, 284th in equity, 258th in net income as a percent of stockholders equity, and 22nd in annual growth in earnings per share. See *Fortune*, June 1973.

[6]1972 *Annual Report.*

[7]This kind of company has some different legal limitations, but the situation regarding charitable contributions, for example, is the same for a corporation or voluntary association.

[8]1972 report to the SEC, Form 10-K, p. 1.

THE COAL COMPANY "The coal company believes that it is engaged in two lines of business: the production and sale of coal and the production and sale of coke[9] . . . ."

> The principal business is the deep mining and preparation of various grades of metallurgical coal for sale primarily to steel producers located in the U.S. and abroad and of steam coal for sale to electric utility companies located principally in the eastern U.S. and Canada. The coal company also sells significant quantities of metallurgical coal and steam coal produced by other mining companies.[10] It operates 18 deep coal mines located in West Virginia and Pennsylvania and is developing an additional mine to go into production in 1974.[11]

EACC, the sixth largest U.S. non-captive coal producer, had an exceptional year in 1970; production reached 14.5 million tons with an all-time high pre-tax income of $22.7 million–growth due primarily to productivity gains, significant price increases, and the heavy influence of Japanese buying that year. Coal production at EACC dropped off to 12.5 million tons in 1972 (up from 11.4 million tons in 1971) and income fell even more dramatically to $10.2 million in 1971 and then to $5.3 million in 1972. These declines since 1970 were due in large part to some rather specialized problems experienced by nearly all underground mining operations. The industry was plagued by an unstable work force due to the turmoil in the Mineworker's Union, unauthorized work stoppages, problems of recruiting and training a new work force, and a lower productivity rate caused in part by the more stringent health and safety regulations which had been instituted.

In general the company was optimistic, stating that EFGA was giving top priority to making its mines both safer and more productive and that the productivity decline of recent years may have been checked. Nevertheless, even the annual report cautioned, "Although Eastern anticipates improved deliveries in 1973, its contracts continue in excess of expected productions."

THE GAS COMPANY Boston Gas Company, the largest gas utility in New England, with 325,000 customers:

> distributes and sells natural gas for residential, commercial, and industrial users in an area which includes the city of Boston (except for one small section . . .), and 46 additional cities and towns . . . gas appliances are sold and rented by the Gas Company incidental to such business.
>
> The territory served by the Gas Company comprises an area of about 783 square miles, having an aggregate population of about 1,600,000. The territory primarily is

[9] In 1972 the Philadelphia Coke plant accounted for 7.2% of coal company's net sales but 24.6% of its income before taxes.

[10] The percentage of coal revenues from brokerage sales declined from 5.4% in 1970 to 1.9% in 1972.

[11] 1972 report to the SEC, Form 10-K, p. 2.

a residential, commercial, and light manufacturing area. The population trend in the area has been characterized by relative stability.[12]

1972 was an especially outstanding year for the Gas Company, which achieved record totals for gas delivered (43.9 billion cubic feet up from 36.5 billion in 1971), revenues ($92.0 million up from $75.5 in 1971), and pre-tax income ($7.9 million up from $5.4 million in 1971).[13]

The *Annual Report* presented the Gas Company as an "innovator in computerized customer service systems, utility applications of modern marketing, use of liquified natural gas (LNG) for supplemental gas supply." In addition to this emphasis on growth and innovation, however, the *Annual Report* acknowledged that constraints limited energy companies in the 1970s and explained how Boston Gas had adjusted to the "energy crisis."

> With the rapidly tightening gas supply situation, Boston Gas revised its merchandising goals and efforts . . . mass media promotional advertising was virtually eliminated to dampen any general impression that gas could be made available in unlimited quantities. No existing gas users were curtailed, and many new customers were added, but when the year's sales goals in commercial and industrial heating sales were reached in early spring, further additions of new customers of this type were suspended for a year.[14]

MARINE OPERATION

> Midland Enterprises Inc. is primarily engaged through wholly-owned subsidiaries in the operation of a fleet of towboats, tugboats, and barges providing barge transportation of cargoes on the Ohio and Mississippi Rivers and their tributaries and the Gulf of Mexico.[15]

The company had 1280 barges, 50 river towboats, and 50 ocean-going barges and tugs, which operated on the Mississippi, Ohio Illinois, and Arkansas River systems and in the Gulf of Mexico and the Caribbean. In addition, the company operated dry bulk commodity terminals on these waterways and a harbor tugboat service in the Port of Boston.

In 1972 the Marine division increased total tonnage to 37.7 million tons (up from 33.2 million tons the year before), took in $69.5 million in revenue (up from $53.7 million), and posted earnings of $11.7 million (up from $7.0 million). Over one-fifth of the total tonnage carried was coal, with much smaller amounts of petroleum, stone, sand,

---

[12] 1972 Report to the SEC, Form 10-K, P. 14.

[13] These figures reflect real growth–and the nearly ideal weather conditions that prevailed–but also result from the gas company's acquisition of three smaller Massachusetts gas companies.

[14] 1972 *Annual Report*, p. 10.

[15] 1972 Report to the SEC, Form 10-K, P. 8.

gravel, phosphate rock, and other materials being hauled. Over 50% of Midland's total tonnage was under long-term contracts with escalation provisions for increased costs, and management expected 1973 to be another good year for the Marine operations.

THE CHIEF EXECUTIVE

> Our central problems are to devise a more just distribution of our increasing quantity of material goods; to meet the demand for a better quality of life by expanding vastly the service sector of our economy; and, by controlling our technology, to develop a consensus on these and other social values and on their relative priorities.[16]

The author of this statement, Eli Goldston, was born in Ohio in 1920, graduated from Harvard College and received advanced degrees from there in both law and business. For many years he was a partner in a Cleveland law firm and came to EGFA in 1961, having become president of Midland Enterprises in Cincinnati which merged with EGFA at that time. He became president of EGFA in 1962 and Chief Executive Officer in 1963. He also maintained close contact with the academic world. In 1971, Mr. Goldston gave the Benjamin F. Fairless Memorial Lectures at Carnegie Mellon University, and in the first half of 1972 he took a sabbatical from EGFA as a Visiting Fellow at the London Graduate School of Business. Not only had he been active personally in cultural, civic, and philanthropic affairs[17] but also, as a company president he had been an outspoken advocate of the social responsibilities of business.

Widely in demand as a writer and speaker, Mr. Goldston's public remarks provided a philosophical background for some of the corporation's actions. His theories did not include a kind of flaccid do-goodism at the expense of profitability. In fact, he emphasized the complexity of the modern business world and the motives which prompted contemporary businessmen. He wrote:

> The businessman has a central concern for the bottom line but he also has a great many other concerns and in most areas he has done much better than he gets credit for.[18]

---

[16]Eli Goldston, "New Prospects for American Business," *Daedalus*, winter 1969, p. 104.

[17]*Who's Who*, for example, listed these activities: director–Arthur D. Little, First National Bank of Boston, Raytheon, John Hancock Mutual Life Insurance Company, Algonquin Gas Transmission Company; member–White House Conference of Fulfill These Rights; chairman–Boston-Kyoto Sister Committee; trustee–Hebrew Union College, Combined Jewish Philanthropies of Greater Boston, New England Aquarium, World Peace Foundation; Board of Directors–International Center of New England; chairman–Boston Project Joint Center for Urban Studies; member–American Academy of Arts and Sciences, Cleveland Bar, Chamber of Commerce.

[18]Eli Goldston, "Corporations Under Attack: Response to New Challenges," speech to American Bar Assocation National Institute, October 1972.

Mr. Goldston noted that the motives of businessmen may be admirable in many cases, but it does not necessarily follow that a "spotless" company results from even the highest ideals. Using himself and his company as an example, he told of students who had protested Harvard's Gulf Oil endowment fund coming to him and stating that instead they wished Harvard to own stock in a progressive company like EGFA. Mr. Goldston made the tongue-in-cheek retort, "But what about our strip mining operations?"[19] explaining that one cannot say simply, "this is a good company" or "this is a bad company" and direct university holdings accordingly.[20] Instead, "You have to say to yourself that you live in a complicated world."[21]

Mr. Goldston also cautioned that business decisions are made in a highly political atmosphere which is not reducible to skeletal mathematic formulation: "No one who has ever participated in the top management decisions of a significant corporation has ever thought that management is a science rather than an art."[22]

On another occasion he elaborated: "What I am suggesting is that the economist should take himself away from the computer, away from the calculator, away from the vector analysis and all those things and get back to the real problems of society."[23]

Mr. Goldston depicted the businessman as serving many, possibly conflicting, constituencies–customers, shareholders, employees, top management, government, society in general, and even the competition. The executive did, however, have some leeway in his efforts to satisfy these groups (and his own conscience), and Mr. Goldston described this area as the space between the floor of what is required by law and the ceiling of what the realities of competition will allow. He argued that it was no longer true (if it ever was) that the executive used this leeway to maximize. Rather than trying to get the most profit out of every single transaction no matter what the consequences, the businessman, operating in a highly complex and political world, "satisfices."

Mr. Goldston wrote: "business management regards itself as having a primary duty of managing to get something done. And if you are going to manage to get something done, you are not maximizing and trying to make the last buck, trying to squeeze the final penny out of every dollar."[24] He contended, however, that this attitude did not mean ignoring profit. Making money in his view was one of the responsibilities of business, too. He continued:

> But if you don't want to spend what little money you have left paying lawyers to defend you from take-over bids, the way our system works, you have to make a

---

[19] *Ibid.*

[20] See *Foundation News*, July-August 1972 for Eli Goldston's more complete rebuttal of such arguments in his "A Review of The Ethical Investor" (pp. 30-36).

[21] Goldston, "Corporations Under Attack."

[22] Eli Goldston, "The Limits of Technology," Diebold Lecture at Harvard Business School, November 1969.

[23] Transcript of Response by Eli Goldston to Professor John Kenneth Galbraith's paper, "Economics as a System of Belief," at the 82nd Annual Meeting of the American Economic Association, December 28, 1969.

[24] Goldston, "Corporations Under Attack."

reasonable amount on the equity. As a consequence, you satisfice . . . but central to satisficing is producing enough money on the equity so that the stock will sell at a decent enough price that you will be able to stay on the job."[25]

Thus, Mr. Goldston saw the corporation as both a social and an economic institution which must translate its responsibilities to the community into operational management practices and decision-making techniques. It needs to be encouraged to respond to human as well as monetary pressures, and Mr. Goldston used the "carrot-stick" image to describe some of the ways an individual company or executive may be so encouraged. It must be worth a company's while, he felt, to act in a socially responsible way, and various incentives could be used as the carrot (or the stick, as in the case of heavy fines for polluting).[26] Mr. Goldston concluded his lectures on *Social Accounting: The Quantification of Concern* with the following five recommendations:

A. First of all we need to reform our Congressional processing of the budget and we need to establish an institution to analyze and publicize the relationship of National Budget decisions to our social problems.

B. The need for such government changes should not cause private business firms to delay in preparing their own sets of social accounts. Initially a firm must make an inventory of what it is doing and not doing on various social accounts that will be necessary.

C. An important strengthening of corporate concern would be the adoption of a sort of anti-trust rule which we might call an anti-lack-of-concern rule which would require divestment of any substantial property or significant operation not visited in person within each 12 months by the executive ultimately responsible for it.

D. I would also unclog the market and profit mechanism by facilitating the removal of managements which failed to provide good earnings.

E. The pressures placed on management by compelling disclosure of some social indicators is obvious; as the costs of noncompliance mount, financial auditors may insist that such disclosure has become essential to the accuracy of traditional financial statements.[27]

EGFA—1962-1972

Mr. Goldston described one of his tasks during the first five-year period (1962-1967) as "beating the business risk down" in what was basically a very heavily

---

[25]*Ibid.*

[26]The concreteness, as well as the appeal, of the carrot is important. Mr. Goldston wrote, "Not an oral moral whip but an enticing economic carrot will make the stubborn business animal get started." "New Prospects for American Business," p. 89.

[27]Eli Goldston, *The Quantification of Concern: Some Aspects of Social Accounting*, Lecture Three, "Social Accounting: Some National Goals and Corporate Purposes Beyond Calibration."

capitalized business.[28] He wanted to do this to justify a leveraged capital structure and then get a substantial return on the residual equity. He instituted a system of controls which included a stringent planning system based on five-year forecasts concerned with such matters as cash flow, operating results, and taxes. An earlier Harvard Business School case commented on the company's development during this period.

> According to management this substantial growth has been the result of a conscious attempt since 1962 to reassess and re-shape the company to fit "new realities" in its product, market, and consumer environments.
>
> Consequently, a five year process of consolidation and restructuring was begun. Each of the closely related existing operations in the company was completely reassessed to select those which by themselves had potential for substantial and stable earnings power. These would be continued and expanded. Any which did not would be sold or dissolved.[29] Meanwhile attempts were made to evolve, in the tradition-bound and conservative industries in which Eastern operated, a management structure which encouraged innovation and entrepreneurial attitudes in operations and which controlled, through a small, highly specialized central staff, goal-setting procedures and selective development of capital and personnel operations. The objective of building a solid as well as an increased earnings base was reflected by the end of this planning period in the development of a federation of market-oriented enterprises in the fields of energy and water transportation, together with numerous long-term contracts with large customers for supplying coal, coke and transportation. In 1967, the emphasis was therefore shifted from consolidation to expansion and profits.[30]

Mr. Goldston's letter to the stockholders in the 1967 *Annual Report*, accordingly called 1967 a "hinge year," and this orientation towards annual growth and profits brought impressive results. For example, the average annual growth rate, compounded, in earnings per share for the 1962-1967 period was 25.28%, a percentage which placed EGFA 22nd in the *Fortune* 500 in this respect.

The changes occurring at EGFA were not limited to the financial. Mr. Goldston's 1967 Annual Letter also included the following statement:

> As modern business managers we cannot operate without a constant sense of accelerating change. All of us–customers, employees, and management–are members of a society looking for better things to come.

Mr. Goldston explained that by that point the company had reached high levels of financial and marketing expertise, but that even with a vigorous and concerned

---

[28]Additional problems arose with the Coal Company, in an industry which is not only very heavily capitalized but also labor intensive. Mr. Goldston said that the Coal Company was, in effect, "going to hell on its productivity."

[29]For instance, EGFA got rid of its involvement in running company stores and in owning part of the Norfolk and Western Railroad.

[30]Eastern Gas and Fuel Associates, Harvard Business School, EA-M 506.

management there was much room for improvement in areas of "human relations." Starting in 1966, the five-year forecasts referred to above included sections on environmental and personnel problems, although Mr. Goldston acknowledged that these did not receive much attention at first. Meanwhile, however, he and the company were beginning to gain a reputation as concerned and progressive members of the community, and the *Annual Reports* provide some of the words to describe these "new directions." For instance, in 1970 there was a special section in the *Annual Report* on "Meeting the Energy Crisis of the 1970s," featuring interviews with top management and statements such as the following:

> Of course there is a very clear trend toward a greater human concern in our society right now and we're definitely going to see its effect on company personnel policies and practices.
>
> (J. T. Cathcart, Sr. Vice President, Administration)

> Like so many other industries, coal is struggling to improve its relations with employees and the public. We've probably overlooked or neglected the human factor; what people want from their work, improved health and safety of working conditions, protection of the environment around the mines and around the places where coal is used.
>
> (Robert Freeman, Sr. Vice President, Coal)

The problem of minority employment at EGFA illustrated how Mr. Goldston helped change his company's work force from virtually all-white to 8-9% black. Mr. Goldston described these events:

> When I first came to the Boston Gas Company I was interested in trying to integrate some blacks into our work force. I first attempted to learn the number of minority employees in the company. There was a total of 1,200 employees and I was told four were from minority groups. Now, four seemed to me a small number, but it seemed about three more than I had seen in several months that I had been around. Persisting, I then discovered that the four included myself, because I was Jewish; an Irish fellow who was dating a Chinese girl; and a black fellow who had retired a few years back. The fourth was never found.
>
> When I set about trying to integrate the work force I discovered two apparent rules. The first was that one could not get a job unless he was Irish. The second rule was that rule one did not apply to the *good* jobs. In order to integrate the work force by hiring blacks, we first had to face the problem of promoting the Irish. Very quickly we had our first Irish vice president. That was when I learned the difference between Protestants from Northern Ireland and Catholics from Southern Ireland because the fellow we had made vice president was a Protestant from Northern Ireland. Very rapidly we had some other Irish vice presidents.
>
> However, as a consequence of our efforts, today we have well over one hundred blacks working for the Boston Gas Company. Each earns about $10,000 representing a million dollars of payroll going into a minority community that

> previously received next to nothing from this particular company, even though there were miles of gas mains and many gas meters and customers within the community.[31]

Other parts of the company showed less spectacular results in this area. In the barge company, for example, the situation was complicated because the employees lived as well as worked together, and much of their travel was through southern states. To a degree, a similar reluctance prevailed in some of the coal company operations, and in places the division between black and white was quite strict.

However, Mr. Goldston explained how integration was achieved in the coal mining communities by starting with the children. For years there had been a company camp, with a number of different sessions each summer for white children at one location and one session for black children at another place. Gradual steps were taken year by year: first the camp staffs were integrated, then all sessions were held at the same place, Japanese children were included, and finally fully integrated camp sessions took place. There were still mines and communities that were almost entirely white, but at least this one instance of outright segregation was changed.

The home office too became involved in efforts to help the minority community and aid black-white relations. Mr. Goldston described one major program, BURP, that EGFA participated in during 1967 and 1968.

> What has come to be known as the Boston Urban Rehabilitation Program (BURP) had its genesis in the early fall of 1967, when the Department of Housing and Urban Development (HUD) decided to conduct a large demonstration of rehabilitation in the Roxbury-Dorchester section of Boston under Section 221 (d)(3) of the National Housing Act of 1961.
>
> The BURP designation was originally limited to describing the allocation of $24.5 million in federal funds to five private developer-sponsors to rehabilitate 2,000 apartment units in 101 buildings. It has since been extended by common usage to cover an almost contemporaneous rent supplement program involving 731 units in 30 buildings, with an allocation of $7.5 million, and two subsequent projects covering 217 units at a cost of $2.7 million.
>
> Inquiries revealed the developers' need for *equity cash* to make their projects go. After extensive negotiations with FHA officials, Eastern Gas and Fuel Associates provided this money by the purchase of equity interests in limited partnerships in a minority of the units. Boston Gas received the fuel commitment by extending its low public housing rates to the buildings, thus meeting competitive fuel costs.
>
> Boston Gas gained its largest single addition to gas load in recent years, while Eastern received the spillover tax shelter benefit. Neither return by itself would

---

[31] Eli Goldston, "For the Rich It Sings: Intra-Industry and Inter-Industry Cooperation and Competition for Socially Responsible Performance," Garrett Lectures on Managing the Socially Responsible Corporation 1972-1973, Graduate School of Business, Columbia University, February 22, 1973.

> have justified our involvement commercially, but together the two showed a respectable profit.[32]

Elsewhere, Mr. Goldston described in more detail some of the difficulties the BURP program encountered and how the company reacted to these:

> Of course there were a lot of problems. Because of the size and speed of the program, there was a minimum of communications with residents of the area. The relocation problems had been underestimated. A perfectly legitimate demand developed for the residents in the community to get a "piece of the action."[33]
>
> They objected to the fact that the program was entirely in the hands of outside owners and developers. We set about to try to find solutions for these problems, and I believe we have made a good start.
>
> Of all our activities in the past few months, perhaps the most significant and satisfying has been our help in putting together an all-black commercially motivated rehabilitation team which has been awarded FHA guaranteed mortgages for a $1 million project as part of the demonstration program. This is the first such award in FHA history.[34]

BURP was completed in 1969 and EGFA was no longer actively involved with the project. As with most housing projects of this nature, along with its successes came continuing problems and criticism. Many complained that there were not enough three, four, and five bedroom units to accommodate the large families in the area. In addition, a study done by a nonprofit group in the area found that the materials used seemed defective in some cases and that a number of the units did not meet the FHA's own standards. As a result, a great deal of continuing repair and upkeep was required, and sufficient money was not alloted for adequate maintainence. An independent study prepared for the Harvard-MIT Joint Center for Urban Studies commented,

> The Boston Rehabilitation Program has been and will unquestionably remain, the object of intense criticism and praise: lauded by its supporters as an extraordinary and ultimately successful effort to revitalize urban housing, condemned by its opponents as a squandering of scarce resources.[35]

---

[32]Eli Goldston, "BURP and Make Money," *Harvard Business Review*. September-October 1969, p. 87.

[33]For instance, at the December 1967 dedication ceremonies, Bryant Robbins, a militant black community leader lambasted BURP, claiming, "The program being dedicated has given no consideration to local developers, nonprofit developers, cooperative ownership or local management. It has been marred by racial discrimination in employment and inadequate relocation procedures."

[34]Eli Goldston, "The Businessman's Role in the Urban Crisis," address to the graduation class of the Program for Management Development, Harvard Business School, May 16, 1968.

[35]Langley C. Keyes, Jr., *The Boston Rehabilitation Program: An Independent Analysis*, the Joint Center for Urban Studies of the Massachusetts Institute of Technology and Harvard University (1970), pp. 4-5.

The report found that criticism centered on three major issues: the lack of community participation, tenant relocation, and communication problems among the various groups involved; but in general it suggested that BURP had benefited from EGFA contributions.

Mr. Goldston's assessment of the program was positive, and he spoke of the community benefits, saying:

> With all its difficulties, BURP was successful by many standards. In 18 months, one-seventh of the black population of Boston was rehoused in renovated units, with no increase in shelter cost. More than 400 black construction workers were employed at one time or another, and the majority of them were given some craft training. Two all-black development teams–contractors–emerged to receive about 10% of the total BURP program.[36]

The area of corporate giving provided Mr. Goldston with an example of the problems–bureaucratic, frustrating, and often petty–that he felt were likely to be encountered by a company trying to investigate its own programs in the social area. Charitable donations were an accepted activity in most large corporations. Few companies approached the legally deductible limit of 5% of pre-tax profit, but many millions of dollars were given away annually. And often, Mr. Goldston learned, given away in a very disorganized and unplanned fashion. At EGFA the money went here or there because it always had, because five years before that had made sense and no one had bothered to see if the situation had changed. Or money went someplace else because a certain officer had personal knowledge of or interest in a particular, possibly obscure, school cause.

Because of the apparently chaotic situation, and in connection with the new planning forecasts being drawn up, Mr. Goldston arranged for outside "experts" to look at the company's policies and see just how EGFA was disposing of its money. He described the situation:

> Years ago when I first came to the company, I was brought a slip of paper to O.K. It seems that in Philadelphia we had given $4500. I think it was to the United Fund and it needed my O.K.
>
> So I signed and I said, "Tell me, why do we give $4500?"
>
> "Well, that's what we gave last year."
>
> So I said, "All right." But that night at home I got to thinking. Why did we give $4500 dollars the year before? We had closed down half of the facility, and did that mean we really should have given half as much because we had half as many employees in Philadelphia? Or because we had thrown a lot of people out of work should we give more?
>
> At dinner that evening I bumped into a chap who was Dean of the Florence Heller School of Philanthropy. So we hired a couple of his crack graduate students to look over what we were doing.

[36] Goldston, "BURP and Make Money," p. 87.

> We didn't know what we were doing. Some of the things that we were doing were absolutely insane. We were giving $2,500 to a church at one of our installations. When I found that out, I asked, "Why do we do it?"
>
> The manager said, "If you don't want to do it, we won't do it."
>
> I said, "No, why do we do it?" And he said, "Well, we were doing it when I came here." I said, "When did you come here?"
>
> "Fifteen years ago."
>
> We never did find out why we started it, but we gave them $7,500 as a three-year terminal gift and got rid of the annual payment.
>
> But as a consequence of that, we decided to think through our charitable giving, and what we then did was we made up a charitable budget. We say that we are going to take about one percent of our pre-tax income and we are going to spend it where we make it.[37]

By 1972 a portion of the decisions on corporate giving were "driven down the ranks;" each of the nine top executive members of the Operations Committee could designate a certain amount (up to $2500, for example) to be given to any charity he wished, provided it was neither religious nor extremely controversial.

PROBLEMS OF GETTING SOCIAL AUDIT INFORMATION

This experience with corporate giving illustrated for Mr. Goldston how little management really knew about much that was going on in the company, especially in areas being scrutinized for their "social impact." Even more alarming than the confusion over charitable donations was the uncertainty regarding matters of health and safety in the coal mines. Accident figures were incomplete or contradictory, the problems about respirators and Black Lung Disease[38] raised a number of complex medical and sociological questions that the company simply did not have answers for. Work on the planning forecasts confirmed that the company did, indeed, look bad (in Mr. Goldston's words) even if there was no way to tell precisely how bad.

In the summer of 1971 EGFA started gathering information. An MBA student was assigned to work under the direction of then Senior Vice President Lawrence E.

---

[37] Goldston, "Corporations Under Attack." Questions and Answers Addendum.

[38] Mr. Goldston wrote of some of these difficulties: "In our coal business, we have been plagued with wildcat strikes for the last year as miners have pressed for greater mine safety and protection from the health hazard, "Black Lung," caused by particles in the form of coal dust. In response we offered complete protection through free respirators, only to stumble against worker resistance to their use. It seemed a miner could prove his manliness by working without a respirator. The problem here remains communications and, I hope, eventual persuasion." (*Limits of Technology*) Mr. Goldston explained that it was difficult for the company to obtain the necessary information on mining health factors. On the one hand, the company learned that heavy use of tobacco was more harmful to the miners than coal dust; yet pressure about "black lung" legislation continued to mount. The company changed its policies at one point, but then discovered that miners often refused to wear respirators–they could not chew tobacco while wearing this device and preferred to go without.

Thompson in an effort to carry out a kind of "audit." (Dr. Thompson at the time was on leave from the faculty of the Harvard Business School and subsequently returned to his position as Professor of Business Administration.) The project was stymied by the very problem it was attempting to solve. The various operating companies were nearly autonomous, and the student had great difficulty getting the necessary information from the appropriate divisions and departments. He could not really do a social audit because he did not have a way to get all the facts.

Nevertheless, this area was still of concern to EGFA top management, who tried approaching the questions of the company's social responsibility from another angle—the shareholders. How, for example did they feel about the company giving away money? How did they feel about mining issues? How, simply, did they feel EGFA "was doing?" Meetings with outside consultants, public opinion researchers, and EFGA executives were held in the fall and winter of 1971 to discuss the idea of a stockholder survey, but this project, too, was abandoned when it ran into the same blank wall—lack of information. How could stockholders be asked their opinions in a vacuum? The same problem emerged. If they really did not know the company's safety record or total social performance, how should they evaluate it?

In early 1972 Mr. Goldston took his leave of absence for six months. Company officials responsible for the audit were reluctant to pursue it during his absence, feeling his support was necessary for its completion. However, by the time Mr. Goldston returned, social responsibility had become an even more important issue, government reporting requirements were stricter than they had been a few years before, and EFGA still had a definite "need to know" about itself and its activities.[39] But the earlier attempts at getting socially relevant information had not worked, and there was a danger in failing to get the information again, of losing credibility. So one of the dilemmas facing Mr. Goldston was: Should EGFA try to do a social audit at the end of 1972, and, if so, how?

---

[39]In the Fairless Lectures for example, Mr. Goldston recommended that firms take some account of themselves socially. And in the *Daedalus* article (1969) he had written: "Perhaps even a social audit could be developed . . . such social accounting will never have the force and precision of the market mechanism and the profit motive, but it will make incentives and controls much more effective."

Exhibit 18-1

PARENT AND SUBSIDIARIES[40]

	State of Organization	*Percentage of Voting Securities owned*
Eastern Gas and Fuel Associates	Massachusetts	
Subsidiaries Consolidated:		
Boston Gas Company (a)	Massachusetts	100.0
Eastern Associated Coal Corp. (a)	West Virginia	100.0
Affinity Mining Company (b)	West Virginia	100.0
Castner, Curran & Bullitt, Inc. (b)	Virginia	100.0
Sterling Smokeless Coal Company (b)	West Virginia	100.0
Eastern Associated Properties Corp.	Delaware	100.0
Eastern Urban Services, Inc.	Delaware	100.0
Midland Enterprises Inc. (a)	Delaware	100.0
Boston Tow Boat Company (c)	Delaware	100.0
Coastal Marine Supply, Inc. (c)	Louisiana	100.0
Chotin Transportation, Inc. (c)	Louisiana	100.0
Coastal Towing Corporation (c)	Texas	100.0
Eastern Associated Terminals Company (c)	Delaware	100.0
Mystic Steamship Corporation (c)	Delaware	100.0
The Ohio River Company (c)	West Virginia	100.0
The Ohio River Company Traffic Div., Inc. (d)	Pennsylvania	100.0
W C M Radio Pittsburgh, Inc. (d)	Pennsylvania	100.0
Orgulf Transport Company (c)	Delaware	100.0
Port Allen Marine Service, Inc. (c)	Louisiana	100.0
Red Circle Transport Company (c)	Delaware	100.0
Unconsolidated Subsidiary:		
Algonquin Gas Company (e)	Delaware	36.8

(a) Separate financial statement filed.
(b) A wholly owned subsidiary of Eastern Associated Coal Corp.
(c) A wholly owned subsidiary of Midland Enterprises Inc.
(d) A wholly owned subsidiary of The Ohio River Company.
(e) EGFA takes up into earnings its proportionate share of Algonquin's undistributed earnings.

---

[40] Source: Report to the SEC for the fiscal year ending December 31, 1972, Form 10-K, p. 23.

Exhibit 18-2

CONDENSED SUMMARY OF CONSOLIDATED INCOME FOR FIVE YEARS

	THOUSANDS OF DOLLARS				
	1972	1971	1970	1969	1968
Net sales and operating revenues	**$331,022**	$291,379	$288,555	$213,513	$197,499
Operating expenses, except depreciation and depletion	**273,130**	237,846	231,304	183,263	168,003
Depreciation and depletion	**23,669**	21,701	16,696	13,674	12,301
	296,799	259,547	248,000	196,937	180,304
Operating income	**34,223**	31,832	40,555	16,576	17,195
Miscellaneous other income (expense) net	**2,129**	2,844	2,608	3,319	2,586
	36,352	34,676	43,163	19,895	19,781
Interest on long-term debt	**12,788**	8,816	7,545	6,729	4,427
Other interest and debt expense	**1,039**	1,785	1,973	1,827	718
	13,827	10,601	9,518	8,556	5,145
Income before Federal income taxes and extraordinary items	**22,525**	24,075	33,645	11,339	14,636
Provision (credit) for Federal income taxes	**5,575**	7,293	11,397	(1,071)	(229)
Income before extraordinary items	**16,950**	16,782	22,248	12,410	14,865
Extraordinary items, net of Federal income tax (Note)	**578**	157	10,423	292	909
Net income	**$ 17,528**	$ 16,939	$ 32,671	$ 12,702	$ 15,774
Common stock:					
Earnings per share and common equivalent share*					
Income before extraordinary items	**$1.75**	$1.59	$2.09	$1.18	$1.41
Extraordinary items, net of Federal income tax	**.06**	.02	.98	.03	.09
Net income	**1.81**	1.61	3.07	1.21	1.50
Stock dividends paid	**3%**	3%	3%	3%	3%

*Reflects average shares outstanding and equivalent common shares of outstanding stock options. 1968–1971 inclusive restated to reflect stock dividends paid in the years 1969–1972 inclusive.

NOTE — The extraordinary items consist of the following: 1972 — tax benefit resulting from sale of Electric Division of Boston Gas Co., net. 1971 — gain on sale of land of $685,000, after applicable Federal income tax of $225,000, and preliminary costs and expenses attributable to discontinued office building project of $528,000, after applicable Federal income tax benefit of $499,000. 1970 — net gain on sales of property of $990,000, after applicable Federal income tax of $681,000, and gain on sale of investment of $9,433,000, after applicable Federal income tax of $4,042,000. 1969— gain on sale of property of $892,000, after applicable Federal income tax of $336,000, and loss on sale of investment of $600,000, after applicable Federal income tax benefit of $214,000; 1968 — gain on sale of land of $909,000, after applicable Federal income tax of $275,000.

Exhibit 18-2 (continued)

Consolidated Balance Sheet

December 31, 1972 and 1971

Assets

	1972	1971
Current Assets:		
Cash	**$ 11,001,588**	$ 11,933,670
Marketable securities, at cost which approximates market	**—**	2,645,233
Receivables, less allowances	**50,552,911**	39,991,527
Inventories, principally at the lower of average cost or market —		
Finished products, principally coal and coke	**4,054,721**	2,790,299
Liquefied natural gas	**1,694,299**	2,358,179
Materials and supplies	**5,789,787**	6,246,827
Federal income taxes applicable to current portion of deferred production payments (Note 3)	**—**	1,910,544
Prepaid expenses and other current assets	**2,374,144**	1,846,275
Total current assets	**$ 75,467,450**	$ 69,722,554
Investments and Other Assets:		
Investment in Algonquin Gas Transmission Company, 36.8% owned (Notes 2 and 8)	**$ 17,968,979**	$ 17,352,174
Unamortized cost of retired utility plant facilities	**3,376,468**	3,906,122
Deferred charges, less amortization	**7,842,340**	6,876,244
Notes receivable — noncurrent	**3,022,812**	3,422,797
Other investments and assets	**16,870,433**	13,407,357
	$ 49,081,032	$ 44,964,694
Property and Equipment, at cost (Notes 2 and 7)	**$550,068,556**	$495,454,811
Less — Accumulated depreciation and depletion	**193,004,147**	171,979,565
Net property and equipment	**$357,064,409**	$323,475,246
Total assets	**$481,612,891**	$438,162,494

Liabilities and Stockholders' Investment

	1972	1971
Current Liabilities:		
Notes payable	**$ 4,100,000**	$ 7,032,700
Current maturities of long-term debt	**5,305,203**	4,950,676
Deferred production payments (Note 3)	**222,831**	4,415,098
Accounts payable	**17,156,300**	17,925,437
Accrued expenses	**14,115,450**	9,661,251
Federal income taxes (Note 6)	**62,231**	—
Other current liabilities	**5,655,928**	4,162,419
Total current liabilities	**$ 46,617,943**	$ 48,147,581
Long-Term Debt, see accompanying summary (Note 2)	**$203,241,282**	$169,419,084
Reserves and Deferred Credits:		
Deferred Federal income taxes (Note 6)	**$ 33,285,631**	$ 31,110,962
Retirement benefits (Note 1)	**5,841,916**	6,008,115
Insurance and other reserves	**6,724,802**	6,518,320
Unamortized job development and investment credits (Note 6)	**11,656,809**	9,087,858
	$ 57,509,158	$ 52,725,255
Commitments and Contingencies (Notes 11 and 12)		
Stockholders' Investment (Notes 4 and 5):		
Common stock, $1.00 par value —		
Authorized — 25,000,000 shares		
Issued — 10,374,000 shares in 1972 and 1971	**$ 10,374,000**	$ 10,374,000
Capital in excess of par value	**83,361,407**	85,566,929
Retained earnings	**107,608,525**	96,095,963
	$201,343,932	$192,036,892
Less — Treasury stock at cost, 989,961 shares in 1972 and 831,484 shares in 1971	**27,099,424**	24,166,318
	$174,244,508	$167,870,574
Total liabilities and stockholders' investment	**$481,612,891**	$438,162,494

Exhibit 18-3

SOURCES OF REVENUES (IN MILLIONS OF DOLLARS)

	1972	*1971*
Coal	$157.4	$149.9
Marine	68.6	52.7
Gas	92.0	75.5
Coke	12.2	12.5
Other	.8	.8
	$331.0	$291.4

(Intercompany revenues eliminated)

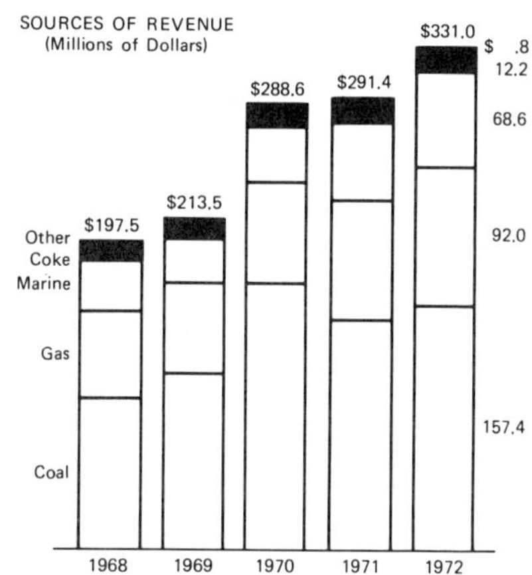

SOURCES OF PRE-TAX INCOME (IN MILLIONS OF DOLLARS)

	1972	*1971*
Coal	$ 5.3	$ 10.2
Marine	11.7	7.0
Gas	7.9	5.4
Coke	1.7	2.5
Equity in Algonquin Earnings	1.7	2.1
Other Items, Net	(5.8)	(3.1)
	$ 22.5	$ 24.1

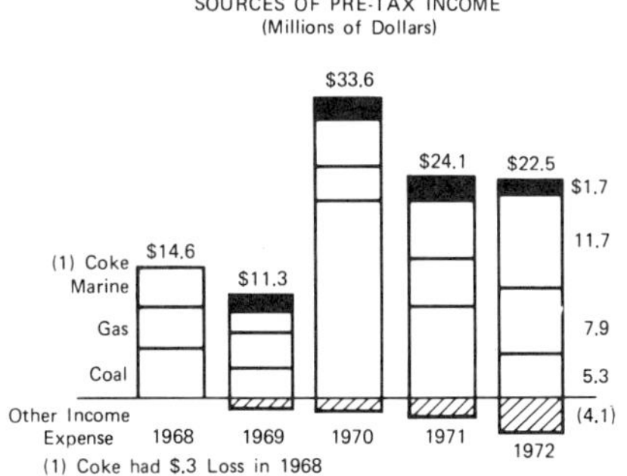

Case Nineteen

Eastern Gas & Fuel Associates (B)

High up in Boston's Prudential Tower, Mr. O. F. Ingram looked at the raw results of the "social audit" of Eastern Gas and Fuel Associates which had been coming in to his desk. So far the corporate staff had been successful in obtaining the information requested, but a number of difficulties loomed in deciding what to do with the data and how to present it. As Vice President of Public Relations, Mr. Ingram had been fully involved in designing and running the project, and now, in February 1973, he was faced with the problem of assimilating and organizing these facts into some sort of report, possibly for publication.

As he focused on the immediate question of whether minority employment figures for the coal company should be averaged or listed mine by mine, Mr. Ingram reviewed the history and timing of this endeavor. In addition to the problems posed by the often rough and unstandardized data, there were larger questions concerning the relationship between headquarters and subsidiary management, as well as between the company and the public. Motives, norms, categories, questions—a complex of variables become specific dilemmas confronting a company once it decides to undertake a social audit.

BACKGROUND

Some of the history and motivation behind the initial EGFA social audit in 1971 was covered in the "Eastern Gas & Fuel Associates (A)" case. Upon Mr. Goldston's return in mid-1972 from a six month sabbatical at the London School of Business, the company committed itself to try another social audit project in spite of the earlier uncompleted attempt.

First, the categories for measurement had to be determined. It was decided that the audit was not to be a questionnaire of the "How are things in general?" variety, but rather a clearly limited and defined attempt to get specific information. One of the reasons for conducting the audit was to inform EGFA management itself about what was going on in the company, in certain social areas. If the performance was bad, the management wanted to know how bad. For the coal company, the gas company, and the marine operations, a solid base of information from which to build strategies, plans, and forecasts was needed.

Four areas were selected—health and safety, minority employment, pensions, and corporate giving. But for a variety of reasons, an obvious candidate—pollution—was not included. Clearly this audit could not cover every important topic, and Mr. Goldston was especially anxious that the facts be both obtainable and meaningful. He explained that EGFA's operations varied greatly with respect to pollution criteria. For example, he said that the gas company would "look like a hero," and there was no point in turning the audit into a pat-on-the-back accolade. The barge operations had been studied by other consultants, and Mr. Goldston commented that he really did not want the survey to get bogged down comparing different types of toilets used on river-going boats. At the coal company, almost the opposite situation prevailed; the question of pollution became too big and undefined rather than too small and picky. It raised all sorts of issues not so much concerning the extraction of coal, but relating to the use of coal in general and its effect on the environment. There seemed to be no good specific question that could be asked that would elicit a factual and quantifiable response.

Accordingly, for this audit, pollution was eliminated as a category. The requests for information were not uniform or standardized; there was no company-wide letter or announcement about the overall project. In some cases the requisite data already existed at corporate headquarters. For example, facts about corporate giving (handled through the Eastern Associated Foundation) were available there, and some information on minority employment was supplied through the personnel office. Stricter government reporting requirements made it easier to get some data, such as that already collected for EEOC filing. This audit also gained some advantages from the earlier summer (1971) effort; some figures (at least for previous years), had been tracked down.

In general, a particular corporate person or group of persons, normally involved in a certain area, was held responsible for collecting the appropriate data. For instance, Mr. H. Brown Baldwin (the Director of Health and Safety) assembled the health and safety figures, requesting by letter the facts from each mine or facility. Mr. Ingram, Mr. J. Thomas Cathcart (Senior Vice President, Administration), and Mr. William L. Helm Jr. (Vice President, Financial Planning) worked on the minority area, often simply telephoning their requests.

The EGFA management collated facts and figures for the past few years for each division, and in one way or another the following questions were covered:

- The frequency and number of accidents and fatalities
- The percentage and level of minority employment
- Corporate giving by category of interest, as compared to forecasted donations, and as a percentage of pre-tax income
- The nature of all pension plans
- The extent of pension plan coverage for both already retired and currently active employees

Mr. Ingram explained that he and his colleagues did not start out with any preset standards or norms with which to measure the incoming data. They were not as concerned with making comparisons (with other companies, industries, or against some more abstract guidelines) as with learning about the company.

The answers came back in late 1972, and Mr. Ingram commented that most of the information appeared to be reasonably complete. Since directions were general rather than specific, sometimes the division had to work out a real problem of interpretation (the barge company, for example, had to decide whether to base its accident rate on a 12- or 24-hour day, since the men lived on the boats even when they were not working).

By the first of the new year (1973) most of the information had been collected. The following sections examine the results from the four categories and the particular difficulties of interpretation and presentation encountered.

HEALTH AND SAFETY

This category was especially important and one in which the coal company was very vulnerable. Over the past decade worries about mine safety had increased, "Black Lung" (the popular name for pneumonoconiosis) had become an important political issue, and serious accidents in any mine led to agonized soul searching and second-guessing throughout the industry.

Goldston noted how difficult getting this information really was: "When we started to get the figures we found that there simply were no very reliable figures industry-wide and that we ourselves didn't have very reliable figures for our own operations. But where there were statistics our figures were worse than the industry's."[1] The results were sobering—an almost 50% rise in lost-time accidents over the past three years. In the coal and coke divisions the number of lost-time accidents per million employee hours had risen from 43 to 78 between 1970 and 1972, from 14 to 30 in the gas company, and from 34 to 43 in the marine division (the company average rose from 36 to 64). During that same period the number of days lost per million employee hours (a measure of accident severity) rose from 2.225 to 3.003. The number of fatalities was too small to indicate a trend; 9 total in 1970, 4 in 1971, and 6 in 1972 (4 of the 6 in coal and coke, the other 2 in the barge company). Although Ingram and Baldwin knew the accident rate had been rising, they had not realized the jump was so large. And the increase was not due simply to a growth in business, because the figures were based on the percentage of lost time accidents per million man hours worked rather than on any absolute numbers.

There were some extenuating factors that modified the severity of the report. For instance, when the figures were compared with the accident rates for time-away-from-the-job in the same area, the company did not look so dangerous. As a whole, too, the coal industry simply is not as safe as many others, and a comparison between EGFA and Du Pont, for example, with its historically exemplary safety record, was bound to be unfavorable. Even within the industry, however, there were questions about definition and the strictness of reporting. If a man finished his day's work after an accident but did

[1] Eli Goldston's speech to the American Society of Corporate Secretaries, June 29, 1973, White Sulfur Springs, West Virginia.

not report the next day, was that an on- or off-hours accident? Moreover, EGFA felt that perhaps its managers were sometimes more attentive in noting accidents or more humane; they might consider something a serious accident and send a man home rather than permit the man to come in if he were unfit for work. Also meaningful comparisons were difficult because there were no standardized reporting norms; inevitably, different mines and different companies meant different things by terms such as "lost-time" accident. Sometimes, too, the data were simply spotty.

However, Goldston was quick to add that these circumstances were just minor excuses. Even if they all influenced the results to a maximum extent, they did not alter the fact that EGFA's record was very poor, especially in the coal mines. Certainly the information could be used to prod the company to work for stricter safety standards, and this orientation was evident in the 1972 *Annual Report* (in the emphasis on safety, and perhaps, too, in the lower income figures from the coal company!). Yet what other use should be made of this information? Should it be made public? Even internally, its effect was hard to calculate. Undoubtedly, it was worse to hide a bad record than to announce it, but Ingram now was forced to think of ways to publicize a bad health and safety record honestly while simultaneously claiming that the company was truly interested in working towards a better society.

MINORITY EMPLOYMENT

Black employment and advancement was a category in which some information had been generated not only by EGFA's own 1971 summer audit but also in response to recent government regulations, one in which Mr. Goldston felt EGFA had made progress in the past. New policies in the gas company particularly had had definite results. Company-wide minority employment had increased numerically but decreased slightly as a percentage of total work force, from 7.9% to 7.5% between 1970 and 1972. The gas company had the best increase (the percentage of minority employment up from 4.5% in 1970 to 7.1% in 1972); the coal company had the sharpest decrease (from 9.2% to 8.0%); and the marine operations recorded a slight drop from 5.9% to 5.8%. These figures were further broken down into the following categories: officers and managers, professional and technical, clerical, skilled, and unskilled. Company-wide, professional, technical, and skilled minority workers were on the increase, while the numbers of unskilled workers and officers and managers dropped and the clerical category held steady. Mr. Ingram commented on some divisional variations here. In the coal company, minority representation seemed to be increasing in the office and manager category but not in the professional and technical area. In the home office and the gas company the opposite situation prevailed, with the increase in professional and technical minority employment due perhaps to the rising importance of the computer field. Exhibits 19-1 and 19-2 show copies of EEOC forms and compilations put together by the MBA student in the summer of 1971.

As the exhibits suggest, the potential ways of displaying this record were many and confusing. In the first place, the very quantity of data was a problem. When does minuteness of detail become meaningless rather than instructive? It was necessary to find a happy medium between the vagueness of generalities and the numbing, endless lists of numbers. Obviously, if the data were to be made public, some averaging and amalgamating was necessary; but some facts were apparent only in detailed reports and would be disguised by averages. For instance, Ingram had figures for the coal company mine by mine, and the divisional record of 8% minority employment included considerable variations here. Some mines were "lily-white" while others had quite high minority representation, and the fairest way to indicate such divergence was unclear. The situation was further complicated, again especially for the coal company, when minority employment was compared with the minority population figures in the surrounding community. Just what is that community? And what if that area is virtually all-white too? The questions and absurdities are numerous,[2] but some decisions had to be reached about the numbers or averages to use and the explanations to give.

PENSIONS

The data about minorities was really only confusing when it was put together or averaged for comparisons. Compared to the data collected about pensions, it was a model of clarity! The audit uncovered the fact that EGFA participated in 23 different pension plans,[3] and there was rampant confusion in the variety of terms binding the company. The results proved an object lesson in what Goldston called "the degree to which things get lost in a big company." Nevertheless, EGFA was involved (one way or another) in a substantial pension plan program, and the audit supplied some important details about the amount involved. In 1972 EGFA paid a total of $4,300,000 in Social Security contributions and $12,553,000 in combined pension plans (up from $8,507,000 in 1970).

Consideration of EGFA's pension arrangements revealed more than just numbers. Some aspects of the coal company's plans especially reflected the changing pressures on business in modern society. Traditionally, contributions to pension funds in the coal company had been linked to production, and over the years the rate had risen from $.40 to $.60 per ton.[4] Yet in 1973 the company was being asked not to raise the rate, but to change the base of evaluation; the emphasis was no longer just on production but on safety and working conditions. Thus, facts, policies, and even philosophies were revealed by EGFA's investigation. Areas needing re-examination became apparent, and, again, the results were there to be selected, arranged, reported, and explained.

---

[2]Some of these all-white mines were in all-white communities, but these had been essentially "company towns," started in another age or by other coal companies later incorporated into EGFA.

[3]Goldston commented that evidence of two more plans turned up after the audit was completed–the company actually worked with 25 different pension schemes.

[4]It went up to $.60 for November 1971, then $.05 more each six months and was to reach $.80 per ton as of November 1974 under UMWA Contract.

CORPORATE GIVING

Eastern Associated Foundation handled the company's major donations, but the information was recorded and classified by division. This topic had been scrutinized, at Mr. Goldston's request, by outside experts in 1964 and 1965, and attempts made to correct some of the inconsistencies and absurdities (see case 18). Also, since 1966 this area had been included in the five-year forecasts, so it was possible to make a comparison between actual amounts given and planned donations.

The total amount of EGFA's charitable giving through the Foundation for 1972 was $216,429, which was just under 1% of its pre-tax income and much higher proportionally than the 1970 figure of $185,442 which was about ½%. The absolute dollar amount had gone up about 15%, but the proportion of contributions rose much more dramatically as earnings declined. Mr. Goldston commented that an earnings decline was not his ideal way of increasing the percentage of income devoted to philanthropy.[5]

In this area, too, variations among the divisions were marked, especially when the amount given was compared to the forecast. In 1972, for example, the coal company's actual earnings of $7 million fell far short of the $19 million forecast. Contributions declined proportionately and remained at less than ½% of actual earnings there. On the other hand, the gas company posted record 1972 earnings of $6.5 million, and its share of corporate donations was over $100,000, almost 2% of its pre-tax profits. Here again the company average hid divisional variations.

It was also important to look at where the money went. Over half of the 1972 donations went to "health and welfare" causes, and the rest was split between higher education and civic and cultural affairs. Specific donees included the United Fund, hospitals, children's activities and groups, NAACP, seminars, and symphonies and ballets.

CONCLUSION

Mr. Goldston had intended that the results should be publicized, but the commitment was not irrevocable nor the form of reporting—if the data were made public—decided upon. Management had learned much about the company's performance that it had not known. However, if the audit were made public, Goldston did not want it dismissed as a publicity gimmick. This meant disclosing a rather poor safety record. Moreover, the question of the proper audience was important. A press release was a simple means of announcing the company's performance. If the stockholders were really the people most concerned, a "Social Report" could be incorporated easily into the Annual Report or mailed separately to them.

---

[5]For instance, in the Fairless Lectures, Goldston commented: "I do not want to suggest that it is unimportant to trv to increase the charitable giving by corporations. If you somehow persuaded corporate management to double its charitable giving from 1% to just 2%, it would be the equivalent of four additional Ford Foundations. Although we are talking about relatively small percentages in charitable gifts, we are talking about important total dollars." Lecture II, "Social Responsibility: Some Corporate Purposes Beyond Maximum Net Profit," p. 42.

These alternatives and others, concerning the arrangement of individual pieces of data and the overall form of publication, were as much a part of EGFA's audit as the surveying activity. And by February 1973, Mr. Ingram realized that time was getting short if anything concerning the audit was to be tied in with the company's Annual Report and proxy statements and to be ready for the April annual meeting.

Exhibit 19-1

Standard Form 100 (Revised)
January 1970
Approved BOB-124-R0002
100-207

EQUAL EMPLOYMENT OPPORTUNITY

EMPLOYER INFORMATION REPORT EEO-1

Joint Reporting Committee

- Equal Employment Opportunity Commission
- Office of Federal Contract Compliance

OHIO RIVER CO
1400 PROVIDENT TOWER
CINCINNATI

Section A - TYPE OF REPORT

Refer to instructions for number and types of reports to be filed.

1. Indicate by marking in the appropriate box the type of reporting unit for which this copy of the form is submitted (MARK ONLY ONE BOX.)

(1) ☐ Single-establishment Employer Report

Multi-establishment Employer:
(2) ☐ Consolidated Report
(3) ☐ Headquarters Unit Report
(4) ☐ Individual Establishment Report (submit one for each establishment with 25 or more employees)
(5) ☐ Special Report

2. Total number of reports being filed by this Company (Answer on Consolidated Report only)

Section B - COMPANY IDENTIFICATION *(To be answered by all employers)* — OFFICE USE ONLY

1. Name of Company which owns or controls the establishment for which this report is filed (if same as label, skip to item 2, this section) — a.

Address (Number and street)	City or town	County	State	ZIP code	b.

b. Employer Identification No.

2. Establishment for which this report is filed.

a. Name of establishment — c.

Address (Number and street)	City or town	County	State	ZIP code	d.

b. Employer Identification No. (If same as label, skip.)

3. Parent or affiliated company (Multi-establishment Employers: Answer on Consolidated Report only)

a. Name of parent or affiliated company: Midland Enterprises Inc.

b. Employer Identification No.

Address (Number and street)	City or town	County	State	ZIP code
1400 Provident Tower	Cincinnati	Hamilton	Ohio	45202

Section C - EMPLOYERS WHO ARE REQUIRED TO FILE *(To be answered by all employers)*

☒ Yes ☐ No 1. Does the entire company have at least 100 employees in the payroll period for which you are reporting?

☒ Yes ☐ No 2. Is your company affiliated through common ownership and/or centralized management with other entities in an enterprise with a total employment of 100 or more?

NOTE: If the answer is NO to BOTH questions, skip to Section G; otherwise complete ENTIRE form.

☐ Yes ☒ No 3. Does the company or any of its establishments (a) have a prime contract with any agency of the Federal Government, a Federally-assisted construction contract, or a subcontract any any tier under any prime Government contract, amounting to more than $10,000; or (b) serve as a depository of Federal Government funds; or (c) serve as an issuing and paying agent of U.S. Savings Bonds and Notes; or (d) hold a Federal Government bill of lading in any amount?

Exhibit 19-1 (continued)

Section D - EMPLOYMENT DATA

374-071

Employment at this establishment-Report all permanent, temporary, or part-time employees including apprentices and on-the-job trainees unless specifically excluded as set forth in the instructions. Enter the appropriate figures on all lines and in all columns. Blank spaces will be considered as zeros. *In columns 1, 2, and 3, include ALL employees in the establishment including those in minority groups.*

Exhibit 1 (continued)

Job Categories (See Appendix (4) for definitions)	TOTAL EMPLOYEES IN ESTABLISHMENT			MINORITY GROUP EMPLOYEES (See Appendix (5) for definitions)							
				MALE					FEMALE		
	Total Employees Including Minorities (1)	Total Male Including Minorities (2)	Total Female Including Minorities (3)	Negro (4)	Oriental (5)	American Indian* (6)	Spanish Surnamed American (7)	Negro (8)	Oriental (9)	American Indian* (10)	Spanish Surnamed American (11)
Officials and managers	125	123	2	1							
Professionals	127	127									
Technicians	33	33									
Sales workers	10	10									
Office and clerical	72	32	40		1						
Craftsmen (Skilled)	217	217		26							
Operatives (Semi-skilled)	96	96		20							
Laborers (Unskilled)	260	260		5							
Service workers	85	57	28	15				1			
1971 TOTAL →	1025	955	70	67	1			1			
Total employment reported in previous EEO-1 report 1970	975	911	64	60							

(The trainees below should also be included in the figures for the appropriate occupational categories above)

Formal On-the-job trainees		(1)	(2)	(3)	(4)	(5)	(6)	(7)	(8)	(9)	(10)	(11)
	White collar											
	Production											

*In Alaska include Eskimos and Aleuts with American Indians

1. NOTE: On consolidated report, skip questions 2-5 and Section E.
2. How was information as to race or ethnic group in Section D obtained?
   1 ☐ Visual Survey   3 ☐ Other - Specify ....
   2 ☐ Employment Record
3. Dates of payroll period used - ....
4. Pay period of last report submitted for this establishment

Section E - ESTABLISHMENT INFORMATION

1. Is the location of the establishment the same as that reported last year?
   1 ☐ Yes   2 ☐ No   3 ☐ Did not report last year   4 ☐ Reported on combined basis
2. Is the major business activity at this establishment the same as that reported last year?
   1 ☐ Yes   2 ☐ No   3 ☐ No report last year   4 ☐ Reported on combined basis

OFFICE USE ONLY

3. What is the major activity of this establishment? (Be specific, i.e., manufacturing steel castings, retail grocer, wholesale plumbing supplies, title insurance, etc. Include the specific type of product or type of service provided, as well as the principal business or industrial activity.

e.

Section F - REMARKS

Use this item to give any identification data appearing on last report which differs from that given above, explain major changes in composition or reporting units, and other pertinent information.

Section G - CERTIFICATION (See instructions G)

Check one
1. ☐ All reports are accurate and were prepared in accordance with the instructions (check on consolidated only)
2. ☐ This report is accurate and was prepared in accordance with the instructions

Name of Authorized Official	Title	Signature	Date
James E. McLaughlin, Jr.	Assistant to treasurer		May 3, 1971

Name of person to contact regarding this report (Type or print)	Address (Number and street)				
Title	**City and State**	**ZIP code**	**Telephone Area Code**	**Number**	**Extension**

All reports and information obtained from individual reports will be kept confidential as required by Section 709 (e) of Title VII

WILLFULLY FALSE STATEMENT ON THIS REPORT ARE PUNISHABLE BY LAW. U.S. CODE. TITLE 18. SECTION 1001

Exhibit 19-1 (continued)

Standard Form 100 (Revised)
January 1970
Approved BOB-124-R0002
100-207

1972

EQUAL EMPLOYMENT OPPORTUNITY

EMPLOYER INFORMATION REPORT EEO-1

Joint Reporting Committee

- Equal Employment Opportunity Commission
- Office of Federal Contract Compliance

OHIO RIVER CO
1400 PROVIDENT TOWER
CINCINNATI

Section A - TYPE OF REPORT

Refer to instructions for number and types of reports to be filed.

1. Indicate by marking in the appropriate box the type of reporting unit for which this copy of the form is submitted (MARK ONLY ONE BOX.)

(1) ☐ Single-establishment Employer Report

Multi-establishment Employer:
(2) ☒ Consolidated Report
(3) ☐ Headquarters Unit Report
(4) ☐ Individual Establishment Report (submit one for each establishment with 25 or more employees)
(5) ☐ Special Report

2. Total number of reports being filed by this Company (Answer on Consolidated Report only)

Section B - COMPANY IDENTIFICATION *(To be answered by all employers)* — OFFICE USE ONLY

1. Name of Company which owns or controls the establishment for which this report is filed (if same as label, skip to item 2, this section)
The Ohio River Company — a.

Address (Number and street)	City or town	County	State	ZIP code	
1400 Provident	Cincinnati	Hamilton	Ohio	45202	b.

b. Employer Identification No. 3 1 0 3 9 7 3 3 0

2. Establishment for which this report is filed.

a. Name of establishment Same As Label — c.

Address (Number and street)	City or town	County	State	ZIP code	
					d.

b. Employer Identification No. (If same as label, skip.)

3. Parent or affiliated company (Multi-establishment Employers: Answer on Consolidated Report only)

a. Name of parent or affiliated company: Midland Enterprises Inc.
b. Employer Identification No.

Address (Number and street)	City or town	County	State	ZIP code
1400 Provident Tower	Cincinnati	Hamilton	Ohio	45202

Section C - EMPLOYERS WHO ARE REQUIRED TO FILE *(To be answered by all employers)*

☒ Yes ☐ No 1. Does the entire company have at least 100 employees in the payroll period for which you are reporting?

☒ Yes ☐ No 2. Is your company affiliated through common ownership and/or centralized management with other entities in an enterprise with a total employment of 100 or more?

NOTE: If the answer is NO to BOTH questions, skip to Section G; otherwise complete ENTIRE form.

☐ Yes ☒ No 3. Does the company or any of its establishments (a) have a prime contract with any agency of the Federal Government, a Federally-assisted construction contract, or a subcontract any any tier under any prime Government contract, amounting to more than $10,000; or (b) serve as a depository of Federal Government funds; or (c) serve as an issuing and paying agent of U.S. Savings Bonds and Notes; or (d) hold a Federal Government bill of lading in any amount?

Exhibit 19-1 (continued)

Section D - EMPLOYMENT DATA

374-071

Employment at this establishment-Report all permanent, temporary, or part-time employees including apprentices and on-the-job trainees unless specifically excluded as set forth in the instructions. Enter the appropriate figures on all lines and in all columns. Blank spaces will be considered as zeros. *In columns 1, 2, and 3, include ALL employees in the establishment including those in minority groups.*

Exhibit 1 (continued)

Job Categories (See Appendix (4) for definitions)	TOTAL EMPLOYEES IN ESTABLISHMENT			MINORITY GROUP EMPLOYEES (See Appendix (5) for definitions)							
				MALE				FEMALE			
	Total Employees Including Minorities (1)	Total Male Including Minorities (2)	Total Female Including Minorities (3)	Negro (4)	Oriental (5)	American Indian* (6)	Spanish Surnamed American (7)	Negro (8)	Oriental (9)	American Indian* (10)	Spanish Surnamed American (11)
Officials and managers	215	211	4								
Professionals	179	179					1				
Technicians	30	30		2			1				
Sales workers	10	10									
Office and clerical	109	52	57	1	1		1				
Craftsmen (Skilled) ...	268	268		42			1				
Operatives (Semi-skilled)	99	98	1	21			2	1			
Laborers (Unskilled) ..	342	342					2				
Service workers	106	75	31	2							
1971 TOTAL →	1358	1265	93	68	1		8	1			
Total employment reported in previous EEO-1 report	1130	1056	74	69	1		2	1			

(The trainees below should also be included in the figures for the appropriate occupational categories above)

Formal On-the-job trainees		(1)	(2)	(3)	(4)	(5)	(6)	(7)	(8)	(9)	(10)	(11)
	White collar											
	Production											

*In Alaska include Eskimos and Aleuts with American Indians

1. NOTE: On consolidated report, skip questions 2-5 and Section E.
2. How was information as to race or ethnic group in Section D obtained?
   1 ☐ Visual Survey   3 ☐ Other - Specify ....
   2 ☐ Employment Record
3. Dates of payroll period used - ....
4. Pay period of last report submitted for this establishment

Section E - ESTABLISHMENT INFORMATION

1. Is the location of the establishment the same as that reported last year?
   1 ☐ Yes   2 ☐ No   3 ☐ Did not report last year   4 ☐ Reported on combined basis
2. Is the major business activity at this establishment the same as that reported last year?
   1 ☐ Yes   2 ☐ No   3 ☐ No report last year   4 ☐ Reported on combined basis
3. What is the major activity of this establishment? (Be specific, i.e., manufacturing steel castings, retail grocer, wholesale plumbing supplies, title insurance, etc. Include the specific type of product or type of service provided, as well as the principal business or industrial activity.

OFFICE USE ONLY

e.

Section F - REMARKS

Use this item to give any identification data appearing on last report which differs from that given above, explain major changes in composition or reporting units, and other pertinent information.

Section G - CERTIFICATION (See Instructions G)

Check one
1. ☒ All reports are accurate and were prepared in accordance with the instructions (check on consolidated only)
2. ☐ This report is accurate and was prepared in accordance with the instructions

Name of Authorized Official	Title	Signature	Date
J. E. McLaughin, Jr.	Assistant to Treasurer		5/31/72

Name of person to contact regarding this report (Type or print)	Address (Number and street)			
	1400 Provident Tower			
Title	**City and State**	**ZIP code**	**Telephone Area Code**	**Number**	**Extension**
	Cincinnati, Ohio	45202	513	721-4000	

All reports and information obtained from individual reports will be kept confidential as required by Section 709 (e) of Title VII

WILLFULLY FALSE STATEMENT ON THIS REPORT ARE PUNISHABLE BY LAW. U.S. CODE. TITLE 18. SECTION 1001

Exhibit 19-2

The following tables were compiled in the summer of 1971 by a Harvard MBA student working at EGFA. Corrections were made later and some of this information re-arranged to fit EEOC reporting specifications.

EASTERN GAS AND FUEL ASSOCIATES AND SUBSIDIARIES SURVEY OF MINORITY EMPLOYMENT[1]

	Total		*EGFA*		*Coal*		*Gas*		*Barge*		*Coke*		*Tow Boat*	
	1970	*1969*	*1970*	*1969*	*1970*	*1969*	*1970*	*1969*	*1970*	*1969*	*1970*	*1969*	*1970*	*1969*
Employment														
Total No. of Empl.	7,537	7,164	105	81	5,652	5,305	1,500	1,495			199	199	81	84
No. of Minority Empl.	538	488	3	3	328	306	96	66			108	110	3	3
Minority/Total (%)	7.1	6.8	2.8	3.7	5.8	5.8	6.4	4.5			54.3	55.3	3.7	3.6
% Minority in Area Population[2]			14.7		5.7		14.7				38.6		14.7	
Minority Index			19.1	25.2	101.8	101.8	43.5	30.6			140.7	143.3	25.2	24.5
Hiring														
Total Hired per Year			15	13							126	N.A.	5	11
Minority Employees			–	1							86	N.A.	–	–
Minority/Total (%)			–	7.7							68.3	N.A.	–	–
Turnover (per 100 empl.)														
Non-Minority Turnover											33.7	N.A.	9.9	14.6
Minority Turnover											79.1	N.A.	–	40.0
Minority/Non-Minority											2.4	N.A.	–	2.7

[1] Based on EEOC Report completed in the spring following each year.

[2] Based on 1970 statistics with respect to Negro and other races as a percent of total population for the respective city in which each subsidiary was predominantly located. (Coal company exception: represents Pittsburgh's SMSA data plus aggregate statistics for the counties in which the mines were located.) Persons between ages 15 and 64.

COMPARISON OF MINORITY EMPLOYMENT WITH AREA POPULATION[1]

		1970		*1969*	*SMSA*[2]	*City*
		Minority/Total	*%*	*%*	*%*	*%*
Total:	Male	500/7115	7.0	N.A.		
	Female	38/422	0.9	N.A.		
	All Employees	538/7537	7.1	6.8		
EGFA:	Male	2/68	3.0	2.9	4.1	13.9
	Female	1/37	2.7	5.7	4.6	15.4
	All Employees	3/105	2.8	3.7	4.3	14.7
Gas:	Male	61/1231	5.0	3.9	4.1	13.9
	Female	35/269	13.0	7.8	4.6	15.4
	All Employees	96/1500	6.4	4.5	4.3	14.7
Tow Boat:	Male	3/79	3.8	3.7	4.1	13.9
	Female	0/2	–	–	4.6	15.4
	All Employees	3/81	3.7	3.6	4.3	14.7
Coal[3]:	Including Office Staff					
	Male	326/5547	5.9	5.9	5.4	8.5
	Female	2/105	1.9	0.9	6.8	19.2
	All Employees	328/5652	5.8	5.8	5.7	9.0
	Mines Only:					
	Male	322/5416	6.0	5.9	3.0[4]	
Barge:	Male					
	Female				11.2	27.4
	All Employees					
Coke:	Male	108/190	56.9	57.6	16.8	30.9
	Female	0/9	–	–	18.5	45.4
	All Employees	108/199	54.3	55.3	17.7	38.6

[1] Based on 1970 Population Census: Persons between ages 15 and 64.

[2] Standard Metropolitan Statistical Area: includes area outside the city's boundaries but which are economically and socially linked to the city.

[3] Male and All Employees area population figures represent Pittsburgh's SMSA or city data plus aggregate statistics for the counties in which the mines were located. Female statistics include Pittsburgh's SMSA or city only.

[4] Aggregate statistic for counties.

SURVEY OF FEMALE EMPLOYEES

	Total		EGFA		Coal		Gas		Barge		Coke		Tow Boat	
	1970	1969	1970	1969	1970	1969	1970	1969	1970	1969	1970	1969	1970	1969
Employment:														
Total:														
Officials & Mgrs.	880		28	22	686	717	158				6	6	2	2
Professionals	208		38	25	41	33	83				5	6	41	43
Technicians	157		–	–	70	60	72				11	8	4	5
Office & Clerical	690		39	34	168	163	469				12	11	2	2
Service Workers	61		–	–	14	15	34				3	2	10	10
All Jobs[1]	7,537		105	81	5,652	5,305	1,500	1,466			199	199	81	84
Female:														
Officials & Mgrs.	7		–	–	4	5	3				–	–	–	–
Professional	18		1	2	5	5	11				1	1	–	–
Technicians	6		–	–	4	3	2				–	–	–	–
Office & Clerical	373		36	33	82	83	245				8	7	2	2
Service Workers	17		–	–	10	10	7				–	–	–	–
All Jobs[1]	422		37	35	105	106	269[2]	243			9	8	2	2
Percent:														
Officials & Mgrs.	0.8		0.0	0.0	0.6	0.7	1.9				0.0	0.0	0.0	0.0
Professionals	8.7		2.6	8.0	12.2	15.2	13.3				20.0	16.7	0.0	0.0
Technicians	3.8		–	–	5.7	5.0	2.8				0.0	0.0	0.0	0.0
Office & Clerical	54.1		92.3	97.1	48.8	50.9	52.2				66.7	63.6	100.0	100.0
Service Workers	27.9		–	–	71.4	66.7	20.6				0.0	0.0	0.0	0.0
All Jobs[1]	5.6		35.2	43.2	1.9	2.0	17.9	16.6			4.5	4.0	2.5	2.4

[1]Craftsmen & Foremen, Operatives and Laborers are omitted here because of the lack of female employees within these categories.
[2]Includes one female craftsman

Case Twenty

Eastern Gas & Fuel Associates (C)

The results of the fall, 1972 audit were published as shown in Exhibit 20-1, as an insert in EGFA's 1972 Annual Report entitled "Toward Social Accounting." This insert, which avoided the legal restrictions and mechanical and timing problems concerning material actually in the proxy statement or Annual Report yet reached the same group of people, also included a stockholder survey. The stockholders were given information and asked for their reactions to the audit. Mr. Goldston commented that one of his reasons for conducting this survey was curiosity. He now speculated on the response to the social audit.

Exhibit 20-1

Toward Social Accounting

TO OUR SHAREHOLDERS:

There has been much talk in recent years of corporate social responsibility and of the need to develop some sort of social accounting to gauge how well a given firm is performing – not just as an economic unit, but as a citizen. Indeed, some have suggested that these measures of corporate performance beyond net profit should be subjected to an independent social audit.

This insert for the 1972 Annual Report of Eastern Gas and Fuel Associates has been designed as an experimental exploration of two aspects of social accounting for "self-auditing" purposes:

(1) What are some internal topics on which management can presently assemble and organize reasonably accurate and coherent data?

(2) Which issues of social accountability are of external interest, and to what extent are shareholders in particular interested, if at all?

To explore the first of these aspects we have gathered statistical information that covers four topics from among the many that are currently of concern to those studying corporate social responsibility:

- Industrial safety
- Minority employment
- Charitable giving
- Pensions

To explore the second aspect we have included, at the end of this insert, a short questionnaire which, if you will mail it back, will serve as a useful measure of shareholder concern with corporate social responsibility and the reporting of it. No generally accepted standards or methods of presentation have been developed for shareholder reporting on such topics nor is there clear evidence as to shareholder interest.

The topics for this first report were not chosen because they are necessarily the most important ones, or the ones that might make us look good, but because they are the most readily measurable, because our goals with respect to them are comparatively simple and clear, and because they lie in areas where management can rather directly influence results. In addition, managerial decisions on these topics can have a significant impact on earnings per share.

In the process of making this first consolidation of social data from our various operations, we found that our records were less complete and less certain than we had believed. We also found that even inadequate disclosure begins to exert a useful pressure on management to comply with new public expectations as to the conduct of large corporations. It may also be some of the best evidence that management is sincerely concerned and making an effort to meet proper expectations.

Four major recurring principles for the quantification of social responsibility have been suggested:

The first is that our priorities have been changing with some rapidity. Many of our political, economic and commercial measures of progress have become obsolescent. We need a new kind of social accounting that goes beyond GNP for the nation and goes beyond net profit for the firm.

Second, while we think of our current economic and accounting measures of GNP and net profit as very precise, when you really get into the nitty gritty of how they are put together, their certainty is delusive.

Third, many proposed imprecise measures of social accounting can be sufficiently accurate to be instructive. They are not hopelessly less accurate than GNP or net profit, and so they can be quite useful, even though they lack precision, for many purposes for which we cannot use GNP and net profit.

And finally, while our efforts to calibrate our concerns by social accounting will reflect this new sense of priorities, without personal observation in the field and a weighing of the figures that we create with moral concerns, social accounting itself becomes only a new numbers game.

As we proceed with these early attempts to develop some form of internal social accounting, we should acquire additional useful insights into this new art.

Eli Goldston

Eli Goldston, *President*

1 INDUSTRIAL SAFETY

Recent legislation has demonstrated that a major current public concern, especially in the heavy industries in which Eastern is involved, is the health and safety of employees.

Our industrial accident record in recent years has not been very good. One standard measurement is the accident frequency rate (number of accidents versus hours worked), and our rate has almost doubled in the last three years, going up most dramatically in gas operations. It is clear that our safety performance has been slipping. In addition it seems that our record is poorer than that of a number of firms with whom we have compared specific records. Just where we stand in our various industries is difficult to gauge because meaningful comparative figures are not available.

ACCIDENT FREQUENCY RATE
(Lost time accidents per million employee hours)

	1970	1971	1972
Coal & Coke	43	61	78
Gas	14	26	30
Marine	34	41	43
EGFA Avg.	36	50	64

Another measure of safety performance is the severity rate, which takes into account time lost as a result of accidents. Here Eastern's record has been steadier, and apparently more in line with other firms for our industries. But much room for improvement remains.

Exhibit 20-1 (continued)

ACCIDENT SEVERITY RATE
(Employee days lost per million employee hours)*

	1970	1971	1972
Coal & Coke	2,948	3,427	4,209
Gas	222	191	303
Marine	1,707	2,015	1,423
EGFA Avg.	2,225	2,516	3,033

*Excluding days charged for fatalities.

Frequency and severity rates, either for a single firm or for an industry, are rather elusive statistics. They may appear worse simply from improved reporting, or may appear better if excessive pressure to improve the record results in variable reporting practices. Comparisons are complicated by numerous variables. Our river towboat crews, for instance, live aboard the boats and so are at their workplace even when not actually working. A greater awareness by both employees and management of the importance of safety may increase the number of reported accidents. Improved benefits could encourage accident reporting. Comparisons are also difficult because of different bases of reporting. We are trying for 1973 to improve both our performance and our ability to supply managers with comparable industry statistics.

Job related fatalities, of course, are the most salient and tragic accidents. We require full reports to top management on all serious injuries and fatalities along with proposals to prevent recurrence. At Eastern we are constantly trying to develop more effective ways to impress on all our people the need to guard against the ever present hazards in their particular line of work. Here is our recent record of fatalities:

FATALITIES

	1970	1971	1972
Coal & Coke	8	3	4
Gas	0	0	0
Marine	1	1	2
EGFA Total	9	4	6

Critics of industry often assume that management has more ability to reduce accident frequency and severity and to eliminate fatalities than may be the case. We do not accept at all the rationalization that "accidents just happen" and we would be the last to suggest that a victim alone is at fault. But it is obvious that we need to be better persuaders and to improve training, motivation and enforcement when it is considered that in at least five of the six 1972 fatalities, the victim was an experienced employee who was clearly violating a standard safety work rule of the company at the time of his death. The need for and difficulty of broad safety indoctrination is evidenced by the fact that 11 employees were fatally injured in 1972 in accidents off the job.

The economics of safety reinforces our social/humanitarian concerns. Compensation of employees injured on the job cost Eastern at least $3,600,000 last year, or about 20¢ in earnings per share.

We are continuing to increase our commitment of men and money to ongoing safety programs in all operations. One of our headquarters officers has been assigned to regular field checks of safety practices and the compilation and analysis of accident statistics. Eastern Associated Coal Corp. has further strengthened its existing safety program by engaging the highly respected safety department of a firm in another industry to help us improve our safety performance in coal operations. In Boston Gas Company, a safety campaign has commenced that focuses not only on safe work habits but also on continuing "defensive" use of equipment and procedures to avoid dangerous situations.

2 MINORITY EMPLOYMENT

An important thrust of Eastern's social concerns effort is to respond positively to the apparently clear national desire to bring an end to discrimination in employment and promotion because of race, religion or other difference from that elusive notion of "the majority."

It is difficult to generalize fairly and judiciously about Eastern's minority employment statistics. Numerically, minority employment in the company has increased in recent years, but has not quite maintained its percentage proportion. This has been particularly noticeable in coal operations, but in this instance, the increased employment has come in areas where there has been a smaller minority proportion in the local population. And it may be that the improving employment prospects for minority members either with our competitors or in fields previously closed to them have reduced the relative attractiveness of jobs with us. Boston Gas has had an excellent record of integrating its work force, but the addition of new territory with a different population mix has appeared to slow the trend.

MINORITY EMPLOYMENT

	1970	1971	1972
Coal & Coke			
Total	5,703	6,050	6,448
Minority	526	544	517
% Minority	9.2%	9.0%	8.0%
Gas			
Total	1,466	1,500	1,611
Minority	66	96	115
% Minority	4.5%	6.4%	7.1%
Marine			
Total Employees	1,077	1,332	1,358
Minority	64	84	79
% Minority	5.9%	6.3%	5.8%
EGFA*			
Total Employees	8,349	8,995	9,526
Minority	659	727	716
% Minority	7.9%	8.3%	7.5%

*Includes Boston Office

Measuring progress in integration is further complicated by the fact that companies were forbidden to record the race of employees until quite recently. Many of our operations are so geographically scattered that it is difficult to determine in many cases if our percentages of minority employment are in line with the minority population in reasonably relevant areas, although this does seem to be true.

MINORITY EMPLOYMENT LEVELS

	1971	1972	1972 Total in Category	1972 % of Total
Officers & Managers	15	12	1,229	1%
Professional & Technical	19	34	648	4.9%
Clerical	58	56	895	6.1%
Skilled	364	398	5,091	7.8%
Unskilled	271	216	1,663	1.3%
	727	716	9,526	

Passing over complicated matters of definition, the figures seem to indicate that Eastern has done a reasonable job but still has some distance to go in reaching a fair proportion of minorities in the work force and in levels of employment. Our effort in recruitment and advancement is to give due recognition to merit and performance while still showing concern for the need to achieve appropriate representation of minorities. There are local instances in our operations which will require continuing attention and prodding if this is to be accomplished.

3 CHARITABLE GIVING

The figures we present below on our charitable giving through The Eastern Associated Foundation are far from complete. Although most charitable gifts of $500 and over have been made by all operations through the Foundation, a good many smaller gifts are made directly from operating funds. In addition, there are expenditures that get classified as personnel expense or sales expense in Eastern that could properly be considered charitable giving. For example, we provide recreation directors for several of our mining communities and we subsidize a summer camp for the children of mine employees. Particularly in the mining areas, equipment is donated or the use of it given to various causes. In addition, company employees are sometimes loaned or assigned to assist in charitable campaign drives or social service projects.

CHARITABLE GIVING BY THE EASTERN ASSOCIATED FOUNDATION

	1970	1971	1972
Total Contributions	$185,442	$210,320	$216,429
1% of Pre-Tax Income	336,450	240,750	225,250
$ per Employee	23.77	23.11	22.78
Earnings per Share	1¢	1¢	1¢

The Federal Income Tax law permits contributions to the extent of 5% of taxable income; many studies, however, have shown that the majority of large public corporations make charitable gifts of about 1% of pre-tax income. We have been using this 1% figure as a guide so far as Foundation gifts are concerned.

We have employed outside professional consultants to help us decide how (a) to respond thoughtfully to the charitable concerns of the communities with which we are related and (b) to balance the interest of numerous applicants. On the basis of their suggestions we have considered it appropriate to channel Foundation giving about one-half to health and welfare, one-fourth to higher education, and one-fourth to civic and cultural causes. Costs of educational assistance to active employees is in addition to this giving.

PER CENT OF FOUNDATION GIVING BY CATEGORY OF INTEREST

	1970	1971	1972
Health and Welfare	56.3%	57.1%	53.8%
Higher Education	26.4	20.7	22.8
Civic and Cultural	17.3	22.2	23.4
Total	100.0%	100.0%	100.0%

Charitable giving budgets are established annually by each of the operations and are reviewed along with our other business plans to be sure they are adequate and balanced. Through a matching gifts program, where the company matches an employee's gift to an educational institution, employees can themselves help determine the scale and direction of company assistance to higher education.

4 PENSIONS

Where at one time company retirement plans had been an accepted, almost competitive, way to attract and keep employees, current thinking turns more to their adequacy of coverage and fiscal soundness. In both of these areas it is virtually impossible to generalize about the pension arrangements for Eastern's employees.

In the matter of coverage, all of our employees are, of course, covered by Social Security, with the employee and the employer paying their equal shares. In 1972 each paid 5.2% of the first $9,000 of an employee's earnings but this has since increased to 5.85% of the first $10,800. In addition, substantially all of Eastern's employees participate in one of the 23 separate formal retirement plans to which the company and its subsidiaries are a party.

Eastern's pension arrangements involve very substantial amounts of money. Total Social Security payments by the company in 1972 amounted to about $4,300,000. The expense for the various types of pension and welfare plans supplemental to Social Security has climbed to more than $12,500,000 annually in recent years. Social Security, health and retirement costs thus add an average of almost $2,000 per employee to the average of $10,000 a year paid to an Eastern employee.

ANNUAL COST OF PENSION & WELFARE PLANS ($000)

	1970	1971	1972
Union Welfare & Pension Plans	$5,814	$5,724	$ 8,904
Other Formal & Informal Plans	2,693	2,967	3,649
	$8,507	$8,691	$12,553

(Costs charged to income in the fiscal year of the company)

Eighteen of the formal retirement plans are maintained by negotiations in collective bargaining with various labor unions. In most of these we have no control over management of the funds or the amount of the benefits. We participate in the control of others to varying degrees.

So far as we know, none of these funds has been challenged as to the competence of its management except the Health and Welfare Fund of the United Mine Workers. Contributions to this fund, based on a per tonnage contribution made by all unionized operators, including our Eastern Associated Coal Corp., have been brought under Federal court jurisdiction because of alleged mismanagement.

So far as fiscal soundness is concerned, we annually charge as an expense against income an amount which reflects the actuarial obligations of the current year. In addition, the past service obligations that existed when various funds were established or resulted from amendments, are being charged to the current year on the basis of 30-year amortization periods.

We have been funding each negotiated plan in accordance with the relevant collective bargaining agreement. In the case of Eastern's Retirement Plan for Salaried Employees, which is non-negotiated and non-contributory, funding has recently been brought up to the level for which concurrent tax deductibility is permitted. This plan is fairly well funded compared to the plans of most companies.

An accrued total liability of almost $35,000,000 is funded by assets in trust with a market value of about $27,000,000. The additional $8,000,000 must be paid to the Trustees or earned through fund investment income in excess of annual expenditures in order for the plan to be considered fully funded.

Exhibit 20-1 (continued)

STATUS OF EGFA SALARIED PLAN FUNDING

Fiscal Year Ending June 30, 1972
($000)

Liability for Retired Employees	$18,872
Liability for Active & Terminated Employees	15,825
	$34,697
Accrued Liability	$34,697
Plan Assets at Market Value	26,671
Unfunded Liability @ Market	$ 8,026

It is difficult to determine how adequately funded the various negotiated plans are since many cover other companies in addition to our own companies and, with continuing changes in benefits, actuarial assumption, and market value of assets, there will be variations which defy simple explanation.

We are regularly reviewing both our negotiated pension arrangements and our salaried plan, using an independent insurance firm as consultants when appropriate. We believe that the expense, the benefits and vesting provisions of our numerous retirement plans are reasonably in line with those of the different industries in which we operate. Since the Health and Welfare Fund of the coal industry is portable within that industry, some of the issues as to portability do not apply to our single largest employee group. There may be continuing pressure to require us and other employers to liberalize vesting and portability. These are, no doubt, desirable pension changes, but they must be recognized as being increases in actual pension cost.

* * * * *

The compilation of this report has helped to clarify Eastern's goals in these areas of social concern.

Our goal in industrial safety is to reverse an unfavorable trend and to significantly reduce the frequency and severity of industrial accidents.

Our goal in minority employment is to achieve full equality of opportunity for all and to adequately reflect in our work force the minority proportion in the population of the areas of our operations without sacrificing performance standards.

Our goal in charitable contributions is to maintain, possibly to increase, a level of about 1% of pre-tax income as an appropriate amount of support for various social causes.

Our goal in our retirement programs is to make certain that company benefits are adequate and that promises to employees are secured through proper funding.

SHAREHOLDER COMMENTS

The attached questionnaire has a number of specific questions and also an opportunity for general comments. We will greatly appreciate your detaching it, filling it in and mailing it to us. We hope to be able to make a preliminary report at the shareholders' meeting on April 26, 1973 as to any significant shareholder opinion.

Exhibit 20-1 (continued)

Questionnaire

1. Should this sort of social accounting report be:
   - ☐ enlarged
   - ☐ continued in about same manner
   - ☐ condensed
   - ☐ omitted

2. Should such reports cover:
   - ☐ Industrial Safety
   - ☐ Minority Employment
   - ☐ Charitable Giving
   - ☐ Pensions
   - ☐ Environment
   - ☐ Female Employment
   - ☐ Consumer Rights
   - ☐ Other (please list)

3. How does our record on industrial accidents seem to you?
   - ☐ Good, taking problems into account
   - ☐ Fair
   - ☐ Mediocre
   - ☐ Poor

4. Should the company continue to move ahead of legal enforcement pressures in the following areas:
   - Employment and promotion of minorities ☐ Yes ☐ Moderately ☐ No
   - Preferential hiring of minorities ☐ Yes ☐ Moderately ☐ No
   - Special counselling, training for minorities ☐ Yes ☐ Moderately ☐ No

5. In charitable contributions, should the company give:
   - ☐ Present level of about 1% as is common practice
   - ☐ Up to permitted tax deductible level of 5% of taxable income
   - ☐ Above 5% even though not deductible
   - ☐ Nothing, letting individuals choose their own charities

6. Should company charitable contributions be:
   - Limited to programs likely to serve our own employees and families ☐ Yes ☐ No
   - Limited to social welfare programs such as hospitals or United Funds ☐ Yes ☐ No
   - Include urban or minority programs ☐ Yes ☐ No

7. Should the company continue its "Matching Gifts" program as a way of bringing employees into charitable giving decisions
   ☐ Yes ☐ No

(continued on other side)

Please add your own comments below:

(continued from other side)

8. Should the company move in direction of the following current proposals for pensions
   - More complete funding ☐ Yes ☐ No
   - Improved vesting and portability ☐ Yes ☐ No
   - Inflationary adjustments for retired employees ☐ Yes ☐ No

Information about respondents

Male ☐ Female ☐ Institution ☐ (Fund, Bank, Trustee, etc.)

Age______

Shareholdings

☐ UNDER 100 ☐ 100-500 ☐ 500-1000 ☐ 1000-5000 ☐ 5000-over

Location

☐ New England ☐ Midwest
☐ Far West ☐ Middle Atlantic
☐ South ☐ Foreign

FIRST CLASS
Permit No. 4188
(Sec. 34.9 P.L.&R.)
BOSTON, MASS.

BUSINESS REPLY MAIL

NO POSTAGE NECESSARY IF MAILED IN UNITED STATES

Eastern Gas and Fuel Associates
2900 Prudential Tower
Boston, Mass. 02199

SPECIMEN

Case Twenty-One

Eastern Gas & Fuel Associates (D)

> I am proud, as an Eastern stockholder, to have a management team "in tune" with and trying to solve some of our basic social problems. Continue to bring the problem areas to light. The solutions will follow in a timely fashion. Cheers.
>
> Increase dividends to 7%.
>
> Hiring and promotion should be on merit only.
>
> I think it is very commendable that you are soliciting opinions on your social accounting. Hope this will help in your decisions.
>
> This evaluation is an excellent experiment—Good Luck!

The quotations above are samples from the over 500 replies received by Eastern Gas and Fuel Associates in response to its questionnaire asking the opinions of its 8,800 stockholders on its experimental social accounting project and report. The earlier cases in this series traced the development of this activity. This case will focus on the aftermath—the stockholders' reactions, the internal reactions, and the options open to EGFA as it confronted the unusual questions of "after an audit, what?" The analysis, based on interviews with EGFA management and on the answers to the questionnaire, shows that, in fact, the consequences of an audit may be even more complex and time-consuming than the audit itself.

Mr. Goldston readily admitted that one of his motivations for surveying the stockholders was curiosity. Just what did its stockholders think of EGFA, especially after they had just been told some rather disappointing facts? For while EGFA's charitable contributions were commendable, its minority employment increasing, and its pension plans at least attempting to respond to new social pressures, its accident record, particularly in the coal mines, was poor—a rise of almost 50% in lost-time accidents in the mines over the last three years. Since no other company had faced a similar situation, there was no way to predict what the response to the publication of these records would be. Goldston commented on some of the management's concerns prior to the survey:

> In our shareholder opinion survey we decided not to set it up so you could really count votes. We were afraid that we in management were—and it is probably generally true—much more liberal in our attitude toward a lot of things than our shareholders. We didn't want to be faced with a clear vote against us, so in our survey we simply asked shareholders to indicate whether they were a large or medium or small shareholder, but not exactly how many shares they had. We also asked for opinions in a multiple choice way rather than by "yes" or "no" votes. In that way we wouldn't get any unwelcome mandates.
>
> We had a number of apprehensions about the survey. One was that the shareholders would get an exaggerated notion of their authority. We didn't want to suggest that if the shareholders voted down charitable giving we wouldn't do it. We were worried that they wouldn't have enough information to vote intelligently, [so] there is a considerable amount of information from our records in it. We were worried that by disclosing some of these things we would stir up some activist groups or the government. We were fretted by our auditors who wanted it clear that they hadn't recommended it and so forth. Nevertheless we went ahead and did it, and we got some very, very interesting results.[1]

Exhibit 21-1 presents the summary answers to the questionnaire and reflects what Mr. Goldston laughingly referred to as the "Lizzie Borden Syndrome." Apparently, people were as impressed with honesty and openness as with performance statistics—Goldston said he got the feeling that this particular sample would have congratulated Lizzie on telling her tale rather than condemned her for her "40 whacks." Certainly EGFA's record was far less gory than Lizzie's, but many shareholders' comments focused on EGFA's willingness to release the figures rather than on the figures themselves. Goldston speculated that perhaps a "straight" record would be suspect and dismissed as a whitewash. One respondent said, "I appreciate the frankness in your report. It is a refreshing departure from the usual corporate nonsense." Many judged EGFA a progressive company not simply on its statistics, but on the fact that it was working "toward social accounting." As the samples quoted below indicate, many favorable comments were directed towards the overall company image rather than in response to specific figures in the report:

> This is an excellent idea. I've learned a lot from it and I suspect you did too.
>
> This report is innovative and progressive. Management is to be commended for considering this adjustment to its annual report.
>
> This questionnaire is a practical and sensible way to develop guidance for management in dealing with corporate-social problems.
>
> Great idea—thanks for making this available. Very educational from all standpoints. Keep up the good work.

---

[1] Goldston, American Society of Corporate Secretaries speech.

> Excellent and honest.
>
> Well-managed company.
>
> Congratulations on soliciting shareholders' opinions on these matters.
>
> Right on!
>
> You are to be congratulated for even including this in your annual report.
>
> I am very pleased with the dynamic activity of the management in all fields mentioned above.
>
> I am proud of what management is doing for EGFA Associates.
>
> Congratulations! Despite my loss of $2000 on your stock, it is heartening to note your humanitarian approach to life.

This last comment suggested the focus of some of the negative remarks–money. Specifically, some stockholders expressed a desire for higher monetary pay-offs. One said, "Why don't you start thinking about the stockholder's welfare," and several echoed the suggestion, "I'd like to see the company give more dividends in cash to the stockholders."

Some of these negative comments were directed toward the company's total philosophy. Typical of this outlook opposing "corporate social responsibility" were such comments as:

> Make money.
>
> Concentrate on EGFA survival, not on sociological recipients and philosophers.
>
> No need for any corporation to develop so-called social attitudes. Our government is well into the social field and we are already heavily taxed to provide such services.
>
> What are you doing to promote an understanding of the private enterprise system?
>
> May I suggest a little less social accounting which makes your executives feel good and a little more in the way of dividends which will make your stockholders feel good.

Most of the respondents, however, applauded the idea of social accounting. Fifty-four per cent felt "this sort of social accounting report" should be "continued in about the same manner" and 16% felt it should be enlarged, whereas 15% felt it should be condensed, and only 11% felt it should be omitted. Such comments as follow reflect on the general idea of social responsibility as well as the company:

> Public opinion and news media make corporate social responsibility a must.
>
> This is a proper step in the direction of corporate responsibility to employees, shareholders, consumers, and community.
>
> I am impressed with the attitude of social responsibility that is implicit in this report. All companies should do the same. I am more likely to hang on to my stock as a result of this.

> I see many annual reports, but none have been as timely to today's conditions as this one on "Social Accounting."

In addition to these general comments on EGFA and social responsibility, other more specific reactions to the various categories were obtained.

INDUSTRIAL SAFETY

In a speech to the American Society of Corporate Secretaries, Mr. Goldston told of some shareholder reactions to the industrial safety portion of the audit:

> The first question for the shareholders on the subject of safety was, 'How does our record on industrial accidents seem to you?' I had wanted to make the first blank 'Awful.'
>
> Well, you have been through this process with counsel and auditors and public relations and all the rest, so you will understand how the first blank became 'Good.' Not 'Bad,' just 'Good, taking problems into account.' Here was this horrendous record that we had disclosed, and when we asked how our record on industrial accidents seemed to them, 38% said, 'Good, taking the problems into account,' and only 9% said poor. Remember, our management group had been telling me, 'We'll be sued! We'll have strikes! We'll be run out of the industry! We won't be able to look our children in the eye when we go home!' Yet 38% of the shareholders said, "that's pretty good taking things into account."

Furthermore, 69% of the respondents agreed that "Industrial Safety" should be included in such a social accounting report. Though this area did not receive as much attention as Goldston had expected, some of the typical comments did indicate concern:

> Industrial accidents: Poor! I am a retired director of industrial safety.
>
> Fatalities seem high.
>
> EGFA can accomplish more in a social sense through a much improved industrial safety record than in any other of the areas mentioned.

MINORITY EMPLOYMENT

Minority employment seemed to be a much more controversial topic. Only 45% (the lowest percentage for any of the topics actually covered) felt it should be included in a social report (but 25% suggested "female employment" as a separate topic.) Goldston pointed out some of the inconsistencies in the shareholder responses in this category:

> We asked if they thought the company should continue to move ahead of legal enforcement pressures in different areas. Almost 3/4 agreed. When we came to preferential hiring, however, a vast majority–about 2/3–disagreed. When we came to special counselling the 2/3 swung around to 'yes.' In effect you could say 3/4 of

> those responding[2] were in favor of moving ahead of the law—which is *satisficing* and not *maximizing* in some of these areas. Two-thirds were against it if you used that phrase "preferential hiring," but 2/3 were for it if you did much the same thing but called it "supplemental counselling."

Sample comments illustrate the general (but not universal) rejection of outright discrimination but also the fear of another kind of discrimination, of hiring only by minority status rather than by qualification:

> It seems important to me that minority groups be helped as much as possible, but I don't believe they should have preferential treatment.
>
> Hiring and promotion should be on merit only.
>
> No special preference for minorities. If they have what it takes, hire and promote them.
>
> Make sure that you don't wind up discriminating against the non-minorities.
>
> No discrimination against any qualified person, regardless of race, religion, or sex. Help for minorities to make them qualified could be good.
>
> Preferential hiring of minorities, subject to qualification to work.
>
> With respect to the hiring of minorities and women, the company's aim should be equity toward each employee and potential employee as an individual.
>
> Minorities my eye. . . . These minorities own cars and are a plague to the good American people. They ruin everything. Not only will it be a waste of money to help them, but a sin.
>
> I am a firm believer in hiring able and trained people whether they are from minorities or not. However, minorities often find it harder to receive training and thus need more help here. Hiring only because of minority background causes worse resentment.

CORPORATE CONTRIBUTIONS

There were several questions in the survey concerning charitable donations, and 53% of the respondents felt this was an important topic for a social report to cover. A large majority (71%) felt that EGFA should continue giving at its present level (about 1% of pre-tax profits), only 12% endorsed raising the amount up to the 5% legally deductible limit, and 1% opted for an even higher percentage of giving. But 13% thought that the company should give "nothing, letting individuals choose their own charities." Sixty-eight percent felt that EGFA should continue its matching gifts program, while 24% felt it should not. Respondents were fairly evenly divided concerning where they thought contributions should be directed. Thirty-seven percent wanted contributions limited to programs "likely to serve our own employees and families" while 41% did not want such

---

[2] In this context Mr. Goldston has lumped together the 29% who said "yes" and the 42% who said "moderately."

a limitation. An approximately equal number (36%) felt that donations should be "limited to social welfare programs such as hospitals or United Funds," and, again, 36% said that they should not be limited in this way. Typical comments reflect the general acceptance of company philanthropy, but with some reminders that it is, after all, the stockholders' money that is being distributed:

> I believe EGFA charitable giving should be a reflection of the shareholder's, manager's and employees' interests. Therefore, as a guide, why not poll these groups?
>
> Contribution to charity should be determined by the employees in each plant location so it will be based upon community needs in place of "national" needs.
>
> Why so much concern about charity? It is stockholders' money. Give it to stockholder and let him/her give to charities of their choice.
>
> Charitable contributions are practiced by both stockholders and employees. So company contributions are a duplication in giving. So cut it out.
>
> Industry-wide contributions, i.e., [I suggest] black lung research in coal industry.
>
> Set up a control formula such as 1% of pre-tax income, plus 8% of any increases in pre-tax income over that of 1972, the maximum not to exceed the IRS 5% of taxable income restriction unless approved by the Board of Directors.
>
> Might consider matching employees gifts—sorry, I see you're ahead of me! The Social Accounting Report is a super idea!
>
> Charitable Contributions: Up to 2% depending upon economic conditions. Endorse your concern with social responsibility.

PENSIONS

Over half (56%) of the respondents thought pension coverage should be covered in a Social Report. Forty-four percent of those answering felt that EGFA should move in the direction of "more complete funding" (26% said no); over half (56%) wanted "improved vesting and portability" (15% did not); and 63% (vs. 17%) recommended inflationary adjustments for retired employees. Sample comments reflect both the majority consensus and some dissent:

> I believe governmental and social pressures will dictate soon total funding, improved portability and inflationary adjustments of pension plans.
>
> Because of the rapid rate of inflation if an employee has been retired after 30 or more years of service with EGFA some periodic inflation adjustment is a just reward for service to company.
>
> No employee should ever receive over $200.00 yearly as a pension. If he is worth more in management's eyes, pay him while he is working. After 65 a person does not need $500.00 or more income from pension. Most over that would only go to government.

> Inflationary adjustments for ex-employees, where pension is less than $5,000 per annum.

OTHER TOPICS

The questions about what should be included in subsequent audits covered topics beyond those in the 1972 audit. Sixty-one percent felt that the area of "the environment" should be included in such a social report, and some commented on this area:

> Depletion of available natural resources. I am apprehensive over environmental pollution.
>
> I would like you to add a section dealing with environmental problems including air and water pollution and strip mining techniques and the company's position relevant thereto.
>
> Company should be more sensitive to the needs of the nation's ecology. With so much land under its control, why not set up wild life preserves, major parks, etc., but retaining deeds.

Forty-two percent approved adding the area of "consumer rights," and one respondent suggested:

> Have one telephone to take complaints. Have more cooperation between departments in Boston Gas as regards customer service and billing, thereby saving duplicate service. Have only qualified people who work a 40 hour week. Have a private detective stationed at Jamaica Plain office and yard at night, to catch thieves and prevent loss of valuable equipment.

Other spontaneous suggestions concerned a topic such as political involvement ("Encourage employees to run for public office, hold appointive positions, and take an active part in the political system.") or employee satisfaction ("I would be interested also in knowing what, if anything, is being done about the quality of jobs [both white and blue-collar] at EGFA–is there any restructuring going on, or any thought of profit-sharing? Is this considered necessary? According to the HEW report 'Work in America' only 43% of white-collar workers said they would choose the same work again. I think this should be included in a Social Accounting.") Miscellaneous recommendations ranged from the very specific ("Perhaps a future questionaire should have a provision for readily making a copy rather than by Xerox so that the respondent can compare his answers year-by-year") to the very general but cryptic ("Neither a Scrooge or patsy be.")

PUBLIC REACTION

As the examples included above have indicated, the overall response to EGFA's endeavor was often unexpected and very candid, but generally approving. The company press release, dated April 26, 1973, the time of the company's annual meeting, is reproduced as Exhibit 21-2.

The project was covered in many newspaper articles (in the *New York Times, Newsday, The San Francisco Chronicle*, for example) and the company generally was applauded for its "social responsibility."

INTERNAL REACTION

Internally, the reaction was a bit more complex. The audit process itself did not seem to cause much resentment, and supervisors, who perhaps had become accustomed to such requests from past efforts, contributed the information willingly enough. However, control of the divisional functions by the central office was a continuing and very open issue, and some tension existed when the issue was encountered. But, in this case, at least, Mr. Goldston felt the balance between headquarters and subsidiary managements did not seem to be seriously disturbed.

Some of the findings did cause some interesting reactions and several novel explanations from subsidiary managers. Mr. Goldston cited the following example in the health and safety area:

> The coal company explained to us that our competitors simply don't list the fellows who get hurt, but let them, as they say, 'ride the bench,' that is, keep them off the sick list by having them at work and doing nothing, or doing very little. Well, you can't keep corpses around very long so if you move from the frequency of accidents to fatalities and your record is worse than other firms, another explanation is needed. The fellow just can't tell you that the competition has mummified the guy and kept him on the payroll.[3]

He cited another similar incident with the gas company:

> Our gas company people explained to me that we count dog bites as industrial accidents. They said: 'We're very conservative. It seems that most gas companies don't count dog bites as industrial accidents, and therefore we look worse, but we really aren't.' I figured out if everybody in the other companies got bitten twice a month we'd still look worse.[4]

Mr. Goldston announced that the audit was not a "one-shot" deal, that those four areas would continue to be monitored and managers evaluated on the basis of performance in these fields, and that different areas would have certain goals or targets by which to judge results (in minority employment, in safety areas, etc.). This continuing audit, unlike the first one, was formally announced to the company. Goldston wrote to the "Operations Committee" as he circulated the tabulations of the shareholder survey:

---

[3]Goldston, American Society of Corporate Secretaries' speech.

[4]Ibid.

> It would seem that several conclusions may be drawn from the results of the survey . . . which, incidentally, no doubt is the first of its kind ever undertaken by a publicly held US industrial firm.
>
> Some of us were apprehensive in advance that providing shareholders with as much detail about matters of social concern could have a variety of disturbing consequences. On the one hand there was the danger that a majority of shareholders would take us to task for being too generous with corporate funds, either through contributions or pension programs, and we would seem to have a mandate against doing what management judgment told us is desirable. On the other hand, the information and invitation could trigger severe criticism by social activist groups or possibly even public agency action.
>
> To date, neither of these extremes has developed. As a matter of fact, we have received a lot of public and private commendations. You will note that statistically, there has been general endorsement by shareholders of company policies in these fields.
>
> Altogether I think we can say that this beginning attempt has encouraged us to go forward with less apprehension about consequences and we can all take pride in having had a part in this project which has already received considerable favorable attention among those interested in the subject.
>
> I have now asked Bill Helm to take a look at the first six months' figures for the same four subjects . . . and in addition to consider how we might add some meaningful accounting of our environmental involvement, particularly in coal but also in our other operations. . . . Working with Bill Helm will be Brown Baldwin, Ozzie Ingram, and perhaps some others. They will appreciate cooperation from you and your colleagues in compiling the data, but will try to keep their requests to a minimum.

As Mr. Goldston reviewed the planning for the new 1973 survey, he remarked, "Having started, it's going to be hard to stop."

Exhibit 21-1

Questionnaire

1. Should this sort of social accounting report be:
- 13% ☐ enlarged
- 56% ☐ continued in about same manner
- 16% ☐ condensed
- 11% ☐ omitted

2. Should such reports cover:
- 71% ☐ Industrial Safety
- 44% ☐ Minority Employment
- 55% ☐ Charitable Giving
- 59% ☐ Pensions
- 59% ☐ Environment
- 25% ☐ Female Employment
- 41% ☐ Consumer Rights
- ☐ Other (please list)

3. How does our record on industrial accidents seem to you?
- 35% ☐ Good, taking problems into account
- 26% ☐ Fair
- 16% ☐ Mediocre
- 11% ☐ Poor

4. Should the company continue to move ahead of legal enforcement pressures in the following areas:

Employment and promotion of minorities
23% ☐ Yes 47% ☐ Moderately 25% ☐ No

Preferential hiring of minorities
8% ☐ Yes 28% ☐ Moderately 57% ☐ No

Special counselling, training for minorities
34% ☐ Yes 39% ☐ Moderately 23% ☐ No

5. In charitable contributions, should the company give:
- 71% ☐ Present level of about 1% as is common practice
- 11% ☐ Up to permitted tax deductible level of 5% of taxable income
- Under 1% ☐ Above 5% even though not deductible
- 14% ☐ Nothing, letting individuals choose their own charities

6. Should company charitable contributions be:

Limited to programs likely to serve our own employees and families ☐ Yes 37% ☐ No 41%

Limited to social welfare programs such as hospitals or United Funds ☐ Yes 38% ☐ No 36%

Include urban or minority programs ☐ Yes 36% ☐ No 33%

7. Should the company continue its "Matching Gifts" program as a way of bringing employees into charitable giving decisions
67% ☐ Yes 26% ☐ No

8. Should the company move in direction of the following current proposals for pensions

More complete funding 44% ☐ Yes ☐ No 25%

Improved vesting and portability 52% ☐ Yes ☐ No 15%

Inflationary adjustments for retired employees 62% ☐ Yes ☐ No 17%

Information about respondents

Male ☐ 78% Female ☐ 13% Institution ☐ 1% (Fund, Bank, Trustee, etc.)

Age Under 35-9%
35-60-43%
Over 60-42%

Shareholdings

☐ UNDER 100 ☐ 100-500 ☐ 500-1000 ☐ 1000-5000 ☐ 5000-over

Location

☐ New England ☐ Midwest
☐ Far West ☐ Middle Atlantic
☐ South ☐ Foreign

Eastern Gas and Fuel Associates

Exhibit 21-2

NEWS FROM EASTERN GAS AND FUEL ASSOCIATES

2900 Prudential Tower Boston, Mass. 02199

Companies and Division

Boston Gas Company
Boston Tow Boat Company
Capital Marine Supply Inc.
Castner, Curran & Bullitt, Inc.
Chotin Transportation Inc.
Coastal Towing Corporation
Eastern Associated Coal Corp.
Eastern Associated Properties Corp.
Eastern Associated Terminals Company
Eastern Urban Services, Inc.
Midland Enterprises Inc.
Mystic Steamship Corp.
The Ohio River Company
Orgulf Transport Co.
Philadelphia Coke Division
Port Allen Marine Services, Inc.
Red Circle Transport Company

For further information call:

O.F. Ingram
262-3500, Ext. 241

April 26, 1973

FOR IMMEDIATE RELEASE

BOSTON, April 26—Shareholders of Eastern Gas and Fuel Associates, Boston-based diversified energy firm, generally support what the company is doing in several areas of current social concern and want it to continue its innovative Social Accounting report initiated this year.

These preliminary conclusions from what is believed to be the first survey of shareholders of a U.S. industrial firm on such topics as minority employment and corporate charitable contributions were disclosed here today at the Annual Meeting of the company's shareholders. Eastern sent to each shareholder with its 1972 Annual Report a detailed report on its performance in industrial safety, minority employment, charitable contributions and pensions, and asked for shareholder reaction.

Eli Goldston, Eastern's chief executive officer, reported that early mail returns from nearly 500 of the company's 8,800 stockholders, showed nearly 85% in favor of continuing to keep them informed of the company's performance in areas where business is often under attack. A majority of the respondents also supported company efforts to move moderately ahead of legal requirements in minority employment, to contribute 1% of pre-tax income to social welfare activities, and to improve pension benefits and funding. A majority also recognized that the company's overall employee safety record needs to be improved.

Responding shareholders indicated a strong interest in having the company add a report to them on its environmental performance, but were not much interested in information about female employment.

"Altogether," Goldston said, "this has been a heartening endorsement by shareholders of progressive programs which management believes are in the public interest as well as forming the basis for long-term financial soundness.

"Comments ranged from those who told us 'Let's stick to business and not sociology,' to 'Congratulations and continue your good work.' Overall, though, there is clear recognition by thoughtful shareholders that business cannot ignore its responsibility to act in and report on areas of public interest."

In the formal action of the meeting, shareholders elected the management slate of Trustees which included William J. Pruyn, president of Boston Gas Company, succeeding C. Russell Walton, former senior vice president of Eastern Gas and Fuel Associates, who retired and becomes an Honorary Trustee.

Announced at the meeting were executive changes voted at a subsequent organization meeting of the Trustees. Eli Goldston, president since 1962, becomes chairman and chief executive officer. John N. Philips, executive vice president since 1969, becomes president and chief operating officer; and Charles A. Coolidge, chairman since 1971, becomes Honorary Chairman of the Board to preside at meetings of the Board of Trustees and shareholders.

The meeting heard reports from the heads of its marine, coal and gas utility operations and a reaffirmation of the company's expectations that depending on anticipated improvement in coal production, continuation of favorable business conditions in barging and approval of proposed increases in gas rates, earnings for the full year should be in the range of $2.00 to $2.50 per share. For 1972 comparable earnings were $1.75 per share.

MARINE

Louis R. Fiore, senior vice president-marine, said that despite current operating difficulties because of flooded Midwest rivers, 1973 should again be a record year for Eastern's transportation operations.

"Although the high water problems will affect our results in the short term," Fiore said, "the bulk of our business is under contract, the commodities await resumption of full operations and we expect to make up practically all of the temporarily lost tonnage over the course of the next few months. In the perspective of the full year, we see no reason to change our expectations that it will again show significant gains and be another record year."

COAL

Robert H. Freeman, senior vice president-coal, reported that Eastern's coal operations share the industry promise of steadily increasing demand for coal while currently experiencing production problems. The company is intensifying training and management development and introducing new equipment into the mines to meet production goals safely.

"I have to say that to date the promise of improvement has not been fully realized," Freeman said. "Coal production in the first quarter was not up to expectations. Wildcat strikes continued at a rate that sometimes approached that of 1972. But with the continuing intensive personnel effort on our part, the success of the new union leadership in establishing control, and the introduction of new equipment we are hopeful that we can better our 1972 performance.

GAS

William J. Pruyn, senior vice president-gas, reported that despite unusually warm weather during the first quarter, results of Boston Gas operations were comparable to those for the same period of 1972. This year, he said, because of an improved supply outlook, the company has resumed an aggressive sales effort, emphasizing new heating sales, particularly in the residential market, although continued attention will be given to non-heating and replacement sales. He detailed arrangements for supplemental gas supplies through imported liquefied natural gas and a new substitute natural gas plant being built in Everett.

"When you match our supply picture with the growth in our company and the changes and improvements in all departments of our operations," he said, "I think there is justification for optimism about the future of the gas operations of Eastern Gas and Fuel Associates."

Chapter Six

The Social Issue Specialist

Responding to social expectations is not merely a matter of changing management attitudes and reordering the priorities governing operating decisions. Adaptation requires the assimilation of new skills, relationships, and information as well. The social issue specialist plays a particularly important part in drawing external demands, corporate policy, and operating decisions together. Through him the organization learns to negotiate with an unfamiliar and sometimes threatening environment.

The question raised by the specialist is one of increasing importance for the management of the large corporation–how should specialized skills be introduced in organizations dominated by generalists? A forceful response to social demands requires strong direction from top management. The specialist is the cutting edge used by the chief executive to narrow the gap between his expectations and operating realities. If this edge is blunted, the chief executive loses a critical source of influence. In fact, without the prior efforts of the specialist, the chief executive would be hard pressed to insist on implementation. On the other hand, permitting the specialist to direct implementation at operating levels himself tends to subvert an otherwise useful general management focus. Were powerful specialist roles created for numerous social issues, the impact on the organization could be dramatic.

In most corporations, this question has not been satisfactorily answered. There is a pronounced tendency among social issue specialists to fail or at least to experience severe frustration in provoking change at operating levels. The specialist usually attributes failure to an intransigent organization that is unwilling to grasp the severity of the social demand and possibly a chief executive who is not sufficiently supportive. Further investigation may reveal incidents that precipitated sharp reversals for the specialist in confrontations with operating management. Feeling let down and convinced that meaningful change is not soon forthcoming, he either leaves the firm or retreats to the safety of the headquarters offices and busies himself with routine matters and external affairs.

The frustrations encountered by the specialist are in part endemic to corporate staff in the divisionalized organization. Yet because of the dynamics of an evolving social issue, the degree of learning required, and the probable resistance among operating managers, the social issue specialist may be in a more tenuous position than his staff counterparts in other functions. If a meaningful specialist role is to survive, three areas must be managed sensitively:

- Introducing the specialist
- Managing the specialist's job
- Designing a corporate specialist capability

INTRODUCING THE SPECIALIST. The specialist's job is virtually certain to be ill-defined at the outset. In general terms, justification for creating the position often eminates from the chief executive's conviction that someone is needed to (a) give emphasis and direction to the social policy, (b) interpret environmental demands and develop a corporate position on them, (c) add substantive skills to the organization, (d) coordinate the response of operating units, and (e) assist senior officers in the performance of their external duties. Despite whatever formal descriptions of the job might be offered, however, a period of uncertainty may be anticipated, devoted to assimilating and defining the specialist's function and, in the process, testing the mandate he has been given to disturb the status quo. His role in the organization is materially influenced by decisions about the criteria for his selection, where he is to report, and what relationship he is to have with the chief executive. A moment's reflection on the alternatives available for each of these choices reveals that designing a new function to facilitate response to uncertain social demands is a complex affair indeed.

The first specialists are often hired specifically for the job and have had considerable relevant experience with social issues through government or activist involvement. Managers with this background have the difficult task of learning how to get along in an unfamiliar organization which, fairly or otherwise, often has them typed as proponents of social causes who probably are fundamentally anti-business. Conversely, they may be selected from within the company and have little detailed understanding of the social issue they are asked to assimilate. Sometimes they are long-service employees nearing retirement, and in other cases, younger managers anxious about the career implications of accepting the position. In either event, the appointment carries with it a variety of personal expectations and established relationships that aid or impede the acceptance of the new function.

The specialist may be placed in an existing corporate staff group or set up in a separate office reporting independently to the chief executive or another senior officer. For example, pollution control may be assigned to central engineering and minority affairs to corporate personnel in one company, while in another a new department may be created to serve these needs. In the latter instance, the specialist may be instructed to engage a number of issues, with the intention that he be a sort of multi-discipline social watchdog. A new department tends to provide greater leverage for the chief executive and more visibility and emphasis for the issue. However, the increased emphasis may cause conflict with the managers of established staff units who feel their territory has been encroached upon. On the other hand, a decision to attach the specialist to an existing staff group raises the further question, which one? For instance, distinctly different patterns of response to environmental concerns are probable if the specialist is part of the engineering rather than the public relations staff or if the OSHA specialist is assigned to personnel, engineering, or the medical staff.

Finally, the chief executive has the responsibility for specifying the relationship between his office and the specialist. The options range from close personal advisor to seldom-seen staff functionary. In the former case, the specialist may appear to garner considerable influence through the visible manifestations of this relationship, to the point that others in the organization feel he speaks the chief executive's mind on matters related to the social policy. It is probable, however, that the more the specialist is viewed as a top management stand-in, the more wary (if not hostile) his ties will be with the operating managers he is supposed to assist. At the other extreme, without tangible chief executive support, the specialist may be dismissed by these same managers as a gadfly without portfolio.

Thus, the design of the position requires careful attention to personal considerations. The specialist must be acceptable to both operating managers and social activists, including government regulators and technical experts. The prognosis for a new department staffed by outsiders with backgrounds and skills related to the issue is generally not very good. Nor is the prognosis much better if a low-ranking manager without prior relevant experience is assigned to a specialist's job in an established corporate staff group.

Ironically, skills as a manager may be a more accurate predictor of the specialist's performance than technical excellence or issue-related reputation. Locating an individual with both qualities is clearly not always feasible. Some companies have surmounted this difficulty by pairing individuals with complementary skills, backgrounds, and cognitive or problem-solving styles.

MANAGING THE SPECIALIST'S ROLE. A source of frustration among specialists is the quest for a clarity and stability in their assignments that in fact may not be attainable. The specialist role is highly ambiguous, a characteristic that in this case may be a benefit to those who can tolerate and utilize it. While they may prefer to view themselves as experts and facilitators, in fact, they may need to be equally politicians and negotiators. Implications for the specialist are found in a diagnosis of the relationships to be managed and the tasks to be performed.

The corporate specialist operates in a web of relationships (depicted in simplified form in Exhibit A) which link external agencies, corporate management, and division management. These relationships should be carefully understood; from the specialist's standpoint they are sources of both danger and influence. In one sense, external demands and corporate commitment provide the initial impetus for change. The more strongly they are stated, the more influence the specialist is likely to have in pressing the operating units to apply resources to lifting the constraints limiting responsiveness. But in another sense, the specialist is implicitly held responsible for keeping social expectations, corporate policy, and operating realities in some sort of balance in a dynamic environment. Although he has little or no authority over any of the parties involved, he has a vital concern in their relationships with one another.

Consequently, the specialist must be a politican; he must manage relationships he cannot directly control. For instance, the environmental control director may want more (or less) attention given to the issue in business plan reviews or in speeches before the Chamber of Commerce. He may attempt to stage the negotiations between social agencies and operating managers. In one instance, an equal employment director even advised the government compliance agency that an audit of one unit would be helpful! To perform this function, the specialist needs an intimate knowledge of the motivations, concerns, and goals of each party to this network. He must know the depth of the chief executive's commitment, the budget problems, and career concerns of operating managers, and the political pressures on the representatives of social agencies (employee leaders, regulators, activists, etc.).

The specialist must also be a skilled negotiator. For if he totes up the mandate given to his office, it generally does not put him in a position to force response on the operating units. At this stage in the process, neither corporate policy nor social demands carry sanctions for noncompliance—he cannot say to operating managers, "do it!" As a result, the specialist must bargain for support and responsiveness. With social agencies he argues the company's case and promises compliance in return for favorable treatment; with operating managers he uses the results of outside negotiations plus technical help to obtain information and personal assistance for the support of his office. The relationships are highly interdependent; if one breaks down, all are likely to suffer.

In each relationship the tenor may be cooperative or advisory; to the extent the latter is chosen, however, the specialist assumes a new set of complexities. Although friends may be difficult to win, enemies can be ill-afforded. As one wise specialist commented, "The point you have to remember is that if you are serious about winning the war, you can't afford to get killed in a skirmish."

The specialist may well ask, "Whom do I represent? The community? The operating managers? The president?" The answer may well be all of them. Hence, the role is ambiguous, a characteristic that the resourceful specialist may use to establish a measure of independence that prevents him from being typed as captive to one set of pressures. Perhaps more than any other manager in the firm, he needs an explicit strategy for the conduct of his department that encompasses both the dictates of the environment and the constraints cast up by the organization.

DESIGNING A CORPORATE SPECIALIST CAPACITY. The role of the specialist changes as the social issue and the corporation's response to it matures. The initiative for action quite rightly passes from his hands to those of operating managers who often employ their own specialists. The social issue specialist, if successful, plays a major part in making this transition possible by two related achievements:

- Sensitizing operating managers to the social demand and providing them with the technical capability to manage it at their level.
- Designing the administrative systems that permit top management to set standards, controls and performance measures.

In effect, these contributions prepare the issue for implementation in a form that is familiar to both operating and corporate managers.

An interesting question comes into focus should the specialist succeed: What is the corporate specialist's function as response becomes institutionalized? There is clearly the danger, both for the corporation and the specialist, that he will cling to a role that was appropriate in an earlier phase of the response process. Such behavior will almost certainly result in confusion and conflict that will probably not long be tolerated. In broad terms, there are two plausible alternatives: (a) the residue tasks of coordinating and managing the reporting system, providing legal and technical counsel, etc. may be reassigned to existing staff units and the specialist's position discontinued or (b) the specialist may retain these residual duties and be assigned other social issues that are then emerging.

The choice determines the configuration of the response mechanism the firm is to maintain at the corporate level. Adopting the first alternative points toward a succession of specialists in temporary positions which exist for perhaps three to six years and are then folded into the traditional organization. The second envisages a multi-purpose social issue specialist whose job is to process issues one after another. Of course, spreading the specialist over a variety of issues may dilute his efforts and over-extend his capability to deal with substantively different responses. There are also obvious implications in this decision for the chief executive as he considers the career aspirations and skills appropriate to those selected as specialists.

Exhibit A

RELATIONSHIPS

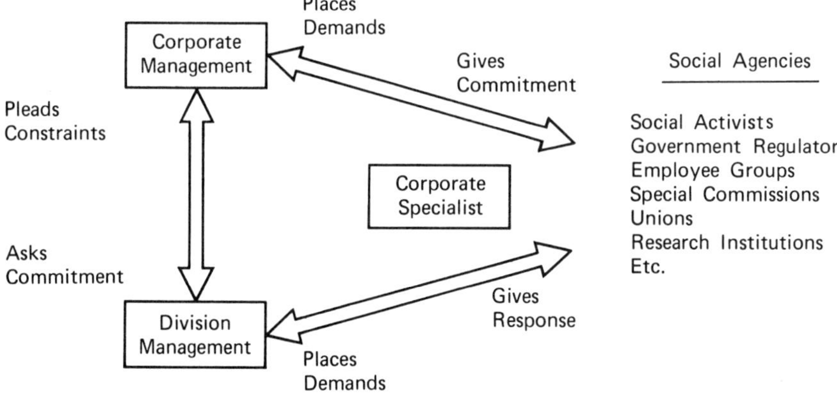

SUGGESTED READINGS

1.–Steiner, George, *Top Management Planning*. New York: McMillan, 1969.

2.–Machiavelli, Niccolo. *The Prince*. New York: Modern Library Edition, Random House, 1950.

3.–Schon, Donald A. *Beyond the Stable State*. New York: Random House, 1971.

4.–Thomas, John M. and Bennis, Warren G., eds. *The Management of Change and Conflict*. Baltimore: Penguin Books, 1972.

Case Twenty-Two

Borden, Inc.

Borden, Inc. was a large divisionalized manufacturing company, noted especially for its food products, with sales (1971) of over $2 billion. The company was divided into four divisions: Foods, Dairy & Services, Chemicals and International. Financial data for the company is presented in Exhibit 22-1, and for the divisions in Exhibit 22-2.

The company moved its administrative headquarters to Columbus, Ohio in 1970-1971 and was constructing a new office building in Columbus to be used for the administrative offices and the data processing center. The executive offices, housing a few top corporate officers, remained in New York City. The new administrative building, in the heart of the downtown area rather than in the suburbs, was seen by some as symbolic of other ways in which the company was changing. In the past few years Borden had committed itself to a new and active program emphasizing corporate social involvement. Internally, change was also apparent in terms of leadership interests, new corporate staff functions, and innovative communication and monitoring efforts.

CREATION OF A PUBLIC AFFAIRS OFFICE

One of the underlying reasons for Borden's actions in recent years was the posture taken by its President and Chairman, Augustine R. Marusi, who became president in 1966 and assumed the additional title of chairman in 1968. However, the more immediate motive underlying its initial steps was the concern that it might be engaged in actions that might be viewed critically. In 1967, Borden had run into considerable trouble with the FDA over its dry milk, Starlac (non-fat dry milk had been identified by the FDA as a carrier of salmonella organisms), and had to withdraw the product at a cost of over $6 million. Company management was anxious *not* to repeat this trouble.

A short time after the Starlac incident, Marusi engaged Carlton E. Spitzer, a consultant and former director of information for the U.S. Department of Health, Education, and Welfare. Spitzer's original assignment was fairly narrow: to consult and provide information/intelligence as to what Borden should worry about vis-a-vis government regulation and specifically, to prevent a recurrence of the embarrassment and expense of the Starlac fiasco. Gradually, the scope of Spitzer's work widened; he began to talk with top management about what Borden *should* be involved in as well as what the company actually was doing. Such thinking and talking began to evolve into something like a public affairs program for Borden, and Spitzer's concerns soon went beyond supplying Washington intelligence.

Simultaneously, social pressures of various sorts were being felt by the company, and a number of new faces appeared at the top of the Borden organization. In 1969-1970 Marusi was becoming increasingly involved in national programs and more visible to the public by, for example, participating in White House conferences and making speeches around the country. He instructed Spitzer to "draw up a plan" for public affairs at Borden. Spitzer began to spend more and more of his time working with this single client and soon realized that he was working on a total concept of involvement for the company, encompassing changes in hiring and recruiting practices, promotional opportunities, the board, and other aspects of the corporation.

When Spitzer presented his plans for the Public Affairs Department in early 1970, Marusi suggested that he run it as vice president of Public Affairs. Spitzer had a number of misgivings and accepted only when he became convinced that Marusi was committed to implementing the plan. Spitzer, trying to "move the company in new directions," felt his ideas both demanded and initiated significant changes of attitude within Borden. He was also convinced that industry had to begin to take some initiative in social developments and hoped, rather forlornly, that business had learned something in the past 30 years and would change its "foot-dragging ways."

Spitzer's task, as he saw it, was to realize his and Marusi's plans and demonstrate to the division managers that, in truth, the character of the company was changing. He commented:

> If you don't lock this whole thing into the machinery of the company and prove or demonstrate the benefits to the division manager of making it a natural part of doing business, if you fail to do that over a reasonable period of time, then it is as fragile as the Chairman's view of it, his own personal conscience about it. The whole area then becomes a terribly unpredictable mushy thing and there is no lasting change built into the character of the company. We're trying to make permanent changes in the corporate character. Otherwise it wouldn't be worth all the effort required and all the flak encountered.

At Borden, with Marusi behind him, Spitzer felt he would be "given the track to run on" to try to meet this "great challenge." Because of this top level support, Spitzer felt that he was properly situated to carry out his plans, but he still needed a structure to engage others. The development of this structure occupied much of his time during the following two years. Through these activities he hoped to create a strong department to direct the public affairs of the company and to help secure a place for its goals among those of the whole corporation.

The former Public Relations Department of 36 professionals and staff had been reduced in size prior to Spitzer's arrival as part of a general effort to cut the size of the corporate staff and strengthen management at division levels. Under Spitzer it remained small, employing six professionals and a support staff of eleven in 1970. This was reduced in 1972 to one professional and three support staff.

COMMUNICATION DEVICES: PRESIDENT'S LETTER AND PRESIDENT'S FORUM

Marusi continued to expand his role as a spokesman on social issues through outside speaking engagements and candid discussion with Borden managers at lower levels who were remote from the executive offices. In spite of some negative reactions within the company, Spitzer was encouraged by Marusi's increased involvement, for it complemented his ideas about how the company and its image should develop.

Nonetheless, even with this support and exposure, Spitzer feared that nothing of substance would occur. It was still necessary to transmit to the organization Marusi's intention to incorporate public affairs into the way the operating managers conducted their businesses. Two communications vehicles were then established to give emphasis and meaning to Marusi's words: the President's Letter and the President's Forum.

The President's Letter was sent out, from time to time, by Marusi to Borden's managers to announce or to explain important developments, often involving corporate social issues or policies. The President's Forum, initiated in 1970, consisted of occasional meetings featuring guest speakers who were often controversial or critical figures. The President's Letter was used to introduce, discuss and recap these sessions. Borden's executives attended the forum because they were specifically invited by the president. The forum forced some sort of dialogue with and response to the speakers. As Spitzer put it, "We've sometimes had to rub their [the Borden executives] noses into special issues where formerly they would have avoided them." The president described these gatherings in his June 1971 letter:

> About a year ago we instituted "President's Forum," a series of informal meetings at which various Borden executives can exchange opinions in a candid way with outside guests whose responsibilities and experience are of particular interest to business and industry.
>
> During the past year we have met with Thomas Williams, director of the Office of Public Affairs of the Environmental Health Service; James Grant, Deputy Commissioner of the Food & Drug Administration; Elizabeth Hanford, Executive Director of the President's Committee on Consumer Interests; and Dr. William Darby, noted nutritionist.
>
> Our most recent guest was Berkeley G. Burrell, president of the National Business League, and co-author of a new book about black-owned and managed business in America, titled "Getting it Together."*

---

*Subsequent guests included Governor John Gilligan of Ohio, Senators Saxbe and Taft of Ohio, and Sherwood Fawcett, President of Battelle.

MINORITY AFFAIRS: THE COUNCIL, THE AUDIT

An important part of the Public Affairs plan was devoted to minority affairs. One especially significant development in this area stemmed from the Forum meeting with Burrell, described above. Marusi's letter continued and described the motivation for the establishment of a Minority Affairs Council and for an attempt at a "social audit." He wrote:

> The conversation with Mr. Burrell was especially stimulating to me, and I would like to share my thoughts with you.
>
> First, the meeting confirmed that many useful activities are under way throughout the Company to hire and train minority workers at all levels of employment, to purchase goods and service from minority enterprises, and to work with minority banking institutions. I was delighted to hear these informal reports of the follow-up action to my most recent President's Letter, and to know that our managers are determined to do all they can to strengthen these efforts.
>
> Second, the meeting confirmed that we have not yet analyzed on a company-wide basis, the full extent and impact of Borden's efforts in minority affairs. We are taking constructive action. But, as Mr. Burrell's book suggests, we aren't "getting it together." We aren't relating or coordinating our efforts. Nor do we really know what they add up to collectively.
>
> To measure progress requires that we have a starting point. We know how many minority workers are now employed by Borden and their job classifications and pay scales. But we need to know much more:
>
> - We need to know about training programs that now exist or are planned.
> - We need to know our present level of activity with minority suppliers and our expectations, including special efforts to help upgrade minority suppliers.
> - We need to know the scope of our program with minority banks and our plans for the future.
> - We need to know about community programs designed to help minority groups.
>
> This is a big task. I have asked our Public Affairs Department to take on the added responsibility of coordinating minority affairs activities throughout the Company and to report to me regularly on our progress. To organize this effort, I have formed a *Minority Affairs Council* and named Carlton E. Spitzer, Vice President-Public Affairs, as its chairman. The Council Secretary and Program Coordinator is Thomas K. Hamall, our Director of Civic Affairs in the Public Affairs Department.
>
> Members of the Council are:
>
> Fred J. Board, Vice President–Personnel
> Bernard Nemtzow, Vice President and General Counsel and Secretary
> John B. Nimons, Vice President–Puchasing
> Howard H. Ward, Vice President–Finance

> Each Council member will designate an alternate Council member who will also serve as a staff coordinator.
>
> I know that these men will have your full support and cooperation in carrying out their assignments.
>
> Minority Affairs is not a contribution program. It is an integral part of doing business and meeting our business goals. It is, at the same time, a sound and proper way for us to help minority workers and minority entrepreneurs.
>
> Knowing what Borden's program is and how it is developing should give added confidence to our line managers who are faced with questions from community, civic, and minority groups. It should help our managers to separate contributions from investments in this area, erase any apologetic or defensive feelings that may now exist, and deal with minority affairs in a constructive, effective, and business-like way.
>
> In recent years, the manager's job has become ever more complicated. His performance in minority affairs becomes one more measure of his professionalism.
>
> I am confident that you and the men who report to you will set a high standard in this area of your responsibility.

Spitzer found that the forum, and then the council, gave managers at Borden a chance to talk, and he met with some support for his ideas about Borden's role in public affairs. But he was also aware that all the talk was merely opinion. There was a real need to find out, in his words, "where we were, in hiring practices, recruiting and training, compliance with the law, community action, education, drug programs, and all the rest of it." So it was decided at the second meeting of the council in June 1971 to conduct a Minority Affairs Audit. Although Minority Affairs was just part of the total picture, it was recognized as an important part and one for which it might be relatively easy to obtain company-wide figures. This survey was designed over the summer and explained in a letter on September 13, 1971 from Spitzer to "all division, plant and profit center managers," as follows:

> All of you have received a copy of Mr. Marusi's letter of June 10 establishing a corporate Minority Affairs Council. Mr. Marusi has charged the Council with the responsibility for monitoring the status and progress of Borden's efforts in minority activities. For the purpose of this audit, the term "minority" refers to Negro, Spanish surname, Oriental and American Indian.
>
> To measure progress requires that we have a starting point. To this end, the attached Minority Affairs Audit form has been developed. We ask that you carefully and completely fill out the attached three-part form and return it to me at the Public Affairs Department, 50 W. Broad Street, Columbus, Ohio, *not later than September 27.*
>
> The data you provide on your programs in minority employment and training, economic development and community action will be compiled with that obtained from all other Borden plant locations. This will provide basic resource data for the Council and assist its membership in establishing guidelines for future activities.

The audit asked about certain aspects of performance and was intended to provide a base line of information for public affairs (see Exhibit 22-3 for a copy of the questionnaire). At this point Spitzer concluded that questions about cost would only have stirred up trouble and that the answers would probably have been meaningless anyway. He viewed such a first-round audit primarily as an attempt to understand and analyze a situation rather than to seek sophisticated cost benefit quantification.

Replies were received from 60% of those sent the questionnaire. The data were summarized and processed through the Minority Affairs Council for transmission to the office of the president. The results, tabulated in Exhibit 22-4, were somewhat rough and incomplete, but nonetheless they constituted a first step in translating ideas into actions. Spitzer felt they provided a useful starting point for Public Affairs work in this area. He also felt this audit had been a learning experience; not only did Public Affairs learn about different departments, but the departments themselves learned how to go about getting this sort of information. Later figures, obtained from a follow-up survey, were both more encouraging and more accurate. For example, in one department the amount "expended with minority companies" jumped from $260,000 to $4,500,000 from 1971 to 1972. This leap reflected not only some increase in spending by the company, but also a great increase in data-gathering skills by the department involved.

Although the audit was hardly conclusive, it enabled Spitzer and the council to proceed with this part of Borden's Public Affairs program. After reviewing the results, the council recommended the following actions:

1.—A positive effort to hire black salesmen. This idea stemmed from the realization that, based on the audit figures, replacement by attrition would not supply the necessary black salesmen. The council stated that it was no longer sufficient merely to make an effort to hire a black where there was a convenient vacancy; in addition, a definite recruitment drive was required.
2.—An assessment program for women in the corporation. It became evident that hiring women wasn't enough; tracking was necessary to see if they were actually advancing as fast as males.
3.—Use of minority MBAs in a variety of ways throughout the company.

At the time, Spitzer hoped that these programs, which provided an organized if modest way of responding to some important social issues, would be seen as a regular part of doing business and their costs seen as regular business costs.

When the question of funding was put to Marusi, he made it clear that although he thought the proposals were good ideas, they would not be subsidized through a separate corporate budget. Immediately, several division vice presidents lamented that surely they could not be expected to absorb the additional expense in their budgets. However, Marusi remained firm. He indicated that these programs and others like them might be jeopardized, but if they were to be funded at all, the money would have to obtained through the regular division budgets. In this context, Spitzer contended that his department's projects must *not* be seen as optional or have a special budget which could be looped off easily.

There were other developments in this area too. After reviewing the audit, the council requested the Employee Relations Department to monitor progress in minority employment. Representatives were to be sent to each division and department manager to help him set his own goals, covering such matters as promotions and salary increases for minority workers. The department was then to be measured against these self-imposed quotas.

The concern for minorities and discrimination was continued in another new policy, promulgated by the president this time, but carried out by the council. Marusi explained his idea on plant site selection in a President's Letter dated June 11, 1972. He proposed:

> **TO THE ORGANIZATION**:
> For some time now, this corporation has been evolving a company-wide program based on its total relationship to our American minorities. Some of these programs, such as Equal Employment Opportunities, have been at least in part legislated. In other areas, like the establishment of the Minority Affairs Council, our actions have been self-initiated.
>
> The council has been given the responsibility for auditing and assessing Borden's total efforts in minority programming; establishing specific goals in employment, training, minority banking, marketing, activities with minority suppliers and involvement in community programs designed to assist minority groups.
>
> There is another area to which we will now direct our attention. In the future, all Investment Proposals for new or expanded installations must contain a report that addresses itself to minority socio-economic issues, i.e., how communities within which a site is viable act with regard to equal employment opportunities (including construction trades) and open housing. A condition for joining a community or expanding Borden's operations within it will be that it qualifies in every sense. We should also use corporate influence to accomplish needed change in communities where we now operate facilities when discrimination exists. Communities that have major racial prejudices and/or other problems do not represent good investments for the future.
>
> I've asked the Public Affairs Department to design a report form for immediate use throughout the company. It will be a part of all Investment Proposals. A copy of the report will be sent to Carl Spitzer, Chairman of the Minority Affairs Council, in advance of Investment Proposal submission to the Office of the President. The Public Affairs staff will, upon request, assist any division and/or profit center develop the data required. The report will be reviewed by the Minority Affairs Council and their comments and recommendations obtained prior to O.T.P. review. There will be no approval otherwise.

This new policy, as yet largely untested, evidently made it impossible for the company to expand or go into a community without the approval of the Office of Public Affairs or the Minority Affairs Council. The wording of Marusi's letter implied that these signatures would be as necessary as the signatures of the Engineering and Technical Departments. Spitzer indicated that if the policy were implemented successfully, the MAC or Public Affairs people would set the criteria on discrimination and judge whether the particular community was the right environment for a Borden's facility.

ANOTHER AREA–THE ENVIRONMENT

Public Affairs was concerned with the physical environment as well as with discrimination and minorities. Primary staff responsibility in this area rested with the Quality and Environmental Control Department, which reported to the vice president of Engineering. This department in turn coordinated certain of its efforts with the Technical Services Department, another component of the central engineering organization. Technical services began sending teams of roving auditors unannounced to facilities in the four operating divisions to pinpoint trouble spots which might result in law suits or plant closings by outside authorities. The auditors had authority to shut a facility down themselves if they believed the circumstances warranted it, though as yet no action of this sort had been taken.

Spitzer commented that "we are now saying 'let's audit every *potential* pollution problem.' " He suspected that the audit program would help operating managers overcome a psychological problem as well. Whereas in the past they may have tended to obscure possible pollution problems, Spitzer now hoped that they would be less reluctant to request funds for pollution control devices. On the other hand, he was aware that the critical test of the program would come when it pointed to the need for expenditures which threatened programs planned by the divisions. As in the case of minority affairs, the costs of pollution control were borne by the divisions, and capital expenditures were processed through the established capital budget and request procedures.

In addition to the auditing teams, there was a way for reports to come in to the corporate offices directly. Crises or problems could be called in to "Operational Alert," a hot line originated by Public Affairs and run by the Quality and Environmental Control Department to speed up corrective action. Although Spitzer was not directly involved with the day to day activities in the environmental control area, he attempted to keep informed of problems and developments in the area.

A SPECIAL CASE–THE PURCHASING DEPARTMENT

Some of the changes in the company spread outside the Public Affairs Department. One of the most "gratifying" developments, according to Spitzer, occurred in the Purchasing Department. In September 1972, the Vice President of Purchasing, John Nimons, set an aggressive policy to purchase from minority vendors which, in Spitzer's view, would have been "unthinkable" two years before. The reason for this turnaround was more complex than merely Nimon's personal conviction. In fact, he needed to be "persuaded" that the president was serious. Spitzer had mentioned earlier to Marusi that Borden's record in procurement did not look good from an affirmative action viewpoint. Marusi immediately sent a letter to the appropriate officers, suggesting that more drastic steps were in order to correct the "flat line" situation, which showed a static number of minority vendors. A new policy was clearly implied.

Once Marusi forced the issue, Nimons responded promptly. Exhibit 22-5 presents the letter in which he announced the new policy concerning minority suppliers.

A way of determining what actually occurred was also developed in the form of quarterly reports on minority vendors to be filed with the Purchasing Office. Spitzer was pleased with the reporting system; it represented the type of control mechanism that he was anxious to see adopted for different programs throughout the company. Through it he hoped that managers would come to see performance in these areas as part of their regular assignments.

UNFINISHED BUSINESS

In the areas of minority affairs, the environment, purchasing, and internal communication, change appeared to have occurred at Borden under the new Public Affairs plan. Spitzer had a progression in his mind; the company's posture would go from having virtually no activities in areas of social concern to having programs, clear enforcement of those programs, and finally goals and measurement built into the whole process. He recognized that progress had not been very uniform thus far, but that Borden's had moved farther along this path since 1970. In most cases, the measurement question had not been tackled, but in matters of discrimination, for example, enforcement procedures were at least being worked on.

Yet in the fall of 1972 Spitzer remained somewhat pessimistic. For with the startup of some new programs had come a clearer appreciation of the formidable problems ahead and the opposition in the organization likely to be encountered in the attempt to solve them. It was with an increased awareness of these difficulties that Spitzer approached the next steps in integrating and strengthening the Public Affairs program at Borden.

Exhibit 22-1

SIX YEAR FINANCIAL SUMMARY

(All dollar and share figures in thousands—except market price and per share statistics)

	1971	1970	1969	1968	1967	1966
SALES, INCOME and DIVIDENDS						
Net Sales	$2,069,667	$1,832,202	$1,896,595	$1,830,474	$1,748,709	$1,707,034
Income before Extraordinary Items	$ 60,533	$ 53,681	$ 50,754	$ 49,147	$ 58,779	$ 61,149
Net Income	$ 60,533	$ 53,681	$ 28,304	$ 46,375	$ 58,779	$ 61,149
Percent of Income before Extraordinary Items to Sales	2.9%	2.9%	2.7%	2.7%	3.4%	3.6%
Percent of Net Income to Sales	2.9%	2.9%	1.5%	2.5%	3.4%	3.6%
Per Share of Common Stock and Equivalent:						
Income before Extraordinary Items	$ 2.00	$ 1.83	$ 1.73	$ 1.68	$ 2.01	$ 2.14
Net Income	$ 2.00	$ 1.83	$ .96	$ 1.58	$ 2.01	$ 2.14
Dividends Declared per—Common Share	$ 1.20	$ 1.20	$ 1.20	$ 1.20	$ 1.20	$ 1.20
Preferred Series A Share	.60					
Preferred Series B Share	.78					
Income Available for Common Shareholders—						
Net Income	$ 60,533	$ 53,681	$ 28,304	$ 46,375	$ 58,779	$ 61,149
Less Dividend Requirements on Preferred Stock	(1,189)	(284)	(284)	(284)	(284)	(284)
	$ 59,344	$ 53,397	$ 28,020	$ 46,091	$ 58,495	$ 60,865
Average Number of Common Shares Outstanding	29,077	28,879	28,854	28,856	28,711	28,065
Income Available per Common Share	$ 2.04	$ 1.85	$ .97	$ 1.60	$ 2.04	$ 2.17

Exhibit 22-1 (continued)

	1971	1970	1969	1968	1967	1966
FINANCIAL STATISTICS						
Capital Expenditures	$ 57,987	$ 60,332	$ 57,689	$ 55,256	$ 67,570	$ 94,158
Depreciation, Depletion and Amortization	$ 42,393	$ 38,725	$ 40,196	$ 37,172	$ 36,074	$ 31,797
Current Assets	$ 611,111	$ 572,258	$ 542,957	$ 506,077	$ 514,622	$ 432,111
Current Liabilities	$ 250,323	$ 246,034	$ 208,836	$ 171,978	$ 171,767	$ 177,548
Working Capital	$ 360,788	$ 326,224	$ 334,121	$ 334,099	$ 342,855	$ 254,563
Current Ratio	2.4:1	2.3:1	2.6:1	2.9:1	3.0:1	2.4:1
Long-term Debt	$ 239.087	$ 219,136	$ 225,594	$ 240,119	$ 253.432	$ 169.257
Debt-to-Equity Percent	34%	34%	36%	38%	41%	28%
Shareholders Equity	$ 696,702	$ 653,524	$ 630,315	$ 638,003	$ 625,660	$ 596,467
Liquidating Value of Preferred Stock	(29,258)	(9,455)	(9,455)	(9,455)	(9,455)	(9,455)
Common Shareholders Equity	$ 667,444	$ 644,069	$ 620,860	$ 628,548	$ 616,205	$ 587,012
Equity per Common Share at Year End	$ 22.94	$ 22.17	$ 21.55	$ 21.79	$ 21.32	$ 20.53
SHAREHOLDERS DATA						
Average Number of Common Shares and Equivalents Outstanding	30,304	29,352	29,327	29,329	29,184	28,538
Outstanding Shares at Year End—Common	29,090	29,048	28,809	28,851	28,897	28,590
Preferred Series A	473	473	473	473	473	473
Preferred Series B	686					
Market Price of Common Stock:						
At Year End	$ 28	$ 27	$ 23	$ 34	$ 35	$ 31
Range of Year	$ 24-30	$ 17-27	$ 22-35	$ 28-38	$ 30-42	$ 28-41
Number of Common Shareholders	70,916	71,886	70,997	71,424	74,508	70,856
EMPLOYEES' DATA						
Payrolls	$ 357,000	$ 333,700	$ 339,800	$ 322,800	$ 303,100	$ 290,600
Average Number of Employees	48,000	45,900	48,300	48,900	47,700	47,900

Exhibit 22-2

SALES AND INCOME BY BUSINESS AREA
(DOLLARS IN THOUSANDS)

	Sales				*Income*			
	1971		*1970*		*1971*		*1970*	
	$	%	$	%	$	%	$	%
Foods	827,234	40	649,170	35	58,976	42	47,335	37
Dairy and Services	590,008	29	586,252	32	31,079	22	32,539	25
Chemical	400,543	19	386,171	21	30,923	22	30,942	24
International	251,882	12	210,609	12	20,483	14	18,666	14
Total	2,069,667	100	1,832,202	100	141,461	100	129,482	100
Other income and expenses not allocable to operations and taxes					80,928		75,801	
Net Income					60,533		53,681	

Exhibit 22-3

MINORITY AFFAIRS AUDIT

DIVISION: DATE:
LOCATION:

EMPLOYMENT & TRAINING

Employment

1. What is the racial composition of your geographic area?
   ________% White ________% Black ________% Other
2. What is the total number of employees in your work force? __________
   (A) Of this number how many are minority employees? ____ or ____ %
   (B) How many minority employees are in supervisory positions?____ or____ %
   (C) How many minority employees are in "middle" management positions?
   ________ or ________ % of work force
   (D) How many minority employees are in "top" management positions?
   _____or_____ % of work force.

   COMMENTS ____

   ____

   ____

3. How many departments (of what total) are composed of less than 10% minority employees?_____ of _____

Training

1. What is the total number of trainees in the work force?__________
   (A) How many minority trainees? _________
2. How many employees are in in-house training programs?__________
   (A) How many are minority employees? _________
3. How many employees in tuition-refund plans? _________
   (A) How many are minority employees? __________

   COMMENTS____

   ____

   ____

Recruiting

1. How many employees were recruited *this year* right out of college?_________
   (A) How many were minority employees?_________
2. How many employees were recruited from vocational education schools?________
   (A) How many were minority employees? _________

3. How many employees were recruited from high school graduating classes? ________
   (A) How many were minority employees? ________________________________

   COMMENTS____

   ____

   ____

Testing

1. List below any paper and pencil tests you give and indicate who takes them and whether they are used in hiring, promotional or transfer decisions, e.g., SRA General Clerical–Clerk Typists–New Hires.

   ____

   ____

   ____

2. (If applicable) list any of the above tests which have been validated.

   ____

   ____

Affirmative Action Plan

Have you prepared and submitted your location's affirmative action plan? Yes______ No _______ If not, by what date will it be submitted? _____________

Exhibit 22-4

MINORITY AFFAIRS AUDIT SUMMARY REPORT

234 of *400* plants and distribution centers responded
(Chemical–48)
(D&S Northern–74)
(D&S Southern–40)
(Foods–72)

Employment

93 facilities have a per cent of minority employment equal to or better than the per cent of minority population within their hiring area.

114 facilities are below the per cent on minorities in their geographic area.

The chart, on page 342, presents a cross section view by division and geographic location.

Minorities in Management

263 minority employees hold supervisory or management positions at *84* installations out of the *234* facilities reporting.

Chemical– *25* installations have *69* supervisors
8 installations have *9* mid-managers
D&S– *29* installations have *78* supervisors
8 installations have *22* mid-managers
2 installations have *3* top managers
Foods– *29* installations have *69* supervisors
8 installations have *11* mid-managers
3 installations have *4* top managers

Training Programs

56 of the *234* facilities reporting have some form of training programs. Most are entry level on-job training. *38* of *56* have minority employees in training.

School Recruitment Programs

45 plants and/or distribution centers have established some form of linkage with local high schools, vocational schools and/or colleges and universities for recruitment purposes. *13* of the *45* installations have used these institutions as a resource in recruiting minority workers.

Testing

Audit results indicate that only *41* installations of *234* reporting use any form of testing program. The *41* use specific skills tests, i.e., typing, shorthand, basic math, driving tests related to jobs applied for. Only *12* use general skills tests and *17* use psychological tests.

Affirmative Action Programs

33 of the plants and/or distribution centers which employ more than 50 had not, at the time of the audit, submitted affirmative action plans.

(Chemical–13 installations)
(D&S–3 installations)
(Foods–17 installations)

Minority Economic Development

55 of the *234* installations reporting expend approximately $260,000 per year with minority companies.

(Chemical–22 installations–$99,000 per yr.)
(D&S–28 installations–$116,000 per yr.)
(Foods–5 installations–$45,000 per yr.)

Below is an overview of types of goods and services provided:

Refuse Removal–11 locations
Janitorial Services–19 locations
Equipment Repair–8 locations
Window Washing–3 locations
Lawn Care–3 locations
Auto Repair–3 locations
Painting–3 locations

EXHIBIT 22-4 (continued)

% MINORITY EMPLOYEES RELATED TO MINORITY POPULATION IN HIRING AREA

Division	*Total # Facilities*	*Above % Below %*	*South*	*Southwest*	*Midwest*	*Northwest*	*Northeast*
Chemical	48	36/12	6/1	3/0	9/4	5/0	13/7
Dairy & Services	114	23/91	3/21	9/7	7/37	0/0	4/26
Foods	72	34/38	6/13	1/3	17/8	5/7	5/7
Total	234	93/141	15/35	13/10	33/49	10/7	22/40

General Repair–2 locations
Physician Services–2 locations
Produce Contracts–2 locations
Water Treatment–1 location
Travel Agency–1 location

Banking

2 accounts totalling *$30,000* are maintained by Southern Dairy & Services.

At the corporate level approximately *$650,000* is maintained in accounts at minority banks in New York, Chicago, and Puerto Rico.

Community Programs

37 of the *234* locations reporting have some involvement in programs related to the minority community.

(Chemical–10 locations)
(D&S–19 locations)
(Foods–8 locations)

These programs include:

NAB or other employment programs–13 locations
Social programs, Settlement Houses, etc.–13 locations
Financial support–6 locations
Product Donation–5 locations
Volunteers and Board members–7 locations

Exhibit 22-5

BORDEN, INC.
50 West Broad Street, Columbus, Ohio 43215
C. E. Spitzer

September 21, 1972

John B. Nimons
Vice President
Corporate Purchasing

TO: ALL DIVISIONAL PRESIDENTS
ALL DIVISIONAL GROUP VICE PRESIDENTS
ALL DIVISIONAL PROFIT CENTER PRESIDENTS
ALL DIVISIONAL PROFIT CENTER PURCHASING AGENTS

Mr. A. R. Marusi, as of September 13, has re-emphasized Borden's sincere dedication and intent to implement the policy of purchasing from minority owned and operated companies.

It is not always enough for top management to simply adopt a policy line. The line and staff organization must realize that management means what it says, and now demands proof that this objective is being attacked.

The same principles must be applied that are utilized in effective programs in Equal Employment Opportunity. A successful Minority Purchasing Program cannot be treated as extra-curricular activity. It must become a function of normal purchasing procedures, just as Equal Employment is an integral part of normal personnel policy and procedures.

The fact that this is not an empty policy constructed only of words becomes very clear. Accountability is being injected, not only as a measurement but as a stimulus to seek and use such suppliers. The record will show the degree of intent, as well as performance.

The majority of minority suppliers are local and are concentrated in businesses that provide services such as janitorial, trash removal, roofing, painting and construction contractors, key punch and data processing, automotive repair and cleaning, office machine services and multiple small products at the wholesaler and jobber level. Because these services and products quite often are not purchased by the purchasing agent, it is imperative that your local minority purchasing policy be communicated to all members of the operating team.

The search cannot be limited to suppliers you deem qualified. The word, instead, is QUALIFIABLE. Firms must be solicited and included that would not ordinarily meet all standards but that can, with encouragement and assistance, become qualified as suppliers of goods and services to Borden, Inc.

The form attached is another one of the many that we must all file. After this is acknowledged, however, it in no way relieves anyone from the requirement to set it up so that it will be filed regularly on a quarterly basis. We will undertake to file a summary report with the OTP.

This Minority Purchasing Program has many built-in difficulties. In the beginning, to identify and encourage the minority business man in the local community will require extraordinary effort. It needs to be reiterated, however, that this effort must be put forth!

The report for the July-September quarter should reach this office by November 1, 1972.

J. B. Nimons

INFORMATIVE

Office of the President

Exhibit 22-6

QUARTERLY REPORT OF GOODS & SERVICES
PURCHASED FROM MINORITY OWNED AND OPERATED BUSINESS

M8–CP–1
10/1/72

DIVISION ____________________   DATE OF REPORT ____________________

PROFIT CENTER ____________________   SIGNATURE ____________________

LOCATION ____________________

Vendor Name	Type of Business	1971 Total	1972 to Date	1972 Outlook	1973 Forecast	Rating

Case Twenty-Three

Omar Industries, Inc.

Omar Industries was a diversified manufacturing company with sales in 1973 of about $1.0 billion. It was composed of eight operating divisions, half producing chemicals and packaging products for industry and the other half consumer durables. In all, the company had over 40 manufacturing locations in the United States and several more overseas under the direction of the International Division. Assisted by one acquisition, corporate sales had grown at a rate of about 10% over the previous decade. Although net profit to sales had slipped from 5.3% to 4.0% during this period, return on equity had held constant at roughly 10% as the company increased its debt to equity ratio from .30 to .67. During 1974 renewed emphasis was placed on improving margins and increasing earnings per share. Moreover, in view of the increased debt levels, the president had made it clear to his division managers that the corporation was going to "live within its means" by not spending more on capital investment than its cash flow after dividends (about $62 million in 1973) justified.

ENVIRONMENTAL CONTROL DEPARTMENT

In 1970, the Environmental Control Department (ECD) was formed to consolidate a number of corporate staff activities related to Omar's concern with the environment. The company was recognized as a leader in the control of air and water pollution in its manufacturing operations, at times pioneering in the adoption of new control technologies. During his years as President, the current Chairman of the Board had stressed the importance of providing "the best pollution control equipment to meet or exceed community criteria."

ECD performed a variety of functions including (a) assisting the operating divisions in achieving compliance with government regulations, (b) keeping the corporation current on changes in regulation or control technology, (c) reviewing capital requests from an environmental viewpoint, and (d) encouraging the divisions to incorporate environmental concerns and potential expenditures in their planning. The department did not, however, have the authority to force action on the operating divisions, though in some respects it shared the responsibility for the implementation of the corporate policy on pollution.

ECD was directed by John Carpenter, who reported to Fred Phillips, an Administrative Vice President for Special Services, a position that included responsibility for several corporate-level technical service groups and various external programs related to environmental affairs. ECD was divided into sections responsible for air, water, testing, and environmental hygiene. This latter section was acquired from the corporate personnel group when ECD was formed on the premise that much of the effort required in the occupational health and safety area was related to engineering rather than personnel.

OCCUPATIONAL HEALTH AND SAFETY

In the summer of 1974, Phillips and Carpenter were becoming increasingly concerned about a growing public interest in the work environment in general and the requirements posed by the Occupational Health and Safety Act (OSHA) in particular. They were especially worried about the 90 dbl. standard for noise included in the Act as the maximum allowable for sustained exposure. Carpenter commented:

> OSHA inspectors have been hammering some of our divisions for noise. We know there are some places where the levels get as high as 130 dbls. – that's way above the new national standard of 90 dbls. I've been going to the technical directors in the divisions to try to get them to write down their existing situation. They're annoyed with me at the moment. They say they don't have the time or the money to spend on worrying about noise at the moment. My argument is that if they get it written down, they can at least, one, ask for money to work on the problem and, two, show OSHA that they're acting in good faith.
>
> The divisions are different. The Chemical Division is doing an excellent job. The Packaging Division is giving us no response. We had a meeting with them a little while ago to discuss it and they took the position, "We hear you but until we have a specific problem, in other words a citation, we're not going to do anything. There are other pollution problems right now that are of more importance to us."

In the first week of July, Carpenter called Fred Bellows, Manager of Plant Construction and Engineering in the Automotive Parts Division, to arrange a meeting to assess the division's status in the areas covered by the Occupational Health and Safety Act—chiefly noise abatement. While he had been working with several of the other divisions on formulating action programs to bring their operations into compliance with the new regulations, Carpenter had had little contact with this division on this particular issue.

The Automotive Parts Division was acquired by Omar in the late 1960's. Its sales had been more or less constant at $90 million since that time and as a result had not been keeping pace with the corporation's overall growth. Profit margins, always tight, had been under increasing pressure in recent years as the division worked to develop new products in a highly competitive field. It operated four general line and two specialty plants in addition to several technical centers.

On July 13, Carpenter, Bellows and Walter Gardner, an engineer who worked for the Director of Environmental Hygiene, met in Carpenter's office. The following discussion ensued:

Carpenter: I wrote to all of the technical directors in the divisions recently outlining goals and objectives for engineering noise out of our operations. We see OSHA inspectors telling us to engineer the noise levels down to the point that employees don't have to wear ear plugs within maybe a two-year time frame. We also have the feeling that if we have programs prior to the time they demand them, they will be willing to accept a more reasonable compliance schedule.

Bellows: We have already had one citation on noise.

Carpenter: (to Gardner) Did you know that?

Gardner: No.

Carpenter: Was the citation given by the state or OSHA?

Bellows: OSHA. They gave us a citation and were going to give us until July 1, 1972 to correct it. That was ridiculous–only four weeks away. I talked with the enforcement officer and told him so. I told him we were spending 5,000 hours of engineering time working on the problem. That's stretching the truth a bit, though we can justify it if they ask us by stretching the description of what our engineers are doing. But we do have mandatory ear protection rules in areas of 100 decibels and down to 85 decibels it's encouraged but optional. On this basis, the inspectors closed the file. On the basis of our efforts–a continuing long-range program–they said O.K. I gave them no numbers, no details, and no schedules, but if they have another complaint, they said, "We'll open it up again."

Carpenter: Let's say they did.

Bellows: We would use the same argument–a long-run argument.

Carpenter: Do you have a schedule with definite programs and goals?

Bellows: No, it's a long-term project but one that falls short of redesigning the machines. We have 250 stamping machines and there just isn't enough money to do it. One of these machines, even running by itself, generates 90 decibels. I don't know how we can do it.

Carpenter: That's what the Chemical Division people told us about the forming machines, but now they have redesigned them so that noise levels have dropped from 114 decibels to 90. You need a schedule and some objectives.

Bellows: But as soon as you have a schedule, you need a budget and people assigned to it.

Carpenter: That's just what I am trying to get you to do.

Bellows: The noise problem is really a problem, no denying it.

Carpenter: Then why don't you want to take out the noise?

Bellows: The noise on a machine is important. That's the way the operator tells if something is wrong. That's the reason I'm not happy with the ear protection devices. The operator with ear plugs in can't listen to the equipment as well.

Gardner: I'd like to see ear protection devices eliminated, too, but you can only do that by eliminating the noise.

Bellows: We've got noise control on all new equipment.

Carpenter: You've put it on the purchase order?

Bellows: Yes.

Carpenter: That's great.

Bellows: No, it's not great. We often need special machines and with these new requirements, some suppliers just won't bid on them.

Carpenter: Not even for money?

Bellows: We didn't say we would pay a million dollars. They weren't sure they could come up with a new technology for what we pay. Somewhere along the line, John, it's got to be economical. You can't put the machine in a room by itself.

Carpenter: That's a point though. Have you thought about shielding?

Bellows: Have you ever run a machine? At some point it's going to be uneconomical to do this. We have got a problem here that won't be solved in your lifetime.

Carpenter: The Chemical Division is going to do it on all their forming machines.

Bellows: What's it going to cost them and how long will it take?

Carpenter: $8 million. They have got a program for doing it that may take six or seven years, but it looks like OSHA may buy that. However, we had another situation at the Wilton plant. The OSHA inspector didn't like what we are doing. She told us to put together a program for meeting the national standards, but said that an eight to ten year time frame would be unacceptable.

Bellows: That's unrealistic.

Carpenter: But at least they are going to have a program which can be used as a basis for moving ahead toward controlling the problem.

Bellows: It's unrealistic for us. We can't replace all those machines. Maybe we'll change the product. We are moving from some lines to others which aren't as noisy on the machinery. But there are no stamping machines like ours in the United States which can meet the OSHA standards. You aren't going to get that to change.

Carpenter: I can't buy the comment that there never will be a machine that can't do it.

Bellows: Sure, you can have what they call administrative controls—putting the machines off by themselves or having them run automatically by a guy at the end of the plant—but we are a low-profit operation. You're going to have to accept some of these unpleasantries in our case to stay in business.

Gardner: Who says this will cost too much?

Bellows: We [Engineering] never say that. Division management does.

Carpenter: Somewhere along the line this decision gets made. Maybe by the division manager.

Bellows: It's the division manager, all right.

Carpenter: The division manager has got to weigh these things and put them all together.

Gardner: Has he been given a program?

Bellows: No, he only knows the problem in general terms.

Carpenter: In fact, you have a new division manager.

Bellows: We haven't talked with the new one about it yet. Look, we know that noise reduction means machine redesign. I could go to him and tell him that. But I don't know the cost. We have never built machines with a design other than the one we have now, so we would need a study project—maybe $200,000 with a two-year time table. Then a replacement project at $100,000 a machine. That's a lot of money. I don't have to present him with that. I know what he'll say—no. Maybe if OSHA says shut the plant down, that will be something else. But for a business grossing $90 million, it's ridiculous to invest $25 million on a replacement basis.

Gardner: I have just been here for a short time, and I don't know much about costs or about the operation. But I have been in government and I know OSHA is tough.

Bellows: They have been good to us so far.

Carpenter: We can't say what your program ought to be . . .

Bellows: John, I don't object to writing a program. It's necessarily going to be a little nebulous and long term. The amount of money involved is going to be nebulous too. We can say we know it's about $25 million in the long run.

Carpenter: Unless you change the product . . .

Bellows: But as far as what happend then . . .

We could put an engineer on design . . . I don't mean to say we aren't trying to control the noise. Maybe we ought to just bumble along as we are. We don't have the capability to redesign.

Carpenter: You have no incentive to do it now. In fact, you have an incentive to do nothing.

Bellows: OSHA told me that Northern Can has the same problem. OSHA made them make a schedule for compliance and so forth. We will probably have to do this next time. But the inspector said, "If no complaint, then you have seen the last of us for four years."

Gardner: But he said that because OSHA has no inspectors. They will have them very soon, however.

Bellows: Actually, we have had another complaint at Middleton by the state control people. I have been away and I don't know any more about it than that. In a way, I am more worried about that one. But we will argue on the basis of our activities as we have with OSHA already.

Carpenter: It sounds like you're just reacting. What you need is a program. Even your current program might do if it were just written down.

Bellows: Actually we have safety committees at each plant now. They're usually chaired by the plant manager. It's new—just started a month ago. I've seen some preliminary reports. They are pretty grim. If OSHA saw them, they would be unhappy.

(For several minutes the three men discussed the makeup of the safety committees. Because of union considerations, all were salaried personnel. They then discussed the sources of noise, department by department.)

Bellows: Everything you say is possible, but it costs money and we aren't prepared to spend much.

Gardner: Unfortunately, OSHA doesn't think much about costs. I have been there and I know how they feel.

Carpenter: On the other hand, the OSHA people have got to see that $25 million is a lot of money for that operation.

Bellows: I am in favor of much of this ecology kick, but I also like TVs and automobiles and so forth. Someone has got to make a decision on where money is to be spent. I really don't think OSHA will be too tough if they're dealing with people who are making an honest attempt to make the plants clean and safe within their ability to do it.

Gardner: I don't think this attitude will continue. The magic number for OSHA is now 90 decibels and there is some talk in Washington about reducing it to 85.[1] OSHA will become tougher. They will come into the plant and test for specific noise levels for instance, and not pay any attention to how clean the place is if that's their mission.

Carpenter: We would really like to know what your general hearing conservation program is.

Bellows: I will send you a copy of our procedures for employee hearing tests. It depends on the size of the plants. In general, the large ones do the testing

---

[1] Decibel levels are calculated on a logarithmic scale; a reduction in the maximum allowed for sustained exposure from 90 to 85 would have a substantially greater impact on the noise level than the percentage reduction in decibels would indicate.

themselves and the smaller ones send employees to local doctors. All employees are tested when they are hired and periodically thereafter.

Carpenter: O.K. That's part of it. Where from there?

Bellows: We issue ear plugs, we test employees again after a period of time. We are looking for deteriorating conditions. It is a very disquieting thing to me. At the Durby plant, I can look at the tests and tell how long the employee has worked there by how much his hearing has deteriorated.

Carpenter: Do the employees have to wear them?

Bellows: Yes.

Carpenter: How often can they leave them at home before they are fired?

Bellows: The warning system varies but in most cases it specifies "repetitive violations."

Carpenter: Tell you what the Chemical Division does. The first time it's a warning, the second time the employee is docked one day, the third time it's three days and after that he is out.

Bellows: My plant managers would have problems with something like that. You think I'm tough to work with, you ought to talk with some of them.

Carpenter: You should see what we have to deal with in other divisions.

Bellows: I really don't think the next five years will be too bad. In the long run I agree with you, but those stamping machines may not be around that long. I don't see spending money on them. The problem may just go away.

Carpenter: You can always change your plan or even put a probability of a change in the plans when you write them, but at least have the goal–85 decibels–and some goals for getting there. Put what it would cost to redesign the machine, but also take a look at alternatives. I don't have the answers, but that sort of program should be saleable to your mangement and by itself it might be enough. . . . In addition to what you're doing with your plant committees, which would also be included, this program should be in the hands of the plant manager so when OSHA people come, he can tell them, "Here's what we are doing."

Bellows: These inspectors are like other inspectors. It depends a lot on how they are handled. If you keep them waiting in a waiting room for two hours, then they won't take kindly to you. But we have got some pretty good people as plant managers. I really don't think we will have a problem. I see where we could have a tough time if we got a series of complaints and we don't show progress in between. . . . Tell you what I can do. I can sit down and dream up something which I can take to management as long as I don't spend anything on it.

Carpenter: That would be very helpful. Who do you work for?

Bellows: Nelson. He is manager of engineering service, I think, though I am not sure of his title. He reports to the division manager.

Carpenter: Well, we have a lot better feel for what's going on in the Automotive Division. People ask me how things are going in various divisions and when I come to yours, I have never had very much to say.

(After five minutes of informal discussion the meeting ended with the following comment by Bellows, speaking softly and looking at the floor.)

Bellows: Do you think I can last for five more years? I will be 60 in October.

After Bellows and Gardner left, Carpenter turned to the afternoon mail. In the pile was a capital request form from the Automotive Division for a $1.2 million stamping line. Carpenter indicated that he wished he had known about this project before the meeting with Bellows. A quick review of the document revealed that the new line was to be used for an important product and involved a change in technology from the existing machinery in the division. No explicit attention had been given to possible noise problems, and it would, as a result, have provided a useful vehicle for discussing the issue in concrete terms. This being a large investment for the division, Carpenter wondered why Bellows had not mentioned it.

The next morning Carpenter called in Ted Hawkins, Director of Environmental Hygiene, and gave him the capital request with the following comment:

> Ted, get on this one fast. Find out the noise levels and what, if anything they're going to do about it. If we wait until the thing is built, they'll say, "The line is already in. We can't afford to do anything about it now."

Later that day, Carpenter discussed the OSHA situation with Phillips in the context of a general review of the department's activities.

Phillips: We know what the major engineering questions are with OSHA. There is a stamping noise, radiant heat, vapors, and noise in areas other than stamping.

Carpenter: We got a capital request from the Automotive Division yesterday that gets into this. It's for $1.2 million–a new stamping line.

Phillips: I had heard about that. How many lines are there?

Carpenter: I don't have the details exactly. I'm not sure whether it's new or a rebuild. Bellows didn't mention it when we talked yesterday.

Phillips: He may not have known about it. Not very many people do–maybe only four people at corporate. It would have to be a new line.

Carpenter: It's a good example. How do we tackle that one?

Phillips: O.K. You've got to give this to someone and get it straightened out now.

Carpenter: Another thing. Hawkins has been talking about going into a plant in the Chemical Division with some mufflers and physically shutting off all compressed air sources that are not absolutely necessary–actually taking the feeder lines out so the operator can't turn the air back on when he leaves. If it is really necessary, he'll put a muffler on it. He says he can cut the noise by 20% or more.

Phillips: He's said that to me, too. I don't believe it–but let's give him a try.

Carpenter: That would worry me. . . .

Phillips: No, let's do it someplace where we know the plant manager–like Richards.[2] He'll let us know if Hawkins gets in trouble so we can yank him before it gets out of hand. Let's call Richards while we're both here. [On phone] Say Pete, we have a young man–Ted Hawkins–here on our staff who's been talking about cutting noise out of plants by eliminating or muffling compressed air sources. If we send him up to you for a while, would you be willing to have him around to see what he can do.

[Richards responds in the affirmative.]

Phillips: [continuing] His position demonstrates that he is a bit naive, but it also reflects that he's interested in doing something. This is a good time to say, "put up or shut up." He may have something and, if so, we should take advantage of it. If it's O.K. with you, I'll let him get together with Williams [Manufacturing Manager at the Akron plant] and John [Carpenter] and work out a program. Then if he gets in trouble, send him home.

About three weeks later, Hawkins, accompanied by a man from the engineering staff, spent three days at Akron. He then returned and wrote a report to the plant manager, including recommendations for reducing noise. Carpenter was upset, however, when he learned that during his visit Hawkins had taken no direct action, such as disconnecting the compressed air sources, to reduce noise levels.

---

[2] Richards was Phillips' replacement as Plant Manager in the Chemical Division in Akron when the latter became Vice President of Operations Services.

Exhibit 23-1

PARTIAL ORGANIZATION CHART

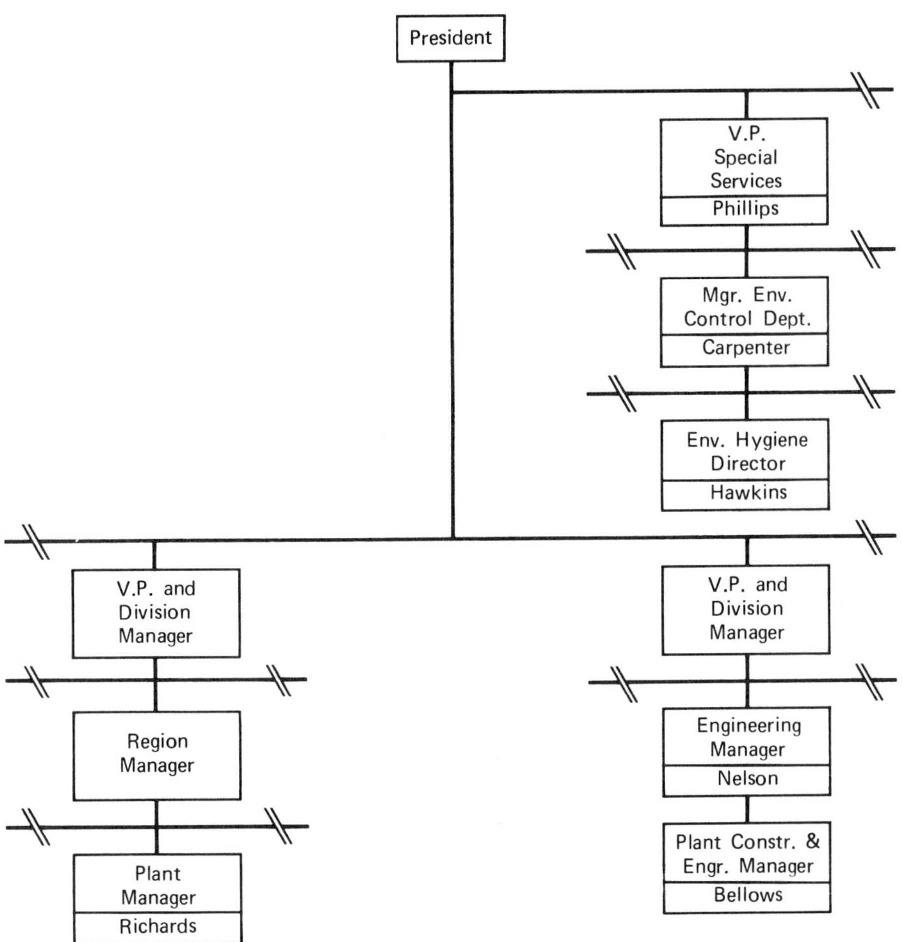

Case Twenty-Four

Affirmative Action at Aldrich

On February 5, 1973, John Cooke, manager of the Evanston Radar Division of the Aldrich Electronics Corporation, was disturbed by his meeting with Frank Stearns, field director of *Progress Now*, a Chicago-based Black Power group. Stearns had demanded that Cooke promote immediately the 23 black women on the Evanston transistor line to the next pay level. Each of the women had more than six years' seniority. Stearns threatened to file suit on behalf of the women with the Equal Employment Opportunity Commission.

Cooke realized that his frame of mind had been fairly negative even before the meeting. That morning he had received a memo from corporate headquarters detailing new procedures for hiring and promoting women throughout the Aldrich organization. The memo also mentioned that a special corporate task force would study all job classification grades and pay scales in order to determine whether women and minorities were being discriminated against, either overtly or covertly.

Cooke liked to think he had come up the hard way. He had made his name at Aldrich initially as chief management-labor negotiator for the Chicago area. He prided himself on being a tough but fair team player, empathetic to labor's legitimate demands. The International Electrical Workers (IEW), who represented 90% of Aldrich's blue collar workers, had a reputation as a hard bargainer; locals were vigilant, insisting upon the letter of the contract. Cooke respected the union's approach; he liked to play by the rules of the game.

After ten years as manager of the Evanston plant, Cooke feared that his job would be very different in coming years, that the old measurement criteria for success in the corporation would probably change. He was not sure, however, what to do.

COMPANY BACKGROUND

Aldrich Corporation, based in and around Chicago, was principally an electronic equipment manufacturer with some 50% of its business in contracts with the Defense

Department. It manufactured components for sophisticated defense systems as well as for civilian uses. The corporation was divided into four divisions: the Radar Division at Evanston, employing 5000; the Equipment Division, specializing in self-contained components; the Guidance Systems Division, making guidance instruments for both defense and civilian aircraft; and the Aerospace Division, designing systems for NASA. Aldrich had total sales of $950 million in fiscal 1971.

The company had achieved its greatest growth immediately after World War II, locating its main midwest plants in six suburban communities that surrounded Chicago. At the time, management felt that this was advantageous because the semi-skilled and skilled labor needed for successful business operations was readily available in these communities. All were within an hour's drive of corporate headquarters in downtown Chicago (Exhibit 24-1 provides basic demographic data for each community as well as Aldrich's employment figures).

THE EVANSTON PLANT

The Evanston plant consisted of three groups: design research, engineering, and manufacturing. Historically, a product was conceived in design research, modified for production in engineering, and then manufactured in the main building of the plant. Cooke had been with the Aldrich Corporation for 34 years, the last 22 having been at Evanston. He had risen to his present position because he was known as a "production man" who had been able to meet production deadlines at least cost. Although Aldrich prided itself on its many technological achievements over the years, often industry giants such as Raytheon or General Dynamics would introduce innovations which required Aldrich to rush a new design into production. Cooke had always done well when the pressure was on.

CONTRACT COMPLIANCE REVIEW AT THE EVANSTON PLANT. Cooke's troubles in the equal employment opportunity area began in November 1971, when one day, with little notice, the Defense Department contract compliance people swarmed over his facility, checking through the details of his Affirmative Action Plan. No other Aldrich plant either before or after had undergone such scrutiny. At the time, in fact, he had felt discriminated against. He told Charles Hogen, Aldrich's Director of Equal Employment Programs, that as far as he could see, he had done everything the corporation had asked him to do in the personnel area. His plant managers had attended the sensitivity training sessions run by Hogen's department; he himself had gone to the senior management seminars where corporate affirmative action programs were discussed. His Affirmative Action Plan had been accepted by Hogen's department. He just could not understand all the fuss.

THE TRANSISTOR LINE PROTEST

The Stearns issue had begun early in June 1972, when three young black female employees in pay grade four had bypassed the normal union-management grievance procedures provided for in the contract to bring a complaint about unequal pay for men and women on their assembly line. They insisted on talking to Cooke personally. They said that only women were assigned to the transistor pre-assembly line and that their pay grades went only from 3 to 7, while men on the intermediate and final assembly lines, who were doing virtually the same kind of work, started at grade 5 and could go to grade 11 (Exhibit 24-2 shows the job breakdown on the transistor line). The women went on to state that the union, the IEW, did not seem to be interested in their problems. The union had said it would consider their problems when the contract was renegotiated in two years. The local president had said that the women had agreed to it when it was signed so they would have to live by it until the next bargaining session. He also noted that any kind of revision would, of course, have to be carefully considered so that it did not work to the disadvantage of other workers. The women said they were not willing to wait that long and wanted some quick action. Cooke had planned to smooth over the incident, relying on the support of the union. But when he happened to mention the incident to Hogen while they were discussing some other matter, Hogen had been very interested, had cut the conversation short, and the next day had brought two corporate lawyers and a job classification specialist to Cooke's office. They urged Cooke to make the women happy. Hogen said that if they took Aldrich to court, the problem could escalate. Much against his better judgment, Cooke called the women back and transferred them to a new all-female line in the wiring department at the next pay grade. It had taken a whole day of heated discussions with the union to explain the extraordinary action. The union reluctantly accepted the shift when Cooke told them about the danger of court and possible government action.

A month later, in early August, he received a memo signed by the 23 remaining black females on the transistor line all with six years' or more seniority, stating that they wished for pay increases without transfers. They were happy on the line, but felt they were doing virtually the same work as the males on the intermediate and final assembly lines who had higher pay classifications. Given the contract seniority system, the women could not transfer without losing all seniority. Cooke told Hogen:

> This is exactly what I feared when you asked me to make those other three girls happy. We had a fine situation here before. The transistor line has been a model of what black workers can do—and women too. Most of my people on that line have been there for ten years or more. We never had any trouble.

Hogen came down, and a series of meetings with the women and the union took place. Cooke thought he and the union had placated the women when Stearns entered the picture in November with the demands he was now voicing.

ALDRICH AND CONTRACT COMPLIANCE

Since Aldrich had such extensive dealings with the U.S. government, management was eager to maintain a corporate posture that would ensure the company's ability to bid successfully on government contracts. Contract compliance was a major component of this posture since a company that fulfills past contracts to the letter of the law has a better chance in the future. In recent years that part of contract compliance which had been of most concern to Aldrich was the Affirmative Action Program required under Order No. 4 (Revised) of the Office of Federal Contract Compliance (OFCC). Other areas of contract compliance, such as safety and security, were not so troublesome. Established procedures had long since been adopted in these areas. Affirmative Action, on the other hand, was a major new thrust of the government. No one knew just what the requirements were, how literally they should be taken, or how they would evolve.

ORDER NO. 4

The Office of Federal Contract Compliance (OFCC) of the U.S. Department of Labor determined contract compliance requirements for all contracting agencies and departments of the Federal Government (e.g., HEW, Defense Department, Atomic Energy Commission). Each agency was then responsible for enforcing the OFCC orders through its own separate contract compliance divisions.

In January of 1970 OFCC spelled out in Order No. 4 what the government contracting agencies required in order to judge the adequacy of contractors' written affirmative action programs. These requirements dealt mainly with the hiring and training of members of minority racial groups. They applied to each prime or subcontractor with 50 or more employees and a contract of $50,000 or more. The contractor had 120 days from the commencement of the contract to develop a written affirmative action compliance program for each of his establishments.

In December of 1971 OFCC published a revision of Order No. 4 requiring contractors to commit themselves to goals and actions to remedy *sex* as well as minority discriminations. Contractors had 120 days to revise existing programs to include the changes under the new Order No. 4.

Written affirmative action programs must contain the following:

1.—A detailed analysis of all major job classifications at the facility, with an explanation if minorities or women were currently being underutilized in any one or more job classifications.
2.—Goals and timetables for affirmative action commitments must be established to correct any identifiable deficiencies.
3.—Such goals and timetables with supporting data and analysis must be compiled and maintained as part of the written affirmative action programs.
4.—Contractors must direct special attention in their analyses and goal setting to specific categories of employees.
5.—These programs must contain among other things:
    a. Identification of problem areas (deficiencies) by organizational units and job classification;
    b. Establishment of goals and objectives by organizational units and job classification, including timetables for completion.
    c. Development and execution of action-oriented programs designed to eliminate problems and attain established goals and objectives.

If, for whatever reason, the contractor was not in compliance, there was a penalty process:

1.—If the concerned government agency chose to prosecute and not accept the company's explanation, a letter asking the company to "show cause" why their name should not be eliminated from the agency bidding list would be sent.
2.—A company had 30 days in which to make a reply.
3.—If the reply was again not judged satisfactory, the regional office could again reject it.
4.—The company would have 10 days to prepare for a hearing in Washington.
5.—At the hearing, if the company again was judged to be grossly negligent, they could be barred completely from all future government contracts.
6.—The company then had access to the courts to try to overrule the decision.

A multifacility corporation was required to have an affirmative action program for each facility; and a "show cause" letter to one plant automatically barred all other plants of the corporation from any government business.

Revised Order No. 4 was the latest step in a process that began in 1965 with President Johnson's Executive Order No. 11246, which called for all government contractors to develop affirmative action plans in "good faith" for the hiring and training of minorities. At that time there was no machinery set up to define what "affirmative action" meant or to make it effective. It quickly became apparent within the Labor Department that rules and regulations were needed to guide contractors as well as compliance officers in the fulfillment of the spirit of E.O. No. 11246. In May of 1968 the Labor Department issued, under Chapter 60-1 of Title 41 of the code of Federal Regulations, rules and regulations regarding procedures that contractors should follow in developing goals as well as a penalty schedule. The major difference between Chapter 60-1 and Order No. 4 (Chapter 60-2) was the fact that under Chapter 60-1 there was no provision that required companies to put in writing their affirmative action plans and goals. This was seen as a major weakness of 60-1 by OFCC and was the main reason for Order No. 4. The political evolutionary process that resulted in Revised Order No. 4 occurred primarily in the Department of Labor with pressure from minorities and women. It was not the result of legislation initiative.

ALDRICH'S RESPONSE TO ORDER NO. 4. In 1970 the responsibility for handling minority affairs and contract compliance at Aldrich was assigned to the Industrial Relations Department (IR). IR handled community relations and legislative lobbying in addition to general labor relations, while the Public Relations Department dealt with press and financial relations. (Aldrich had generally chosen the low-profile approach to public relations and recognized that few nonbusiness-oriented people could identify with what Aldrich was or did.)

Senior management was aware of the potential explosiveness of Order No. 4 in particular and the whole minority hiring situation in general. As a consequence, Hogen was hired in early 1970 to be Director of Equal Opportunity Programs for Aldrich. The new job was placed in IR. Hogen was hired at the personal suggestion of the President and

Chairman of the Board of Directors, Ronald Fleming, a fact that was generally known in the company.

HOGEN AND HIS TACTICS. Hogen had been Director of Human Relations for the Manufacturer's Association of Illinois, a progressive lobbying organization. Fleming had been closely involved with Hogen at the Association and had supported his efforts to educate businessmen that their own self-interest was served by staying ahead of social demands, particularly as concerned human resources.

Hogen came to Aldrich with definite views about the role of corporations as effective agents of social change. He felt that a corporation should try to stay out in front of guidelines and governmental requirements and that in the long run it was "cheaper to lead." He saw his new job at Aldrich as an opportunity to test whether he could be effective in a corporate situation. He was excited because he believed strongly that "Fleming had a deep ethical feeling about life and a commitment that things ought to be better." His immediate boss, M. A. Bergmeyer, the Senior Vice President in charge of Industrial Relations, seemed to hold similar views although his background was quite different. Bergmeyer had risen in the IR department because of his abilities as a labor negotiator. (He and Cooke had entered Aldrich at the same time and worked closely together in early contract negotiations.) He was primarily responsible for Aldrich's history of relatively good labor relations. While other corporations dealing with the IEW had often found it difficult to come to reasonable terms, Aldrich had a history of quick settlements that did not "give away the shop."

In January, 1970, after moving into the Aldrich executive office building in Chicago, Hogen quickly realized that to be effective in creating change in the area of equal opportunity, he would have to work through the established system. He had no staff and no specific line authority. His only influence resulted from his close relationship with Fleming and the general awareness of that fact in the company. He realized that this implicit access would only be effective in the organization as long as he was not publicly overruled. Thus he was very cautious in his initial approach to contract compliance. As he put it:

> Ron Fleming is as sincere about equal opportunity as any man in the U.S. But we have some very conservative divisions here. We have a lot of managers who are very good at production and do not really see the jeopardy. The line people are inclined to say, "If I can produce, you have got the lawyers to keep me out of trouble." No man in the company can get canned for not doing well in the employee relations area. I have Fleming's support, but I use it very judiciously.

Hogen knew Fleming was the type of manager who preferred traditional channels. During his 20 years as chief operating officer, Fleming had built a solid organizational structure with a defined chain of command. He prided himself on not having any "unnecessary frills" at Aldrich. He had placed his managerial stamp on the many charitable and civic organizations in which he involved himself. When something needed to be done by the business community for Chicago nonprofit organizations, Fleming was the one everyone invariably turned to first. Hogen went on to say:

> It was soon very obvious to me that there was little I could do at Aldrich as an individual, unless I could generate some support. I'm a specialist, a counselor, a salesman if you will. So it seemed to me that my first goal was to develop a local competence in this area (Contract Compliance). The best way to do that was through the Industrial Relations Office because it has to deal with Contract Compliance. This is a fixed responsibility for the IR people, and they were nervous about handling it. Instead of selling programs to them, I was supporting them in a function that they already had responsibility for, and I tried very hard to articulate whatever I wanted to have done in a way that took on the appearance of being of assistance to them. That was my general tactic.

ATTRACTING MANAGERIAL ATTENTION. Hogen felt that the first step toward changing Aldrich's attitudes and organization with regard to blacks and women was to focus increased attention by top management on the problem. Change would not come unless it were given a higher priority. Everyone was too busy with day-to-day business to make the necessary additional effort required to alter traditional practices. He decided that the most effective way to obtain increased management attention was to encourage the intensification of affirmative action review by the Defense Department.

Tim Dorman, Contract Compliance Chief for the Defense Department in the midwest area, respected Hogen's intentions and was only too glad to cooperate. Before Dorman came to the Defense Department Contract Compliance Division by way of Army contract compliance, he had been Cultural Attache in the U.S. embassy in India. Previously, he had been executive director of the Urban League in Chicago, where in the early fifties he had run a controversial radio show that dealt with racial matters. Dorman had received numerous personal threats during this period.

Dorman was responsible for all of the 4,700 companies in the midwest area which had contracts with the Defense Department. He preferred to work "nose to nose" with companies in his jurisdiction, seeking to persuade rather than coerce and regarded the "show cause" letter as a last resort. Dorman believed, as did Hogen, that one of the greatest values of the affirmative action programs was the complete self-evaluation process it forced a company to go through. Not only did the company have to identify its weaknesses and deficiencies, it also had to set goals and declare how it planned to achieve them. The company knew the review team would come back and say "why didn't you?" if the goals were not met.

Dorman felt that contract compliance was most effective in the period between 1966 and 1969 when substantial gains had been made in minority hiring at the blue collar level. Since 1969, however, blue collar hiring had remained static, with gains for minorities and women coming mostly at white collar levels. Both he and Hogen knew that during the last five years only six companies in the nation had actually received the "show cause" letter. No company had ever been disbarred from bidding lists or had a contract cancelled. As a member of Dorman's staff remarked:

> Most companies reach an agreement with us before this stage, and in actual fact, if we issued a "show cause" letter to every company not in compliance, the economy would stop in a month.

Hogen gave one example of a review team he had recently dealt with as illustrative of Dorman's style:

> This was an interesting team because it had one old-line reviewing officer who had been with the Defense Department for five or six years under this program but who had a background in labor relations. He was familiar with the whole process of reviewing industry under various legislative and administrative requirements. With him at this in-depth review were two so-called trainees who were new to the Defense Department and part of Tim Dorman's effort to step up the quality of the people he's getting there. One was a girl and one was a young black guy with counseling background. Both were extremely articulate, extremely on the ball, almost overly aggressive. I mean I think they got my dander up a few times by nit picking over what they called "missed opportunities for affirmative action." You know—that's a ball park you could fill any day because there's no limit to the missed opportunities that you have!
>
> But anyway, they lent a very real atmosphere to this thing. They brought it into interracial and female terms. They were defending a cause rather than just being government interviewers. It was a very effective team. We found that, in a way, the veteran review officer was in a position of defending the company quite a bit. He took my role in many cases. "Calm down, Aldrich has been doing this," etc. They worked well together. There was a stepped-up militancy on the part of the group, and I think it's going to continue.

Hogen wanted to demonstrate to senior management that there was a need for defined positions in Aldrich, i.e., organizational structure, to deal specifically with Affirmative Action's plans and minority affairs. He felt, though, that it was important to keep these activities separate in the organization since he was sure that minorities would achieve more gains at Aldrich initially if they had separate definable managers to handle their problems and needs.

With Dorman's cooperation, the process of institutionalization came more quickly than Hogen had expected. In November 1971, at Hogen's initiative, an in-depth contract compliance review took place at the Evanston facility. Neither Cooke nor other members of the corporate staff were aware of Hogen's tactics. The review and disclosures shocked Cooke. Immediately thereafter he told Hogen that he needed a full-time manager of Affirmative Action Programs and requested help in describing the job and finding someone to fill it.

News of the Evanston review passed quickly to other facilities in the Aldrich organization. Some plant managers asked Bergmeyer for advice. He said that each plant would have to examine its own requirements for additional IR staffing.

WOMEN IN ORDER NO. 4. When the Revised Order No. 4 came out on December 4, 1971, Hogen was happy because the revision helped prove his point about the need for specialized positions in the Aldrich organization to deal specifically with changes in affirmative action requirements. The revision demonstrated to senior management that the future could bring more sudden changes in government policy, and that it paid to have an institutionalized means of dealing with these changes.

Hogen said of the change at Aldrich:

> Again, the key to change was pressure from the government. This is the way we respond—to pressure. I've been kind of a mediator between the government and the problems and interests of the IR men at our facilities.

The revision of Order No. 4, as well as the Evanston situation, forced management to focus attention on their women employees.

MINORITY AFFAIRS COMMITMENT

In late 1971, following the affirmative action review at Evanston, Fleming decided that Aldrich should commit itself to a stepped-up minority affairs program. To implement this commitment, he ordered the creation of six new jobs in the company in addition to the Corporate Manager of Minority Manpower Development (reporting to Hogen) which had previously been created in August. The six new positions were as follows: four division managers of minority affairs, one for each Aldrich division, one Special Training Coordinator to report to the Corporate Director of Equal Opportunity Programs (Hogen); and a manager of Minority Vendor Programs[1] (Exhibit 24-3 shows a partial Aldrich organization chart).

Hogen had always contended that the implementation of affirmative action plans should remain distinct and separate from minority affairs functions.

> The maintenance of our Affirmative Action Program entails a great deal of statistical and mechanical work and is increasingly concerned with problems of women employees. I believe that Fleming's action was a commitment to a full-time effort to create an employment climate that would attract and keep larger numbers of minority employees at all levels in the company.

Hogen found that he had difficulty maintaining the distinction between a stepped-up commitment to affirmative action and a stepped-up commitment to minority

[1] Vendor, in this instance, is defined as any minority enterprise from which Aldrich might purchase items. Aldrich's procurement program approached one-half billion dollars and ranged from hardware items for specific products to furniture, window cleaning, leasing, and trucking services. The manager of Minority Vendor Programs had specific authority to seek out and develop more business with minority enterprises in all procurement areas. He reported to the Purchasing Department and was not in Hogen's IR area.

affairs. By August 1972, contrary to Hogen's hopes, three division managers of minority affairs, at the direction of division IR managers, had been told they were responsible for affirmative action programs. While this reflected budgetary pressures at the division level, it appeared that the company had not implemented the commitment by Fleming.

Cooke had been one of the first managers to combine the two positions. Hogen tried to persuade him that it was necessary to keep the jobs separate, since women would represent an increasing problem in the implementation of Aldrich's Affirmative Action Programs. Women comprised 80% of Aldrich clerical workers and 13% of the blue collar workers. Cooke responded, "That is all well and good, but until I am given an increased budget for two extra positions, I will combine them. Besides, I don't feel that blacks should be treated separately. They are treated fairly, and if they don't like the system, they can go somewhere else for work."

WOMEN AND THE COURTS

Aldrich was especially mindful of recent back-pay settlements. Employees at Wheaton Glass Company had recently won a court decision costing $900,000 when they proved that there were dual lines of progression in the organization for men and women in violation of Title VII of the 1964 Civil Rights Act. Executives at Aldrich also knew that courts were no longer ruling that job content had to be "absolutely" the same under the Equal Payment Act in order to prove discrimination in pay but only "substantially" the same. Accordingly, Fleming authorized formation at Aldrich of an eight-person, one-year task force commissioned to look at job descriptions throughout the organization that might tend to discriminate against either minorities or women. Hogen was on the committee that would oversee the task force's work and was of the opinion that substantial revisions in Aldrich's personnel and hiring practices would be needed if Aldrich was to be adequately protected from the possibility of adverse court action. The memo detailing the goals of the task force had arrived on all division managers' desks on February 5, 1973.

POWER NOW AND ITS DEMANDS

Because of its location, the Evanston plant had been experiencing a hard time recruiting qualified blacks to meet its affirmative action goals. As a result, the minorities in the labor force at Evanston (3%) were primarily in low-paying clerical or assembly line jobs.

Power Now, a new Chicago-based Black Power group, had come into existence in order to help publicize and otherwise help minorities in large corporations who felt the system discriminated against them. In articles in the Chicago newspapers Frank Stearns was quoted as saying:

> We see many corporations in and around Chicago practicing overt and covert racism. There is supposed to be machinery in the form of Affirmative Action Programs that is supposed to be helping black people throughout America, but it is a sham. Anyone remotely familiar with Affirmative Action knows that it is another case of big business getting into bed with government to talk a good game but to go on with "business as usual."

Power Now had publicized a number of cases of alleged racism in the Chicago area, but as far as Cooke could tell, no substantive actions either in the courts or through any other agency had resulted.

Stearns had sent Cooke a letter of November 6, 1972, stating that he knew exactly how many blacks were in what positions at Evanston and that their affirmative action plans were a sham to hide Aldrich's racist hiring and promotion practices. He then gave surprisingly accurate figures to prove he knew what he was talking about. He went on to note that a number of black women at Evanston had come to his organization complaining that they were denied promotion and access to high pay scales. Cooke, alarmed at the publicity potential, started to pay more attention to the equal employment program bulletins that Hogen had been sending out. An article in *Business Week* especially caught his eye (see Exhibit 24-4.) He was also aware of Labor Secretary Hodgson's recent decision concerning Bethlehem Steel's Sparrows Point plant where blacks had become concentrated in certain departments with short pay grade ladders and held there by departmental seniority rules. (See Exhibit 24-5.) It seemed to him that Evanston might indeed have the same kind of situation, but he did not know how to proceed.

The meeting with Stearns on February 5 only upset Cooke more. He felt that if there was a problem, it was not his responsibility. Departmental seniority had been a cornerstone of labor contracts for as long as he could remember. He thought he might as well let this task force that Hogen was behind take care of the situation.

Exhibit 24-1

AFFIRMATIVE ACTION AT ALDRICH

	Total Pop. 1970	*% Minority in the Community*	*Aldrich Plant Size*
Oak Park	62,000	4.2	3,800 (Equipment Division)
Evanston	80,000	3.0	5,000 (Radar Division)
Maywood	29,000	4.8	1,600 (Equipment Division)
Evergreen Park	25,000	3.2	2,400 (Guidance System Division)
Skokie	68,000	5.0	3,500 (Guidance System Division)
Dolton	25,000	4.1	2,100 (Guidance System Division)

The Aerospace Division, the only one not located near Chicago, was in Los Angeles, California with one plant of 4,800.

Exhibit 24-2

TRANSISTOR LINE

PRE-ASSEMBLY

Pay Grade	*Seniority Requirements for Grade*	*Males*	*Females*
3 – $2.70	0 – 1 yrs.	–	2
4 – 2.80	1 – 2	–	1
5 – 2.90	2 – 4	–	2
6 – 3.00	4 – 6	–	8
7 – 3.10	6 –	–	23

INTERMEDIATE ASSEMBLY

Pay Grade	*Seniority Requirements for Grade*	*Males*	*Females*
5 – $2.90	0 – 1 yrs.	4	–
6 – 3.00	1 – 2	3	–
7 – 3.10	2 – 4	5	–
8 – 3.25	4 – 6	3	–
9 – 3.40	6 – 8	4	–
10 – 3.65	8 – 10	10	–
11 – 3.90	10 –	15	–

FINAL ASSEMBLY

Pay Grade	*Seniority Requirements for Grade*	*Males*	*Females*
5 – $2.90	0 – 1 yrs.	6	–
6 – 3.00	1 – 2	4	–
7 – 3.10	2 – 4	3	–
8 – 3.25	4 – 6	2	–
9 – 3.40	6 – 8	5	–
10 – 3.65	8 – 10	11	–
11 – 3.95	10 –	13	–

Exhibit 24-3

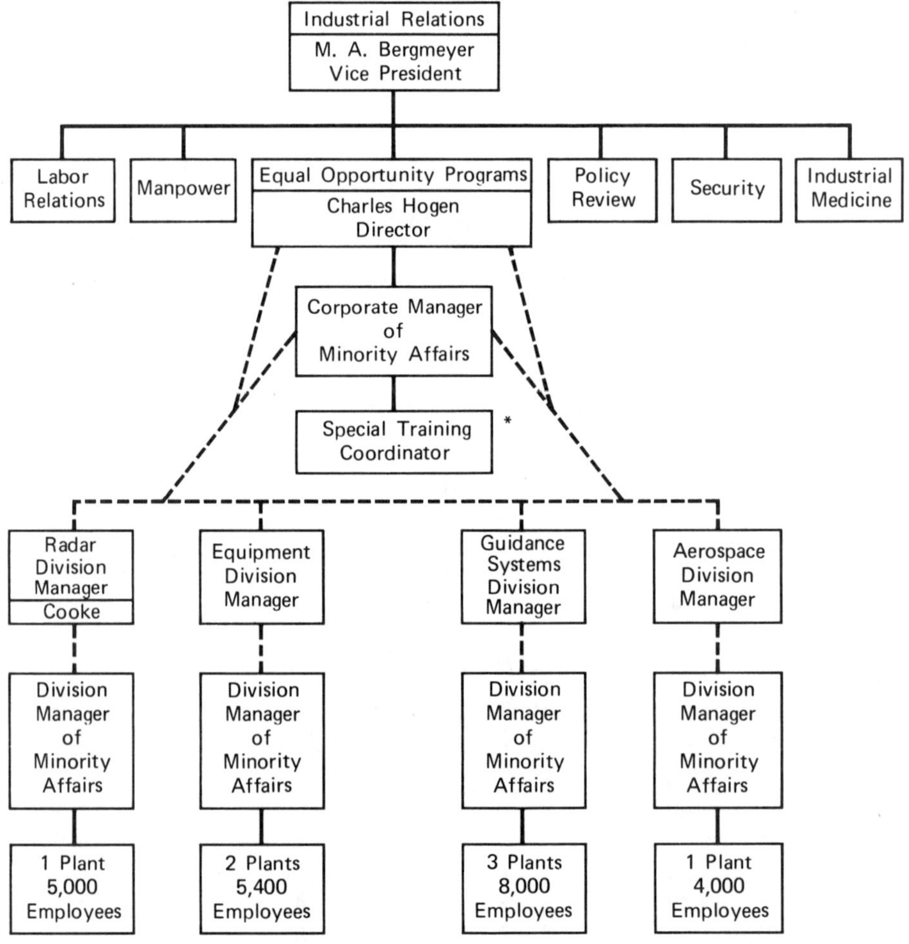

*As of December 1972, this position had not been filled.

Exhibit 24-4

THE COURTS BACK WOMEN ON JOB EQUALITY

WOMEN HAVE WON 178 OF 208 LOWER COURT CASES AND 14 OF 30 APPEALS

Elizabeth G. McDonald, a witty 23-year-old graduate student at California State University in San Francisco, gets a lot of laughs during her Women's Lib show on a cable television station in the Bay area.

The show is called "The Second Sex Scene."

Ms. McDonald may also get some chuckles–including the last laugh–out of a law suit she has filed against 32 companies, many of them nationally known, charging that they refused to interview her for executive trainee and sales openings in 1970, when she was about to graduate from Sacramento State College at San Francisco. She did get an interview with J. C. Penny Co.'s personnel man after she had set up an appointment for "my brother, Edward G. McDonald."

Ms. McDonald is suing Penny, Goodyear Tire & Rubber, Boise Cascade, Phillips Petroleum, Western Electric, and 27 other companies on behalf of herself and other women for allegedly violating the 1964 Civil Rights Act by interviewing only men for the executive trainee and sales jobs. She seeks $640,000 in back pay and compensatory damages, or about $20,000 per company.

Whether or not Ms. McDonald wins her case, other cases filed by individuals and federal law enforcement agencies under the Civil Rights Act and the 1963 Equal Pay Act are producing some distinctly unfunny consequences for company managements. Some of the nation's best-known corporations have lost cases costing hundreds of thousands of dollars in back pay and higher wage scales for women workers. More basic to management policy, court decisions have repeatedly erased hiring and promotion practices designed to keep women out of "men's jobs," whether blue-collar, white-collar, or executive. Every indication points to much more of the same.

WINNING STREAK. All told, some 400 equal pay cases have been filed by the U.S. Labor Dept., and the results should gladden a feminist's heart. The department has won 178 of 208 lower court decisions handed down to date. It has won 14 of the 30 "losers" when they were appealed to higher courts.

The most important decision under the Equal Pay Act–from a standpoint of the money it involved and the precedent it set–was the 1970 U.S. Circuit Court ruling against the Wheaton Glass Co., of Millville, N.J. The court ruled that jobs need not be identical, just "substantially equal," for the equal pay law to apply. It ordered Wheaton to pay close to $1-million in back pay to women inspector-packers. The U.S. Supreme Court refused to hear an appeal, in effect confirming the decision.

This summer Congress broadened the Equal Pay Act to cover an estimated 15-million executive, administrative, and professional employees, and outside salespeople. From 4-million to 5-million of this group are women. Among jobs newly covered are professor, engineer, chemist, buyer, programmer, writer, and editor.

PACE QUICKENS. If the cases involving equal pay appear sure to increase, those involving equal hiring, promotion, and other job patterns appear headed for a quantum jump. Last spring, Congress amended the Civil Rights Act to enable the Equal Employment Opportunity Commission to take employers to court for violations of the fair employment provisions of the act, a change that quickened the pace of litigation considerably. Formerly, only individuals and the Justice Dept. had possessed this power—an arrangement expensive to individuals and apparently uncongenial to the Justice Dept., which had filed only four sex discrimination suits in the eight years of its jurisdiction. EEOC has begun 12 legal actions since receiving its new power last March.

An individual's suit produced the Supreme Court's one decision on sex discrimination under the 1964 rights act: Phillips vs. Martin Marietta. The court forbade Martin Marietta to reject women with preschool children, since the company had no bar against employing men with preschool children. Lower court rulings in cases by individuals included one that opened the job of airline cabin attendant to men.

Of the Justice Dept.'s four sex discrimination cases, three—against Libbey-Owens-Ford, Obear-Nester Glass, and Household Finance—were settled by consent decrees. The first and most important suit charged Libbey-Owens-Ford with keeping women out of supervisory positions and with limiting their overtime work. Justice's fourth case, which is against Philadelphia Electric Co., is in the courts.

In the first of EEOC's 12 legal actions, the commission took Liberty Mutual Life Insurance Co. to court to restore the job of a woman fired after she had filed sex discrimination charges against the company. The court ordered the employee reinstated with back pay, pending an EEOC investigation of her substantive charges against Liberty Mutual. The other cases deal with matters ranging from sex-segregated help-wanted ads to the use of stiffer promotion criteria for women than for men.

THE DELUGE. In a series of tough speeches, EEOC Chairman William H. Brown III has warned employers that these moves are only the beginning. Many more cases will be filed, he says, once the commission's general counsel, William A. Carey, builds up his staff of 57 lawyers to the more than 200 permitted by the EEOC's 50% budget increase for fiscal 1973.

"Many people consider sex discrimination rather comical," says Brown. "But it is not funny—certainly not to the 5,800 people who filed charges of sex discrimination with our commission in fiscal 1971 and the 10,400 who filed charges in fiscal 1972."

Though similar in most ways, race and sex discrimination assume different forms, Brown says. "Today racial discrimination is subtler than in the past," he says. "Women, however, are often excluded by frank, overt discrimination. They are denied certain types of work and those responsible are quite candid about the reasons. They say that women are simply unacceptable in high pressure management, as supervisors, in heavy construction work, or in jobs that require travel.

OFFENDING COMPANIES PAY HEAVILY. MS. McDONALD ASKS FOR $640,000 IN DAMAGES

The same people say that women are good as bookkeepers and switchboard operators and things like that because they are good at detail and don't mind monotony."

When management men act on these preconceptions about the capabilities of women to deny or restrict job opportunities, they are being just as unlawful as when they exclude minorities, Brown stresses. The EEOC chairman notes that some women do reach top jobs even though sex discrimination exists in almost every business in America–"and some people argue that this shows if a woman works hard, she can achieve success as easily as a man." All it really shows, Brown says, is that women may be as competent as men when given the chance.

GUIDELINES. Employers preparing for what apparently lies ahead are finding their handiest guide in the revised version of *Guidelines on Discrimination Because of Sex*, issued by the EEOC last March and often cited in judicial decisions or sex discrimination cases. The guidelines narrow almost to the vanishing point the kinds of jobs for which sex is a "*bona fide* occupational qualification"–BFOQ in lawyers' shorthand.

For instance, the guidelines say that an employer cannot refuse to hire a woman because of the assumption "that the turnover rate among women is higher than among men" or that women are less capable than men of aggressive salesmanship; similarly, a man cannot be denied a job because of "stereotyped characterizations" that men are less capable than women of assembling intricate equipment.

That leaves actor or actresses as examples of jobs for which sex might be a BFOQ. Another example, as one court decision suggested, is wet nurse.

The guidelines also say that state laws barring women from jobs that require lifting loads of certain weights, or barring them from jobs that require night work and overtime work "do not take into account the capacities, preferences, and abilities of individual females," and therefore must yield to the federal antidiscrimination law.

PREGNANCY. The same principle applies to state laws requiring special rest periods and meal periods for women–unless they cover men, too. And any rule restricting the employment of married women is illegal unless it also applies to married men.

The guidelines are equally explicit about fringe benefits. A pension or retirement plan is unlawful if it specifies different retirement ages or benefits because of sex. Disability benefits related to pregnancy must be available "on the same terms and conditions as are applied to other temporary disabilities." A series of cases has been filed against companies (and, on behalf of teachers, against school boards), challenging requirements that pregnant women must quit work by a certain stage of their pregnancy.

The probable outcome of the pregnancy cases is suggested by the action taken last January by General Electric Co. The company responded to a suit by the International Union of Electrical Workers by changing its policy and allowing pregnant women to work for as long as the women's physicians certify that they are physically able to work.

AWARDS IN EQUAL PAY CASES

Wheaton Glass	$901,062	Daisy Mfg.	209,905
G. C. Murphy	648,000	Hayes Industries	206,214
Pacific Telephone & Telegraph	593,457	American Can	149,927
Midwest Mfg.	238,695	RCA	100,432

Exhibit 24-5

LACKAWANNA CASE[1]

Bethlehem's Lackawanna Plant, located near Buffalo, New York, was one of the largest steel-making facilities in the United States. At full capacity, the plant employed about 20,000 people. Covering 5,000 acres, it consisted of several distinct, interrelated operations: receiving raw materials, producing coke and iron, making the steel, rolling it into various shapes and forms, and finishing it. The plant was divided into 74 production and maintenance departments with about 280 seniority units. Associated with these departments and units was a wide variety of working conditions, each demanding particular skills and each involving certain hazards. Consequently, for efficient and safe operations, definite job progressions were established in each unit. In the course of doing a job, an employee acquired the skills and training needed for higher jobs in the same unit. Promotions and, in slack periods, demotions were effected along these lines of progression. Work in one unit was usually different enough from that in another that a transferee to a unit was hardly more knowledgeable than a person recently hired.

Prior to October 1, 1967, it was the unofficial practice to assign newly hired black workers to certain departments in the plant. As a result, about 80% of the blacks ended up in one of eleven departments: brickmason labor, yard, sintering plant, coke ovens, blast furnaces, steelmaking, 44 inch mill, billet yard, bar mills, 28 inch mill, and 14 inch mill. The jobs in these departments were among the hottest and dirtiest in the plant. Almost all of the employees in five of these departments were black: blast furnace, brickmason labor, coke oven, sintering plant, and steelmaking. In the other six departments, more than 20% of the employees were black.

Representatives of the Department of Justice arrived unannounced at the plant on September 7, 1967 to investigate the employment and other personnel practices there. A week later the Assistant Attorney General for the Civil Rights Division wrote the company stating that, in his judgment, its practices were not consistent with Title VII of the Civil Rights Act of 1964. Section 703(a) of Title VII prohibited discrimination against any employee "with respect to his compensation, terms, conditions or privileges of employment, because of such individual's race." Further, employers could not limit, segregate, or classify employees "in any way which would deprive or tend to deprive any individual of employment opportunities or otherwise adversely affect his status as an employee, because of such individual's race." On September 29 the company replied that it was anxious to comply with the objectives and the spirit of the Act and asked about the steps to be taken to bring it into compliance with the Act. Among other things, the company was most cooperative with governmental investigators, opening its records to them, providing them with computerized data, and putting its employees and equipment at the Government's disposal.

---

[1]This exhibit was prepared by Kim Kehoe, Research Assistant, as part of an unreleased case study in 1972.

On December 6 the Justice Department brought action against the company in the federal district court. The following May 15 the United Steelworkers of America and five locals at the plant were named as defendants. At that time the Attorney General alleged that provisions of the collective bargaining agreement served to perpetuate the effects of past discriminatory practices.

In his findings, the judge said in part:

> The court finds as fact that the transfer and seniority system negotiated in the 1962, 1965 and 1968 Master Agreements by the company and the union operates (as described above) in such a way as to tend to lock an employee into the department to which he has been assigned. This lock-in effect becomes stronger as an employee's length of service increases in the department. This means that the longer a Negro has worked in the hot and dirty department to which he was admittedly discriminatorily assigned, the more he has to lose by transfer.

In its order the court expanded the seniority and transfer rights of the employees who had been assigned and limited to the eleven departments mentioned above. All of these employees hired before October 1, 1967 were given priority transfer rights to move into any other department, provided they had the ability and skills requisite for the job. However, the judge did not grant the full relief sought by the government: retention of both their prior pay rate and their seniority for purposes of promotion and demotion. The judge did not grant rate retention and seniority carryover because he held that the present system was not a complete deterrent to transfer and that the changes requested by the Government would disrupt operations and disturb the other employees at the plant. This decision was rendered April 13, 1970.

The Government appealed the decision to the U.S. Circuit Court of Appeals. The case was heard in December and the three-judge panel issued its findings and decree the following June. The court commented on the relationship between the seniority and transfer system and the discriminatory assignment of blacks in the past.

> Although these overt practices were finally discontinued after October 1, 1967, . . . the seniority and transfer provisions perpetuated their effects in two ways. First, they tended to lock discriminatorily assigned employees into their jobs. In order to transfer to a formerly "white" department, these employees were required to suffer an economic penalty: forfeiture of seniority rights and pay levels earned in the "black" departments. The former was due to the use of departmental seniority, the latter to the fact that the transferee's new job was at a low paid entry level in the new department. Thus, to obtain an opportunity that had been denied them because of race, these employees had to be willing to give up what was already theirs because of service in the plant. Second, a transferee to a "white" department would never be able to reach the level of a white employee already there. For example, if a black and a white had been hired at the same time and the latter had been assigned to the more desirable "white" department but the black had not been so assigned, the white started to accumulate department or unit seniority in that department but the black did not. Even if the black were given the chance years later to transfer to the "white" department, the earlier discriminatory job assignment had denied him the chance to earn seniority up to that time in the

> "white" department. Therefore, the use of departmental or unit seniority for purposes of promotion in the formerly "white" department continued the effect of the earlier discriminatory practice.

The court went on to address the question of the effect of the remedy, rate retention, and seniority carryover, on the seniority system and on employee morale. The company and the union had argued that the seniority system insured orderly and efficient job mobility so that "after transfer the employee will advance in his new line of progression in an orderly manner, developing and building on new skills as he moves from job to job." In this way the seniority system served both safety and efficiency. The court went on to say:

> . . . Therefore, the crucial question must be whether the basic goal of the seniority system will necessarily be frustrated by these remedies. It is perfectly clear that this will not be the case. An unqualified worker need not be promoted whether or not he is a transferee under the district court's order. . . . Transferees will not move directly to high or middle level jobs or displace workers from jobs presently held nor jump from low to higher jobs. Under the Government's proposals, a transferee has priority rights only with respect to jobs in formerly "white" departments that are not otherwise filled in the normal seniority procedures. Accordingly, transfers will be to low skilled, entry level jobs. A transferee will be promoted from those jobs in the normal job-by-job fashion, moving up the progression line only as a job immediately above him becomes vacant.
>
> Appellees also argue that the morale of employees who did not suffer discrimination will suffer if rate retention and seniority carryover are ordered. But in the context of this case that possibility is not such an overriding business purpose that the relief requested must be denied. Assuming *arguendo* that the expectations of some employees will not be met, their hopes arise from an illegal system. Moreover, their seniority advantages are not indefeasibly vested rights but mere expectations derived from a collective bargaining agreement subject to modification.

The court returned the case to the district court with the request for a revision of the order. The revised order was to include the following provisions:

> 1.–A transferee shall receive, in his new position, pay equal to the pay in his former permanent position and shall continue to be so paid until he reaches a position whose pay scale is greater. If no job in his new department or unit has a rate as high as his former position, then he shall receive the rate of the highest level job in that department or unit. Because the rate retained is that of the transferee's permanent job, he shall not retain any temporary pay increase if he transfers after a temporary promotion.
>
> 2.–A transferee shall be permitted to exercise plant seniority for all purposes following transfer, except as otherwise set forth herein. When a transferee competes on the basis of seniority for vacancies occurring in the normal course of business, seniority for all bidders shall be computed on the basis of plant, rather than unit or department, seniority. Only workers qualified to fill a higher job may use plant seniority to advance. As workers are recalled after a layoff, all

employees shall assume the same positions relative to each other as they held immediately prior to the layoff.

3.—A transferee's right to transfer with seniority carryover and rate retention may be exercised only once and only during the next two years. If he exercises that right within that period, the transferee's protection of seniority carryover and rate retention shall continue in accordance with the other provisions in the order.

4.—A transferee shall lose his privilege of rate retention if he refuses a promotion in his new unit or department.

The revised order was issued by the district court judge on October 14, 1971.

Chapter Seven

Institutionalization of Social Responsiveness

Social responsiveness is a general management problem. Social issue specialists provide information and skills that are indispensable to the learning process which accompanies the adaptation to new and unfamiliar public demands. However, responsiveness in more than a superficial sense cannot really be claimed until decisions affecting operations bear the mark of the social policy. Institutionalization occurs as organizational commitment to implementation is obtained. By commitment we do not imply some new-found messianic compulsion to behave in one way or another; rather we mean the conviction among operating managers (regardless of how they may feel personally) that responding to social needs is provided for in the conduct of the business. Building and sustaining this commitment in the face of conflicts and questions of priority that are certain to emerge from the encroachment of new constraints on operating decisions are uniquely general management functions. Indeed, without general management support, institutionalization will be painful, slow, and probably costly.

In contrast to the demands placed on social issue specialists, which may call for innovative and untraditional activities, generalists have a task which to them is quite familiar, though certainly no less difficult. The skills that they have to work with are the same ones employed to guide the organization in the attainment of business strategy. Three such skills are of particular importance: the allocation of responsibilities, the design and use of systems to monitor performance, and the management of careers and incentives to shape the decision process and reinforce commitment. While the administrative skills themselves may be familiar, their application involves difficult choices and considerable courage. The stakes are higher and the pitfalls more numerous than the casual observer may recognize.

MANAGING THE RESPONSE PROCESS

The response process, as we described it in Chapter 4, has "top-down" characteristics for emerging social issues. Policy takes shape when the chief executive judges the issues to be of sufficient importance to warrant explicit corporate-wide attention. Implementation is driven by initiatives from this same quarter to acquire the necessary skills and to make room for the response in operating decisions. There may be no practical alternative for getting the job done, particularly if the chief executive wishes to maintain the initiative rather than let it pass to the firm's critics. Overcoming the barriers to social responsiveness in the large corporation—and large institutions more generally for that matter—may call for this sort of leadership.

Yet, there are also serious drawbacks in a "top-down" approach to implementing social policy.

- Without the participation of the organization in establishing standards and shaping programs, sustained commitment may be unattainable. A relapse is probable should pressure for performance wane.
- Centrally directed programs are likely to encounter opposition which, in the final analysis, may severely limit their effectiveness. Middle managers, often with justification, may feel that the corporate staff does not understand the operational implications of their requests.
- The size, influence, and cost of the corporate staff is almost certain to increase, thus negating certain of the benefits ascribed to the divisionalized organization structure. In particular, the clear responsibility for business segments placed with middle-level general managers may be compromised as the weight of social programs increases.

Thus, a major challenge in institutionalizing social policy is the clarification of responsibility for implementation. The corporation stands to benefit from having its key line managers, especially those in middle-level general management positions, take charge of getting the job done, just as they do in the more traditional aspects of running the business. Simply asserting who is to have this responsibility, however, is unlikely to produce acceptable results. A more satisfactory outcome may be reached by identifying how the organization should approach decisions that are influenced by social forces. Until the decision process itself is diagnosed and conditions set for its functioning, formal responsibilities will remain largely abstractions. To say, for instance, that a division manager is responsible for meeting environmental guidelines takes on meaning only as he is able to direct the allocation of resources to pollution control projects.

The pattern suggested below is not foreign to larger corporations. In fact, it resembles the process evident in many firms for making strategic decisions which affect the conduct of on-going business units. This similarity should not be surprising. If responses to social issues are to become integral and natural parts of managing the business, and if adverse side-effects are to be minimized (e.g., wasting resources or needlessly interfering with operations), the decision process should function much as it does when confronted with more traditional problems. Three identifiable activities may be observed in the evolution of decisions in large organizations, each bearing specific attention.

PROBLEM DEFINITION AND ANALYSIS

We have suggested that the breadth of vision necessary to grapple with *emerging* social demands appropriately may be found at the top of the corporation. On the other hand, operating problems are usually perceived and analyzed initially by the managers closest to them—often managers with functional responsibilities down in the operating units. Thus, the marketing organization is expected to scan the environment for new product opportunities and competition threats, manufacturing managers are to be alert to new production technologies, the need for additional capacity, and so forth. They are not passive participants in the decision process who merely act out directives from their superiors. Indeed, the corporation depends on their sensitivity to the environment and initiative in proposing implementation programs. Thus, pressure for concrete action in response to traditional business problems tends to build from the bottom of the organization.

For social policy to be institutionalized, this same sort of upward pressure for social responsiveness is ultimately necessary. We do not, of course, imply that manufacturing managers must become ecologists, for example, or that they should argue for expenditures which compromise the productive capability of their facilities. Yet, if they are not expected to assume responsibility for understanding ecological demands and for formulating corrective programs in line with corporate policy, the firm will have forsaken its most effective means of anticipatory response. This responsibility is unlikely to be discharged by managers at these levels in the organization, however, without certain *quid pro quos* in the form of (a) funding for technical or staff assistance and possibly other resources and (b) some assurance that their efforts will be rewarded.

In essence, a social issue specialist capability is necessary at the extremities of the organization—the sales branches, manufacturing facilities, and division offices as the case may be. An existing functional department may be the logical place to install this capability. For instance, equal employment concerns may accrue to the personnel office, sales practices to the marketing department, and environmental protection to engineering. Unfortunately, there is also a tendency to dump the problem in an already busy department without sufficient attention to questions of organization and substance.

First, what individuals should be given responsibility for problem definition and analysis? Where should they report? And how should they be trained? Constraints of time and money inevitably shape the answers. It may be unrealistic to expect the senior marketing manager to have more than a basic understanding of consumer protection legislation; it may be equally unrealistic to provide for a specialist on such matters in every sales branch. Nevertheless, the degree of emphasis accorded a social issue will tend to be increased by:

(a)—assigning specialist responsibilities to managers with bright career prospects;
(b)—placing whatever full time positions that may be warranted in an accepted promotion ladder;
(c)—providing the incumbent with access to both the division general manager and specialists on the issue at higher levels in the organization.

Second, how should social issues be dealt with in business decisions? Consider the planning that supports the recommendation for a new manufacturing facility. Until recently, it was common for community and ecological impacts to be ignored as the project took shape; if they were considered at all, the impetus came from outsider protests arising once plans were unveiled. To mitigate the expense and delay caused by such protests, some corporations have now attempted to interject social issues earlier in the decision process before choices on location and plant design have solidified. The intent has been to weave these considerations into the standard operating procedures relied upon by the business planners and engineers to guide their analysis. Specific examples of organizations struggling to enlarge the bases for decision making are provided in subsequent case studies including the faculty promotion system at the University of Pennsylvania, and the case in the preceding section on the capital appropriation process at Omar Industries.

COMMITMENT TO ACTION

The strength of the large corporation rests in large measure on the competence of its middle-level general managers. By assuming responsibility for the conduct of their units or divisions, these managers play the lead role in defining and executing strategic plans. They are looked to by corporate-level executives for *commitments* to the achievement of agreed-upon performance goals. Their track record for delivering results has an influence on their ability to secure resources for future projects and on their careers as well. The institutionalization of social policy hinges on the willingness of these managers to extend the scope of activities on which they are willing to make commitments.

Commitments are not entered into lightly by middle-level general managers. They must weigh the demands for performance levied on them from above with the needs of the business represented by their subordinates. The former are typically phrased in terms of results—expected operating profits, return on net assets employed, and so forth—while the latter are in the form of detailed requests or problems stated in operating terms—the proposal for another sales director or a new plant. Middle-level general managers consequently find themselves in the position of bargaining for resources on the one hand while exacting performance targets from their subordinates on the other. They must be alert to what is expected of their unit as they negotiate for capital appropriations and skilled at knowing how hard their organizations may be pushed. When they place their reputations behind plans or project requests, they must be prepared to bear responsibility for the outcome.

Conversely, programs which do not have the general manager's commitment are unlikely to receive the concerted attention of his subordinates. Moreover, such programs run the risk of being poorly conceived or misunderstood. For until the general manager forces proposals to be integrated with the operating plans of the business and elicits or demands the organization's support, there is little incentive to make the programs work, especially if they are thought to threaten some already established objective.

The role to be played by middle-level general managers in the implementation of social policy now becomes quite clear. They should ensure that the issues are identified and incorporated as appropriate in business plans and operating decisions in their units. Moreover, they should assume responsibility for resolving such conflicts between near-term profitability and long-term social benefits as may arise. But most importantly, they should be asked to place their reputations behind the achievement of results in areas of social concern that have been placed in their care and to transmit this commitment to their organizations.

MONITORING THE DECISION PROCESS

Many, probably most, decisions in the large corporation are made without the participation of corporate managers. This is especially true of decisions to do nothing or to exclude alternatives from consideration. In other cases, corporate managers become privy to the decision process only after middle-level general managers have already committed themselves to a course of action and present their recommendations for approval. As we have noted earlier, there are clearly advantages to be gained from this arrangement *provided* the steps taken in the field are in accordance with corporate goals and policy. In fact, without a large and cumbersome staff, the divisionalized firm cannot really be managed in any other manner. And were such a staff created, division managers would in all probability be reluctant to assume full responsibility for their units.

What then does corporate management have to do to extricate itself from the details of social involvement in the far reaches of the organization *without* sacrificing the implementation of the firm's social policy? The remedies are far easier to describe than to execute. As we have said repeatedly, each social issue or family of closely related issues should be approached individually; one must have accumulated a sufficient understanding of both the particular demand and the consequences of alternative responses to it to permit systematic and effective delegation. Nevertheless, a number of generalized areas for response can be readily identified.

The first relates to the articulation of policy. Rarely are policies by themselves elaborate enough to be of assistance to the operating manager faced with an immediate decision—to close a plant rather than request funds for pollution control equipment, to lay off a disproportionate percentage of minorities and women rather than buck the seniority system, and so forth. It would be an unfortunate mistake, we believe, to attempt to rectify this situation by drafting more comprehensive policy statements only to find that they are safely filed in the procedures manual and placed at the far end of the operating manager's bookshelf. Instead, the policy accumulates credence as it is applied to practice; necessarily, it will evolve and be enriched with time as the social demand matures and the organization acquires further experience. A tension is likely between adaptability to changing conditions and consistency of intent. The chief executive has the difficult task of permitting the policy to be amended in the details of implementation while sustaining the integrity of the firm's general posture on the social issue. Thus, he should be sensitive to precedent without being unwilling to countenance change.

Second, continuing attention should be given to the relationship between the response to a social issue and the business strategy of the operating unit (and the corporation as a whole.) The strategy provides the basic organizing device around which the actions and requests of managers in the field are evaluated and interrelated. Whatever can be plausibly and consistently related to this strategy is likely to be given attention and priority. The other side of that coin, of course, is that without such a relationship in evidence, social responsiveness will tend to remain a grudging afterthought for all but the most committed operating managers. Among the remedies, the most powerful is the requirement that a social issue be specifically recognized in the business plan and as a factor in strategic decisions.

Third, requisite planning and control systems are necessary to reflect performance expectations and results throughout the corporation. As several of the later case studies indicate, the information available to management on the organization's posture on an emerging social issue is often scant indeed. As at the University of Pennsylvania, several frustrating and costly years may be required to gather the data, construct a reporting system and sell it to operating management. Where the reporting format is imposed by government regulation, the task would appear to be somewhat simpler, were it not for the fact that regulators, like others grappling with a social issue, display a penchant for expanding and complicating the reporting guidelines. Just as the policy must be adaptive, so also should the planning and control system be constructed to permit modification and elaboration with time.

Planning and control systems do not, of course, guarantee performance; nor can they be expected to substitute entirely for a chief executive's first hand appreciation of the firm's social profile. It would be surprising to find a chief executive who relied exclusively on reports to guide his evaluation; he is more likely to comingle this data with the more tangible impressions gained from observing the number of minority and female faces in management meetings, the opacity of the plume from a plant's smokestack and so forth. While these impressions may prompt immediate action in specific instances, the reporting system provides a more reliable means for achieving consistent response among operating units and meaningful performance trends over time. The need for systematic reporting should be weighed, however, against the danger of saturating both corporate and division management with documentation describing bits and pieces of the unit's overall performance. An acceptable accommodation may be to broaden the base of existing information systems to include social responsiveness.

Fourth, corporate management has the opportunity—some would say the obligation—to build social responsiveness into the performance evaluation process through which rewards and sanctions are distributed and careers are ultimately determined. As we stressed earlier, this process has a profound impact on the middle-level general manager's willingness to commit his reputation to courses of action in his unit.

The chief executive has two problems in deciding whether and how to apply the evaluation process to social responsiveness. The first has to do with preserving the integrity of incentives in the organization. The achievement of strategy is dependent to a considerable degree on disciplined action; support for implementation is obtained through the corporation's promise of rewards for middle managers or the threat of punishment. However, as pressure from government and private action groups increases, the middle manager's personal risks in failing to respond to their demands increases as well. The manager worries about the sanctions these outside groups may levy on him directly; in some cases he may be threatened with legal action as well as adverse publicity.

As these external threats intensify, the corporation tends to lose its hold on some portion of his attention. Consequently, as a means of retaining control over the evaluation process, and thereby over the implementation of business strategy, the chief executive may wish to raise the stakes for social performance in the corporation's system of incentives until they are at least as forceful as the demands placed on middle managers by external agencies.

The second problem relates to the allocation of incentives among the areas in which performance is of importance to the firm. The generation of economic returns has traditionally been the central focus. In the future we doubt that this focus will (or should) change. Nonetheless, social responsiveness is likely to receive a larger share. How the proportions are established among social issues, and between them and economic performance, is by no means clear cut. For instance, should affirmative action be accorded 15 percent of the middle manager's performance review as it is in DESCO, Inc., one of the following case studies? Is this too much or too little? Should additional percentages he allotted to other social issues? To the extent that corporate performance measures directly influence behavior, the chief executive has a sensitive assignment with potentially significant consequences for the firm. The following cases illustrate the dilemmas arising in this situation for managers at both corporate and operating levels.

TOWARD A HUMANISTIC CORPORATION

The institutionalization of social policy, as it has been described above, makes use of the administrative strengths of the divisionalized organization. The upward flow of information and initiative has been carefully provided for, and the distribution of incentives has been based upon systematically measured performance. If successfully implemented, the end result contemplates a decision process in which those closest to the operational impacts of social demands are held responsible for responding to them. Presumably, through these means, the large corporation should demonstrate as much flexibility in adapting to changing social conditions as it has in more traditional competitive and technological areas.

Some readers may raise a real and legitimate objection at this point. We argued in Part One of this book that we are witnessing a secular trend toward a more humanistic society. However, does not the means of implementing social policy fall prey to the same dilemmas that prompted the large corporation to slight social demands in the first place? From one viewpoint the picture we have painted of the response process and the additional suggestions we have made for increasing its effectiveness lead to this conclusion. The middle-level general manager again finds himself in the pressure cooker, only now being held responsible for achieving social as well as economic results without any assured means of resolving whatever conflicts may arise between them. Have we not advocated an accommodation which eventually accentuates the weaknesses as well as the strengths of the divisionalized firm?

If this objection proves valid, the risks to the corporation may be substantial. By their nature, social demands are likely to spawn opposing and often emotional views among people of goodwill. Aside from whatever economic consequences there may be for those involved (e.g., reducing the promotions available to white males in order to increase opportunities for minorities and females), deep-seated values may also be involved. Enforcing a corporate social policy before the issue is generally accepted may invite reactions ranging from raw backlash to the more sophisticated argument that the chief executive's power over the organization is being used unfairly. The result would probably be increased bureaucratization of the firm as middle managers seek to protect themselves against corporate demands, and diminished interest in the pursuit of corporate purpose.

We suggest, however, that a second outcome is possible. If properly managed, the response to social demands may tend to strengthen humanizing forces in the corporation. This contention is based on three opportunities arising from an expanded definition of business obligations.

The first is the opportunity to extend the purpose of the firm—not simply in a philosophical sense (a point by now fairly well established), but in a practical, operational sense as well. Once the basis for such an extension has been established, a greater degree of organizational participation in the formulation of policy may be possible and desirable. The unquestioned acceptance of short run economic goals may be supplanted by a more reasoned debate over the desired purposes of the enterprise and the acceptance of a longer time horizon over which these purposes should be achieved and maintained. That old cliché, "participative management", may finally receive the impetus necessary to make it a reality.

Second, if social responsiveness is to be institutionalized within the framework of the divisionalized organization structure, managers in the field actually need more rather than less autonomy. They are called upon to guide their unit in the achievement of multiple goals without a clear means of arriving at a summary measure of achievement. The checks and balances become more intricate and sensitive, and second guessing from higher levels more tenuous. Under these circumstances, corporate managers may find restraint in the use of power advisable. Rather than stressing controls, they may foster innovativeness among operating managers in response to social demands and exhibit a greater tolerance for untraditional behavior.

Finally, the basis for performance evaluation may be broadened to include a variety of social as well as economic goals. Also, the frequency of measurement and the time horizon adopted for career judgments may be lengthened in recognition of the longer period necessary to demonstrate the achievement of these broader goals. A more comprehensive view of the qualities and performance records desirable in management may then evolve in large corporations. The logical result would be an executive cadre that is more receptive to public and employee expectations and, in all probability, more contented with its own lot.

We do not wish to appear as Pollyannas here; a more humanistic organization will be possible only through continued attention to the governance of large corporations. There is, of course, the chance that firms will become more centralized and authoritarian should chief executives defensively impose and enforce response to a growing array of demands on their organizations. We leave the issue of governance as a final consideration in the administration of social policy, one that in the long run may be the most critical for the vitality and effectiveness of the corporation.

SUGGESTED READINGS

1.–Barnard, Chester L. *The Functions of the Executive*. Cambridge: Harvard University Press, 1968.

2.–Simon, Herbert. *Administrative Behavior*. New York: The Free Press, 1957.

3.–Selznick, Philip. *Leadership in Administration*. New York: Harper and Row, 1957.

4.–Bower, Joseph L. *Managing the Resource Allocation Process*. Boston: Harvard Business School, Division of Research, 1970.

Case Twenty-Five

Foods Unlimited (B)

Don Robbins checked his calendar for the day and grimaced as he realized he had forgotten about a Community Affairs meeting scheduled for 3:00 that afternoon. As he hurried out of the office, he anticipated the reaction of Jack Northrup, Manager of the Vending Operations Department of the FOODS office in Charleston, West Virginia. "There goes Donny Do-Gooder," was the muttered comment last month when Robbins had excused himself from the post-session socializing following a departmental discussion of plans for the vending areas in a new suburban shopping complex.

Robbins had been transferred to West Virginia less than a year before and immediately had been pleased at the opportunities, not only as a first level manager concerned with vending expansions, but also for receiving company support for his interest in volunteer work in the community. Unlike the southeastern area he had left, this north central area had the reputation as the real star in the FOODS crown, leading the five other areas in implementing the recommendations set forth in the corporate Community Activities Manual, as revised in 1973. Since his reassignment, Robbins, with another member of the local Community Activities Group, had become especially involved in working with several high school students and local doctors to set up a Drug Hot Line. This project, plus group meetings and other group endeavors, took up several hours a week. However, Robbins was sure his FOODS work had not suffered as a result—in fact, he felt he was more conscientious than he might otherwise have been—and he expected to put in extra time whenever problems arose, as they generally did just before new installations went into operation. Nevertheless, his first 6-month interim review had not resulted in a recommendation for a raise. Although nothing had been said directly about his Community Activities work, Robbins found himself wondering if that, rather than his job performance, hadn't been the strongest factor in Northrup's rather noncommital appraisal. As he joined the six other group members, low-level management personnel like himself, Robbins was curious to know if some of them had the same problem and, perhaps, had been more successful in coping with it.

BACKGROUND: THE COMPANY

FOODS (Food: Ordering, Operating, Dining and Serving) Unlimited, claiming to feed millions at home, at school, at work, and on vacation, grew from a small cafeteria and food supplier into a billion dollar corporation serving America through a variety of catering, vending, delivery, and franchise operations. Its growth in institutional markets took off in the 1930's when it capitalized on the burgeoning use of vending machines, and, in the years since, FOODS had continued to emphasize the application of automation and technology to the business of feeding people. The research and development for this more technical part of the operations were done at Lexington Laboratories, a wholly owned subsidiary. The other side of the business, FOODS proper, was organized geographically with 156 units scattered across the country and a corporate headquarters and staff at Philadelphia. The ten levels of management, from president to vice presidents, down to managers at area, regional, unit, departmental and supervisory levels, created a closely defined hierarchy for the company's 50,000 employees (12,000 of whom were at the management level). (See modified organization chart–Exhibit 25-1.) FOODS' profits in 1973 were approximately $48 million on sales of just over $1.5 billion, both up almost 10% from the previous year.

For the past several years increased attention had been directed to FOODS' performance in the community as well as on the bottom line. The FOODS (A) case describes the Community Activities Review, one of the techniques the Community Activities corporate staff employed to monitor programs initiated in the field units of the company.

DESIGN AND IMPLEMENTATION: CORPORATE LEVEL

FOODS reorganized its community activities effort starting in 1970 and began to implement this expanded and revamped program throughout the organization. The basic tenets were presented at a meeting of senior management people from the whole company in late 1973; they were given the new Community Activities Manual and instructed in how to apply these guidelines to their own area and state organizations. The basic goal of the program was stated there: "To create public understanding of our role as a provider of important services and as a participating corporate citizen."

The reason for some of this concern was rooted in the conditions and pressures of the late 1960's, when the urban disturbances caused special problems for companies such as FOODS and resulted in an increasing emphasis on "social responsibility" throughout the corporate world. Specifically, FOODS equipment and trucks were vandalized, personnel were increasingly reluctant to travel through or service downtown facilities at night, and so forth. As the '70s wore on, the focus of dissatisfaction shifted; many of the younger employees objected to what they saw as the overly regimented style of the company, and the public complained more and more of poor service and higher prices–of quarters swallowed by machines, of funny-tasting egg salad sandwiches, and of paying $1.25 for a meal that used to cost 75¢.

However, even during the worst riots, some FOODS trucks and personnel were unharmed and permitted to carry on as usual, and some customers, even those hit by higher prices or inconvenience in their convenience foods, continued to write letters of praise and commendation, usually directed to specific employees. The rationale seemed to lie in the relation of the company personnel to the local community. Accordingly, one strong emphasis in the new Community Activities program put together by the corporate people was its grass roots orientation.

Of course, because of the nature of its business, the company had always been in close contact with the public and, in that sense, Community Activities was nothing new. Jonathan Dils, an Assistant Vice President for Public Relations at FOODS headquarters, commented:

> What you should understand is that we have always in this company had something very similar to the Community Activities program. It stretches back over the years. Where the geographical units have been small, like in a town of 10,000, we never really stopped doing it. However, when we started this program again, with the changes in early 1974, in practically none of our metropolitan areas was there anything going on.

Dils indicated that this effort was not initiated solely from altruistic motives; there were sound business reasons for such a company working to improve its relations with the consuming public. He commented:

> We do some things because they are in the interest of the good of the business, some because they are profit oriented, some because we have to do them. They are all a mix. It's always a mixture.

Since the new manual had been presented to the organization in late 1973, the company was adapting its existing structure and traditions to fit the revised guidelines and goals. Dils offered some thoughts as to why and how the program was implemented:

> The implementation of the community relations program was really done because our president and our officers said they would like to have a Community Activities program. Now, you know, they say they would like to have a lot of things, to be honest about it. . . . This one just happened to go well. It may have just been entirely in the way it was presented to the field, that they were open and hungry for it. . . .
>
> The Public Relations Department had two assistant vice presidents. There was one in charge of advertising and public and employee information. Then there was the other one, me, in charge of public affairs, community relations, budgets, personnel, etc. . . we were to provide, in this instance, staff support for all of the line organizations who would be engaged in the Community Activities work. We had a definite charge as to what we were going to do. We had a definite charge as to who was responsible for staff work. We even had a definite charge—maybe secured agreement would be a better word—to the line organization that the Services Division, traditionally the most active in the community, though certainly not the only one with public contact, had been given the responsibility to lead in the implementation in the field—which was to take advantage of their traditional ways. We didn't want to get into an argument about responsibility within the line organization. We just said you've always had that responsibility, we ex-

pect you to stick with it. We expect you to lead the other departments in the formation of these Community Activities groups and to advise us on these activities.

The basis of the Community Activities plan was to be the group, one for each of the 156 unit offices in the company, composed of first and second level management people from the various departments in the unit offices. The members, six to nine per group, were expected to live within the area served by the group. Thus, a first level commercial manager from Wellesley might meet with a second level Systems woman from Newton on the Boston-Suburban West group, under the supervision of another second level manager, to whom none of the group members reported in their regular jobs. The groups (each chaired by a second level person) were given a great deal of autonomy to draw up their own plans and projects and then carry them out. Each could call upon an advisor, a third level manager, and the several advisors in a region met occasionally to discuss the progress or problems of the groups or to help get special funding if needed. By the end of 1974 there were almost 150 groups, organized on paper at least, and many of these were reportedly hard at work on community projects (see Exhibit 25-2 for a description of the group's role).

IMPLEMENTATION AT THE AREA LEVEL

Carl Sheridan, Manager of the north central area (with its 6 regions and 32 units), had been with FOODS in various line capacities for over 20 years. Based on his knowledge of the company and of the new program, he offered some reasons why he felt his area had been able to move quite rapidly and successfully in getting the Community Activities groups operational and useful:

> I think one thing is the delegation of the authority for Community Activities down to the first and second levels in the business, in giving people the opportunity to make a decision as to what we are going to do. It was something we had never had in our business before. Over the years we have tended to become more and more structured and instructions came from the top saying you will do things this way and if you do this you will be rewarded and if not, you're a bad employee.
>
> Well, we turned things completely over and said that the Community Activities group from a geographic area would determine what was appropriate and their program would be their program. They would tell us what they wanted to do and how they were going to do it. We changed our contributions plan. We changed our membership plan in community organizations—things like that—in order to give them some freedom they didn't have before. We tried to turn it into a grass roots situation.
>
> All the people need motivation on an individual basis. Generally the people are pretty enthused. Sooner or later you have to replace a chairman who doesn't seem to care. You have to talk to an advisor. We're constantly replacing group members.

Either they have been moved or ceased to care. Yet those who really don't want to participate, aren't in it. It *is* a volunteer effort, and so far it has worked. No group is nonfunctional because of a lack of volunteers, and the numbers seem to balance out. And, again, we lean a good deal to the local unit. For instance, there are different methods for choosing a leader; sometimes it is automatically the senior person involved or sometimes he or she is appointed from above. And the members serve on a group for differing lengths of time—these administrative details are something we have *not* had to worry about, but have left to the group itself.

You do need a spark sometimes. You have to find somebody to give it to them. Usually in an organization of this size it isn't just one person who provides the spark, because if people won't listen to you, you can just fire and fire away. You have to do a lot of persuasion and I guess you just have to do a lot of things. I don't know how long a list that is, because you just keep doing it until you get it done. Drawing more people into it. Specifically, you have to set up what the problems are, who's involved, the timetable for it, all of the people in the budget, the dollars, and the effect on the bottom line—that's all just applying the rules of good management.

I think we have another management principle at work. It was to cut out some dead wood and to put some people to work who really were not working as hard as they needed to. You know, what we tried to utilize when we got started were the people who had a natural interest in this sort of thing anyway—those who'd been doing a lot of things on their own in an organized way. Those first groups had enthusiasm—we provided the structure for them to proceed with what they had been doing. We gave them recognition for what they had been doing all along and suddenly it was a pretty hot item in the business. That was important. . . .

I'm being honest when I say this, but I did trade off friendships. I have 2 or 3 friends who are in responsible positions who shared my view that it needed to be done. We went there first and got it going. If you can get enough people going, the laggers have to get on the bandwagon because people look at them, saying "Why don't you do it too?"

. . . Once you get it going other people say, "Hey, that really works." It does 2 or 3 things for us. It gets my departments together—and working with other departments—and we're always searching for that. It gives us some impact and we're always looking for how to do that. You use pressure. To get things going for you, you use every technique you can think of. You use political pressure. You use friendships. You use the boss's name, when it's appropriate. You say the president wants you to do that, it's not just me. You get two or three real high quality guys like I had and you go out there and sell the program on its merit—the program really has a great many merits which sell it to 75-85% of the people. So it's just with a few. You always have a problem with a few about how you remove roadblocks. In a few cases where people have resisted, we've been known to hit them with a two-by-four. We've been known to get people transferred. I'm not sure I want to publicize it, but there were some bodies who disappeared from particular places because they were obstacles. I'm not sure I can tell you how it happened. I just know that it happened.

THE REVIEW

Another useful two-by-four Sheridan mentioned was the Review.[1] Under procedures established the previous year, a Review team from headquarters audited local unit Community Activities groups by on-site visits extending over 3½-4½ day periods, followed by in-depth analyses and confidential reporting to those involved. Of course, only a few groups could be visited each month, so theoretically a group might go unreviewed for several years. Nevertheless, the corporate Community Activities staff felt the Review was useful stimulus; even if unused, it reminded the units of the importance headquarters was placing on Community Activities. As they said, the Review was designed to be "a good tool in keeping top management informed of the progress of Community Activities and getting the attention of middle and lower management for the CA effort."

Sheridan explained why he thought the Review was important:

> We used the Review to prove the point that we needed the new program—and we used that as a strategy to get it started. By saying we need it, yet don't have it, this Review proves it, and off we go from here.
>
> Then when we had the program pretty well set up and functioning, we asked ourselves what's going to happen if we stop. There are so many of our PR efforts that die, after the initial blast. We appoint a few people and make a few speeches and then it dies. We said how can we keep it going . . . and so we use the Review function. . . .
>
> Now I want to illustrate to you the reasons for introducing the Review function. One reason is to find out whether the groups are properly organized, whether they are following the principles of the Handbook and general company policy. And the other is to give some credit—and also get a report of what the teams are doing. Since 3 of the 4 Reviews here have been good, this has helped the acceptance problems.
>
> We pulled the Review on a couple of groups. In one particular situation it was especially bad for them. They were simply giving lip service to something. They said they had something and the Review proved they didn't. It was very embarrassing to them. Their regional manager got a report on it, and that didn't jibe with what they'd been telling him. So that was a two-by-four there.

PROBLEMS

The Review also helped highlight some of the difficulties inherent in the Community Activities program. Sheridan commented on one that he felt was particularly important:

> Acceptance at the middle and lower management levels has been somewhat cool . . . There was a middle management lag in putting the proper emphasis on the

---

[1] This device was described in detail in FOODS Unlimited (A).

> importance of CA compared to the measured part of the job at the beginning . . .I hope that lag is starting to disappear.

At FOODS, management personnel were given relative freedom to allocate their time among the tasks at hand. In fact, one reason very few nonmanagement people had gotten involved with Community Activities groups was that they were bound, some by union contract, to a more strict nine to five schedule. Sheridan realized that the "lag" referred to above could harm the individual manager:

> Our basic principle is always that it is up to the individual in management to get the job done, even if it takes 24 hours. You can arrange time in many ways. If you go to a meeting, you go to a meeting. You may have to come back to the office later, but your superior shouldn't complain as long as the job is done . . . I realize it isn't that simple, though, when I put myself in the supervisor's position. Everyone needs people, everyone has too heavy a load. He says, "Here I am—you've just cut my budget, you just cut my force, and now you want to take somebody out of my limited force and let them go make hay and sunshine." But that problem has been in this business ever since I've been here. Our answer is that the manager's job is to structure this situation and control it so that we can accomplish the CA objectives as well as the other. Many of the managers succeed, but some don't. We've got to separate them—those that can't control this kind of situation, we just don't consider them. There is a winnowing effect going on and this is another screen they have to go through.

To try to ensure that there were more managers who could control such situations, Sheridan explained that he was working very hard at trying to get the word down through his area organization. He had met the previous week with the team chairmen for all the groups in the area to go over their plans for the next year. He made sure that newsletters published in the area devoted a lot of space to Community Activities and to involved employees, and he sometimes had the Regional Manager write directly to individuals congratulating them on their work. All of these details contributed to what Sheridan felt was a solid and fairly successful start for the CA program in his area. He claimed with some satisfaction, "After a little more than a year, we think that 70-80% of the groups function very well."

THE GROUP AND THE GROUP MEETING

Don Robbins' group was one Sheridan had singled out for special recognition. From the start, it had had strong leadership from team chairperson Nancy Murphy, Customer Services Manager of the South Charleston Services Department, and had met with an enthusiastic and helpful response in the community. The meeting had already begun by the time Robbins arrived. Several teachers from the local school system were making a presentation on ways that FOODS could contribute to their work at both elementary and high school levels; by supplying material (or even samples) on food and nutrition for science and home economics classes, by arranging more elaborate displays or information centers on jobs within the field for older students, and perhaps by establishing a cooperative, part-time work program for those especially interested. Their presentation was received enthusiastically but took most of the allotted two hours. After the teachers had left, the group members quickly went over the other ongoing projects: the Drug Hot Line Robbins had helped initiate, plans for donating "free" vending machines to a party at a school for deaf children, the more complicated arrangements for a hot lunch program at a neighborhood center for the elderly, and so forth. For several minutes they engaged in a general brainstorming of ideas on ways to encourage recycling of the paper and wrapping materials used in so many FOODS products.

At 6:30, Murphy commented that in closing an already long meeting she wanted to relay to the group her impressions of the meeting the week before with Sheridan and the other group chairpersons. She emphasized that he was certainly supporting the Community Activities program and was most appreciative of all their efforts. Just as he was wondering if he were the only one with a problem in this respect, Robbins heard Bill Stewart, a supervisor in the Systems Department, interrupt and eagerly joined in himself in the following exchange:

Stewart: That may be so, but I feel there's a kind of double standard around here. I get a dirty look every time I mention Community Activities. The area manager may say that Community Activities is of the first magnitude, but the guy who fills out your evaluation says, "To hell with it."

Robbins: In my opinion, the majority of second level and maybe some third level managers think CA work is something you do to get out of work. They don't see what we're doing and they just think we're goofing off.

Murphy: Well, some of your supervisors were at that meeting last week when everyone turned in their CA programs. And they all heard about it. The word came down. There is no question about it–Mr. Sheridan is very much interested in CA and every manager should do what he can to support it.

Stewart: What I'm saying is that I don't think the word has reached everyone. I'm not getting any flak as such, but I'm not getting much support. Most of those second levels think, "So what?" They just don't realize the importance of it.

Murphy: Let me call your supervisors and have a little chat, because the word has been given from Mr. Sheridan.

Robbins: But Mr. Sheridan doesn't rate our evaluations. And it's not what he thinks that gets me or Bill a buck.

Murphy: But let me say this. A person's participation in CA is going to be part of his or her evaluation.

Stewart: But it is the second or third level supervisor who writes that evaluation–it's their opinion as to the value of Community Relations in relation to the rest of the job that determines whether you get a raise or not.

Murphy: Let me make one comment on that. Don't forget it's the second or third level man or woman who writes the evaluation, but it will be read by someone a little further up and they are evaluated on how well they evaluate the people below them. It will be straightened out–don't worry. Of course, CA shouldn't

> mean you don't also do your regular job. It's difficult to find time for everything. But it's difficult enough for a person on a CA group to take care of his regular job plus devote some time to CA without, on top of that, having his boss give him a hard time. If the boss is not encouraging, perhaps a call from me, or our advisor, would help. This isn't the first group that this question has been raised in and we have talked to people on a higher level about individuals and on an individual basis it has been corrected.

As Robbins left he felt somewhat cheered that others had shared his worries and encouraged by what Murphy had said, but nevertheless, some of his original enthusiasm was tempered as he began to realize the truth of her final comments, "Don't forget. We've only been in operation about a year and it takes time sometimes to get the top level organization running the way it should and flowing all the way down."

Exhibit 25-1
ABBREVIATED ORGANIZATION CHART

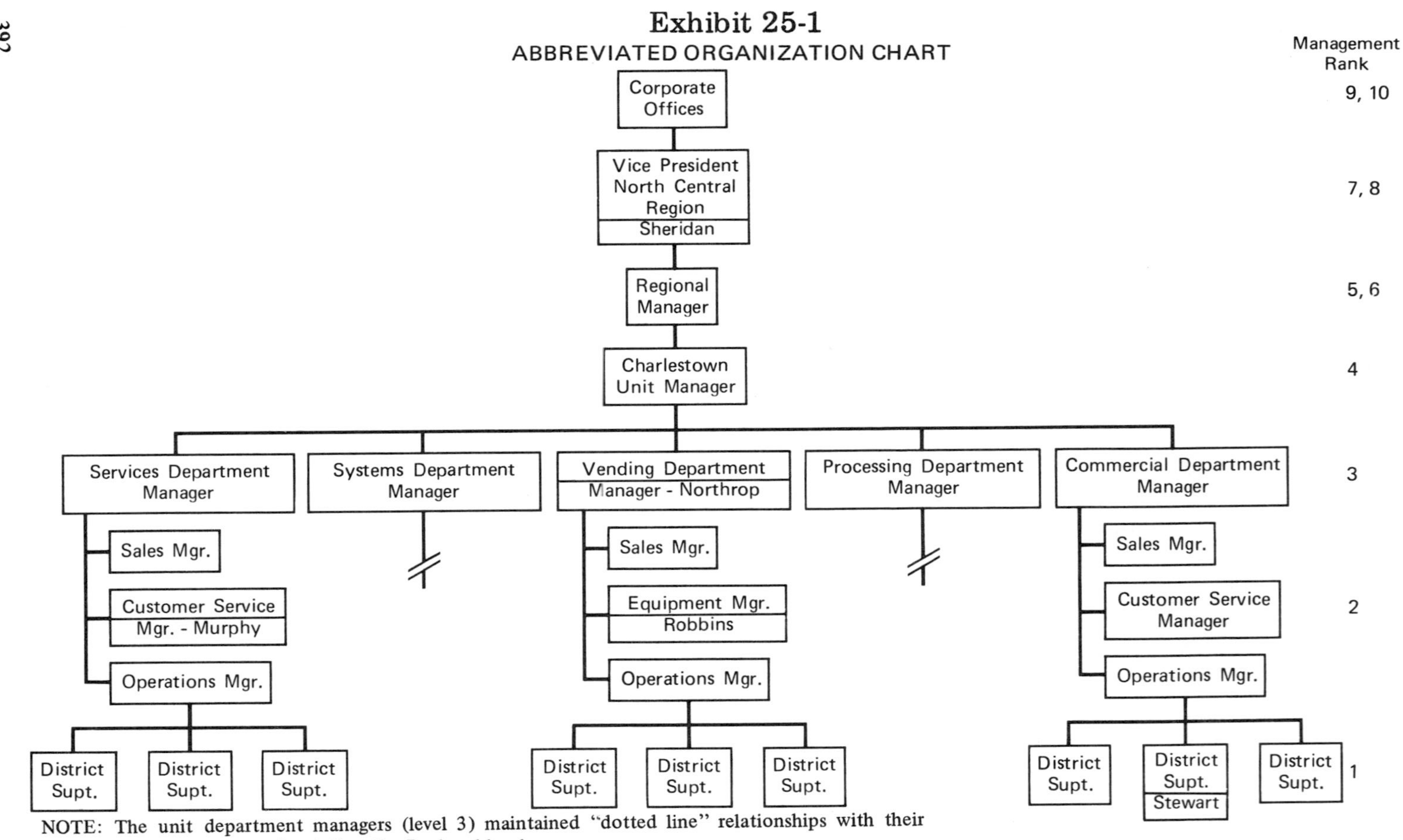

NOTE: The unit department managers (level 3) maintained "dotted line" relationships with their departmental counterparts (level 5) at the Regional level.

Exhibit 25-2

THE ROLE OF THE CA GROUP

I. At first, there was some difficulty in determining the role of the CA group in achieving the CA goal of creating a better understanding and acceptance of our service role and our needs in every community we serve. This problem was resolved when we identified the *informing role* as the primary role of the CA group. The basic elements of the informing role are as follows:

   A. Public Information
      1. Telling our communities what we're doing
         a. Local service improvement projects
         b. CA activities
      2. Stress use of local newspapers and talks
      3. Use radio and TV media as appropriate

   B. "Influentials" Interviews
      1. Identify—at all levels of the community
      2. Get information to them by personal contact

   C. Employee Information
      1. Telling our own people what we're doing
      2. Newsletter
         a. Local service improvement projects
         b. CA activities
         c. Employees who are active in the community

   D. Mobilize Employees Involved in the Community
      1. Identify through a survey
      2. Support their efforts
      3. Establish two-way communication

   E. Company-Sponsored Memberships
      1. Revitalize
      2. Support their club's community activities
      3. Establish two-way communication.

II. The secondary role of the CA group is to demonstrate that we are a participating corporate citizen by *becoming involved in appropriate community activities*. The following guidelines have been most helpful to the CA groups in carrying out this role:

   A. Assume a *supportive* role—support projects of company-sponsored members and employees active in the community.

   B. Become a *coordinator*, a clearing house—not just *doers* of all activities.

C. CA is not meant to replace the Salvation Army or welfare—a mass cash giveaway.

1. Donating used company equipment, i.e., a truck or desk is more effective and long lasting than cash.

III. The necessary ingredients to an effective CA organization.

A. Strong visible top management interest and support for the CA effort.

B. Clearly defined CA objectives based on corporate objectives.

C. A strong Headquarters CA Staff that works directly with the Area Staffs and the line organization, including the CA groups.

1. A good communication and working relationship between the two staff groups is essential to effective CA.
2. Uniform CA training given by a member of the Headquarters Staff is an important factor in a successful CA effort.

D. Adequate CA staff support.

E. Strong CA group chairmen.

F. Dedicated group members.

G. CA Reviews by Headquarters Staff.

1. A necessary follow-up step to improve the effectiveness of the CA effort.

Source: Company document prepared for north central area, "A Focus on Community Activities."

Case Twenty-Six

DESCO, Inc.

In June 1973, John Cunard, north central regional manager of the Industrial Machines Division (IMD) of DESCO, Inc., received the formal write-up of a management practices survey conducted at the Columbus sales branch the previous month by an IMD task force. The survey was part of an effort recently initiated by IMD Division Manager, Carl Wheelock, and his personnel staff to increase the attention devoted to providing equal opportunities for minority and female employees. The Columbus branch was the second of five among the 80 in the division that were to be reviewed in the start-up phase of the survey program.

The stress placed on equal employment opportunities had increased considerably in DESCO during the past year. The company had long been recognized as a leader in efforts to integrate its work force and had frequently been praised for innovative and farsighted attempts to respond to social needs. Nevertheless, the chairman and chief executive became frustrated by what he viewed as insufficient progress in minority advancement to higher management positions, a condition made vividly clear to him from time to time in discussions with young minority managers. Consequently, in 1972 he announced that he expected the performance evaluation of individual managers throughout the company to be related to their record in implementing equal employment goals, though he did not specify how this relationship ought to be determined. Numerical targets for hiring and promotion were established with precision, however, making use of a sophisticated employee information system developed over the previous four years.

Racial balance in IMD, the sales arm of the billion dollar Industrial Products Group, had improved considerably since the first minority recruitment campaign was undertaken in 1968. For instance, at year end 1972, 8.9% of the 4,600 sales workers and 4.9% of the 2,300 officers and managers were minority. On the other hand, the division had been the scene of several acrimonious employee disputes during 1972 and Wheelock was intent on improving both the numerical comparisons and the perceived level of opportunity for minorities and females in 1973. Specifically, he indicated to each of the regional managers and department heads that 15% of the performance appraisal of managers responsible for 20 or more employees was to be allocated to equal employment activities.

His guidelines were communicated in memoranda such as the one received by Cunard and shown in Exhibit 26-1.

Cunard now wondered how the management practices survey on the Columbus branch fit into the division's plans and how he should relate it to his management of the region. A partial organization chart is provided in Exhibit 26-2.

ORGANIZATION FOR EQUAL EMPLOYMENT ACTIVITIES

Although equal employment was recognized as a responsibility of operating management, personnel managers at various levels in the DESCO organization were intimately involved in specifying and directing the supporting programs. Their roles had developed in response to changing needs and conditions: Exhibit 26-3 depicts the reporting relationships as they existed in June 1973.

In 1969, a major reorganization was completed which separated the corporate offices, both physically and functionally, from the divisions. This decentralization was later acknowledged to have had an unintended negative impact on minority-related efforts in progress in the divisions at the time. The momentum of the preceding two years was lost under the pressure of a newly instituted profit planning system and without the day-to-day involvement of the chairman and president in operating affairs. When this lapse was recognized in 1970, a new Corporate Vice President of Personnel, Paul Burnham, was appointed and instructed to place particular emphasis on the implementation of the corporate policy on equal employment. Burnham formed the Human Resources Department in 1971, headed by Jim Bradley,[1] with the express intent that it be the vehicle for encouraging, assisting, and monitoring division activities in this area. Bradley maintained close surveillance of minority and female hiring and promotion figures throughout the company and served as a troubleshooter on specific issues as they arose and were deemed of sufficient importance to warrant corporate participation.

At least one minority relations specialist was included in each division personnel department. In the case of IMD, the position was held by Hank Gibson, who joined the company in April 1972 and reported to the Manager of Manpower Resources, Cliff Wrigley. Gibson's responsibilities included policing the division's affirmative action programs, assisting with employee grievances, and coordinating the assembly of minority and female hiring and promotion targets. Support on technical matters was also available from the personnel research section, directed by Fritz Cole. Most of Cole's time was devoted to performance testing, sales force motivation and compensation, employee attitude surveys, and the like for the 20,000 employees in IMD. However, he had been intimately involved with the company's early initiatives in minority hiring and continued to develop programs in this area, one of them being the management practices survey.

A minority relations specialist had also been assigned to each of the regional office personnel staffs in IMD in late 1971. In the north central region the first incumbent had

---

[1] Bradley was formerly a personnel manager in the western region of IMD.

been promoted to human resources manager of a small division in early 1973 and his place taken by Walter Jennings. At about the same time an assistant was added to provide full-time support in minority hiring for the region's sixteen sales branches. Jennings' time was then available for employee and management counseling, the sorting out of grievances, and work on the various budgets, plans, and reporting requirements prescribed by government agencies as well as his own organization.

SYSTEMS DEVELOPMENT

There were three major ingredients in the DESCO information systems network supporting equal employment activities. The first was the Employee Resources Program (ERP), developed initially in 1970 on a pilot basis and gradually extended throughout the organization. ERP was designed to highlight career needs and advancement opportunities for minority exempt employees. Each employee in this category was covered by the program which monitored individual career paths and aided in matching candidates with job openings on a company-wide basis.

A second ingredient was the "high potential job" concept introduced by Bradley shortly after he bacame Corporate Human Resources Manager. His proposal included the following descriptions:

> If our future plans call for any significant assimilation of minorities into higher level positions, we must take positive and affirmative action to place minorities into positions that normally lead to promotion to those higher level positions. Each major organization has one or more "high potential jobs" which could best be defined in the following manner:
>
> > A high potential job is a job classification in a given department that provides the developmental experience, exposure, and test which, if successfully completed, eventually leads to promotion to a confidential payroll job in a line capacity.
>
> Most high potential jobs have these common characteristics:
>
> - Supervisory responsibility for four or more subordinates.
> - More than 15 of these positions within a given department.
> - Easily lends itself to measurement and evaluation.
> - Usually reports to a confidential payroll position.
> - Has a salary dollar mid-point of approximately $1,300 to $1,600 per month.
>
> The high potential jobs are easily identifiable, for instance, in the field organization of IMD. Promotional avenues "open up" from the zone sales manager (ZSM) and customer service manager (CSM) positions. In fact, this experience could be considered mandatory if an individual wishes to progress within the field organization career path ladder.

Bradley's survey of minority representation in 1970 revealed that less than one per cent of the high potential jobs were held by minorities, a proportion considerably less than their numbers among exempt employees as a whole. Consequently, his recommendation, which was immediately accepted by Burnham, was to place particular emphasis on increasing the minority participation in these positions.

The final ingredient was a comprehensive, computerized affirmative action planning system which was directly tied into the manpower forecast accompanying the annual business plan. For each major job category, the system indicated the number of minorities and females among those currently employed. It also included the openings expected for the coming year, how they were to be filled, e.g., by internal transfer or outside hire, and the resultant force levels at year end. In each instance, the number of minorities and females to be included were specified. The job breakdowns were more detailed than those required in the EEOC reports and highlighted the high performance jobs. The end product was two columns showing the "net additions" planned for minorities and females in each category. A plan was developed for each division and for major components within the division; for example, the north central region plan for 1973 is shown in Exhibit 26-4.

THE PLANNING PROCESS

The affirmative action planning format described above was implemented on a crash basis during a full-scale revision of the 1972 targets. The procedure utilized up to that time called for a determination of targets for hiring and end-of-year work force breakdowns by division personnel departments with the concurrence of line management. The chairman's insistence on more rapid progress on equal employment in early 1972 caused the original plans for that year to be scrapped and the new format, together with significantly higher performance goals, to be adopted under the supervision of the corporate Human Resources Department.

The revised plans were shaped by the Human Resources Department in the part through consultation with a newly established Minority Awareness Council (MAC) conposed of a dozen black emplouees selected by the company to provide feedback to top management on minority affairs. MAC reviewed the data submitted by the divisions and suggested more aggressive targets as well as additional support programs. For the most part, complaints from division management that performance expectations had been changed "in midstream" were put aside by corporate officers. However, on a one-time basis, the Chairman approved a supplemental budget to fund new programs during the remainder of the year without penalty to the division's financial plan.

In the fall of 1972, plans for the following year were assembled in the divisions. Performance expectations were negotiated between the managers of sub-units and the division staff so that by the time the completed documents were reviewed by Human Resources and MAC a considerable amount of discussion about the reasonableness of the commitments had already taken place. Revisions were comparatively modest and took place against the backdrop of a successful effort in meeting the 1972 plan; net additions were 154 and 123% of the targets for overall minority employment and high performance job categories respectively. For the total company, minority representation jumped from 10.7% to 13.4% during the year. Nevertheless, the pace for 1973 was unrelenting; targeted net additions were 25% higher than the actual 1972 achievement.

MANAGEMENT PRACTICES SURVEY

The management practices survey was initially proposed by Fritz Cole, Manager of Personnel Research in IMD, in January 1972. He commented that, "We have to avoid being sucked into the simplistic assumption that minorities are intent only on the numbers—that's only a part of their concern." Perhaps more basic to minority employees, in his judgment, was the perception that performance evaluations, promotions, and training opportunities were equitably administered. From earlier pilot work on salesman selection in several branches, Cole had observed bias to exist in these areas and regional management could not assure him that his findings were atypical. At the same time, Cole was aware that broader issues might also be at stake:

> Much of what we're seeing is a symptom of deep-seated weaknesses in management practices. Our minorities are our best early warning antennae; they are fantastic for sensing when something is off base. Sometimes they reach the wrong conclusion, however, and ascribe it to discrimination, when really the personnel system is just plain dumb and everyone is being hurt.

Cole's proposal called for the appointment of a task force to audit employee practices in the IMD field units. He summarized the objectives of the task force in the following terms:

> The overall objective of the task force would be to audit and better understand management practices with respect to minorities and to develop new and better ways of managing them. This would include, but not be limited to, ways in which regional, branch, and local management make assignments, coach and counsel on a day-to-day basis, and evaluate the performance of minorities. Extensive "third party" analyses and objective methods will be necessary in areas such as assessment of the difficulty level of a minority salesman's territory, the workload of a minority service rep, the work assignments of minority clericals. This in-depth review of management practices would be similar to that conducted recently in New York[2] but would be expanded to major metropolitan areas across the United States in order to prevent rather than respond to future discrimination allegations. Furthermore, it would benchmark such practices against those used with white employees as well as practices in other companies. Considerable emphasis would be placed on supportive actions such as sharing of information with local management and feeding back better ways of managing minorities.

Although receiving immediate support from Bradley, the proposal languished in the division because of budgetary constraints. However, with the chairman's announcement of the supplemental allotments for minority relations activities in June of 1972 and on

---

[2] An employee charge of discrimination in New York had drawn corporate-wide attention in January 1972. In the course of investigating the charges, a joint corporate-region study had been undertaken by Bradley and Wayne Smithers, Vice President of Customer Services in IMD.

the heels of a second discrimination controversy in another IMD field unit (this time in the North Central Region), Wheelock authorized the immediate implementation of the management practices survey program. He agreed with Cole that the task force should be led by a line manager, "someone we can't afford to spare." Because of his previous experience in the investigation of the dispute in New York, Wayne Smithers, IMD Vice President of Customer Services, was persuaded to accept the assignment as an added responsibility. Other members of the team included Cole, Gibson and two representatives from the region office responsible for the unit being reviewed.

The surveys were to be conducted in two phases. The first was a statistical analysis to be completed prior to the field visit. Each minority and female employee in the sales and customer service groups was to be matched with a male Caucasian who had been hired at approximately the same time and had a roughly equivalent amount of prior relevant experience. The subsequent job, salary, and evaluation records of these matched pairs were then scrutinized for indications of systematic bias.

The second phase was to be a day and a half visit to the site by the task force. On the first day, the statistical findings were to be reviewed with branch management and then interviews conducted with a carefully selected cross section of minority, female, and white male employees. That evening, the task force was to analyze its findings and draw up an action program to be discussed with branch management the following morning. The results of the entire survey were then to be placed in a report and circulated to division and regional managers.

Smithers reflected on the sensitive nature of his assignment:

> I walk a thin line. If the survey is seen as punitive, we'll get a lot of scurrying around. But we're not in a punitive role though it's tough to avoid. We gather lots of bits and pieces of data and the branch doesn't know how the results will turn out. It depends on what you want to do–if the intent is to fire somebody, then you will never get good data. We don't get direct action. We make recommendations but have no post completion audits. Follow-up is left to Wheelock; he can take whatever action he thinks is appropriate.

The first management practices survey was conducted in December, 1972, in the Boston branch, one regarded as having a good record in minority relations. A supposedly trouble-free branch was selected to test the adequacy of the survey technique and remove some of the mystery from the process. The findings tended to confirm both the appropriateness of the design and the performance of the branch.

The Columbus branch was the second unit to be audited, in this instance, without firm expectations as to the outcome. An indication of the statistical survey is contained in Exhibit 26-5, an organization chart for the branch in Exhibit 26-6, and a copy of the summary findings and action plan in Exhibit 26-7.

RELATING AFFIRMATIVE ACTION TO PERFORMANCE APPRAISALS. In November 1972, Cunard called his branch managers together for a session on affirmative action. He made it clear that he expected results for the coming year to meet plans and that to emphasize the importance of efforts in this area, 15% of management performance reviews throughout the region were to be allocated to affirmative action.

This percentage was formerly reserved for "individual targets" in both the evaluation and the semi-annual bonus calculation for IMD branch managers as shown in the table below.

BRANCH MANAGER SEMI-ANNUAL BONUS CALCULATION

	Weight		*Rating**	*Weighted Rating*
Revenue budget	.55	X	_____	_____
Expense budget	.20	X	_____	_____
Individual target(s)	.15	X	_____	_____
Credit & collection	.10	X	_____	_____

**Rating*

Exceptional	6	Adequate	3
Consistently exceeds	5	Meets min. req'ts	2
Reasonable, normal	4	Failed	1

BONUS PER CENT GUIDE CHART

Score	1.0	1.1-2.4	2.5-3.4	3.5-4.4	4.5-5.4	5.5+
Bonus% Range	0%	15-17%	18-22%	23-29%	30-35%	36-40%

At the same time Cunard announced an expansion in the responsibilities of the minority relations manager and told his staff that "I am immediately delegating authority to Walter Jennings to speak for me throughout the region with respect to minority relations programs." Another person was added to the staff to specialize in minority recruitment, a step Cunard hoped would permit Jennings to concentrate on advancement, counseling, training, and trouble shooting.

As the table above suggests, the sales targets were of more than passing interest to management. In view of the growth of the Industrial Products Group (averaging 12% over the previous decade), promotion rates had been rapid for those on a "fast track." By the same token, volume targets were always tight, competition among branches keen, and turnover at the branch manager level relatively high. Thus, Cunard's message created apprehension over the way it would affect appraisals and the burden it would add to already heavy work loads. He commented on some of these concerns:

> Very few of our ZSM's (zone sales managers) are minority right now. It's hard to get the branch managers to take the risk and time to change that. The expectation is that he will be willing to put in a black ZSM before he's really sure that the candidate is ready for the job. Then, if I say to the branch manager, "You're in deep trouble if you don't make 100% of revenue plan," he says, "What's going to happen to me if that ZSM doesn't work out?" There is a high turnover among ZSM's—it's a tough job and the failure rate is high. Performance is expected instantly. In six months if a ZSM is at 50% of plan he has trouble not only with his manager but with me. At the same time the branch manager has to depend on him to make plan.

The management practices survey of the Columbus branch provided Cunard with a good deal of additional data about the administration of the personnel function and specifically the equal employment area. He was, however, neither certain about the emphasis that would be given to it by the division manager nor about the weight it should carry in the region. Nonetheless, he was aware that the survey had caused some anxiety at the branch which in some fashion had to be addressed.

Exhibit 26-1

TO: John Cunard Date: February 8, 1973

FROM: Carl Wheelock

SUBJECT: MINORITY/FEMALE EMPLOYEE REPRESENTATION
– 1972 Performance
– 1973 Plans

John, after reviewing our 1972 performance, I am pleased with the results achieved by the North Central Region. I am aware that the female Customer Representative targets were not met. However, in reviewing your total performance, it was a job well done and you and your management are to be congratulated. I trust that your strong performance established during 1972 will continue throughout 1973.

Our plans for increasing minority/female employee representation during 1973 are as equally challenging as they were in 1972. A synopsis of our plan is as follows:

- As mentioned in my memo of January 16, 1973, one of our major objectives is to significantly improve minority representation within our management classification. This objective is to be achieved primarily through promotion from within. In order to properly emphasize the importance of this challenge, the Officials/Managers net add target will have a weighting of 30%. The other five categories will each have a weighting of 14%.
- Although we are presently emphasizing minority representation within our management ranks, it is important to recognize our efforts to improve female representation especially within the Professional, Sales, and Technical categories. From 1972 to 1973, the ratio of female to minority net adds has changed from 1.5:8.5 to 3.0:7.0.
- For those managers who are responsible for twenty or more employees, 15% of their Performance Appraisal or bonus recommendation will be for minority/ female employee activities.

I have attached, for your information and guidance, your final results for 1972 as well as your 1973 objectives which were originally submitted in December, 1972, and which have subsequently been approved. I expect your full support in the achievement of these objectives.

CRW/lmh
Attachment/

c: P. McCarthy
H. Gibson

Exhibit 26-2

PARTIAL ORGANIZATION CHART

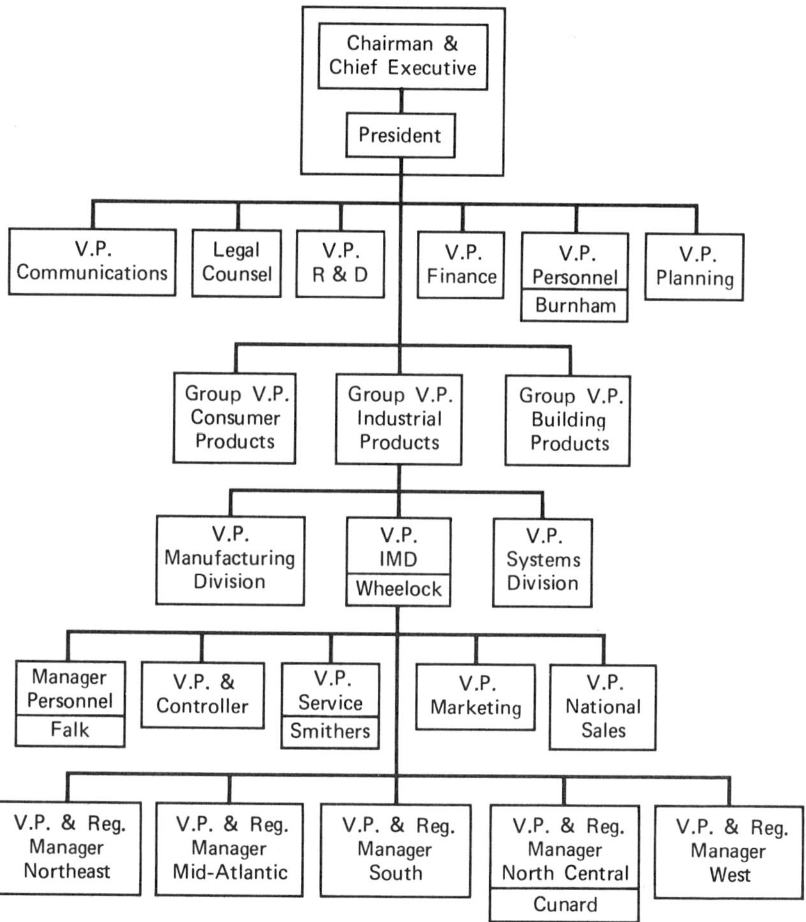

Exhibit 26-3

PERSONNEL FUNCTION REPORTING RELATIONSHIPS FOR EQUAL EMPLOYMENT SPECIALISTS

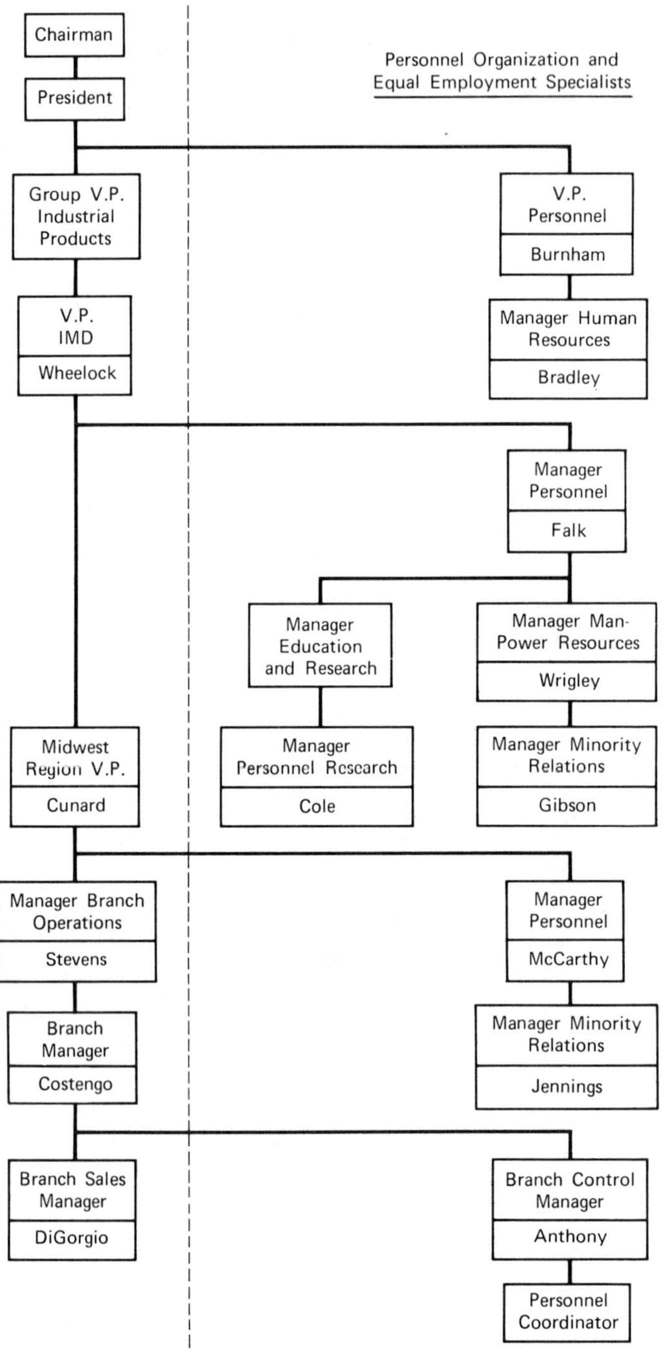

Exhibit 26-4

IMD AFFIRMATIVE ACTION PLAN—WORKFORCE ANALYSIS SHEET—COMPOSITE SUMMARY

Organizational Unit North Central Region

JOB CATEGORY	Workforce Levels 12/31/72					1973 Openings					1973 Promotions/ Transfers-In					1973 Outside Hires					Workforce Levels 12/31/73					MIN NET ADDS	FEM. NET ADDS
	Total	Minority #	Minority %	Female #	Female %	Expand	Turnover Min.	Turnover Fem.	Turnover Oth.	Total	Total	Minority #	Minority %	Female #	Female %	Total	Minority #	Minority %	Female #	Female %	Total	Minority #	Minority %	Female #	Female %		
OFFICIALS/MGRS.																											
Stock Opt Job																											
Branch Mgr.	13	-	-	-	-	-	-	-	1	1	1	-	-	-	-	-	-	-	-	-	13	-	-	-	-	-	-
Other SOJ's*	11	1	9.1	-	-	-	-	-	1	1	1	-	-	-	-	-	-	-	-	-	11	1	9.1	-	-	-	-
SUB TOTAL	24	1	4.2	-	-	-	-	-	2	2	2	-	-	-	-	-	-	-	-	-	24	1	4.2	-	-	-	-
High Pot. Jobs																											
ZSM[xx]	61	2	3.3	-	-	9	-	-	12	21	20	3	15.0	-	-	1	-	-	-	-	70	5	7.1	-	-	3	-
CSM[#]	98	6	6.1	1	1.0	10	1	-	7	18	18	5	27.8	-	-	-	-	-	-	-	108	10	9.3	1	0.9	4	-
Other HPJ's[##]	108	6	5.6	3	2.8	8	-	-	17	25	21	4	19.0	2	9.5	4	2	50.0	-	-	116	12	10.3	5	4.3	6	2
SUB TOTAL	267	14	5.2	4	1.5	27	1	-	36	64	59	12	20.3	2	3.4	5	2	40.0	-	-	294	27	9.2	6	2.0	13	2
Other Mgrs.	34	1	3.0	1	3.0	1	-	-	2	3	1	-	-	-	-	2	1	50.0	-	-	35	2	5.7	2	5.7	1	1
CATEGORY TOTAL	325	16	4.9	5	1.5	28	1	-	40	69	62	12	19.4	2	3.3	7	3	42.9	-	-	353	30	8.5	8	2.3	14	3
PROFESSIONALS																											
High Pot. Jobs	40	1	2.5	1	50.0	-	-	-	4	4	-	-	-	-	-	4	3	75.0	-	-	40	4	10.0	1	2.5	3	-
Other Profs.	2	1	50.0	-	-	-	-	-	-	-	-	-	-	-	-	-	-	-	-	-	2	1	50.0	-	-	-	-
CATEGORY TOTAL	42	2	2.9	1	2.4	-	-	-	4	4	-	-	-	-	-	4	3	75.0	-	-	42	5	11.9	1	2.4	3	-
SALES WORKERS																											
Jr. Reps	93	3	3.2	-	-	11	-	-	7	18	18	2	11.1	-	-	-	-	-	-	-	104	5	4.8	-	-	2	-
Sales Reps	692	75	10.8	26	3.8	80	15	3	111	209	20	3	15.0	2	10.0	189	39	20.6	19	10.1	772	102	13.2	44	5.7	27	18
Consultants	30	1	3.3	-	-	3	-	-	4	7	7	-	-	-	-	-	-	-	-	-	33	1	3.0	-	-	-	-
CATEGORY TOTAL	815	79	9.7	26	3.2	94	15	3	122	234	45	5	11.1	2	4.4	189	39	20.6	19	10.1	909	108	11.9	44	4.8	59	18

*Stock option jobs.

[xx]Zone sales manager.

Exhibit 26-4 (continued)

Job Category	Workforce Levels 12/31/72					1973 Openings					1973 Promotions/ Transfers-In					1973 Outside Hires					Workforce Levels 12/31/73					MIN. NET ADDS	FEM. NET ADDS
	Total	Minority #	Minority %	Female #	Female %	Expand	Turnover Min.	Turnover Fem.	Turnover Oth.	Total	Total	Minority #	Minority %	Female #	Female %	Total	Minority #	Minority %	Female #	Female %	Total	Minority #	Minority %	Female #	Female %		
TECHNICIANS																											
Cust.Rep. 4	243	10	4.1	-	-	20	-	-	4	24	24	4	16.7	-	-	-	-	-	-	-	263	14	5.3	-	-	4	-
C.R. 1,2,3	1042	137	13.1	5	0.5	76	15	-	90	181	-	-	-	-	-	181	41	22.7	7	3.9	1118	162	14.5	12	1.1	25	7
Other Cust.	43	1	2.3	-	-	4	-	-	4	8	6	-	-	-	-	2	-	-	-	-	47	1	2.1	-	-	-	-
SUB TOTAL	1328	148	11.1	5	0.4	100	15	-	98	213	30	4	13.3	-	-	183	41	22.4	7	3.8	1428	177	12.4	12	0.8	29	7
High Pot. Jobs																											
Cust. Reps.	68	8	11.8	68	100.0	-	1	6	-	7	2	1	50.0	2	100.0	5	3	60.0	5	100.0	68	11	16.2	68	100.0	3	-
CATEGORY TOTAL	1396	156	11.2	73	5.6	100	16	6	98	220	32	5	15.6	2	6.3	188	44	23.4	12	6.4	1496	188	12.6	80	5.3	32	7
OFFICE & CLER																											
Grades 6 & 7	122	11	9.0	111	91.0	7	1	8	-	16	8	2	25.0	7	87.5	8	3	2.7	6	66.7	129	15	11.6	118	91.5	4	7
Other Clers	439	96	21.9	426	97.0	23	14	102	-	139	-	-	-	-	-	139	30	21.6	67	56.3	462	112	24.4	446	96.5	16	20
CATEGORY TOTAL	561	107	19.1	537	95.7	30	15	110	-	155	8	2	25.0	7	87.5	147	33	22.4	73	57.0	591	127	21.5	564	95.4	20	27
UNIT TOTAL	3139	360	11.5	542	20.5	252	47	119	264	682	147	24	16.3	13	8.8	535	122	22.8	104	19.4	3391	458	13.5	697	20.6	98	55

Exhibit 26-5

MANAGEMENT PRACTICES SURVEY–COLUMBUS

The Columbus branch employs 232 people of which 29 (12.5%) are minorities and 203 (87.5%) are non-minorities. There are 194 (83.6%) males and 38 (16.4%) females in this branch. The distribution of minority and non-minority employees by occupational group and sex is given below.

		Males		*Females*		*Total*	
Occupational Group		*# in Occup.*	*% in Occup.*	*# in Occup.*	*% in Occup.*	*# in Occup.*	*% in Occup.*
Admin.; Mgrs.; Suprv.	Minority	0	0	0	0	0	0
	Non-Minority	18	100.0	0	0	18	100.0
Sales	Minority	7	10.4	0	0	7	10.4
	Non-Minority	56	83.6	4	6.0	60	89.6
Service Reps.	Minority	15	13.3	0	0	15	13.3
	Non-Minority	97	85.8	1	0.9	98	86.7
Customer Reps.	Minority	0	0	1	20.0	1	20.0
	Non-Minority	0	0	4	80.0	4	80.0
Service/Clerical	Minority	0	0	6	20.7	6	20.7
	Non-Minority	1	3.4	22	75.9	23	79.3
Total: All Occupations	Minority	22	9.5	7	3.0	29	12.5
	Non-Minority	172	74.1	31	13.4	203	87.5

IMD/Personnel Research & Planning
4-29-73

Sales

The Columbus branch has 67 persons employed in sales. Of these, 56 (83.6%) are male Caucasians, 4 (6.0%) are female Caucasians, and 7 (10.4%) are Negro males.

Each minority and female was matched to a male Caucasian who was hired at approximately the same time and had about the same amount of experience in an equivalent sales position. The average or typical minority and matched non-minority salesman is described below.

	A Non-Minority Median	*B Minority Median*	*A-B Median Diff.*
Income			
1. Starting Monthly Salary	750	750	0
2. Current Monthly Salary	614	825	-211
3. Per Cent Salary Increase	NA	NA	NA

	A *Non-Minority Median*	*B* *Minority Median*	*A-B* *Median Diff.*
4. Average Monthly Bonus/Commissions	112	128	- 16
5. Estimated Monthly Income	979	953	+ 26
6. Installation Commission YTD	250	385	-135
7. Supply Commission YTD	0	0	0
8. Total Commission YTD	301	385	- 84
9. Net Add Achievement Bonus YTD	0	0	0
10. Efficiency Bonus YTD	0	0	0
11. Total Bonus YTD	0	0	0
Territory (# Machines) by Product Category			
1. Type # 1	96	102	- 6
2. Type # 2	22	15	+ 7
3. Accessories	8	9	- 1
4. Systems Products	0	0	0
5. Total Machines	157	128	+ 29
DESCO History			
1. Company Tenure (Months)	7	7	0
2. Job Tenure (Months)	7	7	0
3. Last Performance Rating	3	3	0
4. ERP*–Performance	NA	3	NA
5. ERP*–Promotability	NA	3	NA
6. ERP*–Long Range Potential	NA	3	NA
7. Training Programs	2	2	0
8. Average Training Grade	4	4	0
9. Months Before Assigned First Territory	**	6	NA
10. Months in Present Territory	**	1	NA
Personal Background Factors			
1. Age (Years)	26	24	- 2
2. Education: Highest Level Achieved	BA	BA	0
3. Education: Highest Level When Hired	BA	BA	0
4. Previous Full Time Experience (Months)	12	17	- 5
5. Previous Full Time Related Experience (Months)	12	3	+ 9

*Employee Resources Program

IMD/Personnel Research & Planning
4-29-73

Exhibit 26-5 (continued)

Columbus
Partial Summary of Salesforce Statistics

Name	EEO CODE (1)	SEX (2)	AGE	EDUCATION HIGHEST LEVEL ACHIEVED	EDUCATION HIGHEST LEVEL WHEN HIRED	JOB TITLE (ZSR = ZONE SALES REP)	DATE HIRED	MONTHS PREVIOUS EXPERIENCE	MONTHS RELATED EXPERIENCE	COMPANY TENURE (MO.)	JOB TENURE (MO.)	STARTING MONTHLY SALARY	CURRENT MONTHLY SALARY	MOST RECENT PERFORM-ANCE RATING (3)	PER CENT SALARY INCREASE AFTER RATING	ERP PERFORMANCE (3)	ERP PROMOTABILITY (4)	ERP LONG RANGE POTENTIAL (5)	NUMBER TRAINING PROGRAMS ATTENDED	AVERAGE TRAINING GRADE (6)	DATE ASSIGNED FIRST TERRITORY	MONTHS ELAPSED BEFORE ASSIGNED FIRST TERRITORY	DATE ASSIGNED PRESENT TERRITORY	MONTHS IN PRESENT TERRITORY
Gordley, A.G.	5	2	22	BA	BA	ASR	9/72	0	0	7	7	750	825	4	NA	4	5	4	2	NA	NA	NA	NA	NA
Shaeffer, R.P.	5	1	26	BA	BA	Sales Rep.	9/72	6	6	6	6	750	580	3	NA	NA	NA	NA	2	NA	4/73	6	4/73	1
Barfield, D.W.	5	2	24	HS	HS	Sales Rep.	2/68	24	0	62	2	750	580	NA	NA	NA	1	1	2	5	1/73	3	1/73	3
Gorian, C.P.	5	1	39	HS	HS	Sr.Sls.Rep.	8/68	148	148	57	17	450	854	4	7.6	4	4	4	3	NA	8/68	1	12/71	16
Snyder, M.E.	1	1	22	BA	BA	ASR	12/72	4	0	3	3	750	825	NA	NA	3	4	1	2	4	NA	NA	NA	NA
Dupre, S.J.	5	1	25	BA	BA	ASR	12/72	8	8	3	3	800	825	NA	NA	NA	NA	NA	2	3	NA	NA	NA	NA
Ladd, E.H.	1	1	23	BA	BA	ASR	8/72	8	8	7	7	750	825	1	NA	1	2	2	2	4	NA	NA	NA	NA
Testa, R.X.	5	1	31	HS	HS	Sales Rep.	8/72	96	96	7	7	850	NA	3	NA	NA	NA	NA	2	4	4/73	7	4/73	1
Renfro, A.B.	1	1	26	BA	BA	Sales Rep.	10/71	26	18	17	5	750	589	4	NA	3	4	4	3	3	10/72	12	10/72	6

(1) EEO Code: 1 = Negro
5 = Caucasian

(2) Sex: 1 = Male
2 = Female

(3) Performance rating, ERP Performance
1 = Unsatisfactory
2 = Meets minimum performance
3 = Normal, reasonable & expected performance
4 = Consistently exceeds expected performance
5 = Exceptional performance

(4) ERP Promotability
1 = Too soon to appraise
2 = Not promotable within 24 months
3 = Promotable within 24 months after further development
4 = Promotable within 12 months after further development
5 = Immediately promotable

(5) ERP Long Range Potential
1 = Too soon to appraise
2 = No or limited potential
3 = Average potential
4 = Above average
5 = Exceptional potential

(6) Average Training Grade
1 = Poor
2 = Below average
3 = Average
4 = Above average
5 = Superior

Interview Questions–Management Practices Survey

The following general questions are designed to start and sustain a general discussion in the broad area of management practices.

INTRODUCTION: Hi, I'm ____________________ of IMD Headquarters. We're here today in Columbus as part of a Task Force from Headquarters and Region looking at the broad area of management practices. This is the second branch being visited in an effort to obtain an overview of areas in which IMD can improve in its management practices. As part of that effort, we're interviewing approximately 5% of the *Columbus* employees and you're a part of that sample.

As indicated, we're concerned with improving management practices and would appreciate your frank indication of opportunities for improvement. A report summarizing opinions, but of course not identifying names, will be prepared for review of the various management levels. Since we only have an hour for our conversation, I'm sure you'll want to make best use of the time.

For starters, let me ask:

1. How are things going?
2. To what extent is the job what you expected it to be?
3. What do you see as good about DESCO and should be sustained?
4. What do you feel needs improvement?
5. What is in most *urgent* need of improvement?
6. What turns you *on* about DESCO? Off?
7. How do you think others here in the branch feel?
8. If you had to isolate the *three most important* areas for improvement, what would they be?

IMD/Personnel Research and Planning
4/29/73

Exhibit 26-6

ORGANIZATION CHART—COLUMBUS BRANCH

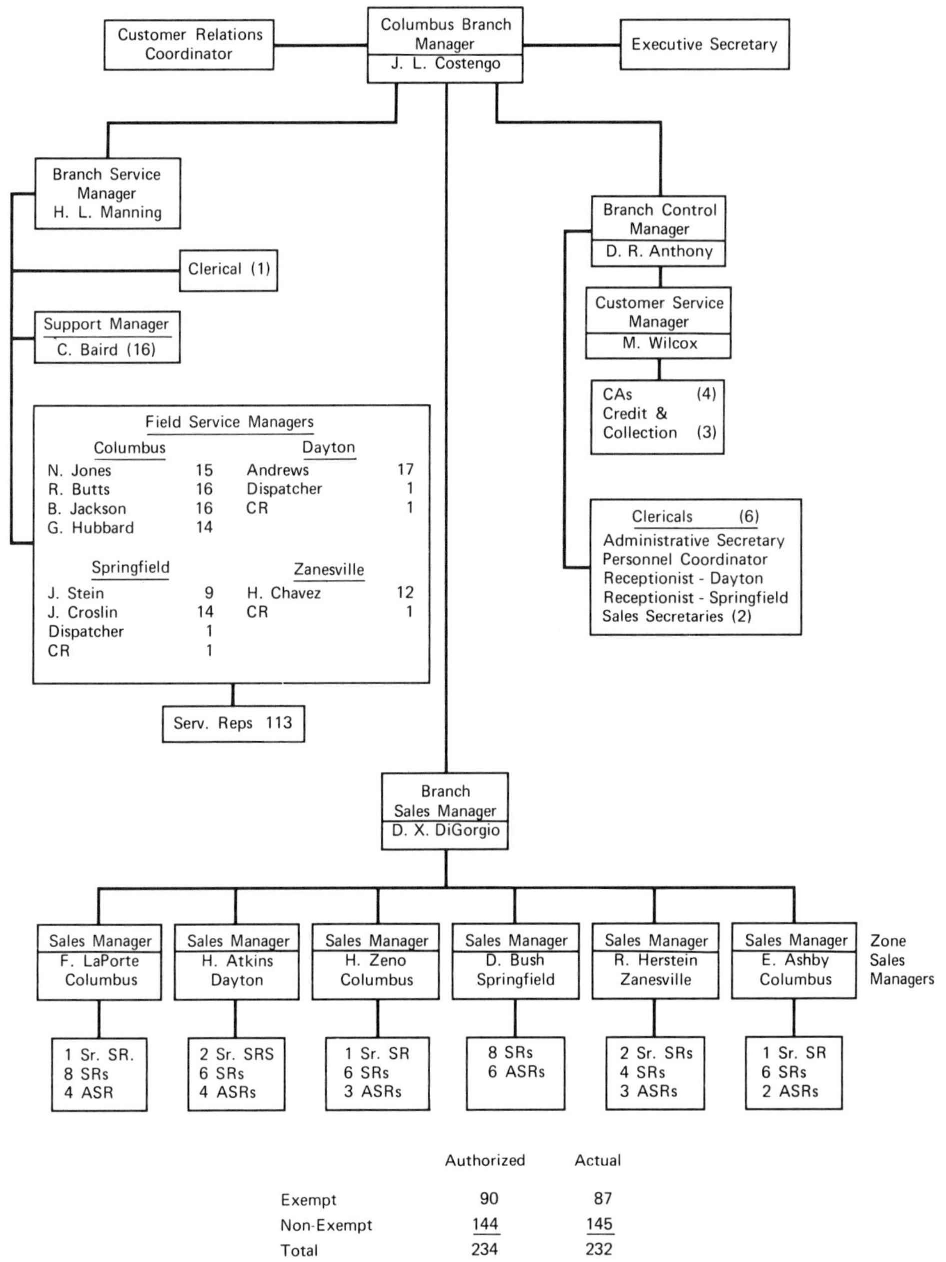

	Authorized	Actual
Exempt	90	87
Non-Exempt	144	145
Total	234	232

Total Branch Revenue - $22,463,000

Exhibit 26-7

TO: Distribution DATE: June 20, 1973

FROM: Smithers

SUBJECT: Management Practices Survey: Columbus Branch Findings

On May 10 and 11, 1973 the second of five scheduled Management Practices Surveys was conducted at the Columbus Branch. The purpose of this survey is to review IMD's general management practices, with specific emphasis on the management of minority and female employees.

As was the case in the previous survey conducted at the Boston Branch, the Task Force spent a day and a half at the Branch completing the following activities:

- 5/10/73 a.m.– Reviewed pertinent data on matched employees with Branch management personnel.
- 5/10/73 p.m.– Interviewed 15 randomly selected employees from Administration, Sales, and Service.
- 5/11/73 a.m.– Reviewed and discussed survey results with Branch management and developed an action plan.

This report will highlight the findings of the Task Force and the resultant corrective actions to be implemented by the Branch, Region, or Division Headquarters.

DATA REVIEW

In reviewing the data that was compiled on the employees in the Columbus Branch, two areas were particularly outstanding:

- Performance Ratings and corresponding salary increases were not always logically related, i.e., 3 rating/6.6% increase; 3 rating/3.0% increase; 4 rating/4.0% increase; 4 rating/9.0% increase.
- Workload point distribution for minority Customer Service Reps was appreciably higher than for non-minority Customer Service Reps.

INTERVIEW FINDINGS

Results of the Task Force's interviews are reported below and include positive achievements as well as problems perceived in the way people are managed throughout the recruitment, training and development, job treatment, promotion, and termination process. General problems are also highlighted.

Positive Perceptions

1. Sales Reps have a strong respect for management.
2. Generally, an openness and willingness to talk about issues exists.

3. Employees are high on DESCO, feel it is a good company.
4. Employees are very strong on feeling of freedom to do job–management delegates responsibility.
5. Customer Service Reps have great pride in their work.
6. Most employees are high on promotional opportunity.
7. Generally, there is a feeling of closeness within groups, i.e., sales teams, service teams; however, most feel there was little closeness between teams and functions.

Recruitment

1. Applicants are made to wait an inordinate amount of time in lobby, and sometimes manager will send a substitute after applicant has waited.
2. Blacks and whites feel that minority recruiting is more of a numbers game; blacks believe better blacks are not recruited due to inadequate salary and pressure to get minorities hired at the last minute.
3. Blacks go thru more interviews (5) than whites (2-3).
4. Inexperienced blacks are used to recruit other blacks. Sometimes the recruiting techniques are questioned.
5. Improper questions are put to female and black applicants:

   e.g., – black: "Can you work with whites?"

   – female. "Too emotional to withstand sales pressures?"
6. Controlling manpower allocations by head count instead of man-months or some other suitable formula puts the branch in the position of having to make rapid selection decisions. Also, the branch doesn't have the opportunity to hire in advance of attrition and its people brought on-board are hurried and rushed through a training program. The perception that leads from this practice is that DESCO is not providing adequate training and advancement programs and in the case of blacks, they perceive this as a short-fall in our commitment to adequately support them.

Training and Development

1. New Customer Service Rep should have experienced Rep with him for a sufficient period of time, rather than the "sink or swim" approach currently being employed.
2. Pre-management training lacking in all areas–(Sales, Service & Administration).
3. Customer Service Rep training insufficient due to lack of manpower available to cover territories (Manpower Pool).
4. Information on competitive equipment must be made available to salesmen by training sessions and documentation.
5. Lack of a good orientation program.

Treatment & Promotion

Standards

– Promotional judgments and career opportunities not clear.

Exhibit 26-7 (continued)

- Some managers not clear on their own and their subordinate goals and objectives.
- Lack of clear career guidance, no "black godfather" who has influence in the system.
- Uncertainty about why all blacks on ERP.

Pay

- Some blacks not clear on their range.
- Customer Service Rep appraisals not related to ratings, and written comments nearly identical for each Rep.
- Quota Club nominee rejected–possibly on race.

Assignments

- Limited opportunity for blacks to sell certain advanced equipment.
- Driving territory to whites first, save blacks for public transportation.
- Feel ZSR and new SR must "pay his dues" to get a decent territory.
- All blacks initially on same team left bad taste.

Communication

- Barriers between sales, service, and administration.
- Strongly felt need for awards banquet.
- Feeling that growth increases impersonality, e.g., 1 sales rep had 5 supervisors in 2 years.

Terminations

- When employees terminate, management goes to great lengths to cut them off from contact with remaining employees, e.g., employee picture was x'ed out on board containing team pictures.
- Terminations work hardship on remaining employees, particularly in Service area, because there are no replacements readily available to fill vacancies.

General Problems

- Backlash–white employees perceive black employees getting advantageous treatment and blacks are hired below standards.
- Inflation problem–Customer Service Reps feel salary is not keeping pace with cost of living.
- Managers feel constrained in speaking up on issues.

Exhibit 26-7 (continued)

MAJOR PROBLEM AREAS/ACTION PLANS

The items identified here and the accompanying action plans were the result of discussions centered on the forestated points between the Task Force, Region Personnel and Branch Management.

PROBLEM	*BRANCH ACTION*	*REGION ACTION*	*DIVISION ACTION*
• Applicants having to wait an inordinately long period of time for interviews.	• Management will formalize a plan to prevent further occurrences including: – Receptionist being given a time parameter for applicants waiting, following which a designated supervisor will be notified. – Interviews will be scheduled and managers will adhere to schedules.	• NONE	• NONE
• Black applicants undergo a high number of interviews as compared to white applicants.	• The number of interviews will be standardized for applicants by function.	• NONE	• NONE
• Blacks are being hired more for quantity than quality.	• Management will review hiring program with region support to develop a plan to insure effective black hiring.	• Region Minority Relations will assist branch.	• NONE
• Female applicants are being asked illegal and improper questions at interview.	• Management will hold a general meeting to review interviewing practices and techniques.	• Arrangements will be made to present & discuss film *51%* to branch management personnel.	• Guidelines will be drawn up delineating the types of questions that are/are not proper in female interviewing.

Exhibit 26-7 (continued)

PROBLEM	*BRANCH ACTION*	*REGION ACTION*	*DIVISION ACTION*
• Job orientation program in administration function is either totally inadequate or non-existent.	• The current programs in use in the sales and service areas will be reviewed to determine adaptability to administration function.	• Region Personnel will draw up a proposal requesting the establishment of a pre-management slot to be responsible for training in the administration area.	• NONE
• Current method of projecting Merit Increase Plan on sub-branch unit basis negatively impacts Performance Appraisal as insufficient budget forces incongruous Appraisal/Increase. A number of employees are unaware of salary range.	• Branch Manager will explore possibility of approaching MIP on total branch basis. • A copy of the Performance Appraisal will be given to the employee with his/her salary range typed on it.	• NONE	• NONE
• Workload point distribution higher for minority Customer Service Reps than for white Customer Service Reps.	• Service function was recently reorganized, workload points now believed to be equitably distributed. Branch Service Manager will review to verify distribution is equitable.	• NONE	• NONE
	• Branch Manager will review methods of determining Customer Service allocations with Region.	• NONE	• NONE
• Career guidance responsibility not clearly spelled-out as to what manager's role should be.	• Management will be briefed on Career Guidance responsibility as prescribed by Region.	• Region Training function will provide data to branch which clearly delineates Career Guidance responsibility.	• NONE

Exhibit 26-7 (continued)

PROBLEM	*BRANCH ACTION*	*REGION ACTION*	*DIVISION ACTION*
• Employees feel that communications between branch functions are too limited.	• Branch management has developed an action plan which is now being implemented that should address this problem.	• NONE	• NONE
• Employees who were interviewed expressed an interest in being apprised of survey results; branch management felt they would like to use survey results as additional communications vehicle.	• Employees who were interviewed will be rescheduled for feedback session in conjunction with regional personnel. • Branch Manager will reinforce need for management follow-up and awareness to communicate minority/female issues.	• Representatives from Region Personnel function will participate in survey feedback sessions.	• NONE

(signed) Wayne Smithers

Case Twenty-Seven

University of Pennsylvania (A)

It was a cold, snowy December day in Philadelphia as President Martin Meyerson was hard at work on his 1971 annual report to the Board of Trustees. He stopped to reflect on his progress during his first year and a half at the University of Pennsylvania. A number of changes had taken place in the University administration, but he was particularly concerned with the progress the University had made in the area of equal employment. When he came to the University in September of 1970, he had hoped to set policy in this area by example. He had brought with him two assistants: Donald Stewart, a black man, and a woman, Veronica von Nostitz. In January 1971, he had created an Office of Equal Opportunity to provide direction for this issue, and Meyerson felt he had made his views known on this subject in speeches and articles. Specifically, he had devoted a significant section of his report to the Trustees the previous January to affirmative action.

But the reality of the University's situation was disturbing. There were only ten fully-affiliated[1] women professors, and the majority were in the medical area. In the College there was not a single woman with a full professorship. For President Meyerson, this was a moral issue. In his judgment, the very nature of a university's purpose dictated that it have a value system that was sensitive to this kind of moral issue. More importantly, he felt that the quality of education at the University would be vastly improved if women and minorities were better represented in both faculty and administrative positions.

Yet, he pondered, "What real support do I have to effect change and what will happen if I don't try or if I am not successful?" The women's group on campus had been vocal in identifying problem areas, but otherwise there was little outside pressure, even

[1] "Fully-affiliated" is a university personnel designation identifying employees in the academic area who held tenure-accruing ranks and other personnel who qualified for the full array of university benefits.

from the government. HEW[2] officials had visited the campus in March, but there had been no word from them since then.

However, other major universities were experiencing considerable difficulty in satisfying government reviewers. The review at the University of Michigan had attracted national attention, and in November, Columbia University had been notified that its eligibility for Federal contracts was in jeopardy because it had failed to meet the legal requirements for equal employment. Since over 20% of Penn's budget came from federal contracts, Meyerson could not afford to take the potential loss of this revenue source lightly, particularly in view of the major deficits the University was experiencing. At the end of 1971 Penn had an accumulated deficit of more than $1.9 million with the prospect that this could climb to over $5 million by the end of 1972.

Although equal employment was an important personal issue for Meyerson, he recognized that the priority it should be accorded and the speed with which the University should move in this area were difficult and complicated issues.

UNIVERSITY OF PENNSYLVANIA–BACKGROUND

A member of the Ivy League, Pennsylvania ranked among the oldest and most eminent educational institutions in the country. The university traced its origin to 1740 with Benjamin Franklin as its founding father and first president of the Board of Trustees. The constitution, which he wrote in 1749, set up a "non-sectarian institution of higher learning founded and run by a board of trustees made up solely of public-spirited citizens"–a unique concept in its time.[3]

With the founding of the medical school in 1765 (the first in North America), the institution became the first "university" in the country, although the title was not officially used until 1791. Other "firsts" credited to the university are, the first comprehensive graduate program in medicine, the oldest psychological clinic, the first department of botany, the first "modern" liberal arts curriculum, the first collegiate school of business, and the first student union.[4]

In 1970 the University was located on a 247-acre campus with 103 major buildings, including two wholly owned teaching hospitals. The main campus was concentrated in the heart of an economically depressed section of West Philadelphia and had an undergraduate population of eleven thousand and a graduate enrollment of eighty-four hundred. The undergraduate College and the College for Women, the graduate programs in medicine, fine arts, law, and business (the Wharton School) were widely acknowledged to be among the finest and most selective in the United States with a student body drawn from all over the country and the world.

---

[2]HEW was the government agency assigned by the U.S. Department of Labor to monitor the Affirmative Action programs of educational institutions.

[3]Faculty and Administration Handbook, University of Pennsylvania, Philadelphia, 1969, p. 6.

[4]*Ibid.*, p. 9.

As prescribed by Franklin, the University was administered by a Board of Trustees, then composed of men of wealth and influence in the leading banking, investment, legal, and manufacturing firms of Philadelphia.[5] The operating affairs of the University were managed by the president, who was the chief executive officer, with the assistance of a Provost who served both as the chief academic officer and vice president. The academic administrators, deans of the twelve schools, and the vice president for health affairs all reported to the Provost, as did those in charge of development, business affairs, etc. The administrative functions also had some direct contact with Meyerson (see Exhibit 27-1). Certain organizational anomalies existed such as in the Wharton School, which granted both graduate and undergraduate degrees in business but also contained social science departments including economics, political science and sociology.[6] Separate schools for men and women were maintained for undergraduate liberal arts.

The University was originally chartered as a private institution, but for 12 years after the Revolutionary War, the school became the first state-aided school in the country. Although in 1791 it again became an independent, privately endowed and gift-supported University, it retained its eligibility for state support.[7] Since 1966 the size of the appropriation from the Commonwealth of Pennsylvania had risen steadily in absolute terms but declined as a percent of the total budget. In 1961 the state contribution represented 9.3% of the university's total operating budget, but by the end of 1971 this had fallen closer to 7%.

The sixties was a period of great expansion for the University, its faculty, and its physical plant. During the presidency of Gaylord Harnell (1954-1970) Penn undertook an intensive self-analysis, referred to as the *Educational Survey*, which began in 1953 and led to the Integrated Development Plan of 1962. This effort resulted in construction of 83 major building projects during the late sixties including classroom buildings, libraries, laboratories, parking garages, athletic facilities, and dormitories. During this period the university was transformed from a largely regional institution to a national university, and the size of the faculty and student body grew approximately 6% a year. In addition, the university became a major research center with federal funds increasing elevenfold from $3,459,000 in 1955 to $41,889,013 in 1970, the latter figure representing approximately 20% of the total budget.[8]

This period of growth was not without its problems. Ties between the University and the local community became strained, and local government and community groups demanded the University support an involvement in responding to the growing problems of urban blight in areas adjacent to the campus. Numerous programs were developed for aiding the community, such as the West Philadelphia Corporation and the University City

---

[5] The trustees were a self-perpetuating body accountable only to themselves. Members were selected by vote of the trustees with the exception of the alumni trustees who are elected by the alumni.

[6] In 1974 the social science departments were moved to the faculty of Arts and Sciences.

[7] *Ibid.*, p. 7.

[8] Progress Report: Observations on Some Current Issues Before the University of Pennsylvania to the Trustees from President Martin Meyerson, covered in three presentations: Long Range Planning Committee, January 14, 1971; Trustees Lunch, January 15, 1971; Founder's Day, January 16, 1971, p. 1.

Science Center. Such programs helped the University avoid major clashes with community groups that other urban-centered academic institutions experienced.

However, 1970 was a critical year, as the University faced grave fiscal problems. There were few options left. Soaring costs and inflation, coupled with no growth in the student body, created a deficit of approximately $2,300,000 in fiscal 1970 and $1,200,000 in 1971. The university's operating reserve of $1,600,000 was exhausted to reduce the 1970 deficit to $700,000. Student fees and tuition were among the highest in the country, alumni giving was increasing but not expected to grow rapidly enough to cover the deficit, and state appropriations were about as high as they could go. It was evident to the Trustees and the administration that stringent cost-cutting measures would be necessary.

PRESIDENT MEYERSON

Martin Meyerson came to Penn in the fall of 1970 at the age of 47 with a national reputation as an innovative and skilled educational administrator. Previously, Meyerson had been president of the Buffalo campus at the State University of New York, and when it was announced that he would be leaving, Warren Bennis reported the following reaction in his book, *The Leaning Ivory Tower*:

> 'Did you see the Meyerson announcement? It's awful, just awful.' Seymour Knox was lamenting Martin Meyerson's decision, announced in January, 1970, to step down from the presidency of State University of New York at Buffalo in order to succeed Gaylord Harnwell as president of the University of Pennsylvania. As chairman of the Buffalo council, Knox had been crucial in bringing Meyerson to Buffalo over the cries of a local faction determined to block the appointment of "that Jew from Berkeley." Therefore, Knox was not happy about Meyerson's decision to move on.
>
> 'I feel like a crumb-bum' he complained. 'Yesterday, in Philadelphia, I ran into an old friend, Bill Day, who is now chairman of the Penn Board of Trustees. Was he gloating! God, it was awful, I felt like he'd stolen my cook.'

Somewhat of an anomaly in academic circles, Meyerson did not hold a doctorate, but a Masters of City Planning from Harvard's Graduate School of Design. He began his teaching career at the University of Chicago and was appointed a full professor at Penn in 1956. He was a leading scholar in urban planning and the author of several important books in the field. From 1959 to 1963 he was the first director of the Harvard-MIT Joint Center for Urban Studies, and then in 1965 after serving as dean of the College of Environmental Design at the University of California at Berkeley, he was named acting chancellor with responsibility for administering to the "reassembled wreckage" of the University after the student upheavals in 1965.

At Buffalo, Meyerson attracted national attention with his plan to build a $650,000,000 campus and radically alter the conventional department-school-and college academic structure. The 90 existing departments were to be restructured into seven new facilities, each with a provost at its head. Within the structure were to be 30 new colleges which would be small enough to be intellectual communities. Fresh new blood was brought into the faculty as he raided the Ivy League schools–Harvard, Princeton, and Yale–for new talent. Although Meyerson left before much of this could be accomplished and it became clear later that it could not be accomplished without him, Bennis reported on the aura that was created:

> Although many faculty members were critical of President Meyerson's administration, nevertheless his administration demonstrated a concern for stature and it promised greatness. It was motivated by a desire to reach a high level of achievement.

Meyerson was equally innovative in the area of employment. He instituted a hiring policy for all major faculty and administrative positions, requiring that the ablest overseas person, minority group member, and woman must be reviewed for each appointment. Although this was in the late sixties and a little before it became fashionable to hire minorities, Buffalo was moving on this issue, and Meyerson felt that the policy had a great deal of respect among the faculty. For his efforts at Buffalo, Meyerson received a citation from the National Organization of Women. His efforts to insure the consideration of minorities and women on an equal basis with men at all levels became part of the recommendation of the Assembly on University Goals and Governance, a national effort to improve higher education, sponsored by the American Academy of Arts and Sciences, for which Meyerson served as chairman.

FACULTY

The University of Pennsylvania faculty was among the most prestigious and well respected in the academic world. A number of top-flight faculty had been added since the mid-1950's, a major recommendation in the *Educational Survey*. In contrast to earlier patterns, the faculty became less inbred during these years. It became a matter of pride in many departments that colleagues were chosen not solely from among past students, but from other major institutions. In this process, faculty members began to seek new appointments under a system that was commonly referred to as the "old boy network." Instead of combing their student ranks, professors contacted colleagues and friends at other "elite" institutions where qualified applicants might be found. Faculty positions were hardly ever advertised or posted, but the word was passed along an academic "grapevine" until a suitable candidate was discovered and successfully recruited. Consequently, the critical search and screening was conducted by department members who selected their own colleagues.

The process varied slightly from school to school within the university. Among liberal arts departments, a person was generally sought for his/her specific expertise, e.g. medieval history or low energy physics. An intensive search was conducted and many vitae collected; once the appointment was made, however, the unsuccessful applications were heaved out. In contrast, others conducted a continuing search. One administrator described the law school process in these terms: "Rarely do they say, 'We need another tax person', then proceed to find a tax specialist. They want the best people they can get, and they figure on the whole they'll come up with enough tax people. Vitae remain on active file for several years. If someone says 'no' one year, they'll ask him/her again next year."

Once selected by colleagues, the candidate's name was forwarded to the dean for approval. In most of the larger schools, specifically the undergraduate college, the dean appointed a personnel committee to review and advise him on these recommendations. It was the dean's responsibility to submit the nomination for approval by the Provost Staff Conference, a group composed of top academic administrators and deans from the major schools. The conference advised on all academic appointments, promotions, and terminations, and the minutes of the meetings became the official employment record for academic personnel. The president and the Board of Trustees were required to give the final stamp of approval. Historically, the faculty operated autonomously in this regard, and the decisions were basically made by the academic departments with the concurrence of the appropriate dean and the school Personnel Committee. The other approvals were normally pro forma.

A similar approval process was used in recommending faculty for tenure, a lifetime guarantee against arbitrary termination. Again, in most instances, the critical decisions were made by the tenured faculty in the department involved with the approval of the dean and the Provost Staff Conference. However, the process, at times, became quite involved. For instance, in the year prior to Meyerson's arrival, a woman who had been approved for tenure by her department was eventually not granted it by the Provost Staff Conference based on the negative recommendations of the department chairman, the Personnel Committee and the dean. The case was opened again in early 1970 after the woman's students submitted a petition praising her teaching and counseling abilities. This time the department voted against tenure, while the Personnel Committee recommended for tenure. The Dean then opposed the woman's appointment and the Provost Staff Conference again denied her tenure. However, the professor in question requested the matter be reviewed by the Committee on Academic Freedom of the University chapter of the American Association of University Professors (AAUP). Based on a strict interpretation of the AAUP guidelines, this committee ruled in her favor and requested tenure be granted, which the provost did on July 22, 1970.

During the period between 1950 and 1970 enrollments increased consistently as veterans and later the post war babies made their way to college. As a result, the university added a large number of young people to the tenured faculty during this period. In 1970 the University had approximately 1700 fully affiliated academic staff members in more than 100 departments. About 65% of the faculty was tenured and a large portion was less than 50 years old. The age and tenure distribution could be tolerated in a period of expansion, but in 1968 enrollments began to taper off and decline. Since all those who might go to college in the following two decades were already born and the population was apparently stabilizing, the University was projecting no growth in enrollments until 1995. With a stable or diminished student body the need for added faculty tended to disappear.

The faculty at Penn was actively involved in the decision-making processes of the university. The Faculty Senate served as faculty forum for discussion of major academic and administrative issues such as grievances, ethics, benefits, etc., that affected the faculty. Senior officers of the Senate were also members of the University Council, the chief deliberative body of the university. The Council was composed of faculty, students, administrators, and staff, including the president and provost, and issues passed in the Council became university policy. In addition, President Meyerson had established the Council of Academic Deans to meet regularly with him and the provost to discuss matters of academic policy.

PERSONNEL DEPARTMENT

Not unlike many Personnel Departments in major universities, the wide variety of functions commonly performed by Personnel Departments were not centralized at Penn, but rather spread out in all departments of the university. The scope of the Personnel Department's job was restricted primarily to record keeping and benefit administration. The department's role was described by one administrator as "passive." Another described the department as an "ineffective abomination." Personnel did not participate in establishing hiring policies and provided few training or career development services for employees. Except for its own employees, it had little involvement in the hiring process at all. Even the hiring of secretarial and clerical help was done in the departments with little aid or encumbrance from the central office.

Although the department provided limited services, its major function, record keeping, was a big job in a University with nearly 16,000 employees, particularly since half of these were part-time and many had non-conventional employment arrangements. Moreover, turnover ranged from 8% to 30% (depending on the employee classification) necessitating that hundreds of new files be created and terminated each year. In the late 60s the personnel records had been computerized, but the major source of information continued to be the hand-typed files maintained by Effie Thompson, a long-time employee in Personnel, and her team of loyal women. Since payroll records were maintained separately, there was little need to consult personnel records except for payment of insurance and retirement benefits. No systems existed for checking the accuracy of the information, since the separate schools maintained their own personnel records and had little cause to request reports from the central office. As a result, the schools also attached little importance to rapidly notifying personnel of employee promotions or terminations. Most administrators felt it was sufficient if the person were taken off the payroll of their own schools. In some instances, the information was never forwarded, and terminated personnel could remain in the active file for years. No one except Blue Cross and Blue Shield and group insurance programs really utilized the records.

Although Personnel maintained a file on all employees, including academic personnel, the authoritative records on faculty were maintained in the provost's office by another long-time employee, Mary Crooks. For nearly 20 years Crooks had recorded the minutes of the Provost Staff Conference and transferred the personnel actions onto 3 × 5 index cards. These cards were considered the official record, and Crooks was responsible for issuing contracts and notifying professors when their appointments were up for review. These files were the ones consulted in the process of issuing, modifying, extending, and terminating several hundred faculty contracts each year.

The inadequacies in the Personnel Department's record-keeping operation were not widely known, but there was considerable dissatisfaction among various groups with the lack of services provided by the Personnel Office. Discouraged by the inadequacies of personnel and the lack of career development opportunities available to nonacademic employees, a group of senior nonacademic officers organized a Task Force in early 1971 to review the role of the administrator in the university. In March of 1971, the Task Force report was issued and one of the major recommendations was that the Personnel Office be reorganized and a training officer appointed. As a result of the report, an Administrative Assembly, similar to the Faculty Senate, but composed of the senior nonacademic administrators who could then participate in the University's decision-making process, was organized.

In response to these employee-initiated recommendations, in October the University named Gerald Robinson, the Dean of Residential Life and Chairman of the Administrative Assembly, to be the new Executive Director of Personnel Relations and gave him a mandate to reorganize the personnel function entirely by integrating the operations of the old Personnel and Labor Relations offices, and establishing a new training program. In addition, the personnel function was elevated in the bureaucratic structure to the same level as the treasurer and comptroller, and reported directly to the vice president for business and financial affairs. Previously, Personnel had reported to the business manager. Robinson was to hire a training officer to institute career development programs for all personnel levels.

Robinson was a graduate of the Wharton School and had served in a variety of administrative positions in admissions, housing, and student affairs including a stint as Dean of Men. At the time of Robinson's appointment, Harold E. Manley, Vice President for Business and Financial Affairs, said the proposals made by the Administrative Assembly under Robinson's leadership, on internal training, promotion ladders, and salary equity had played a major part in his selection for the new post.

HISTORY OF AFFIRMATIVE ACTION AT PENN

In 1965 President Johnson issued Executive Order # 11246 which directed that any organization receiving federal contracts over $50,000 and employing over 50 people "not discriminate against any employee or applicant for employment because of race, color, religion or national origin." This was amended in 1967 by Executive Order # 11375 to prohibit discrimination on the basis of sex. These orders had two components–one requiring the elimination of all existing discriminatory conditions, whether intended or inadvertent, and another requiring all contractors to prepare a written plan detailing how the institution was to act affirmatively to overcome the effects of systematic institutional forms of discrimination. Noncompliance with this order could result in termination of federal contracts. Responsibility for implementation of the order was given to the Department of Labor which issued detailed regulations and delegated the responsibility for monitoring institutions of higher education to the Office of Civil Rights of the Department of Health Education and Welfare.

Until HEW began its investigation for non-compliance at the University of Michigan in 1970, higher educational institutions experienced little governmental pressure to act on equal employment issues: as a result, prior to Meyerson's arrival at the university in the fall of 1970, very little had been done to respond to the substance of the Executive

Orders. In May of 1970, the University Council had established an ad hoc committee on the Status of Women, and the President had appointed a committee on equal opportunity which included faculty and administrators among whom were the university chaplain and the Assistant to the President for External Affairs. However, no policy statements were made and an Affirmative Action plan was not written.

When Meyerson arrived, he soon became aware that Penn, like most major universities, evidenced some inequities in its employment record for women and minorities. For instance, of the 382 fully affiliated faculty in the undergraduate College, there were no women as full professors. Of the 1737 fully-affiliated faculty in the University as a whole, 1550 were men and 187 were women; 59% of the men and 22% of the women held the rank of associate professor or above. Within the administrative ranks, the upper level jobs were filled predominately by men and the secretarial and clerical positions were filled by women. Of the approximately 100 nonacademic top level administrators, only one was a woman. Similar statistics existed for minority employment.

In November, 1970, a group of faculty, administrative, and student women wrote to President Meyerson, requesting a meeting to discuss the status of women at the University. Their letter expressed optimism that problems could be resolved by working together:

> It is our understanding, based upon interviews you have given to representatives of campus newspapers, that you share our concern. In order to facilitate the solution of these difficulties, we would appreciate the opportunity to discuss with you the major problems in this area (i.e. equal opportunity for women) and the necessary plans for future action.

On December 4 the women met with Meyerson and the Provost to discuss means of eliminating discrimination against women, including the nepotism[9] policy, a grievance committee, allocation of special funds for hiring women and adjustments of salary inequities. At this meeting the President asked the women to form a Task Force to make recommendations on a plan for ending discrimination against women. The women agreed and on December 22 they again met with the President and the Provost to present their Affirmative Action Plan (see excerpts in Exhibit 27-2). At that point the President asked them to continue on as a Task Force and stated his intention to include a statement of policy on this issue in his address to the Trustees in January.

In January, 1971, President Meyerson established the Office of Equal Opportunity, reporting directly to the Office of the President, and appointed Jim Robinson to be administrator. Robinson had been associated with the University for several years in the External Affairs Office and, as an articulate black spokesman, had been highly successful in maintaining good relations with community groups during periods of unrest in the late sixties.

---

[9]Previously the University had a policy of refusing to hire two members of an immediate family. In practice, this policy prevented qualified women whose husbands were faculty members from also receiving faculty appointments and vice versa.

In his progress report to the trustees in January of 1971, President Meyerson outlined a six-point program primarily for women, but acknowledging that more work had to be done for minorities:

> I have asked first of all, that the Equal Opportunity Office serve in a staff capacity for a University-wide grievance mechanism on which women are adequately represented. Such machinery should be devised with the advice of the University Council, the Faculty Senate, the Administrative Assembly and other appropriate groups on our campus. This grievance machinery should be established to help assure equality for all groups at our University.
>
> Not because it is required by the Federal government, but for reasons of equity, I have suggested as a second measure, that the office of the President and the Provost and Vice President establish guidelines to assist every budget unit within the University in examining all its members, both academic and non-academic, to ensure that the principle of equal pay for equal work is followed. Academic deans, vice-president, and administrators will be asked to oversee these efforts. The guidelines will apply to all groups and not to women alone. They will apply to black and to white males who may not be adequately compensated. Third, I have requested that the best possible women candidates as well as candidates from other neglected groups be sought out for any existing openings. This request applies to professorial vacancies; it applies to administrative posts, including the top ones within the University. For any opening, without prescribing that a member from a specific group be employed, it is important that the most capable people be considered, whatever their sex, color, or nationality.
>
> I have asked the new Provost and Vice-President to be especially attentive to such criteria. Incidentally, one of the problems in recruiting women for almost all posts is to find and identify the names of the most capable candidates. Women are not part of the network through which most jobs are found.
>
> Fourth, in our graduate and professional schools, I will ask the academic deans to assure that admissions and financial aid criteria are applied equally to men and women. Fifth, we shall revise the University's statement on nepotism; we are now in the process of developing a policy that will provide for the hiring of qualified persons from the same family. Finally, I have asked a group of concerned University women faculty and staff to serve on a Task Force to aid us with these and other questions in the hope that they will agree to this role. I am grateful to them for the assistance they have already given us.
>
> While I have concentrated in this section on women, the emphasis does not mean that the University is not fully aware of its poor record with regard to blacks. For example, we have fewer than 40 blacks at the faculty and upper administrative levels. This figure must be changed and various methods for doing so will increasingly be explored.

In February, 1971, the women at the University, including those on the original President's Task Force on Women, formed a new organization—Women for Equal Opportunity at the University of Pennsylvania (WEOUP). Their stated purpose was to "end discrimination against women at the University and to secure the implementation of an effective affirmative action program." One of the Task Force members, a WEOUP founder, said at the time that, "President Meyerson was all too willing to form a committee to investigate the situation, but, when we came back to him immediately with a specific plan for action, he demurred. His approach was that the University is composed of men of good will and that once a concern for issues such as equal employment was brought to their attention, then you could rely on their good will to implement change." She added, "The women were simply not that sanguine about the extent of goodwill that existed at Penn and felt in order to get something accomplished we needed an organization to push actively for women's rights on the campus at all levels–student, faculty, administrative, clerical and secretarial." During the year, the original 40 members of WEOUP grew to 400 and included women from all segments of the University. A sliding scale for dues was established, based on employment status, and an attorney, Lois Forer, was retained.

The following month a report from the Committee on the Status of Women was issued which documented that there were very few women on the faculty of the University. (See Exhibit 27-3 for distribution of faculty by school, rank, sex.) The report stated in part:

> The general picture which emerges from the data detailed below is a familiar one resembling other universities. In particular,
>
> (1)–there are very few women on the faculty of the University of Pennsylvania: only 7 percent of the fully-affiliated faculty at the professorial level are women. For the College, the single largest school, the figure is only 5.7 percent.
>
> (2)–women are concentrated in the lowest ranks and represent 2.5 percent of the full professors, 7.0 percent of the associate professors and 12.7 percent of the assistant professors. Again, the trend is more striking in the College: full professors include 164 men and 0 women; associate professors, 64 men and 3 women; and assistant professors, 101 men and 17 women.
>
> (3)–there are 14 academic departments with zero women members which should have on the average more than two on the basis of the percentage of women Ph.D.'s available.

In this report the Committee reaffirmed the inadequacies that existed with the University's personnel data:

> Inadequate record-keeping in various parts of the University limited the scope of this study. While our data may be the most accurate presently available, we are under no illusion that it is absolutely correct. Where the same information was obtained from different sources, numerous discrepancies were noted . . . data on salaries and length of time at rank could not be confirmed and the accuracy of this information must remain in doubt. . . . Many departments do not keep complete records on the number of faculty considered for appointment and promotion and the results of such consideration. Extensive data on termination of appointments were apparently unobtainable. It is essential that the University give attention to maintaining accurate records.

About this same time HEW asked for statistics on the employment of women and minorities at the University. At this point, some of the problems in the personnel data base became obvious and hindered the ability of the University to respond. For instance, in the early sixties Penn had collected racial data on all its employees, but in the late sixties when this practice was considered discriminatory, it was discontinued. Jim Robinson reported: "We did the best we could, but we knew we just didn't have very complete data, and what we had was full of inaccuracies. What we submitted was little more than a listing of personnel by sex and where we had it, race. In light of what we learned later the statistics were very crude, but it was all we had."

In March 1971, a HEW site inspection team visited the University, interviewed administration officials, and reviewed the personnel statistics. Robinson commented that, "At that point no one really knew what was needed. The HEW representatives were unclear exactly what they wanted and didn't give us much feedback on how we were to be evaluated. At any rate, they went away to review the data and by the end of 1971 we still hadn't heard from them." Following the HEW inspection, responsibility for drafting an Affirmative Action Plan fell to Robinson and Donald Stewart, Executive Assistant to the President. Stewart was personally concerned about the issue and stepped into the process as a representative of the president's office.

In the spring, the Provost and Vice President, Curtis Reitz, stated the following in a memorandum to all academic deans, directors, and department chairmen:

> The University strives for the highest attainable levels of excellence in its faculty and teaching staff, but can do so only if all candidates, including women and members of minority groups, are fully considered.

During 1971, Jim Robinson and Stewart continued to revise an Affirmative Action Plan which they hoped would serve both as a statement of policy and a guide for action. The plan designated Jim Robinson as responsible for monitoring compliance and providing technical assistance for implementation. Stewart was to serve as coordinator between the Office of the President and the Office of the Provost and the faculty. On September 15 the University issued its first statement on University Employment Policies and Equal Opportunity. This document was intended as a policy statement and dealt with recruiting practices, the appointment process for faculty and administrative personnel, nepotism policy, special recruiting of women, maternity leave, day care facilities, and grievance machinery. It also contained the recommendation that a University Academic Committee on Equal Opportunity be established. It was designed to be an interim document while Stewart and Robinson continued to work on the Affirmative Action Plan.

In a letter to the Provost, WEOUP expressed strong dissatisfaction with the Equal Opportunity Proposal, listing six areas in which the group felt the document was insufficient:

> The document ignores women in A-1, A-3, A-4[10] categories as well as students. In addition, the proposals put forward are quite inadequate for the following reasons:

---

[10]Employment categories at the university were (A-1) administrative, (A-2) faculty, (A-3) secretarial and clerical and (A-4) technicians, craftsmen, operators, and laborers.

1.–No goals or timetables are set; the proposals therefore do not represent affirmative action.
2.–While there is provision for fact-finding, reporting and evaluation, there is no provision for enforcement of any policies, nor are there insurances that women and minorities will play a major role in these functions.
3.–The provisions for accountability leave much to be desired. Male administrators are only *encouraged* to carry out actions which are *required* by law.
4.–There is no provision for adjustment of current salaries and retroactive compensation which must be paid where salary differential because of sex has existed since October 13, 1968.
5.–In general, the statements are vague where they should be explicit. No affirmative action plan will be effective unless backed up by effective grievance mechanisms, and the University statement on grievance mechanisms is the weakest element in a generally weak proposal.
6.–The University proposals on partially-affiliated faculty women are inadequate. This senstive and complicated area requires further study before final recommendations can be made.

Attached to the letter was another Affirmative Action Plan that called for a Women's Advisory group to work closely with the Equal Opportunity Officers, the appointment of women to committees, revisions in admissions policies, a preference to women in faculty and administrative appointments, publishing of job vacancies, and a better training program for women, among others. A major part of this recommendation included an extensive section on the appointment of four Equal Employment Opportunity Officers to examine the status of women. It was suggested that these officers be given staff to oversee the implementation of Affirmative Action and the authority to investigate and resolve grievances. At that time a WEOUP officer stated that "one of our major concerns was that the Administrator in the Equal Opportunity Office did not have faculty status. Without a Ph.D. he did not have complete flexibility in negotiating with all employee groups, specifically the faculty. We also felt that it was important that the Equal Opportunity function to be opened up to women who were tuned in to women's problems."

On October 8 WEOUP filed a complaint with the Human Relations Commission of the Commonwealth of Pennsylvania, alleging two counts of discrimination against women. The first count alleged that Penn denied female employees equal opportunity by "systematically assigning women to job categories which are lower in status, pay and benefits than those assigned to men of equal or inferior education, training and ability", by discriminatory hiring and promotion policies on the faculty, and through maternity leave policies and administration of benefits. The second count alleged that Penn discriminated by denying "accommodations, advantages, facilities, financial aid and privileges to female students and female applicants for student positions." The University responded with a letter from Provost Reitz stating that a set of Affirmative Action proposals was being formulated and circulated for comment throughout the University, and reaffirming the resolutions passed by the University Council requesting that special consideration be given to women in the hiring process. Reitz stated that the president required documentation that women were being sought for every faculty appointment. The letter also included this statement of policy:

> The University is committed to equal opportunity. It has been in the forefront of making higher education available to women. If any discrimination does occur in employment, it is not intentional and can easily be corrected. A major problem in increasing the representation of women and minority group members on the faculty is the small number of positions which become vacant in any one year. Efforts are being made to find qualified women and minority group members to fill vacant faculty and administrative positions.

These series of events from September, 1970, to December, 1971, disturbed President Meyerson. He had hoped the University would have moved more quickly in the Affirmative Action area, but, in view of the events of the last year, he pondered even more seriously what he would recommend to the trustees next month.

Exhibit 27-1

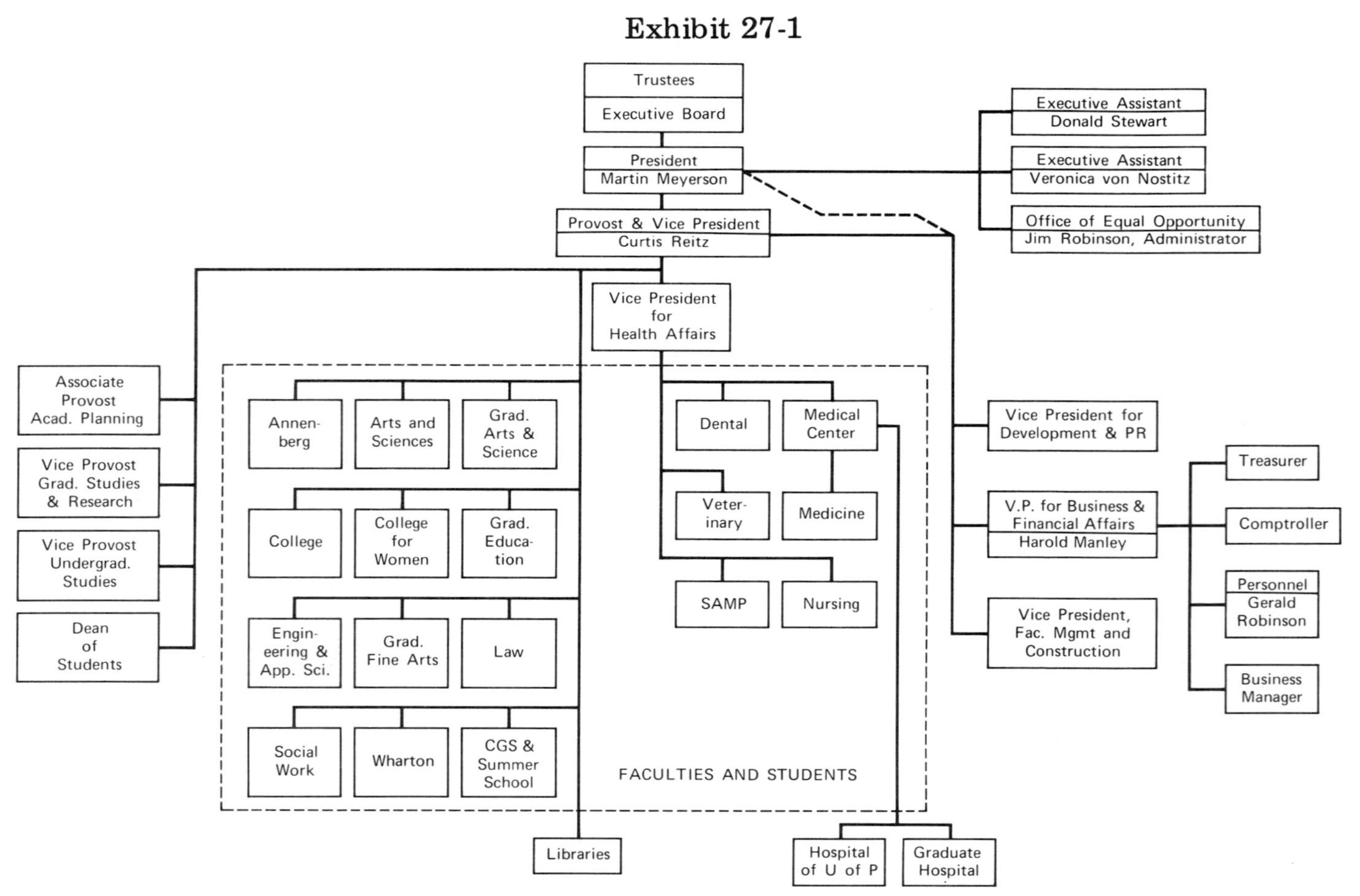

Trustees
Executive Board
President
Martin Meyerson
Executive Assistant
Donald Stewart
Executive Assistant
Veronica von Nostitz
Office of Equal Opportunity
Jim Robinson, Administrator
Provost & Vice President
Curtis Reitz
Vice President for Health Affairs
Associate Provost Acad. Planning
Vice Provost Grad. Studies & Research
Vice Provost Undergrad. Studies
Dean of Students
Annen-berg
Arts and Sciences
Grad. Arts & Science
College
College for Women
Grad. Educa-tion
Engin-eering & App. Sci.
Grad. Fine Arts
Law
Social Work
Wharton
CGS & Summer School
Dental
Medical Center
Veter-inary
Medicine
SAMP
Nursing
FACULTIES AND STUDENTS
Libraries
Hospital of U of P
Graduate Hospital
Vice President for Development & PR
V.P. for Business & Financial Affairs
Harold Manley
Vice President, Fac. Mgmt and Construction
Treasurer
Comptroller
Personnel
Gerald Robinson
Business Manager

Exhibit 27-2

Excerpts from

"A PLAN FOR AFFIRMATIVE ACTION TO ELIMINATE DISCRIMINATION AGAINST WOMEN AT THE UNIVERSITY OF PENNSYLVANIA"

Prepared by the President's Task Force on Women

We strongly urge that the President of the University of Pennsylvania take the following steps:

1.–Instruct the Committee on the Budget and inform the President's and Provost's Staff Conferences that reallocation of funds budgeted to salary for 1971-1972 in all employment categories will be necessary to implement this Affirmative Action Plan, which is designed to enable the University to move toward compliance with existing Federal regulations.

2.–Establish a Women's Commission immediately to oversee the implementation of affirmative action policies toward women at this University. The Commission must have the power to initiate reviews and to investigate grievances concerning partial affiliation, nonappointment, reappointment, promotion and salary. It must have the right of access to records and to personnel; the right to be provided with legal counsel of its own choosing; and the right to make public its conclusions and recommendations.

Initially the Women's Commission should be appointed by the President from a list submitted by the President's Task Force on Women, who will have consulted with all known women's organizations in the University community. It shall be a quadripartite commission consisting of women Trustees (when there shall be any) faculty, students and nonacademic employees. The Commission will, on being constituted, determine its own rules of operation.

3.–Convene a meeting of the President, the Provost, the Academic Vice-Presidents, the Vice-Provosts, all Deans and Department Chairmen and the Task Force on Women to present the following policies with respect to faculty:

a.–Goal: The University of Pennsylvania must have a faculty of the highest quality. It is clear that the University has been deprived of the contributions that could be made by many excellent women who are or may become available. A prerequisite for this goal is that women faculty and women students of the University will agree that all women are being treated fairly here. This will require an active program of recruitment, appointment and promotion. Ultimately there should be no significant difference in the ratio between women and men faculty at the University.

b.–Appointments: To correct the present imbalance it is necessary to give preference to women in the case of equal qualifications. We understand that recently there has been a yearly attrition rate of faculty of about 6%.

Exhibit 27-2 (continued)

Realizing that many of the positions thus vacated must remain unfilled for budgetary reasons, we recommend that women receive 75% on average of all appointments made. This recommendation is independent of the anomalous situation in the School of Nursing, which needs special provisions. The new women are to be appointed at the levels of Assistant, Associate and Full Professor. No appointment of a man should be approved where there are not been a serious search for women to fill the position.

The President should establish a University committee (with a majority of women members) to search for qualified women for Faculty positions.

The committee should also be charged with the responsibility to identify women qualified to serve as Department Chairmen, Deans, etc. This is particularly important because the list of chairmanships issued by the Provost's Office indicates that none of the 119 positions is held by a woman.

c.–Promotions: The present status of women academic personnel at the University must be reviewed by the Women's Commission to ensure that these women have been accorded a rank commensurate with their qualifications. In the case of equal qualifications for future promotion, preference must be given to women in order to correct the present imbalance.

d.–Salaries: First priority in current budget planning must be given to making the mean, median and mode of the salaries of women equal to those of men in equivalent positions. In cases where the numbers of women in such positions are so small that difficulties would arise in applying the statistics, those choices should be made which are most advantageous to women.

e.–Implementation: All departments and schools shall be directed to keep all records on appointments (including the C.V.s of candidates considered), promotion and salaries (including source of salary and special University financial aid). These records shall be coded by sex and shall be open to the Women's Commission. It is understood that strictly confidential matters will be handled in a manner similar to the operations of the Committee on Academic Freedom and Responsibility.

4.–Adopt a positive program of appointment, promotion and salary upgrading for qualified women in nonacademic positions. The goal should be not only to attract outstanding women, but to maintain their interest through substantive work and to advance them to make full use of their growth and experience.

a.–In communications with professional organizations, as well as in advertising, publicize a policy of equal opportunity for women.

b.–Give priority in the 1971-72 budget to bringing the salaries of women to parity with those of men in comparable positions or with comparable qualifications and responsibilities. Pending a review of job classifications, the appended guidelines may be used to determine comparability of A-1 personnel. Special review will be needed to discover and upgrade those A-3 women who carry responsibilities equivalent to A-1 employees.

Exhibit 27-2 (continued)

c.–Give preference in appointments and promotions to women who possess qualifications exceeding those of men. During the period of imbalance between men and women in higher adminsitrative positions, women with qualifications equivalent to those of men should be given preference in promotions.

d.–Identify and begin to train capable women for higher administrative service in "line" as well as "staff" positions. As a modest beginning under the present financial conditions:

(1)–Place women on committees engaged in planning and decision-making, and include them in staff meetings which inform the operation.

(2)–Provide support services for women in administrative positions equal to those available to men.

(3)–Extend to women any privileges of travel, in-service or extramural training, subsidized membership in professional organizations and any other advancement aids that may be available to men.

e.–Communicate the above policies to the Provost, the Vice-Presidents, Vice-Provosts, Deans, Directors and Chairmen who employ women in nonacademic positions. Require them to retain records and make such records accessible to the Women's Commission on request.

f.–Institute a study of current and potential roles for women in administration at the University, calling upon members of the Wharton School, other appropriate faculties and innovative administrators to act as resources. Any in-service education considered for administrative employees should contain subject matter pertaining to women in management.

Initially, the following steps should be taken:

(1)–Examine the Personnel operation to clarify sources of policy toward women and to increase Personnel Office flexibility in hiring and promotion.

(2)–Analyze patterns of promotion, transfer and turnover at the University by age, sex and other factors, to help redefine criteria on hiring and advancement of women.

(3)–Compile listings of University courses which women can attend to improve administrative skill, including the social sciences, operations research and others.

(4)–Identify gaps in the University's offerings on women in business, industrial and institutional management, and encourage the design of new courses by faculty and administrators.

Exhibit 27-3

REPORT OF THE COMMITTEE ON THE STATUS OF WOMEN

APPENDIX I DISTRIBUTION OF FULLY-AFFILIATED FACULTY, PROFESSORIAL RANKS, BY SCHOOL, RANK, AND SEX

School	*Prof.*		*Assoc. Prof.*		*Asst. Prof.*		*Total*		*% Fem.*
	M	*F*	*M*	*F*	*M*	*F*	*M*	*F*	*(%)*
Allied Medical	0	1	0	4	1	3	1	8	(88.9)
Annenberg	7	0	2	0	3	0	12	0	(0.0)
Graduate A. & S.	10	0	15	1	17	1	42	2	(4.5)
College	164	0	64	3	101	17	329	20	(5.7)
Dentistry	14	0	14	1	20	3	48	4	(7.7)
Education	13	1	8	3	4	3	25	7	(21.9)
Chemical Eng.	3	0	5	0	4	0	12	0	(0.0)
Civil & Mech. Eng.	11	0	8	0	3	0	22	0	(0.0)
Electrical Eng.	17	0	16	0	13	0	46	0	(0.0)
Metallurgy & Mtls. Sci.	7	0	4	0	2	0	13	0	(0.0)
Fine Arts	10	2	21	0	8	1	39	3	(7.1)
Law	21	0	6	0	2	1	29	1	(3.3)
Med.-Preclinical	37	2	22	2	24	3	83	7	(7.8)
Nursing	0	1	0	1	1	3	1	5	(83.3)
Social Work	6	2	3	2	8	3	17	7	(29.1)
Vet. Medicine	29	1	25	2	28	4	82	7	(7.9)
Wharton	85	1	51	1	77	4	213	6	(2.7)
Totals	434	11	264	20	316	46	1014	77	(7.0)
% Female, By Rank	(2.5)		(7.0)		(12.7)		(7.0)		

Exhibit 27-3 (continued)

APPENDIX II DISTRIBUTION OF FULLY-AFFILIATED FACULTY, OTHER RANKS, BY SCHOOL, RANK, AND SEX

School	*Lec-turer*		*Instruc-tor*		*Other*		*Total*		*% Fem.*
	M	*F*	*M*	*F*	*M*	*F*	*M*	*F*	*(%)*
Allied Medical	0	0	0	5	0	1	0	6	(100.0)
Annenberg	0	0	0	0	0	0	0	0	–
Graduate A. & S.	1	0	1	0	0	0	2	0	(0.0)
College	2	2	19	3	5	2	26	7	(21.2)
Dentistry	2	0	6	3	9	0	17	3	(15.0)
Education	4	3	0	0	0	1	4	4	(50.0)
Chemical Eng.	0	0	0	0	0	0	0	0	–
Civil & Mech. Eng.	0	0	1	0	0	0	1	0	(0.0)
Electrical Eng.	1	0	0	0	2	0	3	0	(0.0)
Metallurgy & Mtls. Sci.	0	0	0	0	0	0	0	0	–
Fine Arts	1	0	0	0	0	0	1	0	(0.0)
Law	0	0	0	0	0	0	0	0	–
Med.-Preclinical	0	0	5	1	14	6	19	7	(26.9)
Nursing	0	2	1	27	1	12	2	41	(95.3)
Social Work	4	3	0	0	0	0	4	3	(42.9)
Vet. Medicine	0	0	13	0	2	4	15	4	(21.1)
Wharton	23	4	7	0	7	2	37	6	(13.9)
Totals	38	14	53	39	40	28	131	81	(38.2)
% Female, By Ranks	(26.9)		(42.4)		(41.2)		(38.2)		

Case Twenty-Eight

University of Pennsylvania (B)[1]

> Seldom are institutions reorganized or reinvigorated from above alone. The success of transformation and change, of innovation and adaption has always required the continuing interest and energy of the whole community, both collectively and as individuals. My colleagues and I are summoning the campus to join together in this major effort (creating a University Development Plan). We shall need your judgment, concurrence and participation.

Thus Martin Meyerson concluded his Progress Report to the Trustees on January 12, 1972, after outlining a plan for University development in the seventies. In view of the deteriorating fiscal situation, he presented three options for the University: 1) to try to become state related; 2) to cut University activities, salaries, and expenses to a minimum; or 3) to raise more money primarily for qualitative improvements in both programs and personnel. Meyerson strongly recommended the third option and outlined an eight-point program through which the University would emphasize selected educational and research programs with the resources available to it. However, he pointed out that "the pursuit of excellence could not be accomplished by the reallocation of existing funds alone," but that a major Development Fund would be required, and he proposed that a Development Commission, composed of faculty, students, and Trustees be appointed to review his proposals and to recommend new directions for the University. Meyerson cautioned the Trustees:

> Given frequent calls for a "new plan" for higher education, we might be tempted to offer our own grand design encompassing precise goals and means and concluding with a full canvas of a distant future to be realized. I think we must resist that temptation, for such grand visions have a bad habit of turning stale or, at best, of inhibiting necessary improvisations. But we can pursue sharpened goals. We can create opportunities for change, and we can establish a climate hospitable to

[1]For background on the development of the University's Affirmative Action Plan during 1970 and 1971 see University of Pennsylvania (A).

educational innovations of a kind that will make our University the most stimulating one there is for students and faculty alike.

Meyerson commented later, "I felt strongly at that time that in order for the University to make progress in any area, whether it be Affirmative Action or academic pursuits, that our first priority had to be to put our house in order both financially and administratively. Our financial constraints forced us to examine closely our directions and our policies in all areas and to restructure ourselves to meet the challenges of the seventies." In February 1971, Meyerson appointed 15 faculty and three students, including two women faculty members and two women students, as members of the Development Commission. Three Trustees, the Chairman of the Faculty Senate, and the Chairman of the Academic Planning Committee were to be ex-officio members. The Commission was charged with reviewing the Meyerson proposals for future growth and the reallocation of existing funds, using the concept of "selective excellence to strengthen undergraduate education and to promote particularly strong graduate fields to national rank."

That same month Meyerson, acting on a recommendation from the Task Force on University Governance, appointed former Westinghouse vice-president Paul Gaddis to the new University post of Vice President for Management. Previously, the Provost managed the academic affairs and as Vice President was also in charge of all University administrative functions. Meyerson summarized his action by stating, "Our administrative functions had not kept pace with the growth of the University. Our management information systems were not adequate, particularly in the personnel and financial control areas. We couldn't get the data we needed on employees, salaries, and promotions, and even basic operating expenses were difficult to pin down. We needed an experienced administrator who would devote full time to restructuring and updating our management functions." At Westinghouse Gaddis had responsibility for developing information systems, specifically in the public services and hospital fields. This experience was especially relevant to the University since over half of Penn's operating budget went to hospital facilities. Reporting to Gaddis were the three administrative vice presidents: Development and Public Relations, Business and Financial Affairs, and Facilities Management and Construction. In addition, the Office of Equal Opportunity was reassigned from the President's office to a staff function reporting directly to Gaddis (see Exhibit 28-1). Shortly after taking office, Gaddis named Scott Lederman, a Wharton School administrator, as his executive assistant.

FURTHER ACTION ON THE AFFIRMATIVE ACTION PLAN

In mid-January, 1972, the Univeristy began to circulate a working draft of its Affirmative Action Plan for comment by students, faculty, administrators, WEOUP, and others. At that time Gerald Robinson, Executive Director of Personnel Relations, emphasized that the draft was "a point of departure only—an accumulation of input to date, designed to encourage further comment from the campus." Robinson commented later that, "The process as we saw it was to be one of concensus in which we gathered reactions from all segments of the campus. We weren't sure we had addressed the broad concerns of the entire campus, and since HEW had been so vague on what it wanted us to do, we weren't at all sure the plan would meet with government approval. One thing we knew for sure was that our personnel practices were archaic and would need extensive revamping."

The draft included few specific procedures, but called for intensified efforts to develop a wider applicant pool of minorities and women for positions and placed special emphasis on the recruiting process and the development of training programs to qualify protected groups for both entry level positions and for advancement. A more lenient maternity leave policy was included as well as a proposal for the creation of day care facilities. The responsibilities of School and Senate Committees on Academic Freedom and Responsibility were outlined. For most discrimination cases the plan recommended the use of the campus Ombudsman, Chaplain or Equal Opportunity Officer. There was also a section on employment and selection procedures for vendors, contractors, and suppliers.

Gerald Robinson commented on one immediate problem: "One of the areas in which we knew we needed a lot of work was our job classification system. The way our jobs were classified we could not distinguish clearly whether we were paying men and women equally for equal work. As in most institutions the women and minorities were concentrated in the lower-status and consequently lower-paying jobs, and we felt it was important at that time to look closely at the job descriptions and classifications to determine if discrimination was being perpetuated in this form." University personnel were classified into four groups, having the distributions of women and minorities in 1971 shown below:

PERSONNEL CLASSIFICATIONS

	A-1 *Administrative*	*A-2* *Faculty*	*A-3* *Secretarial & Clerical*	*A-4* *Technicians Craftsmen, etc.*
Women	31.9%	12.5%	73.8%	37.5%
Minorities	6.8	9.3	20.9	52.5

As a result, two subcommittees were named by Robinson to study A-1 and A-3 job classifications and the overlap between personnel in the two groups. The A-1 subcommittee was chaired by Alice Emerson, Dean of Students, and the A-3 Subcommittee was headed by Manuel Doxer, Business Manager of the College. The committees were to meet both separately and together to:

1.–Review and approve job gradings of new jobs, revised jobs, and periodically reviewed jobs.
2.–Determine appropriate grades in the event of disagreement.
3.–Determine appropriate salary levels in the event of disagreement.
4.–Monitor administration of the merit salary increase program through reports, statistics, and special studies.

5.–Recommend changes in method, procedure, and policy to the Employee Classification Review Committee.

Traditionally, the University Employee Classification Review Committee, chaired by Harold Manley, Vice President for Business and Financial Affairs, reviewed classifications and approved new jobs. "However," Gerald Robinson stated, "the committee members agreed that if a review of job classifications and a reassignment of job grades was to work, persons from all job levels had to be involved."

No statistical data had been released with the draft plan. So as it was circulated for comment, Equal Opportunity Administrator James Robinson and Gerald Robinson turned their attention to the statistical analysis of the University's employee population. "When we sat down to examine the records closely, it was a shattering experience," Gerald Robinson said. "The personnel files had been put on computer about five years ago and when we ran listings of personnel, we would get alphabetics in numerical fields, missing information and unintelligible entries. It appeared that since there had been so little call for the data, no verification system had been set up to check the information as it was entered. There were so many problems that we just couldn't trust the data." Even more important, the University had not collected racial information on employees since the early Sixties when the practice came to be considered discriminatory, so the racial data was very incomplete. It was decided that a University census was required to get accurate information. Because of the numbers involved, the census was restricted to the 8,000 full-time employees; the extra service personnel (those hired on an hourly basis with no benefits), consultants, and students working for financial aid were omitted. A computer card was run for each employee in the personnel data base containing the person's name and University identification number and sent to each department chairman or administrative unit director who was asked to identify each employee by sex and race by visual survey.

"We had no idea what a hornet's nest we opened up with this project," commented Gerald Robinson. "We anticipated that the entire project could be completed in several weeks, but we soon ran into some strong opposition." A small, but influential and vocal group of faculty members objected to the collection of the racial information. From the beginning these faculty members stated that they were not opposed to the University's Affirmative Action efforts, but that they felt it was an invasion of individual privacy to have this information provided by department chairmen and stored in a central administration file. As eyewitnesses to the tragedies that occurred in Germany in the thirties, these faculty members felt keenly that the collection of racial data was a moral issue which could have devastating effects on individual freedom. The concerned faculty introduced a resolution in the faculty senate which would have prohibited the University from collecting the racial data. Once the issue was raised, the progress of the census was impeded as the various University committees debated the issue. However Gerald Robinson reported that "The majority of the employees at the University understood the purpose of the census and cooperated. There were, of course, a few exceptions such as the department that sent back its cards with all its faculty marked as black."

In addition to the philosophical issue, the census turned up even more mechanical problems with the data base. "There were so many inaccuracies in the personnel cards we sent out, ranging from misspelled names to cards for personnel who left the University ten years ago or were dead," Gerald Robinson said, "many Department Chairmen lost respect for the Personnel Department." Over the next four months most of the cards were returned to Personnel. In the interim an agreement was negotiated with the faculty in which the administration agreed in the future that it would collect racial data only on a self-identification basis. Once the data were collected, they would be stored by employee number on a separate tape which would be kept in a safe in the provost's office. The tape could only be used by authorization of the provost. When needed for Affirmative Action reports, it would be merged into the regular personnel data tape file. Once the reports were finished, the merged tape would then be destroyed, and the original tape returned to the Provost.

By July of 1972 the University had enough data to publish a census (see Exhibit 28-2). "But it was a horrendous summer," Gerald Robinson said. "We had to hire summer personnel to go through all the hard copy files and record information on rank, time in rank, method of entry, beginning salary, current salary, years in service and termination data. All the problems, inaccuracies, etc. were simply listed as 'other'." By the end of the summer the University had compiled some statistical data about the total employee population, and this report along with the draft plan was submitted to HEW. "At that point," Gerald Robinson said, "we weren't exactly sure what all the data meant. There were few totals and no percentages. But we were convinced that the personnel information system needed to be totally revamped and integrated with the payroll systems. However, at that point, University personnel resources and manpower had been allocated to what appeared to be more pressing concerns—job definition and reclassification."

ADMINISTRATIVE CHANGES

In the spring of 1972 the first report from the University Development Commission was issued. The major recommendation in the report was that the University adopt a new budgeting system placing the responsibility for fiscal control on the individual schools. For the first time, Deans would be asked to cover the direct costs of operating their schools with income from tuition, gifts, endowments, grants, etc. The Commission recommended that "fiscal control should go hand in hand with academic review to force the qualitatively poorer parts of the University to improve or vanish, thus raising overall quality." In order to institute such a management system, the Commission pointed out that a more detailed general accounting system would be necessary. One member of the Commission commented, "If academic units were to be responsible for their own expenses, we must have an accounting system which can accurately and fairly allocate income and expenses to the appropriate units. At that time such a system did not exist. I became a wicked double-entry bookkeeper while we were preparing our report. Most of the information we needed simply wasn't available in the form we needed it, and we were forced to sit down and work through the numbers by hand ourselves."

The Development Commission interim report was presented to the Trustees in May of 1972, and the strategy for fiscal independence for the individual schools was endorsed by the Board. The Commission went back to work to finalize a series of recommendations on a broad range of other issues. In the interim Paul Gaddis had begun the reorganization of the management functions at the University and had created a new office of the Assistant Vice President for University Management Information Systems. Previously the Data Processing Department had handled all the University's information systems. There were few programmers on the staff at that time and no personnel trained in systems analysis and design. By September, 1972, the Registrar, Richard Pauman, was appointed to this new office, and he immediately expanded the Data Processing Department and created two new departments–Systems Design and Technical Services. Its first task was to completely revamp the University's accounting system. "The Development Commission Report strongly reinforced our need for a better system for allocating costs," Pauman said. "A new financial information had to be the first priority."

SUBSEQUENT EVENTS IN AFFIRMATIVE ACTION

By late 1972 an ad hoc Affirmative Action Task Force composed of EEO Administrator, Jim Robinson, his assistant, Verrity Powell, Gerald Robinson from Personnel, Scott Lederman, executive assistant to Paul Gaddis, and Bruce Johnstone, executive assistant to President Meyerson, was formed to finalize the Affirmative Action Plan that was to be submitted to HEW. As Don Stewart before him had had major responsibility for drafting a plan, Bruce Johnstone became the unofficial chairman of the Committee. Dr. Johnstone had been an administrative assistant to Sen. Mondale and a project director at the Ford Foundation prior to joining the University staff in mid-1972 to replace Don Stewart, who left to finish his doctorate at Harvard's Kennedy School. Johnstone commented:

> There are probably several good reasons that my office assumed the role of shepherd for the plan. First, at the earlier stages the Affirmative Action effort needed a central thrust. We needed to go about affirmative action in extremely different ways for faculty and non-faculty, and in order to do that effectively the key person must have legitimacy in both areas. The President's office is one of the few places that this legitimacy exists. Since I work very closely with the President, Provost and the Vice President for Management, I could effect some cohesion in these groups. In addition, the visibility of the President's office helps to give authority and immediacy to the issue. As staff in the President's office I have no rights or authority, but have an acknowledged right to be concerned. It doesn't alarm or alienate the various groups on campus that my office is involved and concerned about the issue.
>
> Once I had studied the earlier drafts of the Affirmative Action Plan, it seemed clear to me that what we really lacked were procedures for implementation of the plan–the formal accoutrements of the bureaucracy to get action. The University had put together a marvelous statement of intention, a fine statement of what it thought ought to be done. But the plan lacked instruments or procedures for

> getting the rhetoric out of the Provost's and President's office and down in the day-by-day operation of the University. Administrators, faculty, department chairmen, deans and other academic administrators spent a lot of dysfunctional time agonizing over who should do what—over whose territory was being invaded. My bias is that there is a sense of humaneness in a bureaucracy when it removes uncertainties. It can give personnel a sense of certainty and stability. It can allow them to do those things which are dear to the academic heart without having to fear for territorial infringement.

During the fall of 1972 the Affirmative Action Task Force under Johnstone's leadership and in consultation with various campus groups redrafted the Affirmative Action Plan. (Excerpts from this plan are shown in Exhibit 28-3). The plan was divided into three parts. Part I outlined a University strategy for Affirmative Action, Part II summarized the procedures that needed to be established, and Part III laid out hiring goals for minorities and women during the following three years both for the faculty and for nine administrative areas.

Part I included many of the issues dealt with in the previous plans and stated that the University intended to act affirmatively in five areas: 1) the candidate pool, 2) hiring practices, 3) promotion and retention, 4) compensation, 5) personnel policies. To increase the representation of women and minorities within the candidate pools, the plan stressed advertising for all open positions and an active search in non-traditional areas for women and minorities. In the hiring area, the plan stressed that "In case of virtually equal merit, to avowedly favor women, minorities, or any other previously underrepresented segment of the population" is not at variance with the University's basic premise of nondiscriminatory hiring based on merit. The plan admonished the University to be sensitive to criteria of "merit" which could become a screening device effective in weeding out applicants on the basis of attributes and values which might be quite irrelevant to the skills needed in the performance of the task (i.e. speech patterns, appearance, etc.). In the promotion area, women and minorities were to be accorded the same priority as in the hiring policy. The overall emphasis was to get highly qualified women or minorities into the candidate pools so that a good proportion of the best-qualified people will be women. The plan reaffirmed a policy of equality in pay: "Salaries should generally be the same for individuals with the same qualifications carrying out the same task and bringing the same value to the institution to the extent that these comparabilities can be demonstrated." Personnel policies on maternity leave, part-time work, and nepotism were rewritten to give women more flexibility and to encourage them to continue working. In addition, the strategy called for the University to apply pressure to its contractors and suppliers to adopt their own affirmative action plans.

Part II of the plan dealt with specific procedures for institutionalizing the policy. There were separate sections for faculty and non-faculty personnel. Gerald Robinson stated, "Due to the nature of the University, we were able to formulate and implement specific Affirmative Action procedures for non-academic personnel more quickly. We developed specific procedures for eliminating discrimination in both the hiring and the grievance procedure." Included in the plan were forms to be used in announcing vacancies, where announcements of available positions would be posted, and even organizations such as the Urban League and the NAACP which could serve as personnel resources for protected groups. The plan specified that no personnel action would be complete until a statement of compliance with the Affirmative Action Plan had been filled out by the hiring officer and approved by the Executive Director of Personnel and the Administrator of the Office of Equal Opportunity (see Exhibit 28-4).

A grievance procedure for non-academic staff was also spelled out in considerable detail. Johnstone explained how this procedure related to the organization:

> Acknowledging that the process can be a hassle, we felt strongly that if a legitimate grievance did exist, it was reflective of something seriously wrong in the bowels of the organization. The worst thing that we felt you could do was to go around it and leave it untouched. Each supervisor in the chain needed to be held accountable for his/her actions and to go around the supervisor who allegedly caused the complaint directly to the top may, but in most cases may not, solve the grievant's problem, and it does nothing to alleviate the long-term problems of discrimination which are deep-seated in the bureaucacy. The formal grievance procedure requiring that the complaint be sent up the supervisory chain serves two functions: First, it allows a supervisor to be confronted first with a problem from below, thereby permitting him to clear up the problem and to make accommodations without losing face. If the supervisor is confronted with an accusation of discrimination from above, he may become defensive and intransigent and exacerbate the problem. Second, the bottom up process requires supervisors to account to their superiors for unresolved grievances and redress imbalances in the management structure by putting everyone, not just the President, on notice. Institutionalizing the concern in the existing organizational channels is the only way I knew to get at the heart of the real structural problems.

In the area of faculty appointments and promotions, the plan was less precise but stated in more general terms the types of procedures that needed to be implemented. At that time, these proposals were still under review by a range of faculty groups including the Senate and the University Council. The plan stated that major policy would be promulgated by the Provost, assisted by an Academic Committee on Equal Opportunity and the Council of Academic Deans as well as the University Council and the Faculty Senate. With respect to new appointments, the plan specified:

> Each proposal coming to the Provost's Staff Conference must carry a departmental certification that the nominee was selected after full consideration of all candidates including women and members of minority groups.
>
> Each department should be instructed to retain written records of data obtained concerning candidates considered, and of all application and supplementary material received from applicants, whether successful or unsuccessful, for five years after a position has been filled.

The plan called for the appointment of a Minority Recruiting Officer to assist schools in finding minority candidates for faculty positions. It also affirmed a recommendation of The Development Commission that funds be made available to provide up to one-half of the salary cost (for a maximum of six years) for black faculty members if the department did not have adequate funds in its budget to pay for the position.

As the various pieces of the plan were developed, they were released for review by the University. On December 4, 1972 HEW compliance officers revisited the campus to request additional statistical data on employees. In addition to three new compliance officers, the HEW Regional Office had a new director. Jim Robinson summarized the meeting by saying, "The group was very sharp, but very quantitatively oriented. They felt that our earlier submission of census data was insufficient, but the quantity of information they wanted this time was staggering." HEW requested reports in 15 different formats broken down by faculty and non-faculty and analyzed by full-time and part-time, by rank, by department, by school, and for the whole University. Amanda Poor, a systems analyst added to Pauman's staff the previous month, estimated that over 38,000 different data compilations would be required to collect this information (see Exhibit 28-4). Jim Robinson concluded, "It was a real nightmare. It seemed to us at the time that HEW didn't know for certain what figures they needed, so to be on the safe side, they asked for everything."

As a first step, Poor did an analysis of the data in the Personnel Information System. Due to the objections that were raised when the University conducted its racial survey the previous spring, no racial information had been collected on new hires since that time and the files were consequently already outdated. Other missing data included: 1) discipline or degree which qualified a faculty member to teach in his current department, 2) a notation of the deans and department chairmen, 3) total years of experience, and 4) average annual salary increments. Furthermore, there were no historical data on persons who had been eligible for promotion to tenure and were not granted it. Poor concluded that since the University was considering sweeping changes in its personnel information system, it would not be cost effective either to reprogram the existing files or to hire personnel to sort through all the hard copy files, particularly since the University was uncertain that HEW would require this type of reporting again. On the other hand, by consolidating and simplifying the reports she felt that the volume of data compilations could be reduced from 38,000 to a maximum of 22,125. It was her recommendation that the University use the Statistical Package for Social Sciences (SSPS) to facilitate the compilation of the reports. Since the MIS department had recently set up the program on the University's computer, with only minor reprogramming some meaningful data could be pulled together within two to three months, depending on how long it took to update the racial data.

The University decided to accept the MIS department recommendation, and Poor went to work to generate the reports. Meanwhile, the Personnel Department conducted an update on the racial information. That opened up the issue with the faculty again, and a committee of the Senate was appointed to investigate and recommend a course of action. "In the process of generating the statistics we uncovered any number of new problems," said Gerald Robinson. "First, we had to decide how to divide the University's over 200 job titles into some manageable size groups for comparative purposes. Then, the numerous administrative units had to be broken down," he added. Eventually the job families were reduced to 24 and the administrative units to an equal number. Other sticky questions included how faculty members who held joint appointments in the administration and on the faculty would be counted, what the appropriate size was for aggregating the data so that comparisons would be meaningful but would not be so small that individuals could be identified, etc. Once the employee data were aggregated, then the University faced different problems of disparity. For instance, how could salaries for professors in Neurological Sciences be fairly compared with professors of Folklore?

While the MIS department went to work on the technical aspects of reporting to HEW, the Task Force on Affirmative Action began to address itself to the problem of establishing goals and timetables for action. The Equal Opportunity Office first gathered as many statistics as possible on the number of minority and female Ph.D.'s by the various disciplines. "Information was scanty and not very precise," said Jim Robinson, "but we combed the professional associations, government agencies, foundations, libraries, and directories for data on candidate pools." For academic personnel and senior administrators the University considered the pool to be national in scope, but for middle managers, hourly, clerical, and technical employees, Department of Labor and census information on the Philadelphia metropolitan area was used to determine the size of the candidate pool of minorities and women. Johnstone noted that, "There was considerable resistance among the faculty to the establishment of goals and timetables. Many viewed the goals as quotas which were antagonistic to principles of academic freedom. However, there were schools like Wharton whose faculty and dean understood the purpose of the goals and were very cooperative."

THE WHARTON SCHOOL

In 1973, The Wharton School was composed of two divisions–management and finance–and two departments in the social sciences including the disciplines of sociology, political science, and economics. The Dean, Donald C. Carroll, was a former professor at Massachusetts Institute of Technology's Sloan School and had been named to head the school in September 1972. He was the first dean to be appointed from the outside. Included on Wharton's faculty were two of the few tenured women with full professor rank, Jean Crockett, Professor of Finance and President of the Faculty Senate, and Renée Fox, Chairman of the Department of Sociology.

Carroll described his approach to Affirmative Action:

> When I arrived at Wharton the idea of Affirmative Action was clear, but the techniques for implementation were not. As a professor and department chairman at MIT, I had some experience in this area and was aware of some of the problems to be faced. During my first year at Penn we experienced a lot of groping with the form and substance of Affirmative Action. We tried some things and if they worked, we kept them; if not, we found something else. The procedures evolved almost in a common law way rather than through any intellectual process.
>
> One of the worst problems I faced in the beginning was the availability of accurate data both in the personnel and financial reporting area. The central administration did all the head counting and then sent over the results for verification. The information was simply not accurate. It looked as if they didn't know who was working here. I had to go down the budget sheet and I assumed if we were paying them, they were here. The lack of good accurate data can have some disastrous consequences in the academic area. It is part of every faculty member's contract

that he or she must be notified in writing one year before his or her appointment is up for review. Just last year one of our young professors was not properly notified, and even if we wanted to fire him we would have to give him a one-year reappointment. In other parts of the University I understand some professors have actually received tenure through the same type of slip-ups.

Carroll described his involvement in the goal-setting process in this manner:

All the deans were provided with information on the availability of minorities and women Ph.D.'s. The data were not broken down very finely by discipline. For example, we knew how many women doctorates there were in business, but not finance. But in any case, the percentages were so low—around 1%—that the degree of precision was not terribly important. We were then asked to estimate how many positions would open up during the next three years. Based on an estimation of turnover and our projected growth rate, I predicted that we would have five to six openings a year for a total of 18 new places in the Management division and approximately 13 in the Social Sciences. We are fortunate because Wharton is an expanding school at a time when many parts of the University are shrinking, and we have a greater possibility for acting affirmatively. However, the availability of candidates was so low our goals became only one or two new women and minority group members in each division in the three-year period. I hope we can do better than those goals within that time frame. However, with a limited candidate pool I fear that it will become a process of one Ivy League School raiding another.

During my first year I concerned myself with the need to document in detail the school's hiring and promotion processes. I tried to communicate as strongly as I could that my concern for this issue was real and that tokenism or casual statements to the affect that 'the appointment process was free of bias' were inadequate both legally and morally. In response to my request two distinctly different documentation processes emerged based on the department's style of recruiting.

1)—The prominent departments recruit on a basis of "target of opportunity." Most dossiers from outstanding graduates of Harvard, MIT, Stanford, etc. show up one way or another at the departments. Generally, these departments don't recruit or canvas for faculty members. As someone good came along, he or she was hired. For those departments we have allowed a process description verifying that the search was in compliance with Affirmative Action guidelines to suffice. Such a description might be: 'Thirty-seven names came to our attention and they were all white males. Therefore, we contacted other schools and discovered six qualified minorities for the position. Three were interviewed and one was given an offer. (See Exhibit 28-5 for sample letter utilizing this process.)

2)—Among the less well-known departments an exhuastive search procedure was instituted. It was a tedious and time-consuming process, but it produced an additional black faculty member for the Political Science Department during 1973. The department first developed a list of all available candidates including minorities and women in political science. Names of those in inappropriate sub-disciplines (for instance, the department didn't need anyone that year in Southeast Asian Studies)

> were weeded out. The remaining ones were notified of the job opening and invited to visit the campus. From the group who expressed interest, applicants were selected for additional interviews and several offers made. This process required an extensive national information system which the American Political Science Association was able to provide in that case, but such lists do not exist in sufficient detail for all professional fields.

Carroll concluded:

> No matter which of the two techniques the departments chose to use, I made it very clear to the department chairpersons that I simply would not forward a nomination to the Provost Staff Conference that was not supported by a credible and sincere description documenting that either the process or exhaustive search techniques was used. And on the whole, I must say the faculty has been very cooperative. Most of them complain because it is a lot of work, but there is little resistance to the necessity of avidly recruiting minorities and women for our faculty.

RENEWED CONTROVERSY IN 1973

During the spring of 1973 a final draft of the University Affirmative Action Plan with goals and timetables for the faculty and non-faculty was completed and submitted to HEW for review. The MIS department had succeeded in describing the university population in nine ways broken down by faculty and non-faculty:

1.—By affiliation—either partially or fully.
2.—By salary status—either partially or fully.
3.—By payroll class—A-1, A-2, A-3, A-4.
4.—By race.
5.—By sex.
6.—By race and sex.
7.—By citizenship.
8.—By the 24 job families.
9.—By the 24 administrative units.

Once the description was complete, the statistical analysis was possible using the SSPS package. Bruce Johnstone concluded, "By the end of the academic year 1973 we knew we had taken a giant step forward in institutionalizing affirmative action procedures. We knew where our weak spots were and we had begun to try some new policies and procedures. In the process of examining ourselves, I think we awakened a lot of sensitivities."

Not all groups on the campus were pleased with the University's Affirmative Action Plan, or "Progress Report" as it was officially called, that was submitted to HEW in the spring of 1973. In July of 1973 the president of WEOUP wrote a scathing letter to yet another new Regional Director of HEW indicting the University for its lack of progress in bringing women into its faculty ranks and moving women to senior administrative positions. The letter was also equally critical of HEW for its slowness in completing its investigation of the University. WEOUP contended that the hiring goals outlined for the University would have the net effect of reducing the number of women, not increasing it.

> During the time (1970-73) we have seen the number of women faculty decrease; the ratio of women to men on the faculty decrease; continuation of discrepancies in salaries in some schools; and the filling of faculty positions with male candidates without full review of the qualifications of women applicants for the same position.
>
> Now the University has released a set of goals and timetables calculated to reduce still further both the net number of women and the ratio of women to men on our faculty as the supporting data indicate. [See Exhibit 28-6.]
>
> In our nonfaculty ranks, the number of senior administrators has been increased this past year but no women have been appointed or promoted to senior administrative status during that period. Again, this is the reverse of affirmative action and does not achieve the University's stated goal of increasing the presence of women in decision-making strata of the institution. Individual senior administrators continue to create "unique job classifications" to permit the hiring of young men at salaries higher than those of women already performing the same work with the same responsibilities. They have been found filling positions prior to announcement of openings, and in the increasingly critical area of job elimination have continued a longstanding practice of transfer or promotion of men, but termination of women.

In a letter to President Meyerson the previous month a female professor, Pheobe Leboy, had presented these facts to President Meyerson and asked him to take a leadership role in the revision of the goals. She stated, "We anticipate that most if not all deans and department chairmen will view their goals as maximum rather than minimum targets. It is therefore particularly important that the goals be set high enough to effect change." Copies of all the letters were sent to Pennsylvania's two U.S. Senators, the Chairman of the Academic Committee on Equal Opportunity, the Provost as well as representatives of national women's groups, WEAL and NOW.

Although a number of groups existed on campus to exert pressure on the University on behalf of special interests, the women's group was the best organized and most active (see Exhibit 28-7 Sources of Pressure for Affirmative Action). Each year the group had met with representatives of HEW to present its views and had become discouraged with the lack of response. One activist woman described the situation in this manner: "Each year a new set of faces from HEW appeared on the campus, and we presented our case for women. The compliance officers nodded their heads in astonishment, and went away. We didn't hear from them for a year. It was discouraging that the government was so ineffectual, but we refused to give up."

Another woman administrator added, "We attempted to keep communication channels open and we have received some support from the central administration. However, most of the things that have been accomplished we have done via subtle persuasion and jawboning and few make headlines in the campus newspapers. On several occasions the President and the Provost have intervened on behalf of women either in direct support of a promotion or salary increase. I know of at least one occasion where the President came up with contingency funds to raise a woman administrator's salary up to a comparable level with men in the same position. I think Meyerson's heart is in the right place, but his position is a political one in the sense that he has to juggle conflicting interests. I frankly don't think that the women at Pennsylvania yet have a large enough power base to let him justify acting vigorously in the open on this issue even if he wanted to."

Exhibit 28-1

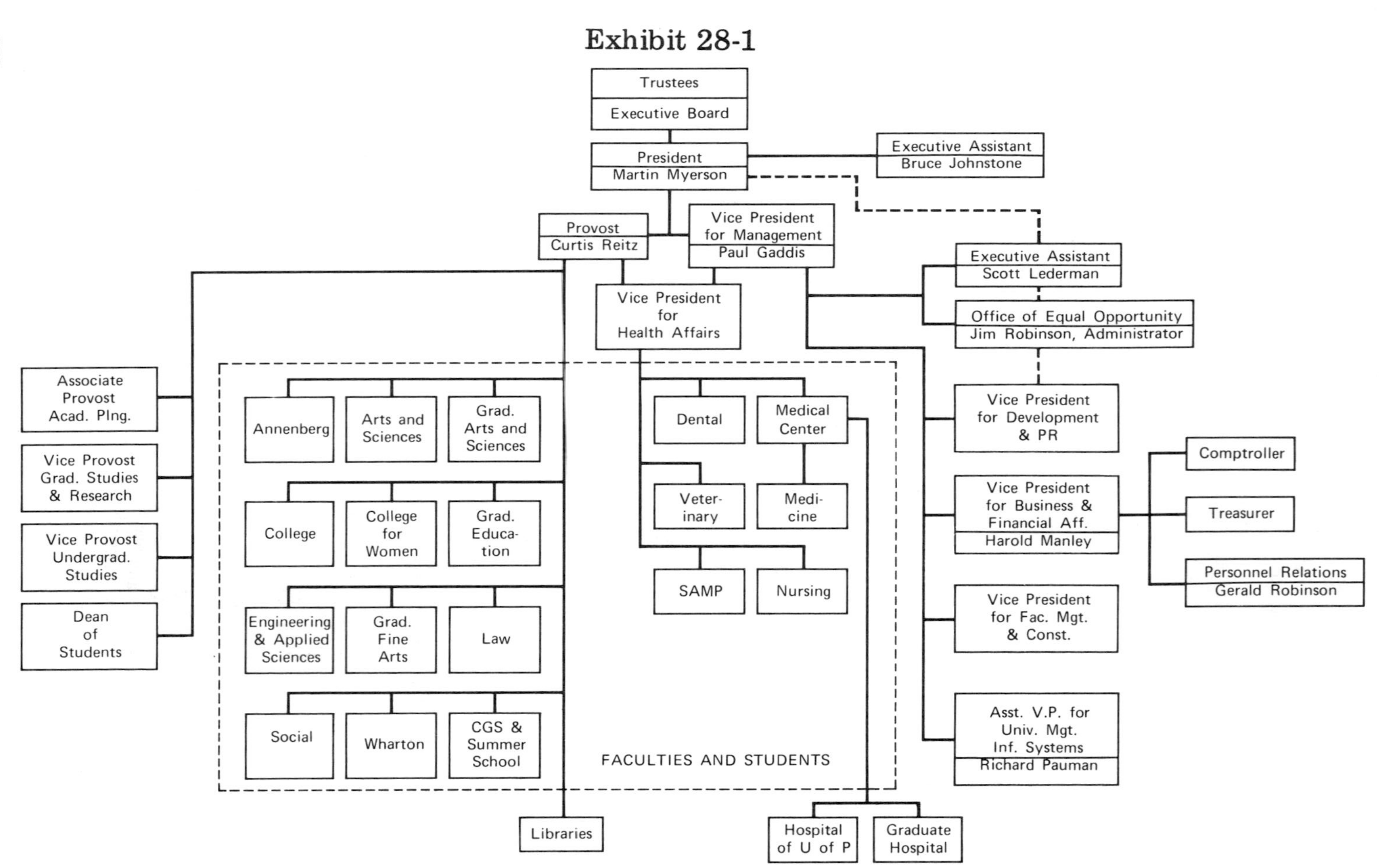
Trustees
Executive Board
President
Martin Myerson
Executive Assistant
Bruce Johnstone
Provost
Curtis Reitz
Vice President for Management
Paul Gaddis
Vice President for Health Affairs
Executive Assistant
Scott Lederman
Office of Equal Opportunity
Jim Robinson, Administrator
Associate Provost Acad. Plng.
Vice Provost Grad. Studies & Research
Vice Provost Undergrad. Studies
Dean of Students
Annenberg
Arts and Sciences
Grad. Arts and Sciences
College
College for Women
Grad. Educa-tion
Engineering & Applied Sciences
Grad. Fine Arts
Law
Social
Wharton
CGS & Summer School
Dental
Medical Center
Veter-inary
Medi-cine
SAMP
Nursing
FACULTIES AND STUDENTS
Libraries
Hospital of U of P
Graduate Hospital
Vice President for Development & PR
Vice President for Business & Financial Aff.
Harold Manley
Vice President for Fac. Mgt. & Const.
Asst. V.P. for Univ. Mgt. Inf. Systems
Richard Pauman
Comptroller
Treasurer
Personnel Relations
Gerald Robinson

Exhibit 28-2

OFFICE OF EQUAL OPPORTUNITY

July, 1972

Class	*T.E.*	*1*	*%*	*2*	*%*	*3*	*%*	*4*	*%*	*5*	*%*	*6*	*%*	*W.*	*%*
A1	882	42	5	29	3	795	90	9	1			7	.8	255	29
A2	4001	76	2	176	4	3613	90	48	1			88	2	606	15
A3	2526	434	17	33	1	2018	80	26	1	1	.4	14	.6	1920	76
A4	648	287	44			357	55	2	.3	2	.3			195	30
University	8057	839	10%	238	3%	6783	84%	85	1%	3	.4%	109	1%	2976	37%

T.E. Total Employees

1 Negroes
2 Orientals
3 Caucasians
4 Spanish Speaking Americans
5 American Indians
6 Other
W Women

Exhibit 28-3

Excerpts from

THE UNIVERSITY OF PENNSYLVANIA AFFIRMATIVE ACTION PROGRAM

A Comprehensive Strategy for Affirmative Action

THE CANDIDATE POOL

One reason for the persistent underrepresentation of women and minorities in many of our institutions–even those most committed to principles of nondiscrimination in hiring–is that the underrepresentation is already in evidence in the pool of candidates under consideration . . . the serious candidate pools may be limited largely to suggestions received by members of the relevant academic or administrative departments or search committees from colleagues at a relatively small number of institutions.

Such a process of co-optation may, of course, perpetuate the backgrounds of those doing the searching. It is not a system likely to give substantial attention to promising candidates from lesser known institutions or from nonacademic professions, to women scholars who have left academe, or to members of minority groups who have not yet entered the mainstream of mobile professors and administrators. Equal opportunity, then,–particularly for academic and administrative appointments–must begin with greater representation of women and minorities within the candidate pools . . .

HIRING

It goes without saying that hiring must be based on merit without regard to race, sex, color, age, religion, or national origin. In fact, there can be no compromise with the principle of hiring by merit, especially in the case of faculty, if the standards of the University are to be maintained. At the same time, the criteria which define "merit" are often difficult to define–much less to quantify, sum, and compare among individuals. Our challenge is to maintain our allegiance to "merit" while critically examining the expressed or implied criteria by which individuals have been judged and the degree to which such criteria have made the maximum use of the skills and talents of women and members of minority groups. We can expect cases to arise when candidates may be judged of virtually equal merit on all but the most trivial criteria. In such cases we believe it compatible with a fundamental allegiance to nondiscrimination and merit, yet responsive to the need to achieve full equality of opportunity, to avowedly favor women, minorities, or any other previously underrepresented segment of the population . . .

The absence of targets, or goals, requires considerable faith on the part of women, minorities, and public and private "watchdog" agencies that a college or university will continue to strive to markedly increase its employment of women and minority group persons. The willingness of institutions to set goals, on the other hand, requires faith on their part that the failure to reach these targets will not be abused or considered in isolation from the special circumstances of a given case. *We believe that colleges and universities should set realistic but challenging goals, with the clear understanding–in accord with Revised Order #4–that these goals will frequently prove unattainable but that performance will be evaluated on the basis of procedure and effort rather than simple proximity to target.*

PROMOTION

Affirmative action at the level of new hiring means very little if the same considerations are not applied to promotions. An aggregate staff census may at times show substantial representation of women and minority group persons, but fail to show those which may be concentrated at entry or near-entry level *positions. Policies and programs to move women and minority group persons up career ladders must be accorded at least as high a priority as those directed toward new hiring.*

A significant new element affecting the promotion of assistant professors to the rank of associate professor with tenure is the virtual cessation of the growth in the overall size of the faculty, coupled with a reduction in retirements and resignations of senior faculty. As a result, promotions to tenure must be limited if the overall ratio of tenured to non-tenured faculty is to remain roughly constant (at about 2:1). Given these constraints, promotions to tenure will increasingly have to be based not simply upon the individual's competence as a scholar and teacher, however demonstrated, but with consideration to the future growth and the present ratio of senior to junior faculty in the department and school. Thus, although we believe the promotion and even the direct appointment of women and members of minority groups into the senior faculty ranks to be of utmost importance to our affirmative action program, we must recognize that the number of promotions to tenure has declined sharply in recent years and may continue to decline or at best remain at a level considerably below the levels prevailing throughout most of the past decade.

RESPONSIBILITY

The final ingredient of affirmative action is the assignment of responsibility. It is important in this respect to distinguish between responsibility for policy and responsibility for the effective functioning of a plan. Policy affecting academic staff or program must reside with the president and the chief academic officer in conjunction with the duly established faculty consultative bodies. Policy affecting support staff must reside with the president and the major nonacademic officers.

However, the effective functioning of an affirmative action program is most dependent upon a different kind of responsibility–the responsibility not to make policy, but to assure the proper workings of the compliance and grievance machinery; to monitor the regulations and directives established by those responsible for policy; and to make certain that the requisite policy decisions are being made by the appropriate individuals or bodies. It is vital to the success of an affirmative action program that one person, in a staff relationship to the president or a chief administrative officer, be held accountable for the effective functioning of the affirmative action program. This individual should generally hold an office and a title such as equal opportunity officer or administrator of an office of equal opportunity.

Exhibit 28-4

TABLE 28-4 HEW REQUESTED FORMATS

Description	*Faculty*					*Non-Faculty*					*Total*
	PF/FT	*Ranks*	*Depts*	*School/ Unit*	*Univ*	*PF/FT*	*Ranks*	*Depts*	*School/ Unit*	*Univ*	
	2	*3*	*200**	*36**	*1*	*2*	*20**	*364**	*60**	*1*	
1. Faculty Utilization by Discipline	X		X	X	X						474
2. Non-faculty Utilization by Job Family						X		X	X	X	850
3. Fac. Distribution by Rank	X		X	X	X						474
4. Fac. Availability by Discipline	X				X						2
5. Non-fac. Availability by Job Family						X				X	2
6. Fac. Utilization Indices	X			X	X						74
7. Non-fac. Utilization Indices						X			X	X	122
8. Academic Promotion Analysis	FT	2	X	X	X						474
9. Academic Tenure Analysis	FT		X	X	X						237
10. Non-acad. Promotion Analysis							X	X	X	X	8500
11. Faculty Compensation Analysis I	X	X	X	X	X						1422
12. Faculty Compensation Analysis II	X	X	X	X	X						1422
13. Non-fac. Compensation Analysis I						X	X	X	X	X	17000
14. Non-fac. Compensation Analysis II						X	X	X	X	X	17000
15. Graduate Ass't Analysis				X	X						37
*Approximate										Total	38,080

Exhibit 28-5

UNIVERSITY OF PENNSYLVANIA
PHILADELPHIA 19104

DEPARTMENT OF SOCIOLOGY
128 McNeil Building

Renée C. Fox
Professor and Chairman

April 13, 1973

Dean Donald C. Carroll
The Wharton School
E-111 Dietrich Hall

Dear Don:

I am writing to you in connection with the prospective appointment of . . . to an Assistant Professorship in the Department of Sociology. I understand that his case has been considered at a recent meeting of the Provost's Staff Conference, and that the information I supplied in connection with the Affirmative Action procedures that had accompanied our recommendation to appoint . . . were not considered adequate. This letter, then, is to supplement the data I've already supplied. I trust that you will transmit a copy of it to the members of the Provost Staff Conference for their reconsideration.

As I wrote to you in my letter of February 14, 1973, officially recommending –'s appointment, the Personnel/Recruitment Committee of the Department of Sociology conducted their search for a young sociological theorist in as conscientious, wide-ranging and equitable way as possible. In keeping with the principles of the Affirmative Action Program of the University of Pennsylvania, we conducted a search for equally qualified persons for this position who belong to minority groups, but did not find individuals with the same kinds of interests and qualifications that . . . possesses–interests and qualifications which the Department needs to increase and diversify its excellence.

Perhaps it would be helpful to all concerned for me to describe how we conduct our search. We are, of course, in contact with respected colleagues in other institutions throughout the country, and in asking them to recommend promising candidates to us, we explicitly request their assistance in identifying talented minority group members. In this connection, for example, I have established a continuing contact with . . . , a prominent black sociologist at Syracuse University, and a member of the Board of Directors of the Social Science Research Council. He has been helping me to locate prospective black colleagues. I have also invited . . . himself to seriously consider the possibility of a professorship at Pennsylvania. As for the recruiting of women, this is obviously less difficult for us, since, as a woman chairperson, I am at the very center of the network of eligible women sociologists of all age groups. I also have the help in this regard from . . . and . . . in our own Department, and from other prominent women sociologists elsewhere, such as ... at Princeton, ... at Goucher, and ... at Stoney Brook. But we do not rely solely on an informal communication system for recruiting minority group colleagues. We have also placed an advertisement in *Footnotes*, the employment bulletin of the American Sociological Association, announcing the jobs that are open in our Department, and the range of competences in which we have a special interest (e.g., theory, methodology, comparative institutional analysis, deviance, race relations, etc.).

So far as our overall recruitment pattern during this academic year is concerned, as you know, the only other appointment that we have thus far made is that of . . . , to an Associate Professorship. She, of course, personifies the feminine minority group (though she by no means represents the only woman whom we are planning to engage). On March 6, 1973, we received . . . , a black Associate Professor of Sociology at . . . , for whom we were about to initiate a formal departmental vote on his appointment, when we received word that he has decided to accept a position at . . . . We are continuing actively to search for a black sociologist. Among our prospective candidates are . . . and . . . , from whom we hope to have visits before this semester ends, or, failing that, by the beginning of the new academic year. Our recruitment process for the academic year 1972-1973 will come to a conclusion in early May. Before then, we will also have visits from two young white sociologists from . . . , the one, a woman, . . . , the other, a man, ... I do not know what the outcome of these visits will be but, once again, the sex distribution involved here, demonstrates the equity principle that we are following in our consideration of prospective candidates.

I hope that this extensive description of our recruiting process will prove helpful to you and the Provost's Staff Conference, and that it will sufficiently meet your approval to allow the appointment of . . . to go through.

My best wishes to you, as always.

Sincerely yours,

(signed) Renée C. Fox

mr

Exhibit 28-6

ANALYSIS OF GOALS AND TIMETABLES—DECEMBER 1972

	Total Faculty	*Women*	*Minorities*	*NEW HIRES*		
				Faculty	*Women*	*Minorities*
Totals as per goals & timetables	1524	192	40	327	60	28
Percentage		(12.6%)	(3.2%)		(18.3%)	(8.6%)
Percentage Untenured	488 (32%)*	142 (74%)**	20?			
1.5% attrition (x 3 yrs)	69	9	2			
Assuming 75% non-promotion rate*						
Loss due to termination (assumes 3/5 of untenured faculty up for promotion by June 1976)	220	64	9?			
Total loss after 3 yrs.	289	73	11?			
Difference between 1972 and 1976				+38	-13	+17
Total Faculty in 1976				1562	179 (11.5%)	57 (3.6%)
Assuming 50% promotion rate						
Loss due to termination	146	43	6?			
Total loss after 3 yrs.	216	52	8			
Difference between 1972 and 1976				+181	+8	+20
Total Faculty in 1976				1705	200 (11.7%)	60 (3.5%)

* Zemsky-Davis-Rubin, ALMANAC, April 10
**From computer print-out, December 1972

Exhibit 28-7

SOURCES OF PRESSURE FOR AFFIRMATIVE ACTION

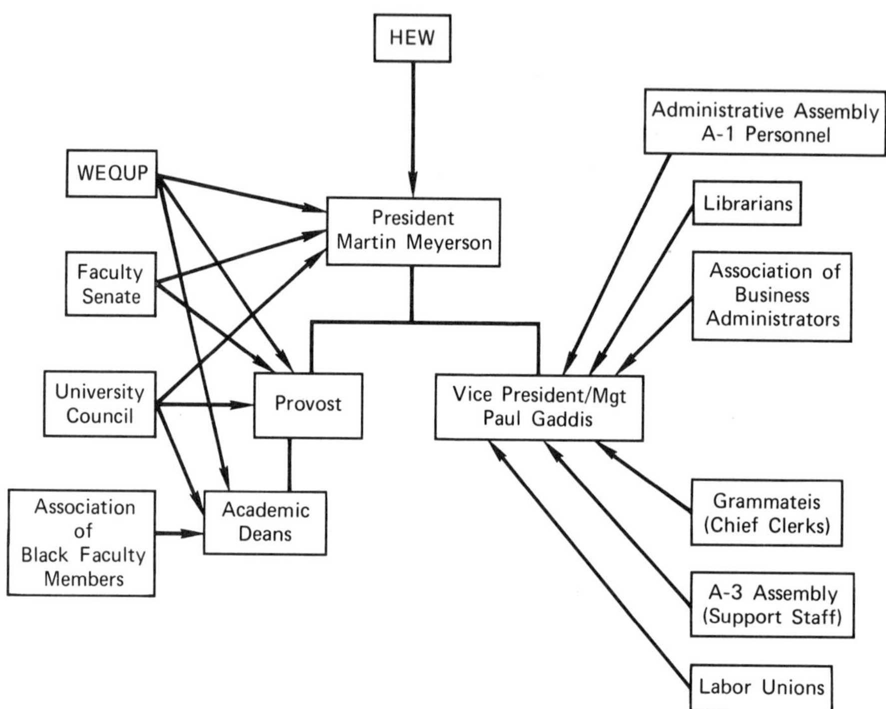

Case Twenty-Nine

University of Pennsylvania (C)[1]

In the fall of 1973 the University received its first reaction from HEW on the Affirmative Action Progress Report it had submitted the previous spring. "At this point HEW seemed more concerned with form than substance," said James Davis, the new Executive Assistant to the Provost. Davis, an associate professor of biochemistry from Oakland University, was on leave of absence at Penn and took his staff position shortly after Eliot Stellér, the former co-chairman of the Development Commission, had been named Provost. In September 1973, HEW asked the University to make some format changes in the report. The goals were to be broken down on an annual basis instead of aggregate over three years, and the job families were to be revamped in the statistical reports to conform more closely with the Equal Employment Opportunity Commission (EEOC). However, the major concern HEW had was the format of the report. "In the interim since we first filed the report," Davis said, "HEW had developed a checklist of points that must be included in any acceptable Affirmative Action Plan. They wanted us to rework our plan in their format." He added, "What they wanted us to do was not particularly difficult, but was time-consuming." By December, the University had revised the Affirmative Action Plan, and it was resubmitted to HEW.

During the academic year 1973-74 the University moved into a second phase of its affirmative action efforts. Bruce Johnstone, Executive Assistant to the President, commented, "In the process of developing a plan we had learned much about the administrative deficiencies of the University. We had devised the procedures, and now we had to make them work. This included developing forms to document the academic appointment process and finalizing an academic grievance process, plus totally reworking our personnel information system."

In the fall of 1973, William Drye, assistant comptroller, was named to head the Personnel Information Services Department and assigned the task of integrating the University's existing payroll and personnel information systems. In addition, his

---

[1] For additional background information on the University Affirmative Action Plan see University of Pennsylvania (A) and (B).

department was to provide counseling services for all University employees on benefits and personnel practices. However, his first priority soon became developing a new personnel information system. Gerald Robinson, Executive Director of Personnel Relations, explained:

> Affirmative Action reporting requirements had caused us to look closely at our data bank back in 1971 and to uncover its problems. But we somehow had managed to collect the data the government needed, as sparse as that was, and I had felt that since a complete new personnel data system which integrated both personnel and payroll data in one bank would eventually be required to operate the department effectively, I had delayed work on the project until some of my organizational and policy problems within the department had been worked out. Although Affirmative Action may have been the impetus in the beginning, a good personnel management system was an over-riding concern of mine.

"We had to start from scratch," Drye learned after only a few weeks on the job. "The payroll records were not in too bad shape, but the system was an antiquated card one. The personnel records were another story. We knew that the records were full of inaccuracies and a complete update on all files would be required." At that point, the MIS Department personnel were fully committed to redesigning the accounting system, so an outside consulting firm, Integral Systems, was retained to provide technical expertise in the redesign of the personnel system. Michael Aherne, a vice president of Integral Systems, had developed such a system for Rutgers University and started immediately to work out a similar program for Penn.

Drye described his approach to his assignment:

> In the beginning we had high hopes that we could have the system up and running by January 1974. We thought we had it all figured out; however, it was impossible to anticipate the problems we ran into and the number of people who had to check every little detail. This did not even include the continuing problem of the collection of racial data. When the Affirmative Action census was taken, Deans had lost a lot of respect for the Personnel records due to the large number of errors. If we were to regain that confidence and cooperation with the new system, we decided to proceed carefully until we were sure the data was correct."

To create a new personnel-payroll system several activities had to go on simultaneously. First, Drye and Aherne had to review the contents of the old data base and begin work on programming a new system. At the same time, procedures had to be worked out for checking the validity of the data that existed and for verifying the accuracy of each file entry with the deans, department chairmen and administrative heads. "We even found dead people on our Blue Cross/Blue Shield rolls," Drye said. Finally, every personnel policy and procedure had to be reviewed and training materials prepared to instruct all personnel in the use and maintenance of the new system. Even the simplest decisions could take weeks. "The University had not looked at its personnel policies this closely for twenty years," Gerald Robinson commented, "and within several months we had resigned ourselves to the fact that the process would simply take a lot of time and would require input from many segments of the University."

By the spring of 1974 the verification of the data in the old system was finally about to occur and Drye and Aherne had mapped out in considerable detail the process required to get the system operating. Exhibit 29-1 is an abbreviated form of their implementation flow chart. Individuals were assigned to the various tasks, and it was estimated that it would take 3,430 person-days of work, not including the time spent by Drye and Aherne, to complete the job. The problem of developing definitions for personnel and payroll terminology alone was estimated to take 188 person-days, or nearly 38 weeks. "With an increased budget and allocation of some temporary personnel, we might have the system operational by January 1975," Drye said.

In the academic area the Faculty Senate and the University Council debated throughout the year on a grievance procedure, and in April 1974 approved the appointment of a Grievance Commission to be selected by the Senate Advisory Committee and composed of 16 persons from the faculty (but was not to include deans, top level administrators, or members of the central administration). Decisions would not be binding, but advisory to the Provost. Working through the Provost Staff Conference, the deans agreed on a standardized form which would constitute a statement of compliance with the Affirmative Action Plan for new appointments. In addition, during the year Assistant Professor Robert Engs also served as Minority Recruiting Officer and developed a file of dossiers on potential black faculty members. Jim Davis said that "although most of the new black faculty members located this year were found by the departments themselves, the visibility of the office (it was located in the Office of the Provost) was tremendously useful for the morale of the black faculty at Penn and for raising the consciousness of deans and department chairmen. The office, coupled with the resources of new Faculty Redevelopment Fund, have made a big difference in our new appointment picture this year." The College hired three new black assistant professors. In Physics one woman was promoted to a tenured professorship.

On April 29 and 30, 1974, HEW representatives visited the campus to review the University's progress with implementation. "We had a very positive meeting with the compliance officers," Davis said, "I think we're moving more toward approval of the plan than confrontation." HEW asked the University to make changes in its plan in four major areas:

1.–To recalculate its goals by a different method so that minority and female populations at the University would approximate candidate pool availability.
2.–To document the applicant flow and terminations for both academic and nonacademic personnel.
3.–To perform a salary analysis to determine if inequities in payment of women and minorities exist.
4.–To describe in detail the chain of responsibility that existed in the implementation of Affirmative Action Plan.

HEW was particularly concerned that the Equal Opportunity Officer did not have a line position.

On June 28, 1974 the University and HEW Office for Civil Rights signed a Memorandum of Understanding in which the University agreed to make the requested changes in its Affirmative Action Plan, and HEW certified the University's eligibility for federal contracts.

Exhibit 29-1

FLOW CHART FOR DEVELOPMENT OF PAYROLL—PERSONNEL INFORMATION SYSTEM

(Excerpted from Detailed Flow Chart Prepared by William Drye and Michael Aherne, Integral Systems)

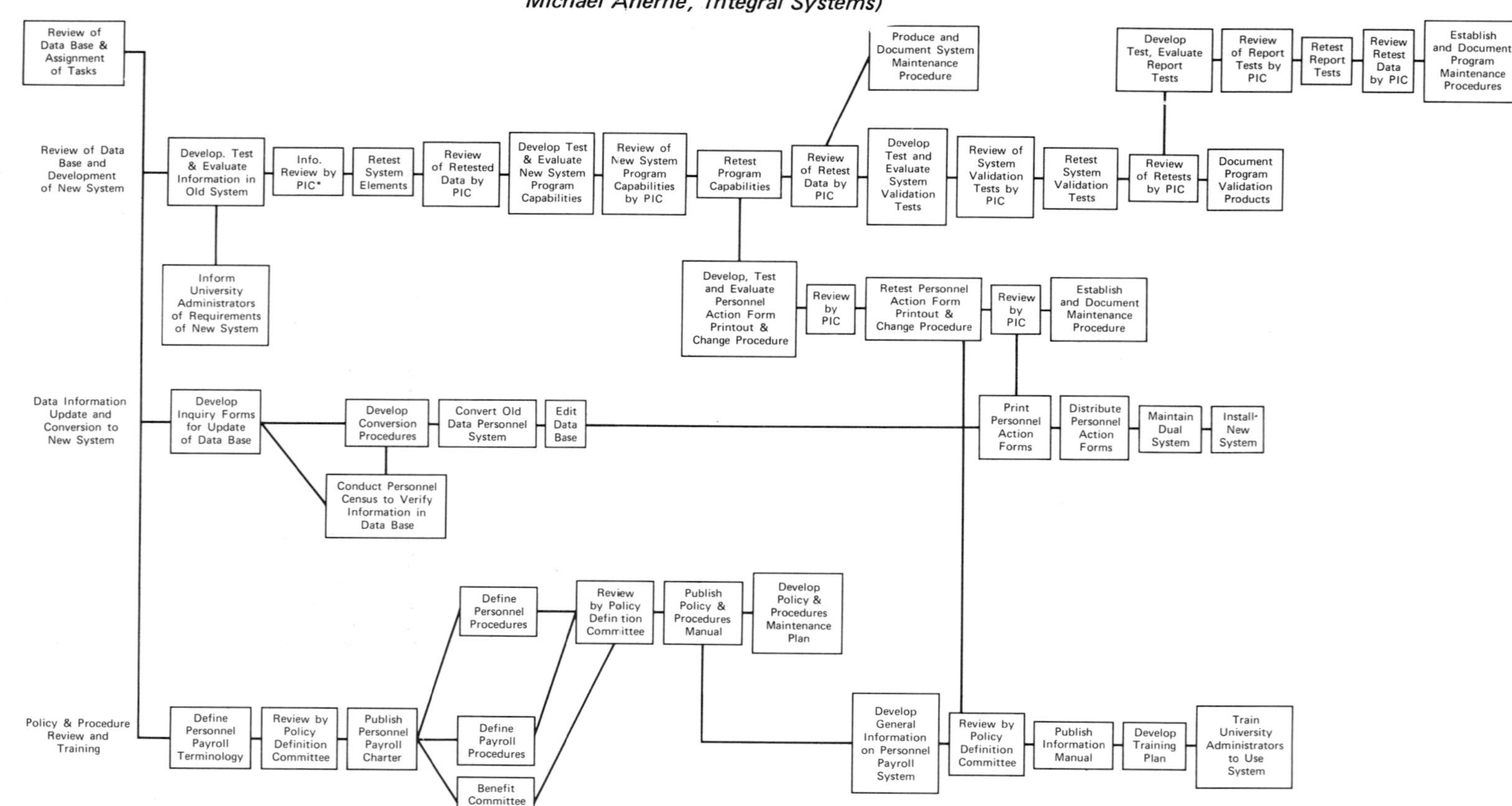

*PIC = Personnel Information Committee. Composed of MIS Department Director and Executive Director of Personnel.

Index Of Cases